MW00415637

1962

A story that needed to be told. Superbly written—by far the most definitive book on the subject. Removes the fig leaves and sets the record straight, something that today's context will profit by emulating.

Dr Y. S. P. Thorat,
former Chairman NABARD and son of General S. P. P. Thorat

From the beginning to the end, the book literally grabs the reader by the throat. Brutally honest, every detail of the conflict with China is laid bare. Sooner or later Indians had to face the bitter reality of what actually happened in the high Himalayas. Perhaps now we can begin to bury the ghosts.

Sam Rajappa,
former editor, *The Statesman*

More than half a century after the Sino-India clash in 1962, the truth emerges… The author, steeped in military matters owing to his own background, is unfettered as he does not wear a rank on his shoulders. The end result is a masterpiece, vital for our understanding if we are not to make the same mistakes again.

M. G. Devasahayam,
former IAS officer

Riveting in both its style and substance, this is the story of an army that was let down by those in power and some senior officers, many of them virtual political appointees. Certain post-1962 reports may still be under the wraps for touching on certain subjects that this book fearlessly exposes.

Ashali Varma,
author of *The Victoria Cross: A Love Story*
and daughter of Lieutenant General Prem Bhagat, VC

Also by Shiv Kunal Verma

Ocean to Sky: India from the Air
Military World Games
The Northeast Palette
Assam Rifles: 1835 to 2010
The Long Road to Siachen: The Question Why
Northeast Trilogy (East of Kanchendzonga, Brahma's Creation and Children of the Dawn)
Courage & Conviction: An Autobiography: General V. K. Singh

1962
THE WAR THAT WASN'T

SHIV KUNAL VERMA

ALEPH

ALEPH BOOK COMPANY
An independent publishing firm
promoted by ***Rupa Publications India***

Published in India in 2016 by
Aleph Book Company
7/16 Ansari Road, Daryaganj
New Delhi 110 002

ISBN: 978-93-82277-97-2

12 13 14 15 16 17 18 19 20

Printed at Parksons Graphics Pvt. Ltd, Mumbai

for my father,
Major General Ashok Kalyan Verma,
and his generation that paid the price

We died, unsuccoured, helpless
We were your soldiers, men of bravery and pride
Yet we died like animals, trapped in a cage with no escape
Massacred at will, denied the dignity of battle
With the cold burning flame of anger and resolution
With the courage both of the living and the dead,
Avenge
Our unplayed lives
Redeem the unredeemable sacrifice
In freedom and integrity
Let this be your inheritance
And our unwritten epitaph

Harji Malik, 'Nam Ka Chu: October 1962'

CONTENTS

List of Maps — *x*
Introduction: Living in the Shadow — *xi*
Prologue: Nam Ka Chu — *xvii*

BOOK I
Undefined Borders

1. Goodbye Tibet, Hello China — 3
2. An Impotent HQ — 29

BOOK II
Blanks on the Map

3. Blanks on the Map — 61
4. The Vanguard — 88

BOOK III
The Valley of Death

5. The Eye of the Storm — 113
6. The Valley of Death — 139
7. Fallback on Tawang — 165
8. When Generals Fail — 189
9. The Battle of Walong — 213

BOOK IV
The War That Wasn't

10. Fortress Se-la — 247
11. The Implosion — 273
12. The Final Countdown — 301
13. The Western Sector — 322

Epilogue: The Missing Links — *373*
Acknowledgements — *395*
Notes — *399*
Bibliography — *414*
Index — *417*

MAPS

Expanding Horizons	2
Indo-China Boundary (Key Areas)	60
Ladakh Overview	76
NEFA (North East Frontier Agency) Overview	84
Morshead-Bailey Survey of 1913	95
Nam Ka Chu (20 October 1962)	138
Bum-la and Tawang	190
Kibithu and Walong	227
Se-la (17-18 November 1962)	278
Dirang Dzong and Bomdila	312
DBO, Chushul and Aksai Chin	349

A Note on Style

Names of people and places have been spelled as per conventions that were in use at the time of the events in this narrative.

Introduction

LIVING IN THE SHADOW

After completing almost three years in the North East Frontier Agency (NEFA, now called Arunachal Pradesh), my father, Captain Ashok Kalyan Verma, was posted to the Indian Military Academy (IMA) in Dehradun as a platoon commander in July 1962. For him, this move would prove to be providential, for within a few months of his departure, 282 of the men and officers he left behind in 2 Rajput would be dead. The others were wounded or overpowered by the Chinese and taken prisoner. Among the handful who succeeded in getting away, some died of cold and starvation, while a few survived weeks of unbelievable hardship and made it back to the plains of Assam through the jungles of the Kameng Frontier Division and Bhutan.

We had moved into one of the spacious bungalows at the IMA sometime in September and I doubt if there could have been a more picturesque or happier place for a little boy to grow up in. Even though I was barely two years old, I have fleeting recollections of the place: Gentlemen Cadets, better known as GCs, running and cycling along the tree-lined avenues, horses being exercised on the polo ground, the commandant's buggy with its coterie of resplendent sowars (mounted soldiers) and ponies, our own bungalow opposite the club and the one time a huge black rat snake suddenly appeared, scaring everyone. I remember the fallen leaves strewn on the ground, the imposing clumps of bamboo and the stunning majesty of Chetwode Hall that dominated the Academy.

Then, suddenly, as the colours of autumn gave way to winter, the Academy, like the leaves on the trees, seemed to shrivel into itself. Even to me, it was obvious that something terrible had happened.

Brigadier (later, Lieutenant General) Premindra Singh Bhagat was then the commandant of the Academy. An Engineer officer, he had been awarded the Victoria Cross in Ethiopia in 1941, making him the highest decorated officer in the Indian Army at the time of Independence. In his mid-forties, Bhagat's receding hairline and bushy moustache gave him a dapper and somewhat avuncular appearance. As was the norm with all incoming officers posted to the IMA, he interviewed my father in early October. Glancing up from the dossier which contained Captain Ashok Kalyan Verma's service record, the commandant asked him if he was happy with his new posting. The usual answer that it was a great honour did not fool the brigadier, who could perhaps sense that the young officer in front of him was holding something back.

The commandant encouraged him to speak freely and the dam burst. My father said he had been posted out of 2 Rajput in July when it was de-inducting from the Lohit Valley where it had been deployed for the last three years. The battalion, under the command of Lieutenant Colonel Maha Singh Rikh, had been on its way to Mathura, but even as the men and equipment were being marshalled onto a special train at Missamari (near Tezpur), it had been ordered to redeploy in the Kameng Frontier Division as part of 7 Infantry Brigade. With barely any winter stores or equipment, the men had somehow made their way across Eaglenest to Bomdila, Dirang Dzong, Se-la and on to Tawang. They had then been pushed further north towards the Bhutan-NEFA-Tibet tri-junction. Military circles had been anticipating an armed clash with China, and under the circumstances the only place my father wanted to be was with the men of his battalion.

Brigadier Bhagat had been the Director, Military Intelligence at Army Headquarters, Delhi, prior to moving to the IMA. Obviously he had a reasonable idea of what was happening in NEFA and asked searching questions about the Kibithu and Walong sectors in the Lohit Frontier Division. Signalling the end of the interview, Bhagat said: 'I know how you feel, but you must now concentrate on training the GCs here—that has to have your entire focus. Let us hope the situation with the Chinese will soon sort itself out and hopefully all will be well.'

Ever since the onset of hostilities between India and China on 20 October, only sporadic news had been filtering through with no clear picture emerging as to what was actually happening. In the last week of November, Brigadier Bhagat called my father to his office. Breaking the news as gently as he could, he said things had gone very wrong for 7 Infantry Brigade and 2 Rajput on 20 October in the Nam Ka Chu Valley. The commandant then said there were hardly any survivors and those who had escaped the massacre were being collected in Ramgarh in Bihar. Being posted back to the battalion was out of the question, but the brigadier suggested my father leave immediately for Ramgarh to find out what had transpired.

Brigadier Bhagat was to later author the famous Henderson Brooks-Bhagat Report that remains classified even today despite successive governments being in power. The report was a detailed study commissioned by Army Headquarters to document the events of October-November 1962 in NEFA but eventually its mandate was limited to commenting on the military reasons for the newly raised IV Corps' defeat. However, at the time, the Henderson Brooks-Bhagat Report was yet to be written; my father, when he returned from Ramgarh, went to the commandant's house and briefed him about what he had seen and heard in Ramgarh. He told him about the haunted looks in the eyes of those who had survived, the smell of decay, every little bit of information… As he sat listening, Bhagat had tears in his eyes. India's senior-most Victoria Cross holder, like so many of his countrymen, could not take the humiliation. By then one thing was evident—life, for all of us, young or old, would never be the same again.

◆

Since then, regardless of where one went, the shadow of 1962 was never very far away. In the early years, not yet familiar with the area, I had no idea of what the terrain looked like or what the situation on the ground really must have been like. Different people left different impressions, but as I grew up, I found myself listening to each and every word that was spoken by the survivors of the conflict and by those who constantly analysed it. I stored away every bit of information that I could lay my hands on.

In 1979 my father was a lieutenant colonel posted in the Cabinet Secretariat in Army HQ in Delhi. We were living in the multi-storeyed apartment blocks on Sardar Patel Marg next to where the Taj Palace hotel would come up subsequently. An elevator with an attendant would ferry people up and down through the day. For a few days, we couldn't help but notice a particular attendant who would always look at my father with a shy half smile. But apart from wishing him very respectfully he would never say anything else. In his early fifties, lean and gaunt, he had the erect bearing of a soldier. The man walked with some difficulty, for he would shuffle away with the help of a walking stick at the end of his shift. A few days later, I happened to be in the lift when my father looked intently at the attendant and asked him if he knew him from somewhere.

The elevator attendant stiffened to attention, but before he could reply, my father had recognized him. 'Har Narayan?' he asked tentatively.

The soldier practically fell into his arms, overwhelmed. Too proud to introduce himself, he had waited for his company officer from the Walong days in NEFA to recognize him. One of the survivors of Nam Ka Chu, Har Narayan had been wounded and taken prisoner. By the time he was repatriated along with the others, he had lost all his toes—they had had to be amputated by Chinese doctors because of frostbite.

After that first encounter a steady stream of retired soldiers started to come and meet my father. A few days later, Har Narayan arrived with a JCO (junior commissioned officer) whose name I cannot recall. Soon enough, the three men were deep in discussion about the NEFA days, talking of comrades who had been so much a part of their lives. After having a couple of stiff rums prepared by the bartender (me), the subedar suddenly looked searchingly at my father and asked, 'Why did it happen, saab?' He then added: 'You remember what was said by General Thorat? You were there,' he said simply.

Seventeen years after the event, this was a name I hadn't heard before, certainly not in the context of what had happened in 1962. After the JCO and Har Narayan had left, I asked my father what all that was about. Lieutenant General S. P. P. Thorat, he said, was the man everybody expected to succeed General K.S. Thimayya as the army chief. That hadn't happened because the defence minister, V. K. Krishna Menon, disliked Thorat and had ensured that Prime Minister Nehru sent the general home. Pran Thapar was appointed chief instead. In early 1960, Thorat, at the time, the Eastern Army Commander, had visited the battalion that was preparing the defences at Walong. The general had been taken around the location and was briefed by Lieutenant Colonel Maha Singh Rikh. My father and the JCO who had visited us had been deputed to escort the general as his liaison team, so they had both been privy to the conversation between the army commander and the commanding officer (CO), Rikh. After making a few suggestions about the siting of certain bunkers and defensive positions, Thorat had stated quite categorically, 'You have three years. The Chinese will come down this axis in October-November 1962. They will definitely come.'

Thorat had then addressed the troops, said much the same thing and departed. 'If the army commander said this in 1960, how come we claim we were not prepared?' I asked incredulously.

'I don't know,' said my father, 'but there was talk of a war game conducted by General Thorat in 1961 where everyone other than the prime minister was supposed to have been present. I think it was called Exercise Lal Qila. There was also some talk of a Thorat Plan that drew a defensive line along the lower reaches that were supposed to be our defensible points. But at our level, all this was just talk.'

Since 1992 I have been working on various films on the history of the Indian Armed Forces. I began to realize then how little information there was about the actual events around 1962. For me, Nam Ka Chu had been the most poignant of them all because it concerned 2 Rajput, the battalion I was born into. But there were so many other units and events that one knew nothing of: 1 Sikh at Bum-la and Tawang, 4 Garhwal Rifles at Nuranang, 4 Sikh LI at Se-la, the Assam Rifles and 5 Guards at Poshing-la, the panic at Dirang Dzong, again 5 Guards at Thembang, 3 JAK Rifles at Bomdila and 4 Rajput at Lagyala Gompa in the Kameng Frontier Division; 2 Assam Rifles at Kibithu, 6 Kumaon at the Ashi Nullah and Yellow Pimple, 3/3 GR at The Ladders, and 4 Sikh at Walong in the Lohit Frontier Division, to say nothing of the Siang and Subansiri Frontier Divisions of NEFA. And then there were the battles fought in Ladakh, extending from the Demchok area to the Spanggur Gap, and then across the Aksai Chin region to the Galwan River Valley and the Qara Qash region to the Karakoram Pass and Daulat Beg Oldi.

Even back then I was aware that if I wanted to tell the story of what happened in that one month, I would have to try and peel through various layers of history, rumour, myths, half-truths and outright lies to understand why events played out the way they did. Even more importantly, I felt that unless one actually visited the locations, the complete picture could never emerge. If that logic was to apply, then apart from the various regions of NEFA, it would mean visiting East Sikkim, the Sikkim Plateau, parts of Kumaon and Garhwal, Lahaul and Spiti and the remotest corners of Nubra, Ladakh and even Zanskar.

It would take me three decades to complete the task.

Prologue

NAM KA CHU

Subedar Dashrath Singh was dying, slipping in and out of consciousness as the blood seeped out of his torn and horribly mutilated body. All around him, the bodies of men from No. 9 Platoon of 2 Rajput's Charlie Company lay scattered—most of them had been torn apart by mortar and artillery fire. The firing had died down hours ago as the last few men, reduced to using stones to fight, were shot through the head at point-blank range. Just a few minutes earlier, Dashrath had fallen to the ground as a Chinese soldier emptied his entire AK-47 magazine into his stomach. 'I felt no pain,' he would recall years later, 'just relief that the nightmare was over. The manner in which we were deployed, we had known for days that we stood no chance if and when the attack came.'

But the end refused to come. Every time he was about to slip into merciful unconsciousness, he would jerk back to wakefulness. Daylight gave way to darkness, during which time many of those, both Indian and Chinese who were still breathing, died. Some went silently, without a whimper, while others begged to be put out of their agony. A soldier propped up against a tree trunk, his legs blown off, moaned for a few hours, then fell silent as he froze to death. Yet, some held on, their bodies defying their wounds and the terrible cold.

What does a dying man think about? Just eleven days ago, on 9 October 1962, Dashrath, along with all the officers and other JCOs of 2 Rajput and 9 Punjab, had been ushered into the presence of Lieutenant General B. M. 'Bijji' Kaul, who had been camping at the Bridge 3 location (at Nam Ka Chu) for the last four days. Flanking Kaul, the newly anointed IV Corps Commander, was Major General Niranjan Prasad, the GOC (general officer commanding) of the Red Eagles, the famous 4 Division of the Indian Army. Others among the red-tabbed brass hats were the commander of 7 Infantry Brigade, Brigadier John Dalvi, and Brigadier K. K. Singh, the BGS (brigadier general staff) of the corps. In addition, the commanding officers of the three battalions that made up 7 Brigade—Lieutenant Colonels Maha Singh Rikh of 2 Rajput, B. S. Ahluwalia of 1/9 Gorkha Rifles and R. N. Mishra of 9 Punjab—were all in attendance.

Even as Kaul outlined an ambitious attack plan to occupy the Thagla Ridge across the Nam Ka Chu, every officer and JCO present at the briefing knew the general's plan was nonsensical. To Dashrath's experienced ears, it sounded like the general was issuing orders for an advance the next morning across the river and up the Thagla slopes on the assumption that the Chinese did not exist. All the officers were sitting in stunned silence as Kaul droned on, using impressive jargon that included terms like 'positional warfare manoeuvre', something neither Dashrath nor any of the others present had ever heard before. Niranjan Prasad was staring at his shoes the entire time, while Dalvi meekly tried to point out a few technical difficulties like limited ammunition, lack of snow clothing, artillery support and other factors. The corps commander, deeming them minor irritants, impatiently brushed them aside.

Having spelt out his objectives, the corps commander asked the assembled officers and JCOs if they had any questions. While the officers were still recovering from the shock of Kaul's master plan, Subedar Dashrath Singh from 2 Rajput spoke up: 'Agar izaazat ho to mein kuch poochna chahta hun (If I have your permission, I would like to ask a question).'

'Haan haan, saab, pooch kya poochna hai (Yes, yes, saab, ask what you want to).'

Dashrath, who had seen five years of close combat with the Japanese in Burma and had then fought in the Jammu and Kashmir Operations in 1948, said: 'Yeh larai to maine pehli bar dekhi hai, saab, jisme hum nalle mein aur dushman upar pahar par (This is the first time I've seen a battle being planned where we are sitting in the valley while the enemy is holding the heights above us).'

'Yeh bhi pehli baar aapne dekha hoga ki koi general front line mein khara ho (This must also be the first time that you're seeing a general on the front lines),' was Kaul's glib response.

'Aapne apni baat to keh di, saab, lekin hamare jawaab nahi diya (You've said what you wanted to, sir, but you haven't answered my question),' said Dashrath. At this point Kaul lost his temper and demanded that the JCO be arrested on the spot and dismissed from service. While Niranjan Prasad and Dalvi tried to pacify the corps commander, Dashrath was quietly asked to leave the conference.

The 'attack' that was launched the next morning came apart the moment the Chinese came forward to meet the 9 Punjab advance towards Tseng Jong. Kaul, his bravado evaporating with every rifle shot and mortar bomb being fired across the river, beat a hasty exit for Delhi, declaring that 'the situation had changed' and he needed to confer with the prime minister. As he watched the retreating back of his corps commander, Dalvi and the commanding officers of the two battalions strung along the riverbed hoped that at least now the reality of the situation on the ground would prevail over political dreams, for it was quite obvious to all present at Nam Ka Chu that the Chinese, by reacting, had ended Kaul's dream of triumphantly leading 7 Brigade onto the Thagla Ridge.

It took a lot of skill on the part of 9 Punjab's Major Mahander Singh Chaudhary to pull his men back to the southern side of the Nam Ka Chu. General Kaul's little thrust across the river was his first real taste of combat where men had died on both sides. However, Kaul's parting instruction to both Dalvi and Rikh was that 2 Rajput, strung out along the mountain stream, should dig in where they were and protect the bridges, although they had no tactical value and were simple logs used by graziers to cross the river.

If the deployment prior to 10 October 1962 had been tactically poor, after Kaul's departure it bordered on the absurd. Despite the fact that the Chinese systematically and openly began to prepare for an attack, neither Niranjan Prasad nor John Dalvi took the initiative to redeploy the Rajputs, the Punjabis or the Gorkhas. Once again, every man in the formation knew that the Rajput positions on the Nam Ka Chu were death traps. Yet, for nine days, none of the commanders showed an iota of common sense, preferring instead to complain about their helplessness rather than prepare the troops to fight if attacked.

No surprise then that when the Chinese attack came at dawn on 20 October 1962, the Rajputs fought valiantly but hopelessly on their western flank. Others, including elements of 2 Rajput at Bridge 3, the Assam Rifles, 9 Punjab at Bridge 2, 4 Grenadiers at Bridge 1, 7 Brigade HQ and 1/9 GR at Tsangdhar either fled or disintegrated in the face of the onslaught by Chinese troops supported by artillery.

In the fighting that lasted but a few hours, the Rajputs, deployed along the Nam Ka Chu, had 282 of their 500-odd men killed. Most of the others were wounded and captured.

Once the firing stopped, the bunkers and crawl trenches would become tombs for the dead. The next morning, not only the Indian casualties, even the Chinese dead were covered with stones and left where they had fallen.

In 1989, an Intelligence officer of an infantry battalion led a patrol into the Nam Ka Chu Valley, the first after the inglorious decimation of the Indian Army twenty-seven years ago. 'There were skeletons everywhere, and we dug out quite a few—especially in the vicinity of Bridge 3 and 4, Temporary and Log Bridge. All the dog tags we found belonged to the dead from 2 Rajput, for they started with the serial number "29". Some were probably Chinese casualties, but we had no way of knowing. There was nothing much that we could do—we just stacked them together, poured kerosene on them, saluted and cremated them. Wherever we dug, we found skeletons. Very few could have survived the carnage.'

◆

But some did survive, simply refusing to die. Subedar Dashrath Singh is today in his late nineties, having served the latter half of his life as the ADC (aide-de-camp) to the Maharaja of Varanasi. Of all the stories of the survivors, his is one of the most incredible. When the JCO finally went down, he had been hit twenty-eight times in the stomach.

'I had no idea how many bullets had hit me,' recalls Dashrath, 'all I knew through the day and then the night was the bitter cold and the maddening thirst. I kept thinking if only the officers had let us deploy on the slopes behind us with just an early warning element at the river, we would have killed many more afeemchis [opium smokers, a derogatory term for the Chinese that was in vogue among the Indians].'

When the Chinese started sifting through the dead and wounded the next morning, Dashrath Singh was, amazingly, still alive, drifting in and out of consciousness. He was placed on a stretcher and laid out along with the others, both Indian and Chinese, who were still breathing. Suddenly, he was aware of a Chinese nurse bending over him. Obviously tasked with assessing the severity of their wounds, the woman had the power of life and death over the hapless men. Speaking to Dashrath Singh in fluent Hindi, she asked him where he was from. Though the JCO was from Etawah, for some inexplicable reason he managed to whisper that he was from Allahabad. The nurse looked at him for just a few extra seconds and then marked him as a hopeful case. The execution party following behind her accordingly bypassed Dashrath.

Strange are the ways of war. The Chinese woman who had decided that his other seriously wounded comrades could not be saved now became Dashrath's guardian angel. Every time the valiant subedar came to, she was right next to him. From the banks of the Nam Ka Chu the surviving

Indians were herded across the Thagla Ridge into Tibet. There, Chinese doctors performed a near miracle, pulling Dashrath Singh from the Danger List to the Critical List, no mean feat when it came to a man who had more than two dozen bullets in his stomach and a collapsed lung. At some point during his recovery, the nurse told Dashrath Singh why she had chosen to save him over the others. It turned out that she had done her nursing training in India, which explained her fluency in Hindi. What she said next almost took the wind out of Dashrath's other lung—the city she had studied in and fallen in love with was Allahabad.

The Chinese nurse would stay by Dashrath's side until he was handed over to Indian doctors at Bum-la where the wounded and the captured men were subsequently repatriated. The officers were separately sent back to Calcutta by air. Even after the formalities were completed and the men handed over, she sought out the Indian doctors so she could explain to them how to keep Dashrath's collapsed lung ballooned. She then turned and was the last to go over the heap of stones that marked the boundary between India and China.

BOOK I

Undefined Borders

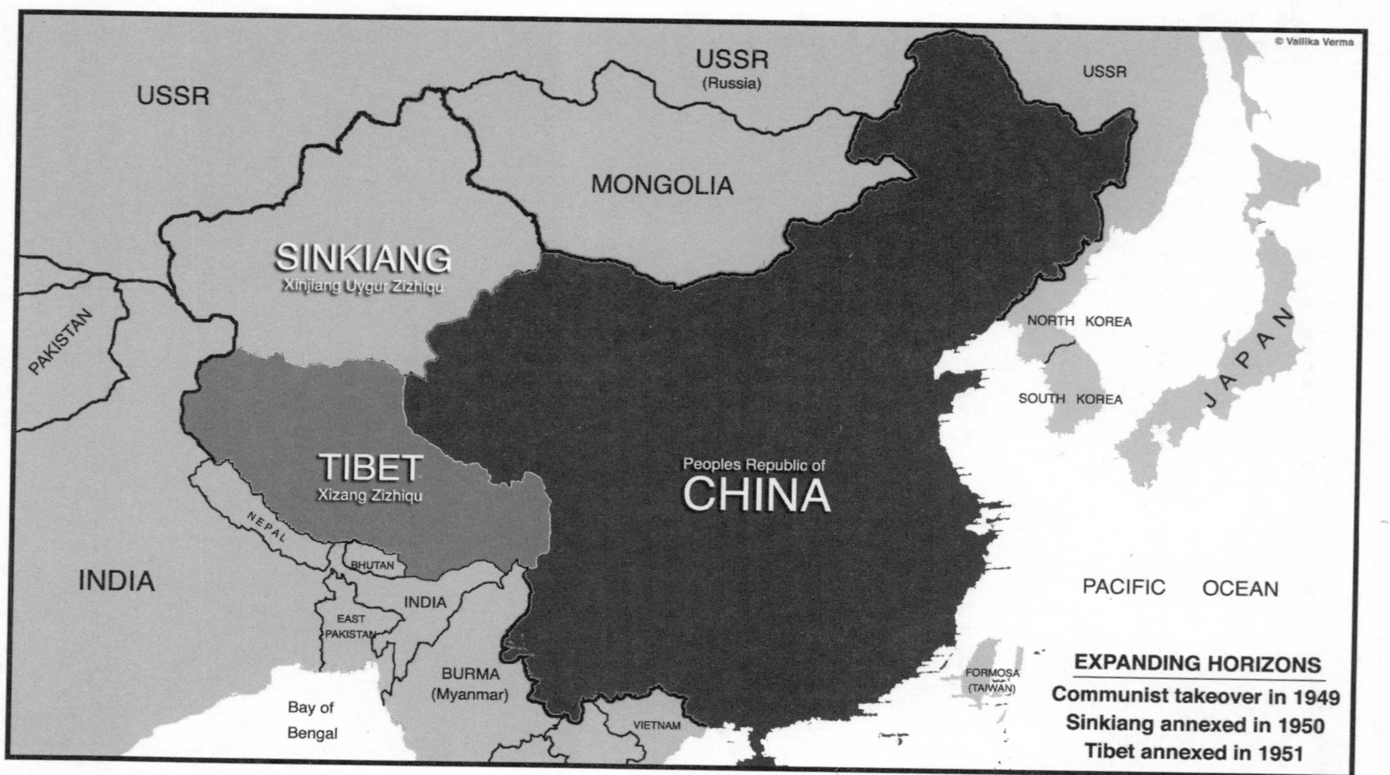

Maps are not to scale and their borders neither verified nor authenticated.

Chapter 1

GOODBYE TIBET, HELLO CHINA

THE DEADLIEST SIN

Jawaharlal Nehru stared angrily out of the car as he made the short drive from Teen Murti, his official residence, to the circular Parliament building in the heart of New Delhi. It was 28 August 1959 and the Indian prime minister was furious at the newspapers for alerting the people of India to the carefully concealed fact that all was not well on the northern border with China. The news report, which blew the lid off the Chinese attack on Indian troops at Longju in NEFA three days earlier, meant that Nehru and his government could no longer conceal the fact that the Panchsheel Treaty signed between India and China in 1954 was dead in the water.

As independent India's first prime minister, Nehru was no stranger to the horrors of war, having presided over the dismemberment of the subcontinent and the subsequent bloodbath that left hundreds of thousands dead. Hardly had the funeral pyres and the graves settled on either side of the newly drawn border than tribal lashkars supported by the Pakistani Army were let loose in Kashmir, leading to more death, rape, and destruction. Even as the country struggled with one domestic crisis after another, the prime minister sought to carve a place for himself on the international stage. He saw himself as the inheritor of Mahatma Gandhi's non-violent legacy and an elder statesman with a global role to play in the postcolonial era. The Ministry of External Affairs, under the stewardship of Nehru himself, was preoccupied with fighting India's Kashmir case at the United Nations while at the same time helping create the platform for Nehru to emerge as the world's leading Afro-Asian leader.

In the early part of 1949, China was not a player as far as India's national security was concerned. The only threat envisaged was from Pakistan, and Nehru airily talked of doing away with an army, claiming that the police was good enough to govern the country and handle external threats.

By 1950, the few eyes that were on China knew that Mao Tse-tung was preparing for a major showdown with the US Army in Korea. Despite China having announced its intention of annexing Tibet, the international community was caught completely unawares when the People's Liberation Army (PLA) boldly moved into Tibet on 7 October. When the Tibetan government turned desperately to India for help, Nehru seemed completely at sea. Appeals for aid were turned down and the Tibetans were advised by India to settle the matter peacefully, whatever that was supposed to mean. The fact of the matter was India had absolutely no clue as to how the situation should be handled.

The Chinese, with this move, had stood all previous policies on their head. They had brushed aside the British concept of Tibet functioning as a buffer state between China and India. 'Frankly, we were like headless chickens,' Major General D. K. Palit would say half a century later. 'Forget about the 90 per cent Indians who did not know where Tibet was, half the people in External Affairs could not pinpoint it on a map either.' Palit had been the commander of 7 Infantry Brigade and later Director, Military Operations during the 1962 conflict. 'To make matters worse, communists in India were celebrating the Chinese move while right-wingers were wanting military intervention with little or no idea what that actually meant on the ground.'

Brigadier John Dalvi further reinforces the point: 'India was in a quandary. The entry of Chinese troops in Tibet had potentially ominous long-term consequences. Tibet had been a buffer zone and had been vital to British India's strategic defence. The abrupt removal of this buffer would alter the geo-political balance, and henceforth India would have a live northern border to reckon with. There was a definite possibility that Tibet could be used as a springboard for aggression against India whenever it suited the communist regime in China.'

At the time of independence, India's official position was that it recognized Tibet as an independent country while also recognizing the fact that it was under Chinese suzerainty. After the annexation of Sinkiang in 1949, Delhi started getting alarmed. Overnight, India had a common border with China in Ladakh. As the communists tightened their hold over China, Chairman Mao declared that henceforth Tibet should be regarded as a part of China. By early 1950 the People's Republic of China (PRC) had made it amply clear that it intended to annex Tibet. In a meeting held in Kalimpong, West Bengal, between the Tibetans and the Chinese, General Yuan Zhongxian, PRC's ambassador to India, had submitted a three-point proposal that clearly said Tibet could either accept Chinese sovereignty peacefully or face the military might of the People's Liberation Army.

B. N. Mullik, the head of India's Intelligence Bureau (IB) at the time, had warned the Government of India that China would almost certainly invade Tibet and had prodded Nehru to consider the option of armed intervention should the situation arise. Accordingly, a meeting was held in the office of the foreign secretary, K. P. S Menon. Along with defence minister, Baldev Singh, and the Commander-in-Chief of the Indian Army, General K. M. Cariappa, India's first ambassador to China, Sardar K. M. Panikkar, was also present.

Mullik argued that by letting the Chinese have their way in Tibet, the equation on India's northern border would change dramatically. The IB chief stated that although neither the United States nor Britain would directly get involved, India could count on their covert support. The Americans, he told the group, had promised air support and were willing to airlift an Indian brigade to Chamdo in Eastern Tibet. Even if preliminary steps were put into place, Chinese Intelligence would surely pass it on to Chairman Mao who would then perhaps think twice before launching troops into Tibet. When Nehru asked Cariappa for his views, he categorically stated that military intervention on behalf of the Tibetans was beyond the capability of the Indian Army.

Cariappa said he simply did not have any troops to spare. If he had no choice but to send troops, only one infantry battalion (approximately 600 men) could be spared from Jammu and Kashmir. This battalion, given the fact that no Indian troops were trained to fight and survive at high altitudes, would have to be inducted into the Chumbi Valley (adjacent to Sikkim on the border with Bhutan and Tibet) over Jelep-la and Nathu-la, and at best one company (about 120 men) could be maintained at Gyantse (in Tibet). Given that the Communist Chinese had the experience of fighting in extremely cold conditions and were better armed owing to the vast quantities of US weapons that were left behind by the retreating Chinese Nationalist Army, the general felt Mullik was being too optimistic. Nehru, who had embarked on a deliberate policy of bringing China onto the world stage, then let it be known that he was not willing to intervene militarily. The Indian prime minister also felt any military offensive by India would severely impact her standing in the eyes of the world. Mullik was to write later in his book, *The Chinese Betrayal*: 'What Cariappa said at that time was indeed very discouraging and disappointing because I had also favoured military intervention in Tibet to save it from China.'

On 7 October 1950, the PLA crossed the Yangtse River at five points with the intention of isolating and capturing the Tibetan Army garrisoned at Chamdo. Commanded by General Liu Bocheng, the Second and Eighteenth Field Armies attacked Chamdo, the capital of the Kham region in Eastern Tibet.

Mullik was not the only one calling for a hard line to be taken against China's expansionist policy. Home Minister Sardar Vallabhbhai Patel, perhaps the only political leader who could challenge Nehru's vice-like grip on the country, also advocated a showdown with China. So did Shyama Prasad Mukherjee (Minister for Industry and Supply) and a host of others. However, practical considerations, along with Nehru's cultivated image of being a 'man of peace' perhaps resulted in India doing absolutely nothing to counter Chinese moves. Sardar Panikkar also advised Nehru not to oppose the Chinese annexation of Tibet. This resulted in a lot of hair-splitting about Tibet's 'sovereignty' and China's 'suzerainty' over Tibet. A few diplomatic notes were exchanged in which India expressed its concern and made the appropriate noises about respecting Tibetan autonomy and settling the issue in a non-violent manner. The Chinese, not quite believing their luck, nodded vigorously and promised to be good boys. The Chinese dragon then replaced the languid Tibetan snow lion on India's northern border.

SARDAR PATEL'S LETTER

At the meeting where General Cariappa had opposed Mullik's suggestion that India consider armed intervention in the event of a Chinese invasion, the most notable missing personality was the home minister. In a letter dated 7 November 1950, Sardar Vallabhbhai Patel, provided a masterly appreciation of the situation on India's northern border after the Chinese takeover of Tibet:

> Their last telegram to us is an act of gross discourtesy not only in the summary way it disposes of our protest against the entry of Chinese forces into Tibet but also in the wild insinuation that our attitude is determined by foreign influences. *It looks as though it is not a friend speaking in that language but a potential enemy.* (Italics mine)

Sardar Patel's assessment of the developing situation left nothing unsaid: with the arrival of Chinese forces at the very gates of India, the Himalayas could no longer be considered an impenetrable barrier. Commenting on the boundary that was drawn up in 1914 between Tibet and India in NEFA,

Patel predicted that the Chinese were highly unlikely to honour any of the previous agreements. He went on to make some critical suggestions that included the need for a detailed appraisal of India's forces and their deployment, especially with regard to the steps that had to be taken to strengthen the northern and northeastern border; the development of roads and communication networks, including rail and air connections; the need to be able to not just move troops but also back them up with enough logistical support that could also, if necessary, support armour; re-examine India's support for the PRC's admission into the United Nations given their blatant aggression in Tibet; and, equally importantly, the need to retain not just the Indian Mission in Lhasa but also maintain the existing military posts at Gyantse and Yatung that secured the traditional trade route.

This letter was written twelve years prior to 1962. Tragically for India, the Sardar died thirty-eight days after sending the letter to Nehru. The general belief in India is that Sardar Patel's words of wisdom went to the funeral pyre with him. That, as we shall see, may not have been the case.

Nehru may have been obsessed with his own image as a champion of non-alignment, but militarily that had not stopped him from eventually taking the right steps when needed, as when Pakistan unleashed its tribal lashkars in Kashmir in October 1947. Even though Nehru made some critical mistakes—going to the UN in 1948 just when a military solution to the problem seemed feasible and then supporting China on the world stage despite it having invaded Tibet—he could not have been unaware about the importance of the country's defence.

Further, the invasion of Tibet on 7 October 1950 had belied Nehru's belief that China would not actually step across the forbidden line. 'Liberate Tibetans from whom?' he would ask whenever anyone prior to the event would suggest that China was preparing to invade Tibet to liberate the Tibetans.

Sardar Patel's letter, apart from spelling out the new ground reality, was also an indirect indictment of India's soft stand towards China on the issue. Nehru, especially sensitive to Sardar Patel's views, acted immediately. Within days of receiving the letter he ordered the setting up of the Himmatsinhji Committee (also known as the North and Northeast Border Committee) in order to survey the problem of defence and security of the northern border. The Chief of General Staff (CGS), Major General Kulwant Singh, was drafted into the committee along with Brigadier Himmatsinhji who was the Deputy Director General, Military Operations in 1950, to study the problems arising out of the Chinese aggression in Tibet and make necessary recommendations.

The committee was to submit its report in two parts. The first part consisting of recommendations regarding Sikkim (which was an Indian protectorate, but retained administrative autonomy), Bhutan, NEFA and the Eastern frontier bordering Burma, was to be submitted in April 1951. The second part containing recommendations on Ladakh, Himachal Pradesh, Uttar Pradesh and Nepal was to be submitted by September 1951. The report was expected to cover not only the army and air force but also civil armed forces like the Assam Rifles which were under the Ministry of External Affairs.

A major part of the committee's recommendations focused on the Assam Rifles, which at the time was the only arm of the government in NEFA. Accordingly, the Assam Rifles was expected to defend the international border, maintain law and order in the tribal areas and take charge of internal defence at times when the police was unable to cope with the situation.

The report noted: 'It will be seen that the whole of the northern borderland is looked after by only two battalions, the 2nd and the 5th. The 2nd alone is responsible for the Siang, Dihang and Lohit valleys and the Tirap Frontier Tract, including the Ledo Road. The 3rd Battalion has the care of Naga areas, both in Assam State and the NEF Agency. The 1st is in the Lushai Hills and the 4th in Manipur. Five platoons, three in the Garo-Khasi Hills are serving outside their normal areas. In Manipur, besides the Assam Rifles battalions, there are the Manipur Rifles, a force of about 400 strong directly under the Chief Commissioner, who also has a police force. For the time being, a detachment from a regular battalion provides guards for the petrol pump, jail, etc. In Tripura State, the Old Tripura Rifles are now being reorganized as the 6th Battalion of the Assam Rifles. The enormous area to be covered in comparison with the limited size of the force has resulted in the wide dispersion in weak detachments. There are no fewer than 70 posts and in many cases platoons have been split to a quarter of their original size to man posts.'

The report suggested: 'In our opinion, the Assam Rifles are not in a position to defend the frontier against mass aggression and the word "Security" instead of "Defence" would better define their duty. We consider also that the "internal border" should not include the border with Pakistan as far as the Assam Rifles are concerned." The report then went on to suggest that "an expansion and the concentration and redeployment of the Assam Rifles are necessary for more effective occupation of the border area'.

By the mid-1950s, the Assam Rifles, in its various avatars, had more or less completed a task which had taken it more than 120 years. It had, by implementing first British India's and then independent India's Forward Policy (not to be confused with Nehru's subsequent Forward Policy), more or less consolidated the entire northeastern region. In the NEFA sector alone, new Assam Rifles posts were established all along the McMahon Line (the boundary between Tibet and India as part of the Simla Agreement, 1914) with extensive patrolling of the border areas. The Government of India believed that the Chinese would not actually go to war with India on the issue of the McMahon Line, and expected that the International Border would stabilize along the Line of Actual Control, that is, the border established by the presence of troops. By then, twenty-four platoons of Assam Rifles were deployed in NEFA, manning posts all along the watershed: Gemchram (13,779 feet), Taksing (10,500 feet), Dom-la (17,060 feet), Karbo (11,811 feet), Dembuen (11,800 feet), Malinye (9,842 feet) Mipidon (5,577 feet) and Jachap (9,186 feet). No government could have asked for more, for these hardy soldiers had always performed way beyond expectation.

In the Western Sector, the IB and the army set up posts in most areas except for Lingzi Tang, Aksai Chin, the Soda and the Depsang Plains as these regions were almost completely uninhabited and nearly inaccessible. Because of its very nature and sheer expanse, the Ladakh region had huge gaps between posts. So an elaborate plan to patrol the various sectors was worked out with the army. At that point, there were hardly any troops in Eastern Ladakh, only a single infantry battalion with its headquarters in Karu was looking after the area up to Chushul.

THE TAWANG SALIENT AND THE TAGIN MURDERS

During the Second World War, a certain amount of road building had begun in the Lohit and Subansiri divisions of NEFA as part of the attempt to administer the area right up to the claimed border as per the Simla Agreement of 1914. However, Tawang and the entire Kameng Division had been left strictly alone after having established the British-Indian claim on Tawang in 1938 by sending the Gordon Lightfoot Expedition to plant the flag.

After 1914, the only known ingress by the Tibetans into Indian territory was in 1942 when they occupied the Tawang salient and the area south of Se-la extending down to the plains near Udalguri. At this time, the British government was fully preoccupied with the Japanese in Kohima and Imphal and, as a result, had ignored Lhasa's incursion. At that point, the British and American governments had been following a policy of appeasement to keep the leader of the Republic of China, Chiang Kai-shek, fighting on their side in World War II. As a result, the security of North Assam had been downgraded. However, once the situation stabilized and it became obvious that the British would defeat the Japanese, the Tibetans had quietly withdrawn. Interestingly, no diplomatic notes were exchanged about the incident—both sides preferring to behave as if the incident never happened.

Immediately after the war, Tibet officially continued to affirm its acceptance of the Simla Convention. In October 1944, Tibet's governing council, the Kashag, had officially written to the Indian government that it 'did not wish to dispute the validity of the McMahon Line', but had requested postponement of the extension of the British administration to Tawang. In 1947, Lhasa accepted the transfer of power in Delhi without any declared reservations. It also tacitly accepted independent India's legal position that as the natural inheritor of all treaties between Britain and Tibet, it would continue to abide by them.

By early 1951, political officers were reporting increased Chinese activity in various parts of NEFA. Most of the Assam Rifles posts were on the McMahon Line, with extended lines of communication running through areas with little or no administrative control. Accordingly, a few posts were set up in the interior to meet tactical requirements. Walong and Hayuliang were established with a platoon each under the command of an officer, while two checkposts were established in the upper reaches of the Siang Valley. However, the governor of Assam, Jairamdas Daulatram, under whose control the Assam Rifles functioned, was most concerned about the Tawang salient where Tibetan dzongpens (local governors) and their henchmen were still exercising control.

Major Bob Khathing, the assistant political officer in Pasighat, was summoned by the governor to Shillong and ordered to take a column of Assam Rifles up to Tawang to establish an administration there. A former Assam Rifles officer, Khathing, with an escort of three platoons from 5 Assam Rifles under the command of Captain H. B. Limbu, reached Dirang Dzong on 1 February 1951. The column then crossed Se-la with considerable difficulty and succeeded in establishing an Assam Rifles checkpost at Jang. Khathing finally reached Tawang, where a representative of the Tsona Dzong dzongpen received him. The local Monpas, in light of the subsequent vengeance let loose on them by the dzongpens for having supported the Lightfoot Expedition in 1938, stayed away from the Indian officials.

Three days later the dzongpen met with Khathing who formally announced that from 'the third day of the Iron-Haired Year, corresponding with 9 February 1951 the administration of Tawang and its monastery would be the responsibility of the Government of India', and that the Tsona dzongpen or any other official of the Tibetan government could no longer exercise authority over the villages south of Bum-la that lay on the McMahon Line. The dzongpen were to cease collection of taxes and any tributes forthwith.

The dzongpen immediately referred the matter to Lhasa, while informing the Indians that they had no idea the area had been ceded to India in 1914. In no mood to wait for Lhasa's reply, Khathing started establishing his own administration by setting up the Assam Rifles post and touring most Monpa villages. He issued orders to the various village chiefs, started building bashas (temporary shelters) and also visited the lamas in the Tawang Monastery. Amusingly, Khathing had to levy an annual house tax of Rs 5 on each Monpa dwelling, for only then were the Monpas convinced that the Indians meant business and that they were, after all, citizens of India.

Though it will remain in the realm of speculation, it is quite likely that the Bob Khathing column into Tawang was Sardar Patel's last gift to the nation. An Intelligence operative who later worked for the IB from Tawang claimed the expedition was the brainchild of Mullik and had the blessing of the home minister who had instructed the Assam governor to bring Tawang under Indian administrative control. Even though the Assam Rifles was under the Ministry of External Affairs, which in turn was headed by the prime minister, there is little doubt that Nehru had not been informed. By the time he found out what was happening, Bob Khathing was already in Tawang.

Nehru was furious. Fait accompli or not, his immediate act was to summon the governor and yell at him. Shaken, the Assam government lost its nerve. On 25 April, when Lhasa responded on the issue, both Delhi and Shillong were imploring Khathing not to do anything 'without consulting us'.

Lhasa instructed the Tsona dzongpen to dig in and hold his ground. Accordingly, the Tibetans ordered all village chiefs to assemble at Tawang. However, by then, Bob Khathing and the Assam Rifles had made a favourable impression on the Monpas. To further underline his authority, Khathing staged a flag march where fifty men with their rifles and gleaming bayonets marched through Tawang. The meeting called by the dzongpen was a failure, with few village chiefs backing the Tibetans. Seizing the moment, Khathing put in an appearance and firmly told the Tsona dzongpen and the other Tibetan officials that they would be escorted to the Indian border post at Khenzemane. Should they venture to cross back into Indian territory without the administration's permission, they would be arrested.

New Delhi now had administrative control over the whole of NEFA. After the incident, Nehru summoned Khathing and vented his anger, demanding to know who exactly had instructed Khathing to take matters into his own hands. Nehru's reaction was fast becoming typical; even on the larger question of China and Tibet, the prime minister, in keeping with his image as a man of peace, refused to publicly castigate China despite the fact that all committees set up to study the situation on the northern border were indicating that a clash with the Chinese was a distinct possibility.

The implementation of the suggestions made by the Himmatsinhji Committee was not always easy. There were continuing intelligence reports that indicated increased covert Chinese activity in various parts of NEFA. As the Indian government moved to expand the administration beyond the 'inner line', there was considerable resentment against 'the intrusion by the plainsmen', and Chinese agents exploited this, with tragic consequences. North of Daporijo and astride the Subansiri River in the Siang Frontier Division was a large pocket of territory that had not been surveyed at the time. Full of deep valleys and dense jungles, the region was inhabited by a fierce and primitive tribe known as the Tagins. In 1953, reports had been received that a number of foreigners—both Chinese and Tibetan—had infiltrated the area and had distributed presents among the villagers while exhorting them to resist Indian administrative control.

A strong column consisting of twenty-three men from 7 Assam Rifles under the command of Major R. D. Singh from the Dogra Regiment was sent into the area to investigate the report. This column was accompanied by 150 personnel including the area superintendent and a political jemadar. On the afternoon of 22 October 1953, the party reached Achingmori where it set up camp. Sentries were posted, but as was usual, a large number of Tagins had collected around the camp, seeking salt and presents that the political officers usually brought with them. The members of the party were unconcernedly going about their various chores when the Tagins, given a signal, attacked the sentries with their dhas and hacked to death most of the members of the column, including Major R. D. Singh and almost all the riflemen. The few who survived the carnage were taken hostage.

It took a major operation in December 1953 involving the army and the air force to bring the culprits to book. Though primarily conducted by the Assam Rifles, this was the first time in independent India that the Indian armed forces stepped into NEFA operationally—three companies of the Parachute Regiment, the mortar platoon of 1 Garhwal Rifles, twenty-two signalmen, six Harwards from No. 17 Squadron, six Spitfires from No. 14 Squadron and five Dakotas from No. 5 Squadron.

PANCHSHEEL AND ITS AFTERMATH

Not only did Nehru continue to ignore the hardliners, but by the end of 1953 India had even initiated fresh talks on the Tibet issue with China. During the six months of discussions, the Indian ambassador to China, P. Nedyam Raghavan, failed to realize that while the Chinese wanted to resolve the Tibet problem quickly, their strategy with regard to the Sino-Indian border was quite the opposite. A memo accessed from the Chinese Foreign Ministry dated 21 October 1953 clearly states that the Tawang issue needed to be kept 'alive' and that it would be beneficial for the Chinese 'to drag on these issues for the time being'.

General Maharaj Kumar Shri Rajendrasinhji had taken over as the Commander-in-Chief from General Cariappa in January 1953. A committee under Major General Kulwant Singh was set up to study the military implications arising from the Chinese occupation of Tibet. The committee clearly stated that Chinese aggression was a distinct certainty in the next five to seven years, that is, between 1959 and 1961. The Kulwant Singh Committee recommended that India should immediately increase the force levels on the Indo-Tibetan border. Despite this, during the run-up to the Panchsheel Treaty, not once was the army asked for its assessment of the situation. Nehru, who viewed Mullik as a hawk and suspected his hand in the Tawang affair also, kept the IB chief out of the loop.

The word 'Panchsheel' denotes the 'Five Taboos' in the ancient Buddhist scriptures governing the personal behaviour of monks. This was suggested by Nehru to Chou En-lai, China's first premier, as the 'Five Principles of Peaceful Co-existence' that would be applicable to international behaviour of modern states. Considering the fact that the future of the Tibetan people who had been subjugated by military force was at stake, the preamble was ironic. The Chinese premier gleefully accepted the treaty which not only recognized China's possession of Tibet but, in fact, legalized it. Additionally, while allowing for trade with the Chinese government in Tibet, the Indians gave up their right over numerous facilities that existed in Lhasa and along the trade route that linked the Tibetan capital to Kalimpong in West Bengal. The Indian infantry detachments at both Gyantse and Yatung and the Indian Mission in Lhasa were to be withdrawn.

Nehru and his team were also under the mistaken notion that if they specified in the treaty the passes through which trade would be held, the boundary between the two countries would be defined. This was not accepted by the Chinese who claimed that all the major passes named in the agreement—Shipki-la, Mana, Niti, Kungri Bingri, Dana and Lipulekh—were well to the north of their claim line.

The reason for India not insisting on reciprocal concessions while recognizing China's suzerainty over Tibet can only be understood in the context of the 'Hindi Chini bhai-bhai' spirit of the 1950s where Chinese and Indian leaders swore 'eternal peace and friendship'. Prime Minister Nehru felt quite satisfied having got a written guarantee of good behaviour from China. The treaty was signed on 29 April 1954 at Peking. This, in hindsight, was a diplomatic coup for China. From India's point of view, it was a disaster, as it mainly served China's interests, although the Indian government's PR machinery heralded it as a triumph for Nehru.

Chinese cartographic aggression began almost immediately after the signing of the treaty. Chinese military garrisons mushroomed all across Tibet, reaching right up to the border with India. Simultaneously, within a couple of months of the agreement, the Chinese began laying claim to areas south of the de facto boundary. It became clear that the Chinese had been misleading the Indians all along. Work on National Highway G219 that was to connect Western Tibet with Sinkiang had begun in 1951 itself. With India having scored a self-goal with the highly vaunted Panchsheel Agreement, to save face, Nehru was left with no choice but to keep the flag of Indo-Chinese friendship flying on the world stage leaving the Chinese free to go about the business of further securing Tibet.

The next phase of the Chinese plan was to stress the fact that the border was not demarcated while at the same time claiming ownership of 36,000 square kilometres in NEFA and another 31,080 square kilometres in Jammu and Kashmir. Nehru broached the subject of the Chinese maps with Chou En-lai when he visited China in October 1954. The Chinese premier dismissed the maps as being of little consequence. Two years later, when it was Chou En-lai's turn to visit New Delhi in November 1956, he once again brushed off the matter. At that time, the Chinese needed another twelve months to complete National Highway G219.

Many observers lay the blame for the 1962 clash at India's doorstep, charging the Nehru-Menon-Kaul troika with provoking the conflict. War with China, even at this early stage, when neither Menon nor Kaul were in the picture, was inevitable. Just as Communist China under Mao had decided that Sinkiang and Tibet were to be annexed for their strategic ends, it had also decided that control over Aksai Chin was a necessity. Nehru proved to be no match for the battle-hardened communist leader. The Kulwant Singh Committee Report—another classified document like the Himmatsinhji Report and the Henderson Brooks-Bhagat Report—not only predicted the clash, it even got the time-frame right. Yet, despite repeated warnings, Nehru would continue to champion China's case for admittance to the United Nations while also preventing a discussion on the annexation of Tibet.

On 17 July 1954, after Chinese troops had crossed the Central Sector passes named in the Panchsheel Treaty, the Consul of China in New Delhi sent the first of many diplomatic notes to the Ministry of External Affairs.

> According to a report received from the Tibet Region of China, over thirty Indian troops armed with rifles crossed the Niti Pass on 29 June 1954, and intruded into Wu-Je [Barahoti] of the Ali Area of the Tibet Region of China. [Wu-Je is about one day's journey from the Niti Pass.] The above happening is not in conformity with the principles of non-aggression and friendly co-existence between China and India, and the spirit of the Joint Communiqué issued recently by the Prime Ministers of China and India. It is hoped that the Government of India would promptly investigate the matter, and order the immediate withdrawal of the Indian troops in question from the above-mentioned territory of the Tibet Region of China. We shall appreciate it if you will let us know at the earliest opportunity the results of steps which you are to take in the above matter.'

On 13 August, even before the Indians had replied, the consul was back with more details of the alleged Wu-Je incident:

> I am to inform you that further investigations reveal that they were a unit of 33 persons attached to the local garrison in U.P., India. The unit was under the command of an officer called *Nathauje* who was a deputy commander of the troops stationing at *Kanman*. Together with the officer, there was a local official named *Sopit Singh* of *Chinal* tribe in U.P., who was also a district magistrate of *Walzanjapur* district. Besides, there were a doctor, radio-operators and soldiers. They were putting up in 17 tents.

It signed off with the same lines about the principles of non-aggression and the spirit of the joint communiqué issued by the two prime ministers.

On 27 August, the Indians replied, denying any such infringement on their part. Countering the allegation, they also made the accusation that Tibetan officials had crossed into Indian territory, and asked China to ensure that this violation was not repeated.

The paper war had begun. Accusations and counter-accusations kept the consulates in New Delhi and Peking very busy.

Thirteen months later, it was the Indians who forwarded a note on 28 June 1955: 'We have now received a report that a party of Chinese are camping at Hoti with 5 tents and 20 horses and that they have entered our territory without proper documents.' They asked once again that China withdraw these troops immediately and refrain from entering Indian territory.

Till mid-1956, the bone of contention was the Barahoti (Wu-Je) region. On 2 May, India objected to the presence of a Chinese officer with twelve men equipped with 'tommy and Sten guns and telescopes' in the Tsang Chok-la area. Then again on 1 September 1956 'a party of about 10 Chinese Army personnel entered and took up positions about 2 furlongs from Hupsong Khad on the Indian side of Shipki-la'.

During his visit to New Delhi in January 1956, Chou En-lai made a pitch for a one-on-one swap between Aksai Chin and NEFA. In talks with Nehru, he said that China had accepted the boundary between Tibet and Burma as the 1914 Simla Agreement defined it. He added that the Chinese government was proposing to recognize the McMahon Line and would be consulting the Tibetans shortly. Later in the day, Chou En-lai suggested to Durga Das, the editor of the *Hindustan Times*, a quid pro quo, once again linking NEFA to Aksai Chin, something that was not acceptable to the Indian prime minister.

UPPING THE ANTE

Nehru had earlier dismissed reports about the construction of a road in Aksai Chin. National Highway G219, however, became a reality when its completion was announced in Chinese newspapers in October 1957. It was later said that part of the reason that India was not aware of the road is that Indian border patrols had never successfully entered the area at that time.

The news of the road's completion, when it was transmitted to New Delhi through its embassy in Peking, stunned Nehru. However, it is not true that the Indians had no inkling of this. On 17 November 1950, a report appeared in *The Statesman* to the effect that the Indian government had been informed of the movement of Chinese troops from Sinkiang to Western Tibet by its agent at Gartok. Whether the Indian government took any action on this report is not known. But the Chinese continued to use this route to supply their troops in Western Tibet. In 1952, Director, IB, B. N. Mullik, had reported that work on a highway linking Tibet with Sinkiang, which cut across the Aksai Chin, had started. In 1955, the Indian military attaché reported to Army HQ that the road was indeed being constructed and the road alignment had been completed. A year later, the same officer reported that work on the strategic highway had commenced and would be completed within two years. This time the letter was copied to the Ministry of External Affairs as well.

Because of the onset of winter, there was no immediate reaction from India to the announcement. Strangely, no one thought of using IAF Canberra to do an aerial reconnaissance of the area. In July 1958, a Chinese patrol had, for the first time, moved across the established line dividing Tibet and Ladakh and occupied the Khurnak Fort which lay well to the west of the boundary line. With the road completed, the Chinese were no longer hiding their territorial ambitions, which had so far been restricted to the Garhwal and Kumaon regions in the Central Sector.

Finally, around the same time that the Chinese occupied the Khurnak Fort, two Indian patrols left Leh to physically verify the presence of the highway. The patrol sent to confirm the southern part of the road sent in its verification by October, but the second patrol commanded by an Engineer officer that had gone to the northern side disappeared. On 18 October, the Indians finally confronted the Chinese:

> The attention of the Government of India has recently been drawn to the fact that a motor road has been constructed by the Government of the People's Republic of China across the eastern part of the Ladakh region of the Jammu and Kashmir State, which is part of India. This road seems to form part of the Chinese road known as Yehcheng-Gartok road or Sinkiang-Tibet highway, the completion of which was announced in September 1957. The road enters Indian territory just east of Sarigh Jilgnang, runs north-west to Amtogar and striking the western bank of the Amtogar lake runs north-west through Yangpa, Khitai Dawan and Haji Langar which are all in indisputable Indian territory. Near the Amtogar lake several branch tracks have also been made motorable.

The note went on to protest that the highway was encroaching into Indian territory, into regions that were well established as Indian for centuries and accepted by the Chinese as Indian territory. It also brought up the issue of the missing patrol and asked China for information on the party and 'any assistance that they may find it possible to give' to ensure that the patrol was able to return. On 22 October 1958, the three officers and eight civilians were 'deported' after being given a severe warning. In its reply to the Indian protest note, the Chinese government predictably charged that it was the Indian armed personnel who had intruded into their territory.

At the same time, India had sent a note to the Chinese government about their maps that showed the India-Tibet border in the east as running along the foothills of NEFA and ignored the McMahon Line altogether. In the west, the Aksai Chin was shown as part of Chinese territory. The Chinese reply to this note was cryptic and claimed that the maps were pre-liberation ones and that a survey had not been undertaken. They assured the Indian government that new boundaries would be marked in consultation with the countries concerned. The Chinese stand only confirmed what Patel had foreseen eight years earlier—the People's Republic of China had thrown out all the past frontier settlements that the Indian government had concluded with Tibet.

On 16 January 1959, India raised the issue of repeated infiltration by Chinese troops. It drew attention to a more recent detachment of Chinese troops that had crossed into the region on 27 September 1958 and later departed towards Tazung Dam in Burma. This was an important landmark in the fast deteriorating relations between India and China, for the Chinese had entered Indian territory in NEFA for the first time.

Nehru was repeatedly being outmanoeuvred by Mao and Communist China. Ever since 1954, the Indian government had been in a reactive role, responding to Chinese moves while keeping the situation hidden from the people of India. Even the news about the construction of the Chinese National Highway G219 through Aksai Chin was kept a closely guarded secret.

By the time General Rajendrasinhji handed over charge as the COAS (with the president becoming the commander in chief, the army chief was now known as the Chief of Army Staff) to General S. M. Shrinagesh in 1955, both the Himmatsinhji and Kulwant Singh reports had been in circulation for a while. The former's recommendations to push troops forward was acted on, while the second report was ignored. Given the prime minister's public stand on China, the Cabinet decided that no military preparation against it was necessary. This would become the cornerstone of India's national policy with regard to China. It was also the guideline for the government, the civil services, the experts, the press and the public.

On 7 May 1957, General Kodandera Subayya Thimayya, better known as 'Timmy' took charge of the Indian Army. Like General Cariappa before him, Thimayya too gave his frank assessment of the Indian Army's fighting capabilities to the government. He said: 'Whereas in the case of Pakistan I have considered the possibility of a total war, I am afraid I cannot do so in regard to China. I cannot even as a soldier envisage India taking on China in an open conflict on its own. China's present strength in manpower, equipment and aircraft exceeds our resources a hundred-fold with the full support of the USSR, and we could never hope to match China in the foreseeable future. It must be left to the politicians and diplomats to ensure our security.'

From Thimayya's statement it was obvious that at the time the Indian Army and the government were under the impression that in the event of a confrontation with India, China would have the full support of the Soviet Union. Thimayya also advocated that should the Chinese penetrate the Himalayan watershed and enter Indian territory, lightly equipped mobile commandos should be used to harass their lines of communication and the Indian Army should stay away from a conventional conflict. Only once the Chinese had entered the plains was the army to 'take advantage of our superior fire power to defeat them'. By this time, Nehru too had begun to realize that sooner or later there would be a clash between the two countries. However, from the various records available from that period, it seemed that the government was expecting only border clashes to take place that were unlikely to escalate further.

By the mid-1950s, over 200,000 PLA troops were stationed in Tibet, resulting in famine conditions as the country's delicate subsistence agricultural system was stretched beyond capacity. Ironically, the Panchsheel Treaty allowed the Chinese to import rice from India to tide over the problem.

By February 1956, a revolt had broken out in parts of Kham and Amdo in Eastern Tibet as local guerrilla forces took on the Chinese troops. The PLA responded by bombing and pillaging monasteries, arresting nobles, senior monks and guerrilla leaders and publicly torturing and executing them to discourage the large-scale resistance they were facing. As refugees from the Kham region began to pour into Lhasa, the Tibetans became increasingly agitated and non-violent resistance increased. Posters denouncing the occupation went up. Stones and dried yak dung were hurled at Chinese street parades. During this period, the directive from Peking was still to woo the Tibetans in Lhasa.

However, the situation continued to worsen, and by December 1958, a revolt was simmering and the Chinese military command was threatening to bomb Lhasa and the Dalai Lama's palace if the unrest was not contained. In March of 1959, the Tibetans feared that the Chinese were planning to abduct the Dalai Lama and take him to Beijing to attend the upcoming Chinese National Assembly. Five thousand Tibetan women marched to the Indian Consulate in Lhasa and presented an appeal for help, while carrying banners demanding 'Tibet for Tibetans' and shouting 'From today Tibet is independent'. As Chinese troops positioned sandbag fortifications for machine guns on the city's flat rooftops and wheeled in heavy guns, the Dalai Lama, wearing a soldier's uniform and with a gun slung over his shoulder, finally slipped out of the city on 17 March and arrived a few days later at the Indian border post at Khenzemane where he was received by 5 Assam Rifles.

Four days later, furious that the Dalai Lama had escaped, the Chinese gunned down hundreds of men, women and children, especially those who were camped around the palace. Two hundred members of the Dalai Lama's bodyguard who had stayed behind in Lhasa were disarmed and publicly machine-gunned. Lhasa's major monasteries, Gaden, Sera and Drepung were shelled—the latter two beyond repair—and monastic treasures and precious scriptures destroyed. Many monks were either killed on the spot, or transported to the city to work as slave labour. In house-to-house searches, any resident found to have any weapon was dragged out and shot on the spot.

On 3 April, Nehru announced that the Indian government was granting asylum to the Dalai Lama. Needless to say, the Chinese were livid.

By then, India's official head-in-the-sand attitude towards China's repeated provocations was starting to change. Incursions in both the Ladakh Sector of Kashmir and in the Lohit Valley clearly indicated that having completed G219 through the Aksai Chin, the Chinese were looking at further expansion. On 23 June, the Indian consul was given a note by the foreign officer in Peking that said: 'According to well-founded report received by the Chinese Government, the Migyitun area in the south eastern part of the Tibetan region of China was intruded, shelled (and) occupied by over 200 Indian troops. These Indian troops, equipped with radio stations and weapons of various types, were building military work around Migyitun.' This was strongly denied by the Indians, but now the obscure village of Longju (near Migyitun), was on the map.

In August 1959, two incidents quickly followed each other—clear indications that the Chinese were now determined to up the ante.

The Ministry of External Affairs recorded that on 7 August approximately

200 armed Chinese soldiers appeared at Khenzemane. An Assam Rifles patrol challenged them and requested them to withdraw to their own territory. Instead of complying, they pushed the dozen or so Indians back almost a kilometre to the Drokung Samba Bridge. After a while the Chinese withdrew and the Assam Rifles followed them back to Khenzemane. The Indians then established a picket there and raised the tricolour. The Chinese once again came back, but the Assam Rifles held firm. There was no firing, though there were plenty of heated exchanges and jostling.

On 25 August, the pushing and shoving war of attrition that had been going on for five years became more serious. In what subsequently came to be known as the Longju incident, a strong Chinese detachment crossed into Indian territory south of Migyitun on the NEFA border and fired without notice on an Indian forward picket. They then tried to arrest the entire twelve-man picket but eight Indian soldiers managed to escape. Thereafter, the Chinese detachment outflanked the Indian outpost at Longju and opened fire at it from a distance of about 700 metres.

The Longju incident made the headlines on 28 August 1959. The newspapers reported that an Assam Rifles post at this small village in the Subansiri division of NEFA was attacked without provocation by the Chinese and the Assam Rifles were compelled to withdraw after suffering casualties. Unable to keep a lid on the deteriorating relationship with China anymore, Nehru was left with no choice but to face Parliament later in the day.

For the first time in twelve years, Nehru was unsure of himself as he rose from the prime minister's seat in the Lok Sabha to face the rest of the House. Clamouring Opposition members who were demanding a statement on the Longju incident fell silent as attention turned to the prime minister. Speaking in his usual clipped style, every word that Nehru uttered stunned the assembled MPs.

For the first time the prime minister admitted to the people of India that serious disputes existed between China and India regarding the India-Tibet border and that several thousand square kilometres of Indian territory in Ladakh, was under Chinese control. He then disclosed the fact that the Chinese had built a highway across the Aksai Chin, adding that the government had thought it fit not to make the disputes public, as that would have made their settlement even more difficult. He then went on to talk of Khenzemane, describing in fair detail what had happened on the border and then finally talked of Longju, where he said that even as he spoke, the problem had yet to be resolved: 'They were in very large numbers, it is difficult to say in what numbers, but they were in some hundreds—200, 300 or even more. They surrounded the picket and apparently apprehended the lot. The outpost is at a place called Longju which is three to four miles from our frontier between India and Tibet as we conceive it.'

Nehru's next announcement was to have far-reaching consequences: 'We have in fact placed this border area of NEFA directly under the military authorities. That is to say it was being dealt with by the Assam Rifles Directorate, which was functioning under the Governor of Assam, and the governor is the agent of the Government of India, in the External Affairs Ministry. ...The Assam Rifles will of course remain there and such other forces as will be necessary will be sent, but they will function now under the army authorities and their headquarters.'

WHOSE LINE WAS IT ANYWAY?

This impromptu reorganizing of India's defence structure was done to reassure Parliament that the prime minister was on the job, and the announcement was met by the thumping of tables by Congress MPs who probably had no idea of the real implications of the announcement. Not only had Nehru ignored Thimayya's views on the availability of troops, he also discounted the dominant view in military circles that believed the Indian Army could only fight the PLA after drawing it to the plains—it is highly unlikely that Nehru had even informally consulted the army chief before making this statement.

Just as the Panchsheel Agreement had forced the government to hide the truth from the people of India, Nehru's unconsidered remark on 28 August 1959 had major national and international implications. The prime minister spoke to Parliament about the Chinese threat and the defence of India's borders for the first time, and also in the same breath declared that the army would be committed for the job. By committing Army HQ, which had no troops of its own in NEFA into the existing defence structure of manning border posts, the prime minister was committing it to a policing role. Any plans for the defence of the region that could be based on a forward line held by the police (Assam Rifles) and an inner line held by the army evaporated.

In his office in South Block, General Thimayya was oblivious of the drama that was being played out in the Lok Sabha less than a kilometre away. Until that moment, the army was not particularly involved with the day-to-day situation with China in either Ladakh or NEFA. Reports in the newspaper that morning had resulted in curious army officers trying to pinpoint Longju in the Subansiri region on the NEFA map. As far as they were concerned, it was just another border incident that involved the Assam Rifles that functioned under the MEA.

Thimayya usually went to his official residence, White Gates, for lunch on Fridays. As he gathered his cap and cane, there was a knock on the door and the Director, Military Intelligence, Brigadier Prem Bhagat, walked into the army chief's office. Without any preamble, Bhagat told Thimayya that the joint secretary in the Ministry of Defence, H. C. Sarin, had just briefed him on the prime minister's statement in Parliament. 'Nehru has finally told Parliament the truth about the northern border. He spoke at length about the National Highway G219 and the loss of the Aksai Chin. He then spoke of both the Khenzemane and Longju incident.'

'It had to happen... I'm surprised it took so long for the press to realize everything isn't quite *bhai bhai* with the Chinese,' said Thimayya, shaking his head.

'There's something else...' Bhagat hesitated, not quite sure if Thimayya was already in on the decision. 'The prime minister has announced that as of today the entire border in NEFA with China is henceforth the army's responsibility.'

The usually calm and unflappable Thimayya now stared at Bhagat, not quite sure if he had heard him correctly. He moved back to his desk and sat down slowly. 'What else did Sarin say?' he asked incredulously.

'Nothing more, really. From his demeanour I gathered the Ministry of Defence had no idea this was coming. If Mr Krishna Menon was consulted by the prime minister, he certainly did not inform anybody else in the ministry.'

After Bhagat left the room, Thimayya smashed his fist on the table in frustration. The prime minister had rarely asked for the army's advice on Tibet and China, but whenever he had had the opportunity, Thimayya had repeatedly tried to impress upon Nehru the futility of trying to take on China in the current state of unpreparedness that the army found itself in. Even though the prime minister had himself commissioned the Himmatsinhji and Kulwant Singh Committees to give their assessment, most of their recommendations had largely been ignored. Now, with not even one soldier in NEFA and just a single infantry battalion in Ladakh, Nehru was handing over a terrible situation to the army. Worse, by announcing in Parliament that the army was now in charge, the carefully orchestrated border moves by the police and Assam Rifles were history. Moving the army in was, for all practical purposes, an act just short of declaring war on China.

Thimayya called in his military assistant and asked him to send a message to his wife, Neena, cancelling lunch. A second message was to be sent to Teen Murti. The chief was on his way to see the prime minister.

◆

The political manoeuvring by Gandhi in 1938 to sideline Subhas Chandra Bose in the presidential race of the Congress Party virtually handed Nehru the prime ministership of independent India. Bose was perhaps the only Indian political leader who understood the significance of armed power as an instrument of state policy while being aware of modern politics. With Bose's exit and Sardar Patel's death in 1950, there was no one who could provide the necessary inspiration for the reconstruction of an army (that had so far served British interests) into an integrated military instrument that could identify potential threats and tackle them militarily.

Nehru, unlike Bose and Patel, veered away from building military power. Although, when cornered, he was not averse to using it—as in the case of Kashmir in 1947-48 and then Goa in 1961—for the most part, he talked disarmament, non-alignment and Panchsheel. In a speech delivered at the Kerala Provisional Conference in 1928, Nehru had spelt out his international assessments: 'No danger threatens India from any direction; and even if there is any danger we shall cope with it.' No surprise then that when the first Commander-in-Chief of the Indian Army, General Sir Rob Lockhart, went to Nehru with a formal defence paper that needed a policy directive from the prime minister, Nehru had exclaimed: 'Rubbish! Total rubbish! We don't need a defence policy. Our policy is ahimsa (non-violence). We foresee no military threats. As far as I am concerned you can scrap the army—the police are good enough to meet our security needs.' It's a different matter that Nehru had to eat his words by the end of October 1947 itself when the tribal hordes invaded Kashmir.

Perhaps Nehru could not have reacted militarily when China invaded Tibet in 1950, but since then he had had more than ten years to prepare, from the time General Cariappa had warned him that the army did not have the capability to face the Chinese. Despite repeated warnings from the army and the various committees, Nehru did very little to address the shortcomings of the army.

The yearlong fighting in Kashmir notwithstanding, Nehru was never comfortable with the armed forces. He would make the right noises at the appropriate forums, but his political indoctrination had consciously or unconsciously instilled in him a desire to downgrade India's officer cadre rather than tap their leadership potential and assimilate them into the machinery of government. This in turn created a vacuum in the decision-making chain, into which the civil servants stepped. They in turn, to protect their own newfound turf, played the game of isolating and dominating the military even further, taking important military decisions that they were not equipped to handle. At a personal level, Nehru was not impressed with most of senior officers and found them shallow, posturing caricatures, generally aping the British in their mannerisms and who had taken no interest in the freedom movement.

To make matters worse, Nehru, along with other politicians, began to develop a deep-seated paranoia about the army. Many other countries that had become independent after World War II fell prey to military coups (the most pertinent example being Pakistan). In view of this, politicians and bureaucrats pushed through mindless measures that systematically downgraded the status and influence of the army.

As he drove from South Block to Teen Murti, Thimayya was acutely aware of the prime minister's deep distrust of the military. Even before he took over from General S. M. Shrinagesh, Thimayya had made no bones about the fact that he was deeply distressed by the continuous neglect of the army. Publicly Nehru was seen to be fond of Timmy; however, behind his back, the prime minister adopted tactics that clearly indicated that he viewed Thimayya as a rival who could challenge his position as the undisputed head of the Indian Union. Given the general's track record in World War II—Thimayya had been the first and only Indian officer to command a fighting brigade in the Arakan where he had been awarded the Distinguished Service Order (DSO)—and the role played by him in the Jammu and Kashmir Operations, Nehru knew he could not browbeat him.

Timmy was universally respected. Not only the officers and soldiers under his command, even the rest of India had eagerly awaited his leadership of the army. The announcement of his impending appointment had led to an editorial comment in the *Times of India*: 'A thrill has just passed through the Army. The signal has gone out that Timmy is on.' In the meantime, just twenty days before Thimayya took charge of the army, Nehru had replaced the defence minister, Kailash Nath Katju, with Vengalil Krishnan Krishna Menon.

Nehru was waiting for Thimayya and for the first time, the normally reticent Timmy exchanged angry words with the prime minister. He told Nehru that his arbitrary decision of making NEFA the responsibility of the army, made public in Parliament, was preposterous and completely against

Indian interests. Thimayya felt that Nehru had completely compromised the army.

Without providing the additional resources required, handing over the borders to the army was a meaningless gesture; this would allow the Chinese the opportunity to claim that the Indians were the aggressors, for they always went to great pains to describe their own troops as border guards. Thimayya asked Nehru to find a way out of the mess in the next couple of weeks, after which he departed. Immediately after Thimayya's departure, the shaken prime minister summoned Krishna Menon to Teen Murti.

Nehru and Krishna Menon knew that the prime minister was in serious trouble. He had got away with the admission in Parliament earlier in the day only because the triple whammy—ongoing clashes on the border, the construction of National Highway G219 across the Aksai Chin and the Khenzemane and Longju incidents—had come as a shock to the members of the House. At any rate, it was unlikely that any of the parliamentarians knew the terrain or understood matters pertaining to the military to raise any meaningful questions. Thimayya wanted Nehru to undo the mistake; but should the prime minister formally withdraw his statement about deploying the army and revert to the previous arrangement, he would be committing political hara-kiri. The threat of Thimayya taking over the reins of government, at least in Nehru's mind, was very real.

Politics is full of subterfuge, and survival, when the chips are down, is perhaps the biggest challenge. Not only did the Nehru-Menon team now have to survive, they had to neutralize Thimayya. Three days later, Krishna Menon sent for Thimayya in 'a highly excited state of mind' and vented his anger at the chief for having approached the prime minister directly, suggesting instead that the matter should have been resolved at his level. Threatening Thimayya of 'possible political repercussions if the matter became public' Krishna Menon ended the meeting. A seething Thimayya returned to his office, and after a brief conversation with his wife, Neena, promptly sent in his resignation letter.

The letter, which was received by Teen Murti on the afternoon of 31 August, was put up to Nehru who promptly sent for Thimayya in the afternoon. By now Nehru was far more assured in his manner, using his authority and personal charm to good effect. After a long conversation in which the prime minister persuaded the army chief to withdraw his resignation letter in the larger interest of the nation, especially since the problem with the Chinese had flared up, the matter of the resignation was deemed closed.

However, after Thimayya's departure, news of his resignation was deliberately leaked to the media while the subsequent rescinding of the letter was held back. Quite expectedly, the Thimayya resignation made banner headlines the next morning. Through the day, there was no formal reaction from the government, as the prime minister was preoccupied with General Ayub Khan, the president of Pakistan, who was in transit through New Delhi. By the evening the Press Trust of India had announced that Krishna Menon had also resigned, only to withdraw its report a short while later.

On 2 September 1959, the prime minister once again rose in Parliament to make a statement. He told the Lok Sabha that he had persuaded the chief to withdraw his resignation. He then went on to speak about the supremacy of the civilian authority over the military and then, had surprisingly, proceeded to castigate Thimayya, saying the issues that led to his resignation were 'rather trivial and of no consequence', and that they arose 'from temperamental differences'. He then chided the chief and reproached him for 'wanting to quit in the midst of the Sino-Indian border crisis'.

Even today, the contents of Thimayya's resignation letter remain a highly guarded secret. Instead, vague stories about Thimayya's resignation were routinely floated where it was said that Timmy had resigned out of pique because of the manner in which Krishna Menon treated him. On careful scrutiny, that doesn't hold water.

The much adored prime minister, who could do no wrong in the eyes of the public, had betrayed General Thimayya. Trapped in this bad situation, the chief had no option but to quietly endure the humiliation and get on with the job of trying to prepare the army to face the Chinese when the need arose.

The prime minister's attitude towards Thimayya was damaging to the chief as well as the army. A whispering campaign started that speculated on the 'rather trivial' reasons for Thimayya's resignation. That the chief was unhappy with the defence minister's insistence on promoting certain officers was a well-known fact and pre-dated the Longju incident. It was hinted that the 'temperamental differences' were a direct result of this difference of opinion. General Thimayya was, by all accounts, a seasoned, disciplined soldier who would hardly have made issues over trifles. Only overriding national interests could have provoked him to take this step. Further, as a disciplined soldier he had accepted his prime minister's assurance and withdrawn his resignation. From the day he had taken charge, Thimayya had been focused on redressing the various problems that faced the Indian Army, especially the evolving civil-military equation where the army seemed quite removed from the decision-making process on matters relating to defence. However, he found himself up against a wall in the form of the Ministry of Defence, which was either indifferent or hostile to his moves. After the resignation drama Thimayya was seen as an alarmist and a defeatist. Having thus weakened the office of the army chief, the prime minister now placed his hope in the man he believed had all the answers. In the corridors of power in New Delhi, it was Lieutenant General B. M. 'Bijji' Kaul whose star was on the rise.

Chapter 2

AN IMPOTENT HQ

GENERAL EXTRAORDINAIRE: THE RISE OF BIJJI KAUL

In 1957, when it was becoming obvious to Nehru that his Panchsheel policy with China was going nowhere, he had turned to Krishna Menon who was described by *Time* magazine as being the second most powerful man in India after the prime minister. As the defence minister of India, his appointment coincided with the elevation of General Thimayya to the top job in the Indian Army. In his younger days, Menon had been one of the founder-editors of the Pelican imprint of Penguin Books in London before he went on to play an active role in the Indian freedom movement, taking a belligerent stance against Western imperialism. This endeared him to the Soviets and vilified him in the West. After Independence, Menon emerged as the spokesperson for India's foreign policy and the architect of the non-aligned policy. His marathon speech before the United Nations Security Council where he outlined India's stand on Kashmir made him a hero in India. During most of the initial talks between Nehru and Chou (until 1956), it was Krishna Menon who was invariably present, supervising the recording of each and every word spoken by the two leaders.

Temperamentally Krishna Menon was a loner, and having had no ministerial or administrative experience, he found it necessary to disguise this deficiency by affecting a perpetual sneer at officialdom. He also sought to dominate the military bureaucracy by trying to make a dent in the solidarity of its senior ranks. In this he succeeded to the extent that Bijji Kaul—basically loyal by nature but emotional, insecure and ambitious—fell for his blandishments and for a time an unwonted relationship was established between the minister and the general officer.

At the same time, Krishna Menon would have probably never have ventured into playing these devious mind games if the signal had not come from Nehru himself. It was Nehru who had built a strong rapport with Kaul; he had allowed this friendship to often overshadow the official relationship, sometimes summoning him for purposes outside the call of army duty, when Kaul was only a lieutenant colonel. In 1953, Nehru entrusted Kaul with the delicate task of overseeing the arrest of Sheikh Abdullah and acting as a political troubleshooter in Kashmir.

Unlike Thimayya and most of the other generals who were army and corps commanders at the time, Kaul had virtually no combat experience. Almost everyone who interacted with Kaul during this period comments on his hypersensitivity about his lack of regimental and active service. After being commissioned into an infantry battalion, Kaul had voluntarily shifted to the Army Supply Corps while he was still a junior officer. Kaul used the term 'national priority' to explain the reason for this shift—a somewhat dubious explanation as no junior officer was likely to be accorded that sort of importance. As a result, Bijji Kaul had not even commanded an infantry company, let alone a battalion, either in war or peace. Though commissioned into the army well before the outbreak of World War II, Bijji Kaul was assigned sundry jobs, none of which had anything to do with combat.

After Independence, his rise had been spectacular and completely at odds with the existing ethos of the armed forces where each appointment in an officer's career is a vital cog in his own training that enables him to take on responsibility at the next level. Back in 1947, Kaul was plucked from obscurity to serve as India's military attaché in Washington DC while also being a member of the quasi-political Armed Forces Nationalisation Committee. In 1948, he was again selected to be the military adviser to the Indian delegation to the Security Council on the Kashmir issue, which was where he first met Krishna Menon.

Nehru then entrusted Kaul with the command of the Jammu and Kashmir Militia, but he had to be withdrawn from this post owing to his differences with Sheikh Abdullah, the then prime minister of Kashmir. By the early 1950s, it was fairly obvious to the rank and file that Kaul was Nehru's trusted man.

After Independence, Kaul repeatedly served under Thorat. The first tenure was in Army HQ when Thorat was posted as the Deputy Director in the Adjutant General's Branch and Kaul was one of his staff officers. 'His posting to Delhi coincided with the feverish political activity connected with the trial of I.N.A. officers in which Congress leaders, including Pandit Nehru and Sardar Patel, were taking active part. It gave Kaul an excellent opportunity to ingratiate himself with them by giving them unauthorised information. He even went to the extent of removing certain papers from official files to which he had easy access and passing them on to defending lawyers.'

Again, in Korea as a brigadier, Kaul was on Thimayya's staff and worked with Thorat in a subordinate position: 'There Kaul had emerged as an ardent admirer of communism and seriously embarrassed Timmy and me by his partiality towards the communist prisoners.' Yet again as a major general commanding 4 Division, he had Thorat as his corps commander. Almost each and every time, despite Kaul's political connections, Thorat would diligently put down on paper that in his opinion, Kaul had reached the limits of his professional competence. Thorat would write later: 'Having known him for so long and so well, I am in a position to assess his good and bad points. On the credit side he was above average in intelligence and had immense drive. He was a tireless worker and good speaker though given to unnecessary dramatization. On the debit side lay his unbridled ambition—in the pursuit of which he was ruthless.' In an army where one bad report usually seals a man's fate, Nehru's intervention kept Kaul's flag flying.

It is interesting to see how the Chinese read Bijji Kaul. General Yang Chengiou, the Deputy Chief of General Staff, had led a PLA team to India in 1957. Apart from visiting ordnance factories and a host of other establishments, 4 Infantry Division (of which Kaul was then the GOC) had put on a demonstration on Indian Army infantry tactics somewhere near Ambala. In a subsequent meeting in Peking, Chairman Mao had asked Yang Chengiou to brief the assembled Chinese leadership on his perception of Kaul.

> Five years ago, I led a military delegation to India. Kaul was then commander of the 4th Division. When he was young he had graduated from the Royal British Military College at Sandhurst. He had probably participated in war in Burma during World War II but he probably has no experience of a real war. His colleagues ridicule him as a General who has never fought a war. During our visit the reason why he put on a demonstration of tactical offensive was, from one point of view, for building up his own image…
>
> …at that time, the demonstration was very well conceived, very tight, as if there was nothing left out. But precisely because of this, I felt that it very much resembled a staged play. Every little detail of whole plan was held in his head. On this point, I admired his intelligence and meticulousness. I did not have much contact with Kaul but generally felt that he was a determined and sensitive person.

> He was inclined to listen to the opinion of his officials and soldiers but not to those of the Generals. That was the fatal flaw in him. He liked music, plays, trekking; he often went on inspection tours of posts in the snow-bound Ji-Jie high mountains. He has experienced danger on quite a few occasions. Those who like him call him a 'brave spirit/devil' a mysterious character in Indian mythology. Last year, he received the Vishisht Seva award 1st class from Nehru himself. That is high merit.

Even if we suspect that the authors, Sun Xiao and Chen Zhibin (both of whom served in the PLA before co-authoring *The Snows of the Himalayas: The True History of the China War*), tailored the quoted conversations, General Yang Chengiou and the Chinese seem to have, in their brief interaction, seen what Nehru and Krishna Menon failed to see for decades. A quasi-political senior officer in the structured confines of any army would threaten its very core. Not surprising then, that when Krishna Menon pushed for Kaul's induction into the decision-making level at Army HQ, General Thimayya tried to put his foot down. 'Every sepoy in the Army knows that Kaul has never been a combat soldier. You cannot hide that sort of thing in the Army. The officers do not respect Kaul.'

This sentiment became the rallying point for the Opposition to question the government's motives in clearing the way for Kaul's promotion, each time twisting the promotion criteria to favour him at the expense of others. In Parliament, Nehru eulogized Bijji Kaul, saying he was one of the best infantry officers in the army. When J. B. Kripalani, leader of the Opposition, questioned this, saying that Kaul's only achievement was Op Amar (an operation where the army built houses in Ambala), Nehru countered by saying that Kaul was an officer who had been in the infantry for twenty-five out of the twenty-eight years of his service. He reiterated his confidence in Kaul as 'one of our brightest and best officers in the army'.

While doors were being opened for Kaul with scant regard to his actual level of competence, both Thimayya and the Eastern Army Commander at the time, Lieutenant General S. P. P. Thorat, had seen the Chinese up close in Korea and had no illusions about their superior fighting capability. The changing equation on the northern border ever since China had annexed Tibet, and the constant friction at the border since 1954 most certainly was of concern to them. Exercise Sheel in 1959 was based on the Western Theatre, where Thimayya had directed the exercise with Lieutenant General P. P. Kumaramangalam acting as the Chinese commander. The conclusion from this exercise was that the available Indian troops and equipment levels were sufficient to contain or even delay the Chinese if they decided to get aggressive in Ladakh.

Around the same time as Exercise Sheel, Thorat forwarded to Army HQ his considered assessment of a likely Chinese attack in Tawang and adjoining areas of NEFA with probable thrust lines and force levels. General Thimayya shared this appreciation with Menon. He followed up with a visit in 1960 to study the Alpine Troops of Europe and on his return gave a proposal to the Government of India to immediately raise specialized mountain divisions for the Indo-Tibet border. But when the recommendations based on Exercise Sheel and Thorat's assessment reached Menon, he shelved them, taking them up only after much prodding. He asked Thimayya to explain the rationale for such a large force as only small numbers had hitherto been involved in the isolated border clashes. The COAS duly did so, only to have Menon declare that it was 'too much' and it needed to be 'pruned down'. Thimayya resisted. And Menon's stance changed from discussion to confrontation.

Krishna Menon was also peeved with Thimayya because he had expressed his unhappiness about the preferential treatment being meted out to Kaul and certain other appointments. Kaul had been promoted to the rank of lieutenant general and brought to Delhi as the Quarter Master General (QMG) in July 1957 against the wishes of Thimayya.

HEAD IN THE SAND

Ever since the Chinese crackdown on the Tibetans in Lhasa and the subsequent escape of the Dalai Lama to India, public opinion in India had been slowly turning against the Chinese. The prime minister's revelations in Parliament on 28 August about China's incursions and establishment of control over the Aksai Chin region further added to the ill-feeling. Angry diplomatic notes continued to buzz between Peking and New Delhi: the Chinese said that the Dalai Lama had been abducted by Chinese rebels and whisked off to India, while the Indians said he was a free man and could go where he liked provided he did not indulge in political activities.

The Khenzemane and Longju incidents in NEFA had added fuel to the fire but in all the clashes so far, there hadn't been any serious casualties on either side. This was to change drastically within the next few days.

On 20 October 1959, the focus shifted dramatically from NEFA to Ladakh when two members of an Indian Police party under Havildar Karam Singh went out on a patrol in the neighbourhood of the Kongka Pass and failed to return by the evening. A search party during the night failed to make contact with the two missing men, so another party was assembled the next morning. According to a note given by the Ministry of External Affairs to the ambassador of China on 23 October in New Delhi, 'another party under the direction of a senior officer, went out to continue the search. This party was surprised by sudden fire from a Chinese armed force entrenched on a hilltop, which used automatic weapons and hand grenades. Apparently, the Indian personnel fired back in self-defence, but were overwhelmed by the strategic situation and the superior strength and firepower of the Chinese troops. According to the latest report, as many as seventeen persons belonging to the Indian party, including the officer-in-charge, have lost their lives and some others have suffered severe injuries.' India also alleged that the Chinese had used mortars for the first time in any border engagement, a fact that was denied by the Chinese.

Through a diplomatic note, the Chinese had subsequently informed the Indian ambassador in Peking that their 'frontier guards' were prepared to turn over the bodies of nine soldiers (just as New Delhi insisted they were border police, the Chinese always referred to them as soldiers) and return ten prisoners. Accordingly, the Indians were handed over on 14 November near Kongka Pass along with their arms and ammunition. The party had by then been in Chinese captivity for more than twenty days and the Indians were extremely suspicious that the prisoners had been subjected to Maoist 'brainwashing' techniques.

At the prisoner return ceremony, the leader of the group, Karam Singh, waved goodbye to his Chinese captors, immediately setting off alarm bells on the Indian side. Around the same time, Chou En-lai, in an interview given to the editor of a leftist publication of the India-USSR Society for Cultural Relations, claimed that Karam Singh had 'confessed' that the Chinese had not used mortars in the clash on 21 October as India had alleged. When this information became public, a wave of anger swept through Parliament and the Indian media.

The issue assumed great importance over the next few days. In the aftermath of the Kongka Pass incident, while India awaited a reply from the Chinese, it had been declared on 1 November that henceforth the Indian Army would take over the border from the border police in the Western Sector as well. Three days after the POWs and the bodies were returned, the Indians issued a formal protest note, stating that while in Chinese custody, the Indians were 'kept under severe living conditions' and subjected to constant interrogation, pressure and threats in an attempt to force them 'to make statements desired by their captors'.

Since the end of August 1959, the defence minister had been taking every possible opportunity to further humiliate Thimayya. As the Karam Singh drama unfolded, Menon decided to further up the ante against the hapless army chief. The announcement on 1 November that the army would take control of Ladakh, akin to the earlier statement made vis-à-vis NEFA after the Longju incident, was perhaps aimed more at Thimayya than the Chinese. For the political survival of both Prime Minister Nehru (and Defence Minister Krishna Menon) it was now important that the dovish image Nehru had so carefully cultivated, even to the extent of lying to his people over half a decade about the Chinese intentions, had to be replaced by a hawkish one.

Indian leaders who had not been blindsided by the Panchsheel Treaty and the 'Hindi Chini bhai-bhai' propaganda had regularly voiced their concern since the early 1950s. In April 1959, after the Chinese crackdown on Lhasa, Ram Manohar Lohia was vocal in saying India simply had to take its head out of the sand: 'When the "Baby Murder" in Tibet took place nine years ago most of the people who today are raising a hue and cry over the second instalment of Chinese assault on the Tibetan people were, as far as I remember, silent. Something ought to have been done then, something ought to have been said. Which, however, does not mean that nothing should be said now. But while saying it, people should not forget their weaknesses; as they say, when the peacock dances it should do well to be aware of its legs.'

But these warnings had fallen on deaf ears. By then, in the corridors of power in New Delhi, there were too many political games being played; games that would all contribute to the fate of the Indian soldiers who were then soon to be committed in both NEFA and Ladakh.

WRONG TROOPS, WRONG PLACE, WRONG TIME

By the end of 1959, 4 Division was on the move from Punjab to the plains of Assam for deployment in NEFA. Structured, equipped and trained for warfare in the plains, its transport and artillery were not suitable for fighting in the mountains, just as its officers and men had no real idea of how to fight even tactical battles in completely different circumstances. Despite the fighting in Kashmir a decade ago, Indian infantry divisions were still designed to fight the Burma campaign in World War II. Already, neither the CGS, nor the Eastern Army Commander nor the COAS were in the decision-making loop—the defence minister preferring to use Bijji Kaul as the sole point of contact instead. Not surprising then, that compelling political pressure forced the deployment of the wrong troops at the wrong place at the wrong time.

4 Division was given the task of defending the entire McMahon Line, extending from Khenzemane near the Bhutan-Tibet-India tri-junction to Kibithu on the Burma border, a distance of more than 570 kilometres as the crow flies. There were no roads worth the name, and lateral communication was virtually impossible. There were no shelters and very little animal transport. Also, with winter setting in, there was actually no urgency to induct troops as the Chinese too would have retired to their secure bases north of the Himalayan watershed to wait out the winter.

As the QMG and the de facto man at the helm of affairs, Kaul was in his element. His job profile required that he be most intimately involved with the maintenance of the troops and all the associated logistical problems. During this time, typically, a meeting would be called with various officers assembled to put forward their demands. Regardless of who was in the chair, everyone would wait for the QMG to show up. When he arrived, Kaul would hardly acknowledge the other senior officers present. Whatever the requirement, he would announce that he could only provide a certain quantity and that was it. He would then look around and say that they would have to 'make do' with what he had said was possible and that he did not want any bellyaching from anyone. Finally, he would announce that he was late for another meeting (either with the prime minister or the defence minister) and would be gone. The chair, even if it was the CGS, would then smile and shrug his shoulders: 'Well, gentlemen, you have heard the QMG; you can all go back and recast your plans accordingly. There is little more that I can do.'

As Kaul's star continued to shine brightly, there were many who were quick to align themselves with him. The senior generals who advised caution and tried to speak up were scoffed at as being alarmist or lacking 'fire in their belly'. Anybody who opposed the Menon-Kaul thought process or tried to speak up was earmarked for elimination.

4 Division had three brigades—of these, 5 Infantry Brigade was sent to Sikkim while its headquarters were to be in Darjeeling. That left 7 and 5 Infantry Brigades to be deployed in the whole of NEFA. The former was earmarked for deployment in the Kameng Frontier Division and its HQ was to be at Missamari near Tezpur in Assam. 11 Infantry Brigade was given the responsibility of looking after the vast area comprising the Subansiri, Siang and Lohit Frontier Divisions. The HQ of 4 Infantry Division was set up in Tezpur. Special trains carrying the troops began to arrive in Missamari.

1/9 Gorkha Rifles, who would subsequently become the vanguard of 7 Infantry Brigade, arrived on 29 November and was soon followed by 9 Punjab.

Normally, an infantry brigade would be made up of three or four battalions (each comprising seven to eight hundred men), all of which function under the Brigade HQ as a cohesive body in mutual support of each other. In the initial move to NEFA, 7 Brigade had two battalions, while 11 Brigade consisted of just 2 Rajput that was being commanded by Lieutenant Colonel Maha Singh Rikh. Travelling on special trains, the Rajputs with their surface transport had reached Missamari from Subathu, from where they proceeded to Lokhra. As part of their induction, they then spent the next few months doing jungle training while getting acclimatized to the conditions in Assam which were a far cry from those in Punjab.

From Missamari the battalion then moved even further east to Tezu, which would become its rear headquarters. In small batches, the men would then be airlifted from the small airfield at Tezu to the advanced landing ground (ALG) at Walong. The rough landing strip on the left bank of the Lohit River could take Twin Otters apart from the Mi-4 helicopters while the workhorse Dakotas used the landing strip as a drop zone (DZ) to drop supplies using reusable parachutes. The only troops ahead of 2 Rajput were a section of 2 Assam Rifles at Kibithu. Despite the chronic shortage of equipment and supplies and the near primitive living conditions, the morale of the troops was extremely high.

Even though almost two decades had gone by since the end of World War II, there were men, now senior JCOs, in the infantry battalions deployed in NEFA who had operated with or seen Chinese troops in action. Though Chiang Kai-shek's Kuomintang troops had mainly operated in the China-Burma-India theatre under the command of the American General 'Vinegar Joe' Stilwell and had been restricted to the northern extremities of the Naga Patkai ranges, Chinese troops were not very highly regarded by the Indians who, as we've noted earlier, referred to them as 'afeemchis'.

The mad rush to send the three brigades east towards the end of November served no operational purpose whatsoever. In a way it was typical of the new manner of functioning in Army HQ. In various offices in New Delhi, maps of NEFA adorned the walls of the big brass with little blue pins showing our troop disposition against the red pins that denoted the Chinese. The entire exercise seemed to have been undertaken so that Nehru could confidently state (mainly in Parliament) that his government had indeed taken steps to prevent incursions by the Chinese.

EXERCISE LAL QILA

Even though the prime minister had committed the army into NEFA after the Longju incident in August 1959, there was no actual movement on the ground to support the statement for three months. However, the incident in Ladakh in October and the government's fresh declaration that the army now had control of the Western Sector as well, forced Thimayya to reluctantly step aside and watch helplessly as Kaul took on the job with a coterie of his hand-picked officers who were loyal to him. Once 4 Infantry Division was asked to unstick itself from Ambala and, along with three of its brigades, move immediately to NEFA, Thimayya discussed the matter with both his Western and Eastern Army Commanders—Lieutenant Generals Pran Thapar and S. P. P. Thorat. The COAS asked Thorat to conduct a full-scale exercise at the Eastern Command HQ in Lucknow. It was Thimayya's last-ditch effort to make Nehru and Krishna Menon see the entire picture and take on the Chinese in a manner where India could have a reasonable chance to defend itself.

Thorat's suggestions dated back to 1958, a full four years before it all fell apart on 20 October 1962 on the Nam Ka Chu. Thorat wasn't some desk officer sitting in an obscure corner of the Ministry of Defence; he was the Eastern Army Commander. Further, he had the army chief, Thimayya, fully backing him. Accordingly, on 17 March 1960, Thorat held Exercise Lal Qila which further elaborated on the magnitude of the threat from China and the vast area over which India would be vulnerable. Though the event was attended by almost all senior officers and others in the decision-making loop, the bottom line was that the warnings from the army commander and the army chief were ignored. Over the next thirty-six months, arbitrary decisions with little or no military logic would be taken that would effectively seal the fate of the army.

Lal Qila was a two-part assessment of the situation vis-à-vis China, with the possible reactions of both West and East Pakistan and the implications of the conflict on Nepal, Sikkim and Bhutan. The first part dealt with the situation on the ground as on March 1960 (the present) and the second part was a projection of the situation in 1961 (the future).

Point by point, under sixty-four different sub-heads, the assessment and outline plan spelt out the situation on the ground and the options available to both sides. Thorat pointed out that while so far the threat had been from Pakistan, now there was no doubt that China also posed an equal threat on the country's northern and northeastern borders. He went on to enumerate the various incidents that had led to this conclusion:

China's refusal to accept the McMahon Line as the international boundary, the various incursions into Indian territory in UP, NEFA and Ladakh, and the fact that diplomatic and political solutions had not worked. He also pointed out that the army might need to render assistance to Nepal and Bhutan as China had laid claim to some of their territories as well. He then listed the army's responsibilities in the area: the setting up and maintaining of strong posts along the border so as to control all routes of entry into India through Tibet and Nepal. While Thorat could not call on Army HQ reserves at this time, he didn't need to consult civil authority in the Naga Hill Tracts Agency (NHTA) before taking military action either. This, at best, would give him a strategic reserve of a brigade if and when the need arose to pull troops out of Nagaland and commit them into NEFA.

Thorat's appreciation of the situation got more and more alarming as he focused on the emerging communication network in Tibet. Ever since the PLA marched into Lhasa in 1950, the emphasis had been on building roads—both strategic and tactical. China was connected with Tibet, Tibet with Sinkiang, Sinkiang with Pakistan and so on, often through areas that were until then considered almost inaccessible. While these were the larger and more prominent arteries that were causing concern in India's Parliament, a smaller but deadlier network was being built and working its way southwards to threaten Ladakh, UP, Nepal, Sikkim, Bhutan, NEFA and even NHTA.

Special Intelligence reports (available not only to the army and the defence minister but also to the prime minister's office) were constantly feeding in information that could hardly be ignored.

Earlier, in October 1959, Thorat had recommended a three-tier defence for the Eastern Sector, specifically NEFA. Subsequently referred to as the Thorat Plan, the suggestion was to establish small outposts as close to the McMahon Line as possible with the sole intention of keeping watch and giving early warning. These outposts were *under no circumstances to get drawn into a battle*, but were to fall back before the Chinese could advance. The second tier was to consist of strong delaying positions, which would force the enemy to halt, deploy and fight. This would lead to a delay, as the Chinese would have to regroup and bring their supply bases ahead before attempting to move forward.

The third tier was to prepare tactical ground of their choosing where the Indian troops could take up positions that would have supply lines that could be maintained from the plains, thus turning the difficulties of the terrain to their advantage. The Chinese then would have absolutely no choice but to fight with their lines of communication extended.

The defensive line was accordingly drawn, extending west to east along Tawang-Bomdila-Ziro-Daporijo-Along-Roing-Teju-Lohitpur-Hayuliang-Jairampur. In his introduction to the exercise, Thorat had commented: 'It must be appreciated that in the early stages of any war the attacker will always have the initial advantage over the defender because he can choose the time and place for the attack and can therefore apply all his strength at any given point. Therefore, he will get into the defender's territory and make penetrations. If this happens the defender must not lose heart because he will have his say when he has located the main thrust and moves his reserves to meet it—very likely on ground of his choosing. There he will give battle, stabilize the situation, and then steadily push the enemy back. This process may take a long time, but there is no other answer to it when one is on the defensive. I make this statement pointedly because I realize that even small-scale penetrations will have great demoralizing effect on the country's morale and may embarrass the government. We must therefore condition our minds to expect and accept these inevitable penetrations in the early stages of the war.

'Even if I were to disperse my force on a "thin red line" all along the border, it will serve no useful purpose for I shall be weak everywhere and strong nowhere. Therefore, I do not propose to do so.

'As the enemy comes further away from his bases on the other side of the McMahon Line, his communications will get stretched. He will find it increasingly more difficult to maintain his forces, and this situation will get worse day by day. A stage will come when his maintenance difficulties will be the same as mine, and it is then that I shall give him the first real fight. The scene of this battle will be a line running east to west through the middle of NEFA which for purposes of this paper, I shall call the Defence Line.'

Frankly, this was not a plan that needed an army commander's input; it should have been obvious to any soldier with the slightest common sense. Unfortunately, the exact alignment of the Thorat Line was flawed as it was drawn off a map. In the Kameng Division, the Tawang-Bomdila axis was actually a line of withdrawal, ignoring Se-la as a possible defensive position. If maintaining the defensive line from the plains was to be the criterion, then the line ought to have run from the Manda-la Heights (the approach to Dirang Dzong running parallel to the Indo-Bhutan border) to Bomdila, which was thirty kilometres to its west. The other problem was that each anticipated point of entry of the enemy needed to be dealt with separately as there was no lateral communication between these points.

THORAT'S DEFENSIVE LINE

In 2006, Major General D. K. Palit, accompanied by a bottle of Black Dog scotch whisky, visited us at home in Gurgaon. I had just got my hands on the Lal Qila file and was extremely keen to go over its contents with the general. Palit had been John Dalvi's predecessor, having commanded 7 Brigade and inducted it into NEFA. Apart from being one of the few officers at the time who had any idea of the ground realities of the Kameng Division, he was also familiar with the terrain extending up to Khenzemane. He had been Director, Military Operations (DMO) during the fateful period in 1962, and had also written a book, *War in the High Himalayas*, which critics rightly felt was aimed entirely at exonerating himself and the Military Operations Directorate in Army HQ that was under his charge.

'Thorat's so-called defensive line was completely at odds with what was being asked for by the government of India,' explained Palit. 'At the time, I too felt he was being a bit vague, and like Thimayya, was being a defeatist when it came to China. Thorat's defensive line did not cut ice with anyone because once the Chinese had chased away our border outposts they could easily halt at the second tier of defence having captured their main objective. It amounted to surrendering our territory without firing a single shot. It was politically unpalatable and no one in India was willing to lose even one square inch of ground.

'I was commanding 7 Brigade and was too junior to be invited to attend the Lal Qila Exercise, but my GOC (4 Division), Major General Amrik Singh, had attended. When he returned, he said the Eastern Army Commander sitting in Lucknow had no first-hand knowledge of the area and had based his appreciation and suggestions based on maps. He wasn't too impressed by Thorat's penchant for making sweeping predictions. He felt Thorat loved playing God. It used to rub a lot of senior officers the wrong way.'

Thorat's biggest blunder may have been to include Tawang in his defensive line. Interestingly, Palit claims that in his report to Army HQ submitted shortly after 4 Division arrived in NEFA from Punjab at the end of 1959, he had pointed out the tactical inadvisability of trying to hold Tawang. He says: 'After my reconnaissance of the Dirang Dzong Valley and the Tawang Salient, I concluded that the key tactical feature in Western Kameng [the vital ground in army jargon] was not Tawang but the spine of the commanding range stretching from Bomdila to Manda-la.

In contrast, Tawang was located on the middle of the Bum-la massif, not on a commanding crest line. Furthermore, there were tracks from Bum-la that bypassed the township and went directly to Jang and Se-la; an invading enemy could easily bypass Tawang. In my opinion these tactical deficiencies made Tawang an unsuitable site for the main defensive position.'

In his subsequent report to Army HQ, Palit was to suggest that: 'For the defence of Kameng FD the "vital ground" was the ridge Bomdila-Manda-la and this was where I intended to arrange the major part of my force. For the defence of Tawang [a subsidiary task] I was prepared to detach one battalion; but to locate the greater part of my force in the Tawang salient, across the Se-la massif, would only invite the Chinese to bypass my position, occupy central Kameng and move down to the plains. Thus, by concentrating my force in Tawang, though I might succeed in my subsidiary task, my main aim—that is, defence of Kameng FD and thus guarding the routes [through it] to the plains—would be jeopardized.'

Palit's assessment, submitted to Army HQ around the time Thorat was beginning to articulate his views on the defensive line, was also faulty. The brigade commander had completely missed the Se-la feature that logically should have been the second line of defence in the sector. At the time, Palit says he dismissed the concept of siting brigade defences at heights over 13,500 feet as being impracticable. Thorat, on the other hand, by recommending Tawang as the second-tier defensive line was violating his own principle of maintaining short communication lines. This allowed Thorat's detractors to accuse the Eastern Army Commander of making grand plans based on theoretical knowledge.

Later, Palit was to concede that it was a big mistake to ignore what Thorat was saying at that time. As the army commander, Thorat subsequently toured the various sectors; to zero in on his lack of ground knowledge in 1959 was grossly unfair. Thorat would have had no choice but to make his entire plan by studying the terrain on a map, for prior to the Dalai Lama's escape from Tibet in 1959, the government refused to entertain his suggestion that responsibility for the NEFA region (very different from manning the border, as announced by Nehru in Parliament in August 1959) be given to the army. There was so much acrimony and controversy over the 'proper border defence' at the time, the very fact that Thimayya supported this suggestion may well have hardened Krishna Menon's stand against it.

However, not one to give up easily, Thorat went and met Krishna Menon in Delhi. In his usual dismissive and sarcastic style, the defence minister said that there would be no war between India and China, and in the most unlikely event of there being one, he was quite capable of fighting it himself on a diplomatic level.

This period also coincided with Nehru's recent new administrative venture in keeping with Verrier Elwin's 'Philosophy for NEFA' that was aimed at protecting the primitive tribal people from a precipitate exposure to the commercial and often venal culture of the plainsmen. The last thing Nehru would have then wanted was to have the army swarming into the region. With the Assam Rifles it was different—the force had always blended in with the local people and was, in fact, an essential part of the tribal experiment.

Delhi's refusal to look north was extremely frustrating for Thorat. 'He knew the army would be left holding the can the moment the balloon went up, and go up it surely would,' said his son, Yashwant, nearly four decades later. 'Father was somewhat influenced by the US Army's tactics in Korea where the 37th Parallel became the sacrosanct dividing line.' Thorat was determined not to allow the enemy to cross the defensive line. He would explain to anyone who was still willing to listen: 'This line will divide NEFA into two halves. The area north of the defence line shall be known as the Northern Sector and the area south of it as the Southern Sector. This is where we must meet and demolish the enemy.' Unfortunately, no one was listening any more.

LAME DUCKS AND PAPER TIGERS

After Exercise Lal Qila, both Thimayya and Thorat came to be known as 'lame ducks'. Thimayya, by letting Nehru repeatedly have his way, was fast losing credibility with the army as well. By then, Krishna Menon was more and more dependent on the QMG, Bijji Kaul, to get things done in Army HQ and would even bypass the Chief of General Staff, Lieutenant General L. P. 'Bogey' Sen, on a regular basis.

The much-maligned Forward Policy of the Government of India, which according to many critics—including the journalist Neville Maxwell—triggered the war in 1962, officially came into being in November 1960, but its genesis probably lay in the Kongka Pass episode. Claiming that B. N. Mullik was the father of the Forward Policy, Maxwell would later say sarcastically that Mullik decided from 'gazing into his crystal ball' that India only had to push forces up to the Chinese pickets, and the latter would retreat. After 1962 most people bought these arguments for by then it was easy to blame the Nehru-Menon-Kaul troika for the fiasco. Some others argue that the Forward Policy may be Nehru's saving grace in a scenario where he had otherwise repeatedly capitulated to the Chinese. The Forward Policy may have contributed to the subsequent military debacle, which is another matter altogether, but to call it the primary reason for the 1962 clash is to buy the Chinese argument entirely.

In fact, on 13 September 1959, Prime Minister Nehru had issued this directive:

> The Aksai Chin area has to be left more or less as it is as we have no check-posts there and practically little access. Any question in relation to it can only be considered, when the time arises, in the context of the larger question of the entire border. For the present, we have to put up with the Chinese occupation of this north-eastern sector of Ladakh and their road across it.

A year later, in November 1960, he said:

> So far as Ladakh is concerned, we are to patrol as far forward as possible from our present positions towards the International Border. This will be done with a view to establishing our posts that should prevent the Chinese from advancing any further and also dominating from any posts which they may have already established in our territory. This must be done without getting into a clash with the Chinese, unless this becomes necessary in self-defence.

In any case, the Forward Policy did not particularly result in troops being 'pushed up to the border'—the border police and the Assam Rifles were already there, had been ever since the mid-1950s when the Himmatsinhji Committee Report's suggestions had been implemented by the Assam government in the east and by the Intelligence Bureau in Ladakh. Critics hold up the Kongka Pass as an example and say that by sending patrol parties into the area, the IB chief (who controlled the border police) acted in contravention of Nehru's orders. This is a deliberate, or perhaps an ignorant assumption on two counts: (1) the incident happened in October 1959 and was perhaps the catalyst for the Forward Policy being put in place a year later, and (2) Kongka Pass, where the Indians were ambushed, was in the area east of Leh, not Aksai Chin, which was the northeastern corner of Jammu and Kashmir.

K. Subrahmanyam, at the time a joint secretary in the Ministry of Defence, in a chapter in the book *Indian Foreign Policy: The Nehru Years* supports this argument: '...what the critics of the so-called "Forward Policy" miss is that the Chinese were constantly moving forward during the years

1959-1961 up to their "claim line". At that stage they put forward two "claim lines", the second one claiming more area than the first. Given the fact that the Chinese were brazenly lying that they were already in occupation of this area, when the Government of India were aware that they were not, it would have been imprudent on anybody's part to accept the second Chinese claim line was a final one.'

By throwing in a second 'claim line' the Chinese were only trying to keep the Indians off balance—a tactic which they adopted regularly with Nehru throughout the 1950s with great success. Physically, the claimed alignment cut across some of the river valleys in the Indus basin and into the trans-Himalayan area of the Karakorams. Though these areas were far removed from the Aksai Chin and Highway G219, the Chinese contention had to be tested by setting up a fresh line of checkposts. The new posts, fell somewhere between the old and new Chinese 'claim lines', and were sited not so much from a tactical point of view but more as observation posts to keep an eye on Chinese movements. Says Subrahmanyam: 'This was the essence of the so-called "Forward Policy". In fact the more appropriate name would be intensive or continuous surveillance policy.'

Nehru, having publically committed himself to defend the Indian border after acknowledging the failure of the Panchsheel Treaty, was at a disadvantage. So long as he single-handedly continued to control Indian policy, the Chinese had a pretty good idea of how India would act. Mao was much too shrewd a campaigner and Chinese intelligence was extremely up-to-date—there was no way that the Forward Policy would be seen as a provocative act. However, having laid the trap by declaring a second claim line, the Chinese promptly branded the Indian counter moves as 'can shi zheng ce'—a nibbling policy—based on the analogy of silkworms eating mulberry leaves until they are fully consumed.

Even today, most Chinese analyses argue that India was planning to take an aggressive stance in Tibet. They have persevered with the theory that India's objective was always to undermine Chinese attempts to rule Tibet so that India could turn it into a protectorate of its own. So long as this assumption continues to be put forth, and the issue is seen only from the Chinese point of view, the Forward Policy will continue to be labelled as India's biggest folly. In reality, the Indians had been patrolling much further forward prior to the directives being issued for the implementation of the Forward Policy. Now they were more or less operating within the Indian border in the area between the two claim lines set down by the Chinese. Maxwell and others who characterize this as the main provocation that hardened the Chinese stance are buying China's argument. That India had security concerns of its own is ignored and the implication is that she was continuing to act on British expansionist policy.

Many Indian writers have echoed Maxwell simply because the Australian journalist, having had access to parts of the secret and classified Henderson Brooks-Bhagat Report, acquired a degree of credibility for 'being in the know'. The hardening of China's stance was more likely to be related to the fact that the Dalai Lama had not only been given political asylum, he had been welcomed with open arms. In addition, the Indian stand on the border issue that no talks were possible unless China first withdrew from the Aksai Chin possibly hardened China's stand. From a Chinese perspective, their own position on NEFA was reasonable while India's rigidness on not wanting to exchange the two areas was unreasonable.

Prime Minister Nehru, having kept his countrymen in the dark over the differences with China for almost half a decade, now found himself manoeuvring through a political minefield of his own making; both in Parliament and with the media he was no longer the man with an unquestioned vision. With the uneasy situation with China now public knowledge, the prime minister had to take steps to ensure that the border stayed strong. Had he not done so, it is quite likely that today India would have neither Arunachal nor Eastern Ladakh under its control.

Says Subrahmanyam in defence of the Forward Policy: 'Those who criticize this policy have not suggested what alternative course the Government of India should have adopted. Do they suggest that the government should have left this area un-patrolled and with no check-posts at all?' It is perhaps worth pointing out that at that time the Chinese claim over Aksai Chin was precisely that—there were no Indian checkposts at Aksai Chin to suggest that the territory belonged to India. The fact that there were no Chinese or Tibetan or Sinkiang checkposts either did not seem to matter to them. After the fateful events of 1962 it is perhaps possible to say that the Chinese appeared to be satisfied after reaching their second claim line—but in 1959, it was impossible to be sure of this.

The problem that arose from having announced the Forward Policy was entirely different. Nehru's tendency to make grandiose statements in Parliament or elsewhere seemed to be aimed at his critics within India and the media, who had started asking uncomfortable questions. Nehru had demonstrated time and again his tendency to announce policy decisions that would leave the concerned establishment running to catch up.

Had Nehru paused long enough to understand the implications of

Exercise Lal Qila and the common sense behind Thorat's defensive line, he may well have still adopted the Forward Policy, but left its implementation to the Assam Rifles in NEFA and Sikkim and the Border Police in Ladakh. These lightly held positions would have, as envisaged in Thorat's plan, fallen back to where the army was waiting for the Chinese. Instead, Nehru brought in the army with the intention of holding ground, in the process forgetting that armies are meant to fight and not just hold ground.

7 BRIGADE DEPLOYS

We shall return to Ladakh in the Western Sector and Walong in the Lohit Frontier Division in subsequent chapters. For the present, our focus must remain on the Bomdila–Dirang Dzong–Se-la–Tawang and Nam Ka Chu areas, which were a part of the Kameng Frontier Division. When looked at from the Chinese side, the closest post in this region was Khenzemane, situated south of the McMahon Line along the north-south flowing Nyamjang Chu that flows into India from Tibet. Khenzemane was dominated by the eastern spur of the Thagla massif, while to its right lay the crest line on which Bum-la was situated. Further downstream, the Nyamjang Chu flowed under the Drokung Samba Bridge after which the Nam Ka Chu coming in at right angles from the west joined it two kilometres south of Khenzemane. After the confluence, the Nyamjang Chu flowed along the side of the Tsangdhar spur before entering the relatively broad valley at Zimithang. The river then passed through scenic jungle, flanked on the right by elevated plateaus, which were cultivated by the Monpa people.

The Nyamjang Chu was joined by the Tawang Chu just south of Lumla, from where the river entered Bhutanese territory and then continued southwards running parallel to the NEFA border before entering Assam as the Manas River. The Tawang Chu, flowing from east to west, separated the Tawang slopes on the northern side while on the southern side, the Se-la massif rose almost vertically. Once across the pass, the tracks dropped down to Dirang Dzong and onto Bomdila, from where one entered the plains of Assam by crossing yet another densely forested ridgeline known as Eaglenest.

Even though General Thorat, the Eastern Army Commander had clearly indicated that for the defence of the Kameng Frontier Division, the Bomdila–Manda-la ridge should be the vital ground, Division HQ kept pushing troops forward although there was little logistical support available. Jeeps and light vehicles could only ply as far as Bomdila, beyond which movement was entirely dependent on porters and hill ponies. The Border Roads Organisation had been tasked with extending the road, but at the time it took seven days to get from Bomdila to Tawang. 5 Assam Rifles, which was previously responsible for the area, had small shelters en route which were used as staging camps.

Major General Amrik Singh, GOC 4 Division, had attended the Lucknow conference where Exercise Lal Qila was held. He had returned to Tezpur echoing the sentiment prevalent in Delhi rather than Lucknow. He let it be known that, in his opinion, the Eastern Army Commander had been rather 'vague' as he did not have any first-hand knowledge of the ground, having 'prepared his assessment off a map'. Though the Thorat Plan suggested keeping the bulk of the troops south of Se-la, Amrik Singh ordered the 7 Infantry Brigade commander, Brigadier D. K. Palit, to locate the greater part of his brigade in Tawang.

Even though General Thimayya still had a year to go as COAS, Amrik Singh's stance as the GOC of a division was most revealing. Not only was the 'Menon-Kaul duo ruling the roost in Delhi, Mullik had emerged as the third, perhaps even more important centre of power. All said and done, Kaul was still only the QMG while Bogey Sen was the CGS, who should have been responsible for all tactical decisions and their implementation. Sen, however, chose to maintain a passive stance and watched wryly as Kaul virtually usurped his role. With Sen refusing to take responsibility, Mullik stepped into the void and became the de facto CGS/DMO. Unable to grasp the logic behind Thorat's 'defensive line', Mullik in his book, *The Chinese Betrayal,* wrote: 'The main objection by the Army [implying the Thimayya-Thorat combine] was that the ground was not suitable for fighting and it must choose its own ground. This was strange logic. Battles are fought on borders, be they suitable or not.'

After Exercise Lal Qila and the failed attempt by Thorat to win the defence minister over, Thimayya and Thorat seem to have washed their hands off the actual deployment of troops in the Kameng Sector. Under normal circumstances, as the Eastern Army Commander, Thorat should never have let Amrik Singh get away with his sycophantic stance bordering on insubordination. However, with the Eastern Army Commander and the COAS being virtual non-entities, there was little anyone else could do. Says Palit, the man directly affected by Amrik Singh's decision: 'I argued against such a top-heavy deployment both for tactical reasons and because of the absence of logistical facilities, but Amrik would not yield. He countered that Tawang could always be maintained by air and the plans for the forward concentration of my brigade must proceed apace... The truth is we were planning and operating in a doctrinal vacuum. I do not recall receiving any operational guidance except a general warning not to become involved in a skirmish with the Chinese or to approach within three kilometres of the border (except where we had already established posts).'

Having pitchforked troops from the plains of Punjab to Assam into NEFA, the last few months in 1960 proved to be anti-climactic. The border remained quiet; there were no infringements. The alarms that had been raised in Parliament and the high drama around the Dalai Lama's escape had begun to fade from public memory. The general belief, among both the civil and the military officers posted in NEFA at the time, was that the events of the past year were all a ploy to give China the bargaining chips it needed to get India to yield to its claim on Aksai Chin. In messes and clubs, people argued that after all Peking had accepted the demarcation of the watershed to delineate the boundaries with Burma, Nepal, Bhutan and Sikkim.

In August 1960, there were reports of a Chinese party having come to a remote monastery in the desolate and bleak area between Bum-la and the Nyamjang Chu Valley that lay to its west. Palit decided to do a detailed reconnaissance of the Tawang salient and he duly set off for Khenzemane via the traditional route that ran from Tawang to Lumla and then north towards the border along the river.

At Zimithang, the valley broadened considerably. The post commander pointed out the stark silhouette of a long flat spur high above to the west. This was Lumpu, a summer habitation for semi-nomadic goatherds who visited the region to graze their animals on the slopes of the Thagla and even across the ridge on the Tibetan side. Proceeding further forward, Palit noted the vulnerability of both the Assam Rifles posts at Chutangmu and Khenzemane for they were located at the bottom of deep valleys that were completely dominated by the heights around them. Backtracking to Zimithang, Palit and his party climbed the near vertical path to the 15,700-foot Chamling-la before proceeding to the Gompa at Taksang (referred to as the T-Gompa by army officers today). There the party spent the night. The head lama confirmed that a party of five Chinese had indeed forced their way in a few days ago. Palit found out that the Chinese had crossed the boundary at a place that he had previously believed to be inaccessible. Now that he realized that there was access via many game trails, he came away convinced that Bum-la, and even Tawang situated further below, were not suitable defensive positions.

Having mentally downgraded the military potential of Bum-la-Tawang Palit decided that the answer lay in fortifying Se-la as a defensive position. The sheer imposing look of Se-la beguiled him into believing that Thorat's defensive line needed to be pushed up from Bomdila–Manda-la to Se-la.

Needing a lot more information, Palit immediately dispatched his DQ, Major Raja Fulay, to reconnoitre Se-la's surroundings. Before Fulay could report back, however, Palit was posted to Army HQ 'with immediate effect'. This meant that Palit, the only senior officer who knew the Kameng Frontier Division first-hand, was no longer in NEFA.

THE CHANGE OF GUARD

General Thimayya retired on 7 May 1961, handing over to General Pran Thapar. Many service officers felt Thimayya should have resigned immediately after Prime Minister Nehru's statements in Parliament in September 1959. The constant eroding of his authority by the Menon-Kaul partnership saw him hang up his boots 'a sad and disillusioned man; his advice regarding China ignored and the Army in the same state of unreadiness for its ordained tasks'. On one of his last visits to some of the formations, he is reported to have said: 'I hope that I am not leaving you as cannon-fodder for the Chinese. God bless you all.'

With Thimayya went Thorat, the Eastern Army Commander. Despite being on the wrong side of the Nehru-Menon clique, many officers still expected Thorat to make the cut on the basis of sheer merit. With the departure of the two most respected officers in the Indian Army, a mass clearing of the stables was undertaken. Lieutenant General Bijji Kaul had already been officiating as the CGS for the past few months. Bogey Sen moved to Lucknow to take over command from Thorat, while Lieutenant General Daulet Singh was chosen to replace Pran Thapar as the Western Army Commander. In Army HQ, almost all key appointments—including the Director, Military Operations and Director, Military Intelligence—were to be staffed by officers who were handpicked by Kaul himself.

With the exit of Thimayya and Thorat, Lieutenant General S. D. Verma, GOC of XV Corps that was looking after Kashmir and Ladakh, also put in his papers. Krishna Menon and Kaul, not just content to see these officers go home on retirement, continued to further discredit other officers who were considered to be Thimayya loyalists. Just before Thimayya's formal retirement, the Menon-Kaul duo even went so far as to institute an enquiry on the charge of treason against the outgoing army chief on frivolous grounds. The charge of 'treason' instituted against Thimayya was symptomatic of the times. The highly respected Verma, who had been expected to take over Western Command, eventually left India to seek refuge in London in order to get away from the vindictiveness of the powers that be. Another officer caught in the crossfire of vendetta was Major General Sam Manekshaw, the then commandant of the Defence Services Staff College in Wellington.

As we've seen, Nehru's guidelines for the Forward Policy issued in November 1960 did not, at first, make any situational difference on the ground either in Ladakh or in NEFA, although excruciatingly detailed protest notes continued to be exchanged between the two countries. After May 1961, with the new command set-up in place—with Thapar as chief and Kaul as the CGS—there was a shift in the pattern of protests as the stakes were raised by the highly publicized Forward Policy. Though there was no major clash in the remaining months of 1961, there was enough activity in both Ladakh and NEFA for the Chinese to give a grim warning in their note of 30 November 'that they would have every reason to send troops across the McMahon Line and enter the vast area between the crest of the Himalayas and the southern foot'.

Meanwhile Nehru continued to put on a brave front. At times it seemed that his statements were all about assuaging the Indian Parliament and the media, which all was well under his stewardship. In October 1959, after the incident in Ladakh where ten Indians had been killed and Karam Singh brainwashed, Nehru had declared in Parliament: 'I can tell the House that at no time since our Independence have our defences been in better condition and finer fettle…' At the same time Nehru was careful to say that India should only operate in areas that were not disputed. It was no secret that he never expected the Chinese to expand the conflict beyond the odd border clash here and there. The state of affairs at the time was that while it appeared as though India had adopted a tough and non-compromising stand with China, in reality, with the few competent senior officers sidelined to make way for those who were rather despairingly referred to in army and governmental circles as the 'Kaul boys', the situation was very shaky.

At other levels, too, changes were taking place that would have far-reaching implications. Palit's successor in 7 Infantry Brigade, Brigadier Ranbir Singh, developed acute asthma that necessitated his immediate removal from Tawang. This created a problem for the MS, Major General Moti Sagar, who had to find an officer best suited to replace Ranbir Singh. Running into Brigadier John Dalvi at the Feroz Shah Kotla Stadium in mid-December where India was playing the third test match against Ted Dexter's MCC, Moti Sagar asked Dalvi if he would consider taking on the responsibility. At the time, Dalvi was on leave in Delhi, for he was posted as the Brigadier Administration in XV Corps overseeing the developments in Ladakh. The offer was accepted at once, even though it meant going from one 'field' posting to another. Though Lieutenant General Bikram Singh, the XV Corps Commander, protested vigorously, Dalvi found himself on the train to Rangiya towards the end of February.

1/9 Gorkha Rifles (GR), commanded by Lieutenant Colonel B. S. Ahluwalia, was stationed at Tawang while 1 Sikh, commanded by Lieutenant Colonel B. M. 'Baij' Mehta, was at Dirang Dzong. The third battalion that made up 7 Infantry Brigade was 9 Punjab under the command of Lieutenant Colonel Byram Master. The Punjabis had been airlifted into Tezpur in December even though there was no apparent reason for this move to have taken place.

Dalvi was taken aback at the complete lack of any real infrastructure despite the fact that 4 Infantry Division had been in the area for two years. The condition of the troops at the 'rear' in Rangiya and Missamari did not inspire too much confidence about the facilities further in the hills. The route from the foothills over which the Line of Communication extended for 7 Infantry Brigade was incredible. There was a steep, almost vertical climb through dense rain forest to Eaglenest at 9,000 feet, then a drop to Chacko and Rupa before another climb from Tenga to Bomdila (10,000 feet); another drop to Thembang and Dirang Dzong (5,500 feet) before negotiating yet another climb to Senge and the windswept Se-la (13,700 feet); once again, after dropping down to Nuranang, the road almost plummeted vertically to Jang (5,000 feet) before crossing the Mago Chu and climbing back to Tawang (10,000 feet).

Just beyond Dirang Dzong was Sapper Camp where Dalvi met the commanding officer of the Tuskers, Lieutenant Colonel Sandhu. The Border Roads Organisation had been hard at work having started surveying the road in 1960 after 4 Infantry Division moved in from the Punjab. Any road cut in the southern slopes of the Himalayas, especially in this region, would take years to settle down. Despite the fact that it had taken Sandhu and his men a few months to reconnoitre and select the final alignment while simultaneously dumping stores and equipment required for the job, in a remarkable feat of engineering, they had completed a fair weather road by the end of 1961. In November, both the chief, Thapar, and the CGS, Kaul, had visited the region and proceeded along the newly laid road up to Tawang. The condition of the road, however, was another matter. Jeeps could barely negotiate the slush-like conditions on either side of Se-la and eventually Dalvi had to walk from Senge to Jang before being picked up and driven to Tawang.

Just before Dalvi arrived in Assam, Kaul had spelt out his plans for Operation Onkar, which was to commence in April 1962. This operation was under the larger umbrella of the Forward Policy, conceived by Nehru's close advisers led by Mullik, to avoid a second 'Aksai Chin'. As such, it is likely that the main thrust of the new policy was primarily meant for Ladakh, even though the Prime Minister's directive of 2 November 1960 had said 'that Indian forces should remain in effective occupation of the whole frontier from NEFA to Ladakh and they should cover all gaps by effective patrolling. No longer should the Chinese be allowed to encroach surreptitiously into our territories not occupied by Indian troops or police'. However, by the time the implications of the new policy were understood, the winter of 1961-1962 had set in. Despite the fact that the Western Sector by itself would require massive logistical support to implement the policy, Kaul expanded its scope to include the Central and Eastern Sectors into the gambit of the new policy. That the eastern sector was an afterthought is supported by the fact that until February 1962, Eastern Command was not aware of Operation Onkar. Secondly, April as the date of commencement was related purely to Ladakh for, until then, it was not possible to airlift the required infantry battalions required for the task.

In the Eastern Sector, there was yet another important change in the command structure—Major General Amrik Singh was posted out just as Operation Onkar was commencing. The new GOC of 4 Infantry Division, Major General Niranjan Prasad, was only due to take over in May 1962. The commanding officer of 9 Punjab was also posted out and replaced by Lieutenant Colonel R. N. Mishra. Although Dalvi as the brigade commander had operational control of the sector on the ground, the Assam Rifles continued to function as a virtual private army of the Ministry of External Affairs. Their administration was under the inspector general based in Shillong and there was no inter-communication facilities between the Assam Rifles posts and the closest army sub-posts. To complicate matters even more, 7 Infantry Brigade was functioning without any useful intelligence.

Meanwhile, the Intelligence Bureau had tabled a detailed report on 17 May 1962, which stated that the Chinese had considerably reinforced their posts all along the Indo-Tibetan border. Krishna Menon gave the order that all gaps still left unoccupied in the border area should be filled up. Even if sizeable forces were not available, he had said, at least a platoon of either the army or police or Assam Rifles should occupy these places. HQ

XXXIII Corps, under the command of Lieutenant General Umrao Singh, protested against the order, prompting Kaul to personally fly down from Delhi in order to cajole them to get on with Operation Onkar. Accordingly, twenty-four new posts were set up in the Eastern Sector. The Chinese did not react to these posts, which were all south of the McMahon Ridge.

One of these posts was 'Dhola' that was to be set up on the Thagla. As per the 'treaty map' that he had, Dalvi suspected that the area was not a part of Indian territory. The brigade commander, along with the commanding officer of 1/9 GR, Lieutenant Colonel B.S. Ahluwalia, had in fact set off for Khenzemane to see the terrain for himself. His suspicion was endorsed by both Niranjan Prasad at the divisional and Umrao Singh at the corps level, the matter being referred to Bogey Sen in Eastern Command at Lucknow, who in turn further back-pedalled it to Army HQ.

The matter was referred to the DMO, Brigadier D. K. Palit, who decided to check with the Director of Military Survey who in turn said the existing maps of the area were 'sketchy and inaccurate'. The file was sent to the Ministry of External Affairs who sent it back to MO with the noting: 'We may permit the Army to extend the jurisdiction, if they have not already done so, up to the line suggested by them.' This was good enough for the CGS, who was getting more and more impatient with what he considered to be stalling tactics on the part of the local commanders. Accordingly, Eastern Command, XXXIII Corps, 4 Infantry Division and finally 7 Brigade were told to go ahead and set up the post anyway.

In the Western Sector, the establishing of the first few posts in Ladakh under Operation Onkar initially seemed to confirm the assessment of the Intelligence Bureau that the Chinese would not like to escalate the situation beyond border incidents. At first, the Chinese simply pulled back, but once they realized what the Indians were up to, the PLA began to encircle the new posts. This resulted in a tit-for-tat reaction from the Indians, resulting in a bizarre tango with both sides being extremely careful to avoid opening fire in a fast escalating scenario.

In Army HQ, no one seemed to have done an appreciation of how the Chinese were viewing the developments. By this time, Kaul had complete and absolute control of operations, logistics and intelligence. Having weeded out all those who could or would point out the obvious drawbacks in what was essentially a politically inspired military policy, not one of the yes men in Army HQ were likely to point out that the Indian moves were likely to provoke a reaction.

In the Kameng Frontier Division of the Eastern Sector, the focus had shifted back to the Thagla Ridge. Dalvi asked Lieutenant Colonel B. M. Mehta to nominate an officer who would command the Assam Rifles platoon that was earmarked for the setting up of the post. CO 1 Sikh suggested the name of Captain Mahabir Prasad (the nephew of the new GOC). Accordingly, the officer reported to Brigade HQ where he was briefed by Brigadier John Dalvi. Dalvi's briefing of Prasad was fairly sketchy since at that point of time there was very little information available. The task given to him was to locate the tri-junction (the meeting of the Indo-Bhutan-Tibet borders) and set up a post to dominate the position. Dalvi didn't know it then, but he had just issued orders that would become the casus belli for the Indo-China conflict a few months later. As per the existing set-up, from that point onwards, Prasad would have no direct link with 7 Brigade HQ, as he was required to report only to the Assam Rifles who in turn were responsible to the Ministry of External Affairs.

Captain Prasad set off in May 1962—proceeding via the Karpo-la axis, he dropped into the Nam Ka Chu Valley by following the trail along Rongla Nullah (later to be known as Bridge 3). Sticking to the game trail on the southern side of the Nam Ka Chu, he and his men moved upstream along the densely forest covered track. Finding the area to be devoid of Chinese troops, he then crossed the stream and took the easier route to Tser Jang Tso, the lake from where the Nam Ka Chu started its short journey to the Nyamjang Chu Valley. Prasad selected a possible site on the northeastern side of the lake and named it Tsangle.

From Tsangle, there was a trail leading up to the Dum Dum-la, from where the Thagla Ridge extended eastwards. Prasad's party made it to the crest line, once again finding the area unoccupied by the Chinese. Prasad now had to take a call; as per his brief, he needed to establish the post on the Thagla Ridge itself. However, the going had been extremely difficult with plenty of snow along the track. In his opinion, this would create severe logistical problems for the new post. After discussing it with the Assam Rifles JCO, Prasad decided it would be more prudent to fall back to the junction of the Nam Ka Chu and the Rongla Nullah. The location they agreed on was sited on a spur, set back 400 metres from the Nam Ka Chu. As far as Assam Rifles posts were concerned, Dhola—as it would henceforth be known—was reasonably well sited from a strategic point of view. Any Chinese activity on the Thagla Ridge could be observed and if the Chinese were to come down the slope, they would be caught on the Nam Ka Chu. Leaving the Assam Rifles to set up the post on 4 June 1962, Captain Mahabir Prasad returned to Tawang where he submitted his report to the Assam Rifles. Incredible as it may seem, he was never debriefed by either Brigadier Dalvi or by 7 Infantry Brigade.

Dhola was the westernmost Indian post and as it lay in disputed territory. It was to be supported by a company that was to be located at Lumpu, separated from the Nam Ka Chu Valley by Hathung-la and Karpo-la, the two passes on the Tsangdhar Ridge. For three months the Chinese did not react, but in early September, the IB reported that the Chinese had occupied the Thagla Ridge.

Despite the MEA having green-lit the setting up of a post at Dhola, the DMO, Brigadier Palit, was not sure of the status of the region. He consulted Dr S. Gopal (the son of the then President of India, Dr Sarvepalli Radhakrishnan) who was the director of the Historical Section of the MEA. Gopal explained to Palit that at the time of the boundary talks with China in 1954, the Government of India was aware that there was some ambiguity in the area of the tri-junction. The depiction on the quarter inch scale map differed from the actual ground position, so the Chinese were given the latitude and longitude reference (91° 40' East, 27° 40' North).

Gopal then made a noting on the file carried by Palit. 'This point was further north of the tri-junction shown on our maps and nearer the point suggested by Army Headquarters. Furthermore, the Chinese had been told that the alignment followed Thagla Ridge, which is also the ridge shown by Army Headquarters in the sketch.' The DMO put this down in the form of a note to HQ Eastern Command and sent it off and, amazingly, did nothing more about it even after the situation escalated dramatically in the next few days. Later, somewhat meekly defending his inaction on this critical bit of information, Palit was to say, 'Dr Gopal never told me the Chinese did not accept our argument in 1954 and had, in fact, claimed the Thagla and Khenzemane to be on the northern side of the McMahon Line.'

◆

Before we move on to the details of the fighting in both NEFA and Ladakh, it is important to understand the historical canvas which was the backdrop to the clashes. In 1947, China was not on India's radar for the simple reason that it didn't share a common border with the subcontinent. To understand the claims and counter-claims, it is important to not only look at events as they unfolded north of the Great Himalayas—involving Tibet, Sinkiang, China, the Soviet Union and Mongolia—but also on the southern side of the mountain chain that involved not just the Indians but a host of others—the British, Sikhs, Dogras, Ladakh, Kashmir, Nepal, Sikkim, Bhutan, the various tribes inhabiting NEFA, Assam, Burma and finally, even the United States.

The border with China even today is an unresolved problem. Unlike the settlement and demarcation of frontiers between Nepal, Bhutan and Burma which also followed the Himalayan watershed principle, Mao Tse-tung did not want the boundary settled with India for the simple reason that with the passage of time, Chinese claims based on—what it wouldn't be inaccurate to call—the whims of its leader then would develop a legitimacy of their own. It is, therefore, even more vital for India's future generations to truly understand the genesis and complexities of our conflict with China—across the mountain border as well as on our side. The country would do well to heed the age-old saying that nations which do not learn from history are doomed to make the same mistakes again.

BOOK II

Blanks on the Map

INDO-CHINA Boundary (Key Areas)

Chapter 3

BLANKS ON THE MAP

THE BOUNDARY

Even today, almost seventy years after Independence, when we talk of the northeastern part of India or the trans-Himalayan regions of Jammu and Kashmir, these vital and integral parts of India are blanks on the map of our collective consciousness. In the 1950s and 1960s, India not only had a leadership that was fairly clueless about geopolitical affairs, its armed forces, which it had inherited from the British, were also in a state of limbo. During World War II, various regiments of the Indian Army had earned their spurs in modern warfare and emerged with enhanced reputations. However, even though the Indianization of the armed forces had begun, the seniormost officers at the time had hardly even commanded infantry battalions, with just one or two having made brigadier by the time the war ended.

Being thrown into a conflict over Kashmir with Pakistan almost immediately, the obvious shortcomings did not show up, partly because the other side had similar problems and the two sides fought each other using similar tactics. When the Communist Party under Mao came to power in 1949 in China after defeating the Nationalist Chinese, it almost immediately annexed both Sinkiang and Tibet. Almost overnight, the military equation on the border changed dramatically, but the Indians failed to grasp the impact it would have on the subcontinent's security. As events unfolded over the next decade, they failed to understand not only China's long-term geopolitical ambitions, which were blatantly expansionist, they also severely underestimated China's operational capabilities.

On the Indian side, the decade-long build-up to 1962 coincided with the somewhat one-sided power struggle that would define civil-military relations in India. Nehru's own insecurities vis-à-vis the generals, combined with the absurd posturing that a non-violent nation did not really need an army, created a situation where the Indian Army was almost leaderless and rudderless. On the other hand, the Chinese had been through some desperate fighting, first with the Japanese and then amongst themselves. Subsequently, the PLA had been involved in a protracted war with the dominant military power at the time, the United States, as they fought it out in the mountains of the Korean peninsula. They had emerged from the clash battered and bruised, but had absorbed the lessons of modern post-World War II combat in terms of operational manoeuvrability. When the time came, Indian commanders, unlike the Chinese, showed themselves to be flat-footed and unimaginative and simply did not know what to do once the enemy went on the offensive.

To understand what happened, it is imperative that we try and get as close to the bone as possible. At times the truth is not palatable, but it needs to be told. Shortage of ammunition and obsolete weapon systems played a role but they were not the defining factors in a conflict that was simply not fought by the Indians as a strong unit. Those who stood their ground and fought extracted a heavy toll from the Chinese who themselves were an army fighting out on a limb. Those who tried to get away were tackled piecemeal by the PLA. The Indian Army allowed the Chinese to bring overwhelming force into play against scattered positions, and mow them down ruthlessly. Therefore, it is also absolutely vital to shake off the traditional Indian indifference towards history so that the real problem is understood in its bare essence.

The Sino-Indian clash in 1962 was the culmination of many factors and many bit players had a role to play in it. At the centre of it all were the Tibetans, but the full cast includes the Chinese, Mongols, Russians, British, Nepalese, Bhutanese, Sikhs, Ladakhis, even the Americans and of course the Indians. At a time when the rest of the world was exhausted from the Second World War and attention was focused on the Cold War, Mao pulled off one of the greatest real estate coups of all time. It was a masterstroke in geopolitical manoeuvring. That India took the brunt of it was partly due to her own inability to think long term. In the end, even though the cast of villains can be long, we only had ourselves to blame. Hopefully, we shall not make the same mistake twice.

THE INDIAN SUBCONTINENT

The Indian subcontinent is a distinct geographical entity with clearly demarcated and defensible borders. The region can be divided into four distinct parts: the massive chain of mountains to the north—2,500 kilometres in length and 250 to 300 kilometres in width—that acts as a formidable barrier against the Tibetan Plateau; the Indo-Gangetic plain that extends from the Indus in Pakistan in the west to the Brahmaputra in the east; the Central Indian Plateau; and finally the Deccan Plateau flanked on either side by the Eastern and Western Ghats and the coastal regions.

The most striking geographic feature is undoubtedly the Himalayan chain that has over 114 peaks that touch heights of over 20,000 feet. The northwestern corner of this forbidding wall is made of sheer rock and ice, a part of the Hindu Kush mountains that adjoin the Karakoram range. Further in, running parallel to the Karakoram are the Ladakh, Zanskar and Great Himalayan ranges, each with their own valleys and plateaus that have formed separate kingdoms in the past. Together this great wall then runs eastwards through Lahaul-Spiti, Kinnaur, Garhwal, Kumaon, Nepal, then on to Sikkim, Bhutan and what was then NEFA (Arunachal Pradesh).

Linked to the Himalayas but running north to south, the Kirthar, Sulaiman and Safed Koh ranges form a massive defensive barrier in the west. In the east the Naga Patkai ranges similarly branch off to the south becoming the Naga Hills and the Manipur Plateau before further linking up with the Chin and Lushai Hills and then the Arakan Yoma before tapering off at Cape Negris in the Bay of Bengal. Collectively, these mountains literally take the shape of a helmet adorning the head of the subcontinent, making ingress into the region rather difficult.

Difficult does not mean impossible, however, especially in the face of a determined invader. Despite their ruggedness and forbidding look, the Western Himalayas have always proved to be rather porous. A succession of invaders, from ancient to medieval times, made their way across passes in the Hindu Kush and the southern ranges that formed the western boundary. Once across the few known and rarely guarded passes, invading armies could follow the linking river valleys into the subcontinent. The most favoured route was along the Kabul Valley into the northern part of the Indus Plain, or through Central Afghanistan through the Kurram, Tochi or Gomal valleys directly into West Punjab (now in Pakistan).

Though the bulk of the landmass then stretches southwards from the mountain wall, life in the upper half of the subcontinent has largely been defined by the Himalayas. The Great Plains are formed by the thick alluvial deposits that are constantly washed down by the three great river systems, extending from the Arabian Sea to the Bay of Bengal.

However, let us confine ourselves to that part of the Himalayan region that protects the subcontinent from the north. Though it was possible for traders and small groups of men to penetrate the Himalayan fortress along the established trade routes, any invading force a la Mahmud of Ghazni in the tenth century, or Tamerlane in the fourteenth century never penetrated the high mountain passes. Hence, in the east, the access to the subcontinent was never across the northern barrier, but followed a gradual and non-violent migration across the Naga Patkai and Naga Hills by races like the Ahom who came into the unoccupied Assam Valley sometime in the mid-twelfth century. The aggressive invasions from the Burmese side were localized and rarely progressed west of the Imphal Valley.

The relationship of the peoples occupying the mountain valleys and hillsides on the southern side of the Himalayan watershed has always been cordial if somewhat aloof. The Bhutia invariably occupied the extreme heights and acted as a buffer between the two regions. The Tibetan plateau was a high altitude desert devoid of rich grazing pastures and arable land, both of which were abundant on the Indian side. Between AD 750 and 850, Tibetan historians claim that their kingdom extended into parts of northern India. Though there is little evidence to buttress this claim, Chinese records suggest that during that period Tibet was militarily quite strong and not too hesitant to advance against Indian Himalayan kingdoms and the Chinese. In AD 787, to stop Tibetan expansion, the Chinese king is said to have entered into an alliance not just with the Indians, but also the Caliph of Baghdad.

Military adventurism against the subcontinent, at the best of times a logistical nightmare, became even less likely from the north with the flow of Buddhism into Tibet. The more primitive Bon (also spelt Phon, traces of which exist in Sikkim even today) form of Buddhism was the national religion of Tibet until the arrival of Padmasambhava (Guru Rinpoche) who immediately got the attention of the people by defeating Chinese 'demons'. With Padmasambhava in the eighth century came Tantrism in the form of Lamaism and Kamalashila, a philosopher from Nalanda, became the head of the metaphysical branch of the Tibetan church.

Buddhism was, at the same time, playing a major role in ancient India's relationship with China. In the sixth and seventh centuries, many Buddhist monks from India made the arduous journey to China—either over the land route that took them first into Afghanistan, on to Sinkiang and then into Han China, or through the regular maritime trade routes that linked South India with Southeast Asia and the southern Chinese ports. All the regions along the route through which the travelling monks transited were also at the time influenced by Buddhism.

Interaction between India and China was frequent during the Tang Period (AD 618-907) and then again during the Song Dynasty (AD 960-1279). Historical records in both countries indicate that the contact between the countries was a two-way street, with Chinese scholars also travelling to India to study and collect Buddhist documents for translation. The most famous visit was the sixteen-year pilgrimage of Hsüan-tsang who entered the subcontinent in AD 630. After his return, he spent the remaining years of his life in the Temple of Great Happiness translating his Indian collection, assisted by twenty monks who were well versed in both Chinese and Sanskrit. During this period, the Chinese scholar-monk recorded in minute detail his travels in India while also translating important Chinese books into Sanskrit that were then sent to Nalanda in AD 647.

Other Chinese chronicles that were written between the sixth and sixteenth centuries meticulously record the visit of every Indian scholar who visited China during that period. Significantly, there is no mention of Padmasambhava or any of the others who visited Tibet and greatly influenced Buddhism there in Chinese texts—a strong indication that through this large span of Chinese history, Tibet was not considered a part of China and, in fact, had little to do with it.

TIBET'S RELATIONSHIP WITH CHINA

Even before 1949 when the Chinese effectively swallowed up Tibet, China had been behaving as if it 'owned' Tibet. But the facts, when looked at closely, tell a different story.

Despite the visits of scholars like Hsüan-tsang in the seventh century, the two civilizations did not have much to do with each other. Even the Opium Wars towards the end of the nineteenth century did not bring the two races face to face. India's interaction was with the Tibetan people. Administratively, it was restricted to exchanges between the British and the Tibetan government once the Sikhs were defeated in the northwest, the Gorkhas in the centre, and the Burmese in the east by the East India Company. As the British Empire expanded, it overpowered Burma, Bhutan, Sikkim, Nepal and Kashmir; as a result of this, it came into direct contact with the Tibetans.

If the great Himalayas acted as a barrier between the Indian subcontinent and Tibet, access from China was equally, if not more, difficult with the Kunlun Mountains bounding the plateau towards the north. Ironically, in ancient times, the easiest approaches into Lhasa were from the south: the Chumbi Valley between Sikkim and West Bhutan, and through Tawang which lay just beyond the eastern extremity of Bhutan. At the other end was the route that linked Ladakh to Sinkiang via Nubra, then through the Aksai Chin to Lhasa. The Chinese pilgrims who furnished us with such valuable insights into early Indian history in the fifth and seventh centuries avoided Tibet, choosing instead to wind around through the circuitous route of Chinese Turkestan and the mountain ranges of northwest India.

The whole of Eastern Tibet, formed by the frontiers of U and Kongbo to the borders of China proper, was known as Kham and the inhabitants as Khampa. It included an enormous expanse of wild mountainous country extending some 1,300 kilometres from west to east and 1,000 kilometres from north to south, and was the catchment area for the Yangtze Kiang, the Mekong and the Salwen rivers. While the northern limit of this region divided the basins of the Hwang Ho and the Yangtze Kiang rivers, towards the south it extended to the frontiers of Assam and Yunnan. Given its immediate proximity to China, the political organization of the region was exceedingly complicated.

Over the centuries, this region appears to have been parcelled out amongst a number of small semi-independent states and nomadic hordes who were ruled by their own petty chieftains; they professed no allegiance either to Peking or to Lhasa. The power struggle between Tibet and China, with the latter every now and then claiming suzerainty, meant nothing as far as the governance of the region was concerned. The appointment of lamas was almost exclusively done by Lhasa, which was forever trying to get Eastern Tibet into its sphere of influence. As for the local Khampas, they feared and dreaded the bigoted rule of the lamas, preferring their own 'half-savage' independence that meant they constantly had to steer a careful course between the Lhasa lamas and the officials from Peking.

Originally the districts that constituted Eastern Tibet extended right up to the western frontier of China proper—to Gansu, Szechuan, and Yunnan—but gradually China had been encroaching upon this region. Ever since China succeeded in establishing a paramount influence at Lhasa, it has been gradually absorbing as much as possible of the border country into its own territory. The result was that over time, large portions of territory that were originally in Tibet and by extension a part of Kham came under the direct control of the viceroys of the neighbouring Chinese provinces. Whilst leaving the native hereditary rulers in actual possession, the Chinese appointed their officials to the various courts to supervise affairs, much in the way the British did by appointing their own residents in the Indian princely states during the Raj.

In the early 1900s, travellers and writers who had visited the region agreed that ethnologically and geographically, Tibet proper extended up to the great Yun-ling Range. The Chinese had maintained their position in Eastern Kham by political adroitness, and only just escaped expulsion owing to the internecine feuds of the numerous petty chieftains and clans. This allowed the Chinese, while holding the Khampas in utter contempt, to maintain an illusion of control over the region and to at least theoretically challenge Lhasa's control over the region.

China's claim on Tibet was a classic case of historical distortion, which was buttressed by the British who double-crossed the Himalayan kingdom in their desire to appease China so that they could further their trade interests. Dismissing Indian arguments on the grounds that post 1947 the Indians were only parroting British imperial policy, the Chinese justified their takeover of Tibet on the grounds that in the twelfth century, Tibet had been briefly incorporated into China when the Mongols under Kublai Khan had established the Yuan Dynasty in China (AD 1271–1368). In reality, the first time China tried to establish political control over Lhasa was in 1720. The Qing Army installed two Chinese resident commissioners (ambans) in Lhasa. For two decades the situation in Tibet had been chaotic ever since the Mongol Lhabsang Khan had notionally assumed the title of King of Tibet in 1697. Around the same time the Tibetan regent, who resented Mongol interference in Tibet, appointed and installed Tsayang Gyatso as the sixth Dalai Lama. Lhabsang Khan accused the new Dalai Lama of 'writing love poems and carousing with women at night in Lhasa'. As relations steadily worsened, Lhabsang Khan, supported by the Qing emperor of China and a number of aristocratic Tibetan families, attacked the regent in Lhasa, who was later executed. This made Lhabsang Khan the king of Tibet in fact as well as in title.

In 1705 the emperor of China sent an envoy to Lhasa and recognized Lhabsang Khan as the king of Tibet under the protection of the Qing Dynasty. By agreeing to pay a regular tribute to the Qing, Lhabsang Khan placed himself (and, by extension, Tibet) in a subordinate relationship with China.

The drama was to continue. With complete military control over Tibet, Lhabsang Khan deposed Tsayang Gyatso by sending him into exile in Peking and placed another monk in his place who came to be known as the 'Fake Dalai Lama'. Tsayang Gyatso in the meantime died en route to Peking and a rumour spread through Tibet that he had manifested in a new body in Litang in the Kham district. Resentment against Lhabsang Khan continued to grow, and in 1717 the monks of the three major monasteries around

Lhasa asked their Mongol followers, the Dzungars, for help. Seven thousand cavalry, aided by scores of Tibetans, then moved on Lhasa and Lhabsang Khan was killed in the fighting. However, the Dzungars also fell out with the Tibetans by looting and executing some Red Hat lamas and failing to bring back the Litang Lama despite having killed the 'Fake Dalai Lama'.

It wasn't just the British who viewed Tibet as a buffer between India and Russia; the Chinese emperor had also seen the Himalayan kingdom as an important buffer between various regions of Western China—Szechuan, Gansu and Yunnan. Kang-Hsi, the Qing emperor, quickly took the Litang Lama under his control and sent an army to wrest control back from the Dzungars. The mobile Mongols annihilated this Qing force and though most Chinese court officials were apprehensive about any further military operations in Tibet, the emperor dispatched a larger army, sending the newly anointed seventh Dalai Lama (Kelzang Gyatso, the Litang Lama—then fifteen years old) with them. By October 1720, the Qing emperor had defeated those opposing him and had complete control over Tibet.

However, the Chinese were not particularly interested in administratively absorbing Tibet into China. Instead, Kang-Hsi created a loose protectorate over Tibet: the Qing Dynasty would protect Tibet from any external and internal threat, and would allow Tibetan leaders it approved of to rule in a manner that was not inimical to Chinese interests. This passive hegemony would work for the rest of the eighteenth century, during which time Chinese armies had to enter Tibet on five occasions.

Despite Chinese intervention, the situation in Tibet simply refused to stabilize. In 1727, civil war erupted. Eventually, one of the ministers, Pholhanas, took control of Lhasa. The seventh Dalai Lama was exiled to Kham and 2,000 Qing troops were garrisoned in Lhasa with another 1,000 men stationed in Chamdo in the Kham region. In addition, the Qing emperor decided to station two Manchu imperial ambans in Lhasa to oversee the garrison in Lhasa and also keep watch on the Tibetan leadership. The ambans would continue to be in Lhasa with varying degrees of importance till 1912.

Even though Tibet found itself substantially scaled down as a political entity, at no stage did it ever lose its identity as a separate kingdom.

Pholhanas proved to be an able administrator and slowly the Chinese ambans had no role to play in the kingdom's affairs. The seventh Dalai Lama was brought back from exile in 1735 and became the religious figurehead. In 1739, Pholhanas was given the title 'Prince of Tibet', which made him the head of the aristocratic family that would henceforth rule the kingdom. Even though unrest was building up towards the end of his reign, when

Pholhanas died in 1747, his second son Gyurme Namgye succeeded him. However, unlike his father, Namgye was openly anti-Chinese and started negotiations with the Dzungar Mongols. When the amban residents in Lhasa found out, they had Namgye killed. In retaliation, Namgye's supporters killed both the ambans. In the ensuing chaos, the Dalai Lama opened the Potala Palace to all the Chinese residents in Lhasa while requesting the Qing emperor for immediate help.

As a reward for his loyalty, the Qing emperor vested in the Dalai Lama extensive temporal power. Various restrictions were then put on the rest of Tibet's nobility, which effectively ended Tibet's brief flirtation with non-religious governance and internecine struggles. Once again the Chinese withdrew, leaving the Dalai Lama in control of Tibet. In 1758, in a remarkably trouble-free succession, Jamphel Gyatso was appointed the eighth Dalai Lama.

Two major events would then occur which would directly impact the China-Tibet-India equation. The first occurred in 1772 when the Bhutanese attacked the neighbouring Cooch Behar kingdom. Warren Hastings, the Governor General of Bengal, promptly engaged the Bhutanese forces. The Panchen Lama, who independently controlled two major districts, offered to mediate, leading to the signing of a pact between the Bhutanese and the British in 1774.

At that time the British were trying very hard to open the Chinese coast for trading, but were being stalled by the Qing emperor who distrusted the western power. Hastings saw the Panchen Lama's intervention in the Bhutanese-Cooch Behar conflict as an opportunity to sponsor trade through Tibet. Accordingly, two British officials made their way to Lhasa where they were firmly told that whole of Tibet was subject to the Qing emperor, and China was unwilling to permit trade. All contact, they were told, had to be through Peking. This would have a deep impact on the British mindset, who would even in later years, continue to harp on Chinese suzerainty even when the Tibetans declared themselves independent in 1912.

The second incident was in 1788 when the Gorkhas, flush with their victory over Nepal and attracted by the monastic wealth of Tibetan monasteries, invaded from the south. In no position to challenge the Gorkhas, the Tibetans sued for peace and promised to pay annual tribute. This was agreed upon, but the tribute stopped after a couple of years, leading to the Second Gorkha invasion in 1791. In desperation, the Dalai Lama once again turned to the Qing emperor who was quick to dispatch a 10,000-strong army to Tibet's aid. The Chinese army not only stopped the Gorkhas, but pushed them right back into Nepal, getting to within thirty-odd kilometres of Kathmandu. The Gorkhas now sued for peace, offering to pay Peking a tribute every five years. The Gorkhas lost the war, and in the process they also succeeded in bringing China into direct contact with the Indian subcontinent for the first time ever.

TIBET'S RELATIONSHIP WITH INDIA

Tibetan links with the Chinese until the 1700s were almost non-existent, but they had an intricate relationship with Indian states with a great degree of trade and religious exchange. Though there had been conflicts and invasions, the topography, with its naturally defined borders, ensured that there was very little friction between the Tibetans and the various Indian states. Apart from Kashmir in the west, the Sikhs, the Nepalese, the Lepchas, the Bhutanese and the various tribes living in the jungles of NEFA, all had common borders with Tibet. In the east, most of the NEFA tribes—the Aka, the Daflas (now known as Nyishi), the Adi and the Mishmi among others—were fiercely independent and acted as a buffer between Tibet and Assam. The fact that these tribes inhabited the dense jungles south of the Himalayan crest line meant that the Tibetans had very little to do with them. The Chinese, needless to say, were nowhere in the picture.

Even Tawang, over which Tibet claimed sovereignty until 1914, was an independent country that was de facto under the control of the lamas and the monks of the Tawang Monastery. It was only towards the latter half of the nineteenth century that Lhasan authorities began to assert their influence over the region and deputed dzongpens to govern the region. Like the Khampa in the Kham province of Tibet bordering China, the Monpa and the Sherdukpen too were caught between the tyranny of the monks and the Tibetan officials. The latter in particular were locally referred to as zakpas meaning 'the plunderers'.

The Tawang belt—better known as the Kameng Frontier Division—ran between Bhutan on the west and the Miji, Aka and Abor (Nyishi) dominated jungles to the east. The northern frontier of this region belt is geographically and culturally separated from Tibet by the Kangto (also known as Sher Kangri) and Gaurichen massif. The crest line also acts as a watershed between the Tsangpo and the Kameng River catchments. Further to its east lies the Bokar region that extends up to the upper reaches of the Subansiri River. So wild and inhospitable was this area that Tibetans on the northern side did not venture across the watershed even for trade.

Between the Subansiri headwaters and the Dibang River catchment lies the main Siang River Valley. The east flowing Tsangpo, after taking a bend to the south, flowed into Abor (Adi) territory. At this point, the Siang Valley is at a considerably lower altitude when compared to the flanking catchments of the Subansiri and the Dibang rivers. This was the natural gateway for trade, but once again the highly aggressive and hostile tribes that inhabited the Assam Himalayas kept the Tibetans away. In fact, even some of the immediate areas on the northern side of the watershed—for example Chumbi that bordered Bhutan and Sikkim and Po-yul that bordered the Mishmi lands to the south—were not under Lhasa or Peking, and considered themselves to be independent kingdoms. The rest of the region was, however, clearly part of Tibet and was governed by dzongpens who operated from their fortified forts (dzongs).

The Po-yul region to the east of the Tsangpo's great bend consisted of two distinct sub-regions: Po-teu and Po-me. The former was bleak country inhabited by lawless herdsmen. Po-me, with its fertile soil, cultivated wheat and pepper, had a flourishing trade in ponies and was noted for its manufacture of blankets, baskets, silver and iron work. This prosperity was due mainly to a number of Chinese soldiers who, on their way to join in the Nepal campaign in 1792, came across this independent country where the writ of neither Lhasa nor Peking held sway. Many of them settled there, married the local women and raised their families.

Finally, lying even further east of Po-yul is the Za-yul region that is Mishmi country. While Tawang was the westernmost trade route between Tibet and Assam, the middle route lay along the Tsangpo (known as the Siang once it crossed the alignment of the watershed on either flank). The Za-yul Chu (Lohit River) afforded the third trade route. The Mishmi were not as warlike as their Abor neighbours to their immediate west. A flourishing barter trade existed with Assam, with the Mishmi acting as the middlemen south of the watershed, and the Popa playing a similar role to the north.

The Chinese, having driven out the Gorkhas, withdrew from Tibet, leaving only two small garrisons at Xigatse and Dingri to keep watch on the Nepalese. They did, however, insist on certain administrative reforms that resulted in the amban being elevated to equal political authority with the Dalai Lama.

General Fu Kangan who had led the Chinese army into Tibet reminded the Dalai Lama in a strongly worded letter of why he needed to be grateful to the Chinese emperor and warned that '[i]f he persists in his old ways of doing things, His Majesty will call back the resident officials and evacuate the Tibetan garrison immediately after the withdrawal of the expeditionary army, and the Court will not come to the help of the Tibet…'

In the immediate aftermath of the Nepalese War, the amban were at their most powerful, yet they made no effort to absorb Tibet into China as a province or in any other manner. Tibet continued to maintain its own language, officials and legal system, and paid no taxes or tribute to China. On the contrary, as pointed out by Melvyn Goldstein in his book, *The Snow Lion and the Dragon*: 'In fact the 1792 reforms included the creation of Tibet's first standing army, the emperor's aim being to enable Tibet to defend itself and thus avoid having to send troops again.'

Meanwhile, the Qing Dynasty faced serious threats from the British in the nineteenth century. Extremely cautious in its dealing with western powers, the Qing had restricted trade to Canton. While there was a tremendous demand for Chinese goods—silk, porcelain and tea—the Chinese were quite self-sufficient and there was no demand for western goods. Qing trade regulations meant that the British and other European traders had to pay for their goods in silver. This created a huge imbalance in trade, resulting in the British flooding Canton with Indian-grown opium. The subsequent Opium Wars (1839-1842 and 1856-1860) further reduced the Qing's ability to deal with internal disturbances such as the Taiping Rebellion (1848-1865).

With the Qing preoccupied with the British, the Tibetans fought wars with Zorawar Singh's Dogras and the Ladakhis in 1841-1842 and with Nepal in 1855-56 without any Chinese assistance. Even the subsequent war with Nepal in 1855-56 saw no Chinese involvement, despite the fact that the Tibetans were forced to pay Nepal an annual tribute and accept a Nepalese resident in Lhasa.

Towards the end of the nineteenth century, the British were the dominant power to the south of Tibet as a string of Himalayan kingdoms (including Nepal and Sikkim) were defeated by them and came under their influence. In their subsequent relations with Tibet, the British would play a major part in hyphenating it with China even after the Qing dynasty was ousted and the Tibetans declared themselves outside the purview of Chinese suzerainty. This factor was to be the biggest contradiction in Britain's Tibet policy, where it dealt directly with the Tibetan government to achieve its ends, but had to constantly turn to China to legitimize them.

All the while there was never any doubt that Tibet was an independent country with its own identity. Even after 1720, at no stage did the Qing dynasty actually try and annex or occupy Tibet. If the threat to the Chinese from the Dzungar Mongols had not been there, it is quite likely that the Chinese would have left Tibet completely to itself. China had already brought under its administrative control the territories that it wanted. As for the southern frontier of Tibet that bordered the Indian subcontinent, the Chinese had little or no interest in it.

After the Bhutanese invasion of Cooch Behar and the subsequent Gorkha invasion of Tibet in 1791-92, it would take the British another hundred years to firm up their Tibet policy. By 1899, the time Lord Curzon was Governor-General of India, British thinking could be summed up in a single statement he made: 'Chinese suzerainty over Tibet is a fiction, a political affectation.' However, in discounting China as a major power and in his Russian fixation, Curzon was to lay his entire emphasis on the wrong country. 'If we do nothing in Tibet we shall have Russia trying to establish a protectorate in less than ten years... This might not constitute a military danger, at any rate for some time, but would be a political danger. The effect on Nepal, Sikkim and Bhutan would constitute a positive danger. We can stop a Russian protectorate over Tibet by being in advance ourselves.'

After Colonel Younghusband's expedition into Lhasa in 1904 had forced the reluctant Tibetans to trade with the British, the border between Tibet and Sikkim was demarcated. In 1913, the Morshead–Bailey expedition was sent to the Tibet-NEFA border to study and map the watershed from the Tibetan side. Both the Chinese and the Tibetan authorities were fully aware of the survey. The following year, when the McMahon Line was drawn up in Simla, the Tibetan representative, Lonchen Gaden Shatra Paljor Dorje, accepted the geographic and demographic arguments of the British based on the expedition's detailed findings. It is also an undisputed fact that Lonchen Shatra had the prior approval of both the thirteenth Dalai Lama and the Tibetan Kashag to help draw up and then accept the McMahon Line.

INDO-TIBET BOUNDARY (WESTERN SECTOR)

The Indo-Tibet boundary was always going to be a problem. Apart from its vastness—extending from the Karakorams in the west to the Lohit River in the east—the actual demarcation had rarely been done. Neither the Tibetans nor the people living in various kingdoms to the south used geographic contours, instead they demarcated regions based on the needs of the people. For example, the Tibetans grazed their yaks and upland sheep in the higher reaches, while the Bhutanese harvested the bamboo that grew at lower altitudes.

But with the twentieth century came modern mapping techniques that began to delineate frontiers on more specific lines. To further complicate the issue, the definition of Tibet itself was somewhat vague; political Tibet (lands controlled by Lhasa) was considerably smaller than its ethnographic counterpart which was close to 2,080,000 square kilometres (almost the size of present-day India).

The majority of the Tibetan population at the time lived in the districts between Lhasa and the Chinese border, but the rest of the country was sparsely populated. The high altitude and harshness of terrain served to isolate it not just from India to the south, but also China to the east and Mongolia to its north. The devastating hordes of Mongols that poured through Central Asia and reduced the Russians and half of Europe to vassalage never entered Tibet, even though it lay at their very doorstep. Even when they attacked India, they chose to bypass Tibet and entered the subcontinent through the easier passes of Afghanistan.

The frontiers were also ill-defined because governmental control in Tibet (and China) remained fairly fluid. Given that both the Chinese and the British were constantly probing and pushing their frontiers forward (the British staying away from the political boundary of Tibet but confining themselves to the tribal belts that acted as a buffer between Tibet and Assam), it was perhaps inevitable that there would be serious differences in opinion between the two once China invaded and annexed Tibet. Later, China would, ironically, on behalf of Tibet, lay claim to areas that the Tibetans themselves had conceded as not being a part of political Tibet.

The only comprehensive attempt at defining the frontier between India and Tibet in a scientific manner was when British and Tibetan officials met in Simla in 1914 to demarcate the boundaries. The third party at the convention—the Chinese—was present to simultaneously demarcate the boundaries between inner and outer Tibet. This convention was later mired in controversy as both the British and the Chinese adopted different stands at different times (as we will see when we deal with the Simla Convention in the next chapter).

Over the last one hundred years since the three parties put their heads together, the Indo-Tibet border has seen many changes as empires fell and new political dispositions came up. To understand the huge, rugged, disputed expanse that runs across the entire width of northern and eastern India, the frontier needs to be broken up into three different regions—the western, the central, and the eastern. Between the central and the eastern section lie the three erstwhile Himalayan kingdoms of Nepal, Sikkim and Bhutan.

◆

The bone of contention in the western section is the boundary that extends eastwards from the Karakoram Pass to the Changchenmo Valley that lies to the south. This was the traditional line that divided the Ladakh region in Jammu and Kashmir from Sinkiang and Tibet, both of which are now under Chinese control. India claims that the huge expanse of the Aksai Chin lies south of the Kunlun mountain range and is therefore an integral part of its territory. Geographically part of the Tibetan Plateau and the Changtang, the region is almost uninhabited and sees little precipitation. Historically, however, the 38,000-square-kilometre Aksai Chin was a part of the Himalayan kingdom of Ladakh until it was annexed by Kashmir in the nineteenth century.

Even by the standards of the Karakorams, the Aksai Chin region is extremely remote, and the boundary between Ladakh and Tibet was never formally settled. After the Amritsar Treaty formally created the kingdom of Jammu and Kashmir, the British abrogated to themselves the responsibility of the state's security, making themselves responsible for Kashmir's northern and eastern borders with Sinkiang and Tibet. The first British attempt, Cunningham's Ladakh Border Commission, failed to delineate the eastern border between Ladakh and Tibet and the northern boundaries between Kashmir and Sinkiang in 1847, which left the British no choice but to rely on an earlier treaty, signed on 16-17 September 1842, between Ladakh and Tibet, which was one of non-aggression rather than a boundary treaty.

The 1842 treaty officially marked the end of hostilities between the two sides: Zorawar Singh's ambitious Dogra venture into Tibet and an equally unsuccessful retaliation that brought the Tibetans to Leh. The Persian and Tibetan texts both agree that India 'shall remain in possession of the limits of boundaries of Ladakh and the neighbours subordinate to it, in accordance with the old customs, and there shall be no transgression and no interference in the country beyond the old-established frontiers'. The Tibetan text in Kashmir's possession was of the same tenor.

What were the old established frontiers? In 1878, when the Chinese once again established their control over Sinkiang, they created a customs post north of Shahidula implying that they considered the Kuen Lun as outside their jurisdiction. However, seeing that there was no effective Kashmiri governance in this area, the Chinese occupied Shahidula in 1890 and two years later moved further westwards and erected a boundary marker at the Karakoram Pass.

This was indeed surprising for, in 1865, William Henry Johnson, who had earlier been involved in the survey of Kashmir and Western Himalayas, had surveyed the Ladakh-Tibet border. As part of the Trigonometrical Survey

of India, he was to draw up the elusive Ladakh-Tibet border extending from Demchok in the south to the 18,000-foot-high Karakoram Pass in the north. Johnson took the Kuen Lun Mountains and not the Karakorams as the natural boundary and thus included the barren Aksai Chin desert into the boundaries of Kashmir.

Leaving the Aksai Chin to the north, the boundary then drops south from the Changchenmo Valley to Spiti that is today a part of Himachal Pradesh. This line passes through Pangong Tso, Chushul and Demchok, all of whom have seen minor boundary disputes over the ages. The entire frontage for the western section is over 1,610 kilometres long; and of the nearly 39,000 square kilometres that is under dispute, the bulk of the territory is today under Chinese control.

The frontier between Ladakh and Tibet can be traced back to the tenth century when a Tibetan prince, Skyid-Ida-Ngeemagon, conferred the Meryal (Ladakh) fief to his eldest son. In 1681 and 1683, the Tibetans, aided by Mongols, invaded Ladakh. In 1684, a peace treaty between the two sides was concluded that read: 'The boundaries fixed in the beginning, when Skyid-Ida-Ngeemagon gave a kingdom to each of his three sons, should still be maintained.'

The peace treaty was scrupulously honoured by both sides for a century and a half. The year 1821 marked the beginning of the Sikh/Dogra expansion northwards when Gulab Singh's mercurial rise under Maharaja Ranjit Singh would make the Dogras under General Zorawar Singh important players in Kashmir and Ladakh. In 1835, Zorawar led his men across the Great Himalayan Range through Umasi-la and arrived at Padam. From here he moved westwards, capturing the Suru River Valley and the small town of Kargil. In the next four years, he had the entire region of Ladakh and Baltistan under his control.

In 1841, Zorawar Singh once again crossed into Ladakh. His 5,000-strong army, supplemented by another 2,000 men from Kishtwar, Ladakh and Baltistan, advanced eastwards along the Indus River and brushed aside all Tibetan opposition at Rudok and Tashigang. By September the Dogras had set up base at Taklakot near the Manasarovar Lake where they hastily constructed a small fort. This location was twenty-four kilometres from the borders of Nepal and Kumaon.

Zorawar Singh's exploits changed the map of northern India and threatened to completely undo the carefully cultivated relationship between Lhasa and the British. While the Tibetans had been at the receiving end militarily, the British had been viewing Zorawar Singh's advance with alarm; from their point of view a direct link between Lahore (the Sikhs) and Nepal (the Gorkhas) was most undesirable, and they had been putting relentless pressure on the Lahore Durbar to press Gulab Singh to recall Zorawar Singh and vacate the Tibetan territory occupied by him.

However, Zorawar Singh had already achieved all that he could in the region. The intense cold and lack of supplies had immobilized his army, and to make matters worse, the Tibetans, aware of the threat to Lhasa, had put together a large force to neutralize the Dogras. Boldly seeking to engage the Tibetans rather than sit back and wait for them to attack him, the Dogras were overcome at Toyu (at over 16,000 feet) on 11-12 December, 1841. Zorawar Singh himself died fighting. The few survivors from this ill-fated campaign escaped into British Kumaon. Gulab Singh, who was himself leading an Anglo-Sikh campaign into Afghanistan, was told of the disaster by Henry Lawrence.

Gulab Singh's prestige was severely dented by the demise of Zorawar Singh and his army, and to make matters worse, the Tibetan Army was now advancing on Ladakh. A force under the command of Dewan Hari Chand was rushed from Jammu to Chushul where it crushed the Tibetan Army, thereby avenging the defeat at Toyu. In September 1842, Diwan

Hari Chand and Wazir Ratnu, on behalf of Gulab Singh, signed a peace treaty with Kalon Surkhan and Depon Pishy on behalf of the Dalai Lama and the Tibetan Government. This treaty 'as recognized by both sides since olden times', accepted the traditional boundary between Ladakh and Tibet.

The village and area around Minsar near Manasarovar Lake that was held by the rajas of Ladakh since 1583 was, however, retained by the Dogras. Indeed the Jammu and Kashmir Government regularly received revenue from Minsar that lies hundreds of miles inside Tibet till 1948. This treaty of 1842 settled the boundary between Ladakh and Tibet in unequivocal terms leaving no cause for any kind of border dispute in this region.

◆

Arguments and counter-arguments have continued to be exchanged for the last one hundred years. The Indians point to a formal communiqué of 1847 that was sent from the British to the Chinese viceroy of Kwangtung and Kwangsi provinces for delimiting the boundary between Ladakh and Tibet. The Chinese at the time had said: 'The borders of the territories have been sufficiently and distinctively fixed.' Subsequently, the stand taken by the Chinese was that the British proposal was rejected, as China at the time was in a weakened state and it was feared the British would have taken advantage of the situation to obtain even more Chinese territory.

An agreement in 1852 further indicated that the boundary was defined, as the operative section reads: 'The boundary between Ladakh and Tibet remains the same as before.' China countered this saying: 'This agreement only referred to the maintenance of the old boundary by the two sides of Ladakh and Tibet, and provided Ladakh should pay annual tribute to Tibet but made no provisions whatever about the boundary between Tibet and Ladakh.'

Almost half a century later, the British Minister to China, Sir Claude MacDonald, again tried to address the boundary issue, suggesting the demarcation of the frontier between Sinkiang and Tibet with Ladakh. Once again China refused to accept the proposal. Subsequently, the Chinese would point to the MacDonald proposal as proof that none of the earlier arguments held any water as the proposal itself proved that the boundary had not been delimited. However, on closer scrutiny, the MacDonald proposal was a major deviation from the earlier established boundary. The new proposal, in fact, drew a line from the Karakoram Pass towards the east—very different from any Indian or British map of that time. Ironically, the MacDonald line would have placed more than half of the Aksai Chin in Chinese territory.

The Chinese refusing to get pinned down was not specific to just the western section of the boundary. Post-independence, with Pakistan coming into play, the Sino-Indian boundary became even more complicated.

INDO-TIBET BOUNDARY (CENTRAL SECTOR)

In the central sector, the area from Spiti to the junction of India, Nepal and Tibet is a distance of 640 kilometres. The main points of dispute between China and India have been in Spiti, Barahoti, and the Nilang region next to the Shipki Pass. These disputes have festered for decades and have never been settled. India's stated stand is that the Sino-Indian Trade Agreement of 1954 defines the boundary line along the axis of six passes in the region. The Chinese claim that the trade agreement had nothing to do with defining the frontier. The Indians also claim Chuva and Chuje, as per the 1684 and 1842 treaties, belong to India. Peking has, in reference to the Western Sector, already rejected these treaties. Wu-Je, yet another area, was first contested between the two countries in 1954. India claims the boundary here was confirmed by the correspondence between 1889 and 1890, and then again in 1914. China says that the boundary was never formally agreed upon.

Known as Kedarkhand or Uttarakhand in ancient Indian literature, the Garhwal and Kumaon regions were a combined political entity. Lying to the east of the Sutlej River catchment, the region extended up to the Sharda or Kali Ganga River that traditionally separated it from Nepal in the east. Towards the north, running from west to east, the watershed is all too obvious as it runs from the Yamunotri group of peaks to Gangotri and then onto the Nanda Devi group. Though the region was invaded and captured by the rampaging Gorkhas towards the end of the eighteenth century—their kingdom extending up to Kangra in the Punjab—this is perhaps the least disputed part of the present day Indo-Chinese boundary.

Ironically, the one region in the Himalayan belt where the border was perhaps the most volatile and the boundary kept shifting during the last two hundred years is today the only completely settled international boundary—the Tibet (China)-Nepal border. Ever since 1788 when the Nepalese first invaded Tibet in modern times, territorial expansion made the watershed of the Great Himalayan Range redundant. Nevertheless, after Chinese intervention and the defeat of Nepal in the 1792 war with Tibet, as per the Treaty of Betrawati, the Himalayan watershed more or less was considered to be the border. However, in the absence of any scientific survey, certain pasturelands remained under dispute.

After invading and annexing Tibet, China diligently worked towards settling and demarcating the China-Nepal border. The boundary agreement was then signed on 5 October 1961 by the king of Nepal and Mao after which the actual boundary line was demarcated physically. During the joint boundary demarcation, there were claims and counter-claims about thirty-two points. These were quickly settled by the Chinese who were also treating the settlement of the boundary with Nepal and Myanmar around that time as a means to show the rest of the world just how reasonable they were. Regarding the question of Mount Everest, the dispute was settled when the visiting prime minister, Chou En-lai, made a statement in Kathmandu that 'Mount Everest belongs to Nepal'.

Hidden from the rest of the world, the days of peaceful isolation of the Lepcha, the original inhabitants of the Teesta River Valley, were numbered, as the door into 'Mayelyang' (Sikkim) was forced open by the Bhutia people who hitherto lived above the clouds to the north. In the mid-seventeenth century, the situation was to change dramatically with the arrival of Tibetan lamas who instituted a monarchy as the protector of the faith. Buddhism and Lamaism, having originated in India prior to flourishing in Tibet, had returned to India. The wheel had turned a full circle. With the coronation of the first Chogyal, Sikkim entered what can best be described as its medieval period.

Sikkim was to play an important role in changing power equations in the years to come; along with the Chumbi Valley that formed a tri-junction with the kingdoms of Tibet, China and Bhutan, it straddled the most important trade routes between India and Tibet. For Sikkim, the Chumbi Valley was the gateway to the north, connecting Tibet over the Nathu-la and Jelep-la passes. Early records indicate that neither Tibet nor Bhutan, or China for that matter, ever held sovereignty over the Chumbi Valley. It almost seemed to exist in limbo.

In the treaty of 1890, Britain's protectorate over Sikkim was recognized by China, and the Sikkim-Tibet border was delineated. Tibet, however, was not party to this agreement and refused to recognize the boundary. This led to a series of events that eventually led to the 1903 Younghusband expedition that brushed all opposition aside and eventually entered Lhasa without waiting for formal approval from either London or Calcutta in 1904. The Dalai Lama fled to Mongolia in the hope of getting the Tsar of Russia's support against the British. To secure the withdrawal of British Indian troops from Lhasa, the Dalai Lama's representative had to agree to Younghusband's terms that were formalized as the Anglo-Tibet Convention of 1904. The agreement recognized Britain's protectorate over Sikkim and gave British India the right to establish trading posts at Gyantse, Gartok and Yadong while at the same time placing restrictions on both China and Russia. A large indemnity of Rs 7.5 million was levied and British troops were to be stationed in the Chumbi Valley adjoining Sikkim. By virtue of these terms, for all practical purposes, Tibet was converted into a British protectorate.

Public outrage in London over the war and the massacre of Tibetans, coupled with the 'unauthorized' capture of Lhasa, resulted in many of the terms being repudiated. London was worried about the Russian reaction to the blatant British aggression, while also being wary of annoying China owing to its own interests in Hong Kong. Not only was the large indemnity reduced to almost a third, it was decreed that British troops would not be stationed in the Chumbi Valley for more than three years. The resultant 1906 Anglo-Chinese Convention modified the 1904 accord, thereby legitimizing Chinese authority over Tibet. It also stated: 'The Government of Great Britain engages not to annex Tibetan territory or to interfere in the administration of Tibet. The Government of China also undertakes not to permit any other foreign state to interfere with the territory or internal administration of Tibet.'

This complicated milieu was to hold good till 1947 with some differences arising over the North Sikkim plateau. With the departure of the British from the subcontinent, Nepal, Sikkim and Bhutan retained their independence and sovereignty.

◆

The Bhutan-Tibet border follows natural features—the watershed of the Chumbi Valley in the northwest and the crest of the Great Himalayan Range of mountains to the north. It was only in the mid-eighteenth century that Bhutanese delegations to the Dalai Lama came into contact with the Chinese representatives in Lhasa, prior to which there never was a tributary relationship with Peking. Relations with Tibet itself, never particularly good, were strained considerably when Bhutan sided with Britain in the early 1900s. Trying to secure its southwestern flank against increasing foreign aggression, China claimed a vague suzerainty over Bhutan in the period just before the Chinese Revolution of 1911. The new Republic of China let the claim lapse, however, and it was never again raised publicly.

Tension in Bhutan-China relations increased with the Chinese occupation of Tibet in 1951 and again rose with the anti-Chinese revolts in eastern and central Tibet between 1954 and 1958. The massive Tibetan uprisings in 1959 and the flight to India of the Dalai Lama, as well as the heightened presence of Chinese forces on the ill-defined frontier, alerted Bhutan to the potential threat it faced, and its representative in Tibet was withdrawn. Included in the territory occupied by the PLA were the eight western Tibetan enclaves administered by Bhutan since the seventeenth century. New Delhi intervened with Peking on behalf of Thimphu regarding the enclaves, but the Chinese refused to discuss what it considered a matter between China and Bhutan. Another problem with China emerged at this time as the result of the flight to Bhutan of some 6,000 Tibetan refugees. The spectre of renewed Chinese claims to Bhutan, Sikkim, and Nepal was raised after China published a map in 1961 that showed alterations of traditional Sino-Bhutanese and other Himalayan borders in Peking's favour. Bhutan responded with an embargo on cross-border trade and forged closer links with India.

INDO-TIBET BOUNDARY (EASTERN SECTOR)

As we've seen before, when the McMahon Line was drawn in 1914 along the crest of the Himalayan ranges separating Tibet from northeast India by following the watershed principle; the Tibetan representative, Lonchen Shatra, had received the consent of the thirteenth Dalai Lama and the Tibetan Kashag before signing the agreement. For the Chinese to dispute this boundary alignment subsequently was a clever distortion of history. After the collapse of the Qing dynasty in 1911, Tibetan troops had driven the ambans out of Lhasa. In a communiqué to the United Nations in 1960, the present Dalai Lama had stated: 'Whatever the position of Tibet may be prior to 1911-1912, in any event from the day the 13th Dalai Lama proclaimed the independence of Tibet, after the invading Chinese armies had been driven out of Tibet, Tibet was not only independent de facto but de jure.'

In the east, the frontier stretches across the rugged Assam Himalayas over 1,100 kilometres, extending from Bhutan in the west to the Sino-Myanmar border in the east. While the Indian position is based on the boundary line running along the crest of the Himalayas, the Chinese claim line runs along the base of the foothills. The entire area between these two lines encompasses 83,000 square kilometres.

As per the Chinese, the area between the foothills and the McMahon Line is divided into three parts: Monyul, Layul and Lower Tsayul. During the time of the second Dalai Lama, the Monyul area had an inseparable alliance with Tibet. In the middle of the seventeenth century, these ties were further strengthened under the fifth Dalai Lama. That was also the time when the Tawang Monastery was expanded and registered in the Dgondeb (register of monasteries). The Tawang Monastery was given definite administrative and religious powers, such as appointing lower ranking officials, levying of taxes and implementing the monk service system (offering the second among three sons to serve as a lama).

The Chinese draw reference to a plethora of Tibetan documents, most of them quasi-religious in nature, that claim the region even south of the foothills in this case. In 1942, the local Tibetan government ordered an inspection tour of the borders. The report said: 'The area from Amra Tala of Tibet to Posale, Lhasding, and the Jomochu River in the south, is a vast uninhabited forest and within two miles of the above-mentioned three places are all our territory. In Water Monkey Year (1932), the British set up a camp about a mile south of the Jomochu in our territory. Eleven years have since passed. About 9 miles south of Jomochu river, we reached the trade mart Udalguri which is one of those places from which Tibet receives land rent. Another 14 miles away is Kubiale, also one of those places where we receive land rent...'

This document, according to the Chinese, shows that at the time the boundary extended up to the south of Amra Tala—which forms the basis of the Chinese claim.

However, none of these Chinese documents talk about the peoples inhabiting the area south of the watershed, who are distinctly different from the Tibetans. The Monpa were settled in the Tawang Valley when waves of migrants entered via Bhutan. Later, the Monpa converted to Lamaistic Buddhism and the establishing of the Tawang Monastery firmly placed the stamp of Buddhism on this region. The Monpa are one of the dominant tribes of Kameng district and are further subdivided into the Tawang, Dahing and Kolan sects.

The Loyul area refers to the Siang River Valley. The Chinese claim that it was always under the administration of the Po-me area, and subsequently under the Pemakoe under the Sela Monastery. As further proof, they point to important documents such as the mandates issued by the local authorities of the Tibet region since the seventeenth century covered the Loyul region. Other examples are given to back the claim that the Loyul area extended up to the Assam plain. In 1921 the Tibetans sent a high ranking official from Pemakoe. All the places beyond Gelling mentioned by the Tibetan

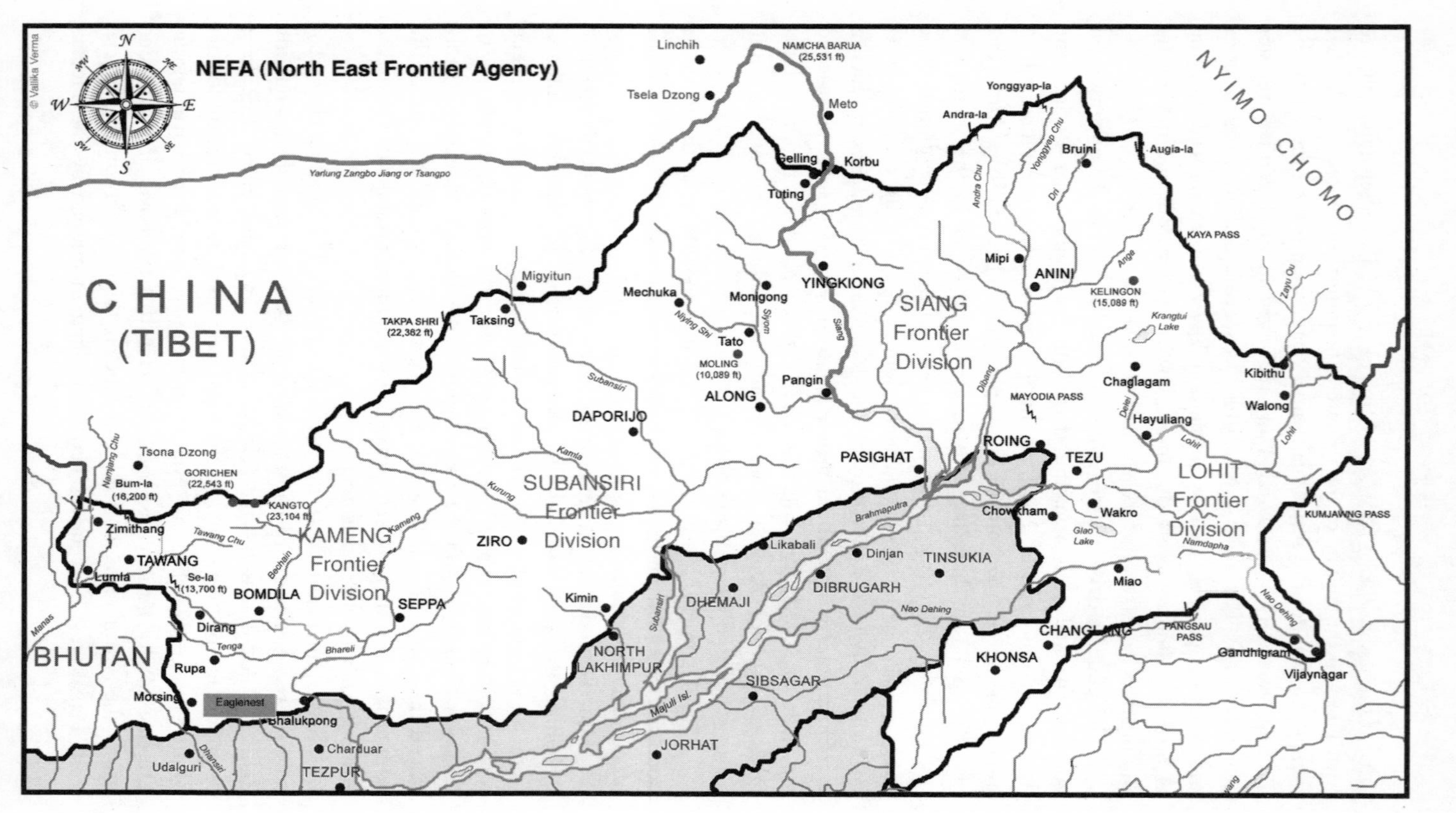
NEFA (North East Frontier Agency)
© Vallika Verma
N
E
S
W
CHINA
(TIBET)
NYIMO CHOMO
BHUTAN
Linchih
NAMCHA BARUA
(25,531 ft)
Tsela Dzong
Meto
Yarlung Zangbo Jiang or Tsangpo
Yonggyap-la
Andra-la
Augia-la
Gelling
Korbu
Tuting
Bruini
Andra Chu
Yonggyap Chu
Dri
KAYA PASS
Mipi
ANINI
Ange
KELINGON
(15,089 ft)
Krangtui
Lake
Zayu Qu
Migyitun
Taksing
TAKPA SHRI
(22,382 ft)
Mechuka
Monigong
YINGKIONG
Niying Shi
Siyom
Siang
Tato
MOLING
(10,089 ft)
Pangin
ALONG
SIANG
Frontier
Division
Dibang
MAYODIA PASS
Chaglagam
Kibithu
Walong
Delei
Hayuliang
Lohit
Subansiri
DAPORIJO
Kamla
Kurung
SUBANSIRI
Frontier
Division
ZIRO
PASIGHAT
ROING
TEZU
LOHIT
Frontier
Division
Chowkham
Wakro
Glao
Lake
Namdapha
KUMJAWNG PASS
Tsona Dzong
Namjang Chu
Bum-la
(16,200 ft)
GORICHEN
(22,543 ft)
KANGTO
(23,104 ft)
Zimithang
Tawang Chu
Kameng
KAMENG
Frontier
Division
TAWANG
Lumla
Se-la
(13,700 ft)
Bechain
BOMDILA
SEPPA
Kimin
Likabali
Brahmaputra
Dinjan
TINSUKIA
DIBRUGARH
DHEMAJI
Miao
Nao Dehing
CHANGLANG
PANGSAU
PASS
Manas
Dirang
Tenga
Bhareli
NORTH
LAKHIMPUR
KHONSA
Gandhigram
Vijaynagar
Rupa
Morsing
Eaglenest
Bhalukpong
SIBSAGAR
Majuli Isl.
Udalguri
Dhansiri
Charduar
TEZPUR
JORHAT

official extending to the vicinity of Pasighat are accordingly part of the Chinese claim.

Once again, the Chinese completely ignore the fact that the area south of Tuting (also called Duding) was essentially all tribal country. To the immediate south of the watershed, Khamba people inhabit the area around Gelling and the Yonggyap Valley. Further to the west, inhabiting the Mechuka Valley, is the other Buddhist tribe, the Memba, who are originally said to have migrated east from Tawang centuries ago. Like the Monpa, they too are deeply religious and virtually every aspect of their life is moulded by their religion. Even though the Memba are followers of Buddhism, they continue to worship some of their pre-Buddhist animistic deities. As a result, their faith is a mix of two different cultures.

The tribes in the region (mainly Abor, now known as Adi) were not only hostile to the British, they were extremely violent to any ingress into their area even from the north. Every British thrust into the region prior to 1910 was met with fierce resistance. Interestingly, beyond the watershed, the people north of the McMahon line, by and large, rarely ventured into these tribal belts, though the tribes themselves would regularly come north to trade, following a barter system. This was also true of the entire Subansiri River watershed, known as the Bokar region, which lay further east of Mechuka and extended up to the Kameng frontier.

South of the McMahon Line the Siang (also referred to as the Dihang River) flows in a north-south direction and forms the nucleus for the dendritic drainage system of the Himalayas. The 'riddle of the Tsangpo Gorge' was one of the world's biggest geographical mysteries until the early twentieth century when Captains Morshead and Bailey confirmed that the Siang was indeed the Tsangpo. After it enters NEFA just north of Gelling, the various subsidiary streams on the NEFA side, all part of the dendritic drainage system, add their substantial volume of water to the mighty Siang. After it debouches into the plains at Pasighat, the river joins the Lohit River that has already merged with the Dibang near Sadiya to form the Brahmaputra.

The southern side of the Loyul area is the main territory of the Adi Minyong tribe. They inhabit both banks of the Siang from the Tuting area to the plains of Assam. The Adi Minyong initially stubbornly resisted British attempts to subjugate this region. But in 1862 the Minyong were forced to negotiate. They accepted British sovereignty up to the foothills but their relations remained strained until 1912.

Towards the extreme east, bordering Burma, the Chinese claim that the Lower Tsayul area (Lohit River Valley) originally belonged to Tibet. In the mandate given by the Dalai Lama in 1896, it was stated that the region of both the Upper and Lower Tsayul, the area would be under the administration of Sangngachos Dzong. In 1910, the minister in charge of Border Affairs in Szechuan and Sikang, set up commissioners at Sangngachos and Tsayul and sent them on a tour of inspection of the Lower Tsayul area, mainly to guard against British intrusion. In the report submitted by the officials in 1911, it stated, 'The dividing line between Tsayul and Lo Lo is along a stream at Yapichulung at the third stage to the southeast. The British are still farther away beyond Adzara. The name of the place is not known.'

Further 'evidence' provided by the Chinese to strengthen their claim in the Lohit River Valley is a subsequent report by a survey team that charted the area up to Yapichulung: 'On the western bank of Lower Tsayul there are 10 households at Sungkung, 7 households at Sama and one household at Waloon [Walong]...'. After the Revolution of 1911, this area was still under the administration of Sangngachos Dzong. According to the Chinese, it was not until 1944 that it was invaded by Britain.

There is little doubt that China, having colonized Tibet at a time when colonialism was on its way out in the rest of Asia and Africa, based its territorial claims along the Himalayan watershed on what can best be described as the limits of Tibetan ethnography. That the claims made by the Chinese—by far surpassing anything the Tibetans themselves ever staked a claim on—was a process driven by strategic interests. Even before China's invasion of Tibet changed the equation in Asia, an equally important development on India's northernmost border had taken place that had almost gone unnoticed. This was the Chinese takeover of Sinkiang on 25 September 1949 when Nationalist Chinese troops stationed there changed their allegiance to Communist China. This immediately brought the vast expanse of the Aksai Chin into play. There can be little doubt that China decided to contest the McMahon Line in the east as a bargaining chip to secure Aksai Chin in the west.

On December 26 1959, Peking wrote to New Delhi stating that China had consistently said that 'an overall settlement of the boundary question between the two countries should be sought by the Chinese and Indian sides, taking into account the historical background and present actual position'. According to an article by Durga Das, the then editor of the *Hindustan Times*, when Chou En-lai visited India in April 1960, he told Nehru that China proposed a 'reciprocal acceptance of present actualities in both sectors and constitution of a boundary commission'. This statement implied that the Chinese would accept the McMahon Line in the eastern region in exchange for India's acceptance of China's position in the western region.

During a press conference in New Delhi, this proposal was confirmed by Chou En-lai: 'We have asked the Indian Government to adopt an attitude towards this western area similar to the attitude of the Chinese government towards the area of the eastern sector; that is, it may keep its own stand, while agreeing to conduct negotiations and not to cross the line of China's administrative jurisdiction as shown on Chinese maps.' This was perhaps the closest the two sides had ever come to an agreement. As is well known, this was not acceptable to Prime Minister Nehru and the Indian government. The boundary issue has continued to sour relations between the two countries.

Chapter 4

THE VANGUARD

ASSAM RIFLES—EARLY HISTORY

Most writers who have commented on the events leading up to the conflict between India and China in October-November 1962 have failed to pay adequate attention to the crucial role played by the Assam Rifles. Quite naturally, the entire focus was on the Indian Army and its failure to stop the Chinese assault when it came. Some observers, including the journalist Neville Maxwell, as well as declassified CIA reports, have zeroed in on Nehru's Forward Policy and tried to lay the blame at India's doorstep. This is a blatantly unfair charge, for the Forward Policy as a whole needs to be understood in its entirety, as it had been in existence from around the early 1900s. The Assam Rifles pushing forward into NEFA was a continuation of British consolidation tactics that had been put into place since 1878. Once the McMahon Line had been drawn and the Himalayan watershed identified as the boundary, it was but natural for the Assam Rifles, the only real arm of the government in the region, to make their presence felt. The army would only come into play much later. However, to get a better understanding of this police force that would play a major role in the events leading up to 1962, one must first dwell briefly on its history.

Infighting among the Ahom rulers of Assam opened the door to the British. In 1792, while the Nepalese were fighting the Tibetans, the events taking place in Assam would influence the course of history for the next 150 years. At the height of the Moamoria Rebellion (1769-1806), the Ahom king, Gaurinath Singha, turned to the rising power in the subcontinent, the British, and appealed for help. At that time the East India Company held sway over most parts of the country with only two major Indian powers hostile to the British still holding out—Tipu Sultan in Srirangapatna (Mysore) and the Marathas. In the east, Bengal had fallen into British clutches after the Battle of Plassey (1757) and the Company at the time wasn't interested in expanding eastwards. But trouble in the Ahom kingdom presented an opportunity which it could not resist.

Moamoria rebels had captured Gaurinath's capital, making his position extremely precarious. After vacillating for a while, Governor General Lord Cornwallis gave permission for the dispatch of a force consisting of 550 men under the command of Captain Thomas Welsh. Three hundred and sixty of them were sepoys from the Bengal Army, while the rest were mainly medics under Doctor John Peter Wade. Captain Welsh's sepoys were armed with the Short-land Pattern .75 calibre flintlock muskets and the India Pattern of the same weapon. This weapon, popularly known as Brown Bess, was used in the Napoleonic Wars with great success. This was a high-performance musket, which was easier to load, and it took about a minute for an expert soldier to fire four rounds. Though the rebel troops had greatly outnumbered the sepoys time and again, the Moamorias were poorly armed and poorly led; they were completely overwhelmed by the show of British strength. Most Moamorias fought with whatever weapon they could find: swords, pikes, pickaxes, spears, and even bamboo sticks. The battles were generally over even before they began. The British withdrew (as per the non-intervention policy of the new Governor General Sir John Shore) but they left an overawed Ahom kingdom in their wake.

After the withdrawal of the British forces, the political situation deteriorated rapidly and chaos prevailed all over again. The Dundiya Rebellion that played havoc with lives and property in western Assam followed the Moamoria Rebellion. The Ahom prime minister, Purnananda Buragohain, managed to bring about some semblance of order, but in order to further consolidate his power, he appointed all his relatives to high office. This brought him into direct confrontation with Badan Chandra Borphukan who was the governor of Gauhati. There was an assassination attempt that was traced to Borphukan. He then fled to Bengal where he petitioned Governor General Lord Hastings for help to overthrow Purnananda Buragohain. The British were still not willing to play their hand, so Borphukan turned to the Burmese king, Bodaw U Waing, better known as Bodawpaya.

Even the Ahom's worst enemies could not have scripted a more undignified end to their six-hundred-year rule. The Burmese were quick to exploit the situation. The first intervention was in 1816, where the Burmese faced the Ahom Army at Ghiladhari on 27 March, resulting in the Ahom Army suing for peace. That suited the Burmese commander, for his main objective was to plunder the country and take the loot back to Burma. Three years later, the Ahoms were at it again, the Burmese-installed

Chandrakanta Singha having been deposed by Purinder Singh. Once again this brought the Burmese into play, and they reinstalled Chandrakanta. This time around, the Burmese had other plans for Assam and they refused to withdraw, imposing a rule of terror on the countryside. This period came to be known as the 'manor din' in Assamese and 'chahi-taret khungtakpa' in Manipuri—seven years of devastation. The situation was soon untenable even for Chandrakanta, who yet again turned to the British for help.

Though outwardly the East India Company appeared reluctant to intervene in Assam's affairs, the Madras and Bengal armies planned a two-pronged assault under the command of Sir Archibald Campbell who then invaded Burma through the Arakan Coast and Rangoon. A third smaller force assembled at Golpara and moved upriver along the Brahmaputra into Assam. The Burmese invasion, a long hard battle of attrition, lasted two years until Bodawpaya sued for peace. As part of the settlement, the kingdom of Assam was handed over to the British (Manipur and Tripura remained independent kingdoms).

After a few years of direct rule, parts of Upper Assam were returned to Purinder Singh. This arrangement was to last until 1839 when the British decided to expand their domain and set into motion a series of annexations. Purinder Singh was deposed on grounds of 'misrule' and Assam became a part of Bengal. It was only in 1919 (under the Government of India Act) that Assam was designated as a separate province. The British, when they moved in, looked at Assam as a unit of India as a whole. This resulted in a more stable administration and more importantly, an infusion of fresh ideas that would transform the region completely. Perhaps the most important step was the planting of the first tea garden by Robert Bruce at the mouth of the Kundil River near Sadiya in 1832. With unlimited land at their disposal, tea planters went to work clearing forests and soon most of Assam was growing tea.

The flat plains of the Brahmaputra and Surma river valleys were hemmed in from all sides by densely forested mountain ranges: the Himalayas to the north, the Naga-Patkai and Manipur Hills to the east, the Lushai Hills to the south and the Jaintia, Khasi and Garo ranges in the centre. Inhabited by tribes of various hues, the plains were at their mercy, as foraging parties would swoop down, looking for loot and hostages. They would leave behind a trail of arson, pillage and terror in their wake.

One of the major reasons why the British had hesitated in getting involved in Ahom politics was the probable quantum of troops that would be required to control such a vast expanse of land. However, Captain

Welsh's six companies of sixty men each had shown that a small body of troops, equipped with the best available weapons, could defeat any enemy, regardless of their larger numbers. It was also obvious that Indian soldiers, when exposed to sordid political machinations, as was the case with the Ahom kingdom, were not too effective as a cohesive fighting force. In addition, the directors of the East India Company were always looking to curtail costs. Maintaining armies was an expensive business and in keeping with Company policy, after the Burmese War, troop strength in Assam was greatly reduced.

The need to protect the fast expanding tea gardens and imported labour now became a major problem. Regular army units had shrivelled to just four regular battalions (forbears of the 6th and 8th Gorkhas). Accordingly, it was decided to raise a levy that would operate directly under the civil government and would be distinct from both the regular army and the armed police. The levy was to be placed on a better military footing than the police so that they could be used instead of regular troops along the tribal border. The initial troops for the levy were to be drawn from the armed Bengal Civil Police and it was to be officered by police officials. Accordingly, the first unit of the new organization, the Cachar Levy, was raised in 1834-35 by Mr Grange, the civilian officer in charge at Nowgong.

Shortly after the raising of the Cachar Levy, the British undertook the first of a series of excursions into Naga territory. While the stated aim of the first expedition into Naga territory in 1839 was to dominate the Naga tribes and restrain them from their frequent raiding, another important factor was that the British had learnt that the king of Manipur was planning to include the Naga Hills in his territory. As the British consolidated their hold on the region, the levy began to emerge as the strong arm of the government. By 1862, the force had been reorganized and renamed 'Frontier Police' and fresh battalions were raised, their name dependent on their place of origin.

By 1878, the British decided to further consolidate their hold on the region. A Forward Policy was adopted and new areas were annexed. The role of the Frontier Police changed from a mainly defensive posture to a positively offensive posture involving punitive expeditions not only in British administered areas but also tribal areas that until then had been strictly off limits. There were a series of expeditions—against the Daflas and the Aka Hill Group in NEFA, the Lushai Expeditions against the Mizos, the annexation of Manipur in 1891, the Chinglong-Naga expedition in 1910-11, and the Kuki Rising between 1917 and 1919. The force also distinguished itself during World War I. This is when its name was finally changed and it began to be known as the Assam Rifles. During World War II, despite the reverses suffered in Burma against the Japanese, the men distinguished themselves, especially during the evacuation of civilians from Burma and subsequently as the secret V-Force that operated behind enemy lines. At the time of independence, the Assam Rifles had a track record that undisputedly made it one of the finest paramilitary forces in the world. For the new Indian government, it was perhaps the only real link between the rest of the subcontinent and the Northeast.

THE SWORD ARM

After the first Burmese War resulted in the annexation of Assam, the British extended their administration up to the foothills all the way from Bengal to Burma. The area to the north, reaching up to the Himalayan watershed, would come to be known as the North East Frontier Agency (NEFA) and was generally referred to as the 'un-administered' part of Assam, the affairs of individual regions being left to the local tribal people.

To the extreme west lay the kingdoms of Sikkim and Bhutan. From the British point of view, the fate of both these semi-isolated Himalayan kingdoms was linked to two major factors: the fallout of the Anglo-Gorkha wars and the degree of trade that would eventually exist with the Tibetans over the established Silk Route. Sikkim being physically closer to Nepal and the proximity of the Chogyals to Tibet resulted in a fair amount of interaction with the British. Bhutan, on the other hand, not only controlled parts of Sikkim and Kalimpong, it shared its southeastern boundary with the Ahom kingdom's northwestern border. At the time of the annexation, there had been a degree of confusion and some Bhutanese settlements had spilled into Assamese territory.

Pushing the intruders back was an immediate priority, adding to the somewhat frosty relationship that existed between the Bhutanese and the British. In 1837 and then again in 1863, missions were sent to Punaka, the Bhutanese capital. Quick to take offence at what was described as the 'high-handed behaviour' of the Bhutanese, the second mission led to a stronger British force moving into the Himalayan kingdom. The first clash took place at Daling, east of Darjeeling and then again at Dewangiri, north of Rangiya. In 1866, the Bhutanese agreed to comply with the British terms regarding the delineation of the border.

The eastern boundary of Bhutan bordered the Monpa and Sherdukpen region of NEFA. At that time the only approach to Tawang was through

Bhutan and hence it was not on the immediate radar of the British government. To the immediate north of Darrang district, the Aka tribe dominated the Kameng River Valley that was further flanked to the east by the Dafla and the Miri tribes. The Abor (now known as Adi) inhabited the hills between Subansiri and the Dibang river valleys while the three Mishmi groups had made the region bordering Burma their home. Though none of these tribes were as hostile to the British as the Naga, Kuki and Lushai that inhabited the Naga-Patkai range of mountains, the British continued to be wary of the NEFA region, their military probes being fairly shallow.

All military expeditions by the British, though labelled as punitive measures to punish the tribes for transgressing outside their area, were in effect part of their attempt to bring the frontier under their control. Though there had been minor incidents involving the Daflas and the Miris in the past, the real trouble started in 1848 when Abor warriors abducted several plains dwellers. The raid had been primarily carried out by the tribe to assert their share in the gold and fish taken from the rivers flowing through their land. Initial measures taken against the Abor (including a punitive raid under Captain Vetch) only resulted in more retaliatory acts, until the British mounted a major military campaign in 1868-69. The first attempt was a miserable failure, but the second time around a stronger force succeeded in making headway against the Abors's carefully prepared defences despite suffering heavy casualties. Finally, only after the last stockade was taken at the point of the bayonet, did the Abor submit.

At that point of time, the Abors controlled the Siang River Valley; of all the NEFA tribes, they were the most hostile towards any transgression in their area. In 1864, it was decided that a fairly large force known as the Lakhimpur Armed Police Battalion (later 2 Assam Rifles) would have to be based at Dibrugarh to look after both the Sadiya and the Lakhimpur districts. In the 1870s, the Lakhimpur Battalion was deployed against both the Abor and Mishmi tribes, but its attention was more towards Northern Nagaland where it was engaged in operations against the Ao and Lotha tribes. In 1893, a 600-strong force (consisting of both the police and the army) under Captain Maxwell supported by 1,500 porters made its way up the Siang River Valley. The expedition, ostensibly to support the political officer who was to 'punish' the Abors for taking slaves, was tasked to push upriver as far as possible, then cross to the east and return along the Dibang River to Sadiya. The mission only partly succeeded, for the Abors succeeded in launching an attack on the expedition's base camp that left forty-five dead and forty-nine wounded.

By now, past experience in other sectors was also reinforcing the belief that the paramilitary usually functioned far more smoothly when it was not saddled with army troops. Not only were mixed expeditions less successful, the cost of using regular army troops was, in relative terms, quite prohibitive. This belief got further reinforced when in 1899 another mixed expedition (eight companies of regular army and sappers plus 200 men from the Lakhimpur Battalion) under Colonel Molesworth moved against the Mishmis. The three-month expedition cost the Government of India Rs 2 lakh. It was widely believed that had only the Lakhimpur troops been used, it would have cost considerably less and the goal would have been achieved more effectively.

As a result, over the next few decades in the run-up to Independence, the paramilitary force that became the Assam Rifles, functioned almost completely independently even though it was officered by army officers on deputation. It evolved its own style of functioning, which made it the ideal first line of defence for Thorat's plan where 'lightly equipped troops' would act as a screen, falling back on the defensive line while all the time harassing the advancing Chinese lines of communication. Despite holding the portfolio of External Affairs under which the Assam Rifles functioned, neither Prime Minister Nehru nor his advisers seemed to understand the importance of the Assam Rifles, which was not only tailor-made for the defence of NEFA, but had already done all the hard work by manning most of the border. Post 1959, after the army began to deploy in the Kameng and Lohit Frontier Divisions, the Assam Rifles became the poorer cousin which, much like the army, had no clear-cut role defined for it.

MAPPING THE FRONTIER: MORSHEAD & BAILEY

In Sadiya, Assam, the buzz around finding alternative routes to Tibet and even South China was gaining ground. British interest in the region beyond the crest of the Himalayas had been renewed when the Qing government sent military forces under General Zhao Ehrfing to establish a Chinese administration in Tibet in 1910. A year later, another large mixed force under General Bowers moved up the Siang River with the intention of finding the overland route. Once again, the troops were almost immediately embroiled in a running fight with the Abor tribes who fought the British force with all the jungle guile they could bring to bear. Casualties were heavy and the expedition had to turn back.

Despite the military reverses, agreements with various tribal leaders had been reached which would allow the British to expand their administrative

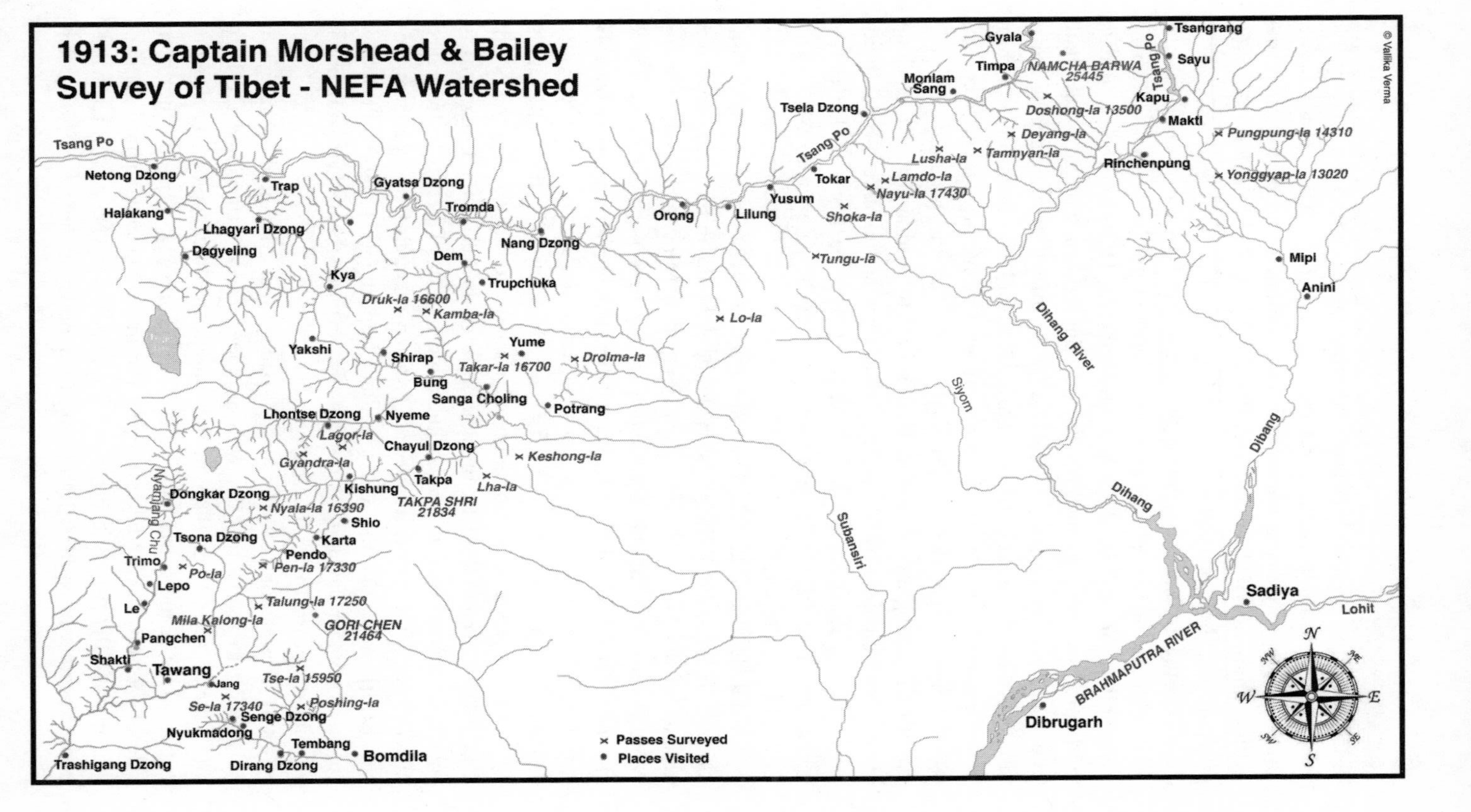
1913: Captain Morshead & Bailey
Survey of Tibet - NEFA Watershed
© Vallika Verma
Tsang Po
Netong Dzong
Trap
Halakang
Lhagyari Dzong
Dagyeling
Gyatsa Dzong
Tromda
Nang Dzong
Dem
Trupchuka
Kya
Druk-la 16600
Kamba-la
Yakshi
Shirap
Bung
Yume
Takar-la 16700
Drolma-la
Sanga Choling
Potrang
Lhontse Dzong
Nyeme
Lagor-la
Chayul Dzong
Gyandra-la
Keshong-la
Takpa
Lha-la
Kishung
TAKPA SHRI
21834
Nyamjang Chu
Dongkar Dzong
Nyala-la 16390
Shio
Tsona Dzong
Karta
Pendo
Pen-la 17330
Trimo
Po-la
Lepo
Le
Talung-la 17250
Mila Kalong-la
GORI CHEN
21464
Pangchen
Shakti
Tawang
Jang
Tse-la 15950
Se-la 17340
Poshing-la
Senge Dzong
Nyukmadong
Tembang
Bomdila
Trashigang Dzong
Dirang Dzong
Passes Surveyed
Places Visited
Gyala
Timpa
NAMCHA BARWA
25445
Monlam
Sang
Tsela Dzong
Doshong-la 13500
Kapu
Tsangrang
Sayu
Makti
Deyang-la
Pungpung-la 14310
Lusha-la
Tamnyan-la
Rinchenpung
Tokar
Lamdo-la
Nayu-la 17430
Yonggyap-la 13020
Yusum
Orong
Lilung
Shoka-la
Tungu-la
Lo-la
Mipi
Anini
Dihang River
Siyom
Dibang
Dihang
Subansiri
Sadiya
Lohit
BRAHMAPUTRA RIVER
Dibrugarh
N
E
S
W
NE
SE
SW
NW

reach into the region. However, this time, there was a lot of negative commentary in the press; both the expense and effectiveness of using army units were openly being questioned. The consensus was that small parties with Lakhimpur Battalion (Assam Rifles) escorts would be far more successful in achieving their objectives.

This theory was soon put to the test in 1912-13 when survey parties with moderate-sized escort parties were pushed up the Siang and Dibang river valleys far into the Abor and Mishmi Hills. These were areas that no outsiders had ventured into before and conventional wisdom would have expected that the survey party would be decimated. Amazingly, the tribes simply let them through. In fact, porters had hitherto been brought from other regions; now they were simply replaced by Mishmis themselves. This was a huge development and a major feather in the paramilitary force's cap. In this changing scenario, it was decided to send a survey team along with a road-building party into the Lohit Valley and explore the possibility of opening a trade route with Southwest China via Rima in Tibet. This group was successful in starting work on a bridle path up to Walong, no mean feat at the time.

Similarly, the Mishmi Exploration Survey of 1912 that included Captains George Bailey and S. F. Morshead, had little difficulty in traversing the lower reaches of the Dibang River and making it to Mipi in the valley of the Matun River, one of the key tributaries that flow north of Anini. There the party ran into a party of Khamba Tibetans who were not only friendly, but even offered to provide guides who would lead them into outer Tibet. Following the ill-fated British military expedition of 1911, the entire region hitherto referred to as 'un-administered' was now to be known as the North East Frontier Tracts (NEFT). In addition, after the fall of the Qing dynasty in China, reports reaching Assam indicated that the Tibetans had expelled all Chinese officials and troops and declared themselves independent. For the British surveyors, this was a godsent opportunity to not only follow the road to Pemako and Po-me but also explore the hitherto unknown reaches of the mythical Brahmaputra bend.

On completion of the survey, Bailey and Morshead were given permission to return to Mipi with an added caveat that should the local and Tibetan authorities allow it, they should try and explore the frontier between the Siang River Valley and Tawang, moving along the northern side of the watershed while surveying the important geographical features. Accordingly, the two British officers doubled back to Mipi with ten hand-picked porters in April 1913. During their previous visit, anticipating that sanction would be given, they had dumped two months' worth of rations at Mipi. The first half of May was spent laying out staging points of rations as far as possible along the route to Yonggyap-la (13,020 feet). Finally, in pouring rain that made progress extremely difficult, the party of twelve along with three local guides set off from Mipi on 16 May 1913.

Given that the McMahon Line was subsequently drawn up based on the findings of this team, it is perhaps worth our while to follow the route taken by them. Making short forced marches (the porters had to keep returning to ferry supplies from the earlier staging points) the party finally made it to a hut below the Yonggyap-la. On 26 May 1913, in swirling mist and falling snow, the party struggled up the last 1,500 feet to the pass which was almost impossible to find, being buried under twenty feet of snow. By then, some of the guides and porters were suffering from snow blindness. In a superhuman feat of extreme doggedness, the party somehow got across to a hut on the northern side of the pass.

After a day's halt that allowed the men to recover from the snow blindness, the party followed the watercourse to Yonggyap Da where the waters coming down from the Pungpung-la (14,310 feet) more than doubled in volume. The stream, henceforth known as the Shumo Chu, then joins the Siang River at Tambu. However, as there was no trail along the river, the only way to get to the Shumo Valley was by crossing over Pungpung-la, which was also covered in twenty feet of snow. The party then dropped down to the Chimdro Valley, where the local dzongpen was persuaded by Captain Bailey to provide porters for the onward journey. This gesture was to set an important precedent for the rest of the expedition. Finally, on 5 June, the party reached Kápu on the Siang River.

Moving downriver, the party came through Gelling village before climbing up to Rinchenjung (just short of Tuting when approached from the Tibetan side) before retracing their steps to Kápu. Moving further upstream, Morshead and Bailey reached Lágung where the dense, humid tropical jungles of the lower Siang region gave way to tall pine and cypress trees and lush grass dotted with a multitude of wild flowers. Unlike the Abor region further downstream of Tuting, the houses in the Outer Tibetan region were built of stone and had peach, walnut and pollard willow growing in groves. Before entering the Po-me Valley, the party was again held up by the authorities and detained at Showa since the British-Indian officials had assured them that the Abor Survey would not penetrate beyond Pemakó. The Tibetans worried that the two officers could be working for the Chinese who had been expelled from the area eighteen months earlier.

Captain Morshead, the trained surveyor in the party, had until then been fairly secretive about his activities that included the clandestine making of a map. Some years previously, a Chinese surveyor had also come to the Po-me Valley. When the local authorities found him suspiciously marching along counting his steps and entering numbers in a book, they promptly sent him back the way he had come. Having made friends with the Tibetan officials, Morshead instinctively decided to not only come clean about his task, but also to demonstrate the use of his instruments to the local authorities. This policy of absolute openness worked wonderfully well, for from that point onwards, all physical readings of the terrain could be taken with pinpoint accuracy and with plenty of willing helpers assisting in the task.

Despite the bonhomie with the local administration, permission to traverse the length of the Tsangpo to its source was refused. So the party left Showa on 28 June and in a couple of days reached the twin villages of Tang tó and Tang me. Most rope bridges having been destroyed by the retreating Chinese, they had to take a diversion to cross the Yigrong Tso by ferry, eventually reaching Trulung on 9 July.

At Trulung, the dzongpen of Tse-la and other officials, who had hurried to Pe on hearing of the arrival of strangers, issued the party with passports that allowed them to enter Inner Tibet. The incredible journey that would directly influence events half a century later continued. From Trulung, the survey party followed the Tibet Road along the Rong Chu via Tongkuk Dzong and the Nyima-la to Pe. The party then moved along the right bank of the Tsangpo to Gyála, where it formally entered Tibet.

The two British officers were determined to survey as much of the Tsangpo as they could. This meant they would have to head east for a while; in the end the survey party could not actually make it to the great bend itself, but they were able to more or less establish the entire course of the Tsangpo.

While returning to Gyála the weather became bright and sunny allowing Morshead to interpolate not just the Namcha Barwa but also some of the triangulated peaks across the river that culminated in the Gyála Peri. By the end of August the party had reached Tsetang, a town of some 300 houses that included a colony of Kashmiri traders from whom they procured critical provisions. From Tsetang they left the Tsangpo and entered Chumda Kyang. They were now in the typical elevated plateau country of Tibet, far above the level of trees or fuel, where in winter no crop would ripen other than a little stunted barley. Villages were few and squalid, and the undulating stony flatlands were void of all detail except when a few black yak-hair tents and scattered flocks indicated the presence of a grazing camp.

The next phase of the expedition was critical, as it would survey the little known area across the Subansiri catchment. While Morshead concentrated on the physical features, George Bailey was involved in a much wider study, collating not only the anthropological data of the region, but making extensive notes pertaining to the vegetation and wildlife of the various areas they were traversing through.

The dense leech-infested vegetation on the NEFA side of the watershed was distinctly different from the arid and dry terrain on the Tibetan side. During the next few days the Subansiri catchment was surveyed in fair detail; the party also visiting Sanga Choling and Migyitun. The last Tibetan village on the Char Chu was Drotang, after which the area was uninhabited. Lopas (Tagins) would come up to barter with the Tibetans through this wild country, but no Tibetan ever ventured into Tagin country. As a result, it proved to be extremely difficult to gather detailed information pertaining to villages beyond the uninhabited stretch of jungle which the party could not traverse either.

Returning to the northern side of the Himalayan watershed, the party made its way to Chayul Dzong from where they proceeded to the Trashi Tongme Gompa. In early October they entered into the head of the Seti Chu, a part of the drainage system of the Nyamjang Chu/Manas River. The Seti Valley was completely uninhabited and the waters cut through an impassable gorge. The track south now had to cross the main Himalayan axis by climbing up to Tulung-la (17,320 feet) before winding down a steep valley to the villages of Nyuri and Dyuri which together made up the remote district of Mago. Once again the river itself was impossible to follow, so there was a steep climb to Chera-la from where a track bifurcated to the west to link up with Tawang. This route was not taken; instead the group crossed Tse-la (15,650 feet) that brought them into the head of a tributary of the Dirang Chu (a part of the Bhoroli or the Kameng River system) that they followed to Poshing-la, situated just above Dirang Dzong. From the camp just below Poshing-la, the plains of Assam were clearly visible.

They were now in the midst of Monpa (spelt by Morshead as Mönba) country, the neat cultivated fields and solid stone houses a pleasant contrast to the barren landscape of Tibet. Marwa, buckwheat, tobacco, chillies and maize were the main crops. During the latter half of October, the Monpas were busy harvesting and stacking both the maize and the chillies, adding spectacular splashes of colour to the villages.

From Dirang Dzong they followed the established route over Se-la before dropping down to Jang and the Tawang Chu, after which they climbed up once again to Tawang. Despite having traversed some of the most daunting territory on the planet for over five months, Morshead and Bailey were not yet finished. The area west of Tawang bordering Bhutan still needed to be surveyed, plus some members of their party had been left behind in Tibet.

The survey party followed the established trade route from Tawang to Lumla, then turned north along the Nyamjang Chu and crossed back into Tibet at Khenzemane. There are some romantic stories about Morshead having been smitten by a Monpa girl. Whatever the actual reasons, they did not survey either the Tsangdhar Ridge or the Thagla Ridge, and erroneously marked the Nam Ka Chu that flowed in from the tri-junction with Bhutan, as flowing north to south rather than west to east. This thin strip, the Nam ka Chu Valley—approximately 14 kilometres in length and entirely uninhabited—would later become infamous. After collecting the remaining members of their party, the expedition retraced its steps, following the route over Se-la and Dirang Dzong before returning to the Assam plains.

There are certain other aspects of the Morshead-Bailey expedition that need to be highlighted. The party set out from Mipi in mid-May and completed the journey in six months. This was most remarkable, for a similar run on the southern side of the Himalayas would simply not have been feasible. While on the Tibetan axis the party had to move along the Tsangpo from Assam, owing to the north-south orientation of all major river valleys—Lohit, Dibang, Siang, Subansiri, Kameng and Manas—getting from one to the other was almost impossible. Hence, should there be a military confrontation with Tibet (or China or Russia), defending the watershed from the south would be a herculean task.

Second, the Chinese shadow would always loom over Tibet, especially the Kham region. Already the Nepal-Tibet and Sikkim-Bhutan confrontations had seen Chinese intervention in the past. Whatever Tibetan sentiments may have been, they simply did not have a geographical barrier like the Himalayas on their eastern flank or the military ability to keep the Chinese out indefinitely.

With the collapse of Chinese authority over Tibet in 1912, the scenario was to undergo a major change. At the time, the thirteenth Dalai Lama was in exile in India and he immediately began to make preparations to return to Lhasa. The last of the Chinese still holding out were granted free passage and allowed to return home via Calcutta. After the Dalai Lama's return to the Tibetan capital via Yatung in January 1913, he issued what the Tibetans regarded as an unambiguous declaration of independence.

To further underline the Dalai Lama's determination to fully separate from China, the Tibetans signed a treaty with Russian-dominated Mongolia that recognized each other's independence. The Tibet-Mongol Treaty was one of the contemporary factors that indicated that the changing equation between the Tibetans and the Chinese required new international agreements. This resulted in the Simla Convention of 1914.

However, at that stage, in keeping with past British policy, it was felt that for the convention to have any meaning, China had to be a party to it. There were primarily two objectives of the convention: the first was to settle the artificial concept of an 'Inner' and 'Outer' Tibet. The second, which did not involve China directly, would be the settlement boundary between British India and Tibet.

The British recognized that they could not possibly come to Tibet's aid in the event of the Chinese deciding to flex their military muscle. It was therefore necessary for them to have two platforms on either side of Bhutan from where they could influence events—the Chumbi Valley to the west and Tawang in the east. Accordingly, there were protracted discussions pertaining to the threat from China between Sir Charles Bell who was assisting Henry McMahon, the British foreign secretary, and the Lonchen Shatra.

SIMLA CONVENTION, 1914, AND ITS AFTERMATH

Strangely, the British government went to great lengths to keep the proceedings of the Simla Convention of 1914 under wraps. So much so that even the Assam government was kept in the dark as to what was decided as the final frontiers of India. The explanation perhaps lay in the earlier 1907 Anglo-Russian Convention. The agreement with Russians had stipulated that both the British and the Russians acknowledge Chinese suzerainty over Tibet and that neither side could sign an independent treaty with the Tibetans. Article II of the section titled 'Arrangement Concerning Thibet' stipulated: 'In conformity with the admitted principle of suzerainty of China over Thibet, Great Britain and Russia engage not to enter into negotiations with Thibet except through the intermediary of the Chinese Government.'

In Simla, both the Lonchen Shatra and Henry McMahon, were extremely well prepared. The Tibetan representative was equipped with virtually every conceivable document—all the sheets were carefully stacked between wooden slats and wrapped in colourful Chinese silk in the customary Tibetan manner. Almost all historical books and documents had exotic names: *The Feast of Pleasure for the Perfected Youths* gave an account of the early boundaries between China and Tibet, compiled at the time of the fifth Dalai Lama. *The Golden Tree, the World's Sole Ornament* gave information pertaining to even older boundaries. There were registers of houses, monasteries, tenants, landlords, taxes, incomes; registers of doorsteps and fireplaces, each doorstep and fireplace connoting a family; bonds of allegiance; military lists, and agreements showing the quotas of troops to be supplied by various districts; laws, regulations, legal judgments and executive orders; these and other proofs of actual administration were brought down from Tibet to support their claims.

The British on the other hand, had most of the territory under their control mapped out. Apart from a plethora of surveys by various expeditions, McMahon had access to Bailey and Morshead's recent survey that painted a clear picture of the situation on either side of the border in the extreme east. The British also had Claude White's equally precise survey of the Sikkim Plateau (where the Teesta River originated), East Sikkim, the Chumbi Valley and Bhutan. While the border with Nepal was well defined, the northern border that stretched from Kumaon all the way to the Aksai Chin was also a relatively known entity. The only unexplored region was the gap between the upper reaches of the Subansiri eastwards to the Kameng River (Bokar region).

On the map, the lower thick line running east-west formed the McMahon Line between India and Tibet on the one hand and India and Burma on the other. A second north-south continuous line indicated the boundary between China and Tibet. The territory lying between the thick line and the dotted line was referred to as Inner Tibet. It is significant to note that when the Chinese later raised an objection to the Simla Convention, it was only regarding the position of Inner Tibet and had nothing to do with the demarcation of the McMahon Line. Interestingly, in the subsequent border agreement with Burma that was signed in Peking in October 1960, the Chinese government accepted the portion of the same McMahon Line—nearly 200 kilometres—that separated Tibet from Burma.

The map attached to the Simla Convention had been initialled by the British representative, Henry McMahon, and signed by the Chinese delegate, Chen I-fan and the chief Tibetan representative, the Lonchen Shatra, on 27 April 1914. However, almost immediately, China refused to ratify the convention. At that stage, both the British and the Tibetan governments agreed that the refusal precluded China from enjoying any of the rights it had been granted in Outer Tibet, and that the agreement would be binding on the British and Tibetan governments.

The most significant factor that needs to be understood is that the Simla Convention of 1914 merely formalized what had in effect been the traditional boundary between the territories of India and Tibet (other than Tawang). It was a recognized and long-established boundary that was not 'created', but only confirmed by treaty. If anything, Captain Morshead had provided the scientific data while Captain Bailey had provided the cultural and demographic information to support the validity of the established frontier. The local authorities and inhabitants of the area as well as the governments of the two sides had for centuries recognized the validity of this boundary alignment, and even the People's Government of China, after they established their control in Tibet, proceeded on the basis that this was indeed the boundary. The same watershed boundary represented by the McMahon Line of 1914 also held good for Bhutan, Sikkim, Nepal, Kumaon, Garhwal and Kinnaur extending up to the Sutlej River. The frontier beyond the Sutlej was also reasonably well established at the time: Lahaul, Ladakh and the Aksai Chin extending up to the Karakorams.

The British hesitation, apart from the reasons listed earlier, to go public with the details of the Simla Convention after 1914 can also be understood. There was still a huge gap on the ground between the administered part of Assam and the McMahon Line. The Mishmis and the Abors had only recently started allowing survey parties through their territories, but for all practical purposes remained uninitiated to modern governance. To the west were the Gallongs, Minyongs, Boris, Daflas, Akas and Sherdukpens, who were also part of the NEFT (later NEFA) area. Besides, almost immediately, World War I had erupted in Europe, resulting in the weakening of the Assam Rifles that had to divert a portion of its trained forces to Gorkha battalions.

The Chinese attack on Eastern Tibet even while the Simla Convention was in effect may have had a major role to play in the Tibetans agreeing to give up certain areas that were under their control. In the exchange of notes attached to the convention, Tawang was made a part of India. Though not formerly acknowledged, the British negotiators did not want to make any direct payment for Tawang, for it would 'make us a party to interference with the integrity of Tibet'. In the agreement with Lonchen Shatra, it was agreed that money would be paid later, 'for some supposedly unconnected purpose'. In the event, a month after the convention was signed and Tawang ceded to British India, the Tibetans were given 5,000 Lee Enfield rifles and 500,000 rounds of ammunition.

The annexation of the Chumbi region into British India did not happen only because at the time it did not have a border with India, flanked as it was to the southwest by Sikkim, and the southeast by Bhutan. The handing over of Tawang to the British did not go down particularly well with the Loseling College of Drepung Monastery which had lost a major source of income. To further complicate matters, London was adamant about the strict adherence to the 1907 Anglo-Russian Treaty. By the time this policy was changed, with fighting breaking out between the Tibetans and the Chinese in 1917, British officers in India had already taken the decision to keep the 1914 Simla Convention under wraps.

The Simla Convention was badly handled by the British. The veil of secrecy that was adopted by them allowed the Chinese to question its very validity. Subsequently, the Chinese even accused the British of having lied about the McMahon Line.

THE BOUNDARY CRYSTALIZES

In the immediate aftermath of World War I, the Assam Rifles continued to build a formidable reputation for itself. The Kuki uprising (1917-1919) was effectively dealt with, as was the crisis in the Chin and Lushai Hills at the same time. Many men had fought with regular army units during the Great War and as they now returned to their parent units, all Assam Rifles battalions found themselves oversubscribed in NCOs and men.

The 1913 survey and the subsequent 1914 drawing up of the boundary had placed Tawang well south of the McMahon Line. Though this was kept a secret even from the Assam government, this was the only region where the Tibetans were exercising control on a non-Tibetan population across the watershed. Perhaps with this in mind, the British decided to raise an additional Assam Rifles battalion, which came into being in June 1920 at Lokhra. Along with 2 Assam Rifles, 5 Assam Rifles would be the other unit destined to play a major role in the events to come.

The new battalion's Area of Responsibility (AOR) included the Kamrup and Darrang borders that faced Aka and Dafla dominated areas. The battalion set up posts (all in the plains) facing North Lakhimpur, Harmati, Dikulmakh, Hathipaithi, Udalguri and Darrang. However, around this time other events were to occur that would put any thoughts of venturing out towards Tawang on the back burner. The time between 1920 and 1922 saw a spike in activity in the struggle for independence following British atrocities in Jallianwala Bagh in 1919 and elsewhere. After Mahatma Gandhi moved a resolution at a special session of the Indian National Congress in Calcutta pledging total non-cooperation with the government, Assamese nationalists instigated riots and organized strikes in the tea gardens. The Assam Rifles, including 5 Assam Rifles, was constantly deployed in an attempt to bring the situation under control.

By 1932, as part of the post-war economy drive, 5 Assam Rifles was disbanded and its men transferred to 2 Assam Rifles to form an amalgamated, composite unit comprising two headquarters and eighteen platoons. In the new deployment, only four platoons were left at Lokhra, which was the gateway into the Kameng Sector.

However, shortly thereafter, the Government of India Act of 1935 necessitated a more accurate defining of the tribal areas in Assam. It was now public knowledge that the frontier of India had been wrongly shown on British maps, and that the Tawang salient was indeed a part of British India. The Assam government was quick to act. The political officer from Balipara, Captain G. S. Lightfoot, was ordered to undertake a 'preliminary and exploratory' mission to Tawang. On 12 April 1938, Lightfoot set out from Lokhra with a force of two platoons (200 rifles) under the command of Major W. F. Brown. The column proceeded into the thick jungle-clad hills, moving along the Bhutan border via Doimara, Shergaon and then across the fir-clad slopes of Manda-la into Dirang Dzong. Despite the difficulties created by the dzongpens, they commandeered enough local villagers and after crossing Se-la the force reached Tawang on 30 April 1932.

At first the Monpa were evasive and not willing to engage with the British officers. However, the men managed to make inroads with the local population that lived in a state of constant terror, exploited by both the lamas from the Tawang Monastery and the dzongpens. The next two months were spent in visiting various scattered settlements, the officers impressing on the people that they were British-Indian citizens who could not be subjugated by the Tibetans. The resentment against years of exploitation soon began to manifest itself and the Monpas began to grow more forthcoming.

On his return to Assam, Captain Lightfoot reported that the inhabitants in both the Sherdukpen and Monpa areas were most willing to come under British administration but they lived in mortal dread of Lhasa and its henchmen. The Sherdukpens, in fact, referred to the Tibetan dzongpens as zakpas, meaning 'the plunderers'. Lightfoot recommended that gradual steps be taken to bring the area under British-India's administration. While the Assam government in Shillong concurred with Lightfoot's recommendations, the Indian government dragged its feet, citing financial constraints. This inaction had its ramifications in the Dirang-Tawang belt, for those who were perceived to have been friendly with the Assam Rifles personnel were subsequently victimized by both Tibetan dzongpens and monastery lamas.

While the Tibetan government strongly protested Captain Lightfoot's expedition, the Chinese stepped up their cartographic offensive. Maps published around that time showed Tawang as a part of Sikang Province and the Tibetan government continued to collect taxes south of the McMahon Line once the Assam Rifles party withdrew. The British-Indian government, ever hypersensitive to Chinese reactions, ignored the issue.

THE 1940S (THE TIBETANS COME CALLING)

Far more dramatic events then took centre stage. The thirteenth Dalai Lama, Thubten Gyatso, died on 17 December 1933 and the long process to find and anoint a successor began. This period coincided with the outbreak of World War II and, suddenly, in the geopolitical scenario, China found itself on the side of Great Britain and the United States of America. The Americans, far removed from the ground realities of Sino-Tibetan relations, began to prod the British at the behest of Chiang Kai-shek to recognize Chinese suzerainty over Tibet. Unable to stand up to US pressure, in the Eden Memorandum of August 1943, the British gave in but threw in a face-saving caveat—that Tibet was to be regarded as 'autonomous'. What the Chinese understood of that word, the world will probably never know.

The organization of Assam Rifles units changed during World War II, bringing them more in line with the regular battalions of the Indian Army. After a gap of ten years, 5 Assam Rifles was re-raised on 1 April 1942. During the war it had served as a training battalion, but was also expected to look after NEFT. There was also a much-required increase in the officer strength. Prior to 1882, the entire leadership had been in the hands of police officers. Subsequently, apart from the commandant and one British sergeant (who were both deputed from the army), each battalion relied on Indian officers who by and large proved to be extremely efficient and resourceful. At the time of Independence, Indian officers, who were on deputation from the army, were running all six existing Assam Rifles units.

In November 1943, 2 Assam Rifles and some platoons of 5 Assam Rifles were removed from the Burma front and were once again placed under the command of the Inspector General of Police, Government of Assam. The main reason for the reversion of the two battalions to the state authorities at the height of World War II was an important step that would have repercussions later.

Though the administration had set up an Assam Rifles post at Rupa in 1941, the presence of a small detachment was meant to protect the

Sherdukpens from their more warlike Aka and Miji neighbours. The detachment was not meant to get into a confrontation with Tibetan officials. The intrusion by the Tibetan Army in November 1942 into the Dirang Dzong area and the Kameng River Valley took the British completely by surprise. The show of strength on the part of the Tibetans was in all probability in response to Captain Lightfoot's earlier thrust into the Tawang salient. The intrusions rattled the British who were used to bullying the Tibetans but were not prepared for any counter aggression. However, with the Japanese sweeping across Burma into Manipur and Nagaland and threatening the Assam Valley itself, the British decided not to react as the last thing they needed then was to open up another front.

The Assam Rifles post at Rupa reported the arrival of Tibetan troops and monitored their presence as they advanced right up to Bhalukpong in the foothills. The timing of their arrival in Tawang and Dirang Dzong in November was significant, as was the route taken by the troops. While one detachment came down the Khenzemane-Nyamjang Chu axis and entered Tawang, another followed the initial route taken by Morshead and Bailey, crossed Tse-la and arrived directly at Dirang Dzong after crossing Poshing-la.

Through the winter of 1942-43, the Tibetan troops encamped in both the Tawang and Kameng regions. During this period, the Tibetans conducted detailed surveys of the various alternate tracks that existed, especially yak trails that could be used to bypass Se-la if necessary. Further south, Bomdila and the tracks around Manda-la were also studied. The Tibetan troops established a camp near Bhalukpong for a while but were then withdrawn from the region by Lhasa.

British officers in Delhi handling the two northern countries felt that the developments in China would inevitably have an effect on Tibet. They were worried that inaction on the part of the British to the Tibetan ingress beyond Tawang might lead to further such incidents. Accordingly, during the next two years, the Assam Rifles set up permanent posts at Karbo, Riga, Pangin and Pasighat in the Siang River Valley, and also at Walong, Changwinti, Hayuliang and Denning in the Lohit River Valley. Even though maintaining these posts, especially during wartime, was a logistical nightmare, it was believed that the presence of Assam Rifles troops in the vicinity would act as a deterrent to any further Tibetan thrust. As the pressure began to ease in the east after the defeat of the Japanese at Kohima, aircraft belonging to the Royal Indian Air Force and the Royal Air Force began to undertake airdrop sorties. This reduced the administrative pressure on the Assam Rifles considerably.

While the Union Jack still fluttered over India, there would be a final twist in the tale. In April 1945, the Tibetan government presented to the British Mission in Lhasa a strongly worded protest that had been passed by the Tibetan National Assembly against British-Indian activities in the tribal areas south of the McMahon Line. Using flowery similes, the Tibetans in their letter talked of the 'big insect' eating up the 'smaller insect' which would cause 'the bad name of the British Government' to 'spread like the wind'.

This letter caused a major flutter in London, New Delhi, Shillong and Gangtok for it looked like the Tibetans were questioning the 1914 Simla Agreement as well. Though the letter didn't say it, there was a hidden threat that the Tibetans might go so far as to denounce the 1914 Convention. In the ensuing correspondence that aimed to draft a logical reply to the Tibetans, it was felt that behind everything was the fact that all Tibetan officials were looking with apprehension to the time when the Dalai Lama would come of age and they would be called to account for having acquiesced in anything which could be considered harmful to Tibet. For thirty years the British government had been inactive and there were doubts whether the British would support Tibet adequately with regard to China.

The 'big insect-small insect' quip resulted in a lot of time being devoted to the drafting of a reply to be communicated to the Tibetans by A. J. Hopkinson, special envoy of the viceroy, during his visit to Lhasa. The British said they had been Tibet's neighbours for 200 years, and had never annexed even a 'scrap of Tibetan territory'; had they indeed been 'covetous of annexing Tibetan territory, they could have easily done so in 1904'. They said firmly that '[w]hile it was true that for many years Britain did not trouble to occupy the territory in question. It made no difference to Britain's right to act as she thinks proper when she thinks proper in her own territory. Their officials have been moving forward to the frontier and will continue to move forward. The armed men who accompany those officers are not troops but a police force (Assam Rifles) for the preservation of peace and order among the tribes who inhabit the area. However, the British will not extend their activities beyond the Red Line; they will not touch one inch of Tibetan territory.'

After World War II, with the collapse of the Empire imminent, the British attitude towards Tibet promptly changed. As the British Raj entered its last few days, its tone and manner towards the Tibetans was quite different from the earlier attitude where British forces would not hesitate to bring down anything that stood in their path. In June 1945, the adviser to the Governor of Assam, J. P. Mills, prepared a top secret paper on the suitability of the Se-la range as an administrative boundary. The governor of Assam in a covering note to New Delhi concurred with Mills.

However, though there continued to be talk of 'adjusting the boundary' to suit Tibetan sentiment, no formal offer was ever made or discussed. The British, for their part, took a considered decision not to rake up the issue unless the Tibetans raised the subject. Hopkinson came to Lhasa and after spending three months holding talks with various officials on a range of subjects, left Tibet on 31 January 1946 via Gyantse and Yatung. On 28 February he filed a lengthy report from Gangtok in which he commented on the handing over of the reply to the 'big insect-small insect' letter of 18 April 1945:

'When I presented the finally approved text of the aide-memoire (cum appendix), both the Foreign Secretaries were present together, the first time for several weeks. Rai Sahib Sonam set it forth paragraph-by-paragraph, sentence-by-sentence, to the Clerical Foreign Secretary, who was new to the subject and genuinely anxious to learn. The lay Foreign Secretary, Surkhang Dzasa, started off, as usual, full of pep, taking copious notes in Tibetan round hand. Then he gradually sagged *(supposedly on opium)*, till he looked like death, a ghastly yellow. Then, after a little snooze, the exposition still proceeding, he recovered sufficiently to cock one eye open, and say to his Clerical colleague, "It is all just a repeat of last year".

'After that meeting, not one word was said to me anywhere about the matter *(McMahon Line)*, and there was not the slightest change in my social relations with the *Kashag* or anyone else, including the Sera representatives, who continued almost heartily friendly to the end.'

This continued to be, more or less, the situation in the North East Frontier Tract until 15 August 1947, when Britain, a depleted super power post World War II, was forced to give up its grip on the Indian subcontinent. Considering the long history of border disputes and the fact that the area was not under army jurisdiction, it's not entirely surprising that the events of 1962 caught India unprepared. Palit was to say much later, 'Frankly, at the time, four-fifths of the Indian Army didn't know where the hell Tibet was.'

TOP LEFT: *Prime Minister Jawaharlal Nehru and Chairman Mao Tse-tung.* TOP RIGHT: *Defence Minister V. K. Krishna Menon.* BOTTOM: *Army Commanders' Conference, New Delhi, 1959; (Left to right) Lieutenant General S. P. P. Thorat (Eastern Army Commander), Lieutenant General Pran Thapar (Western Army Commander), Lieutenant General Kulwant Singh (Southern Army Commander), Jawaharlal Nehru, General K. S. Thimayya (Chief of Army Staff) and V. K. Krishna Menon* (Lieutenant General S. P. P Thorat Collection).

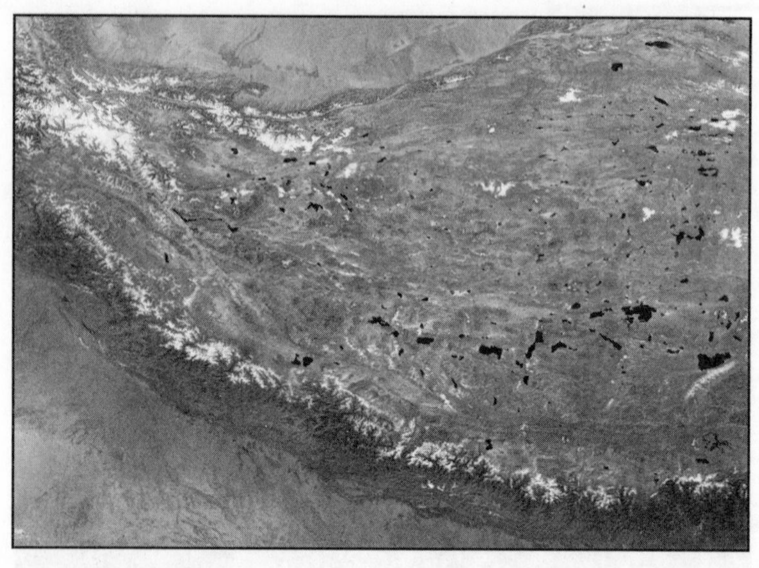

TOP: *Satellite image of the Himalayan sweep with the Gangetic Plain to the south and the Tibetan Plateau to the north.* BOTTOM LEFT: *General K. S. Thimayya, DSO, COAS (8 May 1957 to 7 May 1961).* BOTTOM RIGHT: *General Pran Thapar, COAS (8 May 1961 to 19 November 1962)* (Karan Thapar).

TOP: *Lieutenant General S. P. P. Thorat, DSO, the Eastern Army Commander.* BOTTOM: *Thorat receiving Defence Minister V. K. Krishna Menon in Lucknow before Exercise Lal Qila in March 1960* (Thorat Collection).

TOP: *Prime Minister Nehru with General Thimayya, as Defence Minister Krishna Menon looks on.* BOTTOM: *Chou En-lai, the Chinese premier, with Nehru during the Afro-Asia Conference in Bandung (Indonesia), April 1955.* (Nehru Memorial Foundation)

TOP: *Tibetan monks emerge from the Potala Palace in Lhasa and surrender to Chinese troops during the 1959 unrest.* MIDDLE: *His Holiness the Dalai Lama on his way to India.* BOTTOM: *The Dalai Lama's arrival at the 5 Assam post at Khenzemane.* (Assam Rifles)

Captain F. M. Bailey during the 1912 survey of the Mishmi Hills (Assam Rifles).

The Yonggyap-la with the 25,000-foot Namcha Barua visible in the distance.

TOP: *The 1914 Simla Conference with B. D. Bruce, Chen I-fan, Sir Henry McMahon, Lonchen Shatra and Teichi Trimon* (Assam Rifles). BOTTOM LEFT: *Charles Bell, the man who negotiated the Tawang deal with the Tibetans* (Assam Rifles). BOTTOM RIGHT: *Major 'Bob' Khathing, the political officer who led the Assam Rifles expedition to Tawang in 1951* (Professor Labrang Khathing).

Rare photographs of Major Bob Khathing's expedition to Tawang in 1951. Clockwise: being welcomed at Bomila; holding court in Tawang; the Assam Rifles staging a flag march; and crossing Se-la. (Khathing Collection)

Generals Umrao Singh, Mohinder Pathania, Pran Thapar and 'Bogey' Sen with the governor, General Shrinagesh, in Shillong.

BELOW: *Thapar arriving at Tezpur with Kaul; moving by road to Tawang; ceremonial welcome at the monastery, Kaul, Thapar, Umrao Singh and Amrik Singh inside Tawang monastery; group photograph to mark Thapar's visit to Tawang–Amrik Singh, Lieutenant Colonel B. S. Ahluwalia, Kaul, Thapar, and Umrao Singh.* (Lieutenant General Umrao Singh Collection)

ABOVE LEFT: *Captain G. S. Bhatia and Major B. Avasthy in Subathu prior to 2 Rajput's move to Walong towards the end of 1959* (Lieutenant General Milan Naidu). ABOVE RIGHT: *Thapar being introduced to the staff of 7 Brigade at Tawang.*

ABOVE RIGHT: *Kaul with Umrao Singh sharing lunch;* ABOVE LEFT: *with Lieutenant Colonel B.S. Ahluwalia at Hathung-la* (Umrao Singh Collection). BOTTOM: *Troops on the move in NEFA in 1962* (Rivers of Silence).

The Tser Jong Tso from where the Nam Ka Chu originates; the stream then descends rapidly between the Thagla and Tsangdhar ridges. An Indian Army patrol visited the area in 1989 (Colonel Hunny Bakshi).

An aerial shot of the Nam Ka Chu Valley taken in 2010.

TOP: *Sen, Mohinder Pathania, Thapar, and Umrao Singh in Shillong* (Umrao Singh Collection). MIDDLE: *Niranjan Prasad, John Dalvi and Ahluwalia at 4 Division HQ in Tezpur* (Umrao Singh Collection). BOTTOM: *Second Lieutenant Amarjit Singh 'Tiger' Behl, the GPO, with 17 Field Para at Tsangdhar* (Brigadier Tiger Behl).

Major General Niranjan Prasad (HQ 4 Division)*; Brigadier John Dalvi* (Indian Military Academy)*; Lieutenant Colonel B. S. Ahluwalia (1/9 GR); Lieutenant Colonel M. S. Rikh, Major Gurdial Singh; Major B. K. Pant (all from 2 Rajput), Major M. S. Chaudhry (9 Punjab); Captain G. S. Bhatia and Captain M. S. Mangat of 2 Rajput* (Lest We Forget *and* Rivers of Silence).

Captain Mahabir Prasad (1 Sikh); Lieutenants Bhup Singh and Subhash Chander (2 Rajput), Second Lieutenants Onkar Dubey (2 Rajput); G. P. S. Rao (4 Grenadiers); B. D. Dogra (1/9 GR), Subedar Dashrath Singh and Naik Udai Singh (both 2 Rajput); Sepoy Chain Singh (9 Punjab). (Lest We Forget *and* Rivers of Silence)

The Zimithang Valley with the Tactical HQ of 4 Infantry Division.

LEFT: *Artist's impression of 1 Sikh deployed at Bum-la* (HQ 14 Corps). RIGHT: *Lieutenant Hari Pal Kaushik, the company commander at Tongpeng-la* (Indian Military Academy).

TOP: *A stone slab marks the spot where the 5 Assam Rifles platoon along with 1 Sikh dug in and met the first wave of Chinese attacks on Bum-la.* BOTTOM: *The Tawang Monastery, the birthplace of the sixth Dalai Lama, seen while approaching from Bum-la.*

BOOK III

The Valley of Death

Chapter 5

THE EYE OF THE STORM

DHOLA INCIDENT

In early September 1962, a Chinese patrol came down the Thagla Ridge to Bridge 3 at the Nam Ka Chu and asked the men at the Assam Rifles post at Dhola to withdraw. According to the Chinese, the post was on their side of the border. The post commander held his ground, and the Chinese retreated. On 8 September, at 8 in the morning, a second patrol of sixty Chinese soldiers, armed with AK-47 rifles, came down the same route. Thinking that the Chinese had returned with intent, the JCO panicked and radioed Lumpu and Lum-la that a force of 600 soldiers was closing in on his position at Dhola.

The JCO's exaggerated reaction set in motion events that would eventually culminate in a full-scale attack by the Chinese. A force of 600 men roughly translates into a full-strength infantry battalion, and therefore it was not surprising that alarm bells started ringing, not just in Tezpur, but in Lucknow and New Delhi as well. The JCO's word was not questioned or further verified and even though the Chinese remained on the north bank of the Nam Ka Chu, the damage had been done. 7 Brigade ordered the post to hold its position, while additional Assam Rifles troops from Lumpu and Lum-la were told to move immediately to Dhola.

Brigadier John Dalvi was in Tezpur, from where he was to proceed on leave, which was cancelled and he was ordered to report to Tawang the next day. Other far-reaching decisions were also taken: as we have seen, 1/9 GR having finished its tenure in Tawang was in the process of entraining at Missamari on its way to a well-deserved peace station. It was told to immediately head back to Tawang, while 2 Rajput, on its way to Mathura after completing its three years in Walong, was told to stay put at Charduar and await further orders.

The next day, Major General Niranjan Prasad sent for Lieutenant

Colonel Maha Singh Rikh and told him that 2 Rajput was to move into the Kameng Frontier Division where it was being placed under the command of 7 Infantry Brigade. Rikh protested that his battalion was not prepared to make such a drastic move. Having handed over charge to 6 Kumaon in Walong three months ago, the battalion was in Charduar where it was doing routine training before moving to its peacetime location. The men were not equipped with winter clothing. Apart from crucial items like radio sets, all they had on them were their personal weapons. Prasad, however, insisted that the battalion must move in the next few hours—the time of departure was set for 5 a.m. on 10 September. Transport was at that very moment being requisitioned by divisional staff and they were to get to Dirang Dzong, where they would receive further orders.

Out of an authorized strength of twenty-four officers, the battalion had only fourteen on its rolls; of these, the second-in-command (2IC), Major Gurdial Singh was on leave, Major Rajput, the Alpha Company commander, was on the Senior Officers' Course, Captain Raghbir Sain was on his way to Staff College, Captain Ashok Kalyan Verma was an instructor at the IMA, and Second Lieutenant Bhup Singh was on a Long Range Patrol in the Lohit Frontier Division. That the battalion managed to move at such short notice was a miracle and a lot of credit went to the acting 2IC, Major B. K. Pant.

Dalvi reached Tawang on 9 September and, with his staff, prepared his appreciation of the situation. The next day, Niranjan Prasad visited him, and using a sand model, they went over the various details pertaining to the tactical situation, the quantum of troops required and the logistical details. The assessment, based on the sand model discussion, was forwarded to Lieutenant General Umrao Singh, GOC XXXIII Corps, who in turn passed it on to Eastern Command, cautioning against mounting hasty operations in the Dhola region. Adding his views to Dalvi's appreciation, Umrao Singh said: 'Our ability to reinforce due to lack of troops and roads is limited. Our troops are on restricted scales of rations and have no reserves. Clothing is scanty for the extreme cold. We are short of ammunition and there [are] hardly any defence stores available. We also do not have adequate fire support.'

Umrao Singh further added that 'an attempt on our part to clear the Chinese south of Thagla Ridge will amount to an act of rashness'. To produce even a semblance of the resources required for this purpose, he would have to completely uncover Tawang and also withdraw troops from Nagaland. He pointed out that Tawang was vital ground and its fall into Chinese hands would have far more disastrous consequences than the fall of Dhola. Umrao Singh's cautionary note did not go down well with the Eastern Army Commander, Lieutenant General L. P. Bogey Sen, who until then, had hardly shown any interest in the affairs of NEFA.

Niranjan Prasad reverted to Dalvi with the following directions: 7 Infantry Brigade should be prepared to move to the Dhola area in the next 48 hours (12-13 September) as desired by Eastern Command; 1 Sikh was to remain in Tawang guarding the Bum-la axis; 9 Punjab was to move immediately to Lumpu. He further directed that in the event of a confrontation with the Chinese, the Indians should do the following: First, persuade them to vacate Indian territory; second, if persuasion was not effective then dig in to prevent them from advancing any further and; third, firing to be resorted to only in self-defence. The brigade commander, Dalvi, was to stay in Tawang till 9 Punjab reached Lumpu en route to Dhola.

Sen and Umrao Singh visited Niranjan Prasad at Tezpur two days later. Despite Umrao Singh's clear-headed views, Sen expressed his deep dissatisfaction with the pace at which things were moving. A harried Niranjan Prasad then got on the phone to Tawang and yelled at Dalvi to get a move on, ordering the bewildered brigade commander to move immediately to Lumpu. Niranjan Prasad shouting at Dalvi on the phone was totally out of character. Obviously, GOC 4 Division could see a situation developing which he knew was far from practical, yet he seemed incapable of putting his foot down. 9 Punjab's orders were also changed, asking them to concentrate on Dhola rather than Lumpu. Moving with his Brigade HQ, Dalvi reached Lumpu on 16 October.

The bulk of 2 Rajput also reached Tawang on the same evening. The battalion had, as yet, received no orders. From Charduar, the battalion had made its way to Tenga and then journeyed onto Dirang Dzong via Bomdila. It was then split into two groups—the first group consisting of Alpha, Bravo and Charlie Companies left Dirang Dzong for Senge at 8 a.m. on 12 September under Rikh, while the second, consisting of Delta, Support and Administrative Companies under Major Pant were to follow a day later. The heavier part of the unit baggage had to be left behind at Dirang Dzong under the care of the unit pandit. Lieutenant Colonel Rikh's group reached Senge, just below Se-la Top, at 4 p.m. on 12 September. All vehicles had to be individually towed by a Tusker (Border Roads) tractor over a four-kilometre stretch, which at places was all mud and slush.

After spending a bitterly cold night at Senge, the men now had to march across Se-la as very few vehicles could be taken beyond Senge due to the impossible road conditions. The men, not being acclimatized, found the going very difficult. Some even started vomiting blood. To make matters worse, it started to rain heavily as soon as the first company crossed Se-la. Temperatures plummeted further and it became very, very cold. A large number of the men, who were mainly in cotton clothing, started complaining of headache and fever. Rikh decided to stop at Nuranang, which was a small Tusker camp on the northern side of Se-la. At the time, there was no organized accommodation at the camp. Two companies had to squeeze into the Tusker's sheds, which at least provided some protection from the incessant rain and the elements. The third company slept in the open under improvised shelters made by tarpaulins stretched across vehicles.

On 14 September, the three companies left Nuranang for Jang at about 8 a.m. Due to the large number of men who were sick, the march was very slow. Fortunately, it had stopped raining. Four hours later, dropping down the winding road to Jang, the men were relieved to find decent accommodation at the Tusker camp, which was also known as the convoy ground. Despite the terrible conditions during the march across Se-la, the morale of the battalion remained extremely high and, despite the sickness amongst the troops, not one man fell out. In the afternoon the weather cleared up further, allowing the men the luxury of a bath in the Mago Chu (Tawang Chu) that flowed just below the camp. Across the river, halfway up the forward slopes of Bum-la, the sun was catching the yellow roofs of the Tawang Monastery, which was still another seven gruelling hours away. By 16 September, Major Pant along with the rest of the battalion had also reached Tawang.

Meanwhile, Brigadier John Dalvi and his Brigade HQ were getting first-hand experience of the ground conditions in and around Lumpu, which was entirely reliant on air drops for maintenance. 'I watched air drops at Lumpu and found to my chagrin, but not surprise, that 30 to 40 per cent of the parachutes were not opening out and the drops were total losses. The reason for this waste of air effort was due to our policy of retrieving and re-using old parachutes. For years we had been wasting energy and resources on collecting used parachutes from forward posts.'

The land route to Dhola perforce had to be over the circuitous trails that connected Lumpu to the Nam Ka Chu, for the obvious route along the Nyamjang Chu was under the nose of the Chinese positions on Thagla. Due to sheer cliffs around the confluence of the west-east flowing Nam Ka Chu and the north-south Nyamjang Chu, it was difficult to approach Dhola from Khenzemane. Even the central route over Hathung-la that connected Bridge 1 to Lumpu was under Chinese observation and troops could come under artillery fire while negotiating the steep slopes. Hence, it was felt that the main approach would have to be the track that ran from Lumpu to Bridge 2 via Karpo-la 1.

Dalvi later described the difficult conditions along the route. The occasional huts they came across were the only shelter and could house but a few men. Carrying heavy loads, they were climbing at a height of over 10,000 feet. The descent was very dangerous and a false step meant a broken ankle. Dalvi says he 'reached Bridge 1 exhausted and mentally depressed'. While the route looks a short hop on a map, on the ground it was arduous. 'The turn-around time for loaded men, from Lumpu to Nam Ka Chu Valley was a minimum of 4 days.'

AN EAR TO THE GROUND

Ever since 8 September, when news had reached Army HQ that the Dhola post had reported 600 armed Chinese approaching it, confusion had reigned. Lieutenant General Kaul, the CGS, was away on a holiday in Kashmir, and the DMO, Brigadier Palit, was also away on a naval cruise. The deputy CGS was Major General Joginder 'Jogi' Singh Dhillon, who at the time was officiating for Kaul. As per established norms and procedures, all decisions should have been routed through the Directorate of Military Operations who through the CGS would have advised the COAS on the matter.

Instead, the defence minister, Krishna Menon, called a conference on 12 September to discuss the Dhola incident, to which he invited, along with General Pran Thapar, the Eastern Army Commander, General Bogey Sen. Though there were no records kept of the meeting, it is now fairly obvious that the decision to mount an attack on the Thagla Ridge to clear out the Chinese was taken mainly on the advice given by Sen, who until then had not visited Tawang or any other part of NEFA.

Most officers in Military Operations (MO) were aware of the logistical problems being faced by formations in both NEFA and Ladakh, and the absurdity of the task was obvious right from the very beginning. In the absence of Kaul, the MO Directorate abruptly found itself out of the loop, reduced to the role of merely relaying orders on behalf of the officiating CGS, who, until the Dhola crisis, had no role in any operational matter. Lieutenant Colonel Pritpal Singh (MO-I) was aware that 7 Brigade had been peremptorily ordered to move from Tawang and concentrate post-haste on the Nam Ka Chu, after which they were supposed to push the Chinese back up the hill and across the Thagla feature. As per Krishna

Menon's orders, there were no written records maintained, so it is not known who took this incredible decision. To make matters worse, the army chief's office now instructed the MO to prepare a signal addressed to all formations down the chain of command, ordering the capture of Thagla by 19 September.

The name given to the Nam Ka Chu/Thagla plan was 'Operation Leghorn'. Jogi Dhillon made it very clear that he was not open to any discussion on the issue. He was obviously enjoying his new-found proximity to Krishna Menon, and the chance to deal with operational matters, rather than the humdrum of logistics and other aspects that were actually his job. A Sapper, Jogi Dhillon was a high-profile officer who was otherwise shackled to his desk as Kaul's deputy. To top it off, Dhillon gave Palit a direct order forbidding him from discussing the issue with the COAS, telling him that from now on, the DMO's job was to make sure the orders were simply carried out without any delay.

Not one to give in so easily, Palit sent off a frantic letter to Bijji Kaul imploring him to cut short his Kashmir sojourn and return to Army HQ as there 'had been gross over-reaction to the Dhola incident on the part of all concerned and that his presence at Army HQ was now indispensable'.

The director of the Intelligence Bureau, B. N. Mullik, by then was fully aware that the original report on 8 September emanating from the Assam Rifles JCO had been exaggerated ten times, and the actual strength of the Chinese opposite Bridge 3 was between fifty and sixty. Though previous intelligence reports had placed a Chinese infantry battalion near Le (four kilometres behind the Thagla massif), recent confirmed reports suggested that the Chinese were building up their strength considerably. It was then estimated that between Tsona Dzong and Le, there were at least two regiments (equal to two Indian brigades) in the area. Even though reports of this build-up had been coming in for quite some time, Mullik was quite sure that the Chinese would not cross into Indian territory in large numbers. Mullik's assessment was that if the Chinese did escalate the border issue, there would only be some limited action by them in the Western Sector in the Chip Chap and Galwan valleys.

Mullik, who had the ear of both Menon and Nehru, had shrugged off remonstrations relating to the 'operational extravaganza unfolding on the Nam Ka Chu'. Instead the Intelligence chief had confirmed that it was indeed the Eastern Army Commander, Bogey Sen, who had assured the government of the operation's feasibility at the meeting of 12 September.

Thapar's directive to evict the Chinese across Thagla sent Army HQ into a tizzy. The massive logistical requirement for Dalvi's 7 Brigade was worked out on paper and all coordinating agencies—Air HQ, the railways, QMG's Branch, Eastern Command—got into the act. Dhillon himself took complete charge of the combined effort to support Eastern Command for Operation Leghorn. Movement of equipment and other stocks to Guwahati began almost immediately, while the daily airlift capability was increased from the existing 20 to 30 tons over the next few days. Eighty one-ton vehicles from the Ordnance Depot in Jabalpur were also dispatched during the week to increase the surface carrying capacity in NEFA.

The frenetic pace with which preparations for Operation Leghorn were being carried out in Army and Air HQs gave the impression that everything that could be done to equip Dalvi's brigade for the impending task was being done. The fact that almost half of the drops were ending in disaster because of faulty parachutes was not known at the time. Even when the parachutes did successfully deploy, loads would waft over the ridge at Lumpu and end up in the steep valleys below. The absence of worthwhile maps also meant that no one at Army HQ, including the DMO, Palit, had any idea of the ground conditions.

Lieutenant Colonel R. N. Mishra, the commanding officer of 9 Punjab, met Dalvi at Bridge 1 on the evening of 18 September. The battalion had preceded the brigade commander by a few days and had by then taken a good look around. The quarter-inch maps were based on the Captain Morshead survey and, as we have seen earlier, the Nam Ka Chu Valley had been marked wrongly, giving it a north-south alignment as against the west-east lie of the land. The only other 'map' of the area was a sketch drawn by an Assam Rifles NCO who had accompanied Captain Mahabir Prasad during the setting up of the Dhola post. On this sketch, owing to the fact that the sheet of paper was not big enough, the western extremity of the Nam Ka Chu (the hut at Tsangle) was squeezed into the corner, giving the impression that the upper reaches were just a stone's throw away from Bridge 4. In reality, the distance between Bridge 4 and Bridge 5 at Tsangle took two days of hard marching to traverse.

After reaching the Nam Ka Chu Valley, Mishra had deployed 9 Punjab on the riverfront itself, though a platoon was also occupying the Tsangdhar Ridge that overlooked Bridge 3 and Bridge 4. These were not bridges in the conventional sense, but just logs tied together to help herders get their yaks across and as such had no tactical importance. Battalion HQ along with two companies were at Bridge 2, while one company held Bridge 1. The fourth company along with a platoon of Assam Rifles was holding

Bridge 3 and Bridge 4. The fifty-odd Chinese troops were camping across the river beyond Bridge 3. Sadly, this tactically unsound position would remain the alignment of the Indian defences on the Nam Ka Chu in the days to come.

Tsangdhar had an area that was 110 metres by 36 metres on which Mishra felt the IAF could attempt dropping supplies, as this would cut short the long haul from Lumpu. This flat area was also ideally suited for the deployment of heavy mortars and artillery. The request for an ad hoc DZ (drop zone) to be set up at Tsangdhar was sent back up the chain of command and it went through to the highest echelons at record speed. Within twenty-four hours, this thin strip of land at Tsangdhar was designated as a forward DZ and the IAF was told to start using it immediately. If retrievals at Lumpu were pathetic, the recovery of drops at Tsangdhar was even worse, as most of the loads dumped by the Dakotas and Fairchild Packets fell into the ravines and were not recoverable.

While Mishra was briefing Dalvi about the lie of the ground at Bridge 3, they received the signal issued by Army HQ ordering 9 Punjab to capture Thagla and contain Yumtso-la and Karpo-la 2 by 19 September. The brigade commander immediately countermanded the impractical order. Dalvi then spent the next two days doing a reconnaissance of the area west of Bridge 3, going beyond Bridge 4 up to where Log Bridge and Temporary Bridge would come up later. On 21 September he left 9 Punjab's location and fell back on Lumpu, which he reached at 1 p.m. the next day. By then, the leading elements of 2 Rajput, exhausted from their 400-kilometre journey from the plains, were beginning to arrive.

Dalvi's reconnaissance had helped him arrive at the firm conclusion that 'Dhola was militarily useless, indefensible and dominated by Chinese positions and located in a trap. It had poor approaches, no fields of fire and no mutual support. The Hathung-la and Karpo-la 1 routes could not be defended by one battalion. A secure base for operations was an elementary precaution but could not be established, as our Lines of Communication and the Lumpu dropping zone were vulnerable to a counter thrust. It was impossible even for a brigade to provide its own firm base and assault troops.

'The Dhola area was unsuitable as a forming-up place for mounting any form of attack against the intruding Chinese. I could see the three tiers of Chinese defence positions, the first was on the river bank opposite our own troops; the second half way up the Thagla slopes on Paitsai Spur and the third on the crest of the ridge.' To have any chance against the network of machine guns deployed on the forward slopes and the mortars on the reverse slopes, 7 Brigade would need massive artillery support. At the present time, never mind artillery guns, the brigade did not even have heavy mortars.

So far, the interaction between Indian and Chinese troops had been limited to verbal threats, each trying to convince the other to withdraw from their territory. At times, they were even friendly enough for them to exchange cigarettes across Bridges 1 and 2. Dalvi himself had tried speaking to the Chinese sentries at Bridge 3. This state of affairs was unlikely to last, and the peace was broken on 20 September when a Chinese soldier on the south bank near Bridge 2 threw a grenade at the Indian sentry post a few yards away. In the ensuing firing, two Chinese soldiers were killed and two others wounded, while on the Indian side, five men were wounded. With two armies dug in and facing each other across the Nam Ka Chu, this incident could not be classified as yet another border incident. It was just a matter of time before the situation became very serious.

By 22 September, Krishna Menon had left for New York where he was busy at the United Nations. The prime minister was also not available, so a meeting presided over by the minister of state for defence, Kotha Raghuramaiah, was held. The COAS, Thapar, gave an update of the position in the Bhutan-Tibet-NEFA region and an appraisal of the Chinese reactions to Indian moves in the Dhola area. He stated that in view of our own build-up on the Nam Ka Chu, it was likely that the Chinese would push forward even more troops to supplement the two regiments that were currently reported to be behind the Thagla area. It was also anticipated that the Chinese could broaden the front and strike elsewhere in the NEFA region; and finally, they could retaliate in Ladakh, in which case they would attack our posts in the uncharted region of Chip Chap and Galwan rivers, for that would allow them to reach their 1960 claim line.

The foreign secretary, M. J. Desai, then reiterated Nehru's instructions about our posts in Ladakh and elsewhere—that no infringement of our border in NEFA was to be tolerated. As supplies and forces in the Dhola region were built up steadily, the Chinese had to be evicted even if the action ran the risk of the Chinese retaliating in Ladakh. The foreign secretary said the Chinese reaction in Ladakh was not expected to be beyond the capturing of a few posts.

The army chief then asked for the order to be given in writing.

ANNEXURE 1-A

Ministry of Defence

At a meeting in MMD's [Minister, Ministry of Defence] room, this morning COAS raised the specific question whether action to evict the Chinese can be taken as soon as the Brigade has concentrated. The decision throughout has been, as discussed in the previous meetings, that the Army should prepare and throw the Chinese out as soon as possible. The COAS was accordingly directed to take action for the eviction of the Chinese in the Kameng Division of NEFA as soon as he was ready.

11987/JS(G)/62 COAS of 22-9-62

HC Sarin
Joint Secretary

It seems strange that the army chief should have insisted on a written order at this stage, especially since it would have to originate from a relatively junior bureaucrat. What is even more bizarre is that the final formal decision to take on China militarily was taken by a minister who did not even hold cabinet rank. It would almost seem that Thapar himself had reservations about Operation Leghorn, but he could not afford to come across to the political leadership as a 'meek' chief, especially since the proven war horse, Bogey Sen, was champing at the bit to take on the Chinese.

◆

Headquartered at Shillong was XXXIII Corps, and the first inkling Army HQ would get of the situation on the ground was when the BGS, Brigadier Jagjit Singh Aurora, rang up the DMO and demanded to know why such unreasonable orders were emanating from Delhi. Aurora was emphatic that the brigade, the division and the corps were consistently advising against any offensive action across the Nam Ka Chu that had now become the de facto boundary between Chinese and Indian troops. Obviously, while the orders were flowing directly from Army HQ to the various field formations, their appreciations and replies were being routed through the chain of command and not progressing beyond Eastern Command. The matter was discussed with the officiating CGS, who felt that the GOC Eastern Command had far more operational experience under his belt than the corps commander and that his advice on the issue had to be followed.

The failure to move forward and push the Chinese back over the

Thagla Ridge on 19 September was being interpreted by the Eastern Army Commander, Bogey Sen, as insubordination. He was making it known to the GOC XXXIII Corps, Lieutenant General Umrao Singh, in no uncertain terms, that he felt that GOC 4 Division, Major General Niranjan Prasad, and commander 7 Brigade, Brigadier John Dalvi, were both dragging their feet.

Eastern Command, now with the backing of the government's explicit orders to evict the Chinese, ordered XXXIII Corps to prepare an offensive plan. Umrao Singh now had no choice but to task Niranjan Prasad to move immediately on foot to Lumpu, which he reached on 25 September after an exhausting trek. Prasad was obviously under tremendous pressure, for he had also initially endorsed Dalvi's decision to countermand the Army HQ order to capture Thagla by 19 September. But now the plan for evicting the Chinese by a stipulated D-Day was dominating all thinking. He was acutely aware that unless he could convince Dalvi to produce an appreciation that could be deemed as an attack plan, both he and Dalvi would be branded as cowards.

After reaching Lumpu, Prasad immediately ordered 9 Punjab to move its Delta Company at Bridge 1 to Tsangle, which was across Bridge 5 at the western extremity of the Nam Ka Chu. The Punjabis were to be replaced by 2 Rajput's Bravo Company under the command of Second Lieutenant Subash Chander. Charlie Company was also told to move forward to Serkhim, just south of Hathung-la, and was to be a reserve company if 9 Punjab found itself in need of reinforcements.

Referring to Thapar's orders, Prasad then broached the subject of an attack plan with Dalvi, who predictably exploded, refusing to be part of any such sham exercise. 'My first reaction to the GOC's request for assistance in the preparation of a formal appreciation, for onward transmission to Delhi, for implementing these preposterous tasks, was to refuse point blank. I exchanged some hot words with General Prasad. Chief or no chief, there was no question of evicting the Chinese.'

The three-point guideline for the preparation of the appreciation was along the same lines as before: evict the Chinese from the north bank of the Nam Ka Chu; contain Thagla; and patrol towards Tsangle. Caught in a complete bind, Dalvi and Prasad had only two choices—refuse to execute the order, or prepare an appreciation that would focus on the problems and underline the impossibility of the assigned task.

The first part of the appreciation did just that, underlining the impossibility of trying to maintain troops on the Nam Ka Chu, especially since the logistics routes ran over Hathung-la and Karpo-la 1 at heights in excess of 15,000 feet. Also highlighted was the disparity in existing firepower between the two sides, especially when it came to artillery and heavy mortars. The second part of the appreciation, however, was the critical bit—and here too, the terrain dictated the options. A thrust from the direction of Khenzemane was out of the question as the approach was blocked by steep slopes and guarded by the Chinese. Similarly, a south-north thrust along the middle section of the valley, which was bisected by the Paitsai spur, heavily defended by the Chinese, would mean our troops would be decimated in the form-up areas itself. Hence, militarily, the only possible approach was to push troops up from Bridge 4 to Bridge 5, get to Tsangle in strength, and then try to capture the Thagla Ridge moving west to east.

The appreciation was based on two important premises: one, the route from Bridge 4 to Bridge 5 was along the Nam Ka Chu and two, the strength of the Chinese across the Nam Ka Chu did not exceed that of an infantry battalion. In fact, both these premises were way off the mark. It was not known then that to get to Tsangle, the route would have to be via Tsangdhar and though, on the map, it looked reasonably close it would take the better part of fourteen hours to get there. Secondly, and far more importantly, the Intelligence Bureau's information that there were already more than two Chinese regiments—almost six times the projected force levels—just behind the rear slopes of Thagla, between Tsona Dzong and Le, had not been communicated to either Dalvi or Prasad. For that matter, it is doubtful if the DMO had passed on this important bit of information to either Eastern Command or XXXIII Corps. The withholding of this crucial bit of information by both Mullik, the Intelligence Bureau chief, and by Palit, the DMO, on the assumption that the Chinese would not use this force to actually attack, has to be one of the most bizarre acts of omission in the entire tragedy.

On 26 September, Umrao Singh arrived at Lumpu. He discussed the appreciation with his two subordinate commanders and instructed them to make certain changes. First, he laid additional emphasis on artillery support and, second, he asked Dalvi and Prasad to remove the suggested timeline. The modifications having been made, the appreciation was sent off to Corps HQ who in turn marked it to Eastern Command.

Umrao Singh was in no hurry to leave and spent the next two days studying the ground situation. He also had plenty of time to see for himself the condition of both 2 Rajput and 1/9 GR who by then had or were in the process of reaching Lumpu. After the government's 22 September directive, Bogey Sen had revised his attack plans and had decided to deploy the entire brigade against the Chinese and secure the Thagla feature by the first week of October. Purely from a logistical point of view, it was soon obvious to Umrao Singh that there was absolutely no way that 7 Brigade could be deployed in the Nam Ka Chu Valley in the immediate future and move up to the Thagla ridgeline in the face of Chinese resistance. Despite the massive logistics effort, it was obvious that even if all the airdrops were successfully retrieved and porters and mules assembled to ferry the loads to the Nam Ka Chu Valley, there would barely be enough ammunition to sustain 7 Brigade for one hour's fighting if the attack was to be launched even at the end of October 1962.

Before leaving Lumpu on 28 September, Umrao Singh gave explicit orders that there would be no further concentration of troops ahead of Lumpu until the bare minimum of ammunition and stocks had been accumulated at Tsangdhar, to say nothing of the required artillery support. The earliest any offensive action could be considered, he confided, was the middle of 1963. However, even though Umrao Singh was fully in agreement with his subordinate commanders, he knew that convincing the Eastern Army Commander and the political-military circus in South Block was not going to be easy. Before he left Lumpu, the general had a final meeting with the two commanding officers of 2 Rajput and 1/9 GR, Lieutenant Colonels Rikh and Ahluwalia.

After the conflict, Rikh recorded in his notes: 'When we met the Corps Commander we both felt as if he was saying goodbye to two gladiators who were about to enter the arena never to come out alive. We both assured the Corps Commander that whatever we were called upon to do would be done in the highest traditions of the Army; all we requested was a fair chance of survival and success for our men, and the minimum amount of warm clothing and supplies.'

Even at the initial stages, Umrao Singh had spelt out his misgivings of hustling 7 Brigade into what he considered to be a death trap. XXXIII Corps had suggested withdrawing the Dhola post to Tsangdhar, which was the alignment of the boundary marked on the map. However, should that not be acceptable for political reasons, Umrao had suggested that two battalions be kept in support south of Tsangdhar with the sole purpose of stopping any ingress by the Chinese. Bogey Sen, the Eastern Army Commander, had simply ignored the objections and reconfirmed his earlier orders.

Back in Shillong, the BGS XXXIII Corps and his staff prepared a fresh assessment based on the corps commander's observations during his visit to Lumpu. Relations between Umrao and Bogey Sen were strained ever since the earlier snub given to the corps by the command. Nevertheless, Jagjit Singh Aurora worked out a detailed appreciation that was brutally honest. Once again, unable to break established procedures, it had to be channelled through Eastern Command.

Bogey Sen was openly letting it be known that in his opinion, his three commanders on the ground (Umrao, Prasad and Dalvi) lacked 'fire in their bellies'. Both the Dalvi-Prasad appreciation and the Umrao Singh report reached Eastern Command within a day of each other. Bogey Sen decided to ignore the first part of the Dalvi-Prasad report, focusing only on the section that talked of moving troops up the Nam Ka Chu and then outflanking the central Chinese defences by capturing the ridgeline. The second report, based on an even more detailed study of the situation by the corps commander, was deemed to show the negative outlook of Umrao Singh. Bogey Sen now had the 'positive' Dalvi-Prasad attack plan, and the corps commander's 'negative' report. He asked Thapar to immediately sack Lieutenant General Umrao Singh as the GOC of XXXIII Corps.

Through this entire period, the CGS, Kaul, had been missing from Army HQ, and was continuing his holiday in Kashmir. Even though the DMO had dashed off a personal letter asking the CGS to return, both Krishna Menon and Pran Thapar had decided against truncating the Kashmir sojourn and recalling the most powerful man in Army HQ to Delhi.

FROM THE FRYING PAN INTO THE FIRE

Lieutenant General Bijji Kaul's return to South Block on 3 October coincided with Prime Minister Nehru's return to India from a trip to various African countries. Krishna Menon had also returned from New York on 30 September. The Bogey Sen-Umrao Singh clash had spilled out into the open by then and the impression in most circles was that the XXXIII Corps Commander was the only obstacle in what was seen as a simple operation. The Intelligence Chief, Mullik, on whose advice Nehru depended heavily, was openly suggesting sacking Umrao Singh and appointing a new corps commander. However, removing Umrao Singh from command at this stage, just as the Chinese were about to be evicted across Thagla would have sent the wrong signals to all the officers and men.

Kaul and Thapar were closeted together for the entire day, with frequent conversations with both Krishna Menon and Nehru. The solution that emerged at the end of the day had the classic stamp of the Menon-Kaul (and Nehru) style of functioning. Kaul had been told that Umrao had failed to deliver and the need of the hour was to have a man at the helm who could, and would, forcefully push the Chinese back across Thagla and the McMahon Line. Since sacking Umrao would be politically incorrect at this stage, Menon suggested a sly plan where he would continue with XXXIII Corps in Shillong, but be made responsible only for Sikkim, Nagaland and East Pakistan, leaving the designated officer who was to replace him in NEFA free to concentrate on the job in hand. Not giving Thapar and Kaul any time to react, Menon quickly added that in his opinion, the designated officer could only be the dynamic and forceful Bijji Kaul.

Almost everybody who interacted with Kaul at the time remembers him as being quite extraordinary. Since the 8 September Dhola crisis had begun to unfold, most officers in Army HQ who could see the absurdity of what was happening kept lamenting that in Kaul's absence, the acting CGS and the COAS had completely overreacted and created a situation that was logistically impossible to execute. Given Kaul's penchant to dash off to the front, it was believed that he would have made the effort to get to Niranjan Prasad and Dalvi, which would have allowed him to arrive at a more realistic picture. But then again, all those who had interacted with Kaul also remember him as being pompous and vain, something that would come across even in the briefest of meetings.

The fact that Menon knew Kaul so well allowed him to bait the hook and it was a matter of seconds before the CGS was attached to his line. Nehru did have to make a show of first cajoling and then ordering the general to take on the job. The plan to create an ad hoc formation, IV Corps, to be headquartered at Tezpur was then worked out. Kaul would now be moving down in the hierarchy by two steps by relinquishing the post of CGS and becoming a corps commander. But it was a small price to pay if it allowed him the opportunity to emerge as the hero who had defeated the Chinese. The fact that Kaul would be functioning as the head of a corps that had only two measly brigades under its command was ignored, as was the fact that Kaul would now, at least notionally, be under the command of Bogey Sen.

At 9 p.m. on 3 October, Lieutenant General B. M. Bijji Kaul was formally informed that he had been appointed as commander IV Corps with the specific aim of evicting the Chinese from the Dhola area and pushing them off the Thagla Ridge.

If Kaul had had any reservations, they had evaporated by the morning of 4 October and his vanity had taken over the situation. He started the day by meeting with Prem Bhatia, the editor of the *Times of India*. Soon after Kaul was driven to Palam Airport by his DMO. Wrote Palit subsequently:

'I asked whether he felt justified in vacating the CGS's chair just to go and "take command of a couple of brigades?"... He replied, somewhat defensively, that he would soon be given more troops as other divisions would be sent to him and that eventually his corps would command the whole frontier from the Uttar Pradesh Himalayas to the Burma border... It was a crucial responsibility...given him by the Prime Minister himself. When I expressed my doubts about the feasibility of mounting an offensive in that terrain, Bijji assured me that, according to Thapar, both 7 Brigade and 4 Division had produced workable plans for the attack; it was only Umrao who (he had been told) was being obstructionist.'

Palit then goes on to say: 'I could see that Bijji was greatly pleased with himself and I could imagine why... Here was his chance to make up for the past, to fill in the blanks in his credentials and to give the lie to his detractors. There would be no holding him back.'

Ever since the Chinese appeared at Dhola on 8 September, the DMO had repeatedly lamented the fact that Kaul was missing from the scene. Once he took over the newly created IV Corps, there was an infusion of optimism that ignored reality. Even though fully aware of Kaul's vain and pompous streak, Palit and many others who interacted with him held Kaul's analytical abilities in high esteem, perhaps next only to that of General Thorat.

Yet, on the way to the airport, Palit failed to tell Kaul, who until then was his direct boss, that according to the Intelligence Bureau chief, he would be facing at least two Chinese regiments. Until then (especially since Kaul was basing his optimism on the Dalvi-Prasad appreciation), the assumption was that on the Thagla Ridge and forward slopes there was just the one company of the PLA (equivalent to an Indian infantry battalion). This vital piece of information being held back at this critical juncture must rate as one of the most serious omissions of the war, bordering perhaps on criminal negligence.

The moment Kaul landed at Tezpur, there were many subtle and some not so subtle messages being given to the rank and file of the Indian Army. The Eastern Army Commander, Bogey Sen, received the new IV Corps Commander at the airfield, which in itself was an unprecedented step. This clearly signalled that Bogey Sen and Eastern Command would fade into the background as the only recognized chain of command would now be Kaul-Menon-Nehru. The sidelining of Umrao Singh was an equally clear message—anyone who had the gumption to protest would be unceremoniously shown the door. In the week that would follow, along with Bogey Sen, even the COAS, Pran Thapar, would fade away from the decision-making process.

While Kaul was in Tezpur, locked in conference with Bogey Sen and Umrao Singh, Niranjan Prasad landed at Lumpu, this time by helicopter. Ever since 28 September, there had been no feedback on the appreciation that had been sent to Eastern Command. As soon as Dalvi broached the subject with Niranjan Prasad, the 4 Division GOC's reply was disheartening: 'Look, old boy, no one is interested in your bloody appreciation. They are only interested in your D-Day for evicting the Chinese.' Then came the news that Lieutenant General B. M. Kaul had been appointed the GOC of a new corps to speed up operations. It was obvious that there was no one now who could stand up for the men of 7 Brigade.

While Dalvi was still trying to come to grips with these startling revelations, Prasad delivered yet another gem: he wanted the brigade commander and the commanding officers of 2 Rajput and 1/9 GR out of Lumpu heading for the front immediately. He said Kaul would be furious if he found Dalvi or any of the other senior officers in Lumpu and that the party must leave at once. An indignant Dalvi decided to stand his ground saying he saw no reason to shift his headquarters forward and that there was little dignity in 'senior officers scurrying away like thieves in the night. Who are we more afraid of,' he asked, 'the Chinese or our own superior commanders?' By then, Niranjan Prasad was almost frantic with worry. He 'begged' Dalvi to just head off in the general direction of the front. The GOC said he didn't care if the officers sheltered in the nearest yak shed, but they had to go! By noon the brigade commander and his two bewildered COs were sloshing through ankle-deep slush through grazing meadows as they headed off towards Hathung-la. The night was spent three kilometres north of Lumpu, each man wondering what lay ahead of him.

New Delhi awakened on 5 October to front-page headlines in the *Times of India* that proclaimed Kaul was on his way to NEFA to evict the Chinese from Indian soil. If secrecy was to have been part of Kaul's operational plans, he had already ensured that was not possible. (Army HQ later went through the sham of ordering an inquiry to find the source of the leak.)

The Bell helicopter with the new corps commander on board landed at Lumpu at 2.30 p.m. In the absence of any senior officers, two doctors and the brigade major, Major Rex Kharbanda, received Kaul. 'Where is GOC 4 Division?' was Kaul's first query. 'I don't know, sir,' said Kharbanda, 'sometimes he is in Tawang, sometimes in Tezpur.' The corps commander then asked if all the troops of 7 Brigade had moved to Tsangdhar.

'Not yet, sir,' Kharbanda answered honestly.

'Why not?' Kaul exploded. 'It was my definite order that the troops must be in position by the evening of 7th October.' This was the first time any such order was being mentioned. 'How dare you disobey my orders, you are the brigade major. I have given an assurance to the prime minister that I will carry out the operation. I am not a corps commander to sit in Shillong to conduct the operation. I intend to be present to conduct the operation myself.' The corps commander throwing a tantrum in front of relatively junior officers could not have been a pretty sight. What was even more bizarre, Kaul literally bullied Kharbanda into ordering both 2 Rajput and 1/9 GR to move out of Lumpu on man pack basis (with just enough rations for a couple of days) and pouch ammunition.

Major Kharbanda, showing a lot more gumption than many other senior officers, suggested to Kaul that he should speak to his brigade commander before any troops were moved. Kaul again went ballistic, his every alternate sentence ending with 'I shall get you dismissed'. Kharbanda then pointed out that there were no porters, to which Kaul replied that there was plenty of manpower in Tawang and that he would have them moved to Lumpu immediately. Rations would be no problem, for the general would arrange to have them airdropped at Tsangdhar immediately. Finally, Kharbanda pointed out that since the day was almost over, it would be better to move the two battalions in the early hours of 6 October. Kaul conceded that point. As the helicopter lifted off from Lumpu for Tezpur, Kaul could see the three officers standing next to the helipad—what he obviously could not see was the look of absolute despair and disbelief on their faces. The next morning, as darkness gave way to the grey dawn, 2 Rajput and 1/9 GR were on the move. On 'bayonet strength and on a man pack basis', few soldiers could even afford the luxury of a ground sheet, let alone a second blanket. Most men were still in the cotton uniforms that they had been surviving in ever since they left the plains almost three weeks ago. Even at Lumpu, which on paper was far better stocked, there was little that could be given to the men to battle the extreme cold. Now they were headed for Tsangdhar, two days' march away, where there was even less by way of rations and stores.

The route to Tsangdhar from Lumpu was via the 16,000-foot Karpo-la 1, which was even more difficult than the route that traversed Hathung-la and connected with the lower reaches of the Nam Ka Chu. Since the Hathung-la route was under the observation of the Chinese, they had to take the Karpo-la 1 route. The gradient was almost vertical and the temperatures were well below freezing. Yet, somehow, the two battalions had arrived at Tsangdhar by 5 p.m. on 7 October, within the stipulated time set by the corps commander. However, at Tsangdhar, there was no shelter for the men; being above the treeline, even finding fuel to light a fire was a problem. For the second successive night, the men had to camp out in the open at an altitude of over 14,500 feet. In the absence of warm clothing, tents and bedding, the men bivouacked by sharing—two men huddled together with one blanket below and another wrapped around them. With temperatures plummeting to minus 10 degrees Celsius for the second night in succession, a number of soldiers from both the battalions had to be evacuated due to exposure and pulmonary oedema. Four Gorkha soldiers died during this march to Tsangdhar.

In the meantime, the engineer detachment at Lumpu had worked through the night with Petromaxes to prepare a helipad for Kaul at Serkhim. The corps commander, accompanied by GOC 4 Division, Major General Niranjan Prasad, had landed there on the morning of 6 October. After spending time with CO 9 Punjab and the battalion at Serkhim, the general had been carried piggyback across Hathung-la to Bridge 1 by a local Monpa. The rather unusual sight of the corps commander arriving at the Nam Ka Chu in this undignified manner was Kaul's introduction to the men of 7 Brigade who were deployed at Bridge 1. By 2.30 p.m., Dalvi, along with his two commanding officers, made his way from Tsangdhar to Bridge 1 via Bridge 3 and 2. This was to be Dalvi's first meeting with the corps commander who had by then moved the entire brigade to the Nam Ka Chu. Dalvi asked Prasad, his immediate boss, what orders he had for the two newly arrived battalions that were then assembling below Tsangdhar DZ. Niranjan Prasad confessed that he had no clue, as the entire operational plan was under Kaul's personal control.

ROMMEL OF THE HIGH HIMALAYAS

Kaul used the next thirty-six hours to mull over his various options while sending out lengthy signals to Delhi. First, he would lay out the stark reality of the situation on the ground, but then sign off with grandiose claims that he, Kaul, had the situation under control and he would indeed evict the Chinese. Neither the GOC nor the brigade commander had a clue as to what strategy was brewing inside Kaul's head. All this while he would also talk at length about German Field Marshal Erwin Rommel's hooks and deception tactics against the British in the desert of North Africa amongst various other unrelated things.

On the morning of 9 October, Kaul called a conference that included all officers and JCOs of 9 Punjab and 2 Rajput. Following the same pattern of the lengthy signals to Delhi, the corps commander started by appreciating the impossibility of physically evicting the Chinese from their positions on Thagla or, for that matter, holding on to any gains which the Indians might achieve should they attack. Then he shifted tack, saying that despite the stark facts that indicated that any military offensive would meet with failure, he had no choice since he had been tasked by the Cabinet to make some move by 10 October at the latest. He then proceeded to say that the army commander had told the government that he would evict the Chinese and had set 15 September as the date. This date kept getting postponed giving the impression that the troops of 7 Brigade were stalling and not willing to take on the Chinese. Hence, he, General Kaul, had been appointed to take on this task and lead them into battle. The Cabinet, he added grandly, had let him know that they were willing to lose 20,000 lives if need be, but the Chinese now had to be pushed back.

As a direct assault on Thagla would be impossible, he had decided to do a 'positional warfare manoeuvre' and occupy Yumtso-la, to the west of Thagla peak, which at the time was not occupied by the Chinese. He then gave the order to 2 Rajput to cross the Nam Ka Chu on 10 October and go and sit behind the Chinese by occupying Yumtso-la.

Dalvi aptly describes what followed:

'A variety of astonished gazes greeted Kaul's announcement. The CO of 2 Rajput, looked at me with consternation clearly visible on his strong face. General Prasad looked as if he had been poleaxed. I was stunned and speechless for a few minutes.'

Rikh turned to Dalvi, seething with anger. There was no way he was going to commit his troops into battle in territory that was uncharted, without reconnaissance, a clear-cut military task and basic fire support. He told Dalvi that the order was a mad one and demanded to know what the brigade and divisional commanders planned to do about it. For Dalvi, it was an impossible situation—there was no way he could contradict the corps commander in the presence of all the JCOs and officers. Yet, he had to do something, since Niranjan Prasad, his boss, was unable to speak at all.

'After a while I raised a few difficulties about the Rajput's move to Yumtso-la, even if the Chinese permitted us to do so. When I pointed out the shortage of snow clothing, I was informed that 6,000 sets had been ordered from Canada. On the question of artillery coverage, I was told that determined infantry do not need artillery. The requirement for porters was settled by a promise to send us all the Border Roads Pioneers from Tawang. Everything seemed to be in the future except the move of the Rajputs, which was to be the next day.'

In a last-ditch effort to salvage the situation, Dalvi suggested a strong patrol be sent out before committing the entire battalion. The corps commander reluctantly agreed and it was decided that 9 Punjab would undertake the task later that day. A patrol commanded by an officer would cross the Nam Ka Chu and occupy Tseng Jong that night. 2 Rajput less Bravo Company would move from their assembly area at first light on 10 October and occupy Tsangle, Muksar and Tseng Jong. The Thagla Ridge would then be occupied from the west and 2 Rajput would clear the Chinese to their east until checked. In the final phase, 1/9 GR would pass through the Rajput positions and clear the Chinese from the entire ridge line while 9 Punjab would advance from the Nam Ka Chu and marry up with the Rajputs and Gorkhas.

CHARGE OF KAUL'S LIGHT BRIGADE (TO DELHI)

At the appointed hour, a fifty-man patrol of 9 Punjab under the command of their Delta Company commander, Major Mahander Singh Chaudhary, made their way along the north bank of the Nam Ka Chu from Tsangle near Bridge 5 to Tseng Jong. Meanwhile, 2 Rajput on the opposite bank was preparing two more crossing points just upstream of Bridge 4; these would be known subsequently as Log and Temporary Bridges. At Tseng Jong, the ground was too rocky and hard for digging, so the men quickly constructed sangars while an LMG (light machine gun) section under Havildar Malkiat Singh was told to dig in at the base of Karpo-la 2 from where he could give enfilade fire (strike the enemy from the flank) if the sangars at Tseng Jong came under attack in the morning. The men worked through the night, preparing whatever defences they could.

Just before first light on 10 October, Malkiat drew Chaudhary's attention to the direction of Yumtso-la from where he could see a mass of torches descending towards the Punjabis. After a while, the torches were also visible to the men at Bridge 4. Chaudhary radioed Lieutenant Colonel Mishra, saying that it looked as if the Chinese were concentrating almost an entire battalion against his position.

As dawn broke on the horizon, 2 Rajput's No. 9 Platoon of Charlie Company, led by Subedar Dashrath Singh, also crossed the Nam Ka Chu at the Temporary Bridge and occupied the grazing ground opposite that was marked on the maps as 'Green Patch'. Other than the sound of the river, there was complete silence in the valley. In their assembly area, the rest of 2 Rajput were preparing to move; Charlie Company under Major S. S. Sethi was to lead, with Bravo Company under Captain Ravi Eipe following behind. Alpha Company was to be the third group which would come into play once Thagla had been occupied. They were to be followed by Battalion HQ with Delta Company. The corps commander, GOC 4 Division, the brigade commander, the BGS (Brigadier K. K. Singh, who had also moved up to Nam Ka Chu) were all at Bridge 4, from where they had a commanding view of the unfolding drama.

At 5 a.m., as Charlie Company approached the Temporary Bridge which was the designated crossing point guarded by Dashrath's platoon, the Chinese opened up with a barrage of heavy and medium mortars, directing their fire at Major Chaudhary's patrol that was holding Tseng Jong. Kaul, who had just started his morning shave, was staring open-mouthed across the river towards the flashes of mortar fire and the exploding bombs. 'Oh my god, you are right—they mean business,' was all that he could gasp, as the myth, carefully perpetuated by New Delhi, that the Chinese would not react, came crashing down with the mortar bombs that were falling around the hastily prepared defences of the Punjabis.

The next thirty minutes were to be a watershed of sorts in modern warfare. No commander had so obviously deflated in front of his officers as Kaul did that morning—gone was his bluster of the previous day. Sensing his opportunity, Dalvi prompted Niranjan Prasad to speak to the corps commander again, in the faint hope that even at this late stage, he would see the situation for what it was. For the first time, Kaul actually seemed to be hearing what Prasad was saying, and Dalvi joined in to reiterate what he had said many times before.

Kaul and the others watched the intensive barrage that continued for thirty minutes, while the Chinese infantry tried to close in. The moment the mortars ceased firing, the Chinese put in their first attack. The leading Chinese elements, unaware of Havildar Malkiat's position above and to the west of them, were caught completely unawares by the deadly LMG fire. By now the Nam Ka Chu Valley was completely lit up and the surrounding hills echoed with the sound of gunfire. The Rajputs were strung out in single file and the leading elements were almost at Temporary Bridge while Rikh's party at the rear was approaching Bridge 4.

Kaul then seemed to arrive at a decision. He called Rikh over and announced that 2 Rajput was to advance no further as the situation had changed. He said he was immediately leaving with his staff for Delhi to apprise the prime minister of the serious intent of the Chinese. He turned to Niranjan Prasad and declared that the orders to drive the Chinese across the Thagla were to be held in abeyance until he returned. In the meantime, the brigade was to continue to hold its position on the south bank of the Nam Ka Chu at all costs. The position across the river at Tsangle was also to be held unless it was attacked in strength by the Chinese, in which case he was leaving it to the discretion of the GOC. Turning to Rikh, he repeated his orders, telling the CO that he was to advance no further as the situation had changed. He wanted Temporary Bridge, Log Bridge, Bridge 4 and Bridge 3 to be held by a company of 2 Rajput. Rikh protested, saying these positions were all dominated by the Thagla Ridge and would be impossible to hold in the event of a Chinese attack. Kaul replied that these were only temporary defensive positions and the Chinese would not attack so long as the Indians stayed on the south bank of the Nam Ka Chu. Having said that, Kaul added that not a single inch of territory was to be given up regardless of the cost. He then turned to Dalvi and, nodding in the direction of the hapless Punjab patrol fighting it out at Tseng Jong, declared: 'It's now your battle.' Having said that, Kaul, along with the GOC and his staff officers, left the scene, walking off briskly towards Bridge 3 from where he would exit the Nam Ka Chu Theatre by helicopter from Tsangdhar.

With the abrupt departure of the corps commander, Dalvi, back in command of his brigade, could now focus on the battle raging across the river.

Their first attack having been halted, the Chinese tried to neutralize the LMG section with mortar and MMG (medium machine gun) fire. However, the position had been very well sited in defilade (using natural or artificial obstacles to provide cover) and Chinese fire, though intense and concentrated, could not get at Malkiat Singh's position. While the Chinese continued to engage Major Chaudhary's patrol, the Chinese sent a platoon in a flanking arc towards Karpo-la 2 to try and outflank the LMG section. A splinter had hit Sepoy Suram Chand in the chest, but he refused to give up his weapon and continued taking on the Chinese.

With their ammunition running low, the LMG section had to rejoin the main group. Having seen this, at around 9.30 a.m., the Chinese regrouped and launched yet another determined attack, the third of the morning. They had in the meantime set up their own MMG roughly around the same place where Malkiat's original position had been, and from there they managed to bring some devastating fire to bear on the Indian positions. Major Chaudhary got through to Mishra and asked for mortar and MMG support. Dalvi was now in a dilemma as he felt the Rajput companies strung along the river were extremely vulnerable should the fighting spread beyond Tseng Jong. There was also the danger that Kaul's party might still be within Chinese observation. Though the Mahar gunners had at the time almost 22,000 rounds of ammunition, Dalvi refused to give the order.

Mishra then ordered Chaudhary to fall back if he felt he was no longer capable of holding on to Tseng Jong. The Chinese by then were already coming in for a fourth attack, this time having formed up in the classic wave formation (one line of attack following the other). The two forward sections under the command of Naik Chain Singh and Lance Havildar Ujagar Singh held their fire till the gap had narrowed to almost 100 metres. The Punjabis were desperately low on ammunition by then, and though they managed to cut down a few more Chinese soldiers, the third wave managed to close the gap. In the ensuing hand-to-hand fight, Ujagar Singh was killed. Chaudhary managed to stabilize the situation by launching a counter-attack. Sepoy Kanshi Ram, who had been Ujagar's number one on the LMG, despite being wounded, hurled his last grenade at a Chinese officer and some men who were approaching him. He then jumped out of the sangar and grappled with the officer, killed him and snatched his automatic rifle.

The situation was desperate by then as Chaudhary's men were almost out of ammunition. The Chinese were regrouping and they quickly came again. Once again Chaudhary asked Mishra for mortar and MMG support to cover his withdrawal, but once again Dalvi refused. Malkiat Singh and Naik Chain Singh took up covering positions while the rest of the party fell back towards Green Patch where Dashrath's platoon was waiting to let them through. Malkiat now called out to Chain Singh to fall back while he continued to cover him. Chain Singh didn't get too far; he was brought down by the Chinese, his thigh shattered by a burst of gunfire. Chain Singh now yelled to Malkiat to make a run for it while he held off the Chinese. As Malkiat made his way down, he looked back to see a defiant Chain Singh surrounded by the Chinese, still holding out.

Major Chaudhary brought back the remnants of his patrol and crossed back to the south bank at 3 p.m., followed shortly by Dashrath's platoon. 9 Punjab had lost nine men, eleven of whom had been wounded while two men were reported missing but were later found to have been captured by the Chinese. Dalvi's refusal to support the Punjab troops with the requested fire support must have been seen as a betrayal by the men on the ground. Later, Brigadier Dalvi justified the decision on three counts: (a) shortage of ammunition; (b) the danger of counter bombardment that could catch the Rajputs who were in the open and (c) to ensure the safety of the corps commander who was hurrying back to Delhi to report on the seriousness of the situation, which, in his opinion, was of prime importance.

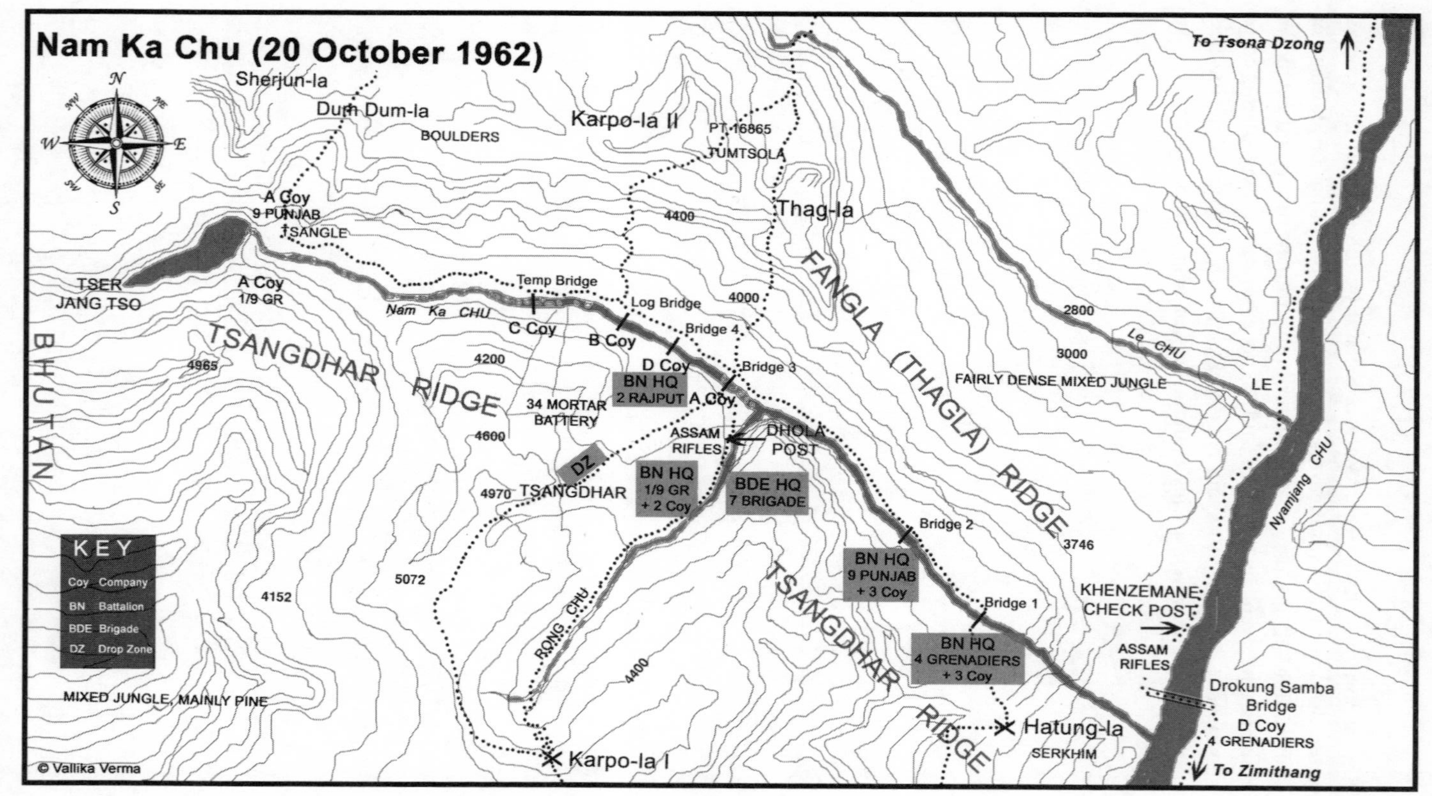

Nam Ka Chu (20 October 1962)
N
E
S
W
To Tsona Dzong
Sherjun-la
Dum Dum-la
BOULDERS
Karpo-la II
PT.16865
TUMTSOLA
Thag-la
A Coy
9 PUNJAB
TSANGLE
4400
TSER
JANG TSO
A Coy
1/9 GR
Temp Bridge
Log Bridge
4000
Nam Ka CHU
C Coy
B Coy
Bridge 4
D Coy
Bridge 3
FANGLA (THAGLA) RIDGE
2800
Le CHU
3000
FAIRLY DENSE MIXED JUNGLE
LE
BHUTAN
TSANGDHAR RIDGE
4965
4200
BN HQ
2 RAJPUT
A Coy
34 MORTAR
BATTERY
4600
ASSAM
RIFLES
DHOLA
POST
DZ
4970
TSANGDHAR
BN HQ
1/9 GR
+ 2 Coy
BDE HQ
7 BRIGADE
Nyamjang CHU
Bridge 2
3746
KEY
Coy Company
BN Battalion
BDE Brigade
DZ Drop Zone
5072
4152
BN HQ
9 PUNJAB
+ 3 Coy
TSANGDHAR RIDGE
Bridge 1
KHENZEMANE
CHECK POST
ASSAM
RIFLES
RONG CHU
4400
BN HQ
4 GRENADIERS
+ 3 Coy
Drokung Samba
Bridge
MIXED JUNGLE, MAINLY PINE
Hatung-la
D Coy
4 GRENADIERS
SERKHIM
Karpo-la I
To Zimithang
© Vallika Verma

Chapter 6

THE VALLEY OF DEATH

A HILLSIDE DOTTED WITH FIRE

In the higher reaches of the Himalayas, October is the golden period. The silt-carrying muddy waters in most of the glacier-fed streams have usually settled down by the second week of September and all the water in the trans-Himalayan arid zone turns aquamarine blue, while in the forest covered slopes on the southern side of the watershed the crystal clear waters appear to be a dark shade of green. Almost all villages, depending on their altitude and location, are either still harvesting or have finished harvesting their crops. Everyone is busy stocking up for the coming winter months, when temperatures plummet to way below zero.

On the night of 19 October 1962, temperatures in the Nam Ka Chu Valley had already dropped to below freezing levels even at the river's lowest point, which was the junction with the Nyamjang Chu just below the Khenzemane grazing ground. With the sun setting early because of the narrowness of the valley, there was no getting away from the cold. As darkness fell, Major Gurdial Singh, the 2IC of 2 Rajput, stood outside his bunker and watched in amazement as the northern slopes of the Nam Ka Chu Valley seemed to come alive with dozens of blazing campfires. Behind and slightly above Major Gurdial Singh's position was the Battalion HQ where the commanding officer, Lieutenant Colonel Maha Singh Rikh, along with three officers—his adjutant Captain Gurucharan Bhatia, Captain Mahavir Mangat and Lieutenant Bhup Singh—was also staring at the amazing display of nonchalance by the Chinese across the river.

The entire valley was lightly forested with bamboo, blue pine, rhododendron and other deciduous vegetation. On the northern side of the valley was the Thagla Ridge that dominated the entire Nam Ka Chu Valley. Due to the forest cover, visibility within the valley was limited to a maximum of 90 metres, though usually it was even less than that. However, further up on the slopes of the Thagla, the treeline thinned out appreciably.

The Thagla Ridge reached higher elevations on its western side (overlooking the Tser Jang Tso) but the slopes to the Nam Ka Chu were more gentle. On the eastern side, towards the Nyamjang Chu junction, the valley was far steeper and the sharp rocky cliffs on the Chinese side made any approach from that direction impossible. From the Chinese deployment, it was obvious that the most vulnerable area was the frontage held by 2 Rajput.

The Chinese defences on the forward slope of the Thagla were in three tiers, the first being virtually on the river within grenade throwing distance of Bridges 1 to 4. A second line was dug in a few hundred yards behind and above them, while the main defences with mortars and MMGs were positioned around 600 metres above the river. Not only did this allow them to dominate the Nam Ka Chu Valley, it also allowed the Chinese to keep their eye on the Tsangdhar slope at the base of which were the Indian positions manned by elements of Assam Rifles, 9 Punjab, 4 Grenadiers, 2 Rajput and 1/9 Gorkha Rifles that constituted 7 Brigade under the command of Brigadier John Dalvi.

The Nam Ka Chu originated from a glacier-fed lake, Tser Jang Tso, situated at an altitude of 13,600 feet. The river flowed eastwards, dropping sharply down to 7,100 feet over a distance of sixteen kilometres, an extremely sharp descent even by Himalayan standards. At various points, the Nam Ka Chu had wooden logs spanning the waters, acting as makeshift bridges across it. These became important features around which the units of 7 Brigade were deployed. At the highest point, after the river flowed out of Tser Jang Tso, was Bridge 5 that had one company of 9 Punjab deployed next to it. Further downstream was Temporary Bridge that had Charlie Company of 2 Rajput less a platoon. However, a platoon from Delta Company brought them back to full company strength. After a gap, Bravo Company was deployed at Log Bridge, followed by the Battalion HQ at Bridge 4. This location was protected by Delta Company that was also at full strength with men from the Charlie Company platoon in its ranks. At Bridge 3 was Alpha Company with an additional platoon of Assam Rifles under its command. The entire frontage of 2 Rajput extended across almost four kilometres, from Temporary Bridge to Bridge 3.

Further downstream, to the right of the 2 Rajput position, was 7 Brigade HQ with a company of 1/9 GR protecting its location. Bridge 2 and Bridge 1 had a larger concentration of troops. 9 Punjab less one company was holding the area around Bridge 2 while 4 Grenadiers less one company was deployed around Bridge 1. Just above the junction of the Nam Ka Chu and the Nyamjang Chu, Khenzemane was the headquarters of 5 Assam Rifles with one wing of ninety men and a company of 4 Grenadiers under its command.

Commanded by Lieutenant Colonel B. S. Ahluwalia, 1/9 GR less three companies was strung out on the forward slope of Tsangdhar in depth to (i.e. behind) 2 Rajput's Alpha Company, which was deployed at Bridge 3. One of its companies was on its way to reinforce the Punjabis at Bridge 5 while another was at the brigade's rear at Tsangdhar itself. Ever since 10 October, the officers of the various units had been trying to maintain the security of the large gaps that existed between these positions by carrying out extensive day and night patrolling. Due to the poor visibility and the nature of the terrain, that was an almost impossible task. The gap between Bridge 5 and Temporary Bridge (the left flank of 2 Rajput) was an astounding nine kilometres, a distance that took eighteen hours to cover along the southern side of the Nam Ka Chu. Apart from the vast frontage being held by the Rajputs, there was no interconnecting support between companies, or even platoons.

Though the battalions worked round the clock to try and improve their defences, they were severely limited on nearly all fronts. There was an acute shortage of even basic items like digging tools. 2 Rajput was particularly handicapped, having handed over the bulk of their equipment to 6 Kumaon at Walong. The men were short on all items; there was no question of snow clothing and each man only had a single blanket, as protection from the cold. The four 4.2-inch mortars deployed on the forward slopes of the Tsangdhar slopes were useless, as they had no ammunition. There were four 81.5-mm (3-inch) mortars with the unit with a total of sixty bombs. There was one Vickers machine gun with limited ammunition. As regards small arms, each LMG had seventeen magazines of ammunition, while each soldier had on him his pouch ammunition along with two grenades. The few 2-inch mortars available were also redundant as there were no bombs to go with the firing tubes.

The 2 Rajput positions had no artillery support. The rest of 7 Brigade had four 75-mm para guns that had been airdropped at Tsangdhar but after they were recovered, only two were serviceable. Two hundred and sixty rounds of ammunition had also been salvaged from the drops, but the artillery could not deploy any forward observation posts, as they did not have radio sets for the observers to control and guide the guns. At the same time, the Chinese were clearly visible, coming and going in large numbers. On 17 October, twelve Chinese 82-mm mortars had been dug in and deployed opposite Bridge 4. To make matters worse, having been forced to occupy defensive positions at the base of the Tsangdhar, practically on the riverfront itself, the men would have nowhere to go after their limited ammunition ran out.

In the crisp cold air of the night, watching the campfires lit by the Chinese on the other side of the Nam Ka Chu, Gurdial Singh felt a wave of anger. No stranger to battle, Guru fumed at the arrogance of the Chinese, who he felt were laughing at the Indians. Having been away on leave, the major had done everything he could to rejoin the battalion just four days ago. Shocked by the near suicidal deployment, he had been visiting the various 2 Rajput positions on the Nam Ka Chu. He was amazed at the incompetence of the senior officers who had insisted on stringing the troops out along the river. From their observation posts, the Chinese had been watching 7 Brigade walk into a carefully laid trap. He was experienced and pragmatic enough to realize that if the Chinese attacked now, not just 2 Rajput, but every other unit would be annihilated.

Gurdial Singh, a clean-shaven Sikh, was originally from 3 Rajput and had replaced Major Brahmanand Avasthy as the battalion's 2IC at Walong. His arrival in 2 Rajput had had an electrifying effect on the battalion, for in the Rajput regimental circle, Gurdial Singh was a living legend. During the 1947-48 Jammu and Kashmir Operations, he had taken a company of Gujjars from 3 Rajput up to the Tain Dhar Ridge near Naushera in support of 1 Rajput's defensive positions that were being attacked by Pakistani raiders. In spite of heavy casualties, the raiders had managed to get past the barbed wire into a picket that originally contained twenty-seven men, of whom twenty-four were either dead or severely wounded. The three surviving men valiantly took on the intruders in a hand-to-hand fight. Two more defenders fell, but the last man, Naik Jadunath Singh, continued to defy the enemy. The few vital minutes gained by this valiant action allowed Gurdial Singh's company to reach the post and regain the position after a desperate battle. If the company had not reached the picket when it did, the Tain Dhar feature would have been overrun and holding Naushera would have been impossible.

The Tain Dhar Battle was immortalized in the annals of military history as Naik Jadunath Singh was awarded a Param Vir Chakra posthumously. A Mahavir Chakra and several Vir Chakras were awarded to others. The rank and file who had fought at Tain Dhar was of the opinion that the unfortunate death of the brigade commander, Brigadier Usman, resulted in Guru not getting the recognition he deserved on that fateful day. Guru always shrugged it off; the respect of the men under his command was far more important to him. He would say: 'The Gujjar boys of 3 Rajput seemed to think being with me was their safest bet in the fighting. They would stick with me.'

Throughout the day on 19 October the Chinese had gone about their preparations for an all-out attack in full view of the Indians. Gurdial Singh wasn't the only one who knew that in their current deployment, they had little to no chance of stopping the enemy. For the men, however, Gurdial was someone who could lead them into battle in a way that would allow them to give a reasonable account of themselves. Over the past four days, time and again, anxious and even frightened men would keep asking him what to expect. He was much too frank a person to lie to the men. All he would say was: 'It seems they want us to lay down our lives here. What purpose that will serve, I do not know.'

The darker the night became, the brighter the Chinese campfires seemed to burn. Over the roar of the Nam Ka Chu, Gurdial Singh could sense the presence of some of his own sentries as the temperature hovered around minus five degrees Celsius. All around him in bunkers men from Delta and Charlie Companies were huddled two or three together to optimize the warmth of their single blankets. Those not on duty had fallen asleep, exhausted by the incessant cold that was causing toes and fingers to go numb. The major knew the time had come—most of these men were in all probability going to die when the sun came up the next morning.

Death he had faced before and it didn't scare him. What was driving him insane was the hopelessness of the situation they were in. 'These men can fight if only we give them a chance,' he had angrily said to Colonel Rikh earlier just as darkness was falling. The CO had just looked away; how could he tell his 2IC that he had more or less said the same thing to the brigade commander an hour ago. Dalvi was to write later: 'The last memory I have of the frustrating day of 19 October is a conversation with Lieutenant Colonel Rikh. He gave me a very clear and lucid assessment of the Chinese in their assembly areas. His last words were, "Don't worry, sir, despite their superiority the Rajputs won't let you down. If you do get back, see to it that those who got us into this mess get their due."'

THE VIEW FROM THAGLA

Over the past twenty days, the Chinese commanders had watched from their position on the Thagla Ridge as India's 7 Infantry Brigade moved into the Nam Ka Chu Valley (the Chinese called it the Kejie Lang region), one battalion following the other and deploying along the length of the river. Not only was this reducing the fighting capability of these troops, but the Indian commander, by getting into the narrow valley, was effectively taking out of the equation the one factor that could turn the tide against the Chinese—the Indian Air Force. Any aircraft in support of the ground troops, even if it could make the turn west from the confluence of the Nam Ka Chu and the Nyamjang Chu, would be vulnerable even to small arms fire, for it would have to fly laterally across and below the Chinese positions.

Accordingly, the Chinese anti-aircraft detachments in support of Regiments 154, 155, 157, 31 and 32 who were poised for the attack across the Nam Ka Chu were positioned on the Thagla Ridge to take on any Indian air strikes which would perforce have to approach through the Nyamjang Chu valley. This left the Chinese with the 308 Artillery Regiment and the 136 Engineer Regiment in support of the five regiments, a total strength in excess of 10,000 men.

On 11 June 1962, after the 'push and shove' incident at Khenzemane, the Central Military Commission (CMC) had set up the Zang Zi 419 (Tibet Force 419) or the Forward HQ of the Tibet Military Command. At the time 31 and 32 Regiments were part of the 11 Infantry Division, but were subsequently shifted to the Tawang sector. Zang Zi 419 was equivalent to a full-strength Indian division, while each 'regiment' in the Chinese army was equal to an Indian brigade. Zang Zi 419 was under the charge of General Ching Hi, a veteran of the Korea War.

From the reports coming in from various Chinese observation posts, it was obvious that the Indian troops were deploying in a scattered form around company or reinforced company-sized units. The defences were mainly bunkers constructed from stone, wood and soil with barbed wire entanglements, abates, bamboo slips and land mines presumably guarding the approaches. The quality of the bunkers was reported as being inferior, though the numbers were comparatively high. The estimates ranged from fifty to a hundred bunkers at each company location. Inter-connected through 'traffic' trenches, it was thought that each bunker could hold three to five men. It was estimated that the structures were convenient to live and fight from, each bunker having one to three firing holes that were visible. Most of these opened towards the front, where the range of vision and field of fire was narrow while the dead angle of firing (blind side) was large. Camouflage and concealment of the bunkers was reportedly very good, some of the structures not being easy to locate. 7 Brigade had more or less completed the defensive structures required for each stronghold in twenty days. One of the OPs (observation posts) was reporting the construction of a 40-metre communication trench that had come up in a single night. The Chinese commanders also noted that in the organization of firepower, the Indians seemingly had a tendency to pay special attention to the front side, *ignoring the rear altogether.*

On 18 October, operational orders were issued from the Forward HQ of the Tibet Military Command to all Chinese units. The Chinese higher command was determined that the first blow should be a decisive one that annihilated the Indian troops of 7 Brigade. The Chinese commanders were not only fully updated on the Indian army units that were facing them; they also had a fair idea of the military traditions and fighting capabilities of the Indians. Field commanders had been cautioned that they were up against elite Indian troops, and though the Chinese army should strategically despise the enemy, tactically they needed to be taken seriously. Tibetan Command also cautioned that the Chinese troops must be prepared to fight a long, hard and adverse battle, and, if necessary, prepare to fight a second and a third battle.

Based on the instructions that they 'must win the first war', Forward HQ of the Tibet Military Command had to consider 'how big the mouth should be opened'. If the mouth was opened large, then it would not be possible to completely annihilate the Indian forces; if it was opened too small, the Indians could pull themselves out of the tactically unsound position they were in on the 'Kejie Lang River Valley (Nam Ka Chu)', regroup and put up a tough fight. Zang Zi 419 now had the option of three combat tactics available to them.

First, carry out a frontal attack on the Indian positions, with subsequent rolling attacks towards the left and right. This method would be akin to locking horns like two bulls, and though the Indians would be wiped out, the Chinese casualties would mount. The second option was to ignore the brigade and capture the heights behind them, thereby cutting off any chance of the troops escaping; the Indians could then be systematically encircled and wiped out. However, here again, it would be risky, as Chinese troops would not only have to fight Indian troops dug in above them, they would also have a large body of Indian troops behind them. The third option would be to attack both flanks—Khenzemane and Tser Jang Tso—while directing the main strike towards the left flank of the middle section (Bridge 4 to Bridge 3 held by 2 Rajput). While pinning the Indians down from the front, they would also assault from the rear after having infiltrated through the positions during the hours of darkness preceding H-hour. This would isolate the Indians into many small sections and these could then be wiped out, thereby ensuring maximum casualties. The plan was sent to Chairman Mao in Peking who gave the go-ahead. The Chinese could now 'gallop up, eat up India's one brigade, that is 7 Brigade, that was lying in front'.

Accordingly, 155 Regiment and one battalion of 157 Regiment were to take on the four Rajput positions and the Assam Rifles post at Dhola, while the main body of 157 Regiment was to simultaneously assault 1/9 GR positions and also cut off the track from Bridge 1 to Hathung-la, thereby trapping 9 Punjab and 4 Grenadiers. While the 2nd Battalion of 31 Regiment was to engage the Rajputs from across the Nam Ka Chu, their role was to pin them down long enough for the attacks to develop from the rear. Finally, 154 Regiment was to launch a battalion-sized attack on the Khenzemane post and the grenadier position at the Drokung Samba Bridge while the remainder of the regiment was to rapidly move down the eastern bank of the Nyamjang Chu Valley and threaten 4 Division HQ at Zimithang.

DALVI'S DILEMMA

On the Indian side, from the humble tradesmen (cooks, dhobis and others) to NCOs, JCOs, officers, battalion commanders, brigade staff up to HQ 4 Division, every man knew the ridiculous deployment along the Nam Ka Chu was a certain death trap. After 10 October, when the realization that the Chinese also had guns had hit Kaul, there had been the unspoken hope that the general's departure for Delhi would finally result in an order that would allow 7 Brigade to extricate itself from the Nam Ka Chu Valley and take up a more realistic defensive position on the northern slopes of the Tsangdhar, if not even further back.

However, as he handed over command of 7 Brigade back to John Dalvi after the firing started, Kaul's orders were unambiguous on one point. Says Dalvi: 'We were to hold our position, that is the south bank of the Nam Ka Chu and ensure the security of the crossings from Temporary Bridge to Bridge 1 at all costs.' The departing general also told Lieutenant Colonel Rikh that the Indian troops were not to advance across the Nam Ka Chu as 'the situation had changed and the enemy was reacting more violently than he had anticipated'.

Kaul's own version of events in his autobiography confirms this: 'I had seen with my own eyes the superior resources of Chinese in the battle that morning, and the untenability of our position in Dhola area located in a hollow. *I was also advised by the Divisional Commander* (italics mine) that I should go to Delhi and ask Army Headquarters and the Government not to press us to "expel" the Chinese from this area, a task which was beyond our capacity and that we should occupy a position where we could be better placed vis-à-vis the enemy. Dalvi had also the same view. I agreed with both the Divisional and Brigade Commander.'

With their respective commands back, Niranjan Prasad and John Dalvi could turn their attention to the serious problems faced by the depleted, half-starved and under-equipped 7 Brigade, problems that they had, in the last few days, watched with dismay and professional discernment grow by the minute. Even as he departed, Kaul had tied their hands with that one final order: that there could be no changes in the ground positions until he himself cleared it. They had no choice but to try and maintain these untenable positions until Kaul's orders changed. To be fair to Kaul, the moment he reached Delhi the next morning, he presented his alarming assessment to Army HQ and to the prime minister. Nehru convened a meeting at his residence, Teen Murti, in the evening of 11 October. Apart from Nehru and Kaul, also present were the defence minister, Krishna Menon, the COAS, General Pran Thapar, the air chief, Aspy Engineer, the cabinet secretary, S. S. Khera, the foreign secretary, M. J. Desai, the Intelligence Bureau Chief, B. N. Mullik, and the Eastern Army Commander, Bogey Sen. Kaul, true to his word, did not change his stance and clearly spelt out the Indian position at Nam Ka Chu. His first-hand account described the situation on the ground lucidly, explaining in detail the overall superiority of the Chinese both in numbers and weaponry; the shortages faced by the Indian troops on all fronts, ranging from clothing to rations to ammunition; the abysmal rate of retrieval of air supplies; and the difficulties posed by the terrain and the cold. He stated in unambiguous terms that it was nearly impossible for the Indian troops to expel the Chinese and advised an immediate withdrawal from Nam Ka Chu to a sounder position that was logistically and tactically defensible.

When Kaul finished speaking, he expected the matter to be settled then and there. As the group digested Kaul's 'new' understanding of the situation, a pensive Nehru said he did not want a situation where Indian troops would be committing suicide. He then asked for suggestions as to what needed to be done in the circumstances.

As we have seen, Bogey Sen, despite commanding the Eastern Army, had never been to Nam Ka Chu. Nor had the COAS, Pran Thapar. Both these officers had in fact been sidelined in what until now was the 'General

Kaul Show'. Perhaps in a bid to reassert their own positions, both Sen and Thapar now argued against Kaul—Sen saying that regardless of the conditions, a full brigade should be able to hold a defensive line even against superior forces. Kaul's earlier bluster now made it impossible for him to speak up against the army commander and the chief, who clearly outranked him in the chain of command.

Nehru and Menon, perhaps loath to invite the criticism that would have followed a pullout from the Nam Ka Chu, for once decided to go against the advice of Kaul and backed Sen and Thapar. Unable to convince the COAS and the government, Kaul returned to Tezpur. The next day Nehru left for Colombo and during a stopover at Madras, made grand statements about 'throwing out the Chinese from our territory'. Both the Indian and the international press, which hailed it as a declaration of war on China, seized upon these remarks. To make matters worse, on 17 October, Menon, Thapar and Sen converged on Tezpur where Kaul now continued to argue for a strategic withdrawal from Tsangle and Bridge 5. After the events of 10 October, the Chinese had nullified the strategic importance of this location. Again Thapar and Sen hardened their stand, and ordered the corps commander to move 1/9 GR to Tsangle as reinforcements. These decisions (11 and 17 October) were not communicated to either 7 Brigade or 4 Division.

While Niranjan Prasad and John Dalvi awaited fresh orders from the top, the Chinese stepped up their activities. From their 7-ton roadhead at Marmang, a few miles from Thagla, they used Tibetan ponies to bring mortars and guns across the ridge and fortified their positions with the thoroughness and skill that had earlier been demonstrated by them during the Korean conflict. Two dozen Indian observation posts were sending in detailed reports to Brigade HQ that was located away from the Nam Ka Chu, in depth behind the Assam Rifles post at Dhola and Bridge 3. They reported all the Chinese activity including the taking of bearings of Indian positions for the silent registration of targets. Dalvi himself observed a jeep reaching the top of the Thagla with a senior Chinese officer on board. On 19 October, the Rajput observation post at Temporary Bridge counted 1,978 Chinese soldiers at Tseng Jong. All this information, along with grid references, was being relayed to HQ 4 Division which had somewhat unceremoniously been shifted to Zimithang from Tezpur so it could be closer to the front.

As all this was going on, 7 Brigade HQ had waited in vain for the one order that would allow them to pull the main body of troops back from their suicidal deployment. Finally, after sundown on 19 October, with the clock ticking away, Prasad called Dalvi and asked him to move the remaining body of 1/9 Gorkhas to Tsangle at first light the next day. Dalvi, shocked, asked the GOC if he had been reading all the reports that had been filed through the day about the Chinese build up.

Dalvi once again pleaded for permission to withdraw from the river. Finally, Prasad gave him the news that Kaul had fallen ill and had had to be evacuated to Delhi on 18 October. The GOC categorically stated that there was no one in the chain of command who could revoke the personal order given by the corps commander.

Asking Dalvi not to do anything rash, Prasad conveyed the brigade commander's appreciation to HQ IV Corps. The three main points were: (a) On 20 October the Chinese would definitely wipe out the Indians at Tsangle (b) Within the next two days, the Chinese would drive a wedge between and through 2 Rajput positions and capture Tsangdhar. When this happened the whole brigade would be overrun, and (c) due to the present dispersal and lack of troops, the Chinese would have a walkover, as they would have to contend with only two or three infantry companies, who, without any artillery support and limited ammunition, would be overrun sooner rather than later.

After a while, a despondent GOC was back on the line. He had conveyed his own and Dalvi's assessment to the BGS IV Corps, Brigadier K. K. Singh. The BGS is the hub around which the entire Corps HQ technically functions. Despite everything Prasad said on the phone, Singh was adamant that Kaul's orders were sacrosanct. He did, however, offer to try and contact the general who was said to be suffering from pulmonary oedema and was bedridden in Delhi. The BGS then said Division HQ and the brigade should not panic, as it was unlikely that the Chinese would do anything big. This was to be the last communication between 4 Division and IV Corps.

Dalvi was getting more and more frustrated and upset. When he got this last call, present in the mess with him were the divisional signals officer, Lieutenant Colonel K. K. Tewari; the brigade major, Major Rex Kharbanda; the DQ, Major Pereira; the OC mortar battery, Major Balraj Nijjar; the Intelligence officer, Captain Tushar Gupta; the signals officer (Sparrow) Captain Lakshman Singh; and Captain H. S. Talwar who had wandered down from 17 Para Field gun position to Brigade HQ. Unmindful of the fact that all the officers could hear every detail of the conversation between himself and the GOC, Brigadier Dalvi said words to the effect: 'I can no longer stand by and watch the massacre of my men. It is time that some senior officer took a firm stand. This is no longer a case of trying to bluff the Chinese by sitting under their noses. If a scapegoat is wanted, I am willing to offer myself and am prepared to accept the consequences, and resign my commission.'

Dalvi's outburst had the strange effect of causing Niranjan Prasad to break down. The general turned fatalistic and said he too had enough, and he might as well go down with the brigade the next day. He said he would stay and die with the men. This was perhaps Prasad's moment of truth. In the absence of Kaul, he was the officiating corps commander. Being fully aware of the situation on the ground he could have concurred and ordered a withdrawal. But yet again he chose to look over his shoulder and ask for instructions. Maybe by then it was already too late, for even as the two most senior commanders on the ground openly expressed their impotence and helplessness, Chinese infiltration parties had already started preparing to ford the Nam Ka Chu and come up behind the Indian positions.

Unknown to Dalvi and the brigade signals team, both 9 Punjab and 4 Grenadiers were also patched in on the line and heard the conversation between the brigade commander and the GOC. The effect of this conversation on the morale of the two commanding officers and the battalions can best be gauged from how events played out the next morning.

THE ENDLESS NIGHT

The bitter cold had seeped into his bones. His feet had now been numb for days and the pain in his hands was quite unbearable. Subedar Dashrath Singh wrapped his blanket tightly around himself and stared into the darkness. To his left was nothing but dense jungle; the next Indian position at Bridge 4 seemed to be miles away. Behind him was the Tsangdhar slope, which further up was held by 1/9 GR. In the open defences, he could make out the shadow of his platoon, each man, like him, straining to look out into the darkness until his eyes watered from the strain. Dashrath was painfully aware of the huge gaps all around him.

The fires on the opposite slope were bothering the JCO. 'I now think,' he later told me, 'that there was nothing haphazard about those camp fires. I think each one was a beacon of sorts that allowed the infiltrating Chinese behind us to get their bearings in the pitch dark. Even at a distance the flickering flames were hypnotizing. It was hard to take your eyes away from the fires.' Earlier that evening, as the Rajputs at Temporary Bridge prepared to face yet another freezing night, a herd of approximately seventy yak had burst through the opposite bank of the Nam Ka Chu, splashed through the river and stampeded through the Rajput positions. It was obvious the Chinese were testing the depth and the flow of the water, while also checking if any wires and mines had been laid by the Indians. 'It could be a deception,' Dashrath had told Major Sethi and Major Pant shortly after the last animal had weaved its way through the Rajput positions. 'Their observation posts know we don't have mines. I also don't think they'll play to our strength by attacking frontally across the river tomorrow.'

Major Pant's presence was reassuring. He was an energetic individual with a forceful way of getting things done. Though he was one of the most educated officers in the unit (having done his masters from Allahabad University) he had not had too many staff appointments. He was, as other officers would say, 'the hard core of the unit'.

To Dashrath's right was the Charlie Company HQ, further flanked by Second Lieutenant Onkar Dubey and Subedar Ramjanam Singh. This platoon was manning defences slightly lower down the slope, overlooking the Temporary Bridge and was the closest to the river's edge. Directly behind them was No. 10 Platoon of Delta Company under the command of Jemadar Jagan Nath Bose.

Downstream, at Log Bridge, the deployment of Bravo Company was similar. The Gujjars were under the command of Lieutenant Subash Chander who had Subedar Mohan Lal with him. Subash Chander had been in the Engineers prior to getting commissioned as an officer and joining 2 Rajput. A sincere, trusting individual, he was an extremely reliable and steady officer. The flanking platoons on either side were under the command of two able JCOs: Jemadar Gian Chand, an outstanding athlete, on the left, and the soft-spoken Subedar Har Lal to the right. No 6. Platoon, under the leadership of Naik Hoshiar Singh, a services wrestler, was positioned just astride the Log Bridge.

Bravo Company's location was relatively better than the defences at Temporary Bridge. Both their flanks were protected and the area had better vegetation from a tactical point of view. Some of the old-timers in Bravo Company had fought in Europe during World War II. Prior to Partition, the Gujjar Company had been a part of 8 Punjab, which on transfer to Pakistan had come to 2 Rajput in exchange for their Punjabi Mussalman component. Among them had been Havildar Kamal Ram, who had won a Victoria Cross in the Sangro River Battle in Italy and Subedar Des Raj who had been awarded the Military Cross in the same battle. Both Kamal Ram and Des Raj had retired just a few months ago.

The remaining platoons of Delta Company (one platoon having moved to Temporary Bridge with Major Pant) were defending Bridge 4 and the left flank. No. 11 platoon under the command of Jemadar N. P. Dass was the closest to the river. Company HQ under the command of Subedar B. C. Roy was situated just above the forward platoon, while No. 12 Platoon under Jemadar Biswas held the upper ground a bit to the left. Flanking the position to the right was the Battalion HQ that contained Lieutenant Colonel Rikh and his adjutant, Captain Gurucharan Singh Bhatia, with Major Gurdial Singh and Second Lieutenant Bhup Singh deployed just ahead. Bhup Singh had returned to the battalion earlier in the day after having completed a detailed reconnaissance of the Dibang Valley as part of Op Onkar. Positioned between Jemadar Biswas's platoon and Battalion HQ was a platoon from 7 Mahar under the command of Jemadar Mohan Lal that had two Vickers machine guns and at least 32,000 rounds of ammunition; the mortar platoon along with the one platoon from Charlie Company was deployed to the right of Battalion HQ. Captain Mahabir Mangat, having only two days ago relinquished command of Alpha Company, was in the communications bunker next to Battalion HQ.

Serious and reserved, Captain Gurucharan Singh Bhatia was due to get married after his NEFA tenure. Every evening the unit gramophone would play love songs while the field telephone was held next to it so that Bhatia could hear his favourite: *'Teri pyari pyari surat ko kisi ki nazar na lage, chashme baddoor'*. The peace station posting he had been patiently waiting for so that he could get married had finally come. At daybreak on 20 October Captain Bhatia was scheduled to bid the men goodbye and leave for Poona.

Popular and vivacious, Captain Mangat was the life of the battalion. He had an endless stock of Sardar jokes, quite a few of them aimed at himself. His letter to his erstwhile roommate at the IMA, Ian Cardozo (1/5 GR, who retired as a Major General) was perhaps one of the last letters to make it out of Nam Ka Chu: 'It looks like it is I who will go first into battle. I am not able to tell you where I am but we are just short of the McMahon Line. The Chinese hold the high ground and seem to be in great strength. Should they attack we will defend our territory to our very last breath. It is very cold out here and we do not have snow clothing but we will give the Chinese a hot reception if they dare to attack. Will tell you all about it, *IF* and *WHEN* we meet again, I don't know where you are but I wish we were better prepared.'

Delta Company was a Bengali Company and the men were acutely conscious of the fact that unlike the Rajput and Gujjar Companies, they were not battle tested. Rikh was aware of this and had decided to keep them close to Battalion HQ.

The sharp exchange of words with Gurdial Singh earlier in the evening after Rikh had returned from Brigade HQ had only added to the feeling of impending doom. Rikh knew the hour of reckoning was at hand. For days he had done what he was trained to do—follow orders despite the impossibility of the task. He had, time and again, given his frank opinion to Dalvi, then watched helplessly as first the brigade commander, then the GOC begged and pleaded with faceless men at the other end of the telephone to extricate the doomed brigade. On 10 October when a visibly shaken Kaul made a hurried exit to 'consult Mr Nehru' both Rikh and Dalvi were certain that it was only a matter of time before they were allowed to pull back and take up more credible fighting positions.

But that order never came.

Rikh had to quickly put all these thoughts behind him and focus on the long night ahead of him. Would the Chinese put in a night assault? It was quite likely. The cards were all held by the Chinese. Now all that Rikh could do was wait and watch. He knew every man in the battalion was where he was supposed to be and all the patrols were out. The officers and JCOs were moving about the defences amidst the men who were on duty, while others were trying to get some sleep. There was no report of any activity. After a while, with nothing more to be done, Rikh retired to his corner of the command bunker to get some much needed sleep.

The last Rajput position was at Bridge 3 where Alpha Company was deployed under the command of Captain Ravi Eipe. This was the original Dhola post. A platoon of Assam Rifles was occupying the top of the spur that overlooked the Rongla Nullah that came down from Tsangdhar. No. 2 Platoon under CHM (company havildar major) Saudagar Singh was holding the ground to the left, approximately 600 feet below the Assam Rifles position. Another twenty feet below, No. 1 Platoon under Subedar Basdeo Singh was just above the river, overlooking the bridge. Company HQ was directly behind and above Basdeo Singh's position, while to its right was No. 3 Platoon under Jemadar Ghanshyam Singh. The last platoon, from its position on the spur, not only overlooked the Rongla Nullah, it covered the track that led to Brigade HQ that was sited a kilometre further behind.

On the same spur, but deployed further up in depth were 1/9 GR. Though downstream of the Rajput positions was Bridge 1 and 2 where 9 Punjab and 4 Grenadiers were deployed, the only exit from the Nam

Ka Chu Valley for 2 Rajput would be through the Rongla Nullah. All the men knew this exit route as they had entered the valley this way. Given the nature of the terrain, any attack on this position would have to come from the west. As a result, Alpha Company was tactically perhaps the best situated.

9 Punjab was at Bridge 2 while 4 Grenadiers, the last entrant into the valley, was holding the position at Bridge 1. One company was deployed at the Drokung Sambha Bridge next to Khenzemane and another company, minus a platoon, was at Serkhim just below Hathung-la. Lieutenant Colonel K. S. Harihar Singh, with Major Oscar Thomas as his adjutant, was commanding the battalion. The Battalion HQ and one company was deployed on the southern bank of the Nam Ka Chu while Major Balbir Singh's company was across the river, below the sharp cliffs of the Thagla which seemed to rise vertically just beyond his position. By the time the river had tumbled down from the icy heights to Bridge 1, the lowest point in the Nam Ka Chu Valley, it had lost considerable altitude.

The Grenadiers were huddled amongst the boulders nearly on the riverbed, all bunched up together. There was a single stone hut in the area, which was occupied by the CO and the six officers. The men had constructed sangars for themselves amongst the boulders, which were the only protection they had from the elements. The Intelligence officer, Second Lieutenant R. S. Kahlon, felt that it was hopeless as a defensive position; limited and cramped, no two positions within the battalion were more than 180 metres apart. Like the Rajputs, the Grenadiers had virtually no support weapons. The men had carried 3-inch mortars all the way from the plains but these were useless as there were no bombs. A single telephone line had been laid out by the Signals detachment that ran from Brigade HQ through 9 Punjab's location at Bridge 2 to Bridge 1 and then onto the Division Tac HQ. Both the 9 Punjab and 4 Grenadier communication networks were hooked onto the same line.

'The fear of the unknown', wrote my father in *Rivers of Silence* (he had been with the men until a couple of months before), 'plays a great part in conditioning the behaviour of men, even if as soldiers they are meant to be able to face uneven odds at times. Those who had earlier combat experience were perhaps even more tense, with images of past encounters in their minds, knowing that they must put up a brave front. Patriotic ideals recede into the background, what now counts is the next man and JCOs and officers. They're in it together and while fear has a numbing effect, a conscious effort has to be made to conceal it.'

KNIFED IN THE BACK

The Chinese had started infiltrating across the Nam Ka Chu on the night of 18 October itself. Small parties had identified the crossing points between and upstream of the Rajput positions, which had large gaps between them. In their version of the battle, the Chinese have perhaps deliberately avoided talking of the crossings, claiming that the 1st and 2nd Battalion of 155 Infantry Regiment under the command of Liu Guang Tong had moved into their forming-up position (FUP) by 4 a.m. on the morning of the 19th and then crossed the Nam Ka Chu under the covering fire of their artillery guns some three hours later. From survivor accounts, the timing of the attack and the description of the crossing given by the Chinese do not quite add up.

The river upstream of Temporary Bridge was easily fordable. Protective screening parties were already in position from the previous night when the Chinese infantry columns started crossing over sometime during the night. The troops were in canvas shoes without socks and their weapons and equipment had been muffled. Holding hands in the dark, the shadowy figures began to cross the freezing river, carefully negotiating the slippery rocks and the fast flowing water. Once across, they darted across the narrow footpath that led up towards Bridge 5, and began to form up in the coniferous spruce and fir jungle where they slipped into dry socks and regular boots. The telephone line that ran along the track was left alone for if it were cut or tampered with, the Rajput positions would be warned. Chinese ambush parties were also in position to intercept any link patrols that may have come along. None did and the crossings were completely undetected.

The infiltration parties that had crossed over the previous evening had moved deeper up the slope, positioning themselves behind the Rajput positions and below the 1/9 GR locations. Others had moved to cut off Hathung-la while other designated parties had moved stealthily into position to launch simultaneous assaults on the Gorkhas, the guns and the heavy mortars deployed there. The three westernmost Rajput company locations—Temporary Bridge, Log Bridge and Bridge 4—were thus completely entrapped.

Rikh was woken up with a mug of tea at 4.30 a.m. while the battalion was at stand-to. It was still pitch dark, with dawn some time away. The temperature was way below freezing and though the Nam Ka Chu was at its lowest, the roar of the river dominated the still morning. The wind would only pick up later in the day. In the command bunker, Adjutant Captain Bhatia was on the field telephone, getting reports from the three other company positions. All of them were reporting no activity in their vicinity;

the night patrols confirming there was no contact with the Chinese south of the river. Across the river, the fires continued to flicker on the hillsides.

With just a hint of grey towards the east, at 5.14 a.m., a series of flashes were seen on the Thagla slopes, the sound of the mortars carrying through a few seconds later. Rikh wrote: 'The enemy commenced heavy shelling of all four company localities simultaneously. The shelling was from 82-mm mortars deployed on the forward slopes of the Thagla, and from heavy 120-mm mortars deployed behind the Thagla feature. The enemy shelling was intense and continued for about an hour. We had no weapon to counter the enemy mortars.' The initial salvos ranged onto their targets, and gradually the intensity increased. Some of the cast iron bombs hit the trees, adding yet another frightening dimension to the deafening explosions that had engulfed the Rajput positions. The noise and the unrelenting shelling succeeded in driving the troops out of the open defences into the makeshift bunkers. The men huddled together, their weapons ready, as they peered out of the firing bays towards the front. They were completely unaware of the impending attack that was building up towards their rear.

The initial casualties all occurred in the first few minutes, as splinters hit some men before they could get under cover. At Battalion HQ at Bridge 4, the moment the Chinese opened up, Captain Gurucharan Bhatia had sprinted across to the mortar platoon while Captain Mahabir Mangat raced off to the communications bunker. Bhatia immediately attempted to engage the Chinese with the battalion's 3-inch mortars, firing at maximum range. However, the rounds landed nearly 300 metres short of the Chinese positions.

The Chinese had clearly marked out the battalion's signal bunker. Having forced the troops to take cover, a couple of 75-mm RCLs (recoilless guns) started firing from across the river. These direct firing weapons opened up on the communication hub of the battalion. The last message from the bunker had been transmitted some fifteen minutes after the first mortar salvos had been fired. The direct hits completely destroyed the signal bunker, killing all the men inside, including the gallant Mangat.

The Chinese, having zeroed in on Bhatia's mortar position, now intensified their fire, and within minutes all the 2 Rajput 3-inch mortars were knocked out. At Log Bridge, disaster struck as the company commander Lieutenant Subash Chander was killed just when the Chinese bombardment was lifting; one of the last few mortar shells hit the cookhouse just above the company command post. The officer had by then realized that the attack was coming from the rear and was out in the open exhorting No.

5 Platoon to get out of the bunkers and face the rear. Burning kerosene and ghee tins cascaded down from the cookhouse, driving the officer back into his bunker where he was burnt alive, much to the horror of his watching troops.

After an hour, the shelling stopped. Anticipating a frontal assault on the heels of the mortar barrage, Charlie Company at Temporary Bridge began firing blindly across the Nam Ka Chu. The company commander, Major Sethi was nowhere to be seen and Second Lieutenant Onkar Dubey and Subedar Dashrath Singh had to calm down the nervous men. Recalled Dashrath: 'There was a gap of some ten minutes or so when nothing was happening. All eyes were straining across the river, and no one was watching our rear. Suddenly, one could hear bugles and whistles on the slope behind us. It then dawned on me that the Chinese were behind us.'

Dashrath yelled at Naik Roshan to quickly move his section out of the defences and head for a prominent bump approximately 140 metres above the platoon's position. As the men got there, out of breath, they could hear the Chinese forming up behind the rocky protrusion. Taking position on the moss-covered rock, Roshan and his men could see a teeming mass of Chinese troops, all bunched up, some forty metres in front of them. The section opened fire. It was the turn of the Chinese to be stunned as they took casualties, but the Chinese troops begun to surge downhill. The leading elements opened up with their AK-47 assault rifles and grenades, while from either side of the protrusion the Chinese troops poured past to attack Dashrath's and Major Pant's positions.

Pant had also realized that the direction of the attack was from the rear; he and Jemadar Bose yelled at the men to get out of the bunkers and prepare to meet the onslaught from the rear. Charlie Company's No. 9 Platoon had barely enough time to pull itself out of the bunkers to face the rear. They could see Roshan's men start firing, but then they were under fire themselves as the Chinese came down the slope, using the tree cover to steadily close the distance. Bursts of automatic fire were punctuated with the sharp retorts of .303 bolt-action Lee Enfield Rifles, LMGs; the choking smell of cordite from exploding grenades filled the air.

Every man in Roshan's section held his ground against the sheer weight of the Chinese attack, and one by one, they died there. The few extra seconds that they gained by slowing the Chinese attack gave both Dashrath and Pant a chance to get their men organized. The initial rush on both these platoons was stemmed as the Chinese took severe casualties. As per Chinese records, the battalion commander leading the assault was also killed during this initial exchange of fire. Once again, though troops continued to be engaged in close-quarter duels, there was a momentary lull as the Chinese took stock.

Pant was everywhere, and he yelled across to Dashrath: 'Ab mein kya karu? Aap to purane aadmi hein (What should I do now? You have been in these situations before)'. Before Dashrath could reply, the second wave of attacks began, pushing the JCO back to his own men where he could be heard shouting instructions over the din of gunfire. Charlie Company's No. 7 Platoon that was closest to the Nam Ka Chu was now at the rear end of the battle.

The moment the firing had started, Second Lieutenant Onkar Dubey grabbed an LMG and along with two men rushed uphill to try and support Roshan's section. By then the Chinese were already streaming past along the flanks and had engaged the other two platoons. Taking up a position on the flank behind some trees, Dubey and his two companions inflicted quite a few casualties. However, they were severely outnumbered by the onrushing Chinese. Both his companions were killed and Dubey was shot in the stomach and chest.

Pant, meanwhile, had been hit in the leg, but he was still exhorting his remaining men to fight on even though most of the platoon had been wiped out. According to Rikh's notes: 'The enemy after having been beaten back started more intensive firing on the locality. During this the officer was again seriously injured in the right leg and stomach. He kept on shouting at and inspiring his men who rose to superhuman heights and broke up the fourth wave of the enemy. The enemy saw that the officer was the main cause for the heavy casualties being inflicted on them, accordingly directed maximum fire on Major Pant who being hit all over his body, succumbed to his injuries.'

Dashrath was badly wounded; bursts fired at close range had ripped into his stomach and he was unconscious when the Chinese finally overran his position. Under the circumstances, as the senior JCO, he had managed to control the Rajput response remarkably well. In all, there were seventy-five fatal casualties, while almost all the others who were overpowered and taken prisoner were wounded.

Dubey had been left for dead, but the next day as the Chinese mopping up teams were looking for survivors, they realized the officer was alive. Along with Dashrath, who was saved from an executioner's bullet by the Chinese nurse, Dubey, perhaps by virtue of the fact that he was an officer, was also taken prisoner despite the severity of his wounds. Thus ended the saga of the westernmost position of 2 Rajput at Temporary Bridge.

TO THE LAST MAN

The Gujjars of Bravo Company were in a state of shock, having just seen their company commander charred to death. However, taking immediate charge of the situation, Subedar Har Lal shouted to the men to get behind the trees and rocks and face the rear slope. 'Make your fire count,' he said, 'and then use the rifle as a lathi to club any Chinese who gets in close.' Jemadar Gian Chand's No. 4 Platoon had also just about managed to turn around when an avalanche of khaki-clad Chinese troops began to pour down on the two platoons.

Subedar Mohan Lal, the senior company JCO, and the men in Company HQ just above the burning bunker of the company commander were killed in the first wave as they had no protection. Both No. 5 and No. 4 Platoon however, using the dense tree cover and firing systematically into the mass of troops bearing down on them, succeeded in temporarily halting the Chinese. But in the confined space the Chinese could only go downhill. After regrouping, they launched a second attack, then a third. In this unequal battle, the men fell one by one until no one was left. Some men, having run out of ammunition, still refused to surrender, only to be brought down by bursts of automatic fire.

As both Har Lal and Jemadar Gian Chand went down in a hail of bullets with their men, the Chinese turned their undivided attention towards Hoshiar Singh's position, which was lower down on the spur overlooking the log bridge. The men, having had a little more time to take stock of the situation as the upper layers of the company had taken the initial brunt of the attack, had watched the firefight develop into hand-to-hand combat as the Chinese repeatedly tried to close the gap. Hoshiar and his platoon were shooting at the flanking Chinese with deadly accuracy, the .303 rifles being extremely effective at that range. However, the bolt action meant a slower rate of fire, which combined with an acute shortage of ammunition, was crippling.

The Chinese on the other hand, when shooting downhill, found their fire plunging and were left with no choice but to close the gap with Hoshiar's men. Here, too, the Chinese were left grappling with individual defenders in close quarter battles that were dominated by bayonets, rifle butts and percussion grenades. Having run out of ammunition, Hoshiar had discarded his rifle and picked up a Sten. However, while kneeling down to change the magazine, he was struck a blinding blow from a grenade that lacerated his upper arms and chest. Thrown backwards, he was pinned down by four Chinese soldiers who realized he was the platoon commander from the binoculars and compass on him. Even then he fought ferociously, refusing to give up. Finally, bleeding profusely and panting from his exertions, he was subdued and taken prisoner. By then, approximately four hours after the first shells had lit up the dawn sky on the Thagla, No. 6 Platoon along with the rest of Bravo Company had ceased to exist.

Rikh's notes after the war said: '...the defensive battle fought by B Company at Log Bridge will also rank as one of the most gallant actions fought against the heaviest odds. The company lost over 80 per cent in killed alone, these included the company commander, two of the three platoon commanders and seven section commanders out of nine. This battle will be recalled with pride by all future generations of soldiers in the regiment, as an epic example of how the Rajputs fought and died...' The bulk of the Indian casualties were bullet injuries in the upper part of the body. The Chinese 7.62 mm low velocity ammunition was not as lethal as the Indian .303, but the ability to spray the target combined with the sheer volume of attacking troops meant the Indians were at a disadvantage. Apart from grenades, the attacking Chinese troops also used flame-throwers extensively, with which they would incinerate any surviving soldiers.

The Chinese referred to the Bridge 4 locality as Kalong. From their point of view, unlike the Temporary Bridge and Log Bridge positions that were isolated and could be approached and assaulted relatively easily from the rear, the Rajput Battalion HQ location at Bridge 4 had to be viewed in conjunction with Dhola, which was held by Alpha Company and elements of 5 Assam Rifles, while Wanbudiu (Tsangdhar) is where a company of 1/9 GR had its defences. Having studied the ground from their dominant positions on the Thagla, the Chinese would have known that the Battalion HQ was the most strongly held position. Once they had identified the main bunker, they would have known where the communication hub was and also the location of the four 3-inch (81.5 mm) mortars.

In the first half hour, as we have seen, the concentrated mortar fire (combined with RCLs) had destroyed the signals bunker and the mortar position of 2 Rajput. As mortar bombs continued to rain down, Major Gurdial Singh, from inside his bunker, scanned the area ahead of him and across the river for any Chinese activity. If the bombardment was a prelude to an attack, by now the Chinese should have been milling around on the opposite bank. However, while the mortars continued to fire with the same intensity from the slopes above, the north bank of the Nam Ka Chu was devoid of all movement. Gurdial now realized that the bulk of the mortar shells were targeting the two platoons deployed behind him flanking Battalion HQ. This could only mean one thing: 'My god, they are going to assault us from the back!'

Disregarding the shelling, Gurdial emerged from the bunker and ran along the communication trench to the Vickers machine gun position, yelling above the noise of the explosions that the attack would be coming the moment the shelling stopped. He told the Mahar gun crew to take the weapon and follow him as the attack was almost certainly going to come from the rear. He himself grabbed the heavy tripod and managed to position it outside, but unfortunately the machine gunners were too dazed to follow him.

Also on the move was the Intelligence officer, Lieutenant Bhup Singh, who like the 2IC had understood that the attack would be from the rear. He quickly sprinted up to Rikh's bunker, passing on the way the communications bunker where Mangat and the rest of the signal crew lay dead.

After a sixty-minute bombardment, the shelling abruptly stopped. Any doubts about the direction of the impending attack were quickly dispelled as whistles and bugles went off on the slopes above them. In a virtual repeat of the tactics used against Charlie and Bravo companies at Temporary and Log Bridge, the Chinese swarmed down. Subedar Ram Chander and Jemadar Biswas barely had time to get the men out of the bunkers when their respective platoons on either side of Battalion HQ were attacked by the Chinese. The three officers in the centre, Rikh, Gurucharan Bhatia and Bhup Singh, had positioned themselves around the rear entrance of the command post. The first wave of attacking Chinese troops was met with a volley of rifle and LMG fire, causing serious damage.

Realizing that the machine gun crew had failed to follow him, Gurdial continued to make his way up, eventually joining the Charlie Company platoon. Despite serious casualties, the Chinese were now bringing everything to bear on these three positions as the defending troops grimly held on. The second wave was also fought off, but only just, as the Chinese were closing in rapidly. The advantage of the AK-47 in close combat was tremendous as the attackers could flood the area ahead of them with fire. The Chinese were also using LMGs and high explosive fragmentation grenades.

As the third wave was bunching up to launch yet another attack on the depleted positions, the Vickers machine gun crew under the command of Jemadar Mohan Lal ducked past Battalion HQ and made their way past the lower platoon. This platoon was perhaps the best equipped to fight it out as they were the only ones with plenty of ammunition. This was seen by the lower platoon and men started abandoning their posts in ones and twos. The senior JCO, Subedar B. C. Roy, then lost his nerve and, instead of looking to support the platoons grappling with the enemy above him, set off for Bridge 3 with the bulk of the surviving men.

Unaware of the hurried exit of the lower platoon from the battlefield, Rikh and the remnants braced themselves for the third wave. Ammunition was all but spent and the men were exhausted, finding it almost impossible to effectively throw grenades uphill. The third assault was two-pronged—from the south and southwest. As the Chinese closed in, Gurdial Singh led out the last remaining men in a counter attack, but the show of defiance was only a desperate symbolic gesture. Gurdial was overpowered and the two platoons were wiped out almost to the man.

Amazingly, the command post with the three officers in it was still holding out. In Rikh's own words: 'Captain Bhatia and I continued to engage the enemy from the doorway of the bunker. When I heard that the firing had stopped from the locality on my left, I came out of the bunker to see what had happened. As I stepped out of the bunker, a Chinese soldier who had crawled up to the side of the bunker threw a grenade at me. This grenade hit my rifle and exploded. My left jaw was broken and my lip cut open. I fell down. Lieutenant Bhup Singh rushed out of the bunker, shot the enemy soldier and pulled me back into the bunker. I got up with the support of Bhup Singh and leaning against the door started firing at the enemy closing in on the bunker. An enemy LMG burst fired into the doorway killed my adjutant, Captain Bhatia, and broke the top of my left shoulder. I had the pleasure of killing the Chinese who shot my adjutant. Finally an enemy bullet hit my left elbow and broke it. Due to the loss of blood, I fell down with my left leg outside the bunker. A Chinese fired a burst into it and broke my leg below the knee. Lieutenant Bhup Singh pulled me in and covered me with a blanket.

'The Chinese were now closing in on the bunker from all sides. Bhup Singh manned the doorway and single-handedly kept the Chinese at bay. By this time all firing outside had ceased. This was the last bunker holding out. The enemy kept firing the machine gun into one side of the bunker while still engaging the doorway. Finally, on the third side of the bunker, they crawled up and blew the side in with a pole charge (exploding explosives fastened to the end of a pole)'. Rikh was in a semi-conscious state, fast losing blood. Bhup Singh was still fighting, manning the doorway. Finally his ammunition ran out. The Chinese, seeing that all the firing from within the bunker had ceased, rushed into it and overpowered Bhup Singh, who was pointing to Rikh and screaming, 'commanding officer… commanding officer'. The Chinese got the message, and did not bayonet the wounded Rikh. After a while, they took Rikh outside and put him on a stretcher. His wounds were then bandaged by a Chinese nursing orderly.

Further downstream, Alpha Company's position at Bridge 3 as well as the Assam Rifles post above had got a heavy, prolonged dose of mortar fire. The Chinese would only get to them after having dealt with Battalion HQ and the defences at Bridge 4. With no danger of accidently hitting their own troops, the Chinese bombardment was more spread out here. Jemadar Ghanshyam Singh, commanding No. 3 Platoon, the easternmost Rajput position, was killed during the early stages of the bombardment and Subedar Phool Singh, the senior company JCO, replaced him.

During the hour-long shelling, the Assam Rifles men slowly melted away, leaving the post completely vacant. When the Chinese arrived from the west, they initially assaulted this position, but finding it abandoned, they turned the full fury of the attack on CHM Saudagar Singh's No. 2 Platoon that got assaulted from above and the western flank. Subedar Basdeo Singh's No. 1 Platoon, sited overlooking Bridge 3, was also soon embroiled in fierce hand-to-hand fighting. Some survivors of No. 2 Platoon would later describe how CHM Saudagar Singh, after grappling with a Chinese soldier, snatched his AK-47 and shot five enemy soldiers before being overpowered.

After the lifting of the artillery fire, the company commander, Captain Ravi Eipe, decided to move up to the Assam Rifles post to get a better picture of what was happening. Moving through Saudagar's No. 2 Platoon, Eipe began climbing towards the Assam Rifles post with his runner where he was greeted by a barrage of small arms fire. Thinking that the Assam Rifles were shooting at them, Eipe shouted to them to hold their fire. Only then did he realize that the troops milling around in the Assam Rifles post were wearing the khaki uniforms of the Chinese. Doubling back, he asked No. 2 Platoon to readjust their positions and face uphill.

Describing the subsequent attack, Eipe says: 'In a short while the Chinese started attacking in skirmish order from the westerly direction towards No. 2 Platoon. Meanwhile No. 2 Platoon had reorganized itself and started taking a heavy toll on the Chinese coming towards the post.' The fighting was bitter, with Saudagar Singh fighting bravely, inspiring the men lying in the shallow communication trenches and behind boulders to keep on fighting. In the meantime, a runner brought the news that Subedar Ghanshyam

Singh had been killed. Eipe recalled: 'I told Subedar Phool Singh (company second-in-command) to go to No. 3 Platoon and take over command. At the same time I saw the Chinese outflanking No. 2 Platoon from the west and going towards No. 1 Platoon on the river line.'

At about 7 a.m. the Chinese started engaging Subedar Basdeo Singh's position. The platoon was expecting the attack and there was a barrage of gunfire as both sides opened up. Though attacked from two sides, the platoon held its own and beat back the first few assaults. Fifteen minutes later, the Chinese reassembled and flowed down from the Assam Rifles post and assaulted No. 3 Platoon. Though the men fought grittily, their numbers were depleted as casualties steadily mounted. Though cut off from No. 1 Platoon, Captain Eipe, wounded by a mortar splinter, decided to pull out with the remnants of No. 2 and No. 3 Platoon and try and move along the Rongla Nullah towards Brigade HQ. By this time the panicky runaways from Bridge 4 also arrived at Basdeo's position by the river. The rest of No. 1 Platoon then extricated itself and joined the exodus. Despite the withdrawal, Alpha Company lost more than half its men.

Of its effective strength of 513, 2 Rajput had 282 killed including 4 officers and 7 JCOs. Eighty-one men, including two officers and three JCOs, were wounded and captured. Ninety others, including three officers and two JCOs, were not wounded but were overpowered; sixty others got away with Eipe.

The exact Chinese casualties will never be known, but there is an indication in Rikh's report that was written after his return from captivity to India: 'As a prisoner of war, I was personally interrogated by the Chinese interpreters in the camp. They asked me on several occasions what were the characteristics of the Rajput battalion as different from the other troops in the Indian Army. I enquired of them the reason why they were asking me these questions. They finally told me that it was the first battle on 20 October 1962 that the Chinese Army had suffered the maximum casualties of all the fighting in NEFA. These casualties had been inflicted on them by my battalion. I felt proud to have commanded such a unit.'

Chapter 7

FALLBACK ON TAWANG

THE GORKHAS AT TSANGDHAR

Brigadier Dalvi's lucid and gripping account of what transpired first between him and Lieutenant Colonel Rikh and then with the GOC of the division, Major General Niranjan Prasad, on the evening of 19 October has unfortunately acted as a smokescreen for his own failure to act decisively. While reiterating that the units were in a death trap, neither the brigade commander nor the GOC of 4 Division, despite being present on the ground, thought of pulling the Rajputs, the Punjabis and the Grenadiers back onto the Tsangdhar–Hathung-la axis, which would have been the most obvious thing to do. Even if Kaul's orders were to have been followed in both letter and spirit (of not abandoning the bridges), screen (covering) positions could have been left at the riverfront.

Despite having had nine days to redeploy his brigade which was strung out at the bottom of the valley, Dalvi was repeatedly denied permission by Prasad to redeploy further back on the Tsangdhar Ridge. The moment of truth was on 13 October when the orders to hold the existing positions were reiterated. Dalvi, at that point, as the commander on the ground, should have countermanded the order, something he had done before, and something that would have given the men trapped in the valley some semblance of a chance. He failed to do so. His dilemma is perhaps understandable, but in the ultimate analysis, inexcusable. He was to write later: 'I was alone and lonely at this crucial stage and, for the first time, felt the full impact of the loneliness of command… I should not have accepted the order to defend all the bridges over the Nam Ka Chu on the 13th of October, but then "It takes more courage to appear a coward than risk being killed".'

He goes on to say, 'If I left on tactical grounds, and the Chinese did not attack, I would be branded a physical coward. I did not have the moral courage to accept this stigma.' Dalvi says he asked Prasad if he had been reading the reports that had been filed through the day by Brigade HQ when the GOC had initially ordered him to move another company of 1/9 GR to Bridge 5. The question is, had he himself read and understood them or was he championing the withdrawal so fervently that he lost sight of everything else? If the Chinese attack was imminent, as he himself repeatedly said, then 7 Brigade should have had gone over the various likely scenarios. Ever since Kaul had departed from the vicinity of Bridge 4 on 10 October, Dalvi, despite having been handed back his command, seems to have frozen, hanging on to the hope that any day the order would come to extricate the brigade from the Nam Ka Chu Valley.

Be that as it may, by 18 October when the Chinese openly began ranging targets and marking the ground, their intent was clear. The brigade major, Rex Kharbanda, asked to meet the Intelligence officers of the three battalions deployed on the riverfront. He said to them, 'You guys are talking about so much Chinese movement opposite you. Let us take stock.' Yet, as the day progressed, nothing was done. The Grenadiers and the Punjab positions at Bridge 1 and Bridge 2 were relatively safe from a frontal attack owing to the steep cliffs on the northern side. Even if he could not take the decision to pull back from the Nam Ka Chu, Dalvi should have reinforced the thinly spread out Rajput positions with some of 9 Punjab's platoons. Surely, given the large gap west of Temporary Bridge, he had to be aware of danger to the flank. The Grenadiers, hopelessly cramped amidst rocks, could have occupied the Punjab positions on Bridge 2. In the prevailing tense atmosphere in Brigade HQ, none of this was done or even contemplated. Even an exit plan to extricate the brigade in the event of an attack was not worked out.

Positioned above Dhola (Che Dong) was 1/9 GR, their defences straddling the track that led from the Assam Rifles post to Brigade HQ and then onto Tsangdhar. The central position was held by a platoon from Delta Company that had its remaining two platoons stationed at Tsangdhar. Charlie Company was slightly further up, to the east of the track, while the right side was held by two platoons of Alpha Company. The third platoon of Alpha Company had been dispatched on 18 October to Bridge 5 to support the Punjabis. Bravo Company was deployed around Brigade HQ.

The 34 Heavy Mortar Battery under the command of Major Balraj Nijjar had been deployed one and a half kilometres north of Tsangdhar. Dalvi had told Nijjar that since they were in a defensive posture, the mortars had to be deployed to cover the bridges on the Nam Ka Chu. Dalvi also expressly told the battery commander that the mortars were not to fire unless he personally gave the order. As a result, Nijjar was in Brigade HQ on the morning of 20 October. But he was unable to establish contact with his battery, which was standing by resolutely. Despite the fact that there were 450 rounds stacked up and ready to fire, not a single heavy mortar was fired in the Nam Ka Chu battle. In fact, other than 2 Rajput and perhaps the 9 Punjab Company at Bridge 5, no one seemed ready for a fight.

On the evening of 19 October, the CO of 1/9 GR, Lieutenant Colonel B. S. Ahluwalia, was certainly not privy to the general assessment that the battle was coming. The Gorkha Battalion HQ situated behind the Tsangdhar Ridge did not have direct visual contact with the Chinese and Ahluwalia himself had not seen the enemy preparations on the banks of the Nam Ka Chu. Lieutenant Colonel K. K. Tewari, the divisional signals officer, had been in the mess bunker during Dalvi's emotional conversation with Prasad. Tewari had then moved to the 1/9 GR position where he spent the night. Yet nothing of the assessment was communicated to Ahluwalia, who continued to be unaware of the impending attack. He was only asked to send a company to Bridge 5 in the morning due to 'orders from above'. From their commanding positions, the Gorkhas too had been watching the feverish Chinese activity, but the CO's assessment was that it was nothing but a show of force to frighten the Indians. On the other hand, his company commanders and JCOs thought otherwise, for they asked the men to prime their grenades in anticipation of a night or dawn attack. When the CO came to know, he ordered the men to un-prime their grenades. The Gorkhas were also told that they must not do anything that would escalate the situation. For good measure, Ahluwalia also issued orders that no sub-unit or individual could open fire without his personal orders.

Despite the relative commanding position of 1/9 GR, their defences were quite perfunctory and far from adequate. Though they were the only battalion to have been tactically sited some 200 metres up the spur from the river, the frozen ground was extremely rocky. Unable to dig in without entrenching tools, the only defences the Gorkhas could muster were low sangars, with no overhead protection other than parachutes salvaged from the drop zone that were draped over the stonework.

Chinese activity through the night remained undetected. The battalion conducted its usual morning stand-to at 5 a.m. One column was about to leave for Bridge 5 when the booming of heavy mortars was heard. The Gorkhas were taken completely by surprise as the shells started to land around their positions as well. As the initial surprise wore off, the 1/9 GR 3-inch mortars opened up, but they were hopelessly out of range. The

Chinese quickly got the bearings of the mortar positions and the battalion's four mortars were silenced.

Once the shelling stopped, the sound of small arms fire and grenades carried through to the Gorkhas from the valley below as the Chinese attacked the Rajput positions. Suddenly there was a burst fired from an LMG close to the Gorkha positions. As the inter-battalion telephone lines were all down by then, Ahluwalia sent his adjutant, Major Sher Pratap Singh Shrikent, to investigate. As the officer neared the Delta Company position, he could see the Chinese forming up to attack the forward position, while two other groups were also getting ready to assault both the flanking Alpha and Charlie Company positions.

By the time Shrikent scrambled back to the command post, the fighting had started in earnest. Those manning the command bunker told the adjutant that the CO had rushed off to Charlie Company as soon as the first shots were fired. The adjutant now sprinted to his own bunker where he found Tewari briefing Dalvi over the telephone on the developing situation. Back in the command bunker, Ahluwalia had returned with the news that a 500-strong force was attacking Charlie Company. The company commander, Major M. M. S. Gambhir, had already been killed, but Second Lieutenant B. D. Dogra, though wounded, was spiritedly holding out. Ahluwalia now told Subedar Major Jit Bahadur Chetri to take all available men from Battalion HQ and reinforce Dogra's position.

As the Rajputs below and the Gorkhas above were simultaneously fighting off the first Chinese waves, an Indian Air Force Dakota appeared at 6.25 a.m., preparing to drop off the first load of the morning at Tsangdhar. The Chinese infiltration parties that were moving between the Gorkhas and Tsangdhar to cut off the Hathung-la route, fired at the incoming aircraft, which banked steeply and quickly cleared out of the area.

The desperate fighting continued, but gradually the Chinese by sheer dint of numbers were gaining the upper hand. Dogra's platoon had been overrun, but despite his own injuries, he was still firing a LMG so that the remnants of his platoon could fall back. Both Ahluwalia and his 2IC, Major Anant Singh Charak, had gone to the Charlie Company location to watch the battle, but they were soon in danger themselves. Subedar Dhan Bahadur Chand had to cover their withdrawal with a LMG.

One last bid to dislodge the milling Chinese at Charlie Company was made by the adjutant; Major Shrikent had managed to collect a dozen men and he tried to go to Dogra's aid. It was hopeless, however, and soon this party was hemmed in from all sides as the company position had more or less been overrun. Somehow, Shrikent managed to break off contact and pull his party out.

Two hours after the first mortar bombs had rained down from the sky, Charlie Company of 1/9 GR ceased to exist and the Chinese now turned their full attention towards Alpha Company and Battalion HQ. A large force had got above and behind the Gorkhas, and this group began to close the gap with Battalion HQ. The Gorkhas were fighting desperately and all the news trickling into the command post was negative. Subedar Jit Bahadur and the thirty men who had gone to reinforce Charlie Company had also been encircled and overwhelmed. Two other officers, Second Lieutenant Mahindra and Captain Mahabir Prasad had been wounded and were missing. Captain Prasad, who was from 1 Sikh and had set up the Assam Rifles post at Dhola, had been attached to 1/9 GR on 4 October. As the fighting around the command post intensified, Ahluwalia had been shot in the right shoulder. Realizing the futility of prolonging the battle, Ahluwalia ordered his remaining officers and troops to pull out and withdraw from Tsangdhar.

That the Gorkhas managed to break contact at all was an achievement of sorts, but in the melee, the withdrawal was confused and disorganized. While the bulk of the men withdrew with Ahluwalia towards the Tsangdhar drop zone, a second lot got separated and took the track down towards Bridge 2, but got only as far as Brigade HQ. The CO was carried in a makeshift stretcher constructed with a couple of rifles and a blanket but it was obvious that he was in terrible pain and in urgent need of medical attention. The surviving Gorkhas had just about got past the Delta Company defences on the ridgeline at Tsangdhar, when the Chinese started their assault on Subedar Harka Bahadur's platoon that was defending the ridge. Ahluwalia further split his group, telling his adjutant, Major Shrikent, to deploy some men and help hold the ridge.

The Chinese assault on the Tsangdhar Ridge began to gain momentum. With his ammunition dwindling, Harka Bahadur with about a dozen surviving men, managed to break contact and withdraw. The survivors from the second platoon of Delta Company, under the command of Second Lieutenant Kutty, also extricated themselves along the Tsangdhar-Karpo-la track. Shrikent decided to take his party and head for the drop zone and the advance medical station, but found the route cut off by the Chinese. He then tried to head for Brigade HQ but was met by the battalion 2IC, Major Charak, who told him the enemy had already overrun the position.

The group by now had been forced off the track, and the going was agonizingly difficult. They were still in the vicinity of the battle and rearguards were constantly engaging the pursuing Chinese. Unable to take any more of the jolting passage and realizing that in trying to save their CO the others were likely to get killed, Ahluwalia ordered Charak to abandon him. Leaving a wounded commanding officer behind was unheard of in the Indian Army, but to the officers in the party it must have seemed like there was no alternative. At that time, no one had any idea of how the Chinese would treat their POWs, but if Ahluwalia was to have any chance of survival, only the Chinese medics could provide him with the required attention. Charak had the stretcher placed on a prominent rock, took a rifle and stuck it into the ground by its bayonet, and then wrapped Ahluwalia's turban around the butt of the rifle. Leaving the CO with a water bottle and a rifleman who was to break off the moment the Chinese saw the wounded officer, the Gorkha party moved on.

Meanwhile, some men had found a hideout just below the drop zone into which the various Gorkha parties and some others congregated. They decided to stay there for the rest of the day, to take stock of the situation. At least seven officers (including Lieutenant Colonel Tewari from the Signals and Captain Mahabir Prasad from 1 Sikh) were either killed or missing, along with three JCOs and 190 other ranks.

In the next few days, small groups tried to take the Karpo-la track but were thwarted by the Chinese. Most of the survivors were too stunned to fight any more, intent only on surviving the elements and evading the Chinese. However, there were some incredible acts of bravery. Subedar Bhab Bahadur Khatwal and fifteen men of 1/9 GR rushed a Chinese MMG with the age-old war cry of 'Ayo Gorkhali'. There was the incessant chatter of the Chinese machine gun and then there was silence, as all the men from the party were mowed down. Small parties did make it through the Chinese encirclement into Bhutan, but most of them died due to the cold and starvation as they had no food or warm clothes or blankets.

Others, like Dalvi's party, wandered around in circles, finding the Chinese already occupying the features they were headed for. Finally, they stumbled into the Chinese just below Hathung-la. Dalvi and the surviving seven members of his party were captured on 22 October. The death struggle of 7 Infantry Brigade would continue as men in small parties and sometimes as individuals continued to battle the elements. Very few made it home.

KHENZEMANE

The Assam Rifles post of Khenzemane was situated on the west bank of the Nyamjang Chu where the river forced its way between the Thagla

Ridge and the spur that dropped down from Bum-la. At Khenzemane, C Wing of 5 Assam Rifles under Major H. P. Singh was deployed along the river in the classic arrowhead Indian defensive position—No. 5 Platoon at the head with No. 2 and No. 3 Platoon deployed slightly behind on the flanks. As Khenzemane could be reached by a mule track, unlike the infantry battalions inside the Nam Ka Chu Valley, the Assam Rifles had a fair amount of defensive equipment like barbed wire and entrenching tools that had been put to good effect. Towards the end of September when the build-up in Nam Ka Chu began, Niranjan Prasad had appointed Lieutenant Colonel Rattan Singh, the commanding officer of 5 Assam Rifles, as the Central Sector Commander (Valley Sector) and located Charlie Company of 4 Grenadiers under the command of Second Lieutenant Gopalakrishna Venkatesa Prasanna Rao, in depth around the Drokung Samba Bridge where the track to Zimithang shifted to the east bank.

On 19 October, Niranjan Prasad and Rattan Singh had visited Khenzemane where the Assam Rifles and Grenadiers were also reporting feverish Chinese activity, especially on the Thagla Ridge that overlooked their position on the riverfront. After a while the GOC returned to his Tactical HQ at Zimithang, but in light of the Chinese build-up, Rattan Singh decided to stay on at the Khenzemane post.

At 4 a.m. on 20 October, almost seventy-five minutes before 2 Rajput and 1/9 GR came under fire, the Chinese lit up the night sky over Khenzemane with star shells, illuminating all three Assam Rifles platoons. Within seconds, Chinese mortars and guns opened up. The shelling was not very accurate, though it almost immediately destroyed the Drokung Samba Bridge. This effectively isolated the Assam Rifles position from the Grenadiers, for the bulk of the defences at the bridge were located on the east bank.

At 4.30 a.m. the mortar and artillery barrage was lifted and Chinese infantry closed in on No. 5 Platoon. The fighting was intense, with Chinese superiority in numbers making the vital difference. The platoon commander, Havildar Som Bahadur, and twenty other riflemen were killed and an equal number wounded. After two hours of bitter fighting and with ammunition running out, the Chinese overran the platoon shortly after first light. This brought them into contact with the other two platoons which carried on fighting equally tenaciously despite the Chinese attacking from the north, west and east. Another three hours of fighting, this time in broad daylight, saw both the section commanders, Subedar Hem Lal and Naib Subedar Shamsher Bahadur Thapa fall to Chinese bullets along with another thirty-six other ranks. Rifleman Bishan Singh, the LMG detachment commander of No. 2 Platoon, was blasted out of his position by a Chinese rocket fired at him. Despite being severely wounded and having lost his weapon in the explosion, the soldier jumped into another LMG pit and continued fighting from there. Once his ammunition was expended, Bishan Singh managed to escape from the post and made it back to Zimithang. The commanding officer of 5 Assam Rifles, Rattan Singh, was wounded and along with H. P. Singh and twenty-three other survivors, was taken prisoner. By 9.30 a.m., Khenzemane was in Chinese hands.

With the Chinese pushing hard on the east bank as well, and the company commander, Lieutenant G .V. P. Rao, having fallen, survivors from 4 Grenadiers at Drokung Samba Bridge started to fall back along the track towards Zimithang, which was about a two-hour march downriver. Two platoons from Bravo Company of 4 Garhwal Rifles were deployed at Chutangmu, which was located between Khenzemane and Zimithang, for the protection of Division HQ. After a brief firefight with the advancing Chinese, the Garhwalis fell back on Zimithang, acting as a rearguard for the retreating men of Assam Rifles and 4 Grenadiers. Niranjan Prasad, seeing the survivors arriving, was only just beginning to grasp the magnitude of what had happened on the Nam Ka Chu: 'Stragglers and walking wounded from Khenzemane and Drokung Samba Bridge began to arrive, followed a little later by escapees from Khenzemane. I was glad to see there was no evidence of panic. All those who had escaped, including the walking wounded, brought their weapons back with them—an indication of their good discipline and morale.' Collecting the third platoon that was deployed around Division HQ, the Garhwalis continued to act as a rearguard for the divisional retreat, arriving at Tawang on the evening of 23 October. By then Tawang had been evacuated, and the company commander, on his own initiative, decided to fall back on Jang via Sakden. They reached Jang on 28 October and married up with the rest of the battalion.

There are some serious questions about the tactics employed that unfortunately don't have any answers. On the night of 19 October, there was still the faint hope in Dalvi and Prasad that the Chinese were bluffing and that there would be no actual engagement between the two armies at Nam Ka Chu. Assam Rifles records are clear that the shelling of the region began at 4 a.m., and that the Chinese attack on No. 5 Platoon started at 4.30 a.m. It is almost certain that this information would have been relayed to Division HQ at Zimithang. Yet this vital information was not passed on to 7 Brigade who, almost forty-five minutes later, were under the first barrage of Chinese mortars and guns. Neither at this point nor subsequently, did the Chinese ever formally declare war.

The Chinese are reported to have severed the communication lines between 7 Brigade and 2 Rajput once the shelling started, but contact between Brigade HQ and Division HQ remained intact at least until 8.15 a.m., when the former was abandoned.

Communication is reported to have been in existence between 9 Punjab and 4 Grenadiers till noon. Yet, even when the Grenadier Company was attacked at the Drokung Samba Bridge, neither Division HQ nor the battalion thought it prudent to send reinforcements to the beleaguered men even though neither the position at Bridge 2 (9 Punjab) or at Bridge 1 (4 Grenadiers) had come under mortar or artillery fire. It is indeed strange that the only time Division HQ chose to speak to the commanding officers of these two battalions, they gave orders to withdraw, even though neither battalion had been engaged by the Chinese.

FLIGHT WITHOUT A FIGHT

The Indian political and military leadership at the highest level set the stage and the famed Red Eagles, 4 Division, played its part in offering up 7 Brigade to the Chinese as a passive target. True, both Niranjan Prasad and John Dalvi had had their hands tied, but once the action started, both commanders failed their men completely. At Bridge 1 and Bridge 2, the largest number of troops was available—almost two battalions, nearly half of 7 Brigade. Both these positions were naturally protected from a frontal assault owing to the steepness of the Thagla slopes, and the troops were at a much lower altitude. A basic assessment of any anticipated attack would have made it obvious that to get to these two units, the Chinese would have to break through the 2 Rajput positions which, despite their poor tactical setting, would put up a fight. Yet, between the division, brigade and the two commanding officers, they sat back and allowed the Chinese to systematically destroy individual platoons piecemeal.

On the Nam Ka Chu, the Chinese easily broke up the front into three parts. The first section, to the extreme west (Bridge 5) was ignored; then according to their strategy, they broke up the remaining area into two halves, allowing them to bring down all their strength on the left portion, including Tsangdhar.

From analysing reports of events on the ground, it's clear to me that the fighting withdrawal of 9 Punjab and 4 Grenadiers recorded in the official history could not have taken place as neither battalion was in hostile contact with the Chinese, who had deliberately left them alone through the entire day. A few mortar rounds had landed on the 9 Punjab position around 8.30 a.m. but that had fizzled out after a while. Both the commanding officers, in the absence of any direction or communication from either Dalvi or Prasad, simply did not know what to do. After a while, the fighting in the Rajput and Gorkha positions had all but died down, with only the dead and dying lying amongst the rocks and destroyed bunkers.

At 9 a.m., Lieutenant Colonel Mishra had sent a patrol along with his Signals lineman towards Rongla to check on the status of the telephone line. The patrol reported that Rongla had most probably been abandoned as Chinese troops were swarming over the entire area. At Bridge 1, the Grenadiers were also completely cut off, though they could hear the din of the battles being fought by 2 Rajput to their west and their own Charlie Company to the north as they fiercely defended the Drokung Samba Bridge. Firing from this direction had also died down except for the odd burst of gunfire every now and then. At midday, Major Oscar Thomas, the adjutant, finally got through to Zimithang by plugging into the brigade-division line, even though the brigade end was ominously silent. Division HQ conveyed the news that 2 Rajput between Bridge 3 and Temporary Bridge had been overrun, as had 1/9 GR at Tsangdhar even though there were still some pockets of resistance. The 4 Grenadiers company at the Drokung Samba Bridge had also met the same fate. Thomas was also told that when last contacted, Dalvi and Brigade HQ were trying to get to Hathung-la where they hoped to take a stand.

At this stage, the conversation was interrupted by the GOC, Niranjan Prasad, who asked to speak to the CO, Lieutenant Colonel Harihar Singh. By then 9 Punjab was also patched into the line, allowing GOC 4 Division to talk to both commanding officers simultaneously. Prasad told Mishra to withdraw his battalion to Hathung-la via Bridge 1. The Grenadiers were to hold their position till 5 p.m., wait until the last Punjab platoon had gone through, then immediately follow the Punjabis to Hathung-la where Dalvi was expected to marry up with them. Oscar Thomas also succeeded in getting through to Delta Company at Serkhim and Jemadar Gian Singh at Hathung-la. He was told by both these positions that there were no Chinese troops in their vicinity at that stage.

In his book, Dalvi goes out of his way to protect his commanding officers, especially Mishra. But it is alleged that Mishra, after speaking to Prasad, did not follow orders. Mishra's first task was to get through to Tsangle, where he spoke to the Alpha Company commander, Major Khanna. The

Chinese, after making some initial moves against the position, had decided to ignore Tsangle. Mishra told Khanna that the area east of him was now in Chinese control. He advised him to take Major Minuwala, the Alpha Company commander of 1/9 GR with him and get out via Bhutan. Mishra then asked if Havildar Malkiat Singh, who along with twenty men was carrying snow clothing for the post, had reached Tsangle. Khanna replied in the negative. Malkiat (who had performed heroically at Tseng Jong just ten days earlier, and his party) was never to be seen again. It can be presumed that they were ambushed and killed by the Chinese somewhere between Temporary Bridge and Tsangle.

Harihar Singh and the Grenadiers waited for 9 Punjab to show up along the track from Bridge 2, but there was no sign of the Punjabis. Unknown to them, Mishra, after advising Khanna to escape from Tsangle, had decided to do the same. He ordered the battalion to extricate itself from Bridge 2 and head straight up through the forested slopes to the heights behind them. The Chinese, who had 9 Punjab under observation, and had been sporadically firing mortars at them since 8.30 in the morning, did not pursue the battalion at that stage. As the battalion began to pull out, the intensity of mortar fire also increased and the Chinese began to hit at the troops as they tried to make their way up. At this the battalion lost all cohesion in its dash to get to the upper reaches.

Breaking contact and withdrawing a large body of men, especially in the mountains, is an intricate, high-risk manoeuvre that requires pre-selection, preparation and occupation of fallback positions. The synchronized leapfrogging backwards from Bridge 2 towards Hathung-la and Lumpu, in broad daylight, would have required a lot of skill and coordination. Obviously, the CO of 9 Punjab decided that his best bet to avoid being further shelled by the Chinese was to get away from the river as fast as he could. He seems to have decided that it was a lost cause and had no intention of fighting it out at Hathung-la or anywhere else. Of all the battalions in the Nam Ka Chu Valley, 9 Punjab was the most battle-hardened. They had been there right from the very beginning and were fully acclimatized; Mishra had taken over the battalion just days before it was moved to Nam Ka Chu and if he as their CO had given them a chance, 9 Punjab would have certainly performed most creditably.

No sooner had the withdrawal started than chaos struck as small parties tried to make their way up cross-country through an area that had no tracks. Devoid of any protection overhead or on the ground, the unit suffered terrible losses. Over the next few hours, quite a few men were killed as they lost their footing and plunged over cliffs. Among them was Major Mahander Singh Chaudhary, under whose command the engagement with the Chinese had taken place on 10 October. The officer slipped and fell near the top of the 18,000-foot Dhola summit, landing on a ledge below a sheer cliff. Both his legs appeared to be broken. Some men tried to tie their turbans together in a bid to extricate him. A soldier tried to lower himself, but the turbans broke and the man plunged to his death. The rest of the men then abandoned the officer.

Seeing no sign of 9 Punjab, 4 Grenadiers decided to pull out at 3.30 p.m. Once again, just as the battalion began to withdraw, Oscar Thomas ascertained from his men at Hathung-la and Serkhim that there were still no Chinese troops in their vicinity.

Bravo Company under the command of Major Balbir Singh was the only company to have deployed a platoon across the Nam Ka Chu between Bridge 1 and Charlie Company's position at the Drokung Samba Bridge. The Chinese engaged elements of No. 5 Platoon with small arms fire in the morning and one of the soldiers had been killed. When Balbir Singh started to extricate his platoon, they had to traverse across the Khenzemane grazing grounds that were covered by a Chinese MMG on the cliffs above. An attached artillery officer, Lieutenant A. S. Balasubramaniam from 51 Mountain Regiment, who had been sent as a forward observer, was killed while trying to negotiate this patch. A nursing orderly who immediately went to his aid was also gunned down.

As the main body of 4 Grenadiers began to withdraw towards Hathung-la, the same MMG post that had killed Balasubramaniam had a section of the track in range. To avoid this patch, Harihar Singh asked his Intelligence officer, Second Lieutenant R. I. S. Kahlon, who was in the lead, to skirt the area. The troops were to move through the vegetation keeping the Hathung-la track to their left, and rejoin it after half a kilometre. Second Lieutenant Kartar Singh of Bravo Company with No. 4 Platoon was to be the rearguard, and was to follow half an hour after the battalion's departure. As the troops started to move through the foliage, Harihar Singh changed the order and told the troops to abandon the Hathung-la track altogether and head straight up the slope like Mishra had a few hours earlier.

Lieutenant Kartar Singh, oblivious of the last-minute change in plan, fell back by rejoining the Hathung-la track. He and his platoon made it to Serkhim without any further incident, which only went to prove that had 9 Punjab and 4 Grenadiers followed the Hathung-la track as ordered, they would have been able to get across the pass in good order. Why Mishra and Harihar Singh acted in this manner is beyond comprehension; had they fallen back as instructed, the remaining two battalions of 7 Brigade might have managed to deploy beyond Hathung-la and fight it out.

The Chinese finally attacked Hathung-la in the early hours of 21 October. Jemadar Gian Singh and the thirty-two-man No. 10 Platoon at Hathung-la fought a grim battle. All the men were killed fighting.

A HANDFUL OF MEN

We must return to Tsangdhar where, by midday, some surviving troops were trying to get out in isolated groups, streaming out of the Rongla Nullah, past the overrun 1/9 GR positions on the Tsangdhar slope and then towards the drop zone where a small bunch of men were still standing firm under the command of a twenty-one-year old second lieutenant, Amar Jit Singh Behl.

By 8 October, a detachment of 17 Para Field from Agra had arrived at Tezpur and moved by road to Tsangdhar, reporting to 7 Brigade. The two serviceable guns that had been airdropped at Tsangdhar were deployed near the drop zone and the track running from Nam Ka Chu went past the left flank of this position. On 16 October, the senior officer in the party, Captain Harjeet Singh Talwar, was asked to proceed to Tsangle at Bridge 5 and do a reconnaissance of the Chinese positions on the Thagla Ridge. His party was to follow Monpa guides who were ferrying loads for the Punjab company at Tsangle. Along the way it started to snow heavily. The Monpas jettisoned their loads and melted away, leaving the disoriented officer and his party to find their own way back.

For forty-eight hours the party wandered around in circles, unable to navigate in the mist and snow. One of the soldiers developed frostbite and for a while it looked as if the entire party would die of exposure. Fortunately, on the night of 18 October, they ran into a flank patrol, which took them back to 2 Rajput's Charlie Company deployed at the Temporary Bridge. Major Sharan Sethi and Subedar Dashrath Singh took the exhausted party under their wing and made them comfortable for the night. By that time Brigade HQ was becoming anxious about the fate of the gunners. The next day, after bidding 2 Rajput's Charlie Company goodbye, Talwar made his way to Brigade HQ (while the rest of party returned to the gun position at Tsangdhar) and into an extremely tense situation. He was present in the brigade when Dalvi spoke to Prasad on 19 October evening. After that Talwar pitched his tent outside the brigade and went to sleep, tucked into a sleeping bag.

After getting the news that the party, which had set off for Tsangle was safe, Behl heaved a sigh of relief. He looked forward to meeting Talwar and getting information on Chinese positions, even though the men who had returned from the aborted trip told him the Chinese were out of the range of their guns. The next morning, Behl watched helplessly as the Chinese attack developed in the valley below and the 1/9 GR positions ahead of him started getting shelled by heavy mortars and artillery. As the minutes went by, there was still no sign of Talwar, who had by then attached himself to Brigadier Dalvi's group. Shells soon started landing all around Behl's gun position as well.

Behl, the GPO (gun position officer), now deployed the gunners in a defensive position around the guns. His men had salvaged some eighty-odd rounds, though unknown to them, another 417 shells were lying at the drop zone waiting for porters. Without specific coordinates to fire at, Lieutenant Behl and his men were helpless spectators as the battle unfolded. As a result, not a single shot could be fired in support of 2 Rajput and 1/9 GR on the morning of 20 October.

In the initial shelling, two of Behl's men, Gunner Avtar Singh and Radio Operator Chamkar Singh, had been hit by splinters. Getting the two casualties across to the medical post was impossible as shells were landing all around them regularly. The young officer poured brandy on the wounds and with his bare hands pulled out the big pieces of shrapnel before patching up the two men with field dressings. By then it was almost 9 a.m. and there was still no communication with anybody. His men kept trying to make contact with Captain Talwar but continued to draw a blank. Without a target, engaging the Chinese was just not possible.

After a while, the gunners saw a Bell two-seater helicopter approaching the helipad. By then Tsangdhar was reverberating with small arms fire, Chinese activity being visible in what was known as the black rock area. The intensity of the shelling had lessened, but was occurring sporadically. There was no sign of the helicopter taking off again, so Behl sent two men to see what had happened. They reported that the helicopter was standing at the helipad, but the pilot and another officer in a red turban were lying dead next to it.

The gunners were not the only ones still standing resolutely at their positions. A soldier started to crawl towards Behl's trench, shouting at them so they wouldn't shoot at him by mistake. He was the battery havildar major (BHM) of the mortar battery that was deployed just ahead of the guns. The NCO wanted to know what the latest position was. Behl had just finished telling the soldier that his communication lines had been cut, when small arms fire killed the BHM on the spot. Realizing that the situation was dire, Behl ordered both the guns to fire at the black rock area. The guns had barely fired ten rounds each, when a second Bell helicopter started approaching Tsangdhar. The gunners could see it sharply bank away as Chinese MMGs from various positions engaged it.

Describing the scene at Tsangdhar shortly after mid-day, Behl said: 'The withdrawal from Tsangdhar and areas below had started along the track which passed from the left of my gun position about 150 to 200 yards [140 to 180 metres] away. Some of the people were yelling at us to hold on and keep the enemy at bay. Surprisingly, some of the officers who passed that way did not bother to stop and ask a young officer if he needed any help. All they wanted from us was to keep on firing at the Chinese so that they do not follow them uninterrupted. I felt ashamed of those who were running away. I felt proud of my troop; everybody wanted to fight it out at the gun position.'

But when the direct firing of guns became impossible, Behl gave the order to dismantle the guns. Although a large number of people from all ranks fled past their position, the gunners of 17 Para Field held on. 'They saw a large number of all ranks running past our gun position but not even one person deserted,' said Behl with justifiable pride, after he retired as a brigadier. At 3 p.m. when they had expended most of their ammunition, they surrendered. They were made to spend the night at Tsangdhar. The next morning, Behl requested permission from the Chinese officer to bury the helicopter pilot and the dead major. Giving them as dignified a burial as he could as a POW, Behl managed to identify the two officers as Squadron Leader Vinod Sehgal and Major Ram Singh of the Corps of Signals.

Within a few hours on 20 October, 7 Brigade disintegrated as a formation. Failure to react to Chinese moves allowed the enemy to bring a large number of troops to bear down on individual platoons and companies. Where the officers and JCOs stood their ground, the men responded superbly. Where the officers (whatever their rationale) upped and withdrew, the men had no choice but to follow, and soon it was each man for himself, with many meeting their end trying to escape.

All this while, the small detachment of Sikh gunners from 17 Para Field was standing firm, with no intention of joining the exodus of fleeing officers and men. Unfortunately, most of the subsequent records relied heavily on the accounts of those who ran, their coloured accounts also determining the gallantry awards that were subsequently handed out. By the time those who fought and survived returned from Chinese captivity, no one was interested in their version of what happened. Lieutenant Colonel Rikh, for example, after his repatriation from China, had recommended Major B. K. Pant for a Param Vir Chakra. The citation was ignored as 'the file was closed'. The same was the case with Lieutenant Bikram Singh of 6 Kumaon in the Walong Sector where his CO, Lieutenant Colonel C. N. Madiah, recommended the young officer for the nation's highest award. The government may have failed to recognize these heroic men, but for the rest of his career in the army, Behl for one was known by the sobriquet 'Tiger'.

ZIMITHANG

As we have seen, GOC 4 Division, Major General Niranjan Prasad, was the officer on the other end of the heated conversation with Brigadier John Dalvi on 19 October. Despite all the signs of an imminent Chinese attack, Prasad had doggedly insisted that a Company of 1/9 GR should move to Bridge 5 the next morning even though he agreed with Dalvi that the move would serve no tactical purpose and would further stretch his supply lines. Prasad kept falling back on the fact that he had 'orders from above', finally ending the conversation almost in tears.

Division HQ received the first report of the Chinese assault on Khenzemane within minutes of the attack. Shortly after, the barrage on the Rajput and Gorkha positions began. Brigade HQ by then had lost contact with 2 Rajput but was in communication with 1/9 GR, 9 Punjab and 4 Grenadiers. From all the records available, it seemed everyone was talking to each other, describing the unfolding Chinese attacks. Shortly before 8 a.m., Dalvi spoke to Prasad and reported that the situation in Rongla was untenable and that Brigade HQ was going to fall back on Hathung-la. Dalvi suggested to his GOC that it might be prudent for both 9 Punjab and 4 Grenadiers to also head for Hathung-la.

No such orders were issued to either of the two battalions at that stage. Obviously, despite the barrage of information that had been pouring in, either the GOC was deluding himself or he was in a state of denial. Had he ordered 9 Punjab and 4 Grenadiers to withdraw after speaking to Dalvi, both these fine units would have had at least a three to four hour head start over the Chinese in the race to occupy Hathung-la. Instead the GOC decided to fly to Tsangdhar in the single engine Bell 47G-2 helicopter. At the very last minute, there was a change of plan. Prasad would later write: 'I decided to go with him [Squadron Leader Vinod Sehgal], not only to keep an eye on the battle while 7 Brigade HQ was on the move, but because I was keen to supervise the Tsangle withdrawal… I called out to Vinod

Sehgal to get his helicopter ready, collected [Major] Ram Singh and set out for the helipad. When emplaning, however, Sehgal raised an objection about the load. While he had no objection to carrying an extra passenger against regulations, he said he just could not risk taking a heavy wireless set and battery in addition.... My first reaction was to tell Ram Singh to wait for the next sortie, but Ram Singh quite rightly argued that establishing the set at Tsangdhar was more important as I would be helpless there without communications. In any case, by then the set and the battery had already been strapped on to the outside carrier frame; Ram Singh argued that it would only take a turn-round of 20-25 minutes to drop it at Tsangdhar and return. This made sense, so I got out of the helicopter and allowed Ram Singh to proceed to Tsangdhar.'

Finally, after one and a half hours, HQ 4 Division woke up to the fact that there were two battalions sitting pretty downriver, waiting for the Chinese to regroup and assault them. The order to withdraw was finally given around 11 a.m., after which it took another hour to get organized. As the two battalions left their prepared defences, the Chinese mortar crews got to work.

Meanwhile Prasad was painfully aware that Sehgal had not returned from Tsangdhar. He ordered Squadron Leader A. S. Williams to rescue Sehgal and Ram Singh. Earlier that day Williams had been recalled to Gauhati from Zimithang. Air Vice Marshal Jaswant Singh was waiting for him on the tarmac. The AVM took him to the Dakota that was parked nearby and showed him multiple bullet holes that it had collected earlier over Tsangdhar. He then gave explicit orders not to fly to Tsangdhar as it was already occupied by the Chinese. When Williams told Prasad this, he refused to believe the squadron leader. The need to go to the aid of Sehgal and Ram Singh overrode all other concerns. When Williams went in for a landing approach at Tsangdhar, small arms fire ripped into the cockpit, hitting not only his instrument panel but also the pilot. Somehow, the crippled machine managed to veer away and get past Lumpu before it crashed near Borkungthang. Williams then returned to Zimithang and reported to Prasad that Tsangdhar was crawling with Chinese troops.

It was bad enough that 7 Brigade had disintegrated on his watch in a matter of hours, there was now a desperate need for the GOC to fall back on Tawang and take charge as it was obvious by then that the Chinese were building up for an attack on Bum-la as well.

◆

Major General Niranjan Prasad's actions were symptomatic of the complete collapse of coherent thinking along the entire chain of command. Lieutenant General Kaul, the IV Corps Commander, was ill. In his absence, the BGS, Brigadier K. K. Singh, had time and again demonstrated that Corps HQ was incapable of taking even the most minor decision; the Eastern Army Commander, Lieutenant General Sen, after insisting at the prime minister's residence on 11 October that 7 Brigade must stand its ground, had also refused to take charge of the situation.

More than a thousand kilometres away, the IB director, B. N. Mullik, sitting behind his desk in South Block, had the most accurate picture of the developing situation in Khenzemane and the Nam Ka Chu Valley. While Military Intelligence was out of the loop, the Directorate of Military Operations was aware that by the time army communication networks coded and decoded their signals, the situation would have changed. The IB operative sitting in Zimithang at Division HQ was privy to all the information that was coming in and was directly communicating the situation to Mullik. By midday, he had informed Delhi that Khenzemane, Dhola and Tsangdhar, after offering brief resistance, had been overrun. Just why and how Niranjan Prasad, sitting a few yards away from the same communication hub, failed to grasp this will always remain one of the unsolved mysteries of 1962.

The loss of both his helicopters had made the situation even more difficult for Niranjan Prasad as he was now without any transport. With 7 Brigade wiped out, the next task was to counter the immediate developing threat to Tawang.

Meanwhile, 4 Grenadiers and 9 Punjab after their withdrawal from Bridge 1 and Bridge 2 continued to climb towards the ridgeline that connected Hathung-la with Karpo-la 1 in isolated groups. The two commanding officers, Lieutenant Colonels Harihar Singh and Mishra, had caught up with each other on 22 October. Concerned only with their own safety, they had made good their own escape to the plains of Assam through Bhutan leaving their two battalions to their fate. In a damning indictment of the two commanding officers, Captain Amarinder Singh writes: 'Unbelievably, that was the last the Battalion saw of them until the main body met up with them again at the Brigade Concentration Point at Ramgarh in Bihar, three weeks later.' It would take another seventeen days for the Grenadiers to get back to India via Bhutan. Under the circumstances, a lot of credit needs to go to Major Oscar Thomas for bringing the unit back with relatively few losses. Some of the courageous Punjabis also made it back, but their losses were much higher.

A FORTRESS CALLED TAWANG

Moving westwards from the Bhutan-India-Tibet junction, the first route into India from Tibet was through Khenzemane along the Nyamjang Chu. The next point of entry, approximately three days' march to the east, was Bum-la, which was the preferred crossing point for traders. This track linked Tawang to Tsona Dzong and was the shorter route to Tawang from Tibet. Heavy snowfall would result in Bum-la closing down for the winter months, forcing any movement then to take place only through Khenzemane and the mule track that proceeded south downriver along the Nyamjang Chu to Zimithang before turning east to go to Tawang.

Until the fateful morning of 20 October, the Indian high command seemed so intent on events in and around the Nam Ka Chu Valley and the Thagla Ridge, that everything else had been more or less ignored. The defence of Tawang and the Kameng Sector had been left in the charge of Brigadier Kalyan Singh, commander of the artillery brigade. On 19 October, Kalyan Singh had arrived at Zimithang to meet General Prasad and had since got caught up in the fast-developing scenario. Niranjan Prasad's reluctance to relocate to Tawang the moment the Chinese attacked was understandable, but it was vital to have sent Kalyan Singh back post-haste. However, with both the helicopters lost, it would take the GOC of the division and the commander of the garrison, Kalyan Singh, the better part of two days to walk back to Tawang.

Ever since 8 September, when the Chinese had appeared at the Dhola post, all the carefully laid plans that were a part of the build-up for Op Onkar had been abandoned. With the diversion of 7 Brigade to the Nam Ka Chu Valley, Tawang, which until then had been declared a 'vital area', was left with just 1 Sikh with 7 Bengal Mountain Battery in support to man its defences. With hardly any real force levels under his ad hoc command, Kalyan Singh could do little other than await additional troops that had been promised to him. By 8 October, the Tawang garrison got a major boost with the arrival of 4 Garhwal Rifles and another mountain battery. This was further reinforced when 97 Field Battery with their 25-pounder guns and a troop of 4.2-inch mortars joined them.

Tawang was a defender's nightmare. Situated on a sloping plateau with the monastery dominating the landscape, it could be assaulted from multiple directions. The most obvious and logical approach was across Bum-la, the pass that straddled the watershed directly to the north. This route would place the Chinese in a very strong position, for their administrative bases supported by roads were just across the McMahon Line. The second line of approach available to the Chinese was the Tawang-Mukdang-la-Geyshe-la axis that would allow them to attack from the east. The third approach was down the Khenzemane-Zimithang-Shakti-Lumla track that allowed them to approach Tawang from the west.

Brigadier Kalyan Singh was an inspiring figure and exuded calm confidence. His absence from Tawang between 19 and 22 October was sorely felt, especially since the Chinese build-up opposite Bum-la was obvious. Since 21 October, commander 62 Brigade, Brigadier Nandi Lal, along with his entire Tactical HQ, had been camping at Tawang. The formation had started from Ranchi with three infantry battalions, but had reached Tezpur with only 4 Garhwal Rifles as the other two units had been diverted to Jorhat. The Garhwalis had subsequently been transferred to 4 Artillery Brigade, leaving 62 Brigade with no troops. Considering that Bum-la was expected to be a classic infantry battle supported by artillery, it would have made sense to not only send the Garhwalis but also place 1 Sikh under Brigadier Lal. This was done on 24 October, but by then the situation had changed most dramatically.

◆

Towards the end of October Bum-la is extremely picturesque, its barren rocky slopes covered with rust-coloured vegetation. The approach from Tawang is along zigzagging tracks that climb sharply up, past a sprinkling of small lakes. The vegetation soon falls away and the pass itself is more of an opening into the flat plateau of Tibet. One platoon under the command of Jemadar A. K. Roy of 5 Assam Rifles was located at Bum-la itself, while various sub-units of 1 Sikh were located on the important features behind them.

The Twin Peaks Hill, two kilometres south of the pass, dominates the entire area and affords a commanding view of the McMahon Line. This rocky escarpment, known as the IB Ridge, made it a tactically perfect position and No. 11 Platoon of Delta Company under Subedar Joginder Singh Sahnan occupied it. The remaining two platoons of Delta Company dug themselves in at Tongpeng-la, three kilometres behind the IB Ridge position. Bravo Company was in the area known as Pamdir with No. 6 Platoon at Samatso. The rest of the battalion under the command of Lieutenant Colonel B. N. Mehta was in defences around Milakteng-la, which was roughly halfway between Bum-la and Tawang, where they were further reinforced by one company of 4 Garhwal Rifles.

The Battalion HQ of 4 Garhwal Rifles was set up in Tawang itself, so it could coordinate with its two companies deployed at Mukdang-la (also known as Landa) and Penkingtang, with a platoon at Geyshe-la. 97 Field Battery with its complement of eight 25-pounders was deployed at the road head to Bum-la while the 7 Bengal Mountain Battery with its mules was deployed in the Milakteng-la area. The troop of 116 Heavy Mortar Battery had deployed on the Sulla-Samatso track.

After the Chinese attack on 20 October, activity across Bum-la started in real earnest. From the Indian observation posts, the Chinese could be seen openly occupying their assembly areas. So cocky were the Chinese of their numerical superiority, they even held morning PT for their soldiers right under the noses of the Indians. The frustration among young artillery officers who were raring to have a crack at the Chinese was evident from Second Lieutenant Darshan Khullar's comment: 'If only our artillery had engaged them, they could have been killed in their hundreds. Orders for opening fire had to come down from the highest authority, in this case HQ Eastern Command, whose intention was not to provoke the Chinese.'

The Chinese on their part were obviously patiently waiting for their column that was coming down the Khenzemane-Zimithang-Lumla route. Niranjan Prasad had finally uprooted himself from Zimithang and made the long trek back to Tawang with the Chinese following closely. To complete the farce that was being enacted at the higher levels of command, he received a message over the wireless appointing him acting IV Corps Commander while he and Brigadier Kalyan Singh were somewhere near Lum-la. But by this time, the general neither had any staff nor any means of communicating with anybody. They finally got to Tawang on the evening of 22 October where they found the Eastern Army Commander. Officers present recall that there was a sharp exchange of words between Niranjan Prasad and Bogey Sen. Sen accused GOC 4 Division of cowardice and 'running away' from Zimithang. It also seemed Sen was least interested in the ground situation and had no words of advice for any of his subordinates. Obviously in Tawang at the insistence of Army HQ, this was General Sen's first ever visit and he seemed extremely anxious for a helicopter to come and take him back to Tezpur.

THE BLIND MEN OF HINDUSTAN

During the two-day trek from Zimithang to Tawang, Kalyan Singh and Niranjan Prasad had arrived at the conclusion that by defending Tawang the Indians would be making the same error that they had made in Nam Ka Chu. Given the tactical unsuitability of the ground, and with the Chinese closing in from three sides, a decision to fight at Tawang would be unsound.

Now Prasad told Sen that he had decided to withdraw from Tawang the next day, as the IV Corps assessment suggested that the Chinese would attack through Bum-la on the morning of 24 October.

Sen exploded, and lashed out at Prasad. The manner in which events unfolded on 20 October had made him and General Thapar look like fools. Kaul had been proved right about the tactical absurdity of holding the riverfront. Sen was astute enough to realize that even though Kaul was the architect of the Nam Ka Chu disaster, during the last phase he had changed his tune and this later assessment had proved true. Sen probably expected that he would now be held accountable. In the heated exchange that followed, Sen told Prasad to hold Bum-la at all costs and await the arrival of additional troops to reinforce Tawang. Sen knew the government would be loath to give up what was seen as the symbol of the entire conflict—the Tawang Monastery.

Prasad was equally firm on withdrawing from Tawang and taking up a fresh position across the Tawang Chu at Jang, leaving Se-la to be defended by the reinforcements that were being rushed up. Sen, despite having the authority to override Prasad, no longer had the confidence to follow his own instincts. Despite having landed in Tawang at 10.30 a.m. that morning, Sen had not felt it necessary to reconnoitre the terrain around Bum-la or its defences. Had he done so, apart from boosting the morale of the men on the ground, it would have been obvious to the army commander that Bum-la was not going to be a walkover for the Chinese and that it was a far cry from the tactically unsound position that 7 Brigade had been in at Nam Ka Chu. On the contrary, the army commander gave the distinct impression that he was not particularly interested in the immediate tactical or strategic aspect of the impending battle.

Prasad also was not fully focused on the impending Bum-la battle. His main concern was that the Chinese column that had been following him would bypass Tawang and make a rush for the bridge over the Tawang Chu. If the Chinese cut the bridge off, the Tawang garrison would be cut off and therefore doomed. In addition, once he reached Tawang he was given to understand by BGS IV Corps in Tezpur that as per the corps' assessment, the Chinese were only expected to launch an attack on Bum-la on the morning of 24 October.

Meanwhile, in New Delhi, the former commander of 7 Brigade, Brigadier D. K. Palit, was now the Director Military Operations and perhaps the only man in Army HQ who had any knowledge of the actual ground conditions in and around Tawang; he was about to play a crucial role.

The speed with which the situation had unravelled on 20 October had dumbfounded almost everybody. The Chief of Army Staff who had backed Bogey Sen's refusal to pull back from the Nam Ka Chu during the crucial meeting at the prime minister's residence on 11 October now had egg all over his face. The IV Corps Commander, Lieutenant General Kaul, remained confined to his sick bed, surrounded on the evening of 22 October by 'Thapar, Menon, Mullik and Sarin who were sitting around his bed in funeral silence'.

When Thorat had expounded the concept of the defensive line, Palit, by his own admission, had taken a stand against its viability on the grounds that a withdrawal from the McMahon Line to Bomdila would be a useless manoeuvre since it would allow the Chinese to take their objective (which was Tawang) and then not bother to actually fight the Indians on the defensive line. At that time, this stance taken by him as the brigade commander of 7 Brigade, had placed Palit firmly in the 'Kaul Camp' that seemed to be on the ascendancy in the power struggle that was going on in Army HQ. As we know, along with Thimayya, Thorat and others who were considered to be of the old school had also departed. Palit's subsequent elevation to the post of Director Military Operations came as a major shock for there were at least two other officers who were considered to be more appropriate for the job. In his own words: 'I had at first been regarded as one of "Bijji's men", in the pejorative sense, and, I suspect, I never totally escaped the imprint.' Once in Army HQ, Palit had changed his opinion, for Thorat's defensive line was not based on a whim but on pure military logic of fighting a war on grounds of your own choosing and playing to one's strengths rather than weaknesses.

Right from the very beginning, Palit was not particularly impressed with Tawang as a defensive location. He says: 'After my reconnaissance of the Bum-la region, I was more than ever convinced that Towang (sic) was not suitable as a defensive locality. Then, for the first time, it occurred to me that the Se-la ridge was a possible alternative. I resolved to make a more detailed survey of the terrain on either side of Se-la Top, where the map indicated a number of tracks, many flat stretches for dropping zones and two small freshwater lakes.' However, Palit's own attempt at studying the ground around Se-la and Nuranang had proved futile owing to a snowstorm and ill health. 'Afterwards I had sent Major Raja Fulay, my DAA and QMG (logistics officer) to reconnoitre Se-la's surroundings for both tactical and logistical assessments of its defensive potential. I instructed him to return via the circuitous northern track from Tawang that bypasses

Se-la, skirts the high Mago region and descends to Dirang valley via Tse-la (pronounced Che-la), Poshing-la and Thembang. This was a possible route for outflanking Se-la and I needed to have a detailed report on it.'

It was a different matter that Niranjan Prasad had also arrived at much the same conclusion. Prasad had never commanded troops at a junior level; in fact, he had been seconded to the RIAF during World War II as a junior officer and had flown the Lysander with No. 1 Squadron before moving on to command No. 7 Squadron. He had moved back to the army and commanded 50 Para Brigade in the Jammu and Kashmir Ops in 1948. There too, his lack of experience in commanding troops at the grass-roots level had shown up, and he was fortunate to have been given a leg-up to the next rank. He obviously had a pleasing personality and was generally well liked, but his tendency of developing a fatalistic and supine attitude on the eve of a battle was liable to create problems.

On 22 October while the drama was being enacted between Prasad and Sen in Tawang, Palit was moving rapidly in Delhi. He first went to Kaul's residence but was unable to get his attention owing to the circle of Thapar, Menon, Mullik and Sarin around him. He then accosted Thapar as he came out of Kaul's residence and told the chief that in his opinion, trying to defend Tawang would lead to another Nam Ka Chu and that the army must immediately withdraw across the Tawang Chu and take up a defensive position above Jang and Se-la. In anticipation of getting this plan approved, Palit, as the DMO, had already issued orders stopping the forward movement of additional troops towards Tawang so that the Jang-Tawang route stayed clear for a possible withdrawal.

Thapar, either unable to comprehend the situation, or perhaps simply unable to counter his articulate DMO, failed to act decisively, instead mumbling that he had 'ordered Bogey Sen' to be in Tawang and that he would consider the suggestion of a withdrawal the next day.

A few hours later, as Thapar slept in White Gates, on the windswept heights of Bum-la, at 5 a.m. on 23 October, the men in the Assam Rifles post switched off the safety catches on their weapons as they watched three red flares light up the still dark sky. The Chinese mortars and guns then opened up, while RCL guns moved up to blast away the stone sangars behind which the Indians were waiting for the main attack to begin. Two kilometres behind the Assam Rifles position, all the men of 1 Sikh occupying the IB ridge were also looking towards the pass.

Chapter 8

WHEN GENERALS FAIL

THE BATTLE FOR BUM-LA

Mao tse-Tung's detailed instructions for the campaign against India directed the PLA leaders to go for 'audacious action' wherever possible. China's initial assault on 7 Brigade was a clear indication that PLA tactics would be based on creating local superiority in the campaign by concentrating strength at decisive points and assaulting from different directions. The Indians, being rooted to defensive positions, would always face overwhelming odds in numbers; else the Chinese would simply not engage the positions.

On the morning of 20 October, Jemadar A. K. Roy and his platoon of Assam Rifles had watched in amazement as a workforce of approximately 1,000 labourers, protected by Chinese soldiers, had suddenly appeared at Bum-la (16,500 feet). Equipped with digging implements, they prepared the ground so that the flat terrain could be used as a forming-up area for assaulting troops. In the afternoon, the JCO had trekked to the 1 Sikh position on the IB Ridge (so named because of an old abandoned Inspection Bungalow), where he apprised Subedar Joginder Singh of the developments. Joginder, in turn, discussed the situation with the Delta Company commander, Lieutenant Hari Pal Kaushik, who was based at Topeng-la. It was decided that a section under Havildar Sucha Singh would return to the Assam Rifles post with Roy while at the same time second line ammunition would be ferried across to the IB Ridge.

Over the next two days the Chinese continued to feverishly build up their force at Bum-la. Just as they had insolently lit fires on the Thagla Ridge to keep themselves warm on the eve of the attack on the Nam Ka Chu, here too they conducted morning PT to emphasize their numerical superiority and send a message to the defenders.

As we have seen in the previous chapter, at 4.30 a.m. on 23 October, three red Very lights preceded a barrage of Chinese artillery and mortar

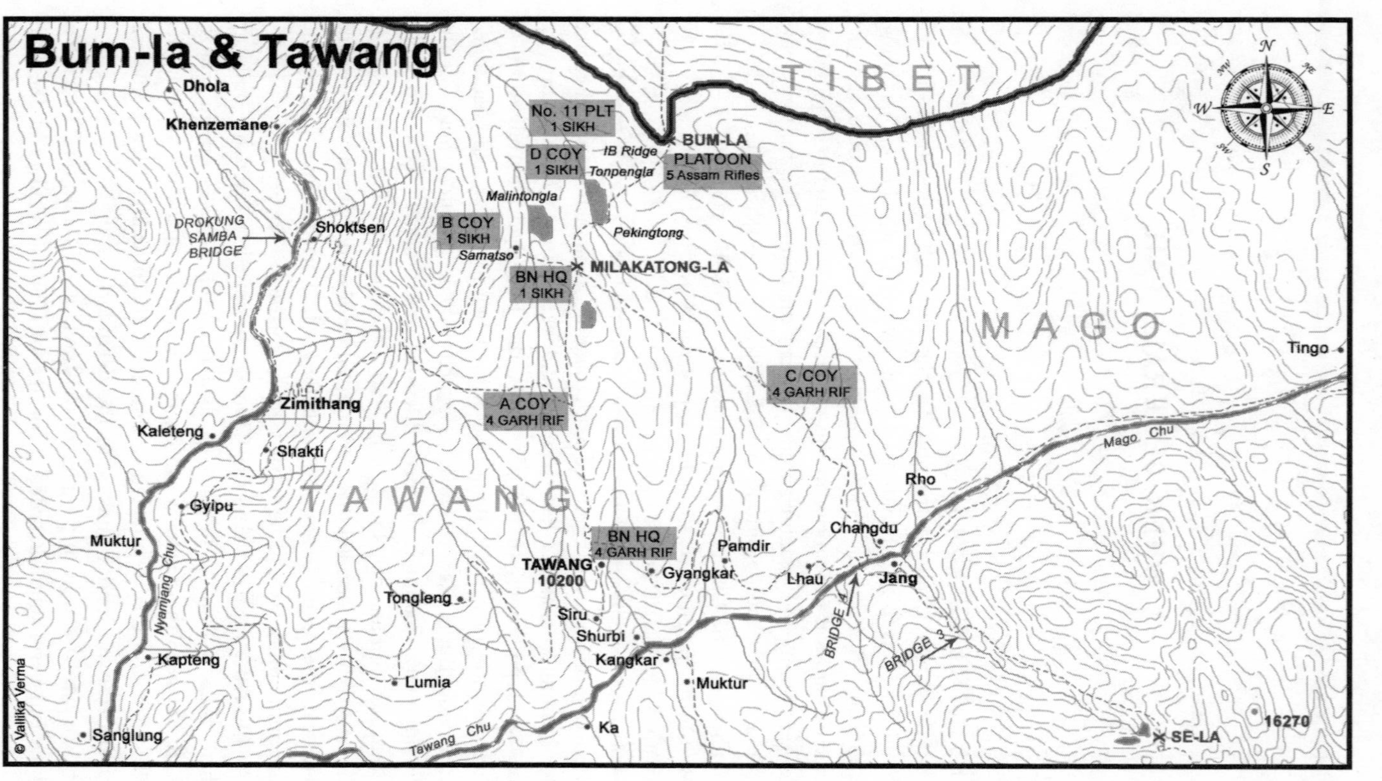
Bum-la & Tawang
Dhola
Khenzemane
DROKUNG SAMBA BRIDGE
Shoktsen
No. 11 PLT
1 SIKH
D COY
1 SIKH
BUM-LA
IB Ridge
Tonpengla
PLATOON
5 Assam Rifles
TIBET
Malintongla
B COY
1 SIKH
Samatso
Pekingtong
MILAKATONG-LA
BN HQ
1 SIKH
MAGO
Tingo
C COY
4 GARH RIF
A COY
4 GARH RIF
Zimithang
Kaleteng
Shakti
Mago Chu
Rho
TAWANG
Gyipu
Muktur
Nyamjang Chu
BN HQ
4 GARH RIF
Changdu
Pamdir
TAWANG
10200
Gyangkar
Lhau
Jang
Tongleng
Siru
Shurbi
BRIDGE 4
BRIDGE 3
Kapteng
Kangkar
Lumia
Muktur
Ka
16270
Sanglung
Tawang Chu
SE-LA
© Vallika Verma

fire on the Assam Rifles post. The Chinese had positioned anti-tank guns behind the fortifications prepared during the last three days, and these now started firing in a bid to destroy the stone sangars. As soon as the shelling stopped, Chinese infantry began to close in on the defenders. The concentrated bombardment amongst the rocks had been terrifying and the men had dug as deep as they could. They were hardly able to breathe as cordite fumes filled the already rarefied air. But the stone fortifications held, despite sections being blown away by direct firing RCLs.

Roy's men and the section of Sikhs under Sucha Singh had no intention of giving in. There were 600 Chinese soldiers crawling towards them through the rocky cover available to them. Supporting mortar fire from the IB Ridge added to the thunderous sound of the Indian weapons within the confines of the pass. However, the Chinese numbers were overwhelming. Roy's men were being silenced one by one by the Chinese. Roy yelled to Sucha Singh to break contact and fall back with his section while Roy and the remaining soldiers would provide covering fire. As the Sikhs and some Assam Rifles men fell back in the dim pre-dawn light, Sucha Singh, at the rear of the column, turned back and looked at the flashes of exploding gunfire and stabbing bursts of small arms fire. The distinct sound of Indian weapons would continue sporadically as the men tried to hold out. Eventually, there was silence; the 5 Assam Rifles platoon had been wiped out and the position had been overrun.

At Bum-la, 1 Sikh's task was to make the pass, and hence the approach to Tawang, impassable. Delta Company held the first line of defence that extended from the IB Ridge to the Twin Peaks and onto Tongpeng-la. Hari Pal Kaushik, then twenty-eight years old, was a hockey player who had been a part of the team that won the gold medal at the Melbourne Olympics in 1956 (he would win another gold at the Tokyo Olympics two years later). Extremely cool under pressure, he had with him an outstanding artillery officer, Captain Gurcharan Singh Gosal, who was to act as a forward observer for the 7 (Bengal) Mountain Battery that would provide artillery cover from their 3.7-inch guns to the Sikhs. Gosal was not only extremely competent, he was also very diligent and methodical in his approach. On his own initiative, he had previously recorded all possible targets in and around Bum-la and set up a firing range, even though there were orders to the contrary. This had allowed Gosal to hone the accuracy of his gun crews who had made all the meteorological corrections that are so critical in high-altitude warfare.

Approximately three kilometres southwest of Bum-la, and west of the foot track, was the feature called Twin Peaks, from which one could observe most Chinese activity across the McMahon Line. Between the Twin Peaks and Bum-la on a stretch of flatland was the Inspection Bungalow. The nearby IB Ridge, roughly two kilometres south of Bum-la, was an ideal position to thwart access to Twin Peaks. No. 11 Platoon of Delta Company, under Subedar Joginder Singh, deployed at the IB ridge, had set up tactically sited bunkers and trenches on the forward slope of the ridge. The IB Ridge dominated the Bum-la bowl, and the climb from the bed of the nullah to their platoon fieldwork was extremely steep; therefore, the Sikhs would be able to mow down the enemy with their Lee Enfield .303 rifles.

Elements of the attacking Chinese force that had bypassed the Assam Rifles post had started to engage Joginder Singh's platoon on the IB Ridge by 5 a.m. The Sikh position dominated the approaches, and the Chinese had no choice but to climb up a nullah to try and close the gap. Heavy mortars engaged the first wave of the Chinese, forcing them to scatter and pull back. For the Sikhs, the main problem was the lack of ammunition. Joginder Singh on the field line once again asked the Delta Company commander, Kaushik, to try and restock his position. By then Tongpeng-la was also in contact with the Chinese, and Kaushik asked Joginder Singh to fall back to the company location.

However, Joginder Singh preferred to fight from his position on the IB Ridge. He told Kaushik his men would hold their position come what may. In reality, despite having broken up the first Chinese attack, Joginder had lost half his platoon owing to the sheer volume of Chinese fire. The Chinese regrouped and launched a second attack, this time from the right flank, which was also stopped. However, by then only a handful of men were still alive to give fight to the Chinese, who were trying hard to hold their own line and put in yet another attack.

Kaushik asked Joginder if he should go 'red over red' which would mean asking the artillery to open fire on 11 Platoon's own position. Without any hesitation, Joginder said, 'Haanji, saab'. Just then the Chinese found and cut off the communication line, leaving the platoon isolated. Joginder Singh had already been shot in the thigh and was bleeding profusely. His platoon now had barely any ammunition. Just as he shouted to the few survivors to take cover, Gosal's guns opened up, devastating the confined area. The Sikhs huddled in their trenches, waiting. Joginder Singh told the surviving men to fix bayonets and they now waited for the Chinese to make their way through the black, blood-splattered rocks towards them. On his command, a final charge was put in but the Chinese automatic weapons that were highly effective at close range cut down most of the men. The wounded Joginder Singh, weak from the loss of blood, was overpowered and captured by the Chinese. While their attention was on the JCO, who would not stop struggling, three surviving members of the platoon managed to slip away. They rejoined the battalion and gave a detailed account of Joginder Singh's last battle.

By then Tongpeng-la was under attack. Kaushik, with the two remaining platoons of Delta Company, thought it unlikely that the Chinese would try to attack his position from the right as it was protected by a huge rock face. From their position on the pass, the Sikhs could see the Chinese making their way towards Tongpeng-la, even as they could hear the intense firing from the IB Ridge. After a brief discussion with the commanding officer, Lieutenant Colonel B. N. Mehta decided to move an additional platoon under Havildar Pratap Singh to protect the right flank. However, even though Tongpeng-la was almost three and a half kilometres behind Bum-la, the Chinese obviously had a fairly accurate idea of the terrain. Hoping to catch Delta Company unawares, they had decided to launch their main attack from the right flank, and were using the rock face behind which they were forming up for the attack.

Captain Gosal, however, had ideas of his own and he directed the guns to engage the Chinese forming up behind the rock face. What followed was a classic example of what a determined and competent forward observer can do. The accurate fire by the 7 (Bengal) Mountain Battery took a heavy toll of the massed Chinese troops. Suffering a large number of casualties, the Chinese were forced to give up any thoughts of launching an attack from the right side.

Gathering their dispersed troops, the Chinese now tried to encircle Tongpeng-la and even tried to use snipers to eliminate the observation post party. The three Sikh platoons, once again aided by accurate fire brought to bear by Gosal's guns, successfully broke up the attack. After a lull, during which time the Chinese collected more troops, a third assault was launched on Tongpeng-la at 11.30 a.m., once again from the right, from behind the rock face. For the third time, the OP officer was alert and the guns thwarted the Chinese yet again. With three attacks having failed, the Chinese decided to bypass Kaushik's position at Tongpeng-la; here too, accurate fire from the Sikhs ensured that there could be no progress towards Milaktong.

Four platoons of the Sikhs and one platoon of Assam Rifles had proved what determined, well-dug-in infantry could do. Despite being confined to fixed defensive positions where eventually both Roy and Joginder Singh's platoons were wiped out, the men repeatedly fought off the Chinese.

WE'LL HOLD THEM AT SE-LA NOW

At the Army House in Delhi, General Thapar was not yet aware of the developments in Bum-la. His mind was preoccupied with what the DMO, Brigadier Palit, had said to him the previous evening. Until now, Tawang had been declared vital ground, but he knew he had erred badly by not allowing 7 Brigade to pull back when Bijji Kaul had rather forcefully stated his case on 11 October. As the COAS, he knew the debacle at Nam Ka Chu would ultimately be laid at his feet. Early on the morning of 23 October, he called Palit and asked him to join the meeting with the prime minister and the defence minister. Palit quickly prepared a written analysis of the tactical alternatives, in case the prime minister or the defence minister asked for it, collected his maps, and presented himself at Menon's office to await the chief.

In the defence minister's room, Nehru, Menon and the foreign secretary, M. J. Desai, were seated around a table where they were joined by Thapar. The COAS told Nehru that his DMO, who had previously commanded 7 Brigade and was well acquainted with the terrain, had some important points to make on the developing Kameng situation. Palit unfolded a map and began to describe the tactical situation in Tawang, in particular emphasizing the tracks from Bum-la that bypassed Tawang and led to Se-la directly. 'What is it that you wish to convey?' a pale and subdued Nehru asked Palit.

'Tawang is not a suitable area in which to site the main defences. The Chinese could entrap the garrison and move into central Kameng without attacking Tawang. What the army desires is permission to withdraw from the Tawang salient and to hold a defensive position further back, because if we continue to hold on to Tawang with the only troops we have available, the Chinese would before long be making for the Brahmaputra plains via the undefended Manda-la.'

Palit stressed that the decision to evacuate Tawang had to be taken immediately. Menon had sat through the briefing with a scowl on his face, showing no interest in the discussion. Nehru turned to Thapar and said: 'It is now for the military to decide where and how they should fight. I have no doubt in my mind that what we lose, you shall eventually win back for us. I cannot lay down conditions about Tawang or any other place on grounds other than military.' Palit left the defence minister's room and proceeded directly to the Ops Room from where he issued orders to stop all forward moves of units belonging to 62 and 48 Infantry Brigades beyond Dirang. He had started to draft a message ordering the evacuation of Tawang when he was called to the chief's office.

Thapar greeted him with a smile and said: 'Well done, Monty, you handled that well.' Between Palit, Thapar and Niranjan Prasad, the stage had been set for the second half of the debacle, the first already having been enacted at Nam Ka Chu. For the men fighting desperately at Bum-la at that very moment, it was perhaps the greatest let-down.

With Thapar having approved the order to evacuate Tawang, Palit rushed back to the Ops Room in Army HQ, where reports of the fighting in Bum-la had started trickling in. Orders were issued for the immediate withdrawal from Tawang.

Even in their wildest dreams, no Chinese commander could have anticipated that the Indians would fold so easily. Right or wrong, the decision to designate Tawang vital ground was taken a year and a half ago, after which thousands of man hours had been used to build up the garrison, to say nothing of the air effort. How, on the whim of a DMO, the COAS could decide to abandon the place, is indicative of the complete collapse of the decision-making process! A tactical withdrawal is one thing, but to fall back the moment the firing starts can only lead to a debacle. It was unfortunate that those who were best suited to fight, like the machine gunners at Bridge 4 and the Assam Rifles at Dhola, chose to leave the battlefield, betraying the sacrifice of those who decided to fight. No amount of post-war rationalizing can cover up the fact that there was a total collapse of command and control.

Palit, as the commander of 7 Brigade who inducted the formation into NEFA in 1959-60, had seen first-hand the huge logistical obstacles. One of the main reasons he did not want to declare Tawang vital ground at that time was undoubtedly the logistics factor. Yet, despite his entreaties, the Tawang garrison continued to be built up. Tragically, when the time came for the troops to buckle down and fight, Palit fell back on his old prejudices and decried Tawang as a defensive position. His timing could not have been worse. Even as he was briefing the prime minister about the need to withdraw from Tawang, one single company of 1 Sikh at Tenglong-la was valiantly holding back the Chinese.

Palit overlooked some fundamental factors when he bulldozed the shaken Indian government and the army chief into taking a decision that would further help the Chinese. It is one thing for forward observation posts of the Assam Rifles to fall back to a pre-determined defensive line as envisaged by Thorat, and quite another for the army to abandon its prepared defences and fall back to a line that exists only on a map. Palit's belated belief that Se-la as a natural barrier would prove to be a natural defensive position, even better suited than Bomdila, might have had merit if Se-la had been prepared for a fight. To move back after the Chinese had attacked was nothing short of suicide. In addition, the following points needed to be considered:

First, had Bum-la been reinforced, the Chinese were not likely to get past determined and resolute Indian troops. 13 Dogra, commanded by Lieutenant Colonel M. S. Oberoi, and 4 Garhwal Rifles were already in Tawang. Had Palit not stopped the forward movement of troops, at least three more battalions or at least some of their leading elements would have been in Tawang by the evening of 23 October, with enough troops to guard and protect the crucial Bridge 4 over the Tawang Chu.

Second, the rapid collapse of 7 Brigade at Nam Ka Chu and the subsequent retreat of 4 Division HQ from Zimithang would have created a major logistical problem for the Chinese who were chasing Niranjan Prasad. The column that could approach Tawang directly from Zimithang would have run into the Garhwalis who were guarding that axis, while 13 Dogra was protecting the route from Lumla to Tawang. Even if the Chinese had made a rush for Bridge 4 (as they did) on the morning of 24 October, Indian troops on either side of the Tawang Chu could have taken them on. One thing is almost certain: the Chinese could not have brought in a large number of troops but would have relied on tactics based on speed.

Third, Tawang was perhaps the best stocked position in the region. It was only after 8 September that the supply drops had been diverted to Tsangdhar; until then, the Indian Air Force had flown tons of equipment, ammunition and other logistical supplies into Tawang. Niranjan Prasad and Palit's decision nullified the entire logistical effort that had been put into place over months. Tawang was being handed over to the Chinese on a platter.

The message to withdraw from Bum-la and Tawang reached the 1 Sikh Battalion HQ at Milaktong-la much to the disbelief of Mehta and the other officers. However, there was no ambiguity in the orders issued by Brigadier Kalyan Singh, Commander 4 Artillery Brigade. The army commander's stance continued to be puzzling, for though he outwardly agreed with the order to abandon Tawang, he privately felt that Tawang should be held, but he neither had the confidence nor the conviction to issue the order himself. As he took off, he told Niranjan Prasad to do as he liked, as it was 'his battle and his command'. However, shortly after landing in Tezpur, Bogey Sen spoke on the phone with Thapar, and after briefing him of the prevailing situation in Tawang, he demanded that Niranjan Prasad be sacked immediately as he had 'run away from Zimithang'.

Back in Milaktong-la, 1 Sikh firmed up its plan for breaking contact with the Chinese and withdrawing to Jang. Delta Company was ordered to hold Tongpeng-la till 3 p.m., after which they were to fall back on Milaktong-la. This was a tricky manoeuvre, but with the help of Gosal's guns deployed at Mi-la, it was executed with precision. Through the day, the artillery had fired almost 600 rounds at the enemy. Delta Company then deployed around Milaktong-la where it would continue to be the rearguard as the rest of 1 Sikh, including Bravo Company and Delta Company, less a platoon of 4 Garhwal Rifles, began to pull back at last light. The Chinese continued to bombard Milaktong-la but were not willing to close the gap with Delta Company again. At 11 p.m., Kaushik's men abandoned Milaktong-la and started the long descent towards Jang. Delta Company of 1 Sikh had shown the Indian Army how to fight. Unfortunately, none of the senior officers were watching.

At 10.30 a.m. that morning, Lieutenant Colonel B. M. Bhattacharjea was chafing at the bit when he received orders to pull his battalion out of Tawang. Even though Delta Company minus a platoon was supporting 1 Sikh at Milaktong-la, neither Alpha nor Charlie Company had reported any contact with the Chinese, even though Tawang was awash with rumours about Chinese columns surrounding the monastery and the town. Alpha Company was immediately ordered to fall back on Tawang and was tasked with holding Tawang till last light, after which it was to fall back on Jang.

By the afternoon, all rear elements were withdrawing from Tawang while Mi-4 helicopters were ferrying women and children out of Tawang and flying them across Se-la to Dirang Dzong. Till that very morning, no thought had been given to evacuating Tawang; within hours, the precipitate withdrawal created mayhem. There were hundreds of men from the Assam Rifles and the Pioneers who, along with civilians and even lamas from the monasteries, now fled towards Jang with whatever they could carry.

Meanwhile, tons of supplies, clothing and ammunition that had been painstakingly ferried into Tawang were now abandoned. Over 1,500 sleeping bags were piled in a corner of the helipad, where a Bell helicopter was left without any crew. The biggest casualty in the withdrawal was the 97 Field Battery—the towing vehicles and the guns got bogged down in the mud below the lower helipad and had to be left behind. Similarly, 116 Heavy Mortar Battery managed to bring the mortars down from Bum-la to Pankentang but could not carry them further. All the mortars had to be spiked and discarded. 1 Sikh too lost a great deal of its equipment during the withdrawal from Bum-la. Two guns of 2 (Derajat) Mountain Battery could not be recovered from Mukdang-la and were abandoned. 7 (Bengal) Mountain Battery, however, was the exception, as it successfully brought all the guns and mules down.

Mukdang-la was at a height of 12,500 feet, over which passed the track from Bum-la to Jang that bypassed Tawang altogether. Charlie Company of 4 Garhwal Rifles under the command of Major Hasta Bahadur Rai was holding this position. On 15 October, with two dozen men and two 3.7-inch guns (without ammunition) the gunners had joined the Garhwali troops on the pine-covered pass where they set up their gun positions amidst grazing yaks. On 23 October the commander of 2 (Derajat) Mountain Battery, Lieutenant Darshan Khullar, woke up to 'the distant sound of artillery fire and realized that battle had broken out at Bum-la. A little later MMG bursts could also be heard. I was vaguely excited. I was certain that the Chinese were being given a bloody nose. I was certain that the Indian Army would, in keeping with its great exploits in the Second World War and the Kashmir operations, stand up resolutely in the face of a Chinese offensive. The thought that we would be asked to withdraw was unthinkable. I was obviously lost in blissful ignorance.'

By 1 p.m., both Rai and Khullar were told to abandon their positions at Mukdang-la at 5.30 that evening and make their way to Jang. Khullar's guns were to be transported back loaded on mules, but the animal transport party was delayed. The mules eventually fetched up at Mukdang-la at 10 p.m., but by then it wore a deserted look with just the two spiked guns holding down the fort. The Chinese were nowhere to be seen either.

Through the night of 23-24 October, troops made their way down from Tawang and assembled at Jang, crossing over the Tawang Chu via Bridge 4. By 5 a.m., the rearguard of 4 Garhwal and 13 Dogra had also reported at Jang. While the Tactical HQ of 4 Division was set up at Dirang Dzong, sixty-four kilometres southeast of Se-la, 4 Artillery Brigade set itself up at the well-appointed officers' mess in Jang which had a telecommunications link with Dirang Dzong and a spectacular view of the Geyshe-la and Mukdang-la forward slopes.

As per 4 Division's assessment of the situation the previous day, the Chinese should have been snapping at the heels of the withdrawing Indians. Accordingly, Charlie Company of 4 Garhwal Rifles under Major Rai was given the task of holding Jang till last light on 24 December. The Engineers had prepared Bridge 4 for demolition while a twenty-man patrol base was established to keep a lookout for any Chinese activity.

'THE TWANG OF A BOW STRING'

Just before dawn, Chinese mortars began their morning bombardment of both Tenglong-la and Milaktong-la while the infantry started closing in on the Indian positions. Strewn amidst the rocks were a number of the dead, as well as those who grievously wounded, a grim reminder of the fierce fighting that had occurred the previous day. However, to the surprise of the Chinese, there was no retaliatory fire from the Indian artillery guns that had played havoc with their troops the previous day. Gradually the mortars stopped firing and probing patrols moved even closer to the Indian defences. Bunker after bunker, position after position, were all vacant. By first light, the Chinese realized that they had captured Bum-la in its entirety, and that the road to Tawang was wide open below them.

On Chinese maps, Milaktong-la is referred to as Dongmen-la. After finding it abandoned, four companies (equivalent to four Indian battalions) of the 3rd Regiment began to cautiously descend towards Tawang. Signs of the hurried departure of the Indians were everywhere; most attempts to burn abandoned equipment had not been very successful, only creating a pall of smoke from smouldering fires. Chinese troops closing in from the direction of Lum-la and by the direct route from Zimithang now found the tracks ahead of them wide open and the advance elements entered Tawang almost simultaneously. No wonder then that the Chinese version of the battle says rather sardonically:

> To the north of Tawang there is high ground, thus it is easy to defend and towards the south is the Tawang river valley, which allows one to look down from a commanding height. Thus from a military point of view, the tactical location is extremely significant. The commander of India's forces on the ground, Major General Niranjan Prasad, referred to Tawang as '4 Division's base for life and death'. Tawang was not only the rear base of Indian forces for occupying Bum-la pass and Dongmen-la [Milaktong-la/Bum-la] regions towards North West but also supported Indian forces in the Kejielang region [Nam Ka Chu], which also played the role of a protective screen for the right flank of Indian forces extending up to the 'McMahon Line'. The Indians had administered Tawang for more than a decade. Various types of military infrastructure were almost perfected and they had built a small military airport with a parking apron for helicopters. Tawang had become

> command centre and supply base for Indian forces that intruded into the Menyu [Kameng] area. However, after the lndian forces at Kejilang and Long bu were annihilated and Bum-la pass was captured by Tibet frontier guards, Indian forces at Tawang were panic-stricken like birds rattled by the mere twang of a bow string.

The Chinese had had the first laugh, as the Indians had so far played the game just as they would have wished them to. Even according to Chinese records, at no stage had there been any action that pitted more than an Indian infantry company against at least four to five times the number of Chinese troops. The Chinese officially admit to 2,419 casualties (722 dead and 1,697 wounded). The figure is quite stunning, given the situation in which each Indian position was asked to fight.

From all accounts, Bogey Sen's presence in Tawang between 22 and 23 October only added to the confusion. Before landing at Tawang, the army commander had flown towards Zimithang to get an idea of the terrain which he was not familiar with at all. Once in Tawang, as we have seen, Sen did nothing to bolster the confidence of the garrison. The meeting with Prasad later in the evening focused on two issues: the Nam Ka Chu rout of 7 Brigade and the immediate withdrawal from Tawang. Bogey Sen opposing a withdrawal only amounted to theatrics, for had he wished, as the army commander, he had the authority to overrule Prasad.

Both officers at the time were unaware that Army HQ, now represented by Monty Palit, was pushing for the same decision. There was a critical difference though—Prasad was planning on falling back on Bomdila with Se-la only playing the part of a delaying obstacle. Palit, on the other hand, based on the one incomplete reconnaissance made almost two years ago, had made up his mind to dig in at Se-la. Thapar having gone along with his DMO, who now had the tacit approval of Nehru, was relegated to the role of a spectator. The Thorat Plan, even though it hadn't been implemented, at least had had some discussions around it and plans had been drawn up. Just as Tawang was abandoned on a whim, Se-la was seemingly chosen arbitrarily by Monty Palit who played the 'cleared by the cabinet' card to ride roughshod over any opposition.

In the coming days, the Indian military high command would take decisions that lacked even the most basic common sense. Even as Palit was coming out of the defence minister's room with Nehru's 'the military must decide where to fight' mandate, Bogey Sen had decided to sack Niranjan Prasad as GOC 4 Division. Less than three hours previously, as he was leaving Tawang, Sen had eventually endorsed Prasad's decision to pull back from Bum-la and evacuate Tawang. Surely, having seen for himself the effect of the headlong retreat from Zimithang on Prasad and other senior officers, Sen was experienced enough to know that to pull back any further would result in losing not just all the supplies and material that had so painstakingly been put together, but a withdrawal without a fight would further sap the morale of the men and officers. So far, after the first couple of hours of fighting on the Nam Ka Chu, Tsangdhar, Khenzemane, and Bum-la, all Indian units that had come into contact with the Chinese were only fighting in penny packets or withdrawing. Had it been decided that Tawang was to be held at all costs, it would have made perfect sense to replace Prasad as the GOC since the army commander felt he had lost the will to fight. But to institute this change after the withdrawal order was given was to add considerably to the existing chaos.

On the evening of 23 October neither Delhi, Lucknow nor Tezpur had any idea where the next defensive line was supposed to be; the only orders given until then were to abandon Tawang and Bum-la and fall back on Jang. When Palit took the draft of the order to hold Se-la to the chief, it was decided that Thapar, Palit and the IB chief, Mullik, would fly immediately to Tezpur and discuss the matter with Bogey Sen in person. From all indications, Thapar was still not fully convinced about the decision to hold Se-la. On his own initiative, Palit put into place steps for the stocking of supplies for Se-la, working on the assumption that five battalions would be required to hold the feature.

As they flew to Tezpur, it seemed Thapar had made up his mind to finally ask Kaul, still confined to his sickbed, to relinquish command of IV Corps. Lieutenant General Harbaksh Singh, who had been Bogey Sen's deputy in 161 Brigade in 1948, was to be appointed in his place the next day. Niranjan Prasad's simultaneous exit would mean a complete overhaul at the top, which would leave Sen as the most experienced of the lot. On landing at Tezpur, the three officers made a beeline for the Ops Room where Sen conducted a briefing. It was soon obvious to all present that the army commander, despite having just returned from Tawang, was unaware of what was going on.

When questioned by Mullik about the strength of Tawang's defences, Bogey Sen stated that, in his opinion, they were adequate to hold out against an attack, but the divisional commander thought otherwise and had decided to withdraw to a more suitable defensive position. Sen said he had not interfered with the divisional commander's plans because by then Bum-la was already under attack and that the Chinese were closing in from all sides. Before an incredulous Mullik could question Sen further, Palit 'unobtrusively pulled him to one side and whispered that the Prime Minister had agreed to a withdrawal from Tawang should the military so decide'.

Sen started to brief the gathering on the operational plans but it soon became obvious that he was familiar neither with the terrain nor with IV Corps's operational plans. His depiction of the threats to Tawang and Bomdila was 'perfunctory and misleading'. Then Sen started to talk of future courses of action, 'waving the pointer vaguely over the sand model, saying he had directed 4 Infantry Division to hold the line of defence Jang-Dirang-Bomdila'. These were the exact words used by General Thorat two years ago and had been the most obvious flaw in his plan, for even then it should have been Mandala-Dirang-Bomdila.

With minimal ground knowledge, Thapar and Sen were torn between regrouping on the defensive line drawn by Thorat in 1960 and the Se-la massif that presented an ideal natural barrier to next engage the Chinese. This confusion is reflected in the barrage of orders that went out pertaining to 4 Artillery Brigade. Initially, they were told to withdraw from Tawang and take up position at Jang. This made no sense as Jang was too close to Tawang and, like Tawang, was on the slopes and not on higher ground. Besides, the logistical problems that had existed in supplying the garrison at Tawang were just as true for Jang. The orders were then changed and the brigade was told to fall back on Bomdila. To Palit, it was obvious that despite his relatively junior rank, he had to speak up before things went too far.

Violating all established protocols, Palit stepped forward. 'I interrupted to protest that what he [Bogey Sen] had just described was not a line of defence but a line of withdrawal. Going up to the sand model I delineated the road from Tawang to the Assam plains. On it, successively lay Jang, Dirang and Bomdila. I forbore from stressing the obvious; instead I pointed out that Se-la was the only geographical feature between Tawang and Bomdila that could constitute a defensive locality. I described in some detail the environment of the pass. I knew the terrain, I said, because I had walked all over it before motor roads ever came to Kameng. I described the main tracks over and around Se-la Top, not all of which were correctly marked on the IV Corps sand model.'

Now Palit took over the briefing in its entirety. 'I could sense hostility from the corps staff, resenting outside interference on tactical matters, but Thapar gave me a look of encouragement and so also, surprisingly, did Sen. He seemed almost relieved that I had taken over. I pressed home the advantage.

'I strongly advocated holding the Se-la massif. I suggested that a brigade sector, later to be built up to two brigades, be established forthwith at Se-la–Senge. As more troops arrived and logistics permitted, a brigade sector could also be established at Bomdila to guard the approach from the north via the Lap Valley and Poshing-la... After some discussions on the map, COAS [Thapar] and GOC-in-C [Sen] agreed to my recommendations and the latter telephoned GOC 4 Division [Niranjan Prasad], who had reached Dirang by then, and ordered him to return to Se-la next morning and, because of my intimate knowledge of the terrain, advise the GOC regarding the layout of defences. The GOC-in-C Eastern Command readily agreed to this suggestion.'

In the history of modern warfare, it is doubtful if there are any generals at the top of a command pyramid who have displayed such collective incompetence as these two officers. Surely, by then, Thapar could see just how muddled Bogey Sen's thinking was, yet he refrained from doing anything about it. On the contrary, on the evening of 23 October, the chief decided to back Sen's decision to sack Niranjan Prasad on the grounds of cowardice. Given that the orders that Prasad had been forced to implement (post 11 October) originated from Thapar and Sen, the sacking of Prasad amounted to making him the scapegoat. But just as Prasad was probably guilty of not standing up and fighting in Tawang, the charge would apply even more to Bogey Sen. That Prasad had failed to instil some backbone into 7 Brigade was bad enough, worse, the GOC failed to grasp that for a tactical withdrawal to happen, there had to be a previously planned alternative. Else, a withdrawal would, sooner or later, become a panicky retreat.

The questions, therefore, that need to be addressed before we move on to subsequent events are: should Tawang have been abandoned? Could Niranjan Prasad have handled things differently? The ifs and buts apart, after the disaster on the Nam Ka Chu and the easy Chinese victories at Khenzemane and Zimithang, the Tawang battle simply had to be fought. Tawang had the potential to be the Kohima of the post-independence Indian Army. Whatever the earlier debates about the suitability of Tawang as a defensive location, there was no question of those arguments coming into play on 23 October after the Chinese had launched their attack on Bum-la.

Palit, far removed from the fighting on the ground, was allowed by Thapar to get Nehru's tacit approval to pull back. Bogey Sen, on the other hand, apparently had no intention of actually landing at Tawang (as his own staff would later confirm) but was forced to do so as his helicopter had a problem. Having set off from Tezpur on 22 October to do an aerial reconnaissance of the Lumla area he was unwilling to leave the helipad despite the Chinese building up to attack Bum-la just twenty kilometres away. The fact of the matter is that all the key commanders on the ground—Dalvi, Prasad and Sen—had mentally prepared themselves to flee rather than to fight. The moment the first escapees from the Nam Ka Chu arrived at 7 Brigade HQ at Rongla, Dalvi, instead of shooting the men for retreating, started preparing to abandon his own headquarters. At Zimithang, besides Assam Rifles and Bravo Company of 4 Garhwal Rifles, Prasad had a company of 13 Dogra. Yet he chose to fall back without offering a fight. By the time the retreating party reached Tawang, the will to hold ground was lost.

OLD WINE, NEW BOTTLES

After Thapar and Mullik returned from Tezpur (Palit was to stay back and orient the commanders with Se-la), the chief issued a series of fresh orders from Army HQ the next morning. Lieutenant General Bijji Kaul was to be replaced by Lieutenant General Harbaksh Singh (from the Sikh Regiment) as IV Corps Commander. Having served as Bogey Sen's deputy in 161 Brigade, which had spearheaded the fight in the Kashmir Valley in 1947, Harbaksh Singh had an excellent rapport with the troops, especially 1 Sikh. Both the battalion and the general had played a pivotal role in reversing the potentially disastrous situation. Having commanded 5 Division earlier, Harbaksh Singh was chief of staff, Western Command, in Simla when he was ordered to move to Tezpur.

Niranjan Prasad was formally relieved of his command as GOC 4 Division and in his place was posted Major General Anant Singh Pathania. The new GOC had an impressive combat record, having been awarded a Military Cross in Burma as a young officer and then subsequently a Mahavir Chakra as the commanding officer of 1/5 GR in the Kargil Sector during the 1947-48 Jammu and Kashmir Ops.

But confusion still reigned. The previous day Tezpur had first ordered the withdrawal to Se-la, then changed the order to read Bomdila. Harbaksh Singh, on taking over IV Corps on 24 October had immediately countermanded the order, telling the Artillery Brigade to dig in at Se-la. Accompanied by Palit, he then left for Dirang Dzong by helicopter, where Niranjan Prasad and Anant Pathania were waiting for him. Even as an ad hoc defensive line, it was fairly obvious that Se-la had some advantages. On the flip side, there were quite a few yak trails that ran from Tawang to Dirang Dzong and Nyukmadong that bypassed Se-la. Furthermore, in 1913 Morshead and

Bailey, by taking the Poshing-la and Thembang route on their way out of Tibet, had shown that Se-la could be bypassed from the east. However, this was a difficult trail for the Chinese to move a large force along, and Palit felt that by securing the heights overlooking the passes, this threat could be tackled.

Other changes were also taking place. General Thapar, in his wisdom, had decided that the only way to reverse the situation in NEFA was to find commanders who had won gallantry awards in the past to take charge. This was one of the most cockeyed decisions of 1962. Most of these officers were comfortably heading towards retirement. They had to be uprooted from their cushy jobs and sent to a windswept Himalayan pass to fight a battle in near arctic conditions. Palit, who had driven Pathania around Se-la in the morning, was struck by his lack of enthusiasm. '…I had received the impression that he seemed dispirited and sluggish. His dejected mood persisted as we continued with our reconnaissance.'

At Jang and Bridge 4, far removed from the drama unfolding at Delhi and Tezpur, there was no sign of the Chinese during the morning hours of 24 October. While Major Rai and his Charlie Company, reinforced with troops from 13 Dogra, scanned the opposite slopes for any activity that would necessitate the blowing up of the bridge, most of the troops who had fallen back from Bum-la and Tawang were sitting around on the convoy ground, waiting for motor transport to take them up the zig-zagging road to Se-la and beyond.

At the convoy ground 'the scene was akin to a cattle fair in India. Hundreds of men with a sprinkling of officers sat around in aimless groups. Some were making up for lost sleep but the enterprising types were brewing tea.' Major General Niranjan Prasad having already relocated to Dirang, the seniormost officer was the 4 Artillery Brigade commander, Brigadier Kalyan Singh, who along with other officers had occupied the Border Roads officers' mess.

Confusion continued to prevail at another level. Niranjan Prasad, while abandoning Tawang, had stated that Se-la would be the next defensive line, whereas Bogey Sen had indicated that it would be Bomdila. Unfortunately, there was no senior infantry officer at Jang, for its natural defensive potential would have been obvious. The steep slopes on either side of the fast-flowing Tawang Chu meant that the distance between the two sides as the crow flies was negligible. If the Chinese got down to the river and crossed over to the south bank, Indian guns positioned further back around Bridge 3 at Nuranang, controlled by forward observers, could extract a heavy toll.

After a dull, uneventful morning and afternoon, suddenly there was a wave of excitement on the convoy ground: a bunch of Chinese soldiers had appeared on the other bank. Sitting in the officers' mess, Kalyan Singh and his officers, who were sipping their evening tea and enjoying their salted almonds, had seen them too. Hurriedly, binoculars were asked for after which Kalyan Singh in his calm manner started describing what the Chinese were doing. Their mortar crews went about systematically setting up the weapons; they then took their compass bearings, aligned and loaded the mortars. Lieutenant Colonel Bhupinder Singh, commanding 22 Field Regiment, who had been an instructor at gunnery school, thought the Chinese performance was commendable.

Describing the scenario further, Khullar says: 'The scene around the convoy ground was equally curious. Most of the men had had no food the whole day and they were bored. The appearance of the Chinese on the other side had helped to break the monotony. A decade plus of peace time unrealistic training against dummy enemy in exercises and camps had dimmed the warlike instincts of our army. I wonder what the Chinese must have thought of us as they waited for the dusk, or last light in the army parlance, to start the fireworks. They must have thought we were the stupidest of donkeys.'

As darkness descended on the Tawang Chu, the first salvos were fired and soon mortar bombs began exploding all around the convoy ground and the officers' mess. 'The Brigade Commander [Kalyan Singh], who had fought against Rommel in the Second World War, jumped off the verandah and took cover in a nearby ditch. Within seconds at least twenty others also jumped in, mostly on top of him. A strong well-built man, he silently rose, shaking off the terrified lot and walked over to his Willis jeep. My CO who otherwise was quite a fidgety person, had kept his cool. He had with him his black Labrador, Quonde, on the leash. He too got into his jeep with his dog, orderly, and Ajit Singh his driver, and drove off behind the Commander's jeep.' A few minutes later, there was a deafening roar as the Engineers blew up Bridge 4. By now, the entire lot of men at the convoy ground had taken to their heels, scrambling up the track in the darkness, in full headlong retreat. Khullar, on foot after abandoning his 1-ton vehicle, 'looked back and found that the Chinese had lit up their camp fires. They must have been very pleased with themselves.'

So began and ended the battle for Bridge 4 at Jang on the evening of 24 October. Needless to say, Jang was abandoned within the hour. So pathetic and feeble was the Indian response, that the authors of the *Official*

History of 1962 felt the need to pad the account with a description of an artillery duel before the bridge was blown up.

SE-LA

The main ridge from the Bhutan border runs west to east linking up with the main Himalayan range at the orographic knot of the Gorichen Glacier and Kangto (23,260 feet), which is the highest peak on the watershed separating NEFA from Tibet. The Se-la Ridge also forms the watershed between the Nyamjang Chu and the Kameng river basins, while also forming the geographical and cultural boundary between the Tawang region and the Dirang Dzong sector. Apart from Se-la, the other prominent passes that run across the feature are Tse-la, Kya-la, Chebra-la and Orka-la, all of them well over 13,000 feet in altitude. From the southern side, the Se-la massif is a sheer escarpment and the pass can only be approached along a lateral road running up from Senge Dzong. Se-la Top is situated at a height of 13,746 feet, which then opens up towards the north like an amphitheatre. The flat area, surrounded on three sides by rugged rocky peaks, harbours two small lakes bordered by patches of rhododendron bushes.

The Nuranang Chu emanates from one of the lakes and is joined by another stream coming in from the direction of Kya-la to the east. Three kilometres to the northwest of Se-la Top, the valley begins to slant down towards Nuranang, which is another seven kilometres away. The crystal clear waters of the Nuranang Chu run down a sharply constricted valley with lightly wooded slopes on either side. The road then begins to drop sharply towards Jang, which is a Monpa village on the northern slopes overlooking the Tawang Chu (also known as the Mago Chu) down below.

The premature withdrawal from Jang after last light the previous day had created a void between the Indian and Chinese positions. 4 Garhwal Rifles, after blowing up the bridge, had climbed up to Nuranang but left most of their heavy equipment behind, including four mortars. The artillery, too, in their headlong rush out of Jang, had left behind critical equipment without which the accuracy of the remaining six mountain guns was seriously hampered. Besides 1 Sikh and the three companies of 4 Garhwal Rifles, there were also elements of 13 Dogra between Nuranang and Se-la Top on the morning of 25 October. Meanwhile, from the southern side, 4 Sikh LI commanded by Lieutenant Colonel R. B. Nanda had also started to arrive at Se-la.

Through the previous day and most of the night, 1 Sikh had been busy with the preparation of defences at Se-la. The arrival of Harbaksh

Singh and the new GOC, Anant Pathania, at Se-la Top during the morning hours sent a wave of excitement through the troops, who were still smarting from being pulled out of Bum-la just when they felt things were getting interesting. By late afternoon, 4 Garhwal had deployed below Nuranang with the 3.7-inch guns positioned next to the battalion's defences. A company of 4 Sikh LI under the command of Captain Rosario, a Goan officer who not only spoke fluent Punjabi but also sported a turban, deployed in the Twin Lakes area.

Harbaksh and Anant Pathania were briefed by Palit, after which the corps commander did an independent reconnaissance of his own with Brigadier Nandi Lal, the commander of 62 Brigade. Harbaksh would have been aware that Bogey Sen, the Eastern Army Commander, as well as the staff of IV Corps, favoured falling back on the Bomdila axis, and that stocking Se-la to take on the Chinese would be a huge exercise in logistics. The BGS IV Corps, Brigadier K. K. Singh, would categorically maintain in later interviews, that it was the COAS, Thapar, and the DMO, Palit, who opted for Se-la as the defensive line against the advice of commanders on the spot.

The erstwhile GOC, Niranjan Prasad, had met Harbaksh at Dirang Dzong and briefed him independently of Palit. By the evening of 25 October, Harbaksh Singh put an end to all ambiguity, stating that the defensive line would indeed be drawn at Se-la. The corps commander then returned to Senge Dzong from where he left for Tezpur by helicopter.

Palit was relieved; his arguments in favour of Se-la had carried the day. Accompanying Palit on the trip to Dirang Dzong and Se-la was Major General Mohinder S. Pathania (Anant Pathania's cousin), who was at a loose end as he waited in Tezpur to take command of 2 Division that was being hurriedly raised for the defence of the Lohit Valley. As soon as Harbaksh Singh had taken off from Senge Dzong, Mohinder took Palit aside and told him that Anant was not at all happy about being stationed at such a high altitude and was in fact considering locating his Division HQ at Dirang, which was at a height of only 4,900 feet.

Palit now had a talk with Anant Pathania to convince him of the tactical sense of staying at Se-la. Describing the scene, Palit says: 'I spoke at length to Anant about the tactical and logistical potential of the Senge-Se-la complex and stressed that the camp we were at was the ideal place for his Division HQ. "You can direct the battle from here as well as keep an eye on the stocking up process. So long as you remain here, sitting astride this road, no one is going to retreat beyond this point. You establish yourself here, Anant, and we will send you all your requirements," I assured him. I cautioned him to secure the heights overlooking the passes he held, such as Kya-la and Poshing-la.'

Ever since the morning of 23 October the army chief had virtually abrogated all tactical decision-making pertaining to NEFA to his DMO—his role seems to have been confined to finding replacements for officers who had to be sacked after the Nam Ka Chu debacle. Showing rare guts in the face of perceived opinion, the chief had taken the decision to replace Bijji Kaul as the IV Corps Commander with Harbaksh Singh. His next choice, however, was not as inspired, for to all officers and men present at Se-la Top on 25 October, one thing was quite obvious: the new GOC of 4 Division, Anant Pathania, did not want to be there. For a GOC of a division to be given a 'pep talk' by a brigadier junior to him would be laughable if it wasn't so tragic.

With 7 Brigade no longer in the equation, a new ORBAT (order of battle) was being drawn up. The moment 1 Sikh and 4 Garhwal Rifles had fallen back on Jang, 4 Division HQ had suddenly woken up to the presence of 62 Brigade HQ which had also fallen back as a part of the general exodus from Tawang. Both these infantry battalions were taken away from 4 Artillery Brigade and placed under 62 Brigade that was, on 25 October, tasked with holding Se-la. However, unknown to the two hapless commanders of 4 Artillery Brigade and 62 Brigade, their fate had been linked to Niranjan Prasad's unceremonious ouster. Brigadier G. S. Gill took over 4 Artillery Brigade from Brigadier Kalyan Singh. Nandi Lal, who had accompanied Harbaksh and been a part of Palit's briefings, was shown the door and replaced by Brigadier Hoshiar Singh. The prime responsibility of 62 Brigade was to hold the new defence line at Se-la. Apart from 4 Sikh LI and 1 Sikh, Hoshiar Singh would also have 13 Dogra, 2 Sikh LI and 4 Garhwal Rifles under his command. Just why Nandi Lal was getting the axe, since at no stage had he any troops under his command, was something no one felt the need to ask.

Thapar's new policy of having only highly decorated soldiers commanding formations in NEFA was absurd. At that point of time, Hoshiar Singh was the Colonel Administration (Col Adam) at the National Defence Academy in Khadakwasla, Poona. By Thapar's specious reasoning, the fact that Hoshiar Singh had been awarded an Indian Order of Merit, the Indian Distinguished Service Medal and the French Croix de Guerre twenty years ago when he was a subedar in the Rajputana Rifles, now qualified him to fight the Chinese at 14,000 feet as a brigade commander. The gallant soldier was given an additional star, and with all the cadets, officers and the commandant lined up at Pashan Gate, the NDA gave Hoshiar a send-off fit for a saviour. On 29 October, Hoshiar Singh reached Se-la Top and 62 Brigade said goodbye to Nandi Lal. The last man there who had a vague idea of the terrain had been told to go home.

While the focus was mainly on the Kameng Sector and the impending battle to be fought at Se-la, Army HQ was grappling with the larger picture. In the northern extremities of Kashmir, the first Chinese attacks in the Daulat Beg Oldi, Chip Chap and Galwan valleys had more or less coincided with the assault across the Nam Ka Chu on 20 October. Here too the Chinese were being allowed to call the shots. Static Indian posts, mostly held by a platoon or a section, were taken out one by one by the Chinese. By 23 October, Indian troops at Srijap on the northern bank of the Pangong Tso were under fire, and the entire sector extending from Chushul to Demchok was being threatened.

In the Eastern Sector, apart from Kameng, the threat of the Siliguri chicken neck being cut off by a thrust down the Chumbi Valley either through Sikkim or Bhutan had to be considered. In addition, there was also a possibility of Chinese attacks in the central part of NEFA where a string of Assam Rifles posts existed. To the extreme east at the tri-junction of China, India and Burma, the Chinese had already launched an attack on Kibithu on 20 October, pushing the Indians back towards Walong. There was now a real danger of an encircling move that would threaten Hayuliang, Lohitpur and Tezu.

The Pakistan factor could not be completely ruled out either. Insurgency in Nagaland had more or less tied down 23 Division plus a number of Assam Rifles troops. General Thapar and Army HQ now had to find the troops to support Harbaksh Singh and Anant Pathania on Se-la. At the commencement of hostilities, 62 Brigade had moved from Ramgarh but had got splintered while still on the move. 65 Brigade (newly raised at Secunderabad; it had only two battalions) had already been moved north.

Bogey Sen was unwilling to move any troops out of Nagaland. The army chief, however, decided to pull out most of 23 Division which was considered to be a reserve formation against the Chinese. Thapar was also willing to gamble that the Western Sector against Pakistan would remain dormant. Accordingly, one brigade of 17 Division was ordered to move post-haste from Punjab to the Siliguri area to be followed by the rest of the division. One brigade from Nagaland was asked to deploy around the Daranga area (bordering southeast Bhutan), while another was moved as a corps reserve to Tezpur. 11 Brigade, then stationed around Imphal, was asked to move immediately to Walong where it would relieve 5 Brigade which in turn would look after central NEFA. A new division was to be set up, headquartered in the Tinsukia area to look after central and eastern NEFA. Finally, Thapar also decided to move armour into the area—he decided to allocate a light regiment equipped with the French AMX-13 tanks to IV Corps while another regiment with the relatively heavier Sherman tanks was to be stationed at Siliguri.

Thapar's decisive and bold approach immediately after the Nam Ka Chu debacle was heartening. He made most of the decisions while he was in Tezpur on 23 October. Officers observing the chief were pleasantly surprised to see him act this decisively, for in Delhi he seemed to be perpetually incapable of taking any firm decision. He also decided to immediately move 20 Division, situated in the Ranchi-Ramgarh area, into Sikkim with its existing two brigades, which was to be further augmented with 202 Brigade from Calcutta. Both 17 and 20 Divisions were to operate directly under Eastern Command as a stopgap measure. XXXIII Corps was to shift its location immediately from Shillong to Siliguri. And in the west, 3 Division was to be raised with 114 Brigade (with four battalions) to be located at Chushul and 70 Brigade (with 2 battalions plus a troop of armoured cars) to be located at Chumathang to look after the Dumti-Demchok area. 163 Brigade was ordered to move up from the Kashmir Valley to Leh for its close defence.

At Se-la, apart from 62 and 4 Artillery Brigade, two more brigades would be placed under Anant Pathania's command. 65 Brigade would also get a new commander in Brigadier A. S. Cheema. This formation consisting of 4 Rajput and 19 Maratha Light Infantry (MLI), was given the task of defending Senge Dzong. Finally, 48 Brigade under Brigadier Gurbaksh Singh, consisting of 1 Madras, 5 Guards and 1 Sikh LI, would be given the responsibility of defending Bomdila in the rear.

Unfortunately, Thapar's forceful behaviour didn't continue into the third day. On 28 October, the Intelligence Bureau chief had let it be known to select officers in the corridors of power that Lieutenant General Kaul was to take back command of IV Corps and Harbaksh Singh would be moved laterally to take over XXXIII Corps from Lieutenant General Umrao Singh. According to the IB chief, Nehru had told Thapar to implement the order as Kaul was to be pronounced medically fit by the doctors in the next twenty-four hours. Thapar had, according to Mullik, agreed without any semblance of protest. The fact that the IB had intimated the government that the troops in Eastern Command, from the ranks to JCOs and officers, all considered Kaul something of a joke, especially after his unceremonious flight from Nam Ka Chu, didn't seem to have changed anyone's mind.

General Pran Thapar's failure to stand up to Nehru on what would prove to be yet another disastrous decision may have had something to do with another rumour doing the rounds—the impending decision to sack both Thapar and Bogey Sen. On the morning of 28 October, Palit, had been called to brief the defence minister. '…just as I rose to take my leave, he abruptly asked, "Do you think we ought to bring back retired generals to take charge of the war?" The question was as unexpected as it was loaded and he had asked it with a sly look on his face. I realized at once what he was alluding to. There had been a great deal of talk as well as suggestions in the press that the government should recall Thimayya and Thorat to service to take command of the army. I pretended to misunderstand his meaning and replied that in times of war it was always open to the government to recall retired officers from the reserve list.

'"I was talking about *generals*," he snapped. "They say we need some retired generals to fight the Chinese."'

Chapter 9

THE BATTLE OF WALONG

THE WALONG SECTOR

The Lohit River Valley marks the eastern extreme of the Assam Himalayas. The river enters Indian territory at Rima, which lies just north of Kibithu, in a comparatively low altitude valley. The river then flows southward to Walong and Hayuliang before curving westwards to debouch into the plains of Assam. The Lohit is joined by the Dibang near Sadiya and, a little further to the west, by the Siang at Pasighat. From this point it is known as the Brahmaputra. Further downstream, the Subansiri and the Kameng add their substantial volume of water before it meets the Manas (Nyamjang Chu) after which it curves south again into Bangladesh where it goes by the name of Jamuna.

The Lohit Frontier Division, unlike Kameng at the other end of the spectrum, was an even bigger logistical nightmare. The 1950 earthquake had completely destroyed the Lohit River Valley, erasing even the existing few footpaths that connected the region to the rest of the world. Without the grassy runway that could accommodate small aircraft on the west bank of the river, it is doubtful if the Assam Rifles would have made any headway in the region.

The Mishmi and the Zekhring are the main tribes of this thinly populated region of less than 20,000 people. Fed by many rivers, this is a fertile area and agriculture is the predominant occupation.

The Digaru Mishmi, popularly known as the Taraon, are concentrated around Tezu, Hayuliang, Chaglagam and Goiliang of Lohit Frontier Division. There is a belief that the Mishmi are in fact indigenous people. This is borne out by the places of origin recited by the priests during the performance of rituals. The Nim-kwey cave is at the confluence of the Lohit and Tidding Rivers, about forty kilometres from Hayuliang and sixty-five kilometres from Tezu. It is sacred and central to their religious beliefs. They are jhum cultivators as well as adept craftsman and weavers. Their settlements are organized clan-wise and they collectively own the village land. Members of the clan can freely cultivate, hunt, fish, gather fruit and firewood on village land. The Mishmis share a physical boundary with Tibet, but other than trade, they had little to do with their northern neighbours who over the ages were quite content to leave them alone.

Previously known as the Meyor, the Zekhring inhabit the Walong and Kibithu circles of the region and have a small population that even today barely touches the four-figure mark. Originally from Tibet they fled their homeland in the wake of the floods that devastated the Chamdo region and also to escape persecution by the Tibetan authorities. Migrating into the Lohit Valley at the beginning of the twentieth century they faced fierce opposition from the Mishmi. Unable to withstand the incessant attacks both in the Dri and Mathun valleys, they extended allegiance to the major clans, paying tributes to their heads. The Imu River was decided as the boundary between the two communities.

In the northeastern corner of the Lohit Frontier Division, the Diphu-la (16,850 feet) is situated some eight kilometres south of the India-Burma-Tibet tri-junction. While in the Kameng Division there was some debate on whether the McMahon Line ran along the Thagla Ridge or the Tsangdhar Ridge east of Khenzemane to the tri-junction with Bhutan, there was never any ambiguity in the case of the Lohit Frontier Division. However, in what was clearly a manufactured controversy, after 1959 the Chinese started claiming that the Dhipu-la itself was the tri-junction. According to this claim line, the crest of the Ndap range branching from Diphu-la then becomes a disputed feature. This spur acts as a dividing line between the valleys of Di Chu and Sat Ti Chu. By laying claim to the crest of the highest range from the northern side and by including Diphu-la in Greater China, approximately 740 square kilometres then become disputed as the Ndap range extends up to Walong.

The entire Lohit Frontier Division is bounded by the Assam Himalayas to its north and east. The McMahon Line running along the watershed divides the Lat Ti Chu on the Tibetan side and the Di Chu on the NEFA side of the crest line. From the Diphu-la, extending southwest and then southeast is the Patkoi Range, a mountain wall that separates the Lohit Division from Burma. To the west, another mountain range acts as the boundary between the Miji Mishmi and the Idu Mishmi, the latter residing primarily in the Dibang River catchment. To the south, a third range hems in the sector, giving the tract a bowl-like appearance from the air.

The surrounding hills around the Lohit River Valley are a maze of spurs, their ridges separating innumerable small streams that flow into the main body of the Lohit. The ridges slope down to either flank of the river, creating lateral natural defensive barriers against any intruding enemy. Each one of these spurs was of tremendous tactical value. With a 2 Assam Rifles post guarding the immediate border at Kibithu, the Indians could optimize their defensive capability considerably by developing delaying defences on these features.

This natural advantage was, however, offset by the logistical difficulties of moving men and supplies into the area. The deadly earthquake of 1950 had decimated the existing primitive trails that existed in the region. In addition, the Lohit Frontier Division was covered with thick forests; dense bamboo forests in the lower reaches give way to broad-leaved evergreen tall trees. As the altitude increases, oak, rhododendron and pine take over, before the advent of spruce and juniper forests in the immediate vicinity of Kibithu.

In the 1860s and 1870s, Captain Cooper had tried to open a trade route to China but had failed. In 1910, a Chinese general had forced the local Mishmi to construct a road to India following the alignment of the Lohit River, but after days of hard labour, gave up the attempt. This resulted in the Rima track being the main line of communication. It ran along the right bank of the Lohit, connecting the Assam plains with Hayuliang with Manikaran and Walong. Steep and narrow, it was difficult going for even pack animals, as many bamboo stairways had to be negotiated before getting to Kibithu. The distance from Walong to Kibithu was thirty kilometres, and from there, the McMahon Line was five kilometres further to the north. Beyond the frontier were two Tibetan villages, Sama and Tattoo, after which lay Rima, a Tibetan administrative base.

On the opposite side of the river was another, more difficult track. In the lower reaches, the gradient was extremely steep and owing to the thick jungles, it was seldom used. Across the river from Walong was a small hamlet called Tinai and further north lay the villages of Dong and Kahoo, the latter being in the Di Chu Valley. Eventually, this track would link up with the western track at Rima. Apart from these two routes, a third track entered the Lohit Frontier Division from Tazung Dam. This track after negotiating the Dhipu-la, dropped down to a lake before reaching Hot Springs in the Di Chu Valley (a two-day march). It would take a further two days to reach Kahoo, from where the track followed the Di Chu to the Sangam at Kibithu where it was connected to the western track by a steel rope bridge.

Kibithu lay 190 kilometres from the road head near Tezu. With even mules stubbornly refusing to negotiate them, both the western and eastern tracks were rarely used either by the Assam Rifles personnel or the army, which inducted 2 Rajput under the command of Lieutenant Colonel M. S. Rikh into Walong towards the end of 1959. The battalion was then a part of 5 Infantry Brigade that had its Brigade HQ in Aalong. A small grass strip had been constructed on the west bank of the Lohit at Walong on which small Otter aircraft could land and take off. These aircraft, along with airdrops by other transport aircraft of the IAF, were the lifeline that supported the entire garrison at Walong and the forward posts at Kibithu.

Captain Ashok Kalyan Verma moved in with the first company of 2 Rajput into Walong after the battalion had detrained at Missamari and spent a few months doing jungle training at Charduar. After a harrowing flight and an equally frightening landing at Walong, he recalls:

> At Walong the river divided the battalion's deployment into two halves. One could only get to the companies on the east side by crossing the 800-foot-wide river suspended upside down on a half-inch thick steel cable. This frightening contraption was called the 'twine' and it consisted of a small wooden piece to which one was lashed onto with raw leather straps.
>
> Having gone ahead of the battalion, the initial reconnaissance of Walong was done by me. I would later be associated with the construction of the defences and bunkers. There was plenty of pine for timber and we had ample time at our disposal. It was great fun toiling with the men. As the other companies started arriving and machine guns got allotted, the work expanded. We also made our own small arms ranges and fired our weapons to stay in practice. Altogether, a very typical period of infantry work. Being separated by the river and the terrain, we officers were left very much on our own.

The most prominent feature in the Walong Sector is Point (PT) 14470, about sixteen kilometres to the northwest. Short of the feature was Trijunction (13,250 feet); to its immediate east were the connecting spurs of Yellow Pimple and Green Pimple—the three features together forming a triangle with Yellow Pimple being the northern apex. While facing north, to the right of Green Pimple were Patrol Base, the Maha Plateau, Mithun and finally The Ladders on the western track to Kibithu itself. On the east bank of the river were High Plateau, Dong Hill, Dong Peak and Dakota Hill.

Other prominent landmarks in the immediate vicinity of Walong were the East Ridge, Yepak Plateau, Avalanche Hill, Mor Post, Firm Base, West Ridge and the landing strip on the west bank of the river. Approximately three kilometres to the north of the Maha Plateau is Ashi Hill, south of which flows the Namti River.

Further to the north on the frontier, northwest of Kibithu is Glei-la (12,820 feet). Across the boundary in Tibet is Sama while a kilometre to the south of Kibithu is the drop zone. On the east bank of the Lohit is the Sangam dominated by the Hump, while to its east is the Dichu Ridge. About half a mile to the north of the Dichu Ridge is the McMahon Ridge, the dominating feature of which is Dome. Along the Kahoo axis up the Di Chu valley, beyond the Hot Springs, was the Jachap post manned by the Assam Rifles.

THE FIGHTING AT KIBITHU

The Chinese had first intruded into the Lohit Frontier Division in October 1957 when troops had come downriver all the way to Walong. On being challenged, the party returned to Tibet. On 28 September 1958, an officer with fifty soldiers advanced into the Di Chu Valley up to Jachap. Subsequently, they continued to send small probing parties into the area, culminating with the official note handed over by the government of the People's Republic of China stating that: 'Monyul, the area of Lower Tsayul including Walong, not only was inhabited by Tibetans, but was always under the jurisdiction of Tibet. British troops unlawfully invaded and occupied Walong in 1944, and it was only after the local Tibet government sent a representative of the dzongpen of Sangacho Dzong to make representations that the troops withdrew.'

This was typical Chinese misinformation. First, the entire belt, though sparsely populated, was the home of the Miji Mishmi with perhaps a scattering of Tibetans, if at all. Second, unlike the Tawang region where the writ of the Tibetan dzongpen carried weight, in the Lohit Frontier Division it had no influence. These incursions, therefore, had prompted Army HQ to move 2 Rajput into Walong to support the single Assam Rifles wing at Kibithu. Even if the Chinese considered Diphu-la to be the tri-junction, as a matter of policy, they did not like to intrude into 'disputed territory'. The intrusions into the Lohit Frontier Division were interpreted as a clear indication that the Chinese would sooner or later try to move troops into the area, just as they had in the Aksai Chin region.

2 Rajput had spent three years in Walong, building and siting the

defences on either flank of the Lohit. The Rajputs, who were to move to Mathura after their two-and-a-half year tenure, handed over to 6 Kumaon, under the command of Lieutenant Colonel C. N. Madiah, towards the end of March 1962. Eastern Command ordered the setting up of three new posts on the surrounding heights, each of which was at an altitude of over 9,800 feet. The first of these guarded the entrance to the Chu Valley and was situated sixteen kilometres west of Kibithu. The Chu post had its own DZ, while the other two new posts were in the Di Chu Valley and had a common DZ. Two additional platoons from 7 Assam Rifles (based in Jairampur) had to be flown in to man these new posts tucked away in the watershed between India and Burma. To further facilitate these changes, a second wing of the Assam Rifles was set up at Hot Springs.

Even before tension started to build up over the Dhola post on the Nam Ka Chu at the other end of NEFA, forward observation posts of the Assam Rifles started reporting a heavy build-up on the Chinese side near both Sama and Rima. Madiah was ordered by Brigadier G. S. Gill, commander of 5 Infantry Brigade, to move to Kibithu with his Tac HQ along with Charlie Company. He would function as the Kibithu sub-sector commander. Madiah immediately decided to deploy Alpha Company on the Dichu Ridge. Bravo Company was ordered to move to the East Ridge while Delta Company was also asked to move out of Walong and take up positions near The Ladders.

Alpha and Bravo Companies of 4 Sikh had started to fly into Walong by end September to fill the void created by the sudden advance of 6 Kumaon to set up the new posts. This battalion, hitherto a part of 62 Infantry Brigade, had moved from Ramgarh to Jorhat along with 2/8 GR, where it was placed under the command of 5 Infantry Brigade. The commanding officer of 4 Sikh, Lieutenant Colonel A. Behl, was appointed the Walong sub-sector commander. Alpha Company was asked to deploy in the Dong area while Bravo took up position on the Maha Plateau with one platoon at The Ladders.

The headlong rush of 6 Kumaon towards Kibithu the moment reports of the Chinese build-up started coming in underlines the lack of cohesive thinking even in early October 1962. The concept of Thorat's defensive line, spelt out so lucidly in Exercise Lal Qila, had obviously not permeated beyond the four walls of the conference room in Lucknow. Brigadier Gill, stationed in Along, would have merely acted as a post office to convey orders to Madiah. By 4 October, Lieutenant General Umrao Singh and with him HQ XXXIII Corps had handed over responsibility for NEFA to the newly founded IV Corps under the command of Lieutenant General Bijji Kaul.

So the question is who gave the order for 6 Kumaon to move to Kibithu? Both Kaul and Niranjan Prasad were embroiled in the events at Nam Ka Chu at this time and could not have given the order for 6 Kumaon's advance. Given the fact that the entire thrust at the time was 'to get a move on' and move forward to the Thagla Ridge and evict the Chinese, the order given to 6 Kumaon was issued in the same spirit of no regard for the actual ground conditions and in all probability originated from the BGS of the newly set up IV Corps, Brigadier K. K. Singh, who was trying to direct the battle from Tezpur.

The area ahead of Walong was being held by the Assam Rifles and Madiah and his battalion should ideally have remained in control of the defences around Walong. Had the Chinese pressed forward, the Assam Rifles platoons and A Wing would have fallen back to where the Kumaonis were waiting in prepared defences. Given the terrain and the narrow boxed-in terrain of the Lohit Frontier Division, regardless of the quantum of force brought to bear by the Chinese, they would have found Walong very difficult to approach, let alone capture.

Instead, Madiah was moved forward into relatively unfamiliar ground to take on the Chinese on the crest lines of the watershed itself. 4 Sikh, flying in and manning battle stations on features they did not know existed until they were physically standing on them, were equally at sea. The thoughtless decision to advance destabilized the entire sector to such an extent that it was almost impossible to recover. The advantage the Indians had as defenders in favourable conditions was squandered even before the first shots were fired.

Eventually, with no effective command and control set up, the ad hoc Kibithu garrison—6 Kumaon and the assorted platoons of 2 and 7 Assam Rifles—would exist in a vacuum. For a sector that was deemed to be as important as the Kameng Frontier Division, Lohit was treated in a most cavalier fashion.

On 18 October (two days prior to the Chinese attack on the Nam Ka Chu) a Kumaoni patrol noticed a Chinese party consisting of two officers and fifty men along with a lama guide occupying PT 10000 to the northwest of Kibithu. Just below this height was PT 9000 where the Kumaonis CO, Madiah, deployed the Assam Rifles platoon. According to the existing 'rules of engagement' only Assam Rifles troops could confront the Chinese, a factor that made the 6 Kumaon move forward even more puzzling. The next day, as the two sides faced off, Madiah decided to reinforce the McMahon Ridge with a platoon from Alpha Company under the command of Major S. G. Naygam. He also asked Delta Company under the command of Captain T. S. Pall to move from The Ladders to Kibithu while Bravo Company under Major B. N. Sharma was told to move from the East Ridge to the Kibithu DZ. Pall would be in position by 20 October while Sharma was expected to reach the DZ on 22 October, thus pulling the entire battalion into Kibithu.

The news of the Chinese assault on 7 Infantry Brigade on the Nam Ka Chu on 20 October combined with the steady build-up of Chinese forces in the area around Sama clearly indicated that the Chinese were preparing themselves for a major assault. An uneasy calm prevailed till 7 p.m. on 21 October when a few Very lights arched into the night sky. A barrage of mortar and artillery fire simultaneously targeted both the McMahon Ridge and The Top in the Dichu Valley. After half an hour of intense shelling, Chinese infantry began their advance on the two Indian posts.

The Chinese were met with both rifle and 3-inch mortar fire, the latter being directed by Naik Bahadur Singh. The Indians were always most effective when they fought the Chinese from their fixed positions, the .303 Lee Enfield rifles taking a deadly toll of the enemy. The first attack on McMahon Ridge fizzled out, but it was followed by a second wave as the Chinese moved forward in overwhelming numbers. Bahadur Singh had by then abandoned the mortars and had grabbed the LMG from the two gunners of his section who had both been wounded. Fighting ferociously, he attracted heavy fire and was hit by a machine gun burst that killed him instantly.

After four hours of fighting, Major Naygam had also been wounded. Surprisingly, at that stage, casualties on the Indian side were relatively light—three killed and six wounded—a phenomenon that was to repeat itself whenever the Indians fought from their prepared defences (1 Sikh at Bum-la and 4 Garhwal Rifles at Nuranang). The fighting had by then spread to a third post, The Hump, which was occupied by a section of Assam Rifles. Naygam then ordered his men to break contact with the Chinese, withdraw to Sangam and regroup on the west bank of the Lohit.

By 7 a.m. on 22 October, Alpha Company along with the Assam Rifles platoon, plus the personnel from Hot Springs and Jachap who had been earlier ordered to fall back on Kibithu by Madiah, crossed the steel wire bridge and then destroyed it. For the time being, this effectively secured the right flank of the Kibithu garrison, for the Chinese could not cross the Lohit.

Others were not so lucky. The Chu post on the western flank, manned by a platoon of Assam Rifles, under the command of Naib Subedar Ao, was also attacked around the same time the previous evening. This post, out on an extreme limb, did not have the means to withstand the Chinese who overran the post, killing most of the men. Those who succeeded in getting away proceeded south, crossed a mountain range and after a month (during which time Subedar Ao died of exposure and fatigue) reached Hayuliang via Minuathang.

Madiah was now in a quandary. The Chu post having fallen the night before, his west flank was exposed. The Chinese were entrenched just northwest of him on PT 10000 from where they were directing accurate artillery fire at his positions in Kibithu itself. The successful withdrawal from the east flank and the destruction of the steel wire bridge had given him temporary respite, but it would only be a matter of time before the Chinese found a way to cross the river. After discussing the matter on the telephone with Brigadier Gill who had arrived at Walong, Madiah asked for further orders. Madiah then received a message telling him that the Walong/Kibithu sector was no longer his responsibility and that IV Corps would henceforth directly issue all further orders to all sub-units. By this time, HQ 4 Infantry Division had virtually ceased to exist and Niranjan Prasad was trekking back to Tawang from Zimithang.

A short while later, 6 Kumaon received orders from HQ IV Corps telling them to withdraw from Kibithu at last light and fall back on Walong.

THE DEPLOYMENT AT WALONG

Madiah now started to withdraw from Kibithu. Just then, Major Sharma's Bravo Company was approaching Kibithu when it was stopped and told to turn back. It would now be the advance guard for the rest of the battalion that was strung out behind them. Despite the enveloping darkness, the Chinese continued to harass the Kumaonis. Charlie Company under Captain P. N. Bhatia was entrusted with destroying all the stores and bringing up the rear. While the rest of the battalion was to go past Ashi Hill into Walong at the end of the twenty-four-hour march, Delta Company was to halt there and take up a screen position, under the command of Lieutenant Bikram Singh.

While the Kumaonis were winding their way back on 23 October, rapid changes were taking place in the ORBAT of IV Corps. As we have seen earlier in the book, Kaul was lying in his sickbed while 4 Division was in the midst of abandoning Tawang and falling back to Dirang Dzong.

The GOC, Niranjan Prasad, had been sacked and his replacement, Anant Pathania was not in on the Lohit Frontier Division loop anymore. It was decided that 5 Infantry Brigade needed to focus on the middle sector (Subansiri and Siang), so Walong had been de-linked from there and put under the charge of Corps HQ, but this was changed the next day and the battalion was placed under 181 Brigade, which at the time was being commanded by Brigadier J. C. Hartley, Military Cross. In less than thirty-six hours, ever since the fighting with the Chinese began, 6 Kumaon had been under three different formations.

Apart from the two companies of 4 Sikh that had been left holding Walong after the Kumaonis had moved up to Kibithu, the airlift of Charlie and Delta Companies had been completed by the morning of 23 October. In addition, the forward elements of 2/8 GR had also started arriving in Walong. With the fallback of 6 Kumaon by the evening, Madiah and Behl could draw up fresh plans for the defence of Walong.

Meanwhile, at Ashi Hill, Lieutenant Bikram Singh was relishing the opportunity to ambush the advancing Chinese. There was a small stream in front of Ashi Hill, known as the Namti Nullah across which there was a suspension bridge. Instead of destroying the bridge, Bikram Singh had his men remove the wooden planks. Men who were with him recall how the officer went about positioning each and every man and sighting his weapon, telling them over and over that no one was to fire until he personally gave the order. Because of the restricted field of fire, Bikram concentrated his entire firepower at the other end of the bridge.

At 3 a.m. on 25 October the Chinese column reached the suspension bridge opposite Ashi Hill. Only one man could traverse it at a time, and the leading Chinese scout started to cross the river. Halfway through, because of the missing planks, he fell into the torrent below. His desperate shouts for help resulted in many Chinese soldiers switching on their flashlights, thereby exposing their positions. Bikram Singh fired a Very light, at which point all the Kumaonis opened fire. Delta Company, supported by mortars and MMGs, turned the tables on the Chinese who were caught unawares at the narrow fording point. It was estimated that at least seventy Chinese soldiers were killed or wounded, while Delta Company had three killed, one wounded and one missing, presumed dead. An hour later, Madiah told Bikram Singh to break contact and fall back on Walong.

On their return, 6 Kumaon had deployed at Walong. 4 Sikh's Battalion HQ had been established on the West Ridge. Alpha Company commanded by Major P. M. Samvatsar was at Dakota Hill; Charlie Company under

Major Sandhu was deployed on the High Plateau while Bravo Company commanded by Major Harbans Singh was holding Maha Plateau with one platoon at Mithun. Delta Company under the command of Major Malik was deployed at Lachhman Ridge, while the battalion mortars were on the reverse slope of Dakota Hill. In addition, two platoons of 2/8 GR had been pushed north to cover The Ladders, while a third platoon was at Maha Plateau with Bravo Company of 4 Sikh. A second Gorkha company was deployed on the East Bank under the command of Madiah. The two wings of the Assam Rifles were patrolling the flanks of the sector.

By the evening, news had filtered in that Lieutenant General Harbaksh Singh had taken over IV Corps from the ailing Bijji Kaul. The officers and men of 4 Sikh in particular were extremely upbeat, for Harbaksh Singh was their Colonel of the Regiment. The new brigade commander, Brigadier Hartley, too was from the Sikh Regiment, which meant that the battalion would be that much more under the scanner. Even though no one in Walong was aware of the full extent of the disaster that had befallen 7 Infantry Brigade, there was a general sense of relief that Bijji Kaul would not be leading them into battle.

Ever since Delta Company's successful engagement at Ashi Hill, the Chinese had been lurking behind it, and they continued to fire at Mithun and the Maha Plateau from there. Two Chinese jitter parties had probed the Walong defences without much success. During the night of 26-27 October, the Chinese launched a determined attack on the Mithun track. The Sikhs were waiting for them and they cut down the advancing enemy with accurate rifle fire. However, the Chinese, desperate for some success in the Walong Sector, attacked again. To meet this developing threat, nineteen-year-old Sepoy Kewal Singh burst out of the defences and, like a man possessed, took on the Chinese in hand-to-hand combat, fighting until he was gunned down. This attack too was beaten back and the Chinese once again withdrew into the lee of Ashi Hill to regroup and reorganize.

Later in the morning, Harbaksh and Hartley landed at Walong in a Mi-4 helicopter. The failed Chinese attack on Mithun had sent the battalion's morale sky high and the officers presented two Chinese automatic rifles that had been recovered earlier in the morning to the corps commander. Meanwhile, the advance party of 3/3 GR (affectionately known as Thud Thud) along with its commanding officer, Lieutenant Colonel Yadav, had arrived in Walong after a gruelling march from Hayuliang; they immediately moved across the river to the eastern side to do their initial reconnaissance of the area.

Meanwhile, Madiah briefed the two senior officers, going over the events in Kibithu. After a quick look around, Harbaksh Singh said that in his opinion, 6 Kumaon, 4 Sikh and the two wings of Assam Rifles were adequate for the defence of Walong, which apparently could be transformed into an impenetrable 'defence box'. According to him, 2/8 GR was surplus, and he issued orders for 3/3 GR to return to Hayuliang immediately.

This decision of Harbaksh Singh is yet another one of those unexplained mysteries of the 1962 conflict. Perhaps the corps commander actually believed that Walong was not defendable. According to the Thorat Plan, the main Indian defences in the Lohit Frontier Division were to have been at Hayuliang. If indeed Harbaksh was looking at fighting the Chinese at Hayuliang, only then is it possible to understand why he not only ordered 3/3 GR to turn back but also gave orders to extricate the two companies of 2/8 GR that were even then engaged in fighting the Chinese at The Ladders with 4 Sikh.

The decision to raise 2 Mountain Division was taken on 24 October in Army HQ. The official history says Major General Mohinder Pathania, until then commanding 23 Infantry Division in Nagaland under XXXIII Corps, had been moved laterally to take over 2 Mountain Division, which was to be a part of IV Corps, on 25 October itself. He is said to have visited Walong the next day. This is most definitely an error, for Pathania along with the DMO, Brigadier Palit, was on Se-la and had only returned to Tezpur later in the day on 26 October. Had he been designated GOC 2 Mountain Division, he would have almost certainly accompanied Harbaksh and Hartley to Walong.

Adding to the confusion, Nehru reinstated Bijji Kaul as GOC IV Corps on 29 October, while Harbaksh Singh was ordered to replace Umrao Singh in XXXIII Corps. On that day itself, Kaul paid a quick visit to Walong. Two days later, Mohinder Pathania was shifted from 23 Infantry Division to 2 Mountain Division, which was assuming command of the Walong Sector with immediate effect. Hartley's 181 Infantry Brigade was also removed from Walong and replaced by 11 Infantry Brigade under Brigadier N. C. Rawlley.

Whoever coined the proverb about too many cooks spoiling the broth may well have been inspired by the haphazard way in which the command structure for Walong was tampered with. This sector, it must be remembered, along with Tawang, was originally set up towards the end of 1959. Three years later, in a period of ten days, with the Chinese having overrun Kibithu, four different command structures were set up at the brigade level, and, incredible as it may sound, under two different divisions.

Mohinder Pathania immediately asked 11 Brigade to set itself up in Walong. Rawlley, the moment he landed in Walong on 31 October, asked for more troops. He also set up his HQ there and made it clear that there would be 'no withdrawal from this place'. The 'surplus' 2/8 GR companies that were fighting with 4 Sikh at The Ladders and Mithun were now to be replaced by 3/3 GR, which had earlier pulled its Tac HQ back to Hayuliang on Harbaksh's orders. Rawlley also had at his disposal a troop each from 62 Para Field Battery and the 71 Heavy Mortar Battery.

Meanwhile, the Chinese, still stuck at the Ashi Hill bottleneck, were launching daily attacks at The Ladders and at Mithun, suffering severe casualties in the process. Unable to retrieve most of their dead, they saturated the killing ground with incendiary bombs during the daylight hours, which set fire to the grass and the vegetation. The Ladders and Mithun was being referred to as Tiger's Mouth.

Soon rumours started floating about radio intercepts of Chinese commanders asking their superiors if they could fall back to Rima. However, the daily attacks and the smoke and the stench of smouldering bodies were part of the Chinese plan to keep the Indian focus on The Ladders while they cut a path up the steep cliffs from Ashi Hill to Green Pimple, Yellow Pimple and Trijunction in an attempt to get above and then behind not just The Ladders and Mithun but Maha Plateau and Lachhman Ridge as well. At the same time, the Chinese were rushing rubber boats to Ashi Hill so that a regiment could be ferried across to attack the Indians on the east bank of the Lohit as well.

Rawlley's instructions to Behl were to aggressively patrol the western flank. On the morning of 3 November, the Sikhs reported some movement in the Green and Yellow Pimple area. Having completed the track from Ashi Hill, the Chinese were in the process of occupying these positions and laying a telephone line that connected them to Ashi Hill.

Ever since 6 Kumaon's Delta Company under Lieutenant Bikram Singh had halted the Chinese advance guard on the Namti Nullah at the base of Ashi Hill, the Indians had the upper hand in the Walong sub-sector. The failure to occupy or even aggressively patrol the high ground above Lachhman Ridge was a tactical blunder. 'We never thought it was possible to get to Green Pimple from the Ashi Hill axis,' said Major Kulwant Singh of 4 Sikh, 'how the Chinese managed to actually get there was amazing. Not having occupied these features was a colossal blunder.'

Two days earlier, Rawlley had ordered another wide recce patrol to set off from the Maha Plateau under the command of Second Lieutenant P. S. Bhandari, who was occupying an observation post of 71 Heavy Mortar Battery. His party, consisting of his own men supplemented by Assam Rifles troops, had camped for the night just below the crest of the West Ridge. The next morning, they skirted past Green Pimple—so named because of the colour of the vegetation that covered it—and spent the night on Yellow Pimple. On 3 November, while dropping down towards Green Pimple, the leading scouts came under heavy automatic fire. Bhandari's party had run into the Chinese who, having occupied Green Pimple, were now moving up to Yellow Pimple. Managing to break contact, the party returned to its base by last light.

The next morning, another patrol was sent out to find out what the Chinese were up to in that area. The 4 Sikh patrol managed to position itself close to the Green Pimple track through which more than a hundred Chinese soldiers passed before they were detected. In the ensuing firefight, both sides took casualties; the patrol had one man killed and seven were wounded. They managed to extricate themselves and fall back on Lachhman Ridge.

With the Chinese having dug themselves in at Green and Yellow Pimple, Rawlley knew the equation had changed. The enemy was now dominating the Walong area and already their artillery fire had become more accurate. Green Pimple in particular dominated not only Lachhman Ridge but also Maha Plateau. Should the Chinese set up observation posts further south along the spur, they would then have complete domination of both the airstrip and the DZ as well.

On the west bank of the river, 4 Sikh was holding most of the defences and 3/3 GR was still arriving at Walong in small groups. In the mountains, especially at heights close to 12,000 feet, the rule of thumb asserts that the attacker must have a 5:1 ratio for any offensive to succeed. Looking at the maps, Rawlley realized that the Chinese, though they had managed to get to Green and Yellow Pimple, were not likely to be in strength. But with each passing day, they would be able to get more and more troops into the area. The east bank at this stage was relatively quiet. 6 Kumaon, after its advance and then withdrawal from Kibithu, had been kept out of the fighting in order to let the men recover from the exhausting ordeal. He decided, against all conventional wisdom, to pull Alpha Company out of the east bank and launch an attack in the hope of dislodging the Chinese from Green Pimple.

Rawlley briefed Captain R. K. Mathur as each man hauled across the

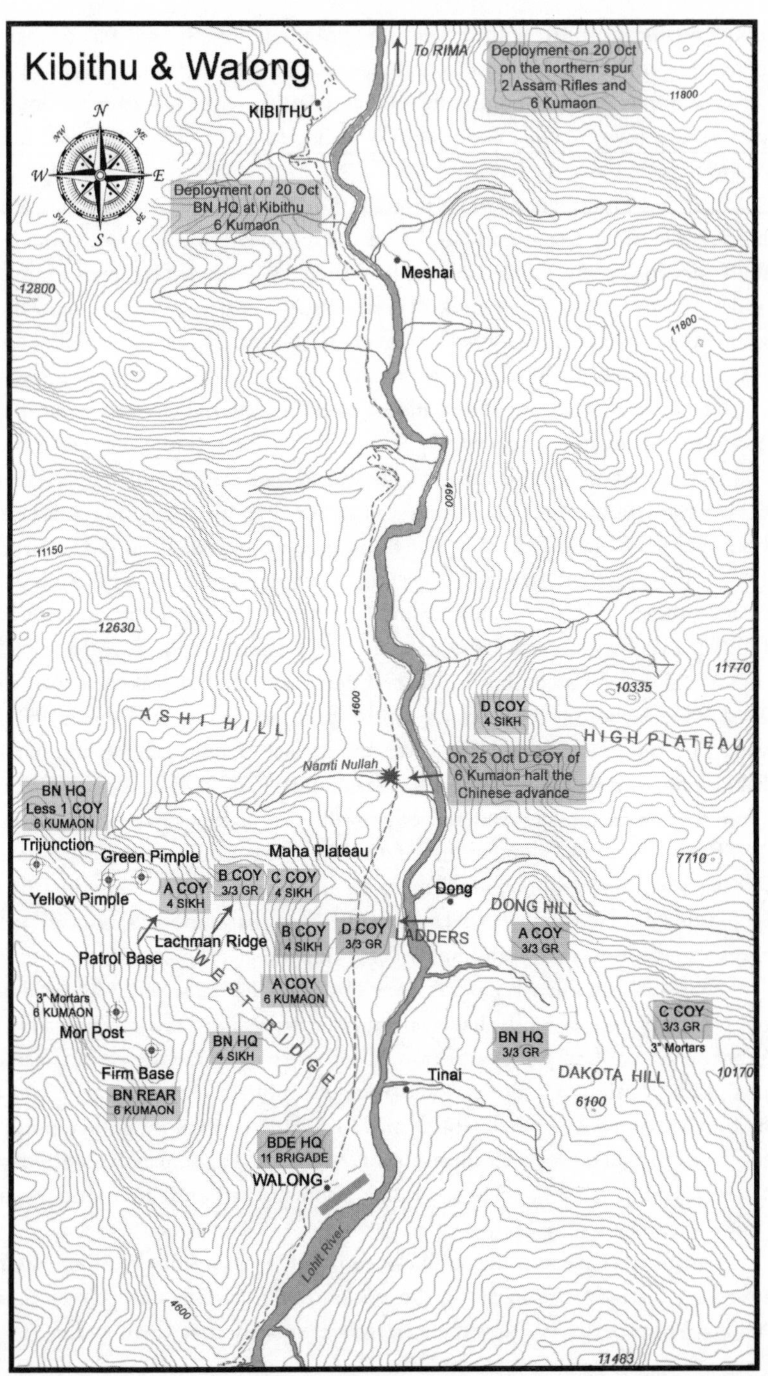

Kibithu & Walong
To RIMA
Deployment on 20 Oct on the northern spur 2 Assam Rifles and 6 Kumaon
11800
KIBITHU
N
NW
NE
W
E
SW
SE
S
Deployment on 20 Oct BN HQ at Kibithu 6 Kumaon
Meshai
12800
11800
4600
11150
12630
11770
10335
D COY 4 SIKH
4600
ASHI HILL
HIGH PLATEAU
Namti Nullah
On 25 Oct D COY of 6 Kumaon halt the Chinese advance
BN HQ Less 1 COY 6 KUMAON
Trijunction
Green Pimple
Maha Plateau
7710
A COY 4 SIKH
B COY 3/3 GR
C COY 4 SIKH
Yellow Pimple
Dong
DONG HILL
Lachman Ridge
B COY 4 SIKH
D COY 3/3 GR
LADDERS
A COY 3/3 GR
Patrol Base
WEST RIDGE
A COY 6 KUMAON
3" Mortars 6 KUMAON
Mor Post
C COY 3/3 GR
BN HQ 3/3 GR
3" Mortars
BN HQ 4 SIKH
Firm Base
Tinai
DAKOTA HILL
10170
BN REAR 6 KUMAON
6100
BDE HQ 11 BRIGADE
WALONG
Lohit River
4600
11483

Lohit on the primitive contraption known as the Flying Fox. His primary objective would be to move to the West Ridge and then climb up to the Green Pimple. After dislodging the enemy from there, he was to reconnoitre the route between Green Pimple and Ashi Hill, and, if possible, try and destroy part of the track.

On 5 November, passing through the West Ridge, Alpha Company headed out. The heavy mortars of 71 Battery were already in action by then and during the daylight hours, they fired 110 rounds on Green Pimple, Yellow Pimple and the left flank of Maha Plateau. Early morning found the men from Alpha Company still short of the objective. For some unknown reason, the mortar fire that was by then expected to be a barrage was conspicuous by its absence. The Chinese could see the Indians advancing, and they opened up from their entrenched positions. Despite the withering fire and severe casualties, the Kumaonis continued to advance, and even cleared the forward bunkers of the Chinese. Mathur and his men fought for an hour, but soon started running out of ammunition. Even if he did overrun Green Pimple, Mathur realized he was in no position to withstand the counter-attack that the Chinese would launch from their positions on Yellow Pimple. Even without any fire support, 6 Kumaon's Alpha Company had performed exceptionally, but it had no choice now but to pull back towards West Ridge where it took up a defensive position against the Chinese who were now pushing forward. However, the arrival of Delta Company under Bikram Singh forced the Chinese to break contact and pull back onto Green Pimple. Alpha Company suffered twenty-three casualties during this attack.

Patrols from 4 Sikh continued to harass the Chinese over the next few days as more troops joined them by the day. 4 Sikh by this time had established a strong base above Lachhman Ridge that considerably restricted the Chinese movements around Green Pimple.

On 9 November, 4 Dogra's Battalion HQ had reached Walong and by 11 November, 3/3 GR had concentrated at Walong. The Battalion HQ along with two companies was immediately deployed on the eastern bank of the Lohit. Alpha Company took over Dong Plateau while two platoons of Bravo Company were deployed on Dong Hill, relieving 6 Kumaon. On the western bank, Delta Company took charge of Lachhman Ridge while Charlie Company took charge of The Ladders that until then had been under command of 4 Sikh.

During this period, the Chinese too had been steadily pushing their troops in a steady stream along the track from Ashi Hill onto Green and Yellow Pimple. By 10 November it was estimated that there was a rifle company plus holding Green and Yellow Pimple.

TRIJUNCTION, YELLOW PIMPLE AND GREEN PIMPLE

The commander of 2 Mountain Division, Major General Mohinder Pathania, wanted to aggressively counter-attack in the Walong sector in the belief that by bringing in even one more infantry battalion, he would be able to push the Chinese back to Rima. The GOC outlined his plan to Bijji Kaul, who, after the reverses on the Nam Ka Chu and Tawang, was hoping to present the prime minister with a quick victory. The BGS in IV Corps HQ, Brigadier K. K. Singh, however, cautioned Kaul against this as intelligence reports were indicating that the Chinese strength in the Rima-Walong area had increased threefold.

Going against the advice of his own Corps HQ, Kaul sided with his subordinate commander. Not only did Kaul green-flag the plan, Rawlley was told by Mohinder Pathania that Kaul wanted both Green Pimple and Yellow Pimple cleared of the Chinese by 14 November, so that 2 Mountain Division could give the prime minister and the people of India a memorable present on Nehru's birthday. The GOC added that both he and Kaul would be present in HQ 11 Brigade by 12 November to supervise the operation.

Rawlley had realized by then that the Chinese, frustrated at Tiger's Mouth, were playing the waiting game. Having established a toehold on the two Pimples, they were not going to fold that easily. Walong's best bet was to fight a purely defensive battle, and try to keep the Chinese above them from advancing further south on the spur. Both Green and Yellow Pimple would have their own supply and logistics problems that could be harassed by aggressive patrolling, making it difficult to maintain. In addition, Rawlley also knew it was but a matter of time before the Chinese launched an attack on the eastern bank of the Lohit. With only part of his reinforcements in Walong, the new proposed timeline for victory was impossible.

On 11 November, a 6 Kumaon platoon under the command of Second Lieutenant A. S. Khatri was to occupy Mor Post further up on the spur and then push on towards Trijunction. This would bring the Kumaonis above and behind the Chinese at Yellow Pimple as they faced off with the Sikh positions below them on West Ridge. The patrol encountered no Chinese troops and, unopposed, found themselves on Trijunction itself. Madiah now ordered the patrol to stay hidden and take up a defensive position. He then rapidly moved his Battalion Tac HQ to Trijunction, where the handful of men consolidated their position during the night. More men joined them in small parties. This entailed climbing up from 6,000 feet to heights in the region of 13,000 feet.

Rawlley was now a man in a hurry. He moved his own Tac HQ to Mor Post and deployed 6 Kumaon's Delta Company plus one platoon under Lieutenant Bikram Singh on the West Ridge. Expecting the Kumaonis to build up sufficient strength through the night, Rawlley now ordered Behl to bring 4 Sikh into play. Hoping to dislodge the Chinese by attacking them from the rear, he wanted to synchronize the Kumaonis attack with a diversion created by 4 Sikh. Accordingly, in compliance with Brigade HQ's order, a patrol under Naib Subedar Gurnam Singh set off while it was still dark with the intention of disrupting the line of communication between Green Pimple and the Chinese firm base at Ashi Hill. The party soon located the telephone line and cut it, after which they laid an ambush and settled down to await daybreak.

Soon enough a small Chinese detachment appeared to repair the telephone line, but they were accompanied by a large protection party. Completely outnumbered, the Sikhs could only hope that they would not be discovered, but the Chinese had no difficulty in locating and surrounding the Sikhs. In the initial engagement itself, two Sikhs were killed and another eight, including Gurnam Singh, grievously wounded. Meanwhile, there was no activity from 6 Kumaon who should have been streaming down on Yellow Pimple. Badly weakened owing to his injury, the JCO realized the only hope his surviving men had was for him to break through the Chinese ring. Picking up a LMG from a dead gunner, Gurnam Singh led the charge while firing from the hip. The wild charge by a few desperate men with the war cry of 'Sat Sri Akal' scattered the Chinese who broke, but not before a Chinese soldier fired a burst at point-blank range into Gurnam's chest, killing him instantly.

From the Trijunction, Madiah could only watch helplessly, as his two companies had not reached the assembly area. By the time Bravo and Charlie minus one platoon had joined up with Alpha Company at the Trijunction, the Sikhs had withdrawn to Patrol Base, managing to extricate their dead and wounded.

Back in Walong, Kaul and Mohinder Pathania had arrived to oversee the operations. As Kaul was to record later, 'I saw the casualties coming back on stretchers. Men had been hit by small arms fire and were in great pain. Before they could be taken back to a hospital, first aid was rendered to them at the Regimental Aid Post. They had been carried for four hours over uneven rocky terrain.' Not only had 11 Brigade failed to synchronize the action between 6 Kumaon and 4 Sikh, there were no helicopters standing by to evacuate the casualties. If the wounded survived the journey back to the airstrip, they were then loaded onto the Otters that were working overtime to bring in additional troops.

Madiah had the entire day to study Yellow Pimple that was being defended by approximately a hundred Chinese troops. Their supporting heavy mortars and mountain guns were positioned on Ashi Hill. For the Kumaonis to have artillery support, the battery of mountain guns needed to be physically hauled up to Mor Post. Also, the Kumaonis troops at Trijunction only had whatever ammunition the men could carry themselves.

The attack was to be launched at 10 a.m. on 14 November using two companies that would simultaneously assault Yellow Pimple. The previous evening, the Indian artillery guns that had been hauled up to Mor Post during the day had shelled Yellow Pimple, but their fire had been sporadic and wayward. After a while, the guns had fallen silent and the officers and men huddled together in the bitter cold, trying to catch some sleep. Two thousand metres below them, to their east, was the Lohit River flowing past the Walong airfield, while to the north, the ground dropped almost vertically to the Namti Nullah.

Before the two companies earmarked for the assault had started to move towards the firm base, an advance party sent to secure the area was fired at by a Chinese patrol. This forced Madiah to advance the time for the attack by half an hour. Alpha Company under Captain B. N. Singh on the left flank began to advance along a narrow spur, reaching Yellow Pimple from above. However, to get to Yellow Pimple, the Kumaonis had to negotiate a dip in the ground, then scramble up the last forty-five metres or so. Despite their determined efforts, the men just couldn't get past this defile. The Indian artillery fire proved to be relatively ineffective and the battalion's 3-inch mortars could not provide fire support.

Bravo Company on the right flank, under the command of Major B. N. Sharma, simultaneously advanced down a shallow valley, which meant that they too would have to climb up the last 180 metres from the southern side to reach the right half of Yellow Pimple. The Chinese reacted violently, bringing down heavy fire on the advancing Kumaonis. On this flank, the battalion mortars were far more effective and the company succeeded in destroying eleven Chinese bunkers. After a while, both Alpha and Bravo Companies were pinned down, around 20 and 150 metres short respectively of the Yellow Pimple perimeter. Unable to either advance or pull back, Sharma asked Madiah for reinforcements. The only reserve that Battalion HQ had was Charlie Company and Madiah decided to commit two of the three platoons on the right flank. Accordingly, Subedars Govind Singh and Surendra Chand joined Sharma around midday. Their arrival allowed the Kumaonis to gain some more ground, but they were again pinned down some forty metres short of the Chinese bunkers.

Subedar Govind Singh made a determined dash with an LMG for the main Chinese bunker that was holding up the advance, but was instantly gunned down. Jamadar Trilok Singh also charged up the slope but was killed. By then, the Alpha Company commander, Captain B. N. Singh was wounded and Second Lieutenant Khatri had assumed command. Once again a stalemate ensued, and after a while the firing died down as the men nursed their limited ammunition. Brigadier Rawlley, who had been watching the attack unfold from the lower slopes of Trijunction, ordered the Kumaonis to hold the ground they had captured and to try and creep forward under the cover of darkness. Meanwhile, 4 Dogra commanded by Lieutenant Colonel R. S. Pathania had reached its full strength with the arrival of its fourth company in Walong earlier in the day. While Battalion HQ and Charlie Company were told to stay on at Walong, Alpha, Bravo and Delta Companies were immediately told to reinforce Trijunction.

However, neither 4 Sikh nor Delta Company of 6 Kumaon deployed on the West Ridge could deter the Chinese from rushing reinforcements up from Green Pimple. As day gave way to night, the Chinese had successfully reinforced the perimeter of Yellow Pimple and at 11.30 p.m., they launched a fierce counter-attack. In the ensuing hand-to-hand fighting, the Kumaonis were compelled to fall back on Trijunction. Alpha Company retained its cohesion and made it back to Trijunction, but Bravo Company dispersed in the dark; some men made it back to Trijunction, while others got to Firm Base and some to the Mortar Post. Of the 200 men who had advanced in the morning towards Yellow Pimple, only 90 returned.

However, for the exhausted men of 6 Kumaon, the ordeal was far from over and for the rest of the troops, strung out from Trijunction to High Plateau on the eastern bank, the fighting was just beginning. While the attention of Kaul, Mohinder Pathania and Rawlley had been on the Trijunction-Yellow Pimple area, the Chinese had been busy inducting an entire division worth of troops who were fully supported by artillery. Already by then, one Chinese regiment (the equivalent of an Indian brigade) had been ferried across the Lohit on boats that had been brought up from Rima.

15-16 NOVEMBER: THE CHINESE COUNTER-ATTACK

The terrain in Walong had resulted in defences that were isolated posts or strongholds. These were not mutually supportive of each other, resulting in a situation where each commanding officer had to fight his own independent battle. By the time HQ 11 Infantry Brigade came into play, the original defence plans had already been unbalanced by the forward move and then withdrawal of 6 Kumaon to Kibithu and back.

The influx of the new battalion (4 Sikh) was mired in confusion with two companies initially being airlifted to Along instead. Part of 2/8 GR was first brought to Walong, then de-inducted shortly thereafter. 3/3 GR first marched in from Hayuliang, was turned around and sent back, then ordered back yet again. 4 Dogra was then flown in, the Otters flying almost fifty sorties for their induction. In all this upheaval, it is important to note that, on an average, one infantry battalion requires close to 10 tons of supplies a day. Wind conditions in the Walong Valley generally restricted the Otter operations to three to four hours a day. The airlift capacity of the five Mi-4 helicopters allotted to this sector and the air drops by DC-3 Dakotas were not enough to meet the fresh requirements, so the troops were surviving on the existing stockpile, which was meagre to start with. As a result, ammunition in particular was in short supply, especially for the artillery.

The unrealistic timeline given to the Kumaonis to force the Chinese out of Yellow and Green Pimple once again resulted in the destabilizing of the Walong defences. Two battalions out of the four available (6 Kumaon and 4 Dogra) were pinned down at or committed to Trijunction. In what must also be a first of sorts in modern warfare, the Walong garrison also had to deal with the presence of the corps commander and the GOC of the division who spent a lot of time sitting in the Brigade HQ, thereby limiting their own overview of the unfolding battle. Quite simply the Chinese could now dictate the course of the battle.

Having withstood the determined assault by 6 Kumaon and successfully pushed them back onto the Trijunction, the Chinese launched their counter-attack at 4.30 a.m. With just one platoon from Charlie Company at his disposal, Bhatia reinforced Trijunction's defences with the Battalion HQ personnel along with the Medical Platoon. As the survivors of the ill-fated assault teams fell back, there was a heavy exchange of fire at the Trijunction perimeter, during which two Kumaonis were killed while both Bhatia and Khatri along with another jawan were wounded. After an hour and a half of bitter fighting, there was a lull as the Chinese withdrew to reorganize themselves.

At 7.30 a.m., the Chinese attacked again. This did not amount to much even though there were casualties on both sides. Throughout the day, the Chinese kept shelling Trijunction intermittently. Despite that, the Kumaonis numbers at Trijunction swelled considerably as small scattered parties managed to return to base. Most of the wounded had been pulled into Trijunction as well, and the Medical Platoon under the RMO, Captain B. C. Chopra, was treating the severely injured. The walking wounded were given basic medical treatment and sent back to man the defences.

Even though the Chinese had succeeded in laying ambushes along the line of communication between Trijunction and Mortar Post, Subedar Ganga Singh, the officiating subedar major, arrived at Trijunction with some ammunition and, equally importantly, cooked food for the men. Two puris were allocated to each man. It would be the last cooked meal that they would get to eat in the Walong Sector.

As darkness fell on Walong, the defenders could see the flashes of gunfire from various other posts in the Lohit Valley below them. However, almost on cue, Chinese artillery began to bracket the Trijunction defences with extremely accurate fire. The Chinese had constructed an elevated observation post approximately 180 metres away from the Kumaonis main defences. Three Chinese soldiers were occupying the post. Havildar Pushkar Singh, known for his accurate shooting, successfully dropped all three. Almost immediately, the shelling died down.

After a brief lull, the Chinese launched another determined attack. Just as the Kumaonis had found it impossible to make any headway against the Chinese defences on Yellow Pimple, the Chinese too were unable to force their way into Trijunction. The first attack was dispersed, only to be followed by a second wave of advancing Chinese that was repulsed as well. Bhatia reported to Madiah that the surviving Chinese troops had gone to ground and were using their own dead as defensive shields. The Indian casualties were also mounting. Madiah once again spoke to Brigade HQ only to be told that 4 Dogra was on its way, but had been held up as the Chinese had cut off the line of communication between Mortar Post and Trijunction.

A third, fourth and fifth attack followed, with the Chinese getting closer and closer to the forward positions each time. Ammunition was now at an absolute premium. Madiah issued orders that only NCOs would handle the LMGs while grenades would be thrown only by JCOs. The Kumaonis were now fighting almost as if in a trance, yet they somehow managed to keep the Chinese at bay. Just before dawn, there was intensive firing from the area between Mortar Post and the Trijunction. The Dogras were desperately trying to break through the Chinese ambushes.

Delta Company of 4 Dogra along with men from Alpha Company, who were acting as fighting porters carrying ammunition, had come under fire from the blockading Chinese. Despite the fact that the battalion had barely flown in and was not equipped for the harsh winter conditions, the men had been climbing through the night in Angola shirts and cotton trousers. Eventually thirty-three men under the command of Captain K. J. S Grewal got through to Trijunction. Their numbers were not even enough to replace the dead in the defences but their arrival was critical—the Kumaonis had all but run out of ammunition.

The next Chinese assault, this time supported by 120 mm mortars, came at 7.30 in the morning. The Dogras were now fighting shoulder to shoulder with the Kumaonis in the forward trenches and twenty-seven of the thirty-three, including Grewal, were killed. The Chinese infantry had been beaten back, but the mortars were taking a heavy toll on the defenders.

Once again, ammunition had all but run out. By then it was obvious no further reinforcements were coming as the remaining Dogras had been pulled into Mortar Post as the fighting spread rapidly. Madiah ordered the RMO to take about thirty wounded men and make a break for Walong. Realizing that his position was now hopeless, Madiah fought on till 9 a.m. and then ordered his men to disengage from the enemy as best as they could and disperse in small parties. The heroic saga of 6 Kumaon, supported in the closing stages by the gallant Dogras, came to a tragic end—Trijunction had fallen.

The Chinese now turned their attention to the West Ridge where Delta Company plus another platoon under Bikram Singh was holding out against the advance. Despite the fact that the Chinese were supported by artillery and extensive MMG fire, the attack was beaten back. Rawlley desperately needed Bikram Singh to hold the West Ridge, for its capture would open up Walong and cut off the 4 Sikh defended localities. Brigade HQ ordered Bikram to hold West Ridge till 11 a.m. 'at all cost'.

After their first attack failed to dislodge Delta Company, the Chinese fanned out and assaulted Bikram Singh's men from three sides. Yet, despite the fact that the men were literally on their last legs, the Kumaonis held out, the young officer roaring like a lion, inspiring his men to fight on. Having held his position beyond the specified time, Bikram Singh asked Brigade HQ for permission to withdraw as he had now run out of ammunition. By then, their position had been completely encircled. One JCO and seventeen other ranks managed to break through the Chinese cordon, but the rest died, all fighting to the end. Bikram Singh was last seen surrounded by the Chinese. Much later, his half-burnt body riddled with bullets was found exactly where he had been last spotted by some of the survivors.

Having overrun the last Kumaoni bastion on the West Ridge, the bulk of the Chinese joined their forward elements that had been harassing and blocking 4 Dogra from reinforcing Trijunction. After a determined effort had allowed the men under Grewal to break through, the rest of the men had fallen back on Mortar Post. Through the night of 15-16 November, the troops had held off the Chinese who were content to keep a loose cordon around the Indian position. After the fall of Trijunction and the West Ridge, the Chinese moved all their troops against the Dogras who were now completely encircled. By then, however, 11 Brigade had issued the order for a withdrawal. Breaking through the Chinese cordon, 4 Dogra headed south towards the Yapak-Lohit junction.

15-16 NOVEMBER: 4 SIKH

Patrol Base that had been set up above Lachhman Ridge by 4 Sikh had been the biggest thorn in the Chinese side. Alpha Company's aggressive patrolling was aimed at threatening the Chinese line of communication between Green Pimple and their rear at Ashi Hill. As a result, there were regular clashes on a daily basis, in some of which the Chinese had been badly mauled. On 15 November, even as the battle for Yellow Pimple was being fought on the slope above, Chinese artillery started intermittently shelling Patrol Base. Not to be cowed down, Major P. M. Samvatsar sent out a patrol to harass the rear of Green Pimple, but the party returned at last light without encountering the Chinese.

At 6.30 p.m. on 15 November, Major Malik, commanding Delta Company on the eastern bank, reported a number of Chinese with torches moving from the north towards Ashi Hill. This message was communicated to all the troops deployed on the west bank. Two hours later, Patrol Base was attacked but the Sikhs were alert and fought off the assault.

Chinese artillery began to pound Patrol Base with a vengeance. The post took a hammering and at 11.30 p.m., the Chinese launched yet another attack. Casualties were mounting and 4 Sikh's Alpha Company commander Major Samvatsar was severely wounded. Yet the men held on grimly. Bleeding profusely, Samvatsar asked for permission to fall back on Maha Plateau. Permission was granted, but the men were not willing to fall back without the company commander and the other wounded.

The Chinese were unrelenting, but the Sikhs refused to yield. Two men in the meantime had got detached from the post. They reported at Battalion HQ and described the situation at Patrol Base. Lieutenant Colonel Behl immediately collected every man he could spare and put them under the command of the unit quartermaster, Captain Inder Jit Kumar, and rushed them to Patrol Base.

Kumar now had a tricky problem. The only hope he had of evacuating Samvatsar from Patrol Base depended on some men volunteering to cover the withdrawal. Three jawans—Lance Naik Santok Singh, Sepoy Tehar Singh and Mela Singh—opted to stay back. It was a suicidal task, but it gave Kumar's party the window it needed to try and get away. Hardly had they left Patrol Base, than a shell landed on Samvatsar, killing him instantly. Kumar was knocked down and captured by the Chinese while the company JCO was also killed. The battered remnants of Alpha Company made it to Maha Plateau. Major Samvatsar, one JCO and twenty jawans were killed while two JCOs and forty jawans were wounded. (Among the dead were four sportsmen who had represented India at the Olympics.)

The Chinese, in a shocking display of brutality, vented their anger on the dead and wounded. After the ceasefire, when an Indian recovery party went to Patrol Base, they found corpses whose hands and feet had been bound with wire. Their turbans were riddled with bullets that had been fired from point blank range.

At Lachhman Ridge, just below Patrol Base, 3/3 GR's Delta Company under command of 4 Sikh had withstood the sporadic shelling throughout 15 November. As soon as Patrol Base fell at 4.30 a.m., the Chinese redirected their heavy artillery fire onto the Gorkhas. Half an hour later, as the shells stopped screaming in, the Chinese infantry launched their attack. In the grey light of dawn, Subedar Kharak Bahadur's forward platoon had held its fire till the Chinese closed in, after which they picked off advancing targets with deadly precision. The Chinese regrouped and launched a second attack at 7.30. When the second attack was also beaten back, they changed tactics and tried to outflank the company. Seeing this, Naik Keshar Bahadur Gurung picked up his Bren and moved to a vantage point from where he kept engaging the enemy. Four waves of the Chinese were repulsed, but each time the survivors would go to ground and the next wave would get in even closer.

The company commander, Captain K. N. Bavadam, could not contact the Battalion or Brigade HQ. So he decided to break through the Chinese cordon on his own and fall back on Maha Plateau. As the withdrawal proceeded, the company was ambushed and outnumbered by Chinese units that had slipped in around them. Naik Keshar Bahadur Gurung was hit on the hip but continued to fight till another round tore into his neck. He was mortally wounded. Havildar Chandra Bahadur Pun took over the Bren and provided covering fire till the last man was able to pull back. Unfortunately he was killed. By then, the Chinese were firing at the withdrawing troops from the abandoned positions on Lachhman Ridge. During the withdrawal, most of the surviving personnel were killed, and Bavadam was captured.

The Chinese attack at 5 a.m. on Maha Plateau had coincided with the assault on the neighbouring 3/3 GR positions on Lachhman Ridge. Charlie Company of 4 Sikh under Major Sandhu fought furiously, taking a heavy toll on the advancing Chinese. Their own casualties, however, were also substantial. Sandhu appealed to Major Harbans Singh, who was commanding Bravo Company at Mithun, for reinforcements. Even though the Chinese had managed to infiltrate the area between Maha Plateau and Mithun and were harassing Harbans's position, a section was immediately dispatched. By the time these men made their way across to Maha Plateau, the survivors from Alpha Company had also reached there. At 7 a. m., the Chinese launched their second attack, and Sandhu was soon overpowered. More than half the Sikhs from Charlie Company at Maha Plateau were either killed or wounded. The few that survived made their way to Mithun where they joined Bravo Company.

Captain Kulwant Singh had been in Jorhat when the battalion was being inducted. He had made his way back to the battalion and had hardly landed in Walong when he was sent to Mithun to join Bravo Company. He had reached the company position on 15 November when the Chinese began firing at the bunkers with 55 mm recoilless guns. Despite the damage, the Sikhs stood firm. At night, the Chinese had managed to send jitter parties into the gap between Mithun and Maha Plateau, keeping the men on their toes. At first light, the Chinese put in an attack but were easily beaten back. In the immediate lull, the company commander dispatched the section to Maha Plateau. The second attack came at around 7.30 a.m., this time from all sides.

Around midday, the orders to withdraw were received and Harbans Singh decided to pull out from Mithun. As Bravo Company moved out, heading down the track that linked up with the western track between Kibithu and Walong, Harbans asked Kulwant Singh to bring up the rearguard. Along with his orderly and an artillery officer, Captain G. P. Bharnagar, who was still trying to direct supporting fire, Kulwant Singh's little group huddled together behind a rock. Fortunately for them, the Chinese did not move immediately to occupy Mithun, instead pulling back to regroup themselves.

'There were still some of the Gorkhas from Lachhman Ridge trying to escape down the track that went through my position,' recalls Kulwant, 'and I was determined to pull out only after the last man had left. The Chinese were shooting at us, so I told Bharnagar that we should wait for an hour or so, and pull out once it got dark. He seemed to nod in agreement, but then he just slumped, shot through the head. In disbelief I turned towards my orderly, who had pulled out the pin from a grenade. He just handed it to me and toppled over backwards, falling off the cliff without making a sound. He was just looking at me, his eyes transfixed. I suppose he had died instantly. I started to sprint and underhand threw the grenade that was live. The blast lifted me off my feet and sent me tumbling and crashing down into the vegetation, coming to a halt on the track below.' Kulwant, badly wounded and barely alive, was found below the track by the Chinese the next day.

16 NOVEMBER: THE LADDERS AND THE EAST BANK

The Ladders gets its name from the steps cut into the rock face on the west bank of the Lohit River as the Kibithu-Walong track negotiates this geographical barrier. Major N. B. Chand, who had placed his main position about a kilometre and a half to the rear, commanded 3/3 GR's Charlie Company. From the company command post, the track ran the distance, about a thousand feet above the river. Once it got to the rock face, the steps took the path onto a plateau. One of the platoons had its defences on the forward end of the plateau, while the other was dug into the vertical cliff itself. These bunkers were like caves on the rock face. Both Delta Company on Lachhman Ridge and Charlie Company were under the command of 4 Sikh, just as the Sikh company across the river on the east bank was under command of 3/3 GR.

The Chinese artillery could not hit the defences at The Ladders from any of their positions on the west bank. The forward platoon was dug in at the top end of the stairway, which allowed it to have an excellent field of fire that completely dominated any frontal approach. As the bunkers were chiselled into the hard rock The Ladders were almost impregnable. About two kilometres to the north was Ashi Hill, from where the Chinese had cut a path to Green and Yellow Pimple. Since 26 October, their guns had been trying to bracket both The Ladders and Mithun, but had not succeeded, while their own casualties were considerable.

The Chinese commander had realized fairly early that to capture Walong his only option was to create a path up the cliff from Ashi Hill on the western flank and get above the Indian positions. On the eastern flank, he would have to get enough troops across the Lohit to capture the Indian positions. Once he succeeded in doing that, he could bring into play his anti-tank 55 mm RCL guns. Delta Company of 4 Sikh was holding the High Plateau on the eastern flank under the command of Lieutenant Yog Raj Palta. So long as the Sikhs held their position, Chand was confident the Chinese could not dislodge his men on The Ladders.

Crossing the river and assaulting High Plateau was always going to be a risky proposition. The Chinese therefore launched a determined assault on The Ladders on the morning of 15 November. Instead of the usual ineffective artillery fire, the Chinese changed tactics and moved up 55 mm RCL guns that opened up in an attempt to soften the Gorkhas. As soon as the firing stopped, the Chinese infantry tried to rush the forward platoon, but the Gorkhas were ready with their deadly accurate .303s and LMGs in the firing trenches. Indian artillery guns and heavy mortars positioned on the eastern bank also came to their support, taking a heavy toll on the attacking Chinese troops. After 9 a. m., the Chinese infantry pulled back and the RCL guns continued to fire at the forward positions. This gradually began to take effect as some of the bunkers were seriously damaged forcing the Gorkhas to vacate them.

By midday, the remnants of the forward platoon on The Ladders were running critically low on ammunition. Naib Subedar Dil Bahadur, the company JCO, succeeded in partly resupplying the positions by braving Chinese fire. At 9 p. m., the Chinese put in yet another attack, but the Gorkhas managed to repulse it; by this time they were running desperately short of men and ammunition. An hour later, Chand radioed Behl asking for reinforcements. But the Sikh CO was fighting a number of battles all around and he was in no position to spare even a single man. After this conversation, the wireless communication between 4 Sikh Battalion HQ and The Ladders broke down. By then, the Chinese too seemed to have shifted their attention elsewhere and there were no further attacks on The Ladders during the night.

Shortly after Lieutenant Palta had warned the companies on the west bank about the Chinese advancing with torches, he had come under heavy bombardment from the guns deployed at the base of Ashi Hills. Convinced that the Chinese would attempt a river crossing under the cover of darkness, he warned his men to prepare themselves for an attack during the night.

Having got sufficient men across, the Chinese launched their first attack on High Plateau at 11.30 p.m. The Sikhs were waiting for them and met the Chinese with concentrated fire. Having got their attention, the Chinese on the slope leading up to High Plateau decided to stay where they were. At the same time a party was sent to cut off the connecting route from Dong Plateau and Dong Hill where Lieutenant Colonel Yadav's Battalion HQ and two companies of 3/3 GR were deployed.

The second attack started at 1.30 a.m. on 16 December. As the Chinese crept up the slope, the Sikhs grimly held their positions. Palta radioed Yadav for reinforcements, then went back to exhorting his men to use their ammunition judiciously and make every round count. All this while, he was moving from bunker to bunker, throwing grenades at the advancing Chinese, while shouting curses at them. The lieutenant was hit once, but his voice did not die down, as he urged his men to hold their positions. Then he was hit again, and this time he did not get up. The company JCO was also killed, leaving Havildar Gurmukh Singh in command.

By that time, the Sikhs had been reduced to eighteen men and a few other non-combatants. Once again, the Chinese attack died down, as they too decided to wait for the light of dawn and additional reinforcements to renew their attack. While the Chinese numbers continued to swell on the riverbank, the commanding officer of 3/3 GR failed to push any troops through to help Gurmukh Singh and his surviving men. Even though the Chinese had laid an ambush on the track, a determined attempt could have been made.

As visibility started to improve at dawn on 16 November, the men at The Ladders could hear the posts above them fighting ferociously, but owing to the nature of the terrain, on the western side they were blindsided completely. On the other hand, Major Chand's Gorkhas had a grandstand view of developments on the river below and the east bank. Chinese troops in rubber boats were still crossing the Lohit in large numbers and were surging up the steep bank to attack Gurmukh Singh's remaining men. From his vantage point, Major Chand could see the Sikhs fighting desperately. At around 7.30 a.m., a small party led by an artillery officer, Second Lieutenant P. S. Bhandari, suddenly appeared at High Plateau and began directing the Indian guns positioned on the rear flank of Dakota Hill. The guns joined the battle with deadly effect. However, by then, the Chinese were mopping up the surviving troops and Bhandari was also killed. By 8 a.m. it was all over for Delta Company—High Plateau had fallen.

Strangely enough, the Chinese did not press on towards Dong Plateau. Instead, they began to physically haul RCL guns up to High Plateau, from where they started firing at The Ladders across the river. The defences in the rock wall that had so far been immune to artillery fire were now repeatedly hit. The bunkers crumbled and the falling dust blinded the Gorkhas. All they could do was move to the forward location that was also intermittently attacked through the day.

THE WITHDRAWAL

On the morning of 16 November, the corps commander, Kaul, and GOC 2 Mountain Division, Mohinder Pathania, had been in Walong, sitting in the Brigade HQ where Brigadier Rawlley and his brigade major, Ashok Handoo, were trying to control the battle. Kaul described the atmosphere in Brigade HQ: 'I overheard several telephone conversations…which gave me the impression that some of our Commanders, despite the resolute attitude of their Brigade Commander, could have displayed greater determination at the time. Soon after 4 Sikh and 3/3 Gorkhas began withdrawing from their positions under pressure. I heard Major Handoo telling several officers in various battalions over the telephone in no uncertain terms that they should give fighting (sic). Some of them did. Others did not.'

Lieutenant Colonel Yadav, CO of 3/3 GR, seems to have frozen. Had he responded to Palta's desperate plea for help, it is unlikely that the outcome of the battle would have been different, but it may have given the remnants a fighting chance. It's evident that the Chinese had not been able to effectively cut off the track between Dong and High Plateau since a small artillery forward observation party managed to get to Delta Company just before the position was overrun. As position after position on both the banks began to fall and Walong began to get shelled, Kaul gave Rawlley orders for battle that were vague enough to absolve the general of having ordered the withdrawal himself. In language typical of Kaul, he and Mohinder Pathania informed Rawlley: '…hold on to your present position to the best of your ability. If the position becomes untenable you are to take up an alternative position and man it to the best of your ability. In the event that also becomes untenable you are to continue to take up a series of layback positions and keep delaying the enemy.'

At noon Rawlley issued the order to all battalion commanding officers to break contact with the Chinese and withdraw. All elements of the brigade were to fall back to the Yapak Ti–Lohit River junction. Troops on the west bank (6 Kumaon, 4 Sikh and 4 Dogra) were to withdraw along the Yapak Ridge while 3/3 GR plus one company of 4 Sikh was to withdraw along the eastern track and link up with the brigade downstream at Hawai, which was roughly halfway between Walong and Hayuliang.

Though all the battalion HQs received the order, it is doubtful that it was passed on to the various sub-units. 6 Kumaon had already disintegrated at Trijunction and Mortar Post and the remaining men had a difficult time getting back to Walong to join the brigade group. As a result they dispersed in small parties, many of whom were subsequently ambushed and killed or captured by the Chinese. Lieutenant Colonel Madiah along with thirty men was also ambushed on the Yepak Plateau on 18 November. Every member of his party was killed while Madiah, who tried to escape by jumping into a lake, was captured and taken prisoner. 6 Kumaon lost 118 men, 113 were wounded and 172 taken prisoner. 4 Dogra, the battalion that had so valiantly jumped into the fray on arrival, lost one officer, 2 JCOs and 107 other ranks.

4 Sikh owed a lot to the Bravo Company commander, Major Harbans Singh, who quickly organized the survivors at Walong and marched them out along the western route. The battalion suffered 180 casualties, of which 82 were killed. On the east bank, there were hardly any survivors from Lieutenant Palta's ill-fated company. Naik Kuldeep Singh, the only known survivor of the High Plateau battle, was perhaps the only one who managed to negotiate the eastern track and make it to Tezu on 4 December.

Delta Company of 3/3 GR at Lachhman Ridge was wiped out to the last man, and Captain Bavadam was taken prisoner. This gallant officer later died in the POW camp. The orders to withdraw were never communicated to Major Chand on The Ladders. He sent Naib Subedar Dil Bahadur who was with the rear platoon back towards Walong to find out what was happening. When the JCO reported that the Walong area was crawling with Chinese troops, Chand refused to believe him. The JCO was asked to take some men with him and go back yet again. As it was getting dark by then, the rear platoon of Charlie Company managed to evade the Chinese and set off for the plains. Major Chand and his remaining two platoons fought on through the night of 16-17 November, before evacuating The Ladders in the morning. Chand fell into the Lohit from where he was fished out and captured by the Chinese further downstream.

The other two companies of 3/3 GR on the east bank and Battalion HQ were virtually unscathed and they set off down the eastern track towards Hayuliang. However, they were relentlessly hounded by the Chinese and suffered heavy casualties during the retreat. The Chinese captured quite a few Gorkhas including Lieutenant Colonel Yadav during the retreat.

Brigadier Rawlley and the brigade group withdrew safely to Hayuliang.

On the morning of 17 November, Kaul, who was scouting around in a Mi-4 looking for survivors, spotted the commander's party and landed on the riverbed. Kaul offered to fly Rawlley out with him, but the commander refused, saying his place was with his men.

Around the same time, Palit in Army HQ in Delhi received a signal sent by Kaul, presumably written just before he took off from Tezpur to look for survivors in Walong. The DMO was to say later 'that he sounded so desperate as to be almost demented. After giving us details of the battle of Walong and warning us of the extreme gravity of the situation, Bijji pushed all circumspection aside and starkly asked for foreign military intervention to save the situation'. When the message was shown to Thapar, he said: 'Bijji has finally lost his mind. He expects us to invite the Americans to fight our battles! We'll have to show this to the PM.' Shortly after briefing Nehru on the situation in Walong and showing him Kaul's message, Thapar and Palit were airborne for Tezpur.

The defences at Hayuliang were subsequently strengthened but the Chinese only advanced up to a post on the high ground north of the town.

BOOK IV

The War That Wasn't

Chapter 10

FORTRESS SE-LA

THE RETURN OF BIJJI KAUL

Towards the end of October, the full extent of the disaster on the Nam Ka Chu was coming through to the country in bits and pieces. Details of the fiasco in which 7 Infantry Brigade of the Indian Army had disintegrated within three hours was stunning everyone. To make matters worse, apart from 2 Rajput, which had stood its ground even as it had been decimated, there was no news of Brigade HQ or the other three battalions at this stage. Some of the men who were not killed or captured by the Chinese would either freeze to death or die of severe frostbite and starvation while trying to escape to the plains of Assam via Bhutan.

In the Kameng Frontier Division, as we have seen, the Chinese tsunami had not been restricted to the Nam Ka Chu Valley; a second thrust along the Nyamjang Chu Valley had smashed past the scanty defences of 4 Division HQ. In the absence of any pre-planned withdrawal plan, the fallback had proved to be nothing but a headlong retreat. So much so that Tawang, built up as 4 Division's vital ground over the last three years, was abandoned in a matter of hours, the decision being taken even before the fighting at Bum-la had begun. The Eastern Army Commander, Lieutenant General Bogey Sen, who had refused to countenance pulling 7 Brigade back onto the forward slopes of Tsangdhar after Kaul had rushed back to Delhi with a realistic assessment of the situation after the 10 October incident, was present in Tawang on 22-23 October and though he was to sack Niranjan Prasad on grounds of cowardice a few hours later, he did nothing to countermand the order to evacuate Tawang.

With Kaul out of the equation on medical grounds, both Eastern Command and HQ IV Corps were championing the Thorat defensive line, wanting to pull the retreating troops back to Bomdila. However, as we know, the DMO at Army Headquarters, Palit, felt Se-la was a far better defensive option to stop the Chinese advance. Palit, who played a critical role on 22 October in getting Nehru's nod for the evacuation of Tawang, had the tacit support of the army chief, General Pran Thapar. After the withdrawal to Jang by the evening of 23 October and a further fallback to Nuranang and Se-la the next day, Thapar finally replaced the indisposed Kaul with Lieutenant General Harbaksh Singh. On 25 October, the new corps commander met Palit and the sacked Niranjan Prasad at Se-la Top, where he and the new GOC of 4 Division, Major General Anant Pathania, were briefed and shown around the area. Harbaksh Singh then declared that Se-la Top, despite the arctic windswept conditions, would indeed be the next defensive line.

Sweeping changes were made at all levels: 1 Sikh, 4 Garhwal Rifles and 13 Dogra along with 4 and 2 Sikh LI were brought under command of 62 Infantry Brigade. The IAF was brought into play almost immediately, as Senge on the southern shoulder of Se-la was well suited to receive supplies by air. Pathania was expected to set up his Divisional Tactical Headquarters at Senge Dzong, from where he was to supervise the battle for Se-la while also plugging the two passes on either flank that could bypass Se-la.

The next five days would see morale on Se-la soar despite the difficult conditions that had to be endured by 1 Sikh and 4 Sikh LI. 4 Garhwal Rifles with 3.7-inch guns in support were deployed further down at Nuranang and they were effectively harassing the Chinese who were still on the northern side of the Tawang Chu below Jang. Though contact with the enemy had been broken with the pullback from Jang on 24 October, patrols from 4 Garhwal and 1 Sikh were in active contact with the Chinese.

On 30 October, news that Bijji Kaul had been declared medically fit and was being reinstated as GOC IV Corps spread like wild fire. Harbaksh Singh was to move as GOC XXXIII Corps where he was to replace Umrao Singh.

Kaul returned to Tezpur on 30 October. Strangely, he declined the offer of a briefing by Harbaksh Singh. Kaul accepted the plan that Palit proposed, even though Palit's earlier reservations pertaining to the deployment of troops in such conditions should have become more valid at this stage. Ironically, even Palit's own notes had expressed his reservations: 'At the time, unaccountably, I disregarded that pre-eminent tactical feature [Se-la]. Possibly this was because at that stage, when the Indian Army was still unfamiliar with the techniques of high altitude warfare, I dismissed the concept of siting brigade defences at heights of 4,000 metres [13,400 feet] and over as impracticable.'

By the end of October, winter had well and truly set in, with frequent white-outs and snowfall at Se-la Top and the surrounding heights. This plan, also accepted by Harbaksh Singh, was based on the five infantry battalions allotted to 62 Brigade eventually defending a compact area at 13,400 feet with additional defensive positions on the two shoulders at around 16,000 feet. HQ 4 Division was to be located at Senge Dzong, just below the southern face of Se-la, with 65 Brigade's two battalions (4 Rajput and 19 MLI) defending the flanks.

Anant Pathania, ever since he took over 4 Division, seemed most reluctant to base himself at Senge, ostensibly on account of high altitude headaches. Kaul's reinstatement gave Pathania the opportunity to request permission to pull back and set up his Division HQ at Dirang Dzong, which at 6,000 feet was appreciably lower in altitude. Without giving it too much thought, Kaul gave Pathania permission. The GOC correspondingly changed the assigned task of 65 Brigade, deploying it with an eye towards protecting his own HQ while considerably reducing the proposed defences on the flank. The fact that Division HQ had been pulled back to Dirang was not known to either Eastern Command or Army HQ, both of which had once again faded into the backdrop with the re-emergence of Kaul.

Apart from the units that had fallen back from Tawang and were now part of 62 Brigade, the new units coming in from the plains were short of blankets, digging tools and critical signals equipment. 4 Sikh LI had been airlifted from Dagshai via Ambala, Agra and Tezpur, and had reached Se-la on October 24; bewildered and tired, they watched the exodus of Tawang's panic-stricken population. These troops, without any preamble or acclimatization, had been deployed ahead of Se-la to guard the approach to Nuranang and the Kya-la-Lunguthang track. Two of their companies were deployed in the Two Lakes area while a third company was in depth behind 4 Garhwal at Nuranang. 2 Sikh LI had moved from Hyderabad without its commanding officer and had reached Se-la Top between 26 and 28 October. Of the battalions that had fallen back from Tawang, 4 Garhwal Rifles were dug in at Nuranang, 1 Sikh was holding Se-la Top and 13 Dogra was responsible for the defence of Senge DZ while also providing depth to the troops deployed at Se-la.

The division plan, as inherited by Kaul, was as follows: 62 Brigade was to guard the frontal approach to Se-la at all costs; Se-la depth and the area around Dirang Dzong was to be the responsibility of 65 Brigade; and the corps's vital ground was to be Bomdila, to be defended by 48 Brigade. While 62 Brigade was mainly being supplied by air with the IAF dropping between 60 to 90 tons at the Senge DZ daily, a fleet of 1-ton vehicles was maintaining 65 and 48 Brigade.

Brigadier Hoshiar Singh, who was now commanding 62 Brigade, exhibited a steely resolve that indicated to the troops that come what may, he was going to dig in and fight it out at Se-la. On arrival, he had declared Se-la to be an impregnable natural fortress. A solid soldier, he went about his job methodically despite all the drawbacks. Over the next two weeks, the battalions worked round the clock, constructing bunkers. Since corrugated galvanized iron sheets were not available, wooden beams were used with shrub branches for overhead cover. Where the ground was frozen solid, stone sangars were constructed. By 15 November, almost all units had completed their defences. However, only a part of the available anti-personnel mines had been laid.

Though the bulk of the guns had been abandoned across the Tawang Chu during the withdrawal, 5 Field Regiment less two batteries under the command of Lieutenant Colonel Budhwar, equipped with 25-pounder guns, had taken charge since his arrival on 27 October. 87 Field Battery under Major Brahm Sat, also armed with 25-pounders, C Troop 34 Heavy Mortar Battery with 4.2-inch mortars and 2 Derajat Mountain Battery minus a section with their 3.7-inch howitzers were also brought under Budhwar. A platoon of 7 Mahar equipped with Vickers MMGs was attached to 2 Sikh LI with one section covering the Kye-la and the other section covering the main road to Nuranang. By 14 November, 5 Field's own 96 Battery had also joined its parent group. However, at this point, 4 Infantry Division had only two-thirds of its projected requirement of seventeen infantry battalions, a third of the required field artillery and a quarter of the required mountain guns and heavy mortars.

Pooled transport was being used to ferry supplies to the battalions from the Senge DZ. Even though all units were deficient in rifles, grenades, 2-inch mortar bombs and had no mortar flares, they had stocked up to two scales of front line small arms ammunition and one week's unbalanced rations.

SPARRING WITH THE CHINESE

The urgency of the first few days had slackened somewhat as the Chinese seemed quite content to stay on the northern side of the Tawang Chu. The opinion expressed by the corps commander, Kaul, was that nothing much was going to happen until the spring of 1963 when he planned to launch an attack to reclaim Tawang. In fact, during his visit to Se-la, he berated one of the commanding officers for spending so much time on the defences, insisting that it was more prudent to stock up for the winter. In keeping with this thinking, the majority of the mines were not laid, for it was felt that in the coming period of heavy snow, they would first get buried and then shift their position.

Having withdrawn from Jang, it was important that 62 Infantry Brigade remain in contact with the Chinese. Across the valley, from the general direction of Tawang, explosions could be heard day and night as the Chinese worked feverishly on a road that would link Bum-la and Tawang. At night, lights illuminating the stretches under construction could be seen, while Chinese movement at the base of the valley was under observation by the Garhwalis. On 1 November Brigadier Hoshiar Singh sent a fighting patrol from 4 Garhwal Rifles under Major H. B. Rai. Accompanying him as the forward observation officer (FOO) was Major Devinder Goswami of 2 Derajat Mountain Battery. The objective of the Garhwal patrol was to destroy the Lao footbridge over the Mago Chu (approximately twenty kilometres east of the Nuranang Falls) and could be used by the Chinese to infiltrate into the Dirang Valley via Jangle.

On reaching Lao, the patrol found the Chinese occupying both ends of the bridge. Rai was not too enthused about taking on the Chinese. The FOO engaged the bridge but the artillery failed to hit the narrow target, though they did cause some casualties to the Chinese troops and damaged the support structure of the bridge on either side of the river. The patrol returned to Battalion HQ on 6 November.

Later that same day, 2 Sikh LI sent out a patrol under Captain M. K. Saxena with four other ranks to reconnoitre the track from Kye-la up to the Mago Chu and observe Chinese activity along the river up to Bridge 3. They were spotted by the Chinese and had to beat a hasty retreat, during the course of which two soldiers were killed. Their bodies could only be recovered four days later. The Chinese had in the meantime taken their rifles. Captain Saxena was recovered by another Sikh LI patrol with severe frostbite on his toes.

1 Sikh sent out a five-man patrol under a JCO towards Lunguthang. They returned and reported no Chinese activity. This was then followed up by another platoon of 1 Sikh on 7 November. This patrol reported more than 500 Chinese troops in the area. The Chinese in the meantime outflanked the patrol and a 200-strong force intercepted the Sikhs near Dzalung-la. Fortunately, 2 Sikh LI mortars firing from Kye-la managed to help extricate the patrol.

Three days later, on 10 November, 4 Garhwal Ops reported a large body of yaks and mules on the move between Rho and Melling. As day gave way to night, reports started coming in of a large number of Chinese having concentrated near 1 Sikh. A Chinese jitter party, which had clambered up an adjoining hill, fired a burst. The Sikhs, unsure of the direction of attack, opened up with small arms and mortars. The field guns, not to be left out, joined in. However, all the firing was at nothing and lasted close to two hours before the officers could bring the situation under control. The panicky reaction of the troops and expending of precious ammunition was a clear indication that the troops on Se-la Top were beginning to get edgy.

While the guns were blazing against an imagined enemy on Se-la, observation posts at Nuranang could see headlights winding their way down towards Tawang from the direction of Bum-la. The road that the Chinese had been constructing had obviously been opened.

Kaul's belief that the Chinese would be quite content to sit out the winter south of the Tawang Chu turned out to be misplaced. Increased Chinese activity in the last few days coupled with 1 Sikh's panic reaction the previous evening did not augur well for the brigade's fighting capabilities.

On 11 and 12 November, alarming reports started coming in from 4 Garhwal Rifles that a large body of Chinese troops—estimated to be in the region of a thousand—were moving from Rho towards Melling in small parties of twenty to thirty men. General Pathania, perhaps influenced by the overreaction by 1 Sikh on Se-la Top, scoffed at the 'impossibility' of the information. The reconnaissance carried out by Brigadier Palit's DQ two years previously had estimated that the Bailey Trail that bypassed Se-la from the east could at best be negotiated by a party of company strength. No one since had questioned this reasoning. Obviously where sixty men could go, there was no reason why a thousand could not. However, the DQ's assessment had been blindly repeated by so many that it had come to be seen as the gospel truth.

Division HQ's doubts were further reinforced when artillery guns tried to engage these groups. The Chinese had taken adequate precautions, having staggered the distances to avoid presenting a bunched target. Also, as the valley was deep, the field guns had to fire at a high angle and met with no obvious success. However, as the reports continued to come in, HQ 4 Division rather belatedly told 48 Brigade at Bomdila to move a company to reinforce the post at Poshing-la. By then it already was a case of too little too late.

On 13 November, a Chinese convoy was seen parked near the district commissioner's office. This clearly confirmed that the Chinese had indeed constructed the link road across Bum-la to Tawang. Again 4 Artillery Brigade tried to engage the target, but failed to do any real damage.

The brigade commander, Hoshiar Singh, was confident that when the main Chinese attack came, he could fight a self-contained battle even if he was cut off and isolated from the rear. Hoshiar Singh repeatedly let it be known to the rank and file that the brigade was going to stand its ground. With Indian patrols generally faring poorly against the Chinese, the brigade commander felt that the troops needed to do something that would boost morale. He announced that the brigade would give a cash award of Rs 1,000 to anyone who captured a Chinese soldier.

4 Garhwal Rifles had been in a supporting role to 1 Sikh in Bum-la. During the fallback from Tawang, Major H. B. Rai had been entrusted with holding Bridge 4, which many junior officers felt had been blown up prematurely the moment the Chinese mortars had opened up. According to all accounts, of all the battalions present on and around Se-la, it was the Garhwalis who had a spring in their step and a glint in the eye as the battalion prepared itself for the coming battle with some aggressive patrolling.

During the daylight hours of 13 November, a 4 Garhwal patrol under Second Lieutenant Vinod Kumar Goswami had moved into the Mago region under the cover of thick vegetation to observe Chinese movements around Rho. Towards the evening, twenty Chinese soldiers approached a hut near the north bank of the Mago Chu and it soon became apparent to the watching Garhwal patrol that the Chinese were settling in for the night. Moving downstream, Goswami, along with seven men, managed to cross the considerably large stream by jamming logs between rocks to construct a makeshift bridge.

In the hut, the Chinese were most relaxed, for, until then, there had been no aggressive intent shown by any of the Indian troops. A lone sentry was on duty a few yards from the hut. It was beginning to get dark and Goswami and two men closed in on the unsuspecting soldier, getting close enough to hit him on his head with the butt of a rifle. Having grabbed the dazed soldier, they started to drag the captured sentry towards the crossing point.

As they approached the water, there were two loud explosions. The Chinese had realized the sentry was missing, so Goswami's rearguard threw two grenades into the hut before making a dash for the logs. The entire area erupted in gunfire, and soon Very lights were arcing skywards, illuminating the river. Halfway across the Mago Chu with his inert prisoner, Goswami had no option but to kill him and save his own party. The Chinese soldier's rifle was, however, sent to Brigade HQ the next day.

Throughout this period, other than the one visit to Se-la on 7 November, Kaul's attention had been entirely on the Lohit Frontier Division. Having declared that the troops should focus on stocking up for the winter rather than worry too much with defences, the corps commander had mentally switched off from the Kameng Sector. With GOC 4 Division also content to sit back in Dirang Dzong, commander 62 Infantry Brigade, Hoshiar Singh, was more or less left alone to counter the developing situation.

Only someone who has been on a Himalayan high-altitude pass can imagine the conditions at Se-la, especially at night. The defensive deployment meant that at any given time there were close to a hundred men out in the raw blistering cold, where the wind chill factor further aggravated the existing arctic conditions. Unfortunately, most of the officers were ensconced in bunkers with bukharis (kerosene heaters) burning to keep them warm instead of being out with the men, where they should have been practising counter-attacks and other battle drills. The reason for this perhaps was Hoshiar's unfamiliarity with the troops he was commanding and also the fact that many officers, including the commanding officer of 2 Sikh LI, Lieutenant Colonel A. R. Irani, were still scrambling to get to their units. Irani had only returned to the unit on 9 November.

Having failed to capture a Chinese soldier, Hoshiar decided to send out a three-company-strong raiding party that would give the Chinese a hard knock. The composite force made up of two companies of 2 Sikh LI and Alpha Company of 1 Sikh plus one platoon under the command of Major S. S. Jaspal, the 2IC of 2 Sikh LI set off for Lunguthang on 15 November to engage any Chinese troops to be found there. The fighting reconnaissance party had enough supplies to sustain themselves for four days. The guns were on standby and a FOO was allotted to the party. Irani, the commanding officer of 2 Sikh LI, moved his command post to Kye-la to watch the progress of the column, code-named Kaua (Crow), which left the battalion HQ at 4.30 a.m.

This plan was flawed right from the very outset. Hoshiar Singh should have known that the Chinese were highly unlikely to present a static target especially south of the Tawang/Mago Chu, where they themselves were infiltrating on the flanks, hoping to draw the Indians out of their prepared defences. Also, somebody in the chain of command should have realized that combining troops from the Sikh and Sikh LI units was a recipe for disaster. Despite Sikhism's tenets forbidding casteism, the reality on the ground was quite different, especially during the mid-twentieth century. The two Sikh

LI units were Mazhabi or low-caste Sikhs. In their villages, they lived in a state of virtual apartheid, dominated by middle-caste Jat Sikhs who made up the Sikh Regiment. Both these regiments of the Indian Army have time and again proven themselves to be outstanding soldiers, but to mix them up was always going to be fraught with danger. In the event, Hoshiar Singh literally blundered into the Chinese trap and the ill-fated and ill-conceived attempt would have the worst possible outcome.

The composite patrol, after crossing the Lunguthang–Kye-la ridgeline, proceeded towards the northeast. Jaspal wanted to get to the highest point in the area, beyond which flowed the Goro Chu. By the evening, the exhausted column reached Dzalung-la, where the Sikh company started establishing a firm base just below the pass, while the two Sikh LI companies continued to probe the area towards Lunguthang, close to which they established a night harbour. The Chinese on their part had been stung by the Goswami incident the previous night and were quite alert. They had been shadowing the Indian composite force from the time they set out while themselves remaining undetected. It was obvious from the way they used the topography of the area that they were familiar with its features. At 2 a.m., after assembling 500 to 600 men, the Chinese launched a simultaneous assault on both the Sikh LI night harbour and the Sikh firm base.

Although 1 Sikh, under the charge of Second Lieutenant Surendra Dagur, was at stand-to when the attack came it was taken by surprise and driven out from the firm base. As darkness closed in, the Sikh LI troops fought a resolute defensive battle against the Chinese for nearly two hours. However, owing to the topography, their radio sets were useless and the FOO could not ask for any fire support. Jaspal then gave the order to fall back and the Sikh LI companies performed a reasonably orderly retreat towards the firm base, only to find that it was occupied by waiting Chinese troops instead of their own comrades. In the pandemonium that followed, Lieutenant M. S. Khaira of 2 Sikh LI was killed along with a JCO and fifty-nine other ranks were either killed or went missing. 1 Sikh had two men wounded.

Badly mauled, those who managed to scatter and regroup started reaching the Sikh LI battalion HQ around 11 a.m. By then, another strong patrol had been assembled and was sent out towards the scene of the catastrophe and they returned by last light having collected some of the wounded men.

Kaua had been a massive disaster. It had also created tremendous bad blood between the Sikh LI and Sikh troops, the former feeling terribly let down by the latter. Even before Kaua, there had already been some minor incidents that underlined the tension between the two units, and obviously the coordination between the two left much to be desired. 4 Sikh LI deployed slightly further away in the Two Lakes area was not affected.

While the remnants of the patrol were staggering back, 4 Sikh LI observation posts were reporting a column of more than a thousand Chinese soldiers moving along the Bhutan border along the Chabra-la–Jangle track. All three batteries at Se-la opened fire, but owing to swirling mist and the wooded terrain where the Chinese were, the column quickly disappeared from sight. 4 Garhwal's Alpha Company that was occupying the forward positions at Nuranang also reported a heavy concentration of Chinese troops across the Tawang Chu. By the evening, the Garhwalis confirmed that there was feverish activity in the vicinity of the Bridge 4 where the demolished bridge was being repaired, the structure having been lit up by vehicle headlights.

CHINESE PLANS

After the clash on the Nam Ka Chu on 20 October, the Chinese had rather effortlessly pushed the Indian troops back to the south of Tawang Chu. The Chinese high command was fully aware of all the changes that were taking place on the Indian side as Chinese Intelligence agencies had set up a web of agents over the last few years to monitor and report on all Indian activity. There was enough reason to suspect that the primitive communication set-up of the Indian Army in NEFA was also compromised and not only were the Chinese listening in, they were also inserting bogus messages at key moments into the chain of command, which helped further unnerve and confuse the Indian commanders.

In 1993 and 1994, two important books were published: the first, *True History of China Border War*, written in the old Chinese script, was authored by Professor Yan Xun of the National Defence University of Beijing; and the second, *China's War of Self Defensive Counter Attack with India*, also written in Chinese, was published by the Academy of Military Sciences. Apart from giving some details of the operations from the Chinese perspective, both these books reveal the extent to which the Chinese had information about Indian deployment, their strengths and weaknesses, and an almost uncanny psychoanalysis of Indian commanders. Almost all Indian accounts, including those of Brigadiers John Dalvi and Monty Palit, mention this fact. Tashi Sonam, the Tawang-based IB agent during the 1962 clash, was categorical: 'The Chinese knew everything, Indian deployment almost to the section and platoon level was known to them. Sometimes they knew what the Indians were going to do even before the decision was taken.'

The head of the Central Military Affairs Commission (CMAC), General Liu Bocheng, was determined to avoid a face-to-face confrontation with the Indian troops. Towards this end, the Chinese plan for phase two of the operations (which started on 17 November) hinged on the Indians deciding to dig in at Se-la. On 23 October, when the decision to abandon Tawang had been taken, both the Eastern Army Commander, Bogey Sen, and BGS IV Corps, Brigadier K. K. Singh, had ordered the troops to fall back on Bomdila as per the Thorat Plan. In fact, at that stage, Bogey Sen had boasted to the political officer, Nari Rustomji, during the lull between the two phases of the war: 'We've got those bastards where we want them now. Just let them move one step forward, and they'll get such a thrashing they'll never forget. Our boys are now in positions where they can fight and show what they're worth. They're just itching for a chance to have a real good crack at the Chinks.'

For Army HQ and the army commander to expect that Se-la would hold out for even two weeks was pure wishful thinking, especially since infiltration routes on either flank had not been studied. Se-la certainly would have been a formidable obstacle had it been selected six months previously and if the Chinese had obliged and assaulted only along the road axis.

One of the key reasons the Chinese did not chase the Tawang garrison across the Mago/Tawang Chu immediately was to lull the Indians into believing that they were happy with the capture of Tawang and would not undertake any further offensive action in the Kameng Frontier Division. Already the Indian leadership had demonstrated to the Chinese just how inflexible they could be. So convinced were they that the Chinese were not going to launch an offensive during the coming winter that even the frenetic construction of the Bum-la-Tawang road (clearly visible from Nuranang) did not shake them out of their complacency.

However, despite everything falling into place for the Chinese, General Liu Bocheng's plan was a bold but dangerous gamble. To outflank Se-la and push his troops behind the garrison onto the Se-la–Dirang–Bomdila road meant that the Chinese troops would have to be self-contained, each man at best carrying a week's ration and limited ammunition. Should the Se-la brigade actually dig in and decide to fight an isolated battle, a face-to-face clash would be inevitable. Following 62 Infantry Brigade's lead, should 65 Brigade close ranks and hunker down at Dirang Dzong, then 48 and 67 Brigade could mop up the Chinese systematically. But then battles are not won by taking timid decisions and the Indians until then had given the Chinese no reason to believe that they had the stomach for a fight. Bocheng was fully aware of the capability of the Indian troops; now he simply had to make sure he got into the minds of the Indian commanders. Even the best troops in the world need to be led and until then the HQs of 4 Division, IV Corps, Eastern Command and New Delhi had not been doing a very good job.

On 29 October, orders were issued by the CMAC to the Tibet Military Region that outlined the attack plans for the battle of Se-la, Dirang Dzong and Bomdila. The major guidelines were to cut off Bridge 1 and Bridge 2 between Dirang and Senge Dzong; concentrate forces and strike at the five battalions holding Se-la from multiple directions; and attack Dirang Dzong and then push towards Thembang and Bomdila. Chinese commanders were told that lack of roads should not hinder troop movements and they should always make sure to protect their flanks as they marched.

Accordingly, Lieutenant General Zhang Gua Hua, the commander of Tibet Military Region, formulated his operational plans. Reporting back to the CMAC, Hua emphasized four key aspects. First, he would carry out multiple attacks on Indian troops ruthlessly. Second, deploy the forces after a careful study of the terrain. Third, identify the command elements at Dirang Dzong and destroy them so that the entire Indian force would be headless and unable to reinforce Se-la. Fourth, even if Dirang Dzong held out, he would get behind the Indian troops with three regiments to cut off their escape towards the south.

This plan was not without its risks and drawbacks. Since some of the routes that the troops would have to take to outflank the Indian positions were long, developing and maintaining effective supply lines would be difficult. Chinese infantry could carry seven days' dry rations themselves while a Tibetan labour force could establish a base with another three days' dry rations. The most damning aspect of this attack would be the numbers. The Indians were known to have seven battalions deployed in the Dirang and Bomdila area. Getting behind Se-la with 10,800 Chinese troops meant that the ratio of Indian to Chinese troops would be barely 1.5:1 which could prove disastrous for the attacking troops. If they managed to overrun Se-la, then the situation could be salvaged but if it held out for even a week, the Chinese campaign would collapse. The assault on the Indian 62 Brigade at Se-la would be launched using four infantry regiments (equivalent to four Indian brigades), supported by three artillery regiments. This was a ratio of 3:1, which was ideally not enough for an attacking force against well-entrenched troops. Outflanking troops moving along the western side of Se-la would have to take care to stay away from the Bhutan border. Though maintaining supply lines along this axis was expected to be easier, there would be less room to manoeuvre.

The CMAC after deliberation gave the Tibet Frontier Command the go-ahead and deployed 419 Tibetan Unit (Division), 11 Division (32 and 33 Regiments), 55 Division (154, 155, 157, 163 and 165 Regiments), the Shan Naan Army with four companies, Artillery (306, 308 and 504 Regiments), five companies of 136 Engineer Regiment plus other service elements bringing the total Chinese strength to approximately 22,000 combat troops. 419 Tibetan Unit with 55 Division was to execute the main thrust against Se-la. 11 Division was to advance along the Tse-la–Poshing-la axis and cut off Dirang from Bomdila while part of the force would attack Dirang and cut off the southern escape routes.

On 15 November, the CMAC appointed Marshal Mi Liu as the commander of the attacking force. Speaking to his subordinates, Mi Liu pointed out that victory could be achieved only by determined and relentless pursuit of the stated objectives. The Indians in front were well coordinated—'the head,' he said, 'is like copper and the tail like tin'. Pointing to the Indian defence posture at Se-la and Senge Dzong he said, 'the right side is like the backbone while the left side deployment is like the stomach. The main thrust towards Se-la and Senge Dzong would be like hitting the Indians in the stomach, which should be comparatively easier than trying to break the backbone.'

The Chinese intent of sweeping across the battlefield was clearly visible from the Indian positions on Se-la. The feverish pace with which they were working on building a Class 9 road (capable of taking 3-ton vehicles) that would allow them to link Bum-la to Tawang was obvious from the very outset. The large Tibetan workforce, dressed in blue, was hard to miss.

However, having declared in public that nothing further was likely to happen in Se-la till the next year, Kaul and his Corps HQ had turned their attention towards Walong. Even though so far Indian patrols had met with little success against a mobile enemy that was not necessarily restricted to the available roads and tracks, both 62 Infantry Brigade and 4 Division's HQs should have known that the Chinese infiltration across the Tawang Chu had begun by 11 November. The Chinese 419 Tibetan Unit had been tasked to move up to Mago, using yaks and ponies to push as much equipment and supplies forward. Then the self-contained and superbly fit troops were given clear-cut objectives with a timetable that had to be adhered to. In small and sometimes large groups, these commando style units began to move across some of the most difficult terrain, towing trolley-mounted mortars and RCLs at a blistering pace.

The 419 Tibetan Unit was commanded by General Chai Hong Tuo. He was in his fifties and travelled on a sturdy grey pony with a couple of extra animals so that he could keep pace with his men. The objective of this unit was to threaten Dirang Dzong and Bomdila by getting to the 9-kilometre and 31-kilometre points on the Bomdila-Dirang road by 17 November. Simultaneously, other battalions of 419 Tibetan Unit were also on the move, with the objective of cutting off both Bridge 1 and Bridge 2 between Se-la and Dirang. While one battalion moved via Chabra-la and Jangle, the other followed the Yonggyap-la and Nyukmadong track.

China's 11 Division, under the command of General Yu Zhi Guo, with its 32 and 33 Regiments, had begun probing the Se-la defences from the direction of Dzalung-la; the Chinese patrols from this unit were tasked with shadowing Indian patrols to determine the exact layout of the Indian defences. Jitter parties were sent out to unnerve the Indians and draw them out into the open where they could be annihilated. Meanwhile, the second battalion of this division was to take on 4 Garhwal Rifles at Nuranang. The main frontal attack on Se-la was to be launched by the Chinese 55 Division that was under the command of General Liu Gueng. D-Day for this was 18 November, and going by the brief fight at Bum-la with 1 Sikh, the Chinese knew that Se-la, should the Indians choose to fight, would be a hard, if not impossible, nut to crack.

ON THE FLANKS OF SE-LA

When 4 Rajput was in Belgaum preparing to move to Sikkim it received orders to proceed to NEFA immediately. Major Trilok Nath was the officiating commanding officer as Lieutenant Colonel Prem Lal had moved as the AAG to IV Corps and his replacement was still with the UN in Laos. On 24 October, a day after detraining at Missamari, Nath was told that the battalion was now a part of 65 Infantry Brigade under the command of Brigadier G. M. Saeed. At the time, there was total confusion in Missamari and with great difficulty and with the help of their erstwhile CO, Prem Lal, the battalion managed to organize transport and started moving towards Bomdila where it was to occupy the left flank while 1 Madras was to situate itself on the right shoulder.

Once they reached Bomdila on 27 October, 4 Rajput was told to proceed to Dirang Dzong, as 1 Sikh LI had been detailed for the defence of Bomdila. Nath immediately left for a detailed reconnaissance of the areas around Thembang, Dirang Dzong, Manda-la and Phudong. Just then 4 Division HQ asked one company of 4 Rajput to immediately rush to Dirang Dzong for undertaking a special task. Delta Company, under Captain P. L. Kukrety, moved forward to Dirang Dzong that same night.

On the morning of 28 October, Kukrety was briefed by Major General Anant Pathania, who was in the process of taking over the division from Niranjan Prasad. Kukrety was asked to occupy the heights guarding the left flank of the division on the India–Bhutan border that covered the approach from Orka-la and Punsum-la. Delta Company would be entirely on its own, and under its command the GOC was allotting a section of MMGs. A local interpreter was provided by the civil administration (he subsequently turned out to be a Chinese officer) and the company was to be entirely air maintained.

The trek to Dangsickpu on the border was supposed to take a minimum of three days, but Kukrety, a mountaineer himself, and the extremely fit Rajput troops, completed the forced march in just one day. Though the distance on the map was thirty kilometres, it was in fact cut repeatedly by small streams that made the going very difficult. Delta Company's lightning move resulted in the men being woefully under-equipped in terms of winter clothing. As had been the case with 2 Rajput and 1/9 GR earlier in the month, each man was in Angola shirts and inappropriate footwear, and had just a couple of blankets. After a couple of days they were joined by a section of 3.7-inch howitzers under the command of Captain Gosal who had performed creditably at Bum-la.

As the rest of the battalion approached Dirang Dzong, a staff officer from 4 Division ordered Charlie Company to detach itself from the battalion and deploy itself at Dirang Dzong for the protection of the Division HQ. By the evening of 30 October, Alpha and Bravo Company along with Battalion HQ had reached Sapper Camp while Charlie and Delta had also been deployed as per orders. Kukrety had sited his position on a vantage point and his men had started to dig in and prepare their defences that would be ready in the next five days. However, no sooner had the Rajputs reached Dangsickpu than survivors from Brigadier Dalvi's ill-fated 7 Brigade along with other refugees from the area started arriving, exhausted and starving, quite a few injured. Also intermingled with them were some Chinese agents, who were segregated and placed under arrest, after which they were marched off to Battalion HQ under escort.

On the night of 29 October, Lieutenant Colonel Brahmanand Avasthy, the new commanding officer of 4 Rajput caught up with the battalion. Avasthy was to have taken over 2 Rajput, but since Rikh was continuing as its CO, Avasthy had been given command of 4 Rajput, a battalion he was not at all familiar with. The new commanding officer brought with him a solid reputation as being one of the best mid-ranking officers in the Indian Army at the time.

The primary task of 4 Rajput was to protect Bridge 1 on the Dirang–Se-la-Jang road, so the battalion shifted its HQ to the vicinity of Sappers Camp. With Kukrety's company watching over the footpaths that skirted Se-la from the west, it was decided that Alpha Company, under Major K. P. P. Nair, would move along the Nyukmadong track to the east to watch over tracks emanating down from Tangyap-la, Kye-la and Se-la.

Once again, GOC 4 Division, Anant Pathania, briefed the company commander, Nair, personally in the presence of both Avasthy and the new brigade commander, Brigadier A. S. Cheema. An officer from 2 Grenadiers who served under him confirmed to me that Cheema, who had commanded 2 Grenadiers in Ambala previously, was considered tactically useless, with a penchant for keeping his immediate superiors happy. The task for Nair's men would be to keep an eye on Chinese troop movement in and around Dzalung-la and deny them the use of the tracks which led down to the Dirang–Se-la road. Taking Nair aside, the brigade commander told the Alpha Company Commander to make sure he had the GOC's orders 'in writing in his own interest'.

On 10 November, Alpha company set off in bitterly cold conditions, with thick fog restricting visibility to around five metres. Nair was to describe the conditions: 'The terrain along the route is mountainous heights varying from 10,000 to 14,000 feet above sea level and covered with dense forest. The area is interspersed with finger-like ridges separated by valleys through which flow streams. The tracks are actually footpaths not more than 3 feet in width. In this sort of terrain it is not possible to maintain a steady marching speed along tracks which in addition to being narrow are tortuous. There are steep ascends and sharp descends. The distances between places are expressed in terms of the time taken to traverse them. In areas where enemy presence is suspected, the ground in front has to be searched while moving forward. Half a kilometre an hour would be a reasonable call of speed of movement.'

On 11 November, the company halted at Dher Gompa where they had to await the arrival of the porters who arrived by midday. The porters refused to proceed any further for fear of the Chinese, so their loads had to be divided amongst the already overloaded and exhausted troops. Alpha Company finally reached its destination, PT 3466, by the next afternoon. Nair was then told by Avasthy on the radio to dig in and start preparing the defences; further instructions would follow.

The second infantry battalion under 65 Infantry Brigade was 19 MLI. Formerly the Kolhapur State Force, the battalion had been earlier deployed in Nagaland from where it had moved to Alipur near Calcutta when it was rushed back to NEFA. By 9 November, it had reached Bomdila from where it was ordered to move further up to Dirang Dzong.

Dirang Dzong was occupied by 4 Division HQ that was housed in a stone building with smartly constructed bashas on the southern bank of the Khouma Chu. Sharing the space was 4 Artillery Brigade, under Brigadier Gurbax Singh Gill. 65 Infantry Brigade was located at Ewang, close to Sapper's Camp. 19 MLI was accordingly ordered to co-locate itself at Ewang where, minus two of its companies, it was deployed for the protection of the Brigade HQ. The remaining two companies were asked to proceed to PT 2090 where they occupied the two banks of the Khouma Chu.

IN THE FOOTSTEPS OF MORSHEAD AND BAILEY

Ever since the decision had been taken to dig in at Se-la, the threat of infiltration along flanking tracks was constantly being discussed at every level. Yet, Anant Pathania did not seem to be taking it seriously. Perhaps he felt that the Chinese could at best send small parties across that would be dealt with by Indian posts sitting on the southern side of the passes through which the tracks traversed. Latching onto the 'small party' factor, right down from Army HQ to corps to division, it was taken as gospel that not more than a Chinese company could negotiate Poshing-la. As noted before, if a company can get across a geographical feature, there is no reason why a battalion or a regiment cannot do the same, especially as the limiting factors are logistical and not physical. The major Chinese thrust, the Indians were convinced, would actually come along the main road between Jang and Nuranang. Having fixated on this, the senior officers displayed a remarkable sense of rigidity and refused to look at other possible approaches that could be utilized by the Chinese.

The Morshead–Bailey report of 1913 had not only suggested but had even demonstrated that a small party of men could get across Poshing-la and drop down directly into Dirang Dzong bypassing Se-la completely. Once the Chinese got across Poshing-la, the track to Thembang was wide open and they could set up road blocks and cut off the Bomdila–Dirang Dzong road.

On their way to join 48 Brigade, 5 Guards under the command of Lieutenant Colonel Jai Singh was still at Missamari when orders were received to send a platoon immediately to Dirang. The platoon, commanded by Captain Amarjeet Singh, reported to 4 Division HQ on the evening of 4 November. It was told to move without any delay to Poshing-la (11,950 feet), which was the last geographical barrier in the event of Chinese troops infiltrating through that route. However, owing to a shortage of porters and ponies, the patrol consisting of one officer, one JCO and thirty-five other ranks could only move out on 6 November. While the patrol had enough rations to sustain itself for ten days, each man was carrying only pouch ammunition.

On 8 November, the patrol was marooned short of Poshing-la as the porters and ponies deserted the group. Wireless contact was made with Division HQ and Amarjeet asked for reinforcements and additional supplies. The next day, the Guards had made contact with four sections of Assam Rifles that were dug in at Tungri, 5,000 feet south of the pass. By 11 November, the Guards patrol started to prepare its defences astride the pass, leaving the Assam Rifles where they were to act as the firm base.

By 14 November, the rest of 5 Guards had moved up to Bomdila from where a JCO and another fifteen men were dispatched to Tungri along with some porters and ponies laden with additional supplies. Around the same time, Captain Amarjeet Singh decided to proceed further north towards Tse-la (15,600 feet) on a reconnaissance. The route from Poshing-la towards the north meant crossing Pang-la (12,950 feet) and Kya-la (12,500 feet) which is stony and desolate country, making the journey extremely difficult. After crossing Kya-la, the party began to climb towards Tse-la through small scrub covered terrain. However, the Chinese spotted the patrol and laid an ambush. On 15 November, the patrol walked into the trap and was cut down by the Chinese.

Four survivors made it back to Poshing-la. Their return coincided with the arrival of the resupply column from Bomdila. Hot on the heels of the escapees, Chinese mortars opened up. After resisting the Chinese for an hour, the remaining troops broke contact and retreated to the Assam Rifles position at Tungri. From Poshing-la the track towards the south first descends sharply for 150 metres after which there is an equally sharp climb towards a rhododendron and fir-covered spur on which the Assam Rifles were deployed. With the Chinese in close pursuit, the combined Guards and Assam Rifles group fought it out till 7.30 p.m. During this period, a situation report was flashed to 48 Brigade at Bomdila, after which Tungri was abandoned and the men fell back on Lagam where they met two more companies of 5 Guards who had been moving towards Poshing-la. The men broke up into small parties to evade the harassing Chinese mortar fire and fell back further towards Thembang and Bomdila.

For the Indian troops deployed at various places to stop Chinese infiltration along the flanks of Se-la, 15 November was proving to be a disastrous day. At the 4 Division HQ, more and more red flags denoting the presence of Chinese troops were appearing as Indian soldiers started making contact with the enemy. Yet, there was an unreal calm in the vicinity of Dirang Dzong. So much so that even then Division HQ had not thought of setting up defences around its own location.

The 1 Sikh patrol had reported from Se-la that there was a large concentration of Chinese troops around Lunguthang. Accordingly, orders were issued to 4 Rajput's Alpha Company dug in at PT 3446 to send a patrol to Yonggyap-la. On the wireless, the 2IC, Major Trilok Nath, told Nair to send the artillery officer, Second Lieutenant Choudhary, along with the patrol under the command of a JCO, Jemadar Rai Singh. The patrol moved out at 7 p.m. in thick fog and after failing to make contact with the Chinese began to retrace its steps towards the company location. At some point, Choudhary insisted on taking a break and brewing some tea. There was an argument between him and Rai Singh who finally detached a section to protect the officer while he continued ahead with the rest of the party. Shortly afterwards, the Chinese, who had seen the fire, quickly closed in and killed the lieutenant and four men of the protection party. Only Sepoy Ganga Din managed to escape the carnage. After wandering around through the night, the soldier eventually got back and reported to Nair on the morning of 16 November.

On the evening of 15 November, 4 Rajput was celebrating its Zojila day (to mark its victory at Zojila in 1948). Major J. R. Saigal who was present at the party describes the scene: '4 Rajput were celebrating their Annual Day with great gusto almost on a peacetime scale, which was difficult to understand in the prevailing situation, more so when Lieutenant Colonel Avasthy was the commanding officer. It was a gala evening to which Major General Pathania and many other officers were invited. I was also there along with Brigadier Cheema.'

The party had just begun to gather steam when a message was brought in to the GOC that two jawans had arrived at Division HQ claiming that the Chinese had overrun the Assam Rifles post at Chang-la and all their comrades had been killed. This brought the celebrations to an abrupt end as Pathania ordered Avasthy to hurriedly put together some men to verify the news. 'Colonel Avasthy along with his Adjutant went out to address the troops which had assembled to proceed on patrolling. His troops heard him with rapt attention and his words of patriotism were inspiring. But one could notice the handicap of the troops going for patrolling. While a few were wearing jungle boots, which is the ideal, others were wearing ammunition boots which made a noise while marching.'

Meanwhile, a second patrol from PT 3446 under Jemadar Man Singh was also dispatched towards the Jalak Pu area. This group came under heavy fire and was extricated with some difficulty. Having realized that Alpha Company was dug in at PT 3446, the Chinese decided to bypass the Rajputs.

Recorded Major Nair: 'We saw them moving down the slope to the east using hand torches, getting on to the next ridge and moving south bypassing my position in area Point 3446. This was a clear example of adhering to the principle of war—maintenance of the aim. The aim of the Chinese column that I confronted appeared to be to get to their assigned position near the road, well behind, to establish a block in order to trap the Indian troops withdrawing along the road from Se-la. When they found that they were being delayed by my troops, they left the track that I was covering, and moved away. I felt gratified that I was able to accomplish my task of denying this route to the enemy. We reached our base in the early hours of 17 November and remained there manning our defences and awaiting further instructions.'

Amidst all the wireless chatter, it was noticed that the Chinese were regularly interfering with the Indian communications. They would at times broadcast misleading messages in Hindi. One such rather simplistic message said 'Stop firing'; on checking, it turned out the message had not originated from any of the Indian networks. Already the confusion and indecision of the higher HQs was messing with the orders that were being given; these often led to unnecessary troop movement. For example, a platoon under Subedar Haribaksh Singh was moved to Labrang. By last light, the platoon was ordered to return to Battalion HQ leaving behind a section. Just what a lone section of bewildered men in the middle of nowhere were expected to achieve was baffling.

On 16 November, all eyes in Division HQ were on 62 Infantry Brigade as the Chinese prepared to launch their attack on the 4 Garhwal positions at Nuranang. At 6 p.m., 4 Division HQ received the news that Poshing-la, held by a section of 5 Guards and Assam Rifles troops under the command of Captain Amarjeet, had been overrun and the combined force had suffered heavy casualties and had been forced to withdraw to the Se-la–Kye-la ridgeline. Division HQ immediately decided to (a) strengthen the Rajput company under Major K. P. P Nair; (b) move 5 Guards to Thembang and recapture Poshing-la; (c) send three companies of 19 MLI divided into two columns to help 5 Guards; and (d) send one company of 1 Madras from Bomdila and two companies of 13 Dogra from Senge to Dirang Dzong for the protection of 4 Division HQ.

By the evening of 16 November, Anant Pathania had realized just how serious the outflanking threat was and that his sending out units piecemeal had barely impacted the Chinese ingress into Indian positions behind him. His other concerns were now dominated by the fact that his own HQ at Dirang Dzong was completely vulnerable. With no defences at all having been prepared there, the overriding concern now was to delay the Chinese for as long as possible while Division HQ was immediately moved further south.

Subsequently, on the same night, two columns of 19 MLI were hurriedly dispatched from Ewang: Charlie Company under the command of Major S. D. Parab, accompanied by a FOO from the artillery, was sent to Tungri via Sangti and Rungza. The Assam Rifles post at Chhang-la had been withdrawn and there had been no communication with a company of 5 Guards that had been sent towards Chhang-la a day earlier. This column made no contact with the Chinese. Shortly afterwards, Parab was asked to withdraw from Rungza and make his way towards Kachow and take up a defensive position there. At 4.45 p.m., the order was further modified by Brigade HQ who ordered Parab to immediately fall back to Battalion HQ as the Chinese had by then established a roadblock between Dirang Dzong and Bomdila.

A second MLI column, consisting of Delta Company less a platoon and a platoon from Bravo Company, was asked to proceed towards Changdor under the command of Major A. M. Shaikh. This group too was accompanied by an artillery observer, Lieutenant Vinay Shankar, and by the morning of 17 November, moving along the Dirang–Munna Camp–Namshu track, they were in visual contact with Changdor where they could see the Chinese milling around. Vinay Shankar called in artillery fire after which the Marathas decided to fall back despite the fact that Shaikh had originally been tasked with digging in and denying the Chinese an infiltration route.

Reports also started trickling in of Chinese infiltration in the area of Nyukamadung. This added considerably to Anant Pathania's fast-growing despondency. He spoke to the BGS IV Corps and sounded out K. K. Singh about an immediate withdrawal from Dirang Dzong. Singh managed to calm down the GOC and strongly advised him to stay put. Nevertheless, Pathania ordered his GSO-2 (SD), Major Ummat, to put together a layout party and proceed immediately for the Tenga Valley and scout around for a new location to set up the Division HQ. Ummat, however, had no intention of stopping at Tenga and made a dash for the plains, where he was subsequently arrested.

One platoon from Major Kukrety's position at PT 3582 was probing northwards when it made contact with the Chinese. In the ensuing firefight, eleven men from 4 Rajput were killed. The platoon had to be reinforced and only then could it break contact with the Chinese and move back into its prepared defences on PT 3582. This developing threat forced Avasthy to get Bravo Company, which had been protecting Bridge 1, to move up and reinforce PT 3582 with one platoon while the rest of the company was to occupy Gompachar to its rear. The Chinese were quite content to let 4 Rajput alone for the time being, having got what they wanted; with Bravo Company out of the way, Bridge 1 would be cut off if the troops at Se-la panicked and made a run for Dirang Dzong. By 17 November, the trap had been set and now all that stood between the Chinese and success was Hoshiar Singh's Se-la brigade.

4 GARHWAL AT NURANANG

The 4 Garhwal defences were located just ahead of Bridge 3 at Nuranang. Two companies, Alpha and Delta, were deployed to dominate the winding road that came up from Jang. Sheer cliffs on either side of the valley protected their flanks that could not be bypassed. Beyond the forward positions, the village of Jang lay some 4,000 feet below. From well sited observation posts, most of the Tawang Chu Valley was visible, while across the river they could clearly observe the forward slopes of Geyshe-la, Rho, Sheo and Lao villages. A little to the left, on the Bum-la slopes, Tawang and its impressive monastery situated on a spur were clearly visible.

The presence of 2 Derajat Mountain Battery's 3.7 howitzers increased the offensive power of the forward defences of 4 Garhwal. This was later further beefed up with the deployment of 25-pounder guns two kilometres behind the forward positions. A company of 4 Sikh LI and a platoon from 13 Dogra had also been deployed for a while with 4 Garhwal and this had helped develop a fine rapport between the men. Most importantly, extremely energetic junior officers were commanding the forward companies. Their enthusiasm and aggressive spirit had communicated itself to the men who were now itching to have a crack at the Chinese.

On 16 November, a group of Monpas appeared near the leading company of 4 Garhwal Rifles. Second Lieutenant Surinder Nath Tandon who was commanding Alpha Company asked Subedar Udai Singh Rawat commanding the forward platoon to investigate. The JCO had got to within thirty metres of the group when he realized they were Chinese soldiers carrying weapons concealed under their Monpa robes. Keeping his wits about him, the JCO threw a grenade at the party and scrambled back into the defences.

This little charade having failed, early next morning the Chinese launched their attack on No. 2 Platoon of Alpha Company that was positioned on the forward right side of the company's defences. This platoon was alerted to the presence of the Chinese when anti-personnel mines around the defences started going off all around them. Chinese mortars opened up briefly, after which they started to attack in waves. For thirty minutes the Chinese tried to close the gap with the three platoons of Alpha Company but the Garhwal troops held their own, shooting down the Chinese with deadly accuracy. The Chinese then pulled back to their forming-up area, to reorganize for a second attack.

A flank patrol of 4 Garhwal which had left the locality on 15 November, came in on the radio at 7.15 a.m., reporting that approximately two infantry battalions were forming up opposite the Alpha Company locality while another large body of troops seemed to heading there from the direction of Jang to further reinforce them. Half an hour later, Chinese artillery and heavy mortars opened up, followed shortly by waves of Chinese soldiers. Owing to the covering fire, the Chinese managed to get fairly close to the Indian defences. The Garhwalis, relying mainly on grenades, broke up this attack successfully and the Chinese withdrew once again.

This was the classic method of defence on which the Indian Army relied and the Garhwalis were in their element. The main problem was that no matter how many men they dropped, the Chinese kept coming—a line of men would replace their fallen soldiers. Sooner or later the well-entrenched Indian troops would run out of ammunition.

The forward platoon under Udai Singh was the most affected as the main thrust of the Chinese attack had been aimed at this platoon. The Chinese were constantly attacking Alpha Company with mortars and artillery fire as more guns were being brought across the repaired Bridge 4. A message was relayed to Battalion HQ asking for more ammunition. Second

Lieutenant Vinod Goswami volunteered to carry the ammunition to Udai Singh. In addition, through the rest of the day, the battalion's quartermaster, Captain P. P. S. Bains, kept up a steady supply of ammunition to replenish the forward positions.

The Chinese had no choice but to try and force their way through Alpha Company to get to the other companies deployed behind them in the narrow valley. Having regrouped, they launched the third assault at 9.10 a.m.; again they were beaten back. Thereupon a lull in the fighting ensued. The Chinese in the meantime seemed to have pushed forward a fairly competent artillery officer to act as the FOO, for accurate counter-bombardment started coming onto the Derajat Battery gun positions. At first some of the gunners broke ranks, but the GPO, Lieutenant Charanjit 'Cherry' Dhillon, quickly brought the situation under control and the guns continued to be fully active.

At 10 a.m., the increased tempo in the shelling suggested that the Chinese were going to attack for a fourth time. Half an hour later, after the bombardment lifted, Chinese infantry launched a three-pronged attack, trying to get at the Indians from the exposed west flank of Alpha Company. They had abandoned their normal tactics of coming in waves, and were now trying to close the gap by crawling through the rocks that were littered with their own dead and wounded. Whatever the limitations of the .303 Enfield rifle, its killing power was tremendous. Both Tandon and Udai Singh stayed resolute and marshalled the Garhwalis superbly. However, the Chinese this time around were getting fairly close to the forward trenches of Udai Singh's platoon. Naik Ranjit Singh Gusain, sensing the danger, came out of his bunker into an open trench from where he started lobbing grenades at the Chinese to great effect.

A bullet hit Ranjit on the head and brought him down temporarily. The Chinese had by then managed to push forward and set up two MMGs within thirty metres of the closest Indian bunker. As the MMGs opened up, specially targeting the Garhwali LMGs, the Chinese resorted to attacking in waves again.

Within seconds, the situation became desperate. Ranjit, though bleeding profusely, was still lobbing grenades at the Chinese, giving a chance for three men to come out of the bunkers and start crawling towards the Chinese MMG positions. Lance Naik Trilok Singh Negi was armed with a Sten gun, while Riflemen Jaswant Singh Rawat and Gopal Singh Gusain were only armed with grenades. Getting to within twelve metres of the Chinese gun positions, they lobbed their grenades and Jaswant sprinted across and leapt into the MMG post. Grabbing one of the MMGs, he started to run back towards his other two comrades when he was shot down. Trilok, while giving Jaswant covering fire, was also killed, but Gopal, though wounded, managed to get back into the bunker with the captured weapon. The Chinese attack once again fizzled out and the wounded men, including the unconscious Ranjit Singh Gusain along with the captured MMG, were sent to Battalion HQ.

Had the Chinese the option of bypassing the 4 Garhwal dug in at Nuranang, they would have done so. Under tremendous pressure to get past Alpha Company, they launched yet another determined attack that was supported by artillery and mortars at 2.50 p.m. Once again, Subedar Udai Singh and his men stood firm. For the fifth time on that fateful day, the Chinese had to withdraw. Though it is hard to confirm the casualties on the Chinese side, almost all records say 300 Chinese soldiers were killed and wounded. Miraculously, at this stage of the fighting, only two Garhwalis had been killed, though many men were hit by shrapnel and were walking wounded.

Around the time the final Chinese attack on Alpha Company fizzled out at around 4 p.m., Chinese artillery fire cut the communication line with Brigade HQ. As attempts were being made to raise Battalion HQ on the wireless, GOC 4 Division took a baffling decision, ordering Hoshiar to withdraw 4 Garhwal. Even though the accepted tactics of the Indian Army at the time suggested that covering troops, after having achieved their objective of delaying the enemy should fall back, it was not a rule written in stone. Now Nuranang was proving to be an ideal defensive position, which by virtue of being boxed in by steep cliffs on either side could not be outflanked. Commander 62 Brigade should have realized that he could now use the hours of darkness to replenish and reinforce this position. Instead, in a repeat of 1 Sikh's fight at Bum-la, Lieutenant Colonel B. M. Bhattacharjea was asked to break contact and withdraw to Se-la at night. They were told 1 Sikh would serve the men a hot meal on arrival at Se-la Top.

Unfortunately, shortly after the first reports of the Chinese attacks started coming in, 4 Division had set a poor example by pulling out two Dogra companies from Senge for its own protection. For all the talk of holding Se-la, after having taken up defensive positions, there was obviously no actual tactical plan in place and the order to 4 Garhwal to withdraw reflects this major shortcoming in the plans of 4 Division. In combat situations, it is extremely hard to speculate on the ifs and buts of any scenario. Yet, the orders to abandon the defences and pull out made no sense whatsoever. Instead of building on the day's success and forcing the Chinese to reinforce failure, the brigade commander threw it away and virtually signed his own and the brigade's death warrant. Until that morning, 4 Sikh LI was deployed around the Two Lakes area between the Garhwalis at Nuranang and the two battalions at Se-la Top. The orders to abandon this position and pull back into a tight square on Se-la Top were a complete reversal of the earlier plan. Had this decision not been taken, 4 Sikh LI could and should have been used as a reserve for 4 Garhwal. As it ultimately panned out, even the other companies of 4 Garhwal had not come into play by last light on 17 November.

From the sublime to the ridiculous! How else can one describe the events that were to unfold in the next few hours as the much-vaunted Se-la brigade imploded with just a little shove from the Chinese. In less than a month since the fiasco at Nam Ka Chu, the shortcomings of senior Indian leadership had once again been completely exposed. By the evening of 17 November, it was quite obvious that 4 Division HQ had once again failed to achieve its objective. Regardless of how well the Garhwalis fought (it's interesting that all Chinese records ignore the fighting on 17 November, claiming that the attack on Se-la started on 18 November) or how things would turn out the next day, Pathania and his staff had already been hamstrung by fear.

Chapter 11

THE IMPLOSION

IV CORPS HQ (17 NOVEMBER - AFTERNOON)

The large silver-coloured Super Constellation of the VIP Squadron lifted off from Palam Airport in New Delhi and set a course for Tezpur en route to Chabua. Inside the cavernous aircraft, only two seats were occupied. The COAS, General Pran Thapar, and the Director, Military Operations, Brigadier D. K. Palit, were headed east to somehow salvage the situation after the fall of Walong the previous day. In Jammu and Kashmir, after the initial Chinese advances in the Chip Chap and Galwan valleys, the situation seemed to be quiet. In the event of a second Chinese offensive resulting in further advances in Ladakh, Army HQ's assessment was that the Chinese were still a long way from posing any threat to either Kashmir or Punjab as their ability to wage war in this sector was limited to trans-border operations. In all likelihood, even getting to Leh would be beyond Chinese capabilities especially if the Indian troops deployed in Chushul fell back across the Chang-la in time.

In NEFA, even though 11 Brigade had ceased to exist as a cohesive body, a Chinese advance along the Lohit River would be extremely limited and could not be considered a major threat to Assam. As for the Kameng Frontier Division, Thapar and Palit believed that with two brigades holding Se-la, there was a good chance of keeping the Chinese at bay even if the odd Chinese column outflanked the Se-la defences and got to the Bomdila road. Even at this late stage, neither the army chief nor the DMO were aware that the GOC, Major General Anant Pathania, had established his HQ at Dirang Dzong and had deployed only one brigade at Se-la. They were also not aware of the large-scale ingress of Chinese troops across Poshing-la and other routes. As a result, the two officers were not particularly concerned with Se-la, their attention being more on Walong and the situation being faced by the newly raised 2 Infantry Division.

The aircraft touched down at Tezpur Air Force Station at 5 p.m. The Eastern Army Commander, Lieutenant General Bogey Sen, and his BGS, Brigadier H. K. Sibal, met General Thapar at the aircraft bay. Both the officers were looking extremely grim. Sen informed Thapar that the Chinese had that morning started their main offensive against Se-la and had attacked 4 Garhwal's forward positions during the day. In fact, even as they spoke, Sen said, the fighting was going on in Se-la.

Thapar decided to stay in Tezpur. He sent a wireless message to Kaul ordering the corps commander to return at once to Tezpur. As the party headed for Corps HQ, Sen filled Thapar in on the details of the events of the morning. The latest information from 4 Division HQ was that the GOC, Pathania, had ordered the battalion to break contact and fall back towards Se-la Top.

Palit, sitting in the front seat of the staff car, thought he had misheard the army commander. Since the chief said nothing, Palit asked Sen: 'Why were they withdrawn? If the Garhwalis had repulsed four attacks by the Chinese surely they should remain at their post?'

Sen was obviously annoyed with the DMO's interjection. He replied sullenly that if Palit wanted an answer to his question he would have to ask GOC 4 Division himself.

Palit, the main architect of 62 Infantry Brigade digging in at Se-la, was not going to be put off. He pointed out to Thapar and Sen the absurdity of the order. If the Garhwalis were to break off contact and pull back, it would leave the main defences unguarded and allow the assaulting Chinese troops to regroup, build up without interference and then launch an assault at points of their own choosing.

Thapar still did not react; he seemed preoccupied and distant, gazing absently at the tea gardens they were speeding past. 'You have to issue immediate orders to cancel the withdrawal of the covering troops,' implored Palit, twisting to look at Sen at the back of the car.

'It is not for me to interfere in IV Corps' battles,' Sen replied coldly.

'Not even in the absence of the corps commander?' As a junior officer, Palit was sticking his neck out, but Sen just ignored his question. Thapar still said nothing. By then the staff car had pulled up outside the IV Corps HQ. It was now completely dark outside.

In the absence of Kaul, BGS IV Corps, Brigadier K. K. Singh, received the chief. Without any preamble, the party proceeded towards the corps's Ops Room where more bad news awaited them. Information had just come in that the fighting had spread to Bomdila. The Battalion HQ of 5 Guards which had moved up to Thembang had reported over the wireless that the Chinese, coming in from the north, had surrounded their location. They had been granted permission to withdraw by 48 Brigade HQ.

Pathania had spoken to the BGS some time ago. He described the situation of 62 Infantry Brigade and his own HQ as very precarious as a result of roadblocks established by the Chinese and had pleaded for permission to withdraw. K. K. Singh had refused, and had advised the GOC to stay put. Thereupon Pathania had rung off.

Palit once again turned in desperate anguish towards Thapar and Sen. He was to write later (and his version was corroborated by others): 'I could scarcely believe what we were being told. None of the commanders seemed to have the heart for a fight. As soon as we were secluded in the corps' Ops Room, I remarked to Thapar, "Everyone seems to be withdrawing! As far as I can make out the Guards have not even been attacked, and yet they are being pulled out of battle. Their withdrawal will mean that the road from Bomdila to Dirang will be exposed to the enemy who would then be free to disrupt 4 Division's line of communication at will. This is a disastrous decision."'

Bogey Sen turned to K. K. Singh, but instead of giving him any definite orders, the Eastern Army Commander told the BGS he was no longer required and dismissed him. As K. K. Singh departed from what was his Ops Room, Palit once again confronted Sen: 'Sir, I hope you will reverse at least this decision. And if it is too late to stop the withdrawal, 48 Brigade commander must be ordered to re-establish a position on Thembang Ridge with fresh troops; or, at least, to position troops somewhere on the lower slopes of that ridge—to deny the enemy easy access to the main Tawang road.'

Bogey Sen said to Palit coldly: 'I've already told you, Monty, it is not my job to interfere in the corps' or the division's battles.'

'On the contrary, in the absence of the corps commander, you, by your very presence, are responsible for the corps' battle. It has reached a critical stage and it is for you to assume command.'

Sen just kept staring at his shoes, stubbornly refusing to say anything.

A desperate Palit turned to Thapar, who had barely even spoken since Sen informed him of the Chinese attack on Se-la: 'Sir, please take over the battle. The army commander disclaims that responsibility.'

Thapar finally reacted. He seemed to shake himself out of a reverie. "A-ho," he replied in Punjabi, and looked at Palit inquiringly. The DMO's first suggestion was that they should recall the BGS to the Ops Room.

Having brought the chief's attention back to the prevailing situation, Palit suggested that Brigadier Gurbax Singh's 48 Brigade in Bomdila be immediately de-linked from 4 Division's command and henceforth be controlled by IV Corps. 'Pathania at Senge must not be made to look back over his shoulder. All his attention must be riveted on the Se-la battle.' Thapar nodded his assent, but the BGS had just realized that his corps commander had not bothered to inform either Eastern Command or Army HQ that he had authorized Pathania to set up 4 Division's HQ at Dirang Dzong more than a fortnight ago. It was incredible—what the entire Chinese Army knew was not known to the Indian high command. It also meant none of the officers in the chain of command was aware of the fact that 65 Brigade was also not on Se-la but had been deployed to defend Dirang Dzong instead. In fact, there were three points that needed to be defended, not two!

Not only was Anant Pathania seventy kilometres from the battle unfolding at Se-la, his position at Dirang Dzong had not yet been fortified. Now that he had realized that the comfortable quarters built by the Border Roads Organisation was not secure, that was all he could focus on. 4 Division HQ had already ordered 13 Dogra to detach two of its companies at Senge Dzong and rush them to Dirang.

Just then, the telephone in the Ops Room rang and Pathania came through on the line. Speaking to K. K. Singh, the GOC said that there were reports of Chinese troops having come around the left flank of Se-la. The road between Se-la and Dirang Dzong could be severed any minute, while the Dirang Dzong-Bomdila road had already been cut off. Pathania added that the line of communication between him and Bomdila already seemed to have been cut, for he was unable to raise Gurbax Singh. Pathania once again asked for permission to withdraw 4 Infantry Division. Just where the GOC wanted to pull back to remained a mystery.

Keeping Pathania on hold, K. K. Singh told Thapar, Sen and Palit what Pathania had said. Neither the chief nor the army commander said anything. Palit told the BGS to firmly tell Pathania there was no question of a withdrawal.

Suddenly, Bogey Sen spoke up, saying that in his opinion, maybe Pathania should be given the order to withdraw. Ignoring the army commander, Palit once again turned to Thapar and implored him to take command of the situation. It was obvious that if Pathania was allowed to withdraw just because the Chinese had appeared on his flanks (an eventuality that had been catered for) the defence of Kameng would collapse and with nowhere to withdraw to, 4 Infantry Division would disintegrate just as 7 Brigade had.

Palit was desperately trying to get Thapar to give a firm decision that would close the issue and put an end to all talk of withdrawal. Anant Pathania was still holding on at the other end of the telephone line as Palit went over the situation with the army chief point by point. Se-la is a strong defensive position; we have a sizeable force holding the pass; all possible encircling moves by the Chinese have been foreseen and plans exist to combat these situations; a withdrawal down a steep road towards Dirang would be un-tactical and could only result in a rout; no alternative defensive positions exist.

Thapar was beginning to see the sense of the argument and the need to take a decision. Holding up his hand to restrain Palit, he finally spoke to Bogey Sen, but instead of taking a firm stand, he started a discussion where he suggested the army commander advise Pathania to stick it out at Se-la. However, Sen had made up his mind and unless the chief gave him a clear and direct order, he was not going to budge. 'If 4 Infantry Division can make a clean break now,' he said, 'it will have a chance of getting away intact.'

An incredulous Palit asked the army commander if 4 Division's operational role was to fight the enemy at Se-la or to keep itself intact? Once again Palit asserted that there could be no question of a pullback, especially since 4 Garhwal had repulsed the initial Chinese attacks at Nuranang. Once again Thapar and Sen got into a long-winded discussion that went nowhere as Sen refused to see reason and Thapar refused to give an order, still trying to gently persuade his army commander. All this while the BGS was standing, holding the telephone with Pathania still on the line.

At this point, there was a diversion as Lieutenant General Bijji Kaul walked into the Ops Room, having arrived from Walong and Chabua.

62 BRIGADE HQ (17 NOVEMBER - AFTERNOON)

At around 3.30 p.m., Brigadier Hoshiar Singh spoke at length on the telephone with the GOC 4 Division, Major General Anant Pathania. Commander 62 Brigade had just returned from Nuranang and he was extremely upbeat, 4 Garhwal having successfully beaten off multiple attacks on their forward defences by an estimated 600 to 800 Chinese soldiers. Not only had the Garhwalis fought most resolutely, as we have noted in the previous chapter, they had only suffered two fatal casualties up to that point. However, by then it was apparent that the Chinese had obtained a foothold on the flanks of 4 Garhwal, for their guns and heavy mortars had

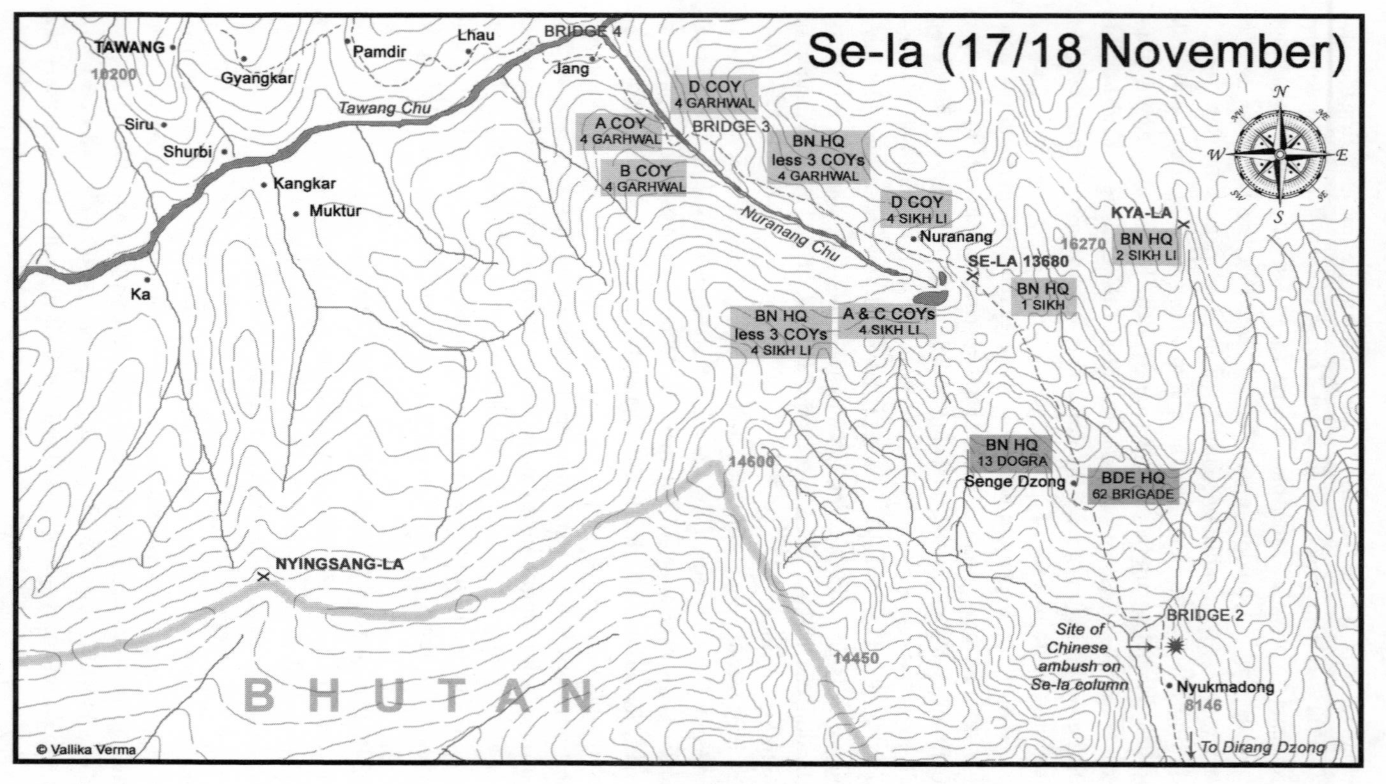

Se-la (17/18 November)
TAWANG
16200
Gyangkar
Pamdir
Lhau
BRIDGE 4
Jang
Tawang Chu
Siru
Shurbi
Kangkar
Muktur
Ka
D COY
4 GARHWAL
A COY
4 GARHWAL
BRIDGE 3
B COY
4 GARHWAL
BN HQ
less 3 COYs
4 GARHWAL
D COY
4 SIKH LI
Nuranang
Nuranang Chu
SE-LA 13680
16270
KYA-LA
BN HQ
2 SIKH LI
BN HQ
1 SIKH
BN HQ
less 3 COYs
4 SIKH LI
A & C COYs
4 SIKH LI
BN HQ
13 DOGRA
Senge Dzong
BDE HQ
62 BRIGADE
14600
NYINGSANG-LA
14450
BHUTAN
BRIDGE 2
Site of
Chinese
ambush on
Se-la column
Nyukmadong
8146
To Dirang Dzong
N
NE
E
SE
S
SW
W
NW
© Vallika Verma

been trying to engage in depth targets as well. Not wanting to withdraw the Garhwalis and anticipating a stronger push either at night or the next morning, Hoshiar Singh had discussed the possibility of reinforcing 4 Garhwal with two companies of 13 Dogra in addition to one company of 4 Sikh LI that had been positioned to cover the pullback.

Unknown to Hoshiar Singh, the GOC had spoken to Brigadier Gurbax Singh, the commander of 48 Brigade, at Bomdila earlier in the day. The news that the Chinese had got across Poshing-la in relatively large numbers and were threatening Thembang was obviously the main topic of discussion. Gurbax had suggested to Pathania that in light of the Chinese move, both 62 and 65 Brigade should immediately withdraw to Bomdila from where the entire divisional resource could be brought into play to halt the Chinese. Gurbax at the time was not aware of the Chinese having attacked Nuranang already. When Pathania told him that the Garhwalis had been fighting since the morning, Gurbax suggested that HQ 4 Division along with 65 Infantry Brigade should fall back, leaving 62 Brigade to fight the Chinese at Se-la. From a tactical point of view, under the circumstances, the second scenario made some sense; however, the suggestion was not acceptable to Pathania.

In between the two telephone conversations (first with Gurbax Singh and then with Hoshiar Singh) Pathania had dispatched his layout party to head for Tenga where he hoped to establish his Division HQ.

On seeing the party leave hurriedly, word spread through Division HQ and the administrative troops that the GOC was planning 'to do a bunk'. However, Hoshiar Singh, at Se-la, was unaware of these developments. His reluctance to ask the covering troops to withdraw from what had proved to be tactically an extremely well sited position was understandable. General Pathania would later claim that by the time he spoke to Brigadier Hoshiar Singh at 3.30 p.m., the latter had already withdrawn 4 Garhwal Rifles, ordered 4 Sikh LI to fall back on to the main Se-la defences and that Hoshiar Singh had asked the GOC to retrospectively sanction his decision.

This testimony was false. On the contrary, Pathania in his conversation with Hoshiar Singh had said that IV Corps had ordained that 'on no account the covering troops were to be sacrificed by delaying their withdrawal in face of superior build up'. Hence, despite his better judgement, Hoshiar Singh withdrew 4 Garhwal Rifles from Nuranang at around 4 p.m., roughly around the time the last Chinese assault was being beaten back. By then, owing to Chinese shelling, the communication lines between 62 Brigade and 4 Garhwal Rifles had snapped and hence Captain Abraham of 4 Sikh LI and another officer were physically sent with the message for Lieutenant

Colonel Bhattacharjea.

In his message, Hoshiar congratulated the battalion commander and his officers and men for 'a very steady and defensive battle'. He also gave instructions for redeploying the battalion. They were to abandon the present defences so as to cross KM 108 on the Jang–Se-la–Bomdila road latest by midnight 17-18 November. The withdrawal had to be coordinated with the FOO stationed at KM 106 so that the artillery guns could then engage the abandoned positions. Battalion HQ minus two companies would redeploy with Brigade HQ at Se-la while the two companies would deploy under 1 Sikh at Se-la itself. The orders were accordingly passed to all sub-units of 4 Garhwal.

Simultaneously, two companies of 4 Sikh LI at Two Lakes were also ordered to fall back and occupy their main positions in the Battalion Defended Area. Ahead of the main defences, one company was to cover the withdrawal of 4 Garhwal and then fall back.

The brigade plan was simple—the covering troops (4 Garhwal Rifles) would henceforth be the brigade reserve while the defences were closed in. At this point, Hoshiar Singh was extremely clear that even if 65 and 48 Brigades were outflanked, 62 Brigade would fight it out. There was absolutely no question of abandoning Se-la and withdrawing from it.

Much as one would like to believe that Anant Pathania was acting purely on the tactical merits of the developing situation, the evidence, including his own statements, are very damning. Most officers who had served with Pathania insist that the man was not a coward, and yet! After ordering Hoshiar Singh to withdraw from Nuranang, the GOC made his call to IV Corps, wanting to speak to Kaul but getting through to the BGS, K. K. Singh, instead.

Anant Pathania's fears, as communicated to IV Corps, were exaggerated. First, at that stage, Hoshiar Singh had definitely not communicated to him that Se-la was being invested from three sides and that his situation was almost untenable. In fact, as Pathania himself admitted after the war, at that stage there was no talk of the Chinese having attacked anything other than Nuranang, though he claims that he did say the situation at Se-la had deteriorated.

Hoshiar Singh had repeatedly underlined his intention to fight it out at Se-la. Apart from repeating this ad nauseam to the men of all five infantry battalions under his command, on 7 November he had sent a letter to all units and sub-units stating: 'The Chinese have ruthlessly attacked our motherland; we must be as ruthless and evict them. This is possible by having an aggressive spirit and a will to win. Se-la is impregnable. We are at a major advantage than the enemy and must be successful: we have a good road, air supply, better and more artillery, and we are fighting on our own soil. Even if the Chinese outflank us and cut our rear, we must not be perturbed. As we are dependent on the air supply, we must hold on to the good defences of Se-la.'

While Hoshiar Singh was not willing to even contemplate a withdrawal, GOC 4 Division was falling prey to the incessant negative talk that seemed to grip staff officers right up the chain of command. Even at the time, it was well known that some senior officers including the BGS, Brigadier K. K. Singh, and the Corps HQ were extremely unhappy with Se-la's selection over Bomdila as the line of defence. In fact, the GSO-1 in 4 Division HQ, Lieutenant Colonel Manohar Singh, had been freely voicing his opinion in favour of a retreat, openly saying the Chinese were invincible, so much so that Pathania at one stage thought of asking for his replacement. This antagonism towards what was seen as 'Palit's plan' seems to have coloured the interpretation of what was said on both sides when Pathania spoke to K. K. Singh.

Despite having failed to get firm orders from Thapar or Sen in the absence of Kaul to withdraw 4 Division, Pathania again spoke to Hoshiar Singh after which the brigade commander called a conference in his bunker at 6.30 p.m. The minutes of the meeting, attended by Lieutenant Colonel Budhwar (OC Field Regiment), Major Bakshi (OC Field Company Engineers), Major Jaidev Singh Datta (BM) and Major A. O. Alexander (DAA&QMG) state:

> The General Officer Commanding 4 Infantry Division had a telephone conversation for about half an hour with the Brigade Commander. According to the General, the situation in the rear was NOT satisfactory. The Chinese have managed to establish a roadblock KM 6 between Bomdila and Dirang Dzong—strength seems to be about one battalion. The General enquired about the situation at Se-la. Commander 62 Infantry Brigade informed him that covering troops of 4 Garhwal Rifles at Nuranang and two companies of 4 Sikh LI had accomplished their job admirably and have been ordered back to Se-la. The Brigade can hold on to Se-la for about a week; if air supply is not affected the Brigade will be quite happy to stay on at Se-la.
>
> The General could not guarantee full air supply to the Se-la Brigade, thus wanted the entire Brigade to fall back on Bomdila rather than lose the whole Brigade at Se-la. If the enemy cuts off

> Se-la, the Division had no reserves to open up the road to Se-la. The General was keen that 62 Infantry Brigade should withdraw on the night of November 17-18 itself, join up with 65 Infantry Brigade and Divisional Headquarters and then bash on to Bomdila. However, Commander 62 Infantry Brigade thought withdrawal on the night of November 17-18 would spread panic and wanted, under these circumstances, to withdraw instead on the night of November 18-19; the General agreed to this proposal. The General also authorized Commander 62 Infantry Brigade to demolish Bridge 1 on the road near Dirang Dzong and Bridge 2 south of Senge. Two companies of 13 Dogras were sent to Divisional Headquarters on the night of November 17-18.

It is obvious that Pathania had already mentally lost the battle for Se-la. Despite having tried his best to get a formal sanction to withdraw 4 Division, he did not have the mandate to pull 62 Brigade out at that point; on the contrary, he was repeatedly being told to stay put. In the long drawn-out conversations, the GOC began to paint a picture that was not quite true. On the other hand, he started undermining the confidence of Hoshiar Singh. If indeed Pathania was so rattled by the Chinese having cut the road behind him, the logical thing for him to have done would have been to collect 65 Infantry Brigade and marry up with 62 Brigade and fight it out with the Chinese. By closing the gap towards Senge Dzong (Pathania also had tanks from 7 Cavalry with him) he could have watched Hoshiar's Singh's back, making sure that air supply would not be affected. The Chinese who could attack from the rear were unlikely to have any artillery. Meanwhile, 48 Brigade would have been left to fight a defensive battle against the Chinese who had come over Poshing-la and other routes. Reinforced by 67 Infantry Brigade, the push towards Se-la for the relief of 62 and 65 Brigade would have stretched the Chinese troops and caught them in a trap of their own making.

Had Pathania moved forward instead of backwards, the story may well have turned out very differently. This did not require any brilliant thinking on the part of the higher command—it was the original concept in the first place in any case. It had got derailed when Pathania had decided to locate his Division HQ at Dirang rather than at Senge. However, it was pretty obvious by then that no one was thinking straight anymore.

Pathania would later claim that he did not 'order' Hoshiar Singh to withdraw, he merely asked him to prepare a withdrawal plan for the night of 17-18 November. Though Hoshiar Singh has come under criticism for agreeing to pull back, it is pretty obvious from existing records that the brigade commander was bullied into accepting Pathania's orders.

IV CORPS HQ (17 NOVEMBER - EVENING)

In his usual dramatic style, Kaul entered the IV Corps Ops Room at 7 p.m. Through the day the corps commander had been at Walong where remnants of 6 Kumaon and 4 Sikh had been trying to fall back along the almost non-existent track towards the Assam plains. Despite the defeat suffered in the Lohit Frontier Division, Kaul was in an upbeat mood. Full of the day's events, the corps commander did not notice the grim faces and the tension all around him. Instead, according to Palit, 'without waiting for preliminaries, Kaul launched into a dramatized blow-by-blow account of events subsequent to the fall of Walong and the part he had played in them: details of 11 Infantry Brigade's withdrawal along both banks of the Lohit; supply dropping missions for the withdrawing troops; 'rescue' missions by helicopter, in one of which Kaul had personally landed 'amidst sporadic enemy fire' and offered to evacuate the Brigade Commander (quite an unprofessional procedure, in my opinion, because the brigade would have been left in the lurch without a commander). 'The Brigade Commander, stout-heartedly, declined the offer.'

For a full thirty minutes, the *Official History of the 1962 War* records, the 'situation in the Lohit Frontier Division was discussed'. Neither Thapar nor Sen tried to stop him. Every time Palit tried to interrupt Kaul 'he would take off on a description of some other hair-raising episode of the Lohit battle, jumping up and down excitedly at the wall map'. Eventually, unable to contain himself, Palit walked over to Kaul and gripped his arm. 'Bijji bhai,' he said firmly, 'forget Walong, the crisis is in Kameng. Your 4th Division is collapsing.'

'What?' he exclaimed, suddenly alarmed. 'What are you talking about?'

Palit then gave him a rundown of what had been happening at Nuranang and Se-la since the morning. Se-la could hold out, perhaps not indefinitely, but surely for at least a week or ten days, but someone had to firmly tell Anant Pathania that pulling out was not an option. In his absence no one had done that and they were now awaiting his arrival so that as the corps commander, he could take that decision once and for all.

It was perhaps the defining moment of the Se-la battle. Palit, assertive and somewhat agitated, yet cool and articulate, had to succeed for the brigade and the division's survival. But just then General Pran Thapar ordered Palit to go and check on the status of 82 Infantry Brigade which was being rushed to 2 Division from Rajasthan. The chief told Palit to make sure the orders were to airlift the brigade and not to send it by train.

During the next thirty minutes, Kaul spoke to both Pathania and Gurbax Singh on the telephone to ascertain for himself the situation in Se-la and Bomdila. While Thapar had relapsed into a brooding silence, Sen was of the opinion that Pathania, as the man on the spot, was best suited to take appropriate action. As per official records, Kaul spoke to Pathania at least twice in quick succession.

Eventually K. K. Singh walked out of the Ops Room to where Palit was sitting with Brigadier Inder Verma, the Brig Adam of IV Corps. Recalls Palit: 'With a somewhat derisive smile on his face he flung a copy of a signal on the desk in front of me and said, "So much for your advice on Se-la."'

The DMO was stunned—he was looking at an operational order from IV Corps HQ to 4 Division granting it permission to withdraw.

'Who has authorized the withdrawal?' Palit asked K. K. Singh curtly, hardly able to believe what he was seeing.

'You can take that up with the corps commander,' replied the BGS, departing from the room.

Turning to Inder Verma, Palit asked him if he could revoke the signal. Being from the Corps of Signals, the Brig Adam was familiar with the communication network where messages from Tezpur to Dirang Dzong had to be relayed through Bomdila. Since messages had to be ciphered, there would be a delay and the message could be stopped provided Verma could quote the DMO's authority to cancel it. Palit agreed and the Brig Adam promptly reached for the phone, saying he would do his best to nullify the signal.

Picking up the message sheet, Palit began walking towards the Ops Room. Coming out of the door was Kaul. Palit stopped the corps commander and showed him the signal, asking who had authorized it. Kaul read the message, hesitated briefly, then said, 'Ask the army commander,' before walking away.

In the Ops Room General Thapar was sitting and staring vacantly at the map on the wall while Sen and Sibal were talking, seated next to him. Assuming from Kaul's remark that Bogey Sen had authorized the signal, Palit thrust the message at Thapar. 'Do you realize, sir, that the army commander has given 4th Division permission to withdraw from Se-la?'

Thapar looked startled and uncomprehending. The contents of the message sheet were obviously news to him. Palit then raised his voice with the intention of getting across to Sen as well, asking the chief 'how it was that when the Corps Commander was present in his HQ, the Army Commander was issuing operational orders—whereas in the former's absence he had refused to shoulder any responsibility.'

Sen looked equally startled as he turned towards Palit and Thapar. He asked Palit what was he was talking about. When the contents of the message sheet were made known to him, he said firmly that he had issued no such orders.

Speaking to both the chief and the army commander, the DMO said: 'We could never face the nation if 12,000 troops, supported by artillery and mortars and stocked for battle, ran away without even facing the enemy. In my opinion, 4th Division is in a position to withstand an attack in strength by the Chinese.'

After some discussion, the COAS ordered that the withdrawal order be cancelled.

At that point, the original message allowing 4 Division to withdraw had not been sent as it was still being encoded. Accordingly, a new signal with Kaul's signature was drafted and dispatched that ordered 4 Division 'to remain at Se-la and to fight it out to the best of its ability and withdraw only if its position became untenable'.

62 BRIGADE HQ (17 NOVEMBER - EVENING)

In an interview more than two decades later, Anant Pathania said he never 'ordered' Hoshiar Singh to withdraw from Se-la. Instead, Pathania claimed, he only 'suggested' to Hoshiar Singh that he prepare a 'withdrawal plan' for the brigade for the night of 17-18 November. This bizarre attempt to pass the buck to his subordinate officer (posthumously) underlines the dangerous state of mind and the guile of a desperate man who has lost his will to fight but is compelled to keep up appearances nevertheless.

On the other hand, there was Hoshiar Singh, quite willing to fight it out at Se-la despite the near arctic conditions at the top of the pass and his own tactical shortcomings. Though he had fallen into the Chinese trap and sent out the composite 1 Sikh and 2 Sikh LI patrol earlier with disastrous consequences, he had mentally prepared himself and the brigade to fight and not once had he shown signs of wavering. For Pathania to have put the seeds of doubt in Hoshiar's Singh's mind by asserting that 'he could not guarantee' air supply was indeed a great betrayal. Although the Indian Air Force had done a tremendous job airlifting supplies to Senge to sustain the Se-la brigade, this was not a guarantee anyone could give. Besides, neither Anant Pathania nor HQ 4 Division had anything to do with the air drops other than forward the logistical requirements. For air supply to have become a reason for abandoning Se-la was indeed most unfortunate, and as much a betrayal to the pilots and airmen who flew sortie after sortie, as it was to the soldiers who had braved the conditions to prepare the defences.

Perhaps one of the reasons why Hoshiar Singh was undermined at a key juncture was the endless debate around the decision to fight at Se-la versus Bomdila. Apart from the BGS IV Corps, K. K. Singh, Anant Pathania himself was most disinclined to fight at Se-la. Kaul, ever since his reappearance, had hardly involved himself with Se-la. In fact in his version of events in *The Untold Story*, the former corps commander doesn't seem to know the difference between Se-la and Tse-la, two distinctly different passes with similarly pronounced names.

HQ IV Corps resented that Se-la as the defence line had been forced on them. That Se-la had its disadvantages was well known and in all probability, to fall back on Bomdila may have been more prudent and in keeping with the Thorat Plan of extending the Chinese lines of communication while shortening our own. But once the decision had been taken to fight at Se-la, there should have been no more debate.

Darshan Khullar, then a second lieutenant who was present at Se-la with 62 Brigade, later wrote: 'The imperative of holding Se-la should not have been in any doubt. The question is of force level and whether it should have been designated as vital ground, or a delaying position strong enough to make the Chinese redeploy and regroup for launching their offensive against the main defences around Bomdila... What it really boiled down to was "After Se-la what?" But this question was never posed or answered.'

Under the circumstances, trying to build the main divisional defences at Se-la to hold the Chinese was a flawed idea on four counts. One, it was too close to Tawang and once the road from Bum-la was constructed, logistically it became all too easy for the Chinese to start thinking of hammering away at the Se-la defences. Two, Indian troops, as Palit himself had earlier noted during his reconnaissance of Se-la, did not at that time have any experience of extreme high altitude warfare. Three, a determined enemy could invest Se-la from all sides. Again, this was a known fact but very little attention was actually paid to blocking or monitoring these routes. Four, too much importance was given to the 'winter is coming' factor. After having decided to hold Se-la on 24 October, the Indian attitude seemed to be that come end November, winter would literally freeze all aggressive options. This was way off the mark, for both Se-la and Bum-la only get blocked with snowfall sometime in the latter half of January, and only for a couple of months.

Anant Pathania was again connected with IV Corps shortly around 10.30 p.m. The 'no withdrawal' signal sent to 4 Division by Corps HQ via Bomdila had reached Pathania an hour ago. In Tezpur, the three generals were at dinner when the call came through. Palit picked up the phone. Even as he waited for Kaul to get to the phone, Palit told the GOC, 'Anant, there is to be no withdrawal. The corps commander will tell you that himself.' Palit then asked Pathania if there had been a frontal attack on the Se-la positions. Pathania said no, there was no contact, but there were reports that the Chinese were active between Bomdila and Dirang and also between Senge and Dirang.

Recorded Palit: 'At this point Kaul took the line from me and a drawn out conversation ensued. There was much reference back and forth to Thapar, who for once was definitive that there was to be no withdrawal. At last Bijji Kaul gave his subordinate commander orders for battle—in words which will surely remain a classic *double entendre* in our military history books. 'Achchha, Anant,' Bijji said in Hindi, 'For tonight you hang on to your defences.' Then in English he added, 'Have another chat with me in the morning!' How far that unconventional enjoinment would stand up as an imperative to a jittery subordinate to stay and fight, I need not comment upon—but it was too late to do anything about it.'

Back on Se-la, subsequent to the conversation with Pathania where the GOC kept emphasizing the deteriorating situation in Bomdila and elsewhere all along the line of communication, Hoshiar Singh seems to have finally lost his nerve. He decided to withdraw 2 Sikh LI into the inner perimeter of Se-la. Orders to this effect were passed to Irani at around 11 p.m. This order was changed shortly afterwards, and the battalion was ordered to go through to Nyukmadong. They were to start withdrawing after 4 Sikh LI had fallen back from the Two Lakes area and occupied their positions within the main defences. The revised order bordered on the ludicrous; Hoshiar Singh wanted a battalion dug in at Se-la Top whose positions were being probed by the Chinese to get up in the middle of the night and withdraw to a place no one was even familiar with. His revised plan also meant clockwork precision involving 1 Sikh, 2 and 4 Sikh LI. Even had this been rehearsed, the coordination required for this task was virtually impossible.

As we already know, 4 Garhwal had been ordered to fall back from Nuranang as it was felt that the covering troops were meant to act as a delaying force as per the Indian Army tactical manual. Yet, in the overall scheme of things, this seemed to be an ad hoc decision, for there were no clear cut defences for it to occupy, either at Se-la Top or at Senge.

If 62 Infantry Brigade had to take the fight to the Chinese, it was imperative for each man, section, platoon, company, battalion to know what was expected of him and their exact position in battle. Equally critical would have been the interdependence and coordination between the battalions. The commander and the commanding officers on the Se-la massif on 17 November did not have to be master strategists to understand this single basic fact; and yet, in the three weeks that were available to them, not once were counter-attacks or strategic withdrawals discussed, let alone practised. 4 Garhwal Rifles, pulling back from Nuranang after the day's fighting, would have expected to occupy preordained defences at Se-la Top. Instead, only once the battalion got there, did it dawn on the officers that there were no defences to occupy. The redeployment of the 'covering troops' had simply not been given any thought!

The 4 Garhwal withdrawal began as per Hoshiar Singh's instructions and the battalion, exhausted after a day's hard fighting and the withdrawal, reached Se-la Top at 3 a.m. Instead of redeploying in prepared defences, the battalion was told to carry on marching towards Senge Dzong. Meanwhile, quite a few stragglers had fallen behind and they were by then much too tired to push on. About fifty men decided to take a break and began brewing tea when the rearguard of the artillery appeared. The battery commander told the men to get moving as the Chinese were hot on their heels, but the men were too fatigued to move.

The Chinese caught the straggler party and mowed them all down. 4 Garhwal, which in the entire day's battle had lost two men, now had more than half a company's worth killed without even the semblance of a fight. The ruthless execution of the Garhwalis out in the open was a clear indication of the Chinese intention to kill as many Indian troops as possible with a view towards completely annihilating 4 Division.

At the time the Garhwali stragglers were being butchered by the Chinese advance elements, half of 62 Brigade was on the move; 4 Garhwal Rifles was marching on towards Senge, 4 Sikh LI after having covered the withdrawal of the main body of Garhwalis and the artillery guns was now heading back towards its main defences. Around the same time, 2 Sikh LI was ordered by its commanding officer to abandon its defences and start moving through the 1 Sikh positions to start its withdrawal towards Nyukmadong. As the Sikh LI troops began to pull out, they were fired upon by Chinese jitter parties.

1 Sikh had not been told that that 2 Sikh withdrawal had been advanced by a day. A wave of panic spread through 1 Sikh at the sudden appearance of 2 Sikh LI amidst its defences. In the process, 1 Sikh troops also began to abandon their defences leading to complete chaos on Se-la Top.

Hoshiar Singh was furious with Irani for having pulled 2 Sikh LI out prematurely from the defences around Kye-la. The early pull-out not only sealed the fate of 4 Sikh LI, it gave the Chinese a walkover on what should have been their Waterloo. Had 4 Sikh LI occupied their defences by the time 2 Sikh LI withdrew, the Chinese troops on their tail would have walked into a death trap.

By the time Hoshiar Singh realized the extent of the damage, 1 Sikh and 2 Sikh LI were milling around in complete confusion. At 4 a.m., Hoshiar Singh spoke to Pathania: 'Something awful has happened. 1 Sikh are withdrawing and Se-la defences are gone. I am going up to stop them.' This was the last time Hoshiar Singh and Pathania were to speak, for line communication between 62 Brigade and 4 Division HQ broke down shortly thereafter. At Se-la Top, the brigade commander realized the hopelessness of the situation. Left with no choice other than to legitimize the withdrawal, orders were given to fall back on Senge-Dzong. By then the leading elements of the Chinese had inserted themselves between 4 Sikh LI (plus elements of 7 Mahar) and the rest of the brigade. Hoshiar Singh had no choice but to abandon the battalion to its fate.

To cover the withdrawal of 4 Garhwal, Delta Company of 4 Sikh LI had been tasked with occupying a screen position at KM 108. This would also allow it to cover the pullback of Alpha and Charlie Companies of its own battalion that were coming down from Tsogiya Lake and re-deploying at Se-la. Accordingly, the Garhwalis went through Delta Company at 2 a.m. and Alpha and Charlie followed at 4.50 a.m., after which Delta Company was also ordered to fall back.

As Delta Company made their way up the Nuranang–Se-la axis, it found Alpha and Charlie Companies astride the road at KM 102. Both these companies had come under heavy fire as they approached their original trenches, which were now occupied by Chinese troops. No. 1 Platoon of Alpha Company under Subedar Nanak Singh put in a bayonet charge and after desperate hand-to-hand fighting, the depleted platoon fell back to rejoin the bogged-down companies.

As daylight lit up the slopes on the southern side below Se-la, all three 4 Sikh LI companies were caught out in the open. Positions on the northern heights that should still have been occupied by 2 Sikh LI were now under Chinese control. Majors G. V. E. Masilamani and S. Rajan, the two company commanders, put in a two-pronged assault to regain the old Indian positions, but they were stopped by the well-entrenched Chinese who were supported by accurate LMG fire from the flanks of the northern slopes. Despite the attack failing, the Chinese lost around thirty men and an officer. Masilamani now ordered the surviving men from the three companies to break south across the Se-la Ridge, go across a saddle and regroup on the other side.

Bravo Company was with the commanding officer on the forward slopes of the left shoulder of Se-la. With the Chinese attacking them from the north, east and west, it was fast running out of options (and ammunition). Firing off the last of their 3-inch mortar bombs and having withstood three attacks, at 9 a.m. the survivors were ordered to break across the ridge to the south as best as they could. 4 Sikh LI by then had broken up into small parties as the surviving men scrambled to get away. The Chinese stayed on their heels and repeatedly ambushed the groups as they made their way down the southern slopes, killing a large number who were by then quite defenceless. One of the company commanders, Major S. Rajan, was also killed in one of the ambushes. The bulk of those who survived managed to get away by escaping into Bhutan.

In a couple of hours, three fighting infantry battalions had been destroyed owing to complete confusion and indecision at the top; another battalion, 4 Garhwal Rifles, had been badly mauled, while the gunners and all other sundry troops found themselves in a headlong rush towards Senge. The main thrust of the Chinese that had been initially halted superbly at Nuranang the previous day was now a distant memory. The defences of Se-la had caved in with barely a push from the Chinese. In the annals of the Indian Army, this had to be its lowest point ever.

PANIC STATION DIRANG (18 NOVEMBER)

Tezpur knew of the Se-la debacle when at 5.30 a.m. Major J. S. Datta, the brigade major, got through to IV Corps HQ and passed on the news that Se-la was being abandoned following the exodus of 2 Sikh LI and 1 Sikh. This was to be the last formal communiqué, after which there was a deathly silence from 62 Infantry Brigade. The information was relayed to Kaul who then spoke to Anant Pathania. Despite the drama of the previous evening, both were stunned by the lightning speed with which events had overtaken them. Pathania again asked for permission to withdraw 4 Division HQ;

Kaul acquiesced without asking the former where he planned to withdraw to. Pathania then said he was closing down his HQ and moving from Dirang Dzong. Thereafter, the lines went dead and there was no further communication between Corps HQ and Division HQ.

In the early hours of 18 November, the situation in Dirang Dzong was outwardly calm. However, after Pathania's conversation with Kaul, the GOC summoned Brigadier Cheema, Commander 65 Infantry Brigade, and other senior officers to the Ops Room for a conference to discuss the situation.

Ever since 16 November when news had first come in that 5 Guards had been overrun trying to defend Poshing-la, Pathania had started becoming more and more worried. The GOC had also realized the folly of not having prepared Dirang Dzong as a defensive position, despite having 65 Infantry deployed around the Division HQ. His immediate reaction was to close ranks around Division HQ and the 19 MLI columns were ordered to fall back on Dirang Dzong. This was a lost opportunity, for both the Maratha columns were well suited to harass the Chinese lines of communication, having done all the hard work of getting into a good tactical position. The MLI columns had plenty of ammunition and were reasonably well stocked. However, on the evening of 17 November they were rather timidly withdrawn. As the first column started to pull back, the Chinese stayed on their heels. On the morning of 18 November, while the exhausted party was brewing tea, it was ambushed near Munna Camp and forty men were either killed or captured, the others barely managing to get away.

Meanwhile, at Dirang Dzong, the divisional conference was not about fighting it out with the Chinese; instead the focus was on the hopelessness of the situation and how best to get out. Strangely, neither the GOC nor the brigade commander seemed to be worried about either 4 Rajput or 19 MLI, so it came as a rude shock when a dishevelled Major Shaikh barged into the 'conference' and announced that the Chinese had ambushed his column and that there was a roadblock at KM 31.

Pathania then gave his last two formal orders as GOC 4 Division. He de-linked 4 Rajput from 65 Infantry Brigade and put it under the command of 62 Infantry Brigade with the job of covering the brigade's withdrawal from Se-la. He then ordered the two companies of 13 Dogra that had arrived at Dirang Dzong from Senge during the night to clear the roadblock, with support from the Stuart tanks of B Squadron of 7 Cavalry.

There were close to 5,000 soldiers present at Dirang Dzong. Apart from Major General Pathania, there were three brigade commanders, two of whom were fast asleep at the time of the conference. The end of the conference was more like the end of a school day when children come tumbling out of their classrooms. 13 Dogra, having just arrived, was told to move for the assault within minutes. With no idea of the geography, it didn't know where to go. By then it was every man for himself and the roads were already getting clogged while senior officers got their personal belongings loaded onto their vehicles.

The bewildered Dogras barely made it to Sagor. Three tanks under Major S. D. S. Jamwal set out with the Dogra troops, but could not proceed any further as the roads were blocked with fleeing troops. The cavalrymen soon abandoned their tanks that were then pushed off the road into the valley below to clear the road. The GOC and his entourage followed in their loaded vehicles to officially 'watch the battle', but at Sagor their small convoy got stuck. 86 Field Battery, located below Sagor, had visual contact with Munna Camp that was by then occupied by Chinese troops. The guns defiantly opened up with their 25-pounders causing substantial casualties among the Chinese. Taken by surprise, the Chinese in turn fired a few rounds of mortars that were sporadic and quite ineffective. Though the Chinese troops were unlikely to have enough ammunition—having come cross country across the passes—the Chinese counter-bombardment convinced the GOC and his entourage to abandon their vehicles and take to their feet, heading for the Manda-la track that bifurcates to the west and then south from Sagor.

Those present in Dirang Dzong during that fateful period say Cheema and Manohar Singh, the GSO-1, were the ones whispering in Pathania's ear, spinning a web of negativity, constantly urging him to make a dash for the plains of Assam before the Chinese surrounded them completely. During World War II Cheema had been a POW of the Italians and was known to be terrified of falling into the hands of the Chinese. The two battalions under his command—4 Rajput and 19 MLI—were strung out defending the various tracks and approaches but the brigade commander rarely, if ever, visited any of the men under his own command, preferring to stick close to Pathania and literally became his shadow. Cheema's professional competence was suspect, yet he was hand-picked by Thapar to command 65 Brigade at this critical time.

Cheema had arrived at the Division HQ for the conference all packed and ready to go. Shortly after Pathania's departure, along with Brigadier Gurbax Singh Gill, commander 4 Artillery Brigade and Brigadier Michael Chatterjee, commander 67 Infantry Brigade (on a reconnaissance trip to Dirang before the induction of his brigade into Bomdila), the convoy of fleeing brigadiers took off after Pathania without so much as a by your leave to any of the troops who were still left in Dirang, to say nothing of 4 Rajput and 19 MLI. As the convoy took off, Cheema was shouting 'Manda-la track, Manda-la track' presumably for the benefit of the vehicles behind him.

THE BIG THREE AT TEZPUR (18 NOVEMBER)

In the morning, Bogey Sen and his BGS, Brigadier Sibal, had dropped in at the Circuit House where the chief had spent the night. All three officers were blissfully unaware of developments either in Se-la or Dirang Dzong. Sen, in fact, was still trying to convince Thapar on the merits of withdrawing from Se-la, when Monty Palit returned from his early morning visit to Kaul and IV Corps HQ.

'4 Infantry Division has pulled out without orders and without offering battle. Sometime between midnight and this morning our forces ran away from Se-la, Senge and Dirang. They seemed to have abandoned all their wireless sets because there has been no further contact with any formation or unit thereafter.'

Both the COAS and the Eastern Army Commander had commanded the Red Eagles during their careers and the stunning news of its disintegration in a matter of hours was a blow. The party made its way to the Ops Room at IV Corps HQ where Kaul was waiting for them. The corps commander brought Thapar and Sen up to date on the developments of the previous night; of Se-la the Corps HQ knew next to nothing other than the fact that the feature had been abandoned, while in Dirang Dzong Kaul said he had agreed to a withdrawal but he had no idea to where; this now left 48 Brigade in Bomdila, commanded by Brigadier Gurbax Singh as the last line of defence.

After Kaul's return from Walong the previous evening, the initial focus had been on Se-la and Dirang Dzong. After the cancellation of the withdrawal order and the dispatch of a new signal telling 4 Division to hold its position, the corps commander had been briefed on the developments in and around Bomdila. The order pertaining to the pullback from Thembang the moment the Chinese appeared indicated that the withdrawal syndrome had also affected Gurbax.

Thembang was perhaps the ideal location to hold as artillery guns positioned further down the road towards Bomdila could create major problems for the Chinese. From a tactical point of view, it was imperative that the Thembang Ridge be reoccupied without any delay. A call was put through to commander 48 Brigade at around 9.30 p.m. Before Kaul could say anything, Gurbax Singh (the son of Sir Teja Singh who built Lutyens' Delhi and the younger brother of the celebrated writer Khushwant Singh) said that 5 Guards could no longer be contacted. The battalion seemed to have disintegrated. There was no question of pushing fresh troops to Thembang because, according to Gurbax, the Chinese had already cut off the approach from Bomdila.

Kaul was intent on re-establishing the line of communication between Bomdila and Dirang. He ordered Gurbax to activate the 7 Cavalry troop of Stewart tanks at Bomdila and lead an infantry column and destroy the Chinese roadblock. For tanks to head off into the dark looking for roadblocks was madness, but obviously Gurbax could not say that to his corps commander. In Burma, the British had evolved techniques to break Japanese roadblocks, but these methods needed fine-tuning and extensive practice. Gurbax protested that it was too dark and he did not want to deplete Bomdila's defences any further.

Not one to be bothered with technical details, the corps commander insisted that a fighting column should step out and patrol the Bomdila–Dirang Dzong road immediately. When Gurbax hesitated, Kaul ordered the brigade commander to move immediately. Kaul reasoned that it was vital to attack the Chinese right away for it was highly unlikely that the blocks were held in strength at this point in time. He also assured Gurbax that he was sending two infantry battalions of 67 Infantry Brigade to reinforce Bomdila. The troops would move through the night and be available by morning. Later in the evening, there was yet another conversation between Kaul and Gurbax Singh who said that even though a fighting patrol had been readied, they were pinned down by defensive fire just 400 metres from the forward defences of Bomdila.

Kaul's briefing on the morning of 18 November was based entirely on assumptions. He presumed that 62 Infantry Brigade was in the process of withdrawing from Senge towards Dirang, and would clear the roadblocks en route. He did not seem to realize the implications of his own earlier orders giving Anant Pathania permission to withdraw from Dirang Dzong. He believed that once the Se-la and Dirang Dzong forces had married up, they would then jointly roll down to Bomdila. Kaul didn't seem to have a real idea of the strength of the Chinese thrust across Poshing-la. In the absence of any actual information, the big three could only speculate and stare at the map in the fond hope that some miraculous solution would fall into their laps.

Coming back to the situation in Bomdila, Kaul informed Thapar and Sen that there had been a delay in the dispatching of two battalions from 67 Infantry Brigade the previous night as vehicles were not available to transport troops forward. These battalions would now reach Bomdila by midday. Kaul also informed them that Gurbax Singh had admitted that the previous night's reports pertaining to the Chinese closing in on Bomdila's defences had proved to be exaggerated. The roadblock between Bomdila and Dirang Dzong was still in place, as the tanks and the infantry were yet to marry up. Kaul once again reiterated that in his opinion, the strength of the Chinese facing Bomdila had to be extremely limited, both in terms of numbers and heavy weapons.

At 11 a.m., Kaul was put through to Gurbax Singh. Once again, he was told that the road-clearing party had not yet left Bomdila. Kaul at this point categorically told Gurbax Singh to send out the column immediately or he would be removed from command.

48 BRIGADE AT BOMDILA (18 NOVEMBER)

Gurbax Singh put the phone down and tried to collect his thoughts. Normally quite cool and collected, he had tried everything to keep the defences of Bomdila intact, but now the corps commander was leaving him no choice. The promised reinforcements from 67 Brigade had not materialized as yet; the previous evening 5 Guards had fought a running battle with the Chinese at Thembang and then gone off the radar after they were told to fall back. His remaining two battalions, 1 Sikh LI and 1 Madras (both minus a company) were deployed around Bomdila, but the brigadier knew that his defences were far from adequate.

In the beginning of November when the focus was entirely on Se-la, 48 Brigade had moved in to occupy Bomdila. With Pathania deciding to set up his HQ at Dirang Dzong and, in the process, deploying 65 Brigade around himself, a second layer of defence had been created between Se-la and Bomdila. This resulted in a false sense of security and pushed the latter's defence requirements further down the priority list. Within a couple of days of the brigade's arrival at Bomdila, Division HQ's focus had shifted to Poshing-la. With the initial dispatch of the 5 Guards column under Captain Amarjeet to block off the pass, it was clear that Thembang would now be the screen position. When the Chinese attack came, it would have to be halted at Thembang with Bomdila being the firm base at the rear.

Unfortunately, ever since Niranjan Prasad had been replaced by Anant Pathania, the prevailing assumption in 4 Division (and IV Corps and Army

HQ) was that with the Chinese having captured Tawang, the 'war' was over. The return of Kaul as GOC IV Corps hardly helped matters. Even though he had been declared medically fit, a family member confirms that 'he fought the rest of the war in great pain'. After his return, Kaul visited Se-la just once, and had made it abundantly clear that he did not expect any major Chinese activity till next spring. Had there existed even the slightest inkling that the Chinese would launch a full-fledged assault within a month of the initial attack on 7 Brigade on the Nam Ka Chu, it is doubtful that Kaul would have allowed Pathania to descend from Senge, headache or no headache.

Pathania certainly did not expect the Chinese to progress beyond the odd skirmish here and there. So set in this view was the GOC that he refused to believe the initial reports from 4 Garhwal that the Chinese were moving men in numbers to outflank Se-la. The very fact that Dirang Dzong had not prepared basic defences to fight the Chinese are clear pointers towards the prevailing mind set.

The mild-mannered Gurbax Singh now regretted that he too had taken the soft option. On arrival at Bomdila, Gurbax had shifted into the comfortable Circuit House and had been quite content to sit back, secure in the belief that Bomdila was too far removed from any immediate threat from the Chinese. The high command expected a linear sequence of events: first Se-la would have to fall, then Dirang, only after that would Bomdila come into the reckoning. On arrival at Bomdila, 4 Sikh LI had been taken away from 48 Brigade and given to 62 Brigade on Se-la. Gurbax was then left with 1 Sikh LI under Lieutenant Colonel M. S. Brar and 5 Guards commanded by Lieutenant Colonel Jai Singh. 1 Madras was then rushed in from Nagaland to reinforce the Brigade.

However, everything changed on 15 November when news filtered in from the Assam Rifles that the Chinese had overrun the small force at Poshing-la. By the evening of 16 November, the bulk of 5 Guards had moved to KM 9 on the road to Dirang, from where they dropped down to occupy Thembang which they reached by 2 p. m. One company had marched through the night and had arrived earlier in the morning. It was decided to locate the battalion's defences in an open patch just below the Thembang village. As the troops began to dig themselves in, their trenches were barely a foot deep when the Chinese were seen coming down from Poshing-la.

Jai Singh immediately sent a screening patrol out, but the Chinese barely paused in their stride and pushed the Guardsmen back into the partly constructed defences. Four 25-pounder guns had been deployed at KM 9 from where they opened fire on the Chinese as they began to form up for an attack. According to a local Sherdukpen, who witnessed the fighting, the effect of the artillery guns was devastating, killing among others a high-ranking Chinese officer on a grey pony. However, showing tremendous discipline, despite the high number of casualties, the Chinese continued to attack 5 Guards. Chinese mortars quickly deployed among the vegetation and began to pepper the Indian position. Second Lieutenant S. S. Choudhary tried to neutralize the Chinese mortars by climbing a tree with an LMG, but a sniper killed him almost immediately.

Despite the reports sent by the Assam Rifles of there being more than a thousand Chinese soldiers approaching Poshing-la, Gurbax and Jai Singh had estimated that at best the Chinese could have pushed 'a few hundred' men across the pass. As a result, 5 Guards was carrying limited ammunition, which by 4.30 p.m. was beginning to run out. With casualties mounting, Jai Singh asked Gurbax if he could withdraw. Permission was granted and in the fading light of the day, 5 Guards neatly disengaged from the Chinese and in single file, began to move down a nullah towards the south that took them to the Gang River.

Around the same time, the 25-pounders had to stop firing as their communication systems broke down. These guns then withdrew along the road to Bomdila. However, two 3.7-inch howitzers of 7 Bengal Mountain Battery under the GPO, Second Lieutenant Akshey Kapila, kept the Chinese at bay for some more time before packing up the guns and moving back to KM 9.

5 Guards in the meantime had reached the Gang River where Jai Singh took stock of the situation. The Chinese, having lost almost a third of their force, were not in a position to follow the Guardsmen. There was a brief discussion between the officers. Jai Singh expressed his concern that the Chinese could have already cut them off. Instead of climbing back and heading for Bomdila, he chose to proceed with the bulk of the battalion towards the east and then south towards the plains of Assam. A couple of officers with some men, however, decided to head back towards Bomdila. They did not encounter the Chinese. However, Major Brij Raj Singh, who was the FOO with 5 Guards, also decided to return to Bomdila and rejoin his guns. The Chinese ambushed his party and all the men were killed.

5 Guards's failure to fall back on Bomdila had serious implications for 48 Brigade. By the morning, Gurbax Singh knew that the Chinese had established their roadblock somewhere near or south of KM 9. Despite

the severe damage done by the guns and the large number of Chinese casualties, it was now clear that the Chinese had got across Poshing-la in far greater numbers than had been anticipated. It was just a matter of time before the Chinese would assault Bomdila. The two battalions from 67 Infantry Brigade that were supposed to have arrived in the early hours of the morning had failed to show up.

Gurbax Singh knew his best chance was to close his troops in a defensive position around Bomdila and let the Chinese come to him. By then, a rough estimate of the Chinese force aligned against 48 Brigade was known. Reports by the Assam Rifles during the fighting at Poshing-la had accurately communicated to Brigade HQ that approximately 1,500 Chinese soldiers were coming down that route; at the time, the numbers were thought to be exaggerated. Gurbax also knew from the gunners (he himself had been at KM 9 earlier in the morning before the Thembang battle) that the Chinese had suffered severe casualties the previous evening. He knew that the Chinese, devoid of artillery and with limited troops, would stand no chance whatsoever of overrunning Bomdila. Even without 5 Guards, the Bomdila garrison had six infantry companies (one Company of 1 Sikh LI was at Phudung, and 1 Company from 1 Madras had been sent to Dirang Dzong to protect Division HQ), along with adequate artillery, a couple of tanks and plenty of ammunition and rations.

However, based on the last information received from 62 Brigade and 4 Division HQ at Dirang Dzong, Kaul assumed that all the withdrawing troops from Se-la and Dirang Dzong were falling back on Bomdila. That is why the corps commander was adamant that the roadblock between Dirang and Bomdila be removed by 48 Brigade. Gurbax Singh had stalled for time with Kaul but now had no choice but to follow orders. Despite the fact that only an advance platoon of 3 JAK Rifles from the promised 67 Brigade had arrived thus far, against his better judgment, at midday, Gurbax Singh gave the mobile column the green light to proceed.

Swirling mist and low-hanging clouds in the valley through the morning had made observation of the Chinese difficult. A patrol from 1 Sikh LI had gone close to KM 9 but returned with no definite information of the enemy. As the mobile column comprising two companies of 1 Sikh LI along with two tanks of 7 Cavalry moved out of Bomdila towards Dirang Dzong, a dense bank of mist enveloped the depleted defences.

The lone company commander left in the Sikh LI defended area, Major Maini, was talking to his JCO when they noticed some people approaching from the direction of the Old Bomdila Pass. Flashes of gunfire followed by the sharp sound of automatic weapons announced the arrival of the Chinese at Bomdila. Maini was hit in the legs and brought down by the initial burst. His men dragged him into a bunker and then six men carried him to the medical station, further depleting the strength of the Sikh LI position.

About a hundred Chinese soldiers had appeared and they were engaged by a determined JCO commanding an ad hoc platoon that held them at bay for a short while. Lieutenant Pran Pahwa of 135 Heavy Mortar Battery, the FOO, immediately asked for fire support from the guns. The shells, fired from close range, exploded among the trees, but unfortunately the Bomdila defences were devoid of even basics like barbed wire and mines. The large gaps allowed the Chinese to manoeuvre their way through them and get into the defences, occupying the vacant bunkers and trenches. Their position having been breached, the ad hoc platoon along with Lieutenant Pahwa decided to make a break for it.

The mobile column had barely covered four kilometres when news came through that the Chinese had attacked Bomdila. The column commander immediately ordered his troops back. As the two tanks tried to reverse in the narrow space, the column came under fire from Chinese jitter parties from the ridge to the left of the road. Though the mobile column at this stage had suffered no casualties, it was already too late, as the Chinese had infiltrated and occupied the Sikh LI defences in reasonable strength. The column was now caught in the open, and the Sikh LI troops turned tail and ran. Gurbax Singh and a couple of other officers came out of their office and tried to stop the troops, but to no avail. With the Indian soldiers out of the way, 6 Field Regiment Battery and the mountain guns began firing over open sights at the erstwhile Sikh LI defences, while the two 7 Cavalry tanks also opened up with their Vickers Browning MMGs and main guns. With the Chinese pinned down in the bunkers, the tanks then took up position in the Circuit House area to guard all approaches from the west.

With 1 Sikh LI having decamped, the only infantry troops left with Gurbax Singh were 1 Madras deployed on the right flank of Bomdila. Until that point, it had been bypassed by the Chinese altogether. Unfortunately, communication between 1 Madras and Brigade HQ had snapped somewhere along the line. Left without any troops to flush out the Chinese and shaken by 1 Sikh LI's flight, the brigade commander got into his jeep and drove off towards Tenga. Shortly thereafter, the rest of the brigade staff followed suit. No clear instructions were issued; word of mouth messages let it be known that a general withdrawal had been sounded.

The guns continued to pound the erstwhile 1 Sikh LI positions for the next two hours. The surviving Chinese either decamped into the hills or just lay low in the bunkers. Having exhausted their ammunition, 6 Field Regiment Battery and the tanks withdrew towards Tenga. Through all this, 1 Madras remained oblivious of the fact that part of Bomdila had been abandoned. By 3 p.m., there was a deadly silence over Bomdila, with the Chinese sweeping the area with sporadic MMG fire every now and then. To all outward appearances, Bomdila had fallen.

TOP: *The bunkers occupied by 4 Garhwal Rifles just north of Bridge 3 flanking the Nuranang Chu. The place is now known as Jaswantgarh. In the background are the slopes on the Tawang side of the Tawang/Mago Chu.* BOTTOM: *Looking down from the Garhwali positions, the village of Jang sloping down towards the river that flows along the base of the valley.*

The Nuranang Valley that drops away to the north, as seen from Se-la Top and Twin Lakes.

LEFT: *President Dr Sarvepalli Radhakrishnan with Anant Pathania and Kaul at Dirang Dzong* (Lest We Forget *and* Rivers of Silence). RIGHT: *Lieutenant Darshan Khullar who was with 2 Derajat Mountain Battery at Se-la.*

ABOVE: *Major General Anant Pathania* (HQ 4 Division)*; Brigadiers Hoshiar Singh* (Wing Commander B. S. Rathee) *and D. K. Palit* (HQ 7 Infantry Brigade). BELOW: *Two Sikh LI battalions (2 and 4) as well as 1 Sikh and 4 Garhwal Rifles were defending Se-la with the support of 25-pounder and 3.7-inch mountain guns.* (Assam Rifles)

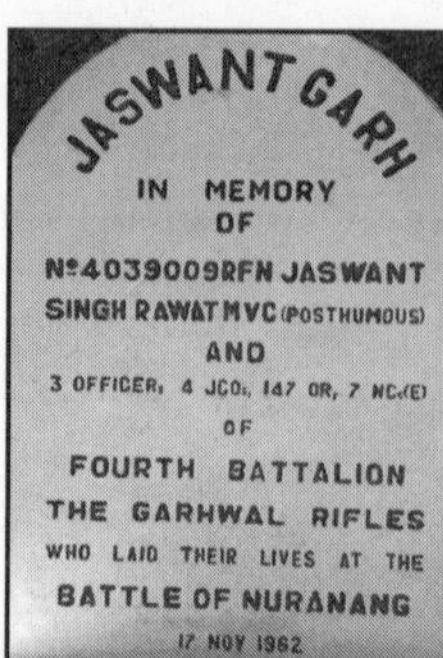

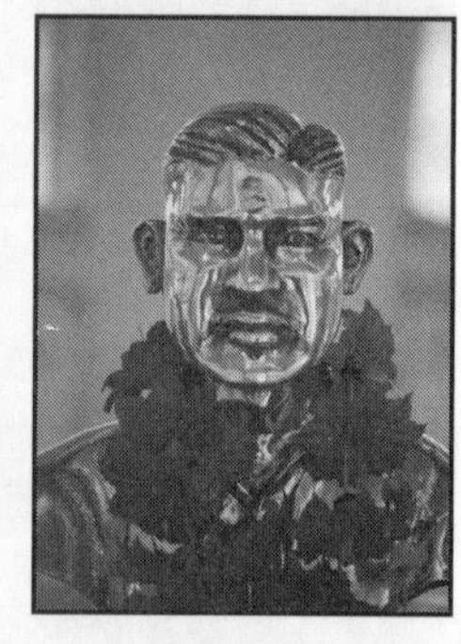

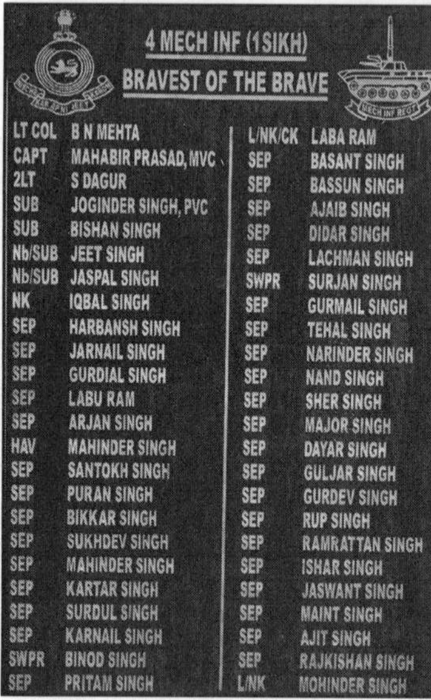

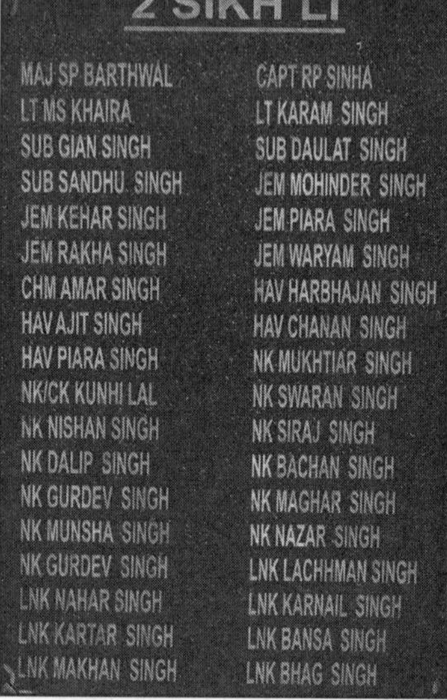

Second Lieutenants S. N. Tandon and Vinod Kumar Goswami, Naib Subedar Udai Singh Rawat, Lance Naik Gopal Singh and Rifleman Jaswant Singh Rawat (4 Garhwal Rifles) (4 Garhwal Rifles).

ABOVE: *4 Division HQ, Dirang Dzong.* BELOW: *Brigadier Gurbax Singh, Commander 48 Brigade.* BELOW: *Lieutenant Colonels Jai Singh (5 Guards), Gurdial Singh (3 JAK Rif) and K. K. Chandran (1 Madras) at Bomdila* (Colonel N. J. S. Pannu). BELOW RIGHT: *Gurbax Singh addressing troops from 1 Madras at Bomdila* (1 Madras).

TOP: *Captain Amarjeet Singh and Lieutenant I. S. Chaudhry (5 Guards); Lieutenant Colonel Brahmanand Avasthy (4 Rajput)* (Indian Military Academy). MIDDLE: *The Lagyala Gompa where Indian troops fought the Chinese after the ceasefire.* BOTTOM: *Brigadier Hoshiar Singh's ashes being brought back by his son* (Wing Commander R. S. Rathee).

TOP: *Major General Kadyan from the Rajputana Rifles salutes the body of Hoshiar Singh at Phudong Village during the funeral* (Wing Commander R. S. Rathee). BOTTOM: *Indian officers as POWs in Chinese captivity before they were repatriated to India in 1963. The two Gurdial Singhs (2 Rajput and 3 JAK Rif) are second and fourth from left; Rikh, Tewari, Dalvi and Ahluwalia are on the right* (Colonel N. J. S. Pannu).

ABOVE: *The view towards Tibet from Kibithu.* BELOW: *Lieutenant Colonel C. M. Madiah and Lieutenant Bikram Singh (6 Kumaon); Sepoy Kewal Singh (4 Sikh)* (Mrs Meena Shyam).

An upgraded version of the rather primitive flying fox across the Lohit (Mrs Meena Shyam).

TOP: *Mishmi tribals with CO 6 Kumaon at Walong* (Mrs Meena Shyam). MIDDLE: *Tri-junction, Green and Yellow Pimple with Ashi Hill in the background*. BOTTOM: *The wing of a crashed Otter at Walong airfield.*

TOP: *Thorat as the CGS in Ladakh in the early 1950s* (Thorat Collection). BOTTOM: *Lieutenant General Daulet Singh, the Western Army Commander, addressing troops* (Lieutenant General Daulet Singh Collection).

TOP: *Daulet Singh sharing a cup of tea with Nehru at Chushul* (Daulet Singh Collection). MIDDLE: *Indian troops patrolling the southern side of the Pangong Tso (Yula Sector) at an altitude of 14,500 feet* (HQ 50 Brigade). BOTTOM: *Soldiers hauling ammunition to the forward posts in the Chushul sector* (HQ 50 Brigade).

TOP: *Chang-la; the Zanskar Range is visible in the distance* (Dipti Bhalla Verma). BOTTOM: *The wounded being evacuated on yaks as an AN-12 lands* (Air Marshal Bharat Kumar).

Shyok River Valley.

ABOVE: *Major General Budh Singh, Brigadier T. P. Raina and Lieutenant Colonel Hari Singh* (Colonel B. R. S. Dahiya). RIGHT: *Major Dhan Singh Thapa and Rifleman Tulsi Ram (1/8 GR)* (Major Sitaram Johri Collection).

Artist's impression of the Rezang-la battle (Battle Honours Mess/Kunal Verma).

ABOVE: *Lieutenant Colonel H. S. Dhingra, Major Shaitan Singh and Sepoy Ram Kanwar Yadav (13 Kumaon)* (Lest We Forget). LEFT: *Retrieving the remains of Charlie Company at Rezang-la after the ceasefire* (HQ 50 Brigade).

TOP: *Captain P. L. Kher, Second Lieutenant S. D. Goswami and Naib Subedar Jangbahadur Gurung* (Lest We Forget). MIDDLE: *AMX 13 tanks at Chushul* (Air Marshal Bharat Kumar). BOTTOM: *Captain A. K. Dewan with the tank crew* (Major General A. K. Dewan).

TOP: *Jemadar Rigzin Phunchok of 14 J&K Militia receives a Vir Chakra as Squadron Leader A. S. Williams looks on* (Thorat Collection). BOTTOM: *The Post War Committee chaired by Defence Minister Y. B. Chavan in December 1962. Thorat is third from left; to his left are the air chief, Air Marshal Aspy Engineer, the COAS, General J. N. 'Muchhu' Chaudhury, and the CNS, Vice Admiral B. S. Soman* (Thorat Collection).

Chapter 12

THE FINAL COUNTDOWN

THE DISINTEGRATION OF 62 BRIGADE (18 TO 23 NOVEMBER)

With 4 Sikh LI having been abandoned to their fate, the remnants of 1 Sikh, 2 Sikh LI and 4 Garhwal Rifles had joined 13 Dogra at Senge Dzong by 9 a.m. on 18 November. The Chinese, though in a position to cut the line of communication with Dirang Dzong, had deliberately held their fire, letting some vehicles coming up towards Senge through to give 62 Brigade the impression that the door to the south was open.

With 13 Dogra having to act as a rearguard, Brigadier Hoshiar Singh realistically only had 4 Garhwal Rifles that was still fit enough to give battle to the Chinese. The plan for withdrawal was accordingly drawn up: the vehicle column under the command of Major Brahm Sat of 6 Field Regiment would move along the road to Dirang Dzong where it would report to Brigadier Gill of 4 Artillery Brigade; following in their wake would be the marching column which, after crossing Bridge 2, would split into two groups—4 Garhwal would follow the track leading to Nyukmadong village and Bridge 1, keeping the main road to their west; the rest would continue to move along the road, 2 Sikh LI leading, Brigade HQ in the middle with 1 Sikh and other minor units bringing up the rear.

This withdrawal plan of Hoshiar Singh's was a tactical disaster. The brigade commander had put his administrative and other soft units at the vanguard of what should have been considered an advance towards Dirang Dzong rather than a withdrawal. With the Chinese on his tail from the direction of Se-la, Hoshiar told Brahm Sat to get an immediate move on. As the column of vehicles began to roll down the road, the weary men of the three infantry battalions hoisted their weapons and packs and started on the march towards Dirang Dzong.

By the time Brahm Sat's convoy reached Bridge 2, he had had a start of almost two hours over the infantry column. Just when it seemed the column would make it to Dirang Dzong, the convoy commander saw his leading vehicles grind to a halt as they came under heavy fire about a kilometre south of Bridge 2. Trapped on the road, unable to even get out of the vehicles and make a run for it, vehicle after vehicle was systematically destroyed by the Chinese. Under orders not to take prisoners, the Chinese herded surviving troops next to burning vehicles and shot them. The entire column was wiped out. The Chinese then withdrew from the ambush site and took up flanking positions—they knew infantry columns were following down the same road.

As the leading elements of 2 Sikh LI reached the site, they were met by the ghastly sight of the dead and the dying littered amongst the remains of burnt and charred vehicles. Hardly had the infantry column reached the spot when it came under withering fire from dominant positions on both sides of the valley. The leading elements stood no chance, completely caught out in the open as it were.

The remainder of the column was hopelessly trapped, left with no choice but to try and push forward along the road towards Dirang Dzong. Using their own 2-inch mortars while calling in 3-inch mortar fire support from 13 Dogra at Senge, the men fought tenaciously and cleared the Chinese from the slopes for about half a kilometre. The column then came under lethal fire from a Chinese post that was situated on a feature below Nyukmadong village. A platoon of 1 Sikh under Lieutenant Surinder Dagur was pushed forward to take on the well-entrenched Chinese. Though the platoon succeeded in its objective, the young officer and most of his men were killed.

As the day progressed, this was the pattern of fighting as a series of Chinese ambushes had to be dealt with. Each time a section or a platoon under one of the surviving officers would move forward. Each time, they would clear the Chinese only to run into yet another ambush. Very few junior officers with the marching column would make it to the end of the day, sacrificing themselves one by one in a desperate bid to break through the Chinese stranglehold on the road. By last light, there was very little command and control left, and as darkness descended, small parties of the surviving troops made for the mountain range south of the Khouma River, hoping to escape across the border into Bhutan.

Chinese troops that had bypassed Se-la and got behind the Indians initially seemed to be under instructions not to take any prisoners. Accordingly, their mopping up parties ruthlessly went about bayoneting the wounded and the dying, while in some cases soldiers who had been captured were lined up and shot in cold blood.

Meanwhile 13 Dogra positions at Senge Dzong were gradually being pushed back by the advancing Chinese troops who were now coming across Se-la. By last light on 18 November Lieutenant Colonel M. S. Oberoi was fully aware that both the vehicle and infantry columns had been completely annihilated. Unable to link up with either 4 Sikh LI or 4 Garhwal Rifles, the battalion, under the cover of darkness, broke contact with the Chinese and in small parties along with elements of the brigade staff made their way down from Senge. The Chinese were, however, waiting for them and had lit up the entire area with Very lights and quite a few men were killed near the Tammapha Chu as they tried to climb the opposite slopes. However, a good proportion of the Dogras managed to get across the southern range into Bhutan. In relative terms, considering the fact that 13 Dogra had been deployed at Zimithang, Tawang and then Se-la, the battalion got out of NEFA in reasonably good order.

On the Nyukmadong-Dirang Dzong axis 4 Garhwal Rifles ran into lighter Chinese opposition, though they too lost a few men and a couple of officers as they were ambushed and harassed by small Chinese parties. The remnants, about 250 men under Lieutenant Colonel Bhattacharjea reached Bridge 1 at 3 a.m., a couple of hours after 4 Rajput had withdrawn from there. Instead of following Avasthy's route towards the Manda-la heights, Bhattacharjea was still looking at linking up with 4 Division HQ at Dirang Dzong. Just short of Dirang, the Garhwalis ran into what they believed to be another Indian column heading in the same direction. However, it soon became obvious that 4 Garhwal had walked into Chinese captivity. The battalion had lost 3 officers, 4 JCOs and 153 ranks during the ill-fated withdrawal after the Battle of Nuranang that had been fought thirty-six hours previously. Five officers including the commanding officer, 8 JCOs and 251 Garhwalis were captured by the Chinese.

Once the decision to abandon Se-la had been taken, 4 Sikh LI found itself cut off. It had fought numerous rearguard actions as it extricated itself from the southern face of the Se-la massif, eventually getting down to the Senge-Dirang road. However, by then, the main body of the brigade had already moved on. At this juncture, the battalion ran into a small Chinese force that it eliminated, even taking a couple of prisoners in the process. However, it was constantly harassed by pursuing troops and continued to take casualties. Finally, at 10 a.m. on 19 November, Lieutenant Colonel Nanda along with five officers, three JCOs and ninety other ranks were killed while trying to clear yet another ambush in the vicinity of Bridge 2. In all, 4 Sikh LI had lost 155 men. After the final battle, the battalion disintegrated into small parties of survivors that then had to dodge their way past Chinese ambush parties as they made their way into Bhutan.

Standing amidst the smoking ruins of his brigade, a large number of his men dead all around him, Hoshiar Singh felt a wave of helplessness. Fate had dealt a cruel hand to this gallant officer. The brigade commander may have been tactically unsuited for the job, but he had the one quality that the other senior commanders all around him lacked—the will to stand and fight. So determined had he been to fight it out at Se-la, he had given no thought to any form of withdrawal. From the moment Anant Pathania refused to let him reinforce 4 Garhwal's success at Nuranang and instead ordered the battalion to pull back, GOC 4 Division had given the Chinese the opening they needed to annihilate his troops. Even now Hoshiar Singh doggedly decided to stay on course for Dirang Dzong, believing he had been ordered to fall back and defend the division locality. After leaving the ambush site, Hoshiar Singh had Lieutenant Colonels Mehta of 1 Sikh and Budhwar of 6 Field Regiment, his GSO–3 and 150 men with him.

The brigade commander and his party continued to push on towards Dirang Dzong for the next forty-eight hours. However, it soon became obvious that the place was crawling with Chinese troops and there was no organized resistance being put up by the remainder of the division's troops. Finally, on 20 November, the decision to head for Dirang Dzong was abandoned and it was decided to turn back and through Manda-la try and head for Bomdila instead. However, this idea was soon discarded as a few local Monpas informed the brigade party that Bomdila too had been abandoned.

By the afternoon of 23 November, the brigade commander's party had been wandering around without any food for more than a week. Having bypassed Phudung, the party was resting in a bamboo jungle near the Phutang Bridge, southwest of Bomdila. Chinese troops belonging to the No. 2 Company of 154 Regiment (419 Unit) had been mercilessly hunting down and gunning Indian stragglers in the region (according to Chinese records, in a total of thirty encounters with Indian troops, they killed 434 and captured 618 Indian soldiers). Earlier in the day they had chanced upon a relatively expensive cigarette stub and boot marks, which indicated to them that the brigade commander's party was just ahead of them. The Chinese now stalked the Indians and approached the party undetected. Hoshiar Singh was at the head of the sixty-man party. He was being given a drink of water by one of the mess boys when he was shot dead. In the subsequent massacre, the three officers with the brigade commander were also killed along with another twenty-nine other ranks while the rest were wounded or captured. None from the party managed to escape.

The Chinese plan had been to capture Hoshiar Singh and the Chinese soldier who killed the brigade commander was severely punished. Realizing who he was from his red collar tabs, the Chinese announced that they had cremated the officer with full military honours. A few days later an officer from the Indian Embassy in Peking was called and the information was conveyed to him. However, this information proved to be incorrect as Hoshiar Singh's body was preserved in Phudung by the local Monpas. Much later, Indian army officers returned to Phudung and cremated the courageous soldier with his eldest son performing the last rites.

4 INFANTRY DIVISION AND 65 BRIGADE (DIRANG DZONG)

Brigadier A. S. Cheema's headlong flight in the wake of his GOC, Major General Anant Pathania, on the morning of 18 November has been documented in the earlier chapter. The brigade comprising 19 MLI and 4 Rajput now remained directionless in the absence of any instructions from its fleeing brigade commander or GOC. With the departure of the 4 Artillery Brigade commander as well, there were now no senior officers left to take charge of the situation in Dirang. The two infantry battalions under 65 Brigade were deployed outside the Dirang Dzong bowl, which by mid-morning was a scene of complete chaos.

There were still over a thousand troops left at Dirang Dzong, almost all of them quite willing to fight, each man awaiting orders which would never come for there was no one left to take charge of the situation. In comparison, there were but a handful of Chinese visible at Munna Camp, who every now and then would lob a few mortar rounds at the Indians hoping to scare them away.

Though the official history goes into the details of Indian counter-attacks, most eye-witness recollections suggest that a lot of it is exaggerated, especially the role played by 7 Cavalry. Major S. S. Brar from the Signals and Major J. R. Sehgal, the DQ of 65 Brigade, did try to rally the troops into a fighting force but without any real success. Towards the evening the two officers realized the futility of staying on in Dirang Dzong. Arming themselves with brand new 7.62 SLR (self-loading) rifles just received from NATO—part of the massive inflow of American equipment (Prime Minister Nehru had hastily abandoned his non-alignment stance)—they too followed in the wake of their senior commanders who had fled in the morning.

Another junior officer, Lieutenant Vinay Shankar, also remained steadfastly at his gun position with his men, awaiting orders that never came. Writes Brigadier Darshan Khullar: 'There was a strange quietude in the atmosphere around him (Vinay Shankar). There was no immediate threat, only a few wary Chinese lurking in the distance, at most a nuisance value. At about 1630 hours, when the Indian defences had acquired a near deserted look, the battery personnel spiked their 25-pounder guns and left Dirang Dzong.' The 4th Indian Division, the famous Red Eagles who had created an aura of invincibility around themselves in North Africa during World War II, and had been commanded by Generals Pran Thapar, Bogey Sen and Bijji Kaul, had ceased to exist within thirty-six hours of the Chinese launching their attack on Se-la.

With the commanding officer of 19 MLI choosing to extricate his battalion rather than fall back to defend Dirang Dzong, he was displaying a behaviour pattern that was alarmingly familiar. So long as the Chinese played the game in a conventional manner, the Indians were in their element, as had been demonstrated by 1 Sikh at Bum-la and 4 Garhwal at Nuranang. However, the moment the Chinese got behind Indian set piece formations, under the garb of a 'withdrawal', most units chose self-preservation over valour. Ironically, during these unrehearsed withdrawals, the mobile and flexible Chinese forces then invariably decimated them.

Initially 19 MLI went westwards towards the Bhutan border, then moved south from Labrang towards Phudung and Morshing, escaping into Bhairabkunda in India from there. In the confusion of the immediate aftermath of the ceasefire, the spotlight was on the higher levels of command; it is a great pity that most of these commanding officers were not tried for cowardice and desertion. Most of these were excellent units with tremendous records—9 Punjab, 4 Grenadiers and 19 MLI—who were let down by their own leadership. The men and junior leadership, bewildered by the turn of events and trusting in their commanding officers can hardly be faulted. Yet it was they who had to collectively pay the price.

Meanwhile, the 4 Rajput Battalion HQ was situated at Sapper Camp, in the vicinity of Bridge 1 while all its sub-units were widely dispersed. Lieutenant Colonel Brahmanand Avasthy had received a series of confusing orders on the night of 17-18 November from GOC 4 Division through 65 Brigade HQ which henceforth placed him under the command of 62 Brigade. At around 8 a.m. on 18 November, just before going off air, 65 Brigade HQ sent a brief signal to 4 Rajput asking them to withdraw to Dirang Dzong. After that, there was total silence from Cheema's HQ. Simultaneously, HQ 62 Brigade had gone eerily silent by then and there were reports coming in from the dispersed Rajput companies that the Chinese were infiltrating into their immediate areas.

Unaware of 62 Brigade's hurried exodus from Se-la, concerned mainly by the wide dispersal of his troops (at dawn, Charlie Company near Labrang had been attacked by the Chinese but it had held firm), Avasthy radioed Major Kukrety, the Delta Company commander, at 8 a.m. on the Bhutan border to rejoin the Battalion HQ at Sapper Camp. However, it soon became obvious that the Chinese were present in reasonable numbers between the Delta Company location and Sapper Camp, so an hour later, the order was modified and Delta Company was told to withdraw to the foothills independently. As per his understanding of the situation, once the Chinese had begun their offensive, 62 Brigade was expected to hold Se-la while 4 Rajput along with 19 MLI were to form the bulwark of Dirang Dzong's defences. It seemed pointless to ask Delta Company to try and fight through to Battalion HQ.

Avasthy had also spoken to Major K. P. P. Nair asking him to hold fast and assume command of all troops to the north of the road and link up with Battalion HQ which would try and get to Dirang Dzong via the northern ridge. According to Nair, he too received a second message from Battalion HQ telling him they were withdrawing shortly thereafter, and that he too should proceed independently to the foothills. After this last communication, wireless contact with Battalion HQ was broken.

Whatever the reality, the bottom line was that by the time the 62 Brigade vehicle convoy reached Bridge 2 and were ambushed, there were no covering troops from 4 Rajput in the immediate vicinity. This allowed the Chinese a free hand, and resulted in the subsequent massacre of the convoy.

Avasthy in the meantime waited in vain at Sapper Camp for Nair to show up with Alpha and Bravo Companies. Finally, after destroying all essential stores that his men could not carry with them, he pulled out of Sapper Camp at 3 a.m. on the morning of 19 November to link up with Charlie Company waiting at Labrang. During the next two days, a few remaining survivors from 62 Brigade and others from Dirang Dzong (including Lieutenant Vinay Shankar) had swelled the ranks of his column considerably. With Dirang having capitulated without a fight and Bomdila having been lost to the Chinese, Avasthy decided his best option was to marshal the men under his command into the foothills via the Manda-la heights, through Phudung and Morshing.

In all likelihood, the Chinese were fully aware of Avasthy's column, which, by the time it crossed Phudung on 21 November, had swollen to almost 600 men. The Chinese had declared a unilateral ceasefire from midnight that day but that had made no difference to the troops on the ground as the killing spree continued unabated. The commander of 154 Regiment (419 Unit) had urged his men to ruthlessly gun down as many surviving Indians as possible. Two days previously, a sizeable Chinese force had crossed Rupa from the direction of Tenga and headed off towards Morshing in the hope of trapping the last remnants of 62 and 65 Brigades that might escape along that route.

In the early hours of 23 November, Avasthy's column reached Priyuding, a tiny hamlet at the mouth of the Morshing village bowl. While the main track led directly to Morshing along relatively flat ground, a track going to the right climbed up to the Lagyala Gompa before dropping down again sharply to rejoin the track at Morshing. At best, it was an additional loop that involved a steep climb to the last monastery that overlooked the old trade route.

At the bifurcation at Priyuding, an arrow indicated that the route to be taken should be via the Lagyala Gompa. There was a hurried discussion, with Avasthy thinking the arrow had been made by the villagers. It was decided that with his Charlie Company, Avasthy would take this route while the remaining two-thirds of the party would go on straight through Morshing. Should the Morshing party be ambushed by any Chinese troops, Avasthy could then cover their flanks. In any case, Avasthy told officers who went on through Morshing, that even if the Chinese were waiting in ambush, they could not be present in large numbers.

The climb to the top of the plateau just adjacent to the Gompa took almost seven hours, by which time the Morshing column had already gone through to safety in the valley below. The Chinese no doubt let them pass without interference because they were aware of the other column closing in on them. At 11 a.m., when Avasthy's party crested the plateau, the Chinese opened fire from well-concealed positions. The Indians went to ground. They now had two options: break contact, scatter back downhill and continue to flee in small groups, or make one last stand despite the fact that they had no artillery or mortars to support them. Fed up with running, and itching for a fight, Avasthy decided on the latter.

After taking stock of the situation, Avasthy split his men into two groups and launched a two-pronged attack on the Chinese positions. Here the tables were turned, for it was the Chinese who were now fighting from within improvised bunkers and concealed positions. The Indians had no choice but to assault the Chinese positions frontally in broad daylight. One after the other, in a battle that lasted over two hours, every last man was killed.

The Indians had fought it out on the plateau, with no quarter asked for and none given. The exact number of men who died at Lagyala Gompa will never be known. Some estimates put the figure as high as 400, but in all likelihood it was close to 170, a number that included seven officers. Along with Lieutenant Colonel Avasthy, among the dead were the two cousins, Lieutenants Manvir Singh and Chattarpati Singh. The latter was the son of Colonel Girdhari Singh, MC Bar and VrC, one of the most decorated soldiers in the Indian Army.

There were no eyewitnesses to the battle and no survivors to tell the tale. The Chinese had also suffered grievously, losing a large number of men whose bodies were initially stacked in the small courtyard of the Gompa. After the action, the Chinese had dug a mass grave and buried the Indian officers and some of the men. On a solitary tree, on a flattened mess tin, they inscribed the names of Avasthy and the others. They took their own dead away, on a long trail of mules and yaks, each animal loaded with three to four dead bodies which were reportedly cremated at Dirang Dzong.

Major Kukrety, the erstwhile company commander of 4 Rajput's Bravo Company on the Bhutan border, would return to Lagyala Gompa after the ceasefire and have some of the bodies exhumed. All the remains had decomposed by then, but from Avasthy's pocket Kukrety recovered a letter written to his wife and a piece of paper with a prayer written on it.

48 BRIGADE (BOMDILA)

Lieutenant Colonel Jai Singh's decision to pull his battalion (5 Guards) out of the fray after the Thembang Battle on the evening of 17 November and the fiasco of sending out a column the next day reduced the battle of Bomdila into a non-event. In the annals of Indian warfare, time and again battles that were being won turned on their head whenever the king was killed. None of the Indian commanders in NEFA—be it Nam Ka Chu, Dirang Dzong or Bomdila—seemed to realize that their departure from the battlefield, whatever the reason, would result in pandemonium. In Brigadier Gurbax Singh's defence, it must be acknowledged that he did try and hold his ground at Thembang on 17 November and then received orders from Kaul which undermined whatever little chance he had of fighting a defensive battle.

The Chinese 33 Regiment had followed the 419 Division across Poshing-la and after Thembang had been taken, their 3rd Battalion had begun probing towards Bomdila in small parties. One column crossed the river and headed for the Manda-la Ridge. The Chinese were expecting Bomdila to be heavily fortified and their other infiltrating groups began to occupy the immediate heights around the town.

As had been the case with Dirang Dzong, the defences of Bomdila were ad hoc, with little or no deployment of barbed wire and mines despite there being no shortage of supplies. It was almost as if the commanders of both these garrisons had lulled themselves into believing that the Chinese would never come this far, convinced that the Tawang Chu would be the dividing line between Indian and Chinese forces.

Once again, official Indian records paint a slightly different picture, giving 1 Sikh LI a generous cop-out by describing in detail the systematic fallback of the mobile column to its forward defences in the face of 'massive Chinese attacks'. This is not only contradicted by the Chinese version of events, the remaining officers in Bomdila have vividly described the situation on the ground where the Sikh LI troops were caught out in the open, the Chinese having got between them and their original defences at Bomdila. Official history would have us believe that the Sikh LI troops had taken up fresh positions near the school building at Bomdila, but this was certainly not the case.

The official version of 48 Brigade's battle of Bomdila is suspect, simply because the timing of the pullback to Rupa is officially shown to be 4.45 p.m., almost three hours after the commander and the brigade staff actually abandoned their positions. The official version claims that Brigadier Gurbax Singh returned to Bomdila on the night of 18-19 November, but even if he did do so (CO 3 JAK Rif, Lieutenant Colonel Gurdial Singh's diary acknowledges that he did), it was in the wee hours of the morning and for a very brief while, which had no effect on subsequent events.

On the ground, Gurbax Singh's hurried departure was the last thing the few remaining troops in Bomdila needed to see, even though some eyewitnesses later claimed the brigade commander had stated that he was going to bring reinforcements. It also did not help matters to see the rest of the brigade staff follow the commander in quick succession. By mid-afternoon, unaware of the developments on the ground, IAF Dakotas arrived over Bomdila and dropped supplies at the DZ. There was no visible activity on the ground, for by then the only troops in Bomdila apart from the isolated and cut off 1 Madras were the advance party of 3 JAK Rifles, a few junior officers along with Lieutenant Colonel Bhupinder Singh, the commanding officer of 22 Mountain Regiment, and some gunners.

Around 3.30 p.m., the telephone in the erstwhile Brigade HQ rang. One of the gunners picked it up to find BGS IV Corps, Brigadier K. K. Singh, on the line from Tezpur, wanting to speak to Gurbax Singh. By then information had trickled down to Corps HQ that Bomdila and 1 Sikh LI positions were under attack. The gunner told K. K. Singh that neither Gurbax Singh nor the brigade staff was anywhere to be found and in fact nothing much was happening in Bomdila, since by then even the artillery guns had exhausted their ammunition and withdrawn. A few minutes later, the telephone rang again, and this time it was the DMO, Brigadier D. K. Palit wanting to speak to the seniormost ranking officer present.

Lieutenant Colonel Bhupinder Singh came on the line and confirmed that 1 Sikh LI had failed to hold the outer perimeter. He also said he had no idea what was happening to 1 Madras and that there seemed to be no communication with the battalion. The artillery officer also confirmed to Palit that the brigade commander had left Bomdila shortly after the Chinese had attacked the mobile column and occupied the outer defences.

An incredulous Palit then asked Bhupinder if he was aware of the overall disposition of the Bomdila defences. Bhupinder replied that he was.

'As the DMO, Army Headquarters, in the absence of the brigade commander, I authorize you to assume command of 48 Brigade.' The DMO went on to say that two battalions of 67 Brigade—3 JAK Rifles and 6/8 Gorkha Rifles—were moving up even as they were speaking and that Bhupinder Singh was to organize the defence of Bomdila to the best of his ability. Should he find the situation in Bomdila untenable, he was authorized to fall back on Tenga and hold that position. The order was acknowledged and Bhupinder Singh said he would do his best.

Darkness had begun to creep in on Bomdila. 1 Madras was still completely isolated, and the Chinese too seemed to have hunkered down for the night, in all probability reorganizing their various scattered sub-units. Around this time, Darshan Khullar recalls: 'It was nearing dusk by then with just a few minutes of light remaining, when suddenly I heard a series of shouts which turned out to be the battle-cry of the Dogra troops of 3 JAK Rif who were marching into Bomdila. The cheerleader was a stalwart JCO with a gold tooth, who straightaway asked me "Chini kahan hai? (Where are the Chinese?)"'

Lieutenant Colonel Gurdial Singh, who had surprisingly failed to meet Brigadier Gurbax Singh on his way up to Bomdila from Tenga, was

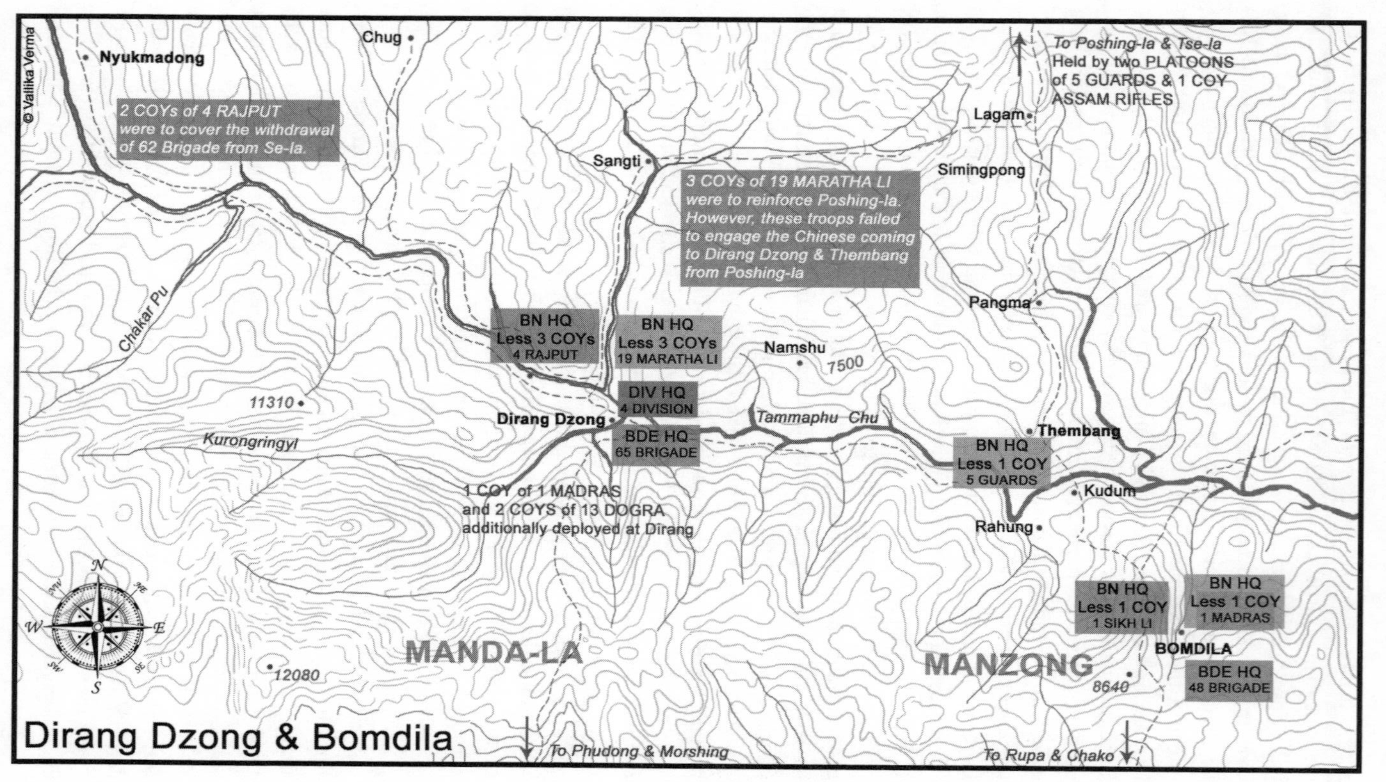

Dirang Dzong & Bomdila

commanding 3 JAK Rif. The battalion was most dismayed to find the town nearly abandoned, and with darkness setting in, there was nothing much that could be done on unfamiliar ground. After a discussion with Bhupinder Singh, the two officers decided they would await the arrival of the Gorkhas and launch a counter-attack in the early morning with the aim of recapturing the forward defences that had previously been held by 1 Sikh LI.

Meanwhile, Chinese passivity in the afternoon on 18 November had created a strange situation. 48 Brigade had abandoned the town, yet it was still occupied by one of its battalions (1 Madras) and another battalion of 67 Brigade (3 JAK Rif). In the absence of Brigadier Gurbax Singh, or any brigade staff for that matter, there was no one present who could effectively take control of the situation. Had some elements of Brigade HQ been present, the logical thing to do would have been to locate 1 Madras, pull them into the town with 3 JAK Rif and then recapture the 1 Sikh LI defences that were now held by a motely group of Chinese troops. With every passing hour, without an Indian counter-attack, the Chinese were being allowed to consolidate their scattered forces who had been probing towards Bomdila.

In the post-war analysis of events, some effort seems to have been made to paint a picture that does not quite add up. Just as Dirang Dzong folded without a semblance of a fight, 48 Brigade, despite holding a very strong hand, simply threw away a chance to give the Chinese forces a bloody nose. Not only did the brigade collapse in the most shameful manner, by making tall claims of Chinese attacks on Bomdila during the afternoon of 18 November, a smokescreen has been thrown up in an effort to obfuscate the truth. As a part of this myth, it was made to look as if 1 Madras was locked in a grim struggle with the Chinese, from which it subsequently broke contact under the cover of darkness and 'withdrew'.

In actuality, all efforts by 1 Madras to establish contact with 48 Brigade HQ had failed simply because the entire brigade staff had virtually abandoned its station the moment the Chinese had been sighted at Bomdila. A probing patrol led by a JCO reported back to Lieutenant Colonel K. K. Chandran that there was no activity in the Brigade HQ. Chandran then realized that the brigade must have withdrawn from Bomdila, leaving them to face the Chinese on their own. Though the Madras officers were completely unfamiliar with the terrain around them, it was decided to extricate the battalion by following the ridge running eastwards to Nafra and then try and head for Kaspi, all points of reference picked off the map. By 11 p.m., the last of the sub-units had also pulled out of their defences. However, as soon as it started moving, the battalion completely lost its bearings and spent that night and the next day wandering around in the jungles. Even at this stage, 1 Madras was relatively untouched and still existed as a cohesive fighting force.

After nightfall, Major Rawat, the brigade major of 48 Brigade along with Major Shashi Dang and Captain Lakhan Pal of 67 Brigade made their way back to Bomdila. Rawat's main objective was to recover some sensitive documents from the abandoned Brigade HQ. Once in Bomdila, Rawat briefed Lieutenant Colonels Bhupinder Singh and Gurdial Singh. All ideas and talk of counter-attacking the Chinese was to be abandoned. Instead, Rawat asked the two colonels to pull out of Bomdila and fall back to Rupa where 1 Sikh LI and 6/8 GR would be waiting for them. The brigade major clearly underlined the fact that these were the orders issued by the brigade commander, Brigadier Gurbax Singh.

The whereabouts of Gurbax Singh on the afternoon and night of 18 November are a mystery. Even more surprising is the claim made to the authors of the official history which records that the commander returned to Bomdila at 9 p.m. after having withdrawn to Rupa only at 4.30 p.m. Darshan Khullar explains: 'It so happened that Brigadier Gurbax had missed 3 JAK rifles because the latter were coming up a short-cut and not following the road. He halted at Tenga valley, got in touch with the Corps Headquarters and allegedly received instructions to head for the foothills. I say "allegedly" because early the next morning Major Nahar Singh, a signals officer from Corps headquarters, arrived with instructions from General Kaul to hold Rupa, about 14 kilometres south of Bomdila (Rupa's importance lay in that it was located at the tri-junction of tracks from Bomdila and Tenga and Rupa valleys; it dominated the tracks that went directly to Chaku via Pirila, and to Padung-Shergaon and onwards to Morshing-Kalaktang-Bhairabkunda). But where were the troops to hold these defences and, more pertinently, where was the time? Would the Chinese allow us the breather?'

By 3 a.m. on 19 November, the few remaining troops in Bomdila had begun to pull out. The Chinese promptly started shelling the withdrawing troops, even opening up with captured 4.2-inch mortars that had been abandoned by the Indians. Amazingly, All India Radio had already announced the fall of Bomdila the previous evening to stunned listeners across the country.

At around 7.30 a.m. on the morning of 19 November, Brigadier

Gurbax Singh was seen with the commanding officer of 1 Sikh LI, the adjutant of 3 JAK Rif and officers from 6/8 GR trying to work out a plan for the defence of Tenga, Rupa and Chaku. 3 JAK Rif was to occupy a defensive position on a feature immediately north of the road to Tenga (the commanding officer, Lieutenant Colonel Gurdial Singh, along with his IO was already reconnoitring the ground on his own) while 6/8 GR would dig in just above Rupa. Earlier, 1 Sikh LI's headlong retreat from Bomdila had only ended when the troops had reached Chaku. These troops were now expected to take up a defensive position in and around Chaku.

1 Madras had all but fallen off everybody's radar, and on 19 November, no one had any idea of the whereabouts of the battalion. The Chinese, in the meantime, had entered Bomdila and found it to be completely deserted. Realizing that the Indians were retreating, the Chinese commander decided to further exploit the situation. His already extended force was now ordered to make a run downhill for Tenga. The rapid movement of Chinese troops was to be a masterstroke. Before either 3 JAK Rif or 6/8 GR could begin to take up positions, the Chinese were onto them, leading to complete panic among the Indian troops who were now strung out between Tenga-Rupa and Chaku. Those who were the last to leave Bomdila were caught on the road near Tenga and gunned down. The two officers from 67 Brigade, Major Shashi Dang and Captain Lakhan Pal were among those who were cut off. While the former was killed, Lakhan Pal escaped by playing dead, lying amidst the bodies of his fallen comrades. So intent were the Chinese on getting a move on, they did not bother to search for survivors among the dead.

The brunt of the Chinese attack around Tenga was felt by 3 JAK Rif. After shooting up the bunched up troops on the road, part of the Chinese force turned its attention to 3 JAK Rif. By 9 a.m., the Chinese had engaged the battalion with 2-inch and 3-inch mortars and LMG fire. The JAK Rif mortar platoons returned fire, but it was at best a perfunctory gesture in the absence of any defences whatsoever. As the casualties mounted, the battalion broke up into small parties and scattered in a desperate attempt to save themselves. By midday, 3 JAK Rif had ceased to exist as a fighting force. While some men managed to fall back towards Chaku, the bulk of the survivors over the next few days had to make their way through the dense jungles directly to Tezpur. Gurdial Singh was taken prisoner, while the battalion lost another ninety-seven men who were either killed, captured or went missing.

Leaving their mortar sections to deal with 3 JAK Rif, the Chinese went after 6/8 GR who were caught in the Rupa gap as they were scrambling back in vehicles for the defence of Rupa. The soft-top vehicles afforded little protection for the Gorkhas, who suffered serious casualties. However, the battalion managed to deploy on the northern track that they held for a while, before falling back with the last two remaining tanks of 7 Cavalry towards Chaku, which they reached by last light.

At Chaku, 1 Sikh LI was hardly a reassuring sight. Recalls Darshan Khullar: 'When in the late afternoon, I reached Chaku, I learnt that a halt had been ordered in the withdrawal. 1 Sikh LI was occupying the feature or rather the lower slopes just above the road. It was no defensive position; they simply sat around because they had no digging implements, only their rifles and brens, weapon scales of ammunition and two 3.7 inch mountain guns.

'...There was no order. People sat listlessly around in groups, with about 20-odd vehicles lined up on the road. Only some enterprising persons, and I was among them, carried some rations. Kapila and I collected some scrap wood and lit a fire and were rewarded by being eased out of it by the arrival of the brigade commander, CO 1 Sikh LI and a couple of others including his Sapper company commander. There was some futile talk of sending for some digging implements and anti-personnel mines. We went back to the so-called gun position by the roadside. It was a starlit night and bitterly cold.'

Besides 1 Sikh LI, the remnants of 6/8 GR were also at Chaku. Shortly after midnight, sentries posted on the lookout reported that the Chinese were advancing towards Chaku from Rupa as they could see a few hundred men on the move with mashals (torches). Accordingly, an officer knocked on the door of the basha in which Gurbax Singh was sleeping to apprise him of this new development. M. S. Brar, the commanding officer of 1 Sikh LI was furious at being woken up for what he considered a trivial matter. Convinced that the mashals were being carried by our own tribals, the colonel wanted to know if the Chinese would be so stupid as to advance down the road carrying torches, and that too in their hundreds.

Official history again is very kind to this officer, attributing the defence of Chaku to him. At 3.45 a.m., when the mashal-lit party opened up with machine guns and tracer bullets streamed through the darkness towards the Indian positions, it started an immediate haphazard exodus. Overall, 1 Sikh LI got away with relatively few casualties—it had sixteen missing, twenty-two killed and thirty-five wounded.

Commanded by Lieutenant Colonel G. S. Kale, 6/8 GR was the last

Indian battalion to be thrown into the Kameng Frontier Division. It had only come into contact with the Chinese less than twenty-four hours earlier at Rupa. Their Bravo and Charlie Company positions were now tested amidst the scramble by the last remnants of 48 Brigade to get out of harm's way. The Chinese, having created panic with their random machine gun fire, now started sending small jitter parties to dislodge the Gorkhas. Given the number of troops available to the Chinese, it is highly unlikely that they would have assaulted the Gorkha positions in strength. As darkness gave way to light on 20 November, both these positions were deserted as the Gorkhas broke contact and pulled back. Chaku was littered with the dead and the dying. 6/8 GR alone had lost 147 men who were either killed, captured or were otherwise unaccounted for.

Around this time, having spent the previous day wandering around in circles, 1 Madras found itself just above the Tenga Bridge. From its position, the entire valley looked abandoned, so Lieutenant Colonel Chandran decided to take the road to Chaku. As the battalion emerged from the cover of the jungle, it came under heavy machine gun and mortar fire from the Chinese who were waiting for them. The 2IC, Major W. N. C. Hensman was killed along with another seven men from the Intelligence Section. Chandran along with 3 officers, 5 JCOs and 187 other ranks plus two non-combatants surrendered to the Chinese and were taken prisoner. In addition, twenty-one other ranks were captured from the company deployed at Dirang Dzong while another thirty-seven men remained missing, believed killed. Those who escaped made their way back to Assam through the dense jungles in small, scattered parties.

At 7 a.m. on 20 November, HQ 48 Brigade reached the foothills. Like 7, 62 and 65 Brigade, it had ceased to exist as a fighting formation. The two battalions of 67 Brigade, sent in to defend Bomdila, were also wiped out. The rout of 4 Infantry Division was absolute. With 11 Brigade having disintegrated earlier in the Walong Sector on 16 November itself, NEFA had fallen. It is highly unlikely that any army in the annals of military history had folded so easily in the face of an enemy who was not particularly numerically superior. Let down time and again by its senior officers, the Indian Army and the people of Assam now lay at the mercy of a handful of Chinese.

HQ IV CORPS (TEZPUR)

Even in their wildest dreams, the Chinese commanders could not have expected the Indians to fold in all the three locations—Se-la, Dirang Dzong and Bomdila—by the evening of 18 November. Ever since the first shots were fired in October, the majority of Indian commanders had time and again demonstrated to the Chinese that the moment they felt their rear threatened, they lost their nerve and the will to fight. The Chinese in turn had taken a huge risk by pushing forward, dangerously stretching their lines of communication. Under normal circumstances, a competent higher headquarters (IV Corps in this case) would have welcomed the Chinese thrust, isolated their already extended troops and then mopped them up. Instead, despite the fact the chief (Pran Thapar), the army commander (Bogey Sen) and the corps commander (Bijji Kaul) were present in the Ops Room in Tezpur, they watched helplessly as all three so-called defensive hubs—Se-la, Dirang Dzong and Bomdila—disintegrated before their eyes.

It was not the Chinese that defeated the Indian Army but the so-called 'senior leadership' of the army; almost all the brigade commanders failed miserably in NEFA, as did the GOCs of 4 Infantry Division. The three ranking officers, who collectively proved to be completely at sea and failed to instil in their subordinates the confidence to stand their ground, further compounded their failure. The shame of the defeat was followed by a surge of public anger, and Nehru, Krishna Menon and Bijji Kaul became the focal points at whose feet India's defeat was laid. In a way, this acted as a smokescreen and most of the culprits responsible for the debacle got away scot-free. None of the senior officers were censored or brought to book.

The collapse is best illustrated by the events that unfolded in the Ops Room of IV Corps on 18 November. While the early morning had been dominated by the stunning collapse of 62 Brigade at Se-la, midday had seen HQ 4 Infantry Division with the Dirang Dzong garrison implode as well. News from Bomdila had not yet come in, but even there the battle was over before it started.

By noon, everyone in the Ops Room knew that there was going to be no miracle that would suddenly reverse the situation in NEFA. Palit later wrote: 'There was a nightmarish quality about the proceedings in the Corps Ops Room. The three senior commanders held a number of discussions in which opinions gyrated freely but were seldom to the point. In the midst of the most acute military crisis the nation had faced in centuries, none seemed able to stretch his strategic horizon to take in the full significance of the situation. Instead, they kept moving round and round in circles of futile argument.'

At that point of time, Bomdila was still under Indian control only because the Chinese had still not showed up. After threatening Gurbax

Singh with a court martial unless he sent out the armoured patrol, there was not much left for Bijji Kaul and the other two senior officers to do.

The DMO then stated that the time had come for them to make a plan for the defence of Assam. 'We must forsee the possibility of the Chinese capturing Bomdila, in which case the whole of the Missamari-Charduar-Tezpur area would be threatened. At the same time, a smaller enemy thrust from Walong must also be expected after a period of build-up.'

Palit was stating the obvious. The army commander, however, was not in any mood for a discussion. Bogey Sen stated that he had no more troops left and therefore he could not make any plans. Palit, by now completely disillusioned by Sen's refusal to take charge, stuck to his guns: 'The Chinese threat to the plains will not materialize immediately,' he said, 'there is bound to be a brief respite during which time we must reorganize and, if necessary, get further reinforcements from the Punjab.'

Fortunately, General Thapar, more to avoid a full-blown argument between his army commander and his DMO, told Palit to go ahead and draw up a plan for further discussion between him, the army commander and the corps commander. A reluctant Kaul then moved to a far corner of the Ops Room to sit down with Palit to do a hurried assessment of the forces available and to indicate guidelines for action.

5 Division had already been earmarked to move from the Punjab and orders were issued for the immediate move by air to Tezpur (leading elements of the division would start arriving the next day). In addition, on the north bank of the Brahmaputra, 181 Brigade along with a squadron of armour was stationed at Daranga while there were close to 6,000 other troops from various support units who could be organized to take on any Chinese raiding parties until further re-enforcements arrived. One brigade from 23 Division was expected to be at Jorhat shortly while two more brigades were on their way to join up with the remnants of 11 Brigade as a part of 2 Division. In addition, there were Assam Rifles and armed police units that could be brought into play if required. Should the Chinese regroup and follow up on their success in the Kameng Frontier Division, these forces would then have to fight a series of delaying actions westwards, backing up towards the Siliguri corridor.

The suggestions having been put on paper, Kaul asked for a helicopter and left his Corps HQ to see if he could find any trace of the withdrawing 62 Brigade that he believed was still fighting its way through towards Dirang Dzong. However, as a helicopter was not available, the corps commander went towards Missamari by road instead. The departure of Kaul meant that

Palit had to approach Sen and Thapar who were 'sitting dejectedly on chairs drawn up near a map, staring at it silently, as though waiting for the oracle on the wall to provide a solution to their problems. I managed to break into their reverie only after my second or third attempt.'

Palit briefed Thapar about the orders he had issued for the immediate airlift of 5 Division and obtained the chief's post facto approval. He then suggested that plans be drawn up to oppose the Chinese should they reach the foothills.

The army commander interrupted the DMO: 'Nothing can be done. I have no troops available.'

With Thapar saying nothing, there was a real danger of Sen's pessimism further affecting an already despondent chief. Palit listed the forces available on the north bank of the Brahmaputra. He argued that given the speed and extent of the Chinese advance, there was no way the enemy could muster enough troops for a concentrated thrust. 'There is plenty that we can do—and will do,' Palit said.

However, Sen wasn't buying any of the arguments. Turning to Thapar, he said: 'Sir, there is no option left for us but to ask for a ceasefire!'

'What?' blurted out an incredulous Palit, 'Surrender?'

'If it comes to that, I suppose, yes.'

The Chief of Army Staff looked grimly at the Eastern Army Commander. He had nothing to say. Everybody else in the Ops Room just stared at the two officers.

Finally, it was Palit who found his voice: 'Never,' he said, 'if the Chinese come down into the plains, that's the time to get our own back at them—not put our hands up!'

Just then news came that the Chinese had engaged Bomdila and that there had been casualties among 1 Sikh LI that was manning the defences. Palit took the telephone and was put through to Bomdila but at that point no one could tell him where Gurbax Singh was. It was 3.30 p.m. and Thapar had had enough—he said he had to return immediately to Delhi and ordered Palit to get the aircraft ready. Palit asked to stay on in Tezpur but Thapar refused. Just before leaving, Palit got through to Lieutenant Colonel Bhupinder Singh, the commanding officer of 22 Mountain Regiment at Bomdila.

At the Tezpur airfield, Kaul who had returned from his foray into the foothills saw off Thapar. He told Thapar that he had gone to Foothills Camp and had appointed the corps's chief engineer, Brigadier Madhav Rajwade, MC to collect as many stragglers and other troops as he could muster and take up a defensive position should the Chinese suddenly appear.

Just as they boarded the Super Constellation IAF aircraft, Palit 'enumerated for him his corps' order of battle on the South Bank and stressed that he had sufficient forces there—logistically supported by a large, well-stocked supply and ordnance base at Gauhati—to foil any Chinese attempt to cross the Brahmaputra.'

Kaul had none of his staff officers with him, so Palit gave him his own notes, after which he boarded the aircraft. As they started to taxi out, Kaul was already making his way back towards Foothills Camp. There he learnt that 48 Brigade had abandoned Bomdila. The corps commander then issued orders for Gurbax Singh to hold Rupa at all costs and returned. He then made his way back to Corps HQ in Tezpur. Lying next to him were the notes made by Palit for the defence of the Brahmaputra Valley. These were now forgotten; instead the staff was asked to work out plans to evacuate Tezpur instead. It was quite dark by then. Across the subcontinent, the airwaves were carrying All India Radio's announcement—Bomdila had fallen!

Chapter 13

THE WESTERN SECTOR

LADAKH

The Western Sector, to a great extent, unlike NEFA was a 'known' region, as the fighting in 1947-48 with Pakistani tribal lashkars had extended almost up to the Leh airfield. After Prime Minister Nehru had announced in August 1959 that the army had taken over the NEFA border, there was initially very little movement on the ground, perhaps owing to Thimayya's reluctance to induct troops into the inhospitable Himalayan region. The Karam Singh episode towards the end of October 1959 (where an Indian patrol had been captured and then allegedly brainwashed), however, galvanized the Indians into action, who now frantically started pushing men and equipment into both Ladakh and NEFA, with little or no thought to the fact that the winter months were only going to compound their problems.

The Western Army Commander at the time was Lieutenant General Pran Thapar and Lieutenant General S. D.Verma commanded the subordinate XV Corps, under whose watch lay the expanse of Zanskar and Ladakh. Verma, like Thimayya and Thorat, was of the school that counselled caution and restraint and adherence to the basic principles of war and was hence a marked man in the eyes of Menon and Kaul.

It was obvious by then that Nehru was making statements in Parliament to placate a hostile Opposition and the few journalists who knew of Ladakh or NEFA. The government's instructions were at best confused—this was no different from the orders issued by Army HQ through 1960-61, which were perfunctory and vague. The discussions were of 'limited defence measures to contain Chinese incursions into Indian territory' giving 'parsimonious financial experts a chance to hinder, delay and block proposals for reorganizing the Army'. Operational planning was based entirely on available airlift capability, and on the assumption that the Chinese would not react to any Indian move. Numerous small posts with poor military effectiveness were established across a massive front with a wide dispersion. Financial and manpower ceilings laid down by the Cabinet were not modified after the handing over of the northern and eastern borders to the army and border formations were expected to make do with whatever was given to them. The funds available were residual amounts after allowing for the Third Five Year Plan, which, in the wisdom of politicians and bureaucrats, remained supreme.

There were hardly any roads worth the name and the newly established Border Roads Organisation (BRO) was awaiting road building equipment from abroad. Besides Leh, the only other functional airfield was at Chushul, which had limited use as it was situated right under the nose of the Chinese in the Spanggur Gap. There were landing strips at both Fukche and Daulat Beg Oldi, but these were difficult to operate from. The Indian Air Force was desperately short of aircraft, but like the BRO, lived in the fond hope of inductions from abroad. Just how and how much was known only to the defence minister and a few select bureaucrats in the Ministry of Defence. With Bijji Kaul as the Quarter Master General (QMG), the entire focus seemed to be on keeping up appearances rather than actually solving problems on the ground.

Even as the troops in Ladakh braced themselves for a second intense winter in October 1960, there was hardly an administrative set-up in place and the scanty posts were entirely dependent on airdrops. Vast quantities of kerosene was required to keep the life-saving bukharis (oil stoves) burning, hence the IAF was hard-pressed to ferry even essential survival supplies, leaving no room for war-like stores. There was hardly any snow clothing, a chronic deficiency of tinned milk (owing to a shortage of foreign exchange) and even cooking staple food like dal was a problem. There were no pressure cookers, without which it is well-nigh impossible to cook food at high altitudes. Local commanders were at their wits' end about how to convince 'Finance' to sanction these vital and essential items. 'Finance' on the other hand, seemed to live with the paranoia of sanctioning any item that could then become a 'precedent'.

Food supplies and accommodation apart, the other major problem pertained to the evacuation of casualties. There were no field hospitals and with the posts so far apart, any medical emergency could only be met with helicopters that were in very short supply at the time. No wonder then, that Nehru's statement announcing that '…necessary preparations have been made for the defence of Indian territory' was met with raised eyebrows and an incredulous shake of heads by those lower down the chain of command. It hardly mattered, though, for it seemed nobody at the top was listening anyway.

Kaul as the QMG, as we have seen, allocated quotas as he pleased without any real understanding of ground realities. General S. D. Verma, the XV Corps commander, tried reason with Bogey Sen, but the CGS made it amply clear that he was not likely to rock the boat. Verma was equally adamant and demanded to know how he could achieve anything in the way of operational readiness since the airlift tonnage allotted by the QMG barely allowed for the maintenance of existing garrisons. After allowing for survival loads, there was no room for weapons and ammunition, let alone additional troops. When Military Operations was confronted with this unpleasant math, they didn't seem unduly perturbed as 'the Chinese were not likely to start a war'. As a result, it was impossible for XV Corps to have any overall strategic or tactical plan. All they could think of at that stage was to set up a few lightly armed air-supplied posts, and then somehow keep those men alive.

In February 1961, the prime minister in a statement to the Lok Sabha implied that the army could take on the Chinese in Ladakh: 'The situation has broadly changed in our favour, not as much as we want it, but is a fact that in areas which they have occupied progressively, the situation has been changing from the military point of view and other points of view, in our favour.'

This was pure wishful thinking and bore no resemblance to the actual situation on the ground. A lesser man would have kept quiet for it was never easy to contradict Nehru, yet Verma protested to Thapar, his immediate boss in the chain of command. In a strongly worded letter, he said that the prime minister's remarks were optimistic and misleading and that his letter should be placed on record with Army HQ. By then, Thapar must have had enough indications to know that it was he, and not Thorat, who was slated to take over the army from Thimayya. Not surprisingly, the Western Army Commander refused to endorse his corps commander's views. On the contrary, he tried to get Verma to withdraw his letter saying the situation in Ladakh was well known and the prime minister's remarks were only meant for the general public. Verma refused to withdraw his letter. Thapar then made sure that the letter did not reach Nehru, the only man who mattered in the eventual analysis. Why antagonize the man?

Till mid-1961, so long as Thimayya and Thorat remained at the helm of the Indian Army and Eastern Command respectively, there was still some semblance of sense in the tactical deployment of the army. Thorat, for example, was not willing to commit his defensive line beyond Bomdila, adhering to the theory that should China attack, the logistical problem of the southern slopes would be 'his rather than ours'. But all this was simply marking time; in April 1961, with Thimayya retiring, out went Lieutenant General S. P. P. Thorat and Lieutenant General S. D. Verma, both resigning within hours of the new structure being announced. As we know, Pran Thapar was the new COAS while Bijji Kaul was to be the CGS. Bogey Sen moved to Eastern Command while Lieutenant General Daulet Singh took over the reins of Western Command.

The new Western Army Commander, like Bijji Kaul, carried the same chip of not having any real combat experience. He was an armoured corps officer who had commanded a squadron of 18 Cavalry. After heading the Armament Group in the Armoured Corps Centre and School in Ahmadnagar, he had commanded the 2nd Independent Armoured Brigade after which he was given charge of the 1st Armoured Division. After the command of a corps, Daulet Singh was entrusted with the command of the Western Army that at the time was headquartered in Simla (now Shimla).

Daulet Singh was fascinated by the Ladakh Sector and rarely missed an opportunity to visit the barren and moon-like landscape, going to some of the remotest posts to get a feel of the prevailing conditions. As a result, unlike his eastern counterpart, Daulet Singh was far more rooted in reality. Not having to deal with a corps commander who only dealt with the prime minister also helped make Western Command a more cohesive organization.

Replacing Verma at the helm of XV Corps was Lieutenant General Bikram Singh. Daulet Singh had complete confidence in the 'havildar major', a sobriquet earned by the corps commander's obsession with discipline. Originally from the Frontier Force Rifles, Bikram Singh had commanded 4 Rajput and then two different brigades in Jammu and Kashmir after Partition. After two stints with Eastern Command, Bikram Singh returned to take over the JAK Division. By the time he was elevated to a three-star rank and given charge of XV Corps, Bikram Singh knew not just Kashmir, but the entire Ladakh region like the back of his hand. He had trekked to the remotest corners, be it Rezang-la, Daulat Beg Oldi, or Chip Chap. The officers under his command knew that come what may, both the corps commander and the army commander would back them to the hilt.

'I will accept battle casualties,' Bikram Singh had told his staff, 'but I will not accept frostbite cases.'

Around this time, the land route over Zojila was made operational, considerably changing the equation. Despite the logistical nightmare of maintaining troops in the expanse of Ladakh and Nubra, XV Corps' logistic arm headed by Brigadier J. M. Das rose superbly to the occasion. Initially commissioned into the Army Supply Corps, Das had shifted to the armoured corps. Along with a small band of officers, he took pains to understand the terrain and the logistical support that was required.

CHINESE CHECKERS

By 1955, it was obvious to the Chinese that a road link to Lhasa from either eastern or northern Tibet would be problematic. Hence, they had turned their attention to the west. However, in this region bordering the Indian state of Jammu and Kashmir, it was felt that militarily India had the upper hand. Keeping the Indians off balance in NEFA was possible from Chinese military bases in Yunnan, but for them to be tackled in Jammu and Kashmir (specifically in Nubra and Ladakh) China had to develop a road linking Sinkiang and Western Tibet along an existing caravan track that passed through Haji Langar (Aksai Chin) exiting Indian territory at a point about thirty kilometres to the northeast of Lanak-la.

Sinkiang had always been strategically important; for the Russians it was the buffer between themselves and the expanding power from the east—the Japanese. The Chinese on the other hand were keen to subjugate Sinkiang to settle part of their own fast expanding population. The discovery of large reserves of thorium and uranium in the region further strengthened China's desire to control the region administratively and militarily. Not too surprisingly, Mao's first move on overthrowing Chiang Kai-Shek was to annex Sinkiang. At that point of time, Sinkiang was connected to China by a 1,000-kilometre caravan route that crossed the Taklamakan Desert, any part of which could have been cut off by the Russians.

We've seen earlier the confusion on the boundary between India and China. This allowed the latter to build the road through Aksai Chin, quite convinced that when the time came, Nehru could be persuaded to accept it. The construction of the road was not a major engineering feat, for there were no culverts or bridges required; just the blasting of rocks and the clearing of debris. However, having constructed the road, the Chinese now had to station troops to protect it.

It was estimated that one infantry division would suffice to meet any threat that might develop from the Indian side. Small roads were then made to connect their forward outposts, which ensured that apart from being well supplied, they were also linked by road to their headquarters at the rear.

As part of their overall policy, the Chinese also adroitly set about working on the local populations; they knew there had been boundary disputes between Tibet and Sinkiang to the north of the Karakoram Range. To appease the people of Sinkiang, a large tract of Tibetan territory north of the Kongka Pass–Lanak-la line was granted to them while political officers went around the Muslim population working up anti-Hindu sentiments against the Indians. Historically, there had been plenty of hostility between Tibet and Ladakh. A large number of Tibetan youth were therefore conscripted into the Chinese PLA and these units were deployed from Kongka Pass southwards, extending up to the Demchok Sector, where it was known that only Ladakhi troops were stationed.

For the security of the Sinkiang-Tibet road, the Daulat Beg Oldi Sector that lay to the west of Aksai Chin and south of the Karakoram Pass was extremely important. To the south of Aksai Chin were two massive brackish water lakes—the Pangong and Spanggur Tso—and the Indians had an airfield at Chushul next to the Spanggur Gap which allowed them to ferry men, equipment, ammunition and even heavy armament right up to the front lines. In the Chushul Sector, despite the Indian airfield, the Chinese were still at an advantage as a motor road to Rudok, a major military base, linked it to Tibet.

The Chinese plan was simple—as soon as the road network was completed, a series of outposts were to be established, reinforcing the existing positions. These posts were manned by Chinese Frontier Guards, irregular troops, who were given the task of probing the area ahead of them and occupying the dominating physical features in their area. If the need to cross the existing border arose, they were to do so but were to keep the commanders in Sinkiang and Gartok informed.

Prior to the Chinese attack in October 1962, the Chinese deployment opposite Nubra and Ladakh was divided into four sectors. The Northern Sector consisted of one regiment (equivalent to an Indian brigade) deployed in the DBO and Galwan areas with the headquarters at Qizil Jilga in Aksai Chin. The Middle Sector comprising the Changchenmo Valley was looked after by another regiment with its headquarters some 130 kilometres north of Rudok and east of Lanak-la. In these two sectors, Chinese troops were to only handle the supporting arms, while Sinkiang Muslims or the Tibetans, as per the area allocated to them, would act as the assaulting troops. A third regiment with its headquarters at Rudok was deployed opposite the Pangong-Spanggur sector, its area of responsibility extending up to Chang-la. In this region, Chinese troops were to be used for the actual fighting.

All three sectors came under the command of a divisional headquarters, based at Shahidulla in Sinkiang.

A smaller force under the Western Tibetan Command based in Gartok was stationed in Tashigang, to operate in the Demchok area if the need arose. The Demchok Sector was to be otherwise handled entirely by Tibetan troops.

The Chinese had an extremely efficient intelligence network and were fully aware of almost all Indian moves. Ironically, the Indians were not far behind. Apart from the IB which had its own network, IAF Canberra aircraft from 106 Squadron regularly made low-flying sorties, photographing all Chinese movement on the other side. In Tibet, the PLA simply did not have the means to intercept these aircraft which had a free run of the skies. Squadron Leader J. M. 'Jaggi' Nath, who first photographed the Aksai Chin highway sometime in mid-1959, claims that he would regularly take off from Agra, cross over into Chinese airspace near the Karakoram Pass, then head all the way to NEFA keeping the Great Himalayan Range to his right, before re-entering India along the Lohit Valley. 'We regularly gave them (Air HQ) detailed photographs of Chinese deployment and movement. The Army Commander Western Command commended me, so where is the question of the top brass not knowing what was going on across the border.'

In 1961, 14 J&K Militia commanded by Lieutenant Colonel Nihal Singh had been given charge of the entire Nubra Valley and the DBO Sector. The battalion headquarters was initially situated at Thoise (Partapur) and its six wings (of approximately forty men each) were guarding the Indo-Sinkiang trade route. After the Kongka incident involving Karam Singh and his men, more importance was given to this sector and the Battalion HQ was relocated to Panamik while DBO was transformed into a base with a garrison of militiamen. By 1962, a dirt runway had been created at DBO, which was capable of taking C-114 Fairchild Packet aircraft. To take off from the strip, the aircraft were fitted with jet packs, which allowed them to handle the extremely rarefied atmosphere at those altitudes.

By the summer of 1962, it was obvious to both Generals Daulet Singh and Bikram Singh that the Chinese meant business. For the past few months, ever since the Forward Policy had been put into place, Kaul (now CGS), had been pushing Western Command to set up new posts. Most of these locations seemed to be picked by Kaul and the Intelligence chief, B. N. Mullik. Both Daulet Singh and Bikram Singh were frequent visitors to Delhi and often discussed logistical difficulties with the CGS.

However, perhaps mindful of what had happened to Verma, neither of them was quite willing to openly oppose Kaul. In 1960, XV Corps had earmarked five battalions for the defence of Leh—three infantry and two militia. Two years down the line, the total force levels in Ladakh were still short of this minimum target.

The Chinese were slowly and steadily upping the ante; by April they had intruded into the Pangong-Spanggur, Hot Spring, Qara Qash and DBO sectors where they had established military strong points. The Chinese were now well beyond the line they had claimed in 1959. Still believing that the Chinese were playing mind games and an armed conflict was unlikely, Army HQ decided to airlift 5 Jat, commanded by Lieutenant Colonel Bakhtawar Singh, into Ladakh. Moving from Uri to Srinagar, Alpha Company arrived in Leh on 21 May while Bravo Company, the last to reach, finally landed at the Leh airfield at the end of August 1962. In between, Charlie Company under the command of Major Bhairon Singh, was flown to DBO in Fairchild Packets, arriving there on 23 July, two days after there had been a skirmish between the Indian militia and the Chinese.

The Jats were allowed just three days to acclimatize at DBO, which was at a height of 16,000 feet. They then took over the outposts, situated at even greater heights, from 14 J&K Militia in the Lungnak Lungspa Valley. By the end of July, the total concentration of Indian troops in the Northern Sector consisted of Charlie Company of 5 Jat with one section of 3-inch mortars, nine platoons of Militia, one platoon of Mahar troops with MMGs and a medical detachment. The area of responsibility for the Militia extended up to the rear depots at the Shyok-Galwan river junction.

The area designated as the Middle Sector is a vast region with varying topological variations. The Galwan River Valley forms the northern part, lying cheek by jowl with the western part of Aksai Chin. Part of the Shyok River Valley also comes under this sector, as do the Changchenmo and Qara Qash rivers. Then comes the massive expanse of Pangong Tso further to the south, separated from the Spanggur Tso by a mountain barrier. Another mountain barrier then separates the Spanggur Tso from the waters of the Indus, astride which lie Rezang-la and Tsaka-la. The Chushul airfield served as the supply base for the entire sector, allowing 114 Brigade commanded by Brigadier T. N. Raina to exercise control from both the logistical and operational points of view. The Tactical HQ of the brigade was established in the Chushul village itself.

As part of the Indian mobilization in Ladakh, 1/8 Gorkha Rifles commanded by Lieutenant Colonel Hari Chand was the first to arrive in

Chushul in March-April 1961. Battalion HQ with Bravo Company (less one platoon that was sent to occupy Rezang-la) dug in next to the Chushul airfield while the remaining three companies spread out to occupy as much ground as possible. Alpha Company was headquartered at Phobrang, with a platoon each at Kongma, Changlung Valley and the Galwan Valley; Charlie Company also moved into the Galwan Valley while Delta Company occupied the northern and southern banks of the western edge of the Pangong Tso.

Despite the Chinese build-up on the other side, a year was to pass before 5 Jat began to arrive. A week after arriving in Leh, Battalion HQ along with elements of Alpha, Bravo and Delta Companies moved by surface transport to Zingral, the roadhead five kilometres short of Chang-la. Moving on foot from Zingral, the Jats tried to get to Darbuk, which in Ladakhi means the 'gateway to hell'. The Chang-la crossing was a nightmare, with most animals transporting the battalion's stores dying from sheer exhaustion and the bitter cold. This delayed the movement of the troops, but eventually more animal transport was commandeered and the Jats got across, all the men completely exhausted. After reaching Darbuk, the battalion was split up even further.

Bakhtawar Singh, along with the company commander of Bravo Company, Major Ajit Singh, met Raina in Chushul. While HQ 114 Brigade was at Leh and was looked after by Raina's deputy, Colonel Karandikar, the Tactical HQ was at Chushul since May 1962. The task for 5 Jat, Raina explained, was to show the flag to the Chinese, across as wide an area as possible. The Middle Sector was not only geographically massive but also perhaps the most inhospitable region in the world. The Chinese, who were on flat ground, had relatively fewer logistical problems especially since their road network had already come up.

Alpha Company, commanded by Major H. S. Hasabnis, took another week to get to Chushul on foot, where they joined the rear elements of 1/8 GR in building barracks from sun-dried mud bricks. Battalion HQ reached Chushul a few days later, at which stage Alpha Company proceeded to Phobrang in 3-ton vehicles that had driven up via the Indus Valley axis via Nyoma and Dungti. From Phobrang the Jats had to cross the Marsmik-la and establish a base at Hot Springs. There they waited for Bravo Company to show up and proceed into the Galwan River Valley to relieve 1/8 GR who had been there for over a year. Delta Company was also pushed up to Phobrang from where one of its platoons relieved the Gorkhas from the Kongma picket.

It was mid-September by the time the Jats began to replace 1/8 GR troops in the Galwan Sector. Small groups of Gorkhas, concentrated at Hot Springs and hampered by the lack of animal transport, could only start their move towards Chushul by 16 October. Hence, by mid-October 1962, only two battalions (less one company of the Jats which was in the DBO Sector) manned the forward pickets of the Middle Sector including the Galwan Valley. Quite a few of 1/8 GR platoons were in the process of falling back on Chushul.

There was nothing ambiguous in the assessment of HQ Western Command of 114 Brigade's fighting capability. There were very few troops on the ground, and these too had been dispersed over a massive area. Daulet Singh remained apprehensive about the penny packet deployments in the name of the Forward Policy. In a letter dated 17 August 1962, the general expressed his reservations in writing. 'Our forward posts in Ladakh are nowhere tactically sited, whereas the Chinese everywhere are'. He went on to state categorically that our deployment was dictated by political considerations, and that he would be failing in his duty if he did not draw attention to the size and shape of the potential threat.

Despite being repeatedly told what the situation was and what the shortcomings were, the operational arm of Army HQ under Kaul refused to be shaken from the belief that there was little chance of any real fighting with the Chinese. How could all the warning signs have been ignored?

However, despite the sluggish approach of Army HQ, some steps were taken. Orders had been passed for the setting up of the 3 Himalayan (later Mountain) Division that was to be commanded by Major General Budh Singh, MC. Till the end of September, 114 Brigade was responsible for the whole of Ladakh, but with the setting up of a Division HQ, the brigade's area of responsibility was to be Chushul and the Northern Sector only.

Despite the developing threat, even the induction of additional troops into Ladakh remained haphazard. On 23 September 1962, 13 Kumaon, commanded by Lieutenant Colonel H. S. Dhingra, was engaged in a brigade tactical exercise in Baramulla. On its way back in the afternoon, the battalion was told to move one company immediately to Ladakh. Accordingly, Major G. N. Singh moved to Leh poste-haste, arriving there on 25 September. Just then news came in that the Chinese were getting even more aggressive in their stance, so two days later the rest of the Kumaonis were ordered to move to Leh. Accordingly, the battalion marched to Srinagar (fifty-four kilometres away) from where it was transported to Sonamarg. By 3 October it had reached the outskirts of Leh, having made the exhausting road journey over Zojila and Kargil. Finally, on 12 October its Delta Company was flown into Chushul while Bravo Company followed the next day by road via the Kiari-Dungti road axis. On 24 October, Charlie Company and Battalion HQ also reached Chushul by road.

Similarly, 1 Jat, commanded by Lieutenant Colonel M. S. Jaspal, was deployed in the Uri Sector at Chhota Kazinag, situated at an altitude of 10,500 feet. As these troops were acclimatized, the battalion was ordered to move to Ladakh on 18 October 1962. However, owing to early snowfall, Zojila was closed till 3 November. By then the first phase of fighting in Ladakh was over. The battalion moved to Srinagar on 6 November from where it was airlifted directly to Chushul.

CHINI AYA

In the DBO Sector, the Chinese had occupied the dominating heights that they considered to be the last ridge on the Chinese side. However, once they got there, they realized they had to advance further into Indian territory to dominate the Indo-Sinkiang trade route. This created a problem because the Chinese had previously acknowledged that the route and even the Karakoram Pass was part of Indian territory.

Accordingly the Chinese decided to occupy a line that would link three heights (PTs 19080, 18630 and 18475) in the Lungnak Lungspa Valley and the western extremities of Spur II and Range I to the south of the Chip Chap River. To accomplish this task, the Chinese would have to take on eleven Indian pickets, which though lightly held, would not be easy. Three strong positions were held by 18 J&K Militia—Bishan (one platoon), Chandni (two platoons less a section commanded by Lieutenant Chhewang Rigzen with Subedar Sonam Stopdan as his 2IC) and Takkar (two platoons and a section) while the others were even smaller posts. The Chinese commanders came to the conclusion that infantry attacks at heights exceeding 16,000 feet would be useless and they would rather try and blast the Indians out with sustained artillery and mortar fire.

The terrain to the south of the Chip Chap River was markedly different with the two ranges, Spur I and Range I, making troop movement against the Indian posts Takkar and Jodha difficult. However, both these positions were situated at quite a distance from the supply posts at DBO, Pramodak and Chandni, and were thus vulnerable if their supplies could be cut off. The Chinese on the other hand, had a road running from Qizil Jilga right up to the Chip Chap and Lungnak Lungspa River junction. Hence, it made sense for them to launch their main attack on the northern and middle part of the DBO sector.

There were twenty militiamen, mostly non-combatants, at Chandni and Hongshongtou drop zones, when on 19 October 1962 the Chinese opened fire with medium and heavy mortars at 11 p.m. These unarmed men, employed to collect drops and ferry them to nearby posts, were in no position to fight back. Quite a few were killed while the others managed to escape to Chandni. The next morning the DZs were abandoned and ablaze.

The Chinese also targeted the observation posts at Bishan, Pramodak and Jodha, while also firing sporadically at Bijoy, Trikoni, Pakwan and Takkar through the night. Pramodak II (all observation posts are marked as II) was the main target and at dawn, the Chinese, presuming that all the men had been killed in the bombardment, started to close in on the Indian post. Commanded by a naik, the five Indian soldiers fought tenaciously. All of them were eventually killed, but not before they had exacted a heavy toll on the Chinese. The attacking troops were all Sinkiang Muslims and it is estimated that more than a hundred of them were killed or wounded; after this incident, the Chinese only approached Indian posts when they were convinced that there were no survivors.

At Chandni, the post commander, Lieutenant Rigzen, had been wounded and at first light, his men had evacuated him to DBO. The medical officer of 14 J&K Militia had been killed, but almost all posts, other than Pramodak II and Chandni II, that had been attacked were holding out. At 12.10 p.m. on 20 October, with the fighting still going on, a C-114 Packet landed at DBO. On board were Brigadier Das and another staff officer from XV Corps, Major Chaudhry. The aircraft was on the ground for forty minutes, long enough for the Intelligence havildar of 14 J&K Militia, Kishan Singh, to give the Brig Adam a detailed rundown. During this period the Chinese fired thirteen mortar shells at the aircraft, which then took off with the wounded, including Rigzen on board. Before leaving, Das gave clear orders that all posts in the outlying areas in the Qara Qash Sector were to be vacated and the troops should fall back on DBO.

On arrival at Srinagar, the wounded were shifted to hospital and Das briefed the corps commander, Bikram Singh, on the DBO situation. Immediate orders to set up a Tac HQ in Partapur were issued.

Meanwhile, back in DBO, at 4 p.m. an Indian observation post reported the arrival of a Chinese convoy consisting of eighty trucks—mainly 5- and 3-ton vehicles—ferrying nearly 1,500 troops, heavy and medium mortars along with machine gun crews.

The newly inducted troops were thrown into action almost immediately, forming up in lines and assaulting Jodha II, Pakwan and Bishan II. As a result of this massive attack, all three posts were overrun by 7 p.m., all defenders having been killed except for two men who managed to escape and fall back on Pramodak I (Tr Jn), the largest base in the DBO area that was now converted into a defended locality.

Meanwhile at Takkar, Subedar Diwan Chand, the post commander, ordered the men at two smaller posts to fall back on his position that was under sporadic, though somewhat inaccurate fire. At 8 p.m., the Chinese launched a simultaneous assault on Bishan, Chandni, Trikoni and Pakwan posts. The fighting was intense and bitter, the Chinese advancing despite casualties, hoping that the Indians would eventually run out of ammunition. Bishan fell after an hour's fighting, but the JCO commanding the position smartly took up an alternative position that deterred the Chinese from taking on Pramodak I. By 10.30 p.m., all the other posts were also silenced. The fight put up by the militiamen had been of the highest calibre. Chandni was in the charge of Subedar Sonam Stopdan who had fifty men with him. They fought with everything they had, but, one by one, most of them were killed. Eventually, Stopdan was also fell. The few remaining men then pulled out under cover of darkness. Takkar post was still holding out, but the main Jodha post had been vacated with two radio operators being taken prisoner. Strangely, the Chinese did not occupy the Indian position and withdrew instead. The post commander, Subedar Rigzen Phunchok, along with the remaining three survivors, reoccupied it. They would hold the position till 28 October until they were finally ordered to pull out.

North of the Chip Chap River, the Chinese had crossed the river and positioned a MMG opposite Bhanu post that was manned by 5 Jat's Charlie Company. They started firing at first light on 20 October after they noticed Naik Bare Singh go across the river to relieve himself. The NCO managed to scramble back and organize his men who immediately engaged the enemy. Chinese mortars also joined in and kept up an intermittent barrage through the day. Sepoys Arjun Singh, Badan Singh, Jai Lal and Tale Ram were killed.

The Jats have always been extremely tough nuts to crack—as the Sinkiang Muslim troops were finding out the hard way. However, without ammunition there is little anyone can do and the rest of the men started pulling out to Arni I and Arni II, the two northernmost Indian positions. Naik Bare Singh along with Sepoy Bahadur Singh and Salu Singh stayed back to cover the withdrawal. However, when it was their turn to pull out, the Chinese surrounded them. Bahadur Singh was killed, while the other two were taken prisoner. Shortly thereafter, Salu Singh managed to escape, and he made his way to Arni I. By 6 p.m. on 20 October, Bhanu post had ceased to exist.

Arni I was being commanded by Naik Chand Singh. The terrain combined with the altitude gave the Indians the advantage. The Chinese kept out of small arms range and peppered the post with mortar and MMG bursts through the day. The arrival of a few extra men from Bhanu post further strengthened the resolve of the men to fight. Through the night, the Chinese kept up a steady barrage in which three Indian soldiers were killed. By first light on 21 October, the Chinese had taken up positions on three sides of the post, but the Jats were not ready to give up. Chinese infantry too was reluctant to advance further, so through the morning they continued to fire heavy and medium mortars. Unable to crack Arni I and Arni II, the Chinese turned their full attention on Dabu post that was defended by ten men. The quantum of fire brought to bear on Dabu forced the defenders to pull out under the cover of darkness. However, there were no casualties at Dabu post.

With Dabu in Chinese hands, on the morning of 22 October, Arni I and Arni II were now isolated. There had been no let up in the bombardment and every now and then Chinese jitter parties would open fire with MMGs. Ammunition was soon running low and Chand Singh sent out an SOS to Second Lieutenant Harish Chandra Gujral, commanding Arni II. Not wanting to expose his men, Gujral handed over charge of Arni II to Havildar Dharam Singh and personally made five runs in a Willy's jeep between Arni I and Arni II. Despite the Chinese targeting him, incredibly, they failed to bring him down. On the return journey, each time he ferried the wounded to Arni II. This display of bravery only raised the morale of the stubborn Jats further. Finally, under cover of darkness, the Jats broke contact with the Chinese and fell back on DBO.

Another post occupied by the men of Charlie Company of 5 Jat was Filter II. This post was also subjected to continuous mortar fire, but in this case the Chinese made no attempt to assault it. This post was also abandoned on the night of 22 October. By 25 October, the last straggler had fallen back on DBO.

THE SAGA OF 14 J&K MILITIA

Reports coming in from various posts clearly indicated to Major S. S. Randhawa, the 2IC of 14 J&K Militia and the overall sector commander for DBO, that the Chinese were trying to dislodge the Indian troops from their posts. Around the time Brigadier Das landed at DBO, Randhawa was moving from Murgo towards Tr Jn with the intention of reinforcing the defences there. Once it was confirmed that Bijoy and Trikoni Posts had fallen, the line of communication to Sultan Chushku became vulnerable. Orders were then passed to all posts in the Sultan Chushku area to withdraw either to Tr Jn, DBO or Burtse.

On 22 October, the BBC flashed the news that DBO had fallen to Chinese forces. Randhawa immediately sent a message to the XV Corps Tac HQ saying that if DBO had indeed fallen, Tr Jn must be held at all costs. This message created some agitation in the Corps HQ for it implied that the Chinese had crossed their 1960 claim line and had cut off the axis between Tr Jn and DBO.

Bikram Singh discussed the matter with Raina who suggested both DBO and Tr Jn be abandoned and the troops pulled back to Sasar Brangza. The corps commander then spoke to Daulet Singh who confirmed the order subject to Randhawa's discretion. Late in the evening on 22 October, the order to withdraw if required was passed to all concerned. At the same time, the army commander also gave orders to fly additional mortars, mines, jeeps and ammunition to Tr Jn.

As it turned out, quite a few posts had held out; most of them would break contact only later that night. The Chinese, on the other hand, having succeeded in clearing the Indians from the heights, never assaulted or occupied DBO or Tr Jn. On 23 October, after burning the five trucks and four jeeps and destroying the fuel dump, the rest of the troops at DBO fell back with the Jats to Murgo. (They would subsequently get to Thoise from where Charlie Company of 5 Jat was flown to Chushul to link up with the rest of the battalion.)

Seventy men of 14 J&K Militia were lost in the fighting. Those who were at DBO withdrew with the Jats, but Major Randhawa's group from Tr Jn chose to follow the Chip Chap–Shyok River route. Once they entered the glaciated region, they lost complete contact with Battalion HQ but were fortunately spotted by a reconnaissance aircraft a day later. The column reached Sasar Brangza safely, with Randhawa having also withdrawn his other troops from Burtse, Sultan Chushku and the Galwan–Shyok River junction.

The Qara Qash sector was perhaps the remotest part in what was already the back of beyond. This plateau, with the lowest point of 15,400 feet and the surrounding features all in excess of 20,000 feet, was the area where the Murgo Chu, Qara Qash, Galwan and Nachhu Chu originated; all the river valleys were above 16,000 feet. There were two camps in this sector—Sumdo and Sultan Chushku. Not only was the sector geographically forbidding, with the main Karakoram Range passing through it, most explorers in the past had given it wide berth. The Survey of India (and the Kashmir State) records were scanty and most features were not marked accurately.

This dreary, cold and isolated region had a single track running through it, linking Qizil Jilga in the north to Samzungling in the south, which was made into a motorable road by the Chinese. In April 1962, Major Randhawa along with Captain D. S. R. Sawhney, Lieutenant Chhewang Rigzen, fifteen militiamen and seventeen porters with forty yaks and ponies had started from Sultan Chushku to establish forward posts in the vicinity of Sumdo. The route was dotted with glaciers; blizzards made the going extremely difficult, but Randhawa persevered, eventually setting up three pickets. The main post was code-named Jyotish, and a DZ was established there so it could be supplied by air. A second picket was a staging camp while the third, at 17,700 feet, was an OP from where all Chinese posts in the Sumdo region were clearly visible. By the time the party returned to DBO, twenty-nine of the forty animals had died of cold and exhaustion.

Lieutenants Rahim and Surat Singh, Captain Chatterji (the medical officer), three JCOs and forty-four militiamen were manning the three pickets when the Chinese opened fire with mortars on the night of 19 October 1962. Though Jyotish was the larger camp, all three officers were at the higher observation camp when the bombardment started. Owing to the difficulty faced by the Sinkiang troops in ferrying ammunition to those heights, the firing was sporadic and there was no question of the Chinese putting in an infantry attack. However, it was also obvious that the Indians could not hold out indefinitely, especially if the DZ was under fire. At 3 p.m., Rahim received Das's orders to withdraw. The Indians moved out at nightfall, and made it to Sultan Chushku after six days, exhausted and in need of medical aid. Fortunately, there were no casualties in the Qara Qash Sector, which by itself was a tribute to the staying ability of the militiamen.

Technically, the Galwan River Valley was a part of the Middle Sector, but geographically not only was it contiguous with the Qara Qash region, it was also equally forbidding and harsh. The Galwan theatre of operations extended over eighty kilometres in length with an average breadth of twenty-four kilometres. The highest peak in the area was 22,220 feet and the Galwan River's source itself was at 19,000 feet, dropping down sharply through the Galwan Basin to the Shyok River junction at 14,700 feet. Fast-flowing tributaries of the Galwan had cut deep gorges across the landscape, which were devoid of even animal tracks. The major characteristic of the Galwan Valley was that the river cut through the main Karakoram Range, which sloped towards the left bank of the Shyok River for almost forty-eight kilometres. Hence to approach the Aksai Chin–Lingzithang Plateau from the west, troops would have to ascend this expanse. Unlike in DBO and the Qara Qash, it was almost impossible to find a level piece of ground in the Galwan Valley, even more so in the smaller valleys through which flowed the tributary streams. So inaccessible was the region even from the Chinese side that the PLA had initially left it alone.

Other than a few graziers from the Nubra Valley, all explorers to the Depsang-Aksai Chin-Lingzithang region had stayed away from the Galwan Valley. However, Charlie Company of 1/8 Gorkha Rifles had established a post named Galwan FDL in May-June 1962. Using the few basic tools available and their bare hands, the Gorkhas succeeded in constructing a helipad that became their lifeline. Towards the end of August they had also established Ration Party, a post to the south of Galwan FDL, in the hope of establishing a link with Indian positions in the Shyok River Valley. Towards the north they established two more OPs to keep a watch on Chinese activities at Samzungling, which was the Battalion HQ and the extent of Chinese presence in the area.

By the end of June, 32 Gorkhas left Hot Springs under the command of Captain G. Kotwal, tasked with creating a land link with Ration Party and Galwan FDL from the southern side. On 3 July, having established the Nullah Jn post, Kotwal pushed forward along the Changlung Valley, leaving a JCO and 9 Gorkhas to man Nullah Jn. Two days later, the party established Patrol Base, from where Kotwal sent out reconnaissance parties to find a route that would link him with Ration Party.

Meanwhile, on 6 July 1962, as part of their policy of occupying remote areas and then claiming them as their own, the Chinese sent a patrol into the northern part of the Galwan Valley. To their chagrin and complete surprise, they ran into the Gorkhas who were firmly entrenched there.

Until July 1962, as had been the case with the entire expanse of the Aksai Chin in the 1950s, the Chinese had usually succeeded in entering an unoccupied isolated area and New Delhi had been reduced to sending notes of protest to Peking asserting that the territorial integrity of India had been violated. From the Chinese point of view, the presence of Indian troops in the Galwan Valley created a serious problem that required some deft footwork, even if reality had nothing to do with Chinese claims. Accordingly, on 8 July, Peking sent a protest note to New Delhi claiming that an Indian patrol had entered Galwan on 6 July and had 'attempted to cut off' an established Chinese post in the lower reaches of the valley.

Even as India refuted the Chinese claim and pointed to the existence of Galwan FDL, on 10 July at 9.30 a.m. a party of twenty-five Chinese soldiers deployed 180 metres from the Indian post. Within the hour, fifty more men had joined the initial group and cut off the track to the helipad. By nightfall, 300 more Chinese soldiers had joined their comrades who not only encircled the Gorkhas, but occupied positions sixty-five metres from the post.

With the Chinese all around them, the Gorkhas continued to hold their ground. Commanded by Naib Subedar Jang Bahadur Gurung, the Indian post held its fire through those nerve-racking hours. In the next few days, the Chinese deployed two of their companies to the north and northwest of Galwan FDL, their forward position being around 180 metres from the Indian post's defences. Another company was deployed even closer, at about 90 metres, to the east and southeast of Galwan FDL. On the diplomatic front, Peking kept up the shrill rhetoric, claiming through protest notes that Indian troops had opened fire on 19 July, 16 August, 2 September and then again on 3 October.

By mid-July, Captain Kotwal's reconnaissance teams sent out from Patrol Base had reported that it was almost impossible to reinforce Galwan FDL by the land route. The only way then for 5 Jat, earmarked to replace the Gorkhas at Galwan FDL, to move into the Galwan Sector was by helicopter. Twenty-five men from 5 Jat's Alpha Company under Major S. S. Hasabnis were finally inducted into Galwan FDL by IAF helicopters that started landing at Helipad from 4 October. The Gorkhas, having lived cheek by jowl with the Chinese for more than two months, were ferried out by returning Mi-4 helicopters over the next four days.

THE BATTLE FOR GALWAN

On the morning of 20 October, Galwan FDL under the command of Major Hasabnis and Subedar Hoshiar Singh was being held by two sections of 5 Jats' Alpha Company. A section was deployed at each of the two OPs, while Ration Party was being held by a platoon. Helipad had a handful of men, while the Galwan-Shyok river junction was the responsibility of Subedar Balraj Singh who had two sections of 14 J&K Militia under his command. Though the IAF helicopters were keeping the lines of communication open, the Chinese knew that once the fighting started, the unprotected Mi-4s would have to abandon the troops. Not only was the quantum of Indian troops facing the Chinese minuscule, it was also obvious that there would be no reinforcements.

In their overall scheme of annexing and then linking Tibet and Sinkiang, the occupation of Aksai Chin was a critical factor. After having built National Highway G219 it was equally important to put the Indians in the immediate vicinity of the Karakorams in a strategically difficult, if not impossible position.

The main characteristic of the Galwan theatre when compared to DBO and Qara Qash was that the Karakoram Range in this area is geographically far better defined. The Galwan River pierces through this imposing natural barrier forty-eight kilometres to the east of the Galwan-Shyok river junction. To the south, the Karakoram Range then splits into two—Karakoram I separating the Kugrang River from the Changlung while Karakoram II, also known as the Nischu Mountains, runs along the left bank of the Changlung River. The slope from the crest line of the Karakoram to the Shyok River was too far for the Chinese to dominate the Shyok route. For once, their usual strategy of occupying the highest range would serve no tactical purpose. Therefore, if the Indo-Sinkiang trade route had to be dominated by the Chinese, they had no option but to descend towards the Shyok River, in the process occupying the entire Galwan Basin.

B. N. Mullik, the man who actually worked out the positing of Indian troops (even after Nehru's handing over charge to the army) read the situation in the Galwan Valley correctly. Once tasked with occupying the Galwan Valley, the tenacity of 14 J&K Militia and then 1/8 Gorkha Rifles saw the men on the ground succeed in doing the impossible. Unfortunately, Mullik's, and by extension the government's, belief that the mere presence of Indian posts in the area was enough and the Chinese would do nothing, eventually turned the few soldiers in the region (one infantry company minus a platoon) into cannon fodder for the PLA.

Having got over the shock of finding the Indians already in the Galwan Valley, the Chinese intent was obvious after they not only encircled Galwan FDL but dug in where they were. The occupation of the Galwan Basin was obviously critical to them; neither Sinkiang Muslims nor Tibetan troops were deployed against the tiny Indian presence.

On 20 October, coinciding with the time Chinese artillery and mortars attacked in Nam Ka Chu in distant NEFA, heavy and medium mortars began a devastating barrage on all Indian positions in the Galwan Valley. Almost immediately, Hasabnis decided to abandon OP2 and pull the men into Galwan FDL. Helipad, with hardly any defences, was the first to fall. When the barrage lifted, Galwan FDL, Ration Party and OP1 all came under small arms and machine gun fire. OP1 was virtually wiped out with most occupants being killed, the wounded taken prisoner and a couple of men managing to escape.

At both Galwan FDL and Ration Party, the Chinese despite their hand-shaking proximity to the Indian positions, seemed hesitant to put in an infantry attack, hoping instead to blast out the Indians from their stone sangars. That the two battles lasted more than twenty-four hours was a tribute to the sheer doggedness of the Jat troops. At the Galwan FDL, Subedar Hoshiar Singh was inspirational—moving from bunker to bunker, he held the men together until, at 6 p.m., a mortar bomb killed him. The Jats still held on, fighting till the next morning. By 10 a.m., after more than thirty hours of intense bombardment and fighting, the last message from Galwan FDL was sent to HQ 114 Brigade, saying that the Chinese were now advancing on the Jat position. Hasabnis was wounded and thirty-six of the sixty-eight men had been killed. Again, a few managed to break contact and make a dash for the Galwan-Shyok river junction. The story at Ration Party was much the same with the fighting ending with the death of the commanding JCO.

Shortly thereafter, two Mi-4 helicopters flew over Galwan FDL and were fired at by the Chinese from their locations. The pilots reported that they had not seen any sign of activity at Galwan FDL or Ration Party. Bikram Singh now turned his attention to the Changchenmo Valley and ordered HQ 114 Brigade to pull back the remaining troops of 5 Jat from Patrol Base to the Nullah Junction. By then, Patrol Base was already under intense artillery fire. However, under cover of darkness, the platoon, under Naib Subedar Umaid Singh began to pull back, leaving a section strength party behind to cover their withdrawal and wait for the men who had gone towards Galwan FDL to lay a telephone line. The next morning, the Chinese tried to occupy the post but were met with heavy resistance. Subedar Amar Singh, commanding the post, fought till the Chinese killed him along with the last man.

Nullah Junction with one section of ten men under the command of Naib Subedar Kanhya Lal, further reinforced by the Patrol Base troops, continued to hold the Chinese at bay throughout 22 October, thereby preventing them from spilling out into the Changchenmo Valley and threatening Hot Springs. The Chinese continued to fire at Nullah Junction but did not put in any determined infantry attack. Though casualties continued to mount—the section commander had his legs blown off from under him—and communication with Hot Springs had been cut, the Indians hung on gamely. Two men were then sent to Hot Springs to ask for further orders.

By 23 October, almost all the men who had survived the initial Chinese onslaught in the Northern Sector and in the Galwan Valley, were on the move, trying as best as they could to fall back on Nullah Junction and then on to Hot Springs. However, there were a few exceptions. Skalzang Dorge, a Ladakhi serving with 14 J&K Militia had been wounded at DBO. Somehow, as the rest of the Indian troops pulled out, Dorge was left behind. Finding himself abandoned, the militiaman crawled into a bunker, dressed his own wounds and settled down to wait, firm in the belief that his comrades would return soon. Living off dry rations and burning kerosene to keep warm, Dorge stayed alive through the next six months until he was rescued in April 1963. With the Chinese also staying clear, Dorge ensured that DBO remained in Indian hands.

The Kongka incident of 1959 had adversely affected public opinion against the Chinese, so much so that even pro-Chinese Marxist parties within India had reacted negatively. To placate public opinion, the Chinese had acknowledged that the Hot Springs area was indeed Indian territory. At the same time they had also declared that Kongka-la and the Lanak-la were Chinese territory. By clearing the Galwan Basin of Indian troops and having occupied the western slopes of the Karakorams, the Chinese forces decided to tailor their objectives in the Hot Springs region accordingly. They therefore decided to leave the middle and lower portions of the Changchenmo Valley in Indian hands while securing Kongka-la and the upper portion of the Changchenmo Valley. This also meant that the Chinese could declare they did not cross their 1959 claim line in the region.

Major Ajit Singh was the commanding officer at Hot Springs. On the morning of 23 October, the situation was extremely critical. Nullah Junction was not only valiantly holding out, it was acting as a block, preventing the Chinese from spilling into the Changchenmo Valley. The Hot Springs theatre of operations extended from the Indo-Tibetan boundary in the east to the Shyok River in the west. To the north, separated by the Karakoram I Range of mountains was the Galwan Valley, while to the south the Karakoram II Range separated it from the waters of the Pangong Tso. There were four major passes that linked the Hot Springs to the other regions—Changlung-la and Kongka-la to the north, Lanak-la in the east and the Marsmik-la to the south, which was the most frequented route into the Changchenmo Valley. The average altitude in the Hot Springs area was 14,700 feet and, unlike the Galwan Valley, the gradient towards the Changchenmo River was wide and gentle. Only towards the western exit of the sector did the valley narrow sharply, after which the Changchenmo flowed into the Shyok River.

The Tsogstsalu post was the closest to Marsmik-la, and it came under harassing fire on 23 October. Both HQ 3 Division and 114 Brigade, when informed, presumed that it would be a matter of time before the Chinese cut off Hot Springs from the south. Raina therefore suggested to Major Ajit Singh that he leave a small party behind and withdraw over the Marsmik-la to the 5 Jat Battalion HQ at Phobrang. Ajit Singh was vehemently opposed to any withdrawal, firm in the belief that the defences at Hot Springs could be held. Besides, he further argued, if he had to abandon Hot Springs, he would much rather move downstream along the Changchenmo and link up with Randhawa's men pulling back from DBO and the Galwan Sector.

Ultimately, it was Raina's call, and the brigade commander had to weigh his options carefully. The southern slopes of the Marsmik-la were defended by the Kongma and Kongma I posts, which were the last positions held by a platoon from Delta Company of 5 Jat commanded by Subedar Surjit Singh. Geographically, the Kongma tract that embraced the southeastern slope of the Marsmik Massif was a part of the Pangong-Spanggur region. The Kongma positions were opposite Anne-la where three Chinese pickets marked their claim line. A motorable road connected the pass with the Chinese rear HQ at Dambu Guru.

The Chinese had engaged the two Kongma positions on 22 October. As the bombardment began at 2 p.m., Surjit Singh ordered the men from Kongma I to fall back on the main post. Owing to the intensity of mortar and machine gun fire, the withdrawing section had to go to ground amidst the rocks. Despite being hopelessly outnumbered, the Jats doggedly held on through the day and the night. However, towards last light on 23 October, there were no men left as all of them had been killed or wounded. Surjit Singh was thought to be among the dead, but he was badly wounded and captured by the Chinese. Only four out of the thirty men managed to escape from Kongma.

By then, Raina knew the fate of Kongma, yet he agreed to back the younger man's instincts, for after all, Major Ajit Singh was the man on the ground.

After eliminating the Kongma positions, the Chinese spent the morning of 24 October harassing Tsogstsalu, after which they withdrew. However, news of fresh Chinese activity in the vicinity of Marsmik-la now prompted Raina to order Ajit Singh to withdraw from Hot Springs. Unable to ignore a direct order, Ajit Singh left a section to hold Hot Springs, after having sent a section earlier to Nullah Junction to reinforce the position there. Then with a column of eighty men, he started for Marsmik-la and reached Tsogstsalu at noon the next day. The fact that the Chinese were free to intercept the route to Phobrang prompted him to retrace his steps and head back down the Changchenmo Valley where he hoped to also link up with the other survivors of his battalion and 14 J&K Militia.

Once the party entered the narrow gorge of the Changchenmo, the bitter cold and freezing conditions got further amplified owing to having to sometimes wade through the river and its tributaries. Though IAF helicopters were regularly searching the area, because of the narrowness of the gorge, the party could not be spotted. Despite almost all men suffering from frostbite by then, Ajit Singh managed to keep his party alive and together, finally emerging at the track junction from where a goat track proceeded to Phobrang.

At this stage, the column was divided into two. Ajit Singh ordered Subedar Umaid Singh to take forty men and head for Phobrang while he would proceed to the Changchenmo-Shyok junction in the hope of finding stragglers from DBO and Galwan. The Phobrang column would take three days to reach its destination. Without exception, every man was suffering from the extreme cold and severe frostbite.

Ajit Singh's party in the meantime had reached the Shyok junction where they found another forty men who had escaped from the Chinese. Many had frozen to death and it was obvious to Ajit Singh that none of the rest could proceed any further unless resupplied from the air. Taking two men with him, the major once again headed back to the track junction from where he made it to Phobrang on 5 November. The next day IAF aircraft dropped supplies and eventually all the men made it back with no further casualties.

Nullah Junction, Hot Springs and Tsogstsalu would remain under Indian control. In all, 5 Jat had 58 killed and over 200 men hospitalized, with the bulk of them returning to active duty within weeks. Despite being split into miniscule sub units the battalion had performed exceptionally well.

THE PANGONG-SPANGUR SECTOR

1/8 Gorkha Rifles, having de-inducted from the Galwan and Changchenmo Valley during the second week of October, were at full strength (minus one company) in the Pangong-Spanggur theatre of operations, and also the mainstay of 114 Brigade for the defence of Chushul. Referred to as the Middle Sector, it included both the brackish water lakes and the watersheds that surrounded it on all sides, creating a bowl-shaped tract. To the north lay the mountain range that separated the Pangong Tso from the Changchenmo, their southern sides sloping towards the lake. Towards the east, were the Pangong and Rezang ranges, running north to south, more or less forming the International Boundary. To the west and south was the Ladakh Range that separated the waters of the Spanggur Tso from the waters of the Indus, which flowed from east to west further to the south. The lakes themselves were at 14,000 feet, while the Pangong and Rezang ranges had a maximum altitude of 19,750 feet.

On the northern bank of the Pangong Tso, facing the Chinese to the east, was the Srijap Sector while on the southern side of the lake, touching the International Boundary was the Yula Sector. The Indians had been using assault boats that had been flown in by the IAF to maintain the line of communication. The point of embarkation was Tokung, the 1/8 GR Battalion HQ, where the relatively small Chushul Chu flowed into the Pangong Tso, while on the northern shore the boats would dock at Srijap East and also on the southern shore at Yula I and Yula II. Though Phobrang, also on the northern side of the Pangong Tso, had been linked to Chushul by a motorable road, ferrying supplies and ammunition to Srijap further to the east from the road heads was not feasible. The Chinese, on the other hand, had built a road from the Khurnak Fort linking their positions in the Srijap area to the rear as was their usual practice. This road had been completed on 27 August 1962. In addition, the southern Spanggur track had also been made into a regular highway. This allowed them to move medium artillery, RCL guns, heavy mortars and even tanks from their rear headquarters at Shingshang and Rudok.

On 26 June 1962, a section of 1/8 Gorkha had crossed the Pangong Tso and established Srijap West. Eight days later, Major Dhan Singh Thapa arrived with reinforcements and the picket became the headquarters of Charlie Company. By the middle of July, Srijap East, Srijap Jamini and Srijap Screen (an observation post) had been established. Simultaneously, on the southern shore of the Pangong Tso, Yula I was established. By the middle of July, to give depth to Yula I, Yulla II and a small observation post, Jamini Tilok had been established.

With the establishing of each post, the names would be stencilled onto the maps and little blue pins added in Command HQ and Army HQ to indicate the forward extent of the Indian positions. In reality, these were created as and remained mere defensive positions that at best could hold out for forty-eight hours. On 20 October, twenty-eight men were holding Srijap

West under Dhan Singh Thapa; Srijap East had one platoon less a section; Srijap Jamini had three men; and Srijap Screen had a section consisting of ten men. On the southern side of the Pangong Tso, Yula I and Yula II were being held by a section of Gorkhas plus a section of engineers each; while Jamini Tilok had a section. A third post, Yula III was deployed as a listening post further to the south and was more contiguous with the Chushul Sector. This roughly meant that there were eighty Indian soldiers in the Srijap Sector and another fifty in the Yula Sector.

The Chinese objectives at this stage become quite clear, especially when looked at in conjunction with their moves in the Northern Sector. The Srijap Valley had to be secured and the Indo-Tibetan boundary pushed forward to meet their interpretation in line with Kongma. If Yula I and Yula II were also taken, then the extension of the boundary to the south would automatically place the entire Spanggur Tso in Chinese territory. For the time being, they decided not to broaden the frontage and did not engage Indian posts on the Rezang Range.

On 20 October, news of Chinese attacks all along the Northern Sector vindicated Daulet Singh's stand that the Forward Policy would explode in India's face if the Chinese decided to get aggressive. By then, reports from both Srijap and Yula sectors indicated that the Chinese were preparing to launch attacks. Accordingly, Srijap Jamini was ordered to fall back on Srijap West while Srijap Screen, Yula II and Jamini Tilok were to fall back to Chushul. Raina issued the orders at midnight but before any of the posts could react, the Chinese opened up at 6 a.m. with artillery and mortars on all posts.

In the Srijap area, the Chinese had deployed around 300 men against each Indian picket. The Chinese held their infantry back, preferring to keep up the bombardment from artillery, direct firing RCL weapons and mortars. Under the cover of darkness, the telephone line from Dhan Singh Thapa's post to the battalion's rear headquarters at Tokung had been cut. Among the earliest casualties at Srijap West was the wireless set. After two and a half hours of relentless bombardment, the Chinese realized that Srijap Jamini had been abandoned.

The next to fall was Srijap East, as the entire section had been killed except for Rifleman Tulsi Ram. As the Chinese overran the position, they found the lone Gorkha survivor sheltering behind a rock. The 1/8 GR party at Tokung reported to Battalion and Brigade HQ that they could hear heavy firing from both the direction of Srijap and Yula. By 11 a.m. the Chinese had consolidated their position in Srijap Jamini and Srijap

East, and they marched Tulsi Ram off to the Khurnak Fort.

Even though 5 Jat and 14 J&K Militia deployed in the Northern Sector had been under attack since the previous morning, Raina was very concerned about the developing situation in the Sirjap and Yula positions. Army HQ until the previous day had resisted all pleas from both Bikram Singh and Daulet Singh for additional troops, blindly repeating the Kaul mantra that the Chinese would not react and, in any case, our airlift capability to induct fresh troops was limited. That argument having collapsed, orders for the airlift of at least one Kumaoni company to Chushul were being hastened. This meant that the entire Chushul Sector, contiguous with Yula, would continue to be defended by just the one battalion, 1/8 GR minus Alpha Company, that was still in Srinagar, recuperating after being pulled out of the Galwan Valley. This effectively meant there was absolutely no scope to reinforce any post or sector if it came under attack.

After the initial two-and-a-half hour bombardment at dawn, the first attack on Dhan Singh Thapa's men at Srijap West had come at 8.30 a.m. The Gorkhas, using their relatively lighter 3-inch mortars and well positioned MMGs, halted the Chinese in their tracks, forcing them to regroup. At 11.15 a.m., the Chinese opened fire again with medium artillery, heavy and medium mortars. After thirty minutes of intense and fairly accurate bombardment, Chinese infantry, their numbers tripled after the capture of Srijap Jamini and Srijap East, closed in from three sides. Thapa ordered his men to hold their fire. Despite severe casualties, Charlie Company did not waver, opening up with all weapons at short range, forcing the Chinese to break contact yet again.

Raina in the meantime had asked Lieutenant Colonel Hari Chand to get a volunteer who could take a storm boat from Tokung and find out what was happening in Srijap and Yula. Naik Rabi Lal, despite the inherent dislike of Gorkhas for water, immediately volunteered. As he approached Srijap East, the boat was fired at from three or four positions, including Srijap Jamini that was by then under Chinese control. After reporting on the Srijap situation, the NCO headed east, keeping the southern bank of the Pangong Tso to his right. Here too he could see both Yula I and Yula II under heavy enemy fire. Rabi Lal returned to Tokung by 11.45 a.m.

The third assault came at 4 p.m., with a dozen Chinese tanks supporting the infantry. Every Gorkha at Srijap knew by then that he was going to die, but to surrender the post was unthinkable. Thapa was wounded, but so long as his men could see him, they fought on. Eventually, he was brought down and by 9 a.m. on 22 October, the Chinese had captured

Srijap West. In the fight for Srijap East and Srijap West, forty-one men had been killed. Of these, sixteen had been wounded but were taken alive by the Chinese. To the horror of an eyewitness who had been captured, fifteen of the sixteen wounded men were executed. The only casualty who had been spared on account of his rank badges was Major Dhan Singh Thapa who was amazingly still alive.

Both the captured riflemen, one each from Srijap East and Srijap West, managed to escape from the Chinese and make their way to Chartse, an Indian supply point. Three more survivors eventually joined them. All the men claimed that the company commander had been killed in the fighting. Much later, after the Indian government had conferred a Param Vir Chakra posthumously to the officer, Radio Peking would announce that Major Dhan Singh Thapa was in fact alive and was a POW.

In the Yula Sector, the Chinese, on 20 October had dispatched a column of 200 men along with yaks and porters that would bypass Jamini Tilok and Yula II and attack Yula I further to the west. They hoped for a quick capture of Yula I that would then cut off the other two posts. A second Chinese column started firing mortars at Yula I at first light on 21 October. At 7 a.m. the section at Jamini Tilok could see the Chinese approaching their screening position. As per their operational procedure, the ten men at Jamini Tilok were not expected to put up much of a fight, they were only meant to delay the Chinese assault on Yula II. Opening fire with deadly accuracy, they successfully achieved their objective, falling back on Yula II by mid-afternoon. However, by then, all the men at Yula I had been killed. Apart from one JCO and nineteen men from 1/8 GR, there were two NCOs and nine sappers from the Engineer Regiment among the dead.

Unable to reinforce his besieged positions, Hari Chand was in a desperate situation. He ordered Tokung to launch two boats and try and evacuate the men from Yula II. Naik Rabi Lal Thapa set out to try and rescue the stranded men. At the landing point he found a dozen Gorkhas and two sappers. After taking six men in his boat, he put the other eight in the second vessel. However, during the return journey, the second boat capsized, taking all nine men on board with it. Finally, at 8 p.m. on 21 October, Rabi Lal Thapa reached Tokung with six survivors from the entire Yula Sector.

THE BATTLE FOR CHUSHUL

In the opening round in Ladakh, the Chinese had more or less achieved all their objectives. Flush with their success against the ill-equipped and tiny Indian dispositions, Radio Peking announced rather grandiosely on 24

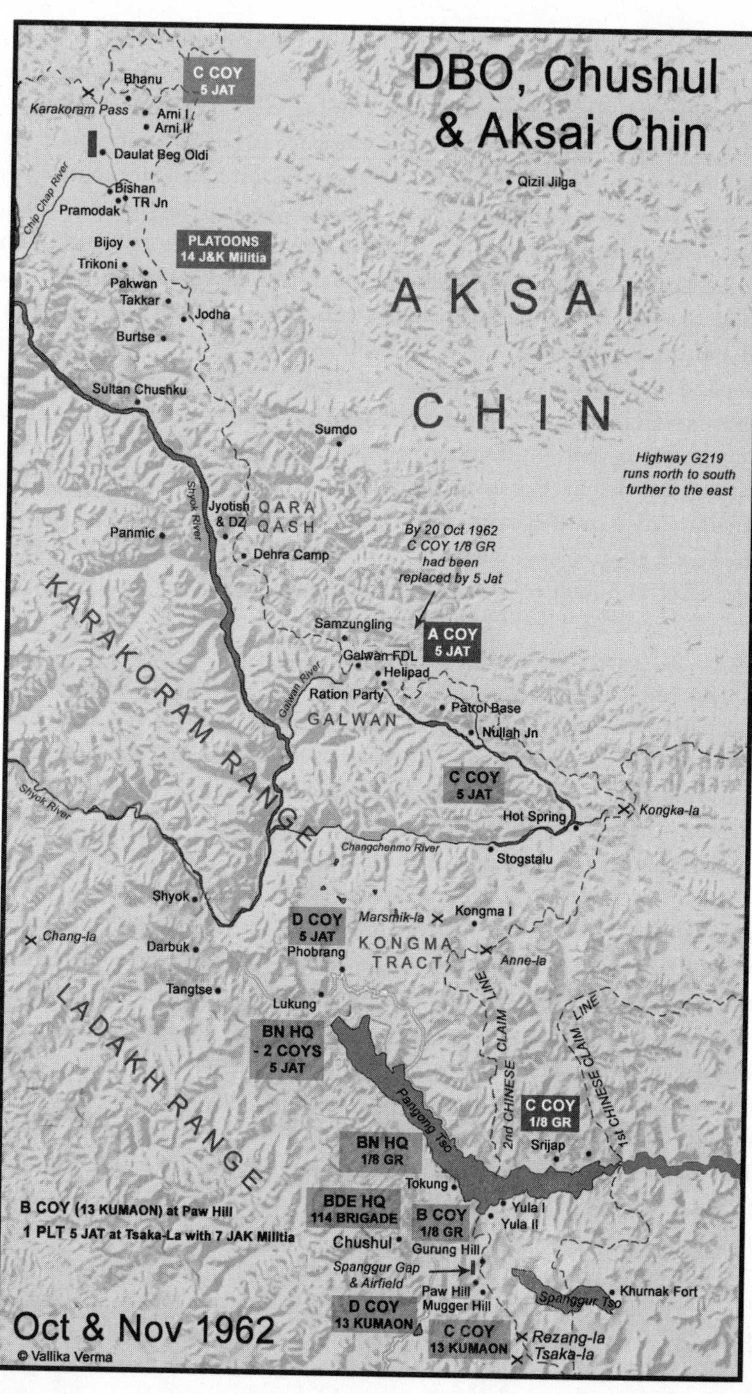
DBO, Chushul & Aksai Chin
C COY 5 JAT
Bhanu
Karakoram Pass
Arni I
Arni II
Daulat Beg Oldi
Chip Chap River
Bishan
TR Jn
Pramodak
Qizil Jilga
PLATOONS 14 J&K Militia
Bijoy
Trikoni
Pakwan
Takkar
Jodha
Burtse
AKSAI
CHIN
Sultan Chushku
Sumdo
Highway G219 runs north to south further to the east
Shyok River
Jyotish & DZ
QARA QASH
Panmic
Dehra Camp
By 20 Oct 1962 C COY 1/8 GR had been replaced by 5 Jat
KARAKORAM RANGE
Samzungling
A COY 5 JAT
Galwan FDL
Helipad
Galwan River
Ration Party
Patrol Base
GALWAN
Nullah Jn
C COY 5 JAT
Kongka-la
Hot Spring
Changchenmo River
Stogstalu
Shyok
D COY 5 JAT
Marsmik-la
Kongma I
Chang-la
Darbuk
Phobrang
KONGMA TRACT
Anne-la
Tangtse
Lukung
LADAKH RANGE
BN HQ - 2 COYS 5 JAT
2nd CHINESE CLAIM LINE
1st CHINESE CLAIM LINE
Pangong Tso
C COY 1/8 GR
BN HQ 1/8 GR
Srijap
Tokung
B COY (13 KUMAON) at Paw Hill
1 PLT 5 JAT at Tsaka-La with 7 JAK Militia
BDE HQ 114 BRIGADE
Yula I
Yula II
B COY 1/8 GR
Chushul
Gurung Hill
Spanggur Gap & Airfield
Paw Hill
Mugger Hill
Spanggur Tso
Khurnak Fort
D COY 13 KUMAON
C COY 13 KUMAON
Rezang-la
Tsaka-la
Oct & Nov 1962
© Vallika Verma

October that the Chinese would now capture the Chushul airfield.

From the Yula Sector, the Chushul Sector ran southwards along the Rezang Ridge which extended up to Gurung Hill. Thereafter, there was a gap in the Rezang Ridge, known as the Spanggur Gap through which the Chushul region was linked to the Spanggur Sector. Extending southwards from Yula III, the main Indian posts on the Rezang ridge were Ration Party, Gurung Hill, Trench Hill, Foot Hill, Paw Hill, Gompa Hill and, south of the Spanggur Gap, Rezang-la and Tsaka-la. The Chushul airfield was the designated vital ground. The area south of Tsaka-la was the Demchok (or Indus Valley) Sector.

The reported use of armour against Srijap West had underlined the true extent of Chinese preparations. Intelligence reports were also confirming the presence of tanks in the Spanggur area. On 22 October, the XV Corps commander, Bikram Singh, visited Raina and informed him that Chushul airfield needed to prepare itself to receive some heavy equipment. Indian Air Force pilots flying transport planes into Chushul said there was a three-kilometre-long column of Chinese military vehicles moving into the Spanggur area. At 1 p.m., Bravo Company of 1/8 GR on Paw Hill also relayed the same information to HQ 114 Brigade.

By 24 October, 13 Kumaon had completed its induction into Chushul. Gurung Hill, Trench Hill and Foot Hill remained with the Gorkhas while Paw Hill and Rezang-la were made the responsibility of the Kumaonis. A battery (six guns) of medium artillery from 13 Field Regiment and a Mahar MMG platoon arrived, but all eyes were now on the IAF that was expected to do the impossible the next day—fly in the armour.

Six AMX-13 light tanks, weighing 14.5 tons each, belonging to 20 Lancers were loaded onto AN-12 aircraft at Chandigarh. This had never been done before and it was not known how the aircraft would behave on take off or landing with such a heavy load. The Chushul runway was situated at 13,700 feet and to compensate for the weight of the aircraft, it was decided to fly with partial fuel. PSP (pierced steel plank) strips fabricated from corrugated iron made up the landing surface and even aircraft with lighter loads were known to bounce about after touchdown. The unknown factors were many and as apprehension mounted, Squadron Leader Chandan Singh volunteered to be the first pilot to take off with an AMX-13 on board.

Chandan Singh got airborne from Chandigarh and after an uneventful flight, touched down smoothly at Chushul at 11.10 a.m. on 25 October. He had fifteen minutes to offload the tank and take off, clearing the way for the next aircraft. By the time the last aircraft approached, 400 feet of the runway had become unserviceable and Squadron Leader D.W. Chauhan would have been well within his rights to abort the sortie. The urgency of the situation was such that he decided to land, displaying superb flying skills.

The arrival of the armour gave a major fillip to the Chushul defences. Western Command, now faced with the real problem of having to defend Leh, decided to induct nearly a division worth of troops into Ladakh mainly by milking the formations that were facing Pakistan. The IAF, while also dealing with a similar situation in Se-la in the east, was flying round the clock. At the same time, even the first line transport from units and formations was being withdrawn to form ad hoc motor companies to facilitate induction.

Also on 25 October, Brigadier R. S. Grewal, MC, arrived in Leh with 70 Infantry Brigade HQ and took over responsibility of the Indus Valley Sector on the same day. Major General Budh Singh officially raised 3 Infantry Division on 26 October 1962 at Leh. His mandate was the defence of Leh. 114 Infantry Brigade HQ, responsible for the Chushul and Phobrang Sectors, remained under the control of XV Corps.

THE DEMCHOK SECTOR

Originating close to the Manasarovar Lake in Tibet, the Indus flows eastwards, entering India to the northwest of Tashigang at 12,700 feet. Bound by the traditional Indo-Tibetan border to the north, east and south, its western flank is marked by a ridge that separates the waters of the Hanle from the various small streams that feed into the Indus. In this region, the Indus flows from the southeast to the northwest, through a valley that is fairly broad. To the north of this sector is the Chang Pass, to the northeast the Jara-la (both around 16,500 feet) and in the south the Charding-la (17,000 feet).

The Indus at this point is quite placid, languidly flowing along for 130 kilometres before entering the gorge beyond Mahe. The north bank of the river is a broad plain almost three kilometres in width while on the south bank the terrain is rockier. On both banks there were bridle paths that connected Tashigang with Leh. Indian Army vehicles used the southern bank where the ground was harder. At Fukche, there was a PSP airstrip that was used by the IAF to ferry supplies into the sector. Dungti was the main base, from where army Engineers had built a road to the north to link Chushul.

Demchok was a small hamlet inhabited by a few families living on the southern side of the Indus, tucked into the valley of the Demchok stream that originates from the Charding-la. Prior to Independence, the Kashmir State Forces and since 1948 troops of 7 J&K Militia had been performing the duties of the Frontier Police. The battalion, made up of three wings, was headquartered at Koyul and was being commanded by Lieutenant Colonel R. M. Banon. Old Demchok was the rear base and it also served as a staging post for the B-Wing troops guarding Jara-la, Oga, Chang Pass and Dumchole. C-Wing was responsible for Tsaka-la and Dungti while A-Wing's area of responsibility was the International Border Post, Old and New Demchok and High Ground.

On the Chinese side, the area south of their base at Ruksum was part of the Tibetan Western Command. Ruksum had an infantry battalion as did Tashigang, both reporting to the Regimental HQ in Rudok. The Chinese had been relatively inactive in this area, being content with building a motorable road up to the Chang Pass. However, their intention now was to cross the range in the north and occupy the southern and western slopes up to Dumchole and the Indus River. Therefore they needed to occupy the entire area to the east of the Dumchole-Koyul line enveloping the crest of the Hanle Ridge extending up to Charding-la.

The Demchok Sector showed no signs of Chinese activity as of 20 October. However, the invasion of Indian territory in the Northern Sector resulted in XV Corps issuing orders to two patrols—one operating towards Charding-la and the other along the Indus Valley—to immediately fall back on the International Border Post after which they were to withdraw to High Ground that was under the command of Major S. K. Sharma. This had been completed by the evening of 24 October. High Ground had a total of five platoons, two sections of 3-inch mortars, two sections of MMGs and four RCL guns, which by Indian standards was almost six times the force levels deployed at any one post in Ladakh. In addition, a party of sappers had also arrived and succeeded in not only strengthening the defences but also laying out barbed wire and anti-personnel mines. On 26 October, Sharma informed Banon in Koyul that he was ready for the Chinese.

Banon decided to send a few more troops to High Ground, Jara-la and Chang Pass. Charding-la was to remain undefended. In the event of an attack, the troops at the Chang Pass were only to delay the Chinese and fall back on Dungti. The men at Dumchole were also to fall back on Koyul, after which the entire garrison was to withdraw to Dungti that was being prepared as a strong base.

The Chinese took their time before launching five columns into the Demchok Sector, mainly because some of the troops had to be brought down from the Srijap and Yula Sectors. On the morning of 27 October at 5.45 a.m., ten vehicles mounted with MMGs followed by about 200 Chinese soldiers could be seen advancing on Chang Pass. Jemadar Ishe Tundup, a Ladakhi, had two sections under command and he watched the Chinese move steadily towards his positions.

Tundup let the Chinese close in until they were 300 yards from the pass. He then fired the first shot with his 2-inch mortar. This was the signal for the two LMGs and rifles positioned on the pass to open up. Some of the leading vehicles received direct hits and started burning, while the bunched Chinese troops took quite a few casualties. This forced them to fan out amidst the rocky terrain from where they started creeping up on the Indian positions. The MMGs, dismounted from the trucks, were then brought into play, pouring voluminous fire at the Indians. In the next two hours of fighting, one militiaman was killed, while Tundup and four other men were wounded.

Unable to hold the Chinese at bay any longer, Tundup ordered his men to take the wounded and break contact while he stayed and provided covering fire. The men would make it back to Koyul, but Ishe Tundup was killed and the Chinese captured Chang Pass by 9.45 a.m. However, the two sections on the Chang Pass had inflicted enough damage on the Chinese to delay their assault on Dumchole, which the depleted Chinese force could now only approach at 4 p.m. Here too, the one section of 7 J&K Militia made them pay heavily before they disengaged and fell back on Koyul. The Chinese finally occupied Dumchole at 5 p.m.

A second Chinese column of 200 men could be seen approaching Jara-la shortly after daybreak. As there was no road but only a small track leading up to the pass, the Chinese were mounted on ponies. The two sections that were being commanded by an NCO, Havildar Satigian Phunchok, opened fire with 2-inch mortars, LMGs and rifles. The animals scattered and the Chinese went to ground. Despite outnumbering the Indians 10:1, without heavy weapons and fighting from lower ground, the Chinese, for once, were in an uncomfortable and unfamiliar situation. As darkness fell, Phunchok took stock of the situation. A few Chinese soldiers had cut off his position from behind. He had one man dead and a few wounded. Low on ammunition and reserves, it was a matter of time before the Chinese would overrun his position, so he decided to break contact and withdraw his men.

The third Chinese column approached High Ground via the Indus Valley. While some troops established an ambush at Lagankhel, the main party assembled on the Leh road at a point called the loop, where they assembled their mortars and fired at High Ground. The first mortar bomb landed at 7.30 a.m.

Through the day, the Chinese kept bombarding High Ground, intermittently infiltrating the Indian positions and exchanging fire with the defenders who were well entrenched. As the day wore on, the situation began to wear on Major Sharma's mind. News of the Chinese having established roadblocks near Lagankhel and the fact that there would be no reinforcements convinced him that should he dig in and fight he would definitely be overwhelmed. Sharma was also aware of a fourth Chinese column that had captured Charding-la earlier in the morning. Should this column also arrive at High Ground, he and his men would be caught in a pincer.

The officer lost his nerve and chose to extricate his men; once again the Chinese were not tested against reasonable defences. Sharma left High Ground with 150 men under the cover of darkness, leaving Lieutenant Siddhu, an Engineer officer, to destroy all the equipment and get the seriously wounded out in the handful of vehicles at his disposal. Sharma's failure to keep the men under his charge together resulted in a lot of confusion and he was the last man to be rescued in the middle of November from Hanle where he was hiding. Fortunately, almost everyone made it back to Koyul.

The last to leave High Ground was Lieutenant Siddhu. After Sharma's departure, he meticulously went about destroying all the equipment. After loading as many men as he could into the three 3-tonners, he dispatched the remaining men with instructions to follow the Koyul Chu until they got to Battalion HQ. He then got into the leading jeep, having fitted LMGs on all the vehicles. His convoy, driving without lights, fired in all directions and bashed through the Chinese barricades once it reached the Lagankhel area.

Siddhu's arrival at Koyul in the early hours of 28 October and his first-hand account of the Chinese ingress gave Brigadier Grewal a fair assessment of the situation in his new command. At dawn, the Indians could see the Chinese, who having occupied Dumchole at night, were preparing their defences across the Indus from Koyle and Fukche. Accordingly, Grewal ordered Banon to fall back on Dungti and concentrate on its defences. The orders for the 70 Brigade commander were clear; there would be no further fallback from Dungti. There would be no further activity on the part of the Chinese in this sector, who also stayed clear of the Hanle region.

THE BATTLE OF REZANG-LA

By the middle of November, feverish Chinese activity in the Chushul sector indicated that an attack was eminent. Yula III, the northernmost Indian position on the Rezang Range was being held by two platoons of 1 Jat's Delta Company, the third platoon being deployed on the Tokung Ridge along with a section each of MMGs and 3-inch mortars. Bravo Company of 1/8 GR had a platoon each on Gurung, Trench and Foot Hills while Alpha and Charlie Company were deployed around the airfield, primarily guarding it from being attacked through the Spanggur Gap. Paw Hill was with Bravo Company of 13 Kumaon who also had a detachment from the Jats, a section manning 3-inch mortars and two RCL guns; Mugger Hill was with the Kumaoni Delta Company while Rezang-la was with the battalion's Charlie Company. In addition, there was a platoon of 5 Jat at Tsaka-la which was attached to 7 J&K Militia under 70 Infantry Brigade. Similarly, to the north, Nullah Junction, Hot Springs, Lukung and Phobrang were being held by 5 Jat, its men having recovered sufficiently from the fighting in the DBO Sector in early October.

At the end of the first phase of fighting, the Chinese declaration on Peking Radio that their next aim was to capture the Chushul airfield was, in all probability, a red herring. Peking had until then never staked a claim on Chushul. However, leaving the Indians in control of both the Rezang Ridge and the Gurung Hill feature would mean letting them dominate the Spanggur Sector. As it were, Indian posts on both Rezang-la and Gurung Hill were on the Spanggur side of the watershed. By forcing the Indians to defend the Spanggur Gap and the airfield as well, not only did the Chinese split Raina's forces, they also took the attention away from their actual objectives—Rezang-la and the crest of Gurung Hill.

Apart from diverting attention from their immediate strategic objectives, the Chinese announcement also implied that the PLA would have no hesitation in pushing beyond even their second claim line. Therefore, as a part of their psychological warfare, it firmly planted the seed in the Indian mind that Leh could be the ultimate target.

Among the various troops being moved into Ladakh were 1 Jat, 9 Dogra, 3/4 GR and 3 Sikh LI. Of these, only 1 Jat was allocated to Chushul, while the rest were deployed post-haste for the defence of Leh. On 27 October, the corps commander formally turned down Raina's request for additional troops for the defence of Chushul on the grounds that Leh must remain secure at all cost. All possible routes to Leh were to be held in strength. In the north, two battalions were being deployed to hold Saser-la, Sultan Chushku, Shyok, and the Galwan-Shyok river junction. The route passing over Chang-la was defended at the pass itself and also at Darbuk. Giving depth to the Chang-la defence were the troops deployed at Phobrang and Chushul with some artillery support. In the Indus Valley Sector, 70 Brigade blocked the axis at Dungti, Chumathang, Kiari and areas further back. In Leh proper there was nearly a battalion worth of troops to defend the surrounding hills.

Chinese preparations to take on Gurung Hill and Rezang-la had begun in earnest since July 1962 when they began fortifying their two posts at Military Base and Jechiung. Indian patrols had since reported the setting up of a Chinese OP to the immediate west of Jechiung. Ever since then, Indian troops regularly reported that the PLA was feverishly stocking these positions with ammunition while preparing the necessary gun positions.

A solitary goat track connected Rezang-la to Tsaka-la that was six and a half kilometres to its south. The base camp was almost three kilometres from the forward defences, and Battalion HQ was another ten kilometres from the base. The post was on a telephone line that connected it to Tsaka-la, from where messages were relayed to Battalion HQ. All other posts in the Chushul Sector were too far away to support Rezang-la.

Unfortunately, Raina's 114 Brigade had failed to do anything about the isolation of Rezang-la. Even though the Indian post had been in existence since May 1961 and had been manned by 7 J&K Militia and then 1/8 GR, there were no bunkers or trenches owing to the rock hard terrain. Indian troops had instead built stone sangars that only had tin roofs for protection. There were no sandbags or even mud to cover the tin, which made the sangars death traps if exposed to artillery or RCL fire. The stone used for the construction was brittle and tended to splinter, magnifying the casualties. 13 Kumaon's Charlie Company under the command of Major Shaitan Singh had moved in and replaced 1/8 GR at Rezang-la on 6 November. Point 18300 dominated the pass in the north and another peak, in excess of 18,000 feet, towered over it to the east. To the south and to the west there was a drop of around 1,900 feet. The pass itself was situated at an average height of 16,000 feet and its northern shoulder was higher than the southern side.

When the original defences had been laid out by 7 J&K Militia, it had been presumed that the Chinese could not approach Rezang-la either from the northwest or the east because of the high features and the fact that any movement in the PT 18300 area would be detected by Indian patrols. However, originating from the northeast of the pass was a stream that flowed to the north, where it joined another small stream that then flowed into the Spanggur Tso. This depression was known as Valley West and as per the Indian appreciation, considered to be the most likely approach if and when Rezang-la was to be attacked. The approach from the south was dominated by Tsaka-la while to the west lay the Chushul Valley.

Accordingly No. 8 Platoon, commanded by Naib Subedar Hari Ram, occupied the area of the main pass, No. 7 Platoon, under Naib Subedar Surja Singh, was deployed on a high spur jutting out on the left bank of Valley West and No. 9 Platoon, commanded by Naib Subedar Ram Chand, was positioned in between. All three localities individually were sited to dominate Valley West, but unfortunately, none of them were mutually supporting. Shaitan Singh's own command post was situated to the west of No. 8 Platoon, while the 3-inch mortar section was situated another 150 yards beyond Company HQ. All three platoons laid their fixed line of fire along Valley West, as did the mortar detachment.

On the morning of 17 November, Rezang-la reported some activity towards the north and a message was relayed through Tsaka-la to the 13 Kumaon Battalion HQ asking for reinforcements. Towards the evening, another column comprising over a 100 yaks, their handlers and some troops were seen south of PT 18300. Not expecting a Chinese assault from that direction, Shaitan Singh came to the conclusion it was an Indian column that was approaching in response to his call for support earlier that morning.

However, what the Kumaonis had seen was in fact the first of four Chinese columns that had been dispatched against Rezang-la. Accompanied by an artillery forward observer, it began to climb the northern slope of PT 18300 in the dark and then move along a small stream to get to the dead ground (blind spot) ahead of the Kumaonis to the south of the mountain before first light. At the same time, a second column, also accompanied by an artillery observer, was climbing along the left side of Valley West with the intention of linking up with the first column. A third column was proceeding directly, while a fourth column was also making its way towards the upper part of Valley East, from where it hoped to cut across the depression and get behind Rezang-la. All the columns were to exploit the topography that afforded plenty of cover, and set up mortar and MMG positions as close to the three Kumaonis positions.

At 1 a.m., Naik Hukum Chand, the 2IC of No. 8 Platoon took out a patrol in front of his position. After two hours of being on a listening watch, the men could hear noises that suggested a large body of men was on the move. Hukum Chand fired a red Very light that illuminated a Chinese column slowly moving towards his platoon position. The patrol commander immediately sent a man to inform Shaitan Singh. The patrol fell back to its defended locality, where every man had by then been put on stand-to.

Meanwhile, when the Very light had been fired, No. 7 Platoon had also reported seeing some movement in front of their position. They too were on stand-to, their weapons at the ready. Shaitan Singh also alerted Naib Subedar Ram Chand of No. 9 Platoon, who asked his own patrols to fall back immediately. Hence by 4 a.m., all three Kumaonis platoons were in position, peering into the darkness for signs of the Chinese. Some additional men had arrived the previous day for a routine Cadre Test (for promotion) and were billeted at the company location. They had brought with them 2-inch mortars that were now available with the company commander. Shortly thereafter, Shaitan Singh fired an illumination flare that lit up the entire area. In front of No. 8 and No. 7 Platoon, the Chinese could be seen preparing to launch their attack. All three Kumaonis platoons opened fire simultaneously, causing heavy Chinese casualties and forcing them to go to ground.

Mugger Hill was the closest post to Rezang-la and was manned by Delta Company under Major Jatar Singh. He immediately reported the sound of gunfire from the direction of Rezang-la and by 4.30 a.m. had dispatched a four-man patrol under Naik Roop Ram to ascertain the actual position.

At Rezang-la, the Chinese were taking casualties, so they prematurely called for artillery support while it was still dark. Their guns opened up, as did their MMGs and mortars that had been positioned earlier in the night. However, the firing was ineffective as the forward observers were unable to guide the guns accurately. As the battle raged, at 6.30 a.m. the Delta Company patrol reached the area through which the Chinese had advanced and where they had kept their reserves. The patrol was spotted and the Chinese opened fire, killing Roop Ram and two others instantly. Sepoy Ram Singh, despite being hit by splinters, managed to duck into the rocks. With the attention of the Chinese on Rezang-la, Ram Singh slipped away after a while.

The original H-Hour for the Chinese to open fire on all the Indian positions in the Chushul sector was 6.30 a.m. The batteries in support of the troops at Rezang-la had been forced to open fire early, and Chinese guns had also engaged Bravo Company of 13 Kumaon at Paw Hill an hour earlier, but now the entire front came alive. The barrage on the Gorkha positions on Gurung Hill, Gurung Hill (Crest), Trench Hill and Foot Hill was particularly severe.

The Chinese bombardment across all positions meant Rezang-la was not only isolated, it was also on the back burner as the commanding officers, Lieutenant Colonel H.S. Dhingra at 13 Kumaon HQ and Raina at 114 Brigade HQ grappled with more immediate issues. As the light improved at Rezang-la, the Chinese forward observers came into play and the bombardment became far more effective. With clearer visibility, the Chinese threw everything at their disposal to blast out Shaitan Singh's men. Apart from heavy artillery that systematically blew up the stone sangars, the Chinese lined up 132 mm rockets, 120 mm heavy mortars, 81 and 60 mm medium mortars, and 75 and 53 mm RCL guns in a direct firing role. Throughout the barrage not one Kumaonis soldier wavered, each man holding his position until he was killed.

As the bombardment intensified, the Chinese threw in their infantry reserve, which joined those who had taken cover when the Kumaonis had opened up. Both No. 7 and No. 8 Platoon had been overrun by 7.30 a.m. hours, but those still alive continued to fight.

With two of his platoons all but wiped out, Shaitan Singh along with his company havildar major, Phool Singh, and two other men decided to join up with No. 9 Platoon, some 550 metres away. Hardly had they covered quarter of the distance when the company commander was hit in the stomach by an MMG burst. Between them the three men managed to somehow evacuate the mortally wounded officer. At 16,000 feet it required a superhuman effort, yet they managed to get to within 800 metres of the unoccupied Rezang-la Base Camp.

Shaitan Singh was still conscious and coherent. He ordered the men to stop, leave him where he was and return to No. 9 Platoon that was still holding out. Phool Singh and the two men did as they were told. All three of them returned to No. 9 Platoon and were killed shortly afterwards. Major Shaitan Singh remained where his men left him, too weak to move, eventually breathing his last amidst the stony, desolate wilderness. He had done enough to carve not just his own name, but also the names of all the men under his command into the pages of Indian history. Five men had been disabled and captured; two died of their wounds in captivity. One man survived—Havildar Ram Singh. He was badly wounded. The Chinese threw him into a sangar where he lay till 4 in the morning. He then crawled out in full view of the Chinese who watched him go, no one moving to stop him. After a few hours, as he made his way towards the rear, a jeep from his own battalion picked him up. The men in the vehicle were unable to recognize the burnt and bleeding figure, refusing to believe who he was until he actually started naming them. At 9 a.m. Ram Singh was escorted into Battalion HQ—reported to the adjutant, narrating the details of the Rezang-la battle.

THE GORKHAS ON GURUNG HILL

For the Chinese, along with Rezang-la the capture of Gurung Hill was of vital importance. As per their assessment, should they successfully capture the Gurung Hill Ridge, the entire Chushul bowl would then be at their mercy. After the initial barrage lifted, waves of Chinese infantry put in a direct attack from the direction of Black Hill, which had been anticipated by the Indians. However, the Chinese tactic was not for the infantry to grapple with the defenders, but to creep in closer to be able to position their MMGs and mortars that would allow them to blast the defenders in their bunkers, trenches and sangars.

However, the bombardment of Gurung Hill was not a one-sided affair. The three Gurung Hill posts were each held by a platoon of 1/8 GR's Bravo Company. In addition, Trench Hill was supported by a section of MMGs and two RCL guns while Foot Hill had a section of 3-inch mortars. An artillery forward observer, Second Lieutenant S. D. Goswami, was positioned with the Gorkhas at Gun Hill, and he was directing retaliatory fire from the Indian guns positioned at High Ground further in depth. Gun Hill was under the command of Captain P. L. Kher.

Twice in the next couple of hours, 600 Chinese soldiers tried to advance in waves, only to be stopped by the Indian artillery and the small arms fire of the Gorkhas, forcing the advancing Chinese to seek cover where they were. At 9 a.m., the Chinese launched a fresh attack with 500 more soldiers. As they moved slowly forward under covering MMG fire, their ranks started to swell as troops from the earlier two attacks began to join them. The nerve-racking phenomenon of the Chinese numbers doubling as they advanced was enough to shake the confidence of any troops. However, Kher was keeping the spirits of his men up, seemingly present everywhere.

Meanwhile, to get a better view of the Chinese, Goswami had crawled forward from where he was directing the lone Indian battery. At this point, both Kher and Goswami were wounded. While Kher was pulled back and evacuated from the post by his men, no one could get to the artillery officer who was trapped in the no-man's land between the defenders and the attackers.

With the two officers incapacitated, Naib Subedar Teghbahadur Gurung assumed command of Bravo Company. The JCO kept moving from one position to another, encouraging the men to keep fighting. It was but a matter of time before a Chinese MMG burst hit him in the chest. Even though he was dying, he refused to be evacuated.

Orders to withdraw from the post were received shortly thereafter. Apart from Gurung, twelve Gorkhas were dead while Kher and another eleven men were wounded. The Gorkhas broke contact and pulled out and the Chinese overran the picket, but abandoned it shortly thereafter. Later in the evening another reserve platoon of the Gorkhas reoccupied the post. The next day, the Chinese once again bombarded the picket intermittently, but failed to launch an attack. Once again orders were received in the evening of 19 November to abandon Gurung Hill. At 5 a.m. on 20 November, the Gorkhas pulled out again. The Chinese, however, never occupied the post.

The second Gorkha picket on the Gurung Hill feature overlooked the Spanggur Gap. On 19 November, at the base of Trench Hill, the Chinese brought up their tanks briefly, but at no stage did they try and rush through the gap. One troop of the AMX-13 tanks under the command of Captain A. K. Dewan was also in the vicinity, supplementing with their guns the accurate fire from 13 Field Regiment's 25-pounders which probably deterred the Chinese from pushing forward with their armour.

The exchange of fire continued throughout 18 and 19 November. With both the airfield and the village under constant artillery fire, reinforcements and supply of the forward positions was proving to be a problem. Rezang-la having fallen, 114 Brigade faced the danger of the Chushul-Dungti-Leh axis being cut off. To further complicate matters, Chinese shelling had snapped all communications between Gurung Hill and Brigade HQ. The only way to get to the Gorkha positions was to cross the flat tract of land and run the gauntlet of Chinese fire. As a result, even though the fighting was raging in front of them, Brigade HQ was not fully aware of the situation.

Accordingly, despite the successful defence of Gurung Hill, Raina ordered the withdrawal at 6 p.m. on 19 November. Contact was broken during the night and by first light on 20 November Trench Hill had been abandoned. Six men in this position had been killed and four wounded. The story at Foot Hill, more of a staging camp for the troops manning the ridge, was much the same as that of Trench Hill. By the time this post was abandoned, the platoon had lost nine men, with one wounded.

After the withdrawal of the Gorkhas, the Chinese once again made no move to occupy these two positions.

Bravo Company of 13 Kumaon under the command of Captain Chauhan was holding Paw Hill that guarded the approach to the eastern perimeter of the Chushul airfield. In terms of both men and firepower, the Paw Hill post was by far the most strongly held. In support of the Kumaonis troops, there was also a section of 3-inch mortars, one section of anti-tank guns (two RCLs) and a platoon of MMGs. This post was the first to come under Chinese bombardment on the morning of 18 November and like Trench Hill and Foot Hill, continued to exchange fire with the Chinese. However, despite the shelling and the occasional probe to test their defences, Chinese infantry did not directly attack either Paw Hill or Mugger Hill.

On the afternoon of 19 November Bikram Singh and Raina held a conference at Brigade HQ amidst the shelling. All junior officers were pleading for a chance to counter-attack the Chinese and take back Rezang-la. However, still anticipating a major Chinese attack through the Spanggur Gap to capture the airfield, the corps commander pointed out that Chushul was a screening position and that the defence of Leh was of paramount importance. Accordingly, the corps commander ordered 114 Brigade to pull back from the entire line of defence and occupy fresh defences along the range west of Chushul. 114 Brigade was tasked with moving all heavy equipment out of the area so that it would not fall into Chinese hands.

During the entire battle of Chushul, 13 Field Regiment had played a major, if not crucial part. While one troop was deployed at High Ground near Brigade HQ, the second troop was deployed in support of Mugger Hill. After the battle of Rezang-la, the Chinese came down from that direction with the intention of neutralizing the Indian guns. Even as the decision to withdraw was being taken, the guns were attacked. The gunners fired over open sights directly into the mass of the assaulting Chinese, forcing them to quickly pull back. As they were withdrawing, the Indian gunners saw some Chinese self-propelled guns moving into the Spanggur Gap. In what would be the last act of defiance in the Chushul sector, the gunners engaged the Chinese guns, blowing one of them to bits with a direct hit.

THE FINAL SLAP (NEW DELHI) 18-19 NOVEMBER

For General Pran Thapar, it was the end of the road. As the gigantic 4-engined IAF Super Constellation flew westward towards New Delhi, Thapar sat with Brigadier Palit in grim silence. The DMO was busy putting down from memory the notes he had handed over to Kaul at the Tezpur airfield. After a while, the chief motioned to Palit to sit closer to him. Stepping across the aisle, he sat down on the armrest of the seat. Thapar reached across and clasped the younger man's hand, tears rolling down his cheeks. For a few minutes, the two officers just sat quietly, sharing their misery and distress. The 4th Indian Division, on whose shoulders the entire defence of NEFA had been entrusted, had folded up and withdrawn without even facing the main thrust of the Chinese.

After he had composed himself, Thapar sought Palit's advice, asking him point-blank if he should 'step down'. Palit did not immediately reply. 'I consulted Bijji this morning,' Thapar added, 'he was emphatic that there was no call for me to resign—and that I must not think of taking such a step. Now I am not too sure; and I would like your frank opinion.'

'Sir, all of us—the Prime Minister, the government, Army HQ and the generals in the field—all must shoulder the blame for the operational trap into which we led ourselves. Our forces could not have stopped the Chinese at the Nam Ka Chu or at the Chip Chap or at Walong and should never have been sent there for that purpose. But the fact remains that at all these places the army did its best and made the Chinese pay a price for their gains. Only at Se-la have we betrayed our trust. There, where we could have stopped them, we ran away without fighting—and the tragedy is that the betrayal came not from the troops but from the generals in command.

'You asked me for a frank opinion. I think that all three generals—Pathania, Kaul and Sen—would be deemed remiss in battle; but you were also there. You elected to be present at Corps HQ—and you did not succeed in preventing Pathania's defection. So my answer is "Yes". I think it's appropriate that you should accept the responsibility for the disaster at Se-la. If I were you, I would go straight to the Prime Minister when we arrive at Delhi, explain frankly what happened and why, and offer my resignation. I hope that he will not accept it; but as the Chief you have to take all the blame on your shoulders.'

Palit felt that his advice notwithstanding, Thapar had already made up his mind by then. By all accounts, Thapar was an upright and conscientious officer, but a lacklustre personality who did not have the combat experience of Thimayya, Thorat or even Sen for that matter. No one, perhaps Thapar included, had expected him to be elevated to the top post.

Now it was almost as if the wheel had turned a full circle. After going over Palit's recast notes for the defence of Assam, Thapar asked his DMO who in his opinion should succeed him: 'Muchhu' Chaudhuri, the then Southern Army Commander, or General Thorat, who had retired?

In his list of general officers who he felt needed to shoulder the blame, Palit was aware that there was another name that needed to be added—his own. Even though he was a brigadier, he was the DMO and the most important cog in the operational chain that was controlled by Army HQ. Palit was also acutely aware of the circumstances under which Thapar and Kaul had emerged as the front runners by sidelining Thimayya and Thorat. As CGS, Kaul had hand-picked Palit for the DMO's job, and what was more, Palit had initially been fairly critical of Thorat's defensive line, even though he had subsequently seen its merits. Palit admits that he made a big blunder at the time. He would write later: 'I fear that mindlessly I gave him the wrong answer. Perhaps because I did not know Thorat well, I replied that I did not consider it advisable to bring back a retired general officer as the next Chief. I added that I did not think that "it would go down well with the army", an expression of prejudice rather than a remark sustainable by either logic or precept.'

After landing in Delhi, Thapar drove off immediately to meet the prime minister while Palit went to additional defence secretary H. C. Sarin's house to bring him up to date and to discuss the plans to defend Assam should the Chinese spill into the plains. But first he telephoned the Military Ops Room in Army HQ, only to be informed that HQ IV Corps had by then reported the actual fall of Bomdila.

After briefing Sarin on the events that had led to the capitulation of Se-la, Dirang Dzong and Bomdila, Palit focused the attention back on Assam. In everyone's perception, Se-la and Dirang Dzong were still deep inside NEFA, while Bomdila was literally the last barrier between the Chinese forces and the rest of India. Even after all these years, it is actually quite amazing as to how such a level of paralysis could have gripped the Indian leadership. Had it just been talk, it would have been understandable, for the further one is from the scene of action, the worse the situation sometimes looks. However, at a time when IV Corps should have resolutely gone about the business of reorganizing the troops, by ordering the evacuation of Tezpur, Kaul and Sen had just given up.

Ever since the fall of Walong, Kaul had been sending frantic messages to Nehru imploring him to ask the United States and Britain to send their air force to stop the Chinese. It perhaps did not even occur to Kaul that India herself had air power that until now had only been used for logistical support. However, it was now Palit's turn to look towards the skies when all else seemed to have failed. He 'impressed upon Sarin that if the fighting spread to the Assam plains, there would be no choice other than to commit the air force, both for ground support roles and interdiction missions in the mountains and on the Tibetan plateau, even if such an extension of the war resulted in Chinese bombers attacking some of our cities'.

Sarin replied that we would use our air force only if we could ensure adequate air defence of our north Indian cities. He then mused, as if thinking aloud, that perhaps we might seek the help of the US or British air force. Palit's cutting remark that we could hardly do that with any justification when we had kept our own fighters on the ground did not elicit any further comment.

Meanwhile, the news of the debacle in Bomdila was sending shock waves through the highest levels in the government. Prime Minister Nehru, stunned by the news, asked to meet General Thorat who, after his retirement, was living in Kolhapur near Poona. The former Eastern Army Commander received the news with some trepidation, for he had parted company with the prime minister under strained circumstances. Thorat quickly dug out two sets of papers in preparation for the meeting: an assessment of the Chinese threat that he had prepared in November 1959 and Exercise Lal Qila which had been held on 17 March 1960 and had been attended by all army commanders and principal staff officers in Army HQ—which included Lieutenant Generals Thapar, Kaul and Sen.

The headlines in the morning newspapers announced the fall of Se-la and Bomdila. General Thapar had briefed the prime minister on the situation in NEFA the previous evening and had asked that his resignation be accepted. He had also recommended that Assam be evacuated immediately.

Flying to Delhi in a special IAF aircraft early in the morning, Thorat was driven straight from Palam to South Block. When he entered the prime minister's office, Thorat saw a haggard looking Nehru sitting at his desk with a vacant look on his face: 'It was indeed a pathetic sight. He was holding an unlit cigarette in one hand and a pair of scissors in the other with which he was cutting the cigarette into small pieces. With clouded eyes he looked up and signalled me to take a seat.'

After a brief silence, Nehru looked up and said: 'Thorat, how could this have happened? You were in Eastern Command; did you have any inkling of the disaster?'

'Yes, sir,' said Thorat, 'the possibility had occurred to us in Eastern Command and the Ministry was warned.'

Nehru said: 'Of course I knew that we were having trouble with the Chinese over some border incidents, but I never thought it would come to this.'

'Sir, the Army had foreseen this possibility and given a warning,' said Thorat.

'When?' asked Nehru sharply.

Thorat said he had signed the note on 8 October 1959 and sent it to General Thimayya who in turn had marked it to the defence minister. 'It was never shown to me,' Nehru snapped after which he went through Thorat's papers. He first read the paragraphs indicated to him by Thorat, after which he went through the folder outlining the details of Exercise Lal Qila.

After twenty minutes or so, Nehru asked why the files had not been shown to him previously.

'You may like to address this question to Mister Krishna Menon, sir,' said Thorat, with ill-concealed sarcasm.

'Menon! Menon!' exploded Nehru. 'Why have you got your knife into him? You people do not realize what an intellectual giant he is!' Even at this stage, with the Chinese threatening to spill into the Brahmaputra Plains, Nehru was not willing to listen to any criticism of his former defence minister. Sitting in front of him was the man who would have been the chief if it hadn't been for the political machinations of the defence minister and Nehru himself. Menon had time and again refused to listen to the warnings of both Thimayya and Thorat. Nehru then asked Thorat if the Chinese would take the Brahmaputra Valley. Thorat replied candidly that he didn't think so; in his opinion, they had already penetrated further than they should have. Thorat further elaborated that owing to the mountainous terrain and lack of roads they were not able to bring up any heavy weapons such as tanks and artillery and it was highly unlikely that they would want to stretch their lines of communication that far. All that Nehru could say was: 'I hope so! I hope so!'

There being nothing more to be said, Thorat took his leave and left the office. Nehru barely noticed that the general had left the room.

At 10.30 a.m. there was an operational briefing by the MO directorate. At the last minute the prime minister decided to go to Parliament instead, taking H. C. Sarin with him. Among those present at the meeting were the COAS General Thapar, the newly appointed CGS, Lieutenant General Moti Sagar, the Western Army Commander, Lieutenant General Daulet Singh and his chief of staff, Major General Joginder Singh, and Lieutenant General K. Wadalia. The DMO quickly summarized the various events that had led to the collapse of 4 Infantry Division during the previous forty-eight hours. He then moved on to the immediate problem at hand: the defence of Assam. Even as Palit spoke, IAF AN-12 and Fairchild Packets had started to land in Tezpur with 5 Infantry Division. Air HQ had indicated that the airlift would be completed by last light on 20 November. Though 5 Division was without artillery support, heavy weapons or vehicles, it was better equipped than any leading Chinese troops could be at this stage should they spill out into the plains.

In addition, the IV Corps reserve, 23 Division, was also on its way from Nagaland with six infantry battalions to supplement the existing troops on the North Bank. General Thapar already seemed to have made up his mind that both banks of the Brahmaputra Valley had to be evacuated while IV Corps with all remaining forces should fall back on Siliguri to the west. Improbable as it may sound, it seemed the army chief had mentally accepted Bogey Sen's bizarre suggestion to surrender Assam. The meeting ended inconclusively.

Thapar then asked Palit to accompany him to his office. This would be the last formal meeting between them. In his meeting with the prime minister after their return from Tezpur, where he offered to resign, Thapar said he had deliberately not recommended replacing the Eastern Army Commander. If his resignation was accepted, he felt it would be more prudent for his successor to take whatever steps he deemed necessary.

Before leaving Thapar's office, Palit made one last attempt to get the chief on board for the defence of Assam: 'If we were to withdraw from the South Bank we would literally be deserting the Assamese people, for which they would never forgive us. It is even possible that parts of Assam would be lost to India forever whether or not the Chinese crossed the Brahmaputra, because the Pakistanis might decide to share in the spoils of war and occupy the Garo and Jaintia Hills or even the whole South Bank including the oil wells of Digboi.'

The colour drained from Thapar's face. Obviously, he had not fully thought through the implications of a withdrawal. The facts now seemed to overwhelm him. 'I told the PM last night that I may have to withdraw from Assam. But I agree with you—it would be an unimaginable disaster. I'll think it over.'

However, it was already too late. The decision to let Thapar go had been taken and the chief, who had throughout his tenure functioned as a lame duck in the shadow of Kaul was now a non-entity. To keep some sort of fig leaf in place, he was told by the government that he should resign on grounds of ill health and not over the NEFA debacle.

Back in Tezpur, Kaul was adding considerably to the spreading panic by making absurd and wild statements while characteristically zipping around in a helicopter from one valley to the other. Quite used to taking decisions without having to refer either to Eastern Command or Army HQ, his two sensational statements—that the Chinese were streaming down from the mountains and that Chinese paratroopers were about to land in North Assam—sent even the most stout-hearted citizen scurrying southwards to cross the Brahmaputra by bridge or by ferry. It is highly unlikely that he even once glanced at the notes given to him for the defence of Assam; instead he ordered the immediate evacuation of Corps HQ. That the civil administration would follow hard on the heels of the army was but natural. These tragic events culminated with Kaul heroically staying back in Tezpur on the night of 19 November with just his BGS, K. K. Singh, for company after sending everyone else away. In his mind, Kaul had played the role of 'the boy who stood on the burning deck' perfectly.

If all this wasn't bad enough, Prime Minister Nehru was to add his touch to the sordid and humiliating drama of 19 November. Three events bear recounting. First, despite the magnitude of the disaster, the prime minister continued to vacillate on the question of who should now lead the army. What was needed was a self-confident, mentally secure, professionally competent chief who would with a firm hand inspire intrepidity and determination in the rank and file he commanded. The defeated army needed to be jolted out of the compliant and irresolute ways into which it had sunk. One of the main reasons for this state of affairs was Nehru's own insecurities. Unfortunately, even after all that had happened, those prejudices continued to weigh him down. Krishna Menon had been replaced as the defence minister on 1 November, with Nehru himself taking charge of the ministry. Interestingly, a few days before the Nehru-Thorat meeting, Menon had suggested to Nehru that should Thapar be removed, Thorat would be the ideal choice to replace him.

According to unconfirmed sources, even at this stage, Nehru wanted to appoint Kaul as the COAS. However, President Sarvepalli Radhakrishnan made it clear that he would not endorse that decision. The next option was the Western Army Commander, Lieutenant General Daulet Singh, who was sounded out but politely refused. Thorat being summoned by Nehru to Delhi indicates that on the morning of 19 November, the prime minister was still weighing the various options available to him. Thorat's sarcastic retort about Krishna Menon had sent Nehru, a man of strong likes and dislikes, into a fit of rage. It is quite likely that the prime minister in that very moment decided in favour of Lieutenant General Joyanto Nath 'Mucchu' Chaudhuri. With the loss of NEFA and the threat to Assam, the prime minister knew that sooner or later there would be calls for his head.

To keep the new man in check, Nehru decided to appoint Chaudhuri the 'officiating chief' who would continue to serve in his current rank, that of a lieutenant general. He was told to report at once to Delhi and take charge on 20 November. Though put out by the slight, Chaudhuri decided not to make an issue of it and agreed to operate as a three-star officiating Chief of Army Staff.

Second, by the evening of 19 November, the foreign secretary, M. J. Desai, and additional defence secretary, H. C. Sarin, were putting the final touches to a top secret letter from Prime Minister Nehru to the President of the United States, John F. Kennedy. Sarin had hinted that the government was contemplating asking the USAF and the RAF to come to India's aid when he spoke to Palit the previous evening. In the latter half of the day, the DMO, along with Joint Secretary (Air) John Lall, was summoned to Sarin's office. Without any preamble, the additional defence secretary handed over the draft of the letter and asked Palit and Lall for their comments, especially to confirm if the demand for the number of aircraft was adequate.

Nehru, the architect of India's non-aligned policy, was openly asking for the intervention and active participation of the United States and Britain for the defence of India. As per the draft, Nehru was telling Kennedy '...the situation in NEFA Command has deteriorated still further. Bomdila has fallen and the retreating forces from Se-la have been trapped between the Se-la Ridge and Bomdila. A serious threat has developed to our Digboi oilfields in Assam. With the advance of the Chinese in massive strength, the entire Brahmaputra Valley is seriously threatened and unless something is done immediately to stem the tide, the whole of Assam, Tripura, Manipur and Nagaland would also pass into Chinese hands.

'The Chinese have poised massive forces in the Chumbi Valley between Sikkim and Bhutan and another invasion from that direction appears imminent... In Ladakh, Chushul is under heavy attack and the shelling of the airfield at Chushul has already commenced. We have also noticed increasing air activity by the Chinese Air Force.'

After pointing out that hitherto India had 'restricted our requests to essential equipment' [most likely a reference to an earlier communication dated 29 October 1962] and thanking the US for the assistance 'so readily given', the draft went on: 'We did not ask for more comprehensive assistance, particularly air assistance, because of wider implications...in the global context and we did not want to embarrass our friends. The situation that has developed is, however, desperate. We have to have more comprehensive assistance if the Chinese are to be prevented from taking over the whole of Eastern India. Any delay in this assistance reaching us will result in nothing short of a catastrophe for our country'.

India's request for comprehensive aid, especially 'immediate support to strengthen our air arm sufficiently to stem the tide of the Chinese advance' goes into minute detail, and is prefaced by the statement: 'We have repeatedly felt the need to use our air arm in support of our land forces but have been unable to do so because in the present state...we have no defence against retaliatory action by the Chinese.' In this context his specific demands were for: '[A] minimum of 12 squadrons of supersonic all-weather fighters' and 'modern radar cover [which] we don't have'. The draft further added that USAF personnel 'will have to man these fighters and radar installations while our personnel are being trained'. Among other things, Nehru was pleading for twelve squadrons of Lockheed F-104 Starfighters and two squadrons of Canberra B-57 bombers.

Both Palit and Lall asked Sarin why the air chief, Air Marshal Aspy Engineer, was not being consulted. Sarin said that apart from him, the foreign secretary and the prime minister, no one else knew of the letter. These two officers were clearly not qualified to answer the question and at best could make only an educated guess. They both agreed that since the Pakistan Air Force had inducted the F-104 and the B-57 and operated these aircraft from airfields that were similar to ours, they could justifiably be asked for.

So shocking were the contents of the letter that the Indian ambassador to the US, B. K. Nehru, contemplated holding it back and not passing it on to the White House at the time. Later, the Government of India denied the existence of these two letters and another communication sent a month earlier by Nehru to Kennedy. In 1965, the then Prime Minister Lal Bahadur Shastri categorically denied that the letters existed in either the Prime Minister's Secretariat or the External Affairs Ministry. However, many years later when the JFK Library declassified the letters, Inder Malhotra, one of India's most respected journalists, accessed them.

The third big blunder was that despite his conversation with Thorat, Thapar's suggestion for evacuating Assam was weighing heavily on the prime minister's mind. In Parliament, even his own party MPs had avoided looking at him while the Opposition had been shocked into silence. A keen student of history, he should have assessed the mood of the nation—this was the moment for a Churchill-like 'Dunkirk' speech.

However, unlike Churchill during World War II who assured his people that they would fight the enemy 'on the beaches...the landing grounds...in the fields…in the streets …in the hills; we shall never surrender', Nehru's broadcast to the nation sounded like a pathetic apology to the people of Assam for deserting them. In his address on AIR on 20 November 1962, Nehru said: 'Huge Chinese armies have been marching in the northern part of NEFA. We have had reverses at Walong, Se-la and today Bomdila, a small town in NEFA, has also fallen. We shall not rest till the invader goes out of India or is pushed out. I want to make that clear to all of you, and, especially our countrymen in Assam, to whom our heart goes out at this moment.'

That the army needed a firm hand at the helm to steady the ship would be to state the obvious. The same applied to the prime minister who, along with Kaul and Thapar, seemed to have lost all sense of proportion. Nehru's actions over the next forty-eight hours, between the evening of 18 and 20 November, should have been his moment of truth. Here, the prime minister of India was to fail miserably, his panic stricken actions culminating with his speech to the nation and the letter to Kennedy, both damning testimony to the fact that he had completely lost control.

As we've seen, Nehru's own insecurity with regard to the armed forces reduced the senior Indian military leadership to a bunch of political appointees that proved to be professionally incompetent. It is ironic that the two men that Nehru decided to thrust greatness upon—Thapar and Kaul—in his need to cut Thimayya and Thorat to size, should be the two who would so blatantly let him down. Whatever else Thapar may or may not be guilty of, his final advice to the prime minister to evacuate Assam must rank as one of the lowest points in the history of post-independence India.

The unkindest cut, of course, was that the Chinese premier, Chou en-Lai, called the Indian Charge de Affairs in Peking on 19 November and briefed him that China would be calling a ceasefire at midnight on 20 November. Had the Indian embassy in Peking shown some common sense and urgently communicated this message to New Delhi, the Indian government would have been spared the humiliation of having taken two steps that were alarmist in the extreme. That the government should first hear of the unilateral Chinese ceasefire on the morning of 21 November through the media while its own embassy had known of it thirty-six hours earlier is yet another aspect of the events of 1962 that defy belief.

In the Western Theatre of operations, by first light on 20 October, all Indian positions had been vacated. The entire ridge of Gurung Hill, Paw Hill, Mugger Hill and all other support positions were abandoned. Later in the day, all heavy equipment including the tanks were formed into a convoy that left for Leh as the troops moved back to occupy their new defences. The Chinese shelled the column as it approached Tsaka-la, but fortunately only one vehicle was hit while the others got through. The Chinese made no attempt to follow the withdrawing Indians.

In NEFA, the Chinese did not cross the last ridge of what they called the foothills. By last light on 22 October, Tezpur was a ghost town and the North Bank was completely abandoned. Through the day Kaul had been flying endlessly with the IAF, frantically looking for survivors. Once it got dark, he went and stood at the end of the dispersal area, next to a parked Dakota that was earmarked to fly him to Gauhati. 'There were no staff officers or ADCs. The whole atmosphere was depressingly calm. The silence was broken only by the croaking of frogs and chirping insects and the occasional sound of a helicopter taking off or landing far on the other side of the runway. It was a dismal sight of a Corps Commander, standing alone in the atmosphere of defeat—a broken man, on his own with no friends or sympathy.'

At around 6.30 in the evening, a helicopter landed with Major General Anant Pathania, GOC 4 Division, who had been picked up just before sunset. As those present on the tarmac watched, Pathania 'slightly drooping, in a crumpled uniform, walking slowly with a long stick as high as himself, dragging his feet as if he was in no hurry and had no particular place in mind to go to' moved towards Kaul, who was still standing there. When he was a few yards from Kaul, Pathania 'came to a slow stop and looked up with a detached expression. He stood and looked up at him for a little while in this fashion and turned his face away as if the man in front of him was better left alone, and deserved no feelings of rancour or words of sympathy.'

On paper the Chinese said they were withdrawing to the line which was under their control prior to 8 September 1962 and would demilitarize the areas occupied by them subsequently. However, in reality, the Chinese continued to stick to their aggressive posture in Ladakh, establishing six new posts in the region: Shenhsienwan on the northern slope of the Karakoram Pass, Tienwentian near Chip Chap-la, a post each at Kongka-la, Nyagzu, Khurnak Fort and also at Spanggur itself. The Chinese call these 'civilian checkposts' and retain the abrogated right to object if there is ever any activity on the Indian side. On 3 March 1963, Pakistan ceded to the People's Republic of China the 5,800-square-kilometre Shaksgam Valley 'pending the settlement of the dispute over Kashmir' with the Indians.

But then that is quite another story.

Epilogue

THE MISSING LINKS

NEHRU'S MAO SHADOW

Chairman Mao pulled off many a miracle in his lifetime and was one of the most if not *the* most influential personalities of the twentieth century. Where India was concerned, he repeatedly displayed the uncanny ability to second-guess Prime Minister Nehru, so much so, that when one looks back at the events, it's almost as if the Chinese knew how the Indians would react to each and every move of theirs.

As we have seen, after coming back from the dead, Mao's Communist Chinese defeated the larger and vastly better equipped army of the Kuomintang. Realizing that the West was both physically and emotionally drained from World War II, and fully preoccupied with containing the Soviets, Mao pulled off what was perhaps the biggest post-War real estate coup by bringing both Sinkiang and Tibet into the Chinese fold. India, which was directly affected by this blatant Chinese expansionism, was the unknown entity in Mao's scheme of things. Yet somehow, not only did the Indians quietly go along with the Chinese moves in Tibet, Mao even managed to get Nehru to endorse the Chinese takeover. The next logical step was to force the Indians onto the back foot, for the threat of the United States jumping into the fray was always a real one. Therefore, to keep the Indians off balance, Mao created a border dispute with India where previously none existed.

With Nehru walking into the Chinese trap despite all the warnings (Sardar Patel died exactly thirty-eight days after writing his famous letter spelling out the Chinese intent) the game was over before it had even begun. The Chinese played their cards in such a manner that the Indians lost what should have been at best a defensive war by not fighting it at all. And finally, to top it all, after the conflict, the Chinese actually managed to convince almost everyone that Nehru was solely responsible for the clash between India and China in 1962.

Right from the very beginning the Chinese played Nehru. Just as the Chinese General Yang Chengiou read Lieutenant General Bijji Kaul like an open book, Mao understood Nehru and with well thought-out moves, made the Indian prime minister and the men around him look like a bunch of bungling amateurs.

Unlike Mao, whose rise to power was through extreme violence, having to carry the cross of non-violence after India gained independence in 1947 further hampered Nehru. He wrote in *The Discovery of India:* 'He (Gandhi) knew, of course, that there were many elements in the country, and even within the Congress, which did not have that faith in non-violence; he realised that a government of free India was likely to discard non-violence when questions of defence were concerned and build up military, naval and air power. But he wanted, if possible, for Congress at least to hold the banner of non-violence aloft, and thus to train the minds of the people and make them think increasingly in terms of peaceful action. He had a horror of seeing [India] militarised. He dreamt of India becoming a symbol and example of non-violence, and by her example weaning the rest of the world from war and the ways of violence. Even if India as a whole had not accepted this idea, Congress should not discard it when the time for trial came.'

In an interview with the *Times of India* in 1968, while discussing the Chinese invasion, Krishna Menon said: 'We did not realize that whenever China had had a powerful government she has been expansionist. Secondly, China had come into power through violence and force and nothing else; she had been at war for thirty or forty years, and the bulk of the world's people were in sympathy with the exploits of the Red Army. Thirdly, China wanted to show both us and the world that she was the largest nation.' On the other hand, Menon was to admit that during this period 'the pressure upon me from all sides was not to increase the Army efficiency and strength but to cut it down'.

Half a century after the events, most of India's popular media is obsessed with the Henderson Brooks-Bhagat Report, which remains classified even today despite the fact that there have been non-Congress governments at the centre on more than one occasion. In the immediate aftermath of 1962, it became a clever ploy for the government to deflect the blame from itself onto the army. As we know, after General Thapar's resignation, Nehru continued to play petty political games, appointing Muchhu Chaudhuri as Chief of Army Staff while holding back his elevation to a four-star rank.

Chaudhuri had taken the initiative to appoint Lieutenant General

Henderson Brooks and Brigadier Prem Bhagat to make an independent analysis of the war. Chaudhuri's initial brief to Brooks and Bhagat was all-encompassing in its scope, but the chief had to back down quickly when it was pointed out to him by the DMO, Brigadier D. K. Palit, that this would allow the two officers to access all the files pertaining to governmental policy decisions. Obviously, if the Henderson Brooks-Bhagat Report was to have teeth, its level would have to be raised beyond Army HQ. When the matter was taken up with the new defence minister, Y. B. Chavan, the government let it be known that 'it did not wish to institute an enquiry into high-level policies and decisions'. So instead of the committee being upgraded to widen its scope, it remained as it had been originally constituted, while its terms of reference were changed. The two officers were ordered to confine themselves to analysing IV Corps' operations only.

Chavan then indulged in some sleight of hand, so common in democracies where those in power need to cover their own follies. Once completed, the report was locked up and few individuals outside the Cabinet were granted access to it. In a subsequent low-key statement in Parliament, Chavan ascribed the debacle in NEFA entirely to the 'failure of military commanders and to the tactical mishandling of troops on the ground'. The defence minister thereby succeeded not only in diverting any criticism from Nehru's government, he also created the impression that the Henderson Brooks-Bhagat Report was a definitive review of the entire Sino-Indian conflict, which was certainly not the case.

Though most of the report's content is known, there continues to be an aura of mystery around it as some critical parts have not yet been 'leaked'. However, those who have been privy to it are emphatic that there is nothing that is not known. It continues to remain under wraps only because despite their brief, the two officers hint at the skewed decision-making system that existed then.

By the end of the 1950s the civil-military equation had become so warped that a man of General Thimayya's stature could be reduced to a virtual non-entity. Success and survival in the military hierarchy depended on falling in line with the 'Chosen One' or at best by keeping one's mouth shut and sailing with the wind, as was the case with General Pran Thapar and Lieutenant General Bogey Sen. As I have pointed out earlier, with General Thimayya went Lieutenant Generals Thorat and S.D. Verma. Even Major General Sam Manekshaw was not spared. After the fall of Tawang on 23 October, the new crop of officers who took over 4 Division and the various brigades in the Kameng Sector were all personally selected by

General Pran Thapar. They failed to show even the slightest semblance of a fight when, three weeks later, the Chinese push became a shove.

In 1953, General Kulwant Singh's report not only looked at the entire India-China border from a military point of view, it warned that the Chinese would go in for limited military action any time after 1961. Throughout this period while Nehru privately expressed his misgivings about the Chinese, in public he was adamant that there was no threat from them. In the east, had it not been for Jairam Das Daulatram, the Governor of Assam between 1949 and 1956, NEFA might have been lost to the Chinese, like Aksai Chin. It is a well-known fact that when Major Ralengnao Bob Khathing came to meet Nehru in New Delhi after his expedition to Tawang, Nehru was furious with him and wanted to know who had authorized the expedition.

The Panchsheel Agreement, signed between India and China, reflected Nehru's idealism that was far removed from the world of realpolitik. At that stage, India at least held some cards, the most important perhaps being the physical access to Lhasa. Nehru chose to discard them without getting in return any concessions from the Chinese in Tibet. Not only that, the Government of India then began to hide from its own people Chinese transgressions on the border. There too the Chinese played it perfectly–engineering trouble in the Middle Sector in the vicinity of the Niti Pass while staying well clear of the Northern and Eastern sectors. After having established that the border was indeed disputed, who ever heard of Barahoti (or Wu-Je as the Chinese called it) again?

Before I end this study of 1962, a quick summary of the whole affair would be in order In 1957, the arrival of General Thimayya at the helm of the Indian Army was hailed as a new beginning. Timmy was quite popular with Nehru (or he would never have been made chief) but to clip his wings the prime minister appointed the firebrand Krishna Menon as the defence minister. A lot of post-war venom has been directed at Menon for his role and style of functioning, but Menon was simply doing what Nehru wanted him to do, as was the case with Kaul. Nehru's interest in Kaul's career and his subsequent rise to the top had begun as far back as 1947; from being considered a 'failed officer', he was posted to the United States as the military attaché after which he returned to India and became Nehru's key man in Kashmir. The Menon-Thimayya clash eventually took place when the army chief put his foot down when Kaul was to be placed in Army HQ on promotion as the QMG.

Thimayya could not have been more categorical in his official assessment of Kaul, yet it was Thimayya who paid the price for his loyalty to his country and his prime minister. Nehru, despite his stature and reputation, showed that he was not above playing petty politics and with Menon as a cat's paw, he contrived to not only sideline Thimayya, but used him and the Indian Army as a smokescreen to get himself out of the Aksai Chin highway mess. If that was inexcusable, how should we regard the prime minister's statement in Parliament the day after he had unilaterally announced the army's taking over of NEFA, that Thimayya was petulant, then begin focusing on the need to maintain civil supremacy over the military.

THE HOLY GRAIL OF THE FORWARD POLICY

Much has been made of the McMahon Line, with some commentators even mentioning the thickness of the pencil used to demarcate the area west of Khenzemane extending up to the tri-junction with Bhutan, thereby implying that the Nam Ka Chu Valley was indeed on the Tibetan/Chinese side. Also, the fact that the Nam Ka Chu is erroneously marked as flowing north to south on the Morshead-Bailey map has little to do with the alignment of the boundary. These are ridiculous arguments, for they ignore the undisputed boundary line that extends eastwards from the Namgyan Chu towards Bum-la. Geographically, it is the Thagla Ridge that is contiguous and not the Tsangdhar Ridge, as claimed by the Chinese. To also dismiss the McMahon Line as some sort of arbitrary demarcation by the British shows a complete lack of understanding of the watershed principle. The Morshead-Bailey survey was extensive and apart from surveying and mapping the geographical features, the recommendation for the boundary line also took into account all the demographic factors.

Tibet's representative, Lonchen Shatra, had arrived in India for the Simla Conference in 1914 armed with every minute detail pertaining to the Assam-Tibet frontier. As a negotiator, he was no pushover. Furthermore, the British were extremely cautious in their dealing with the Tibetans, as they were with the Chinese. There is little doubt that Tawang was indeed the subject of intense discussion. Eventually, in exchange for the weapons and ammunition required by the Tibetans (5,000 Lee Enfield Rifles and 500,000 rounds of ammunition), Lonchen Shatra was authorized by the Dalai Lama to agree to the boundary alignment suggested by McMahon. This secret deal on Tawang could hardly be discussed with the Chinese.

At the time, China's Qing Dynasty had collapsed and the Chinese had been expelled even from Eastern Tibet. The drawing up of the Indo-Tibetan frontier was of little interest to China. The subsequent refusal to ratify the treaty had everything to do with the Inner and Outer boundaries between Tibet and China, and nothing to do with the McMahon Line. Sardar Patel, who had warned Nehru about this in his letter, had anticipated that the Chinese would go back on all existing treaties between the Tibetans and British India. The subsequent interpretation of the Indo-Tibet boundary by Mao's Communist China was dictated purely by China's perceived strategic requirements. Once the Chinese had Nehru trapped with the lofty idealism of the Panchsheel Agreement, the Indo-China border dispute became the focal point and within four years Tibet's annexation was put on the back burner.

Blaming Nehru's Forward Policy for the conflict is to view the situation with blinkered glasses. If anything, the failure was in not implementing it forcefully enough. Indian troops, especially the paramilitary and police forces, had every right to be in the area that India was seriously claiming as its territory. Until 1947, troops from the Kashmir State Forces regularly visited the Aksai Chin area and even maintained a post at Shahidula. Post Independence the practice was discontinued. End result: Mao's Communist China simply took over the entire region and India found out about it in 1957. Critics claim Aksai Chin was never really a part of Kashmir, and it was 'gifted' to the maharaja by the surveyor Johnson, who was considered to be a rogue. Even if that point was ceded, the question that begs to be asked is what did China (or even Tibet or Sinkiang for that matter) have to do with it? The absence of Indian posts in the Aksai Chin made it low hanging fruit. Militarily, the Chinese needed it; so they simply took it!

The Indian failure perhaps lay in putting too much trust in the 'legal' position, rather than looking at the developing situation on the ground. China's practice of 'occupying the last ridge from the China side and creeping up on the first ridge on the Indian' side meant the borders and claim lines would always keep shifting. After the capture of every objective, the Chinese line moved that much more forward. It is partly because of this tactic that the Chinese definition of the Indo-Tibet and Indo-Sinkiang border changed between 1959 and 1960; yet again in September 1962 and once more after the operations in November. In 1965, an altogether different scenario emerged.

The failure lay not in the Forward Policy but in forgetting the famous dictum 'he who carries the big stick rules the roost'. Given Nehru's vague idea about asserting Indian rights in Tibet, the pushing forward of posts in the NEFA area by the Assam Rifles through the 1950s was indeed most commendable. Unfortunately, given Nehru's conflicting views on China, the Government of India did not do enough to build on these posts.

B. N. Mullik understood this aspect, and it was at his constant goading that the Forward Policy was finally declared in 1961. Mullik is today branded as a villain in l'affaire 1962, but that is perhaps unfair. True, he believed the Chinese were not likely to get into a full-fledged war and he was proved wrong in the end. However, that was his perception and he was willing to voice it after looking at all the data that was available at the time. The same information was also available to officers at Military Operations and Army HQ. They refused to even apply their minds to the situation, preferring to queue up behind the flamboyant and totally irresponsible General Kaul instead.

Mullik remains an enigma, the only person who along with Nehru had a role to play in the 1962 affair right from the very beginning. In September 1948, he became the deputy director of the Intelligence Bureau with charge of Kashmir, and was elevated to director on 15 July 1950, a position he would hold till 1964. Outside of Mullik's own book, *My Years with Nehru*, very little information is available on the work done by the covert agencies during this period. However, two things are clear: the United States through its Central Intelligence Agency (CIA) had a presence in the region even in 1950 when there was talk of the Americans and the British flying an Indian brigade into Tibet. Obviously, with Nehru wanting to project a 'non-aligned' face to the world, Mullik was the point of contact with the Americans through the 1950s, during which time the CIA kept the Tibetan resistance going in Eastern Tibet. After the Lhasa disturbances and the Dalai Lama's escape to India in March 1959, declassified CIA files state: 'The Chinese leaders recognized, or were made aware, shortly after the August 1959 clashes, that Nehru's advisors might use these skirmishes to push him and the entire government further to the "right" i.e. towards a militant anti-China policy and a willingness to accept some degree of American support in this policy. The practical strategic danger such a development posed was that the arc of US bases "encircling" China would be extended through India.'

In the CIA's assessment, Mao and other Chinese leaders believed that elements in the Indian establishment 'particularly those in the Ministry of External Affairs and including General Thimayya, were "rightists" who wanted to exploit the border dispute to help the US "isolate China". On the contrary, Thimayya, as we have seen, was dead against any military adventurism against China, or the deployment of the army in either NEFA or Ladakh. By a process of elimination, this only leaves Mullik and Kaul, as the two hard-nosed hawks on the Indian side who, once having got

Nehru to officially endorse the Forward Policy, began to push for and implement an aggressive stand that could not have been matched by the available logistical support on the ground.

In the build-up to the events of October-November 1962, Kaul's ominous presence seems to have been everywhere. As QMG between the second half of 1959 until 1961, it was his responsibility to create the supply lines that would be required to sustain Indian troops in both Ladakh and NEFA. But his cavalier attitude towards logistics combined with Bogey Sen's refusal to step in meant that very few 'warlike' supplies could be ferried to the men who were asked to set up posts in areas that were almost impossible for human habitation.

Kaul's elevation to the post of CGS coincided with Nehru ordering the army to implement the Forward Policy. In the second half of 1961, Kaul told Brigadier D. K. Palit 'that in Ladakh where we are not in occupation of territory we claimed, it was imperative to demonstrate a presence in the empty spaces, even if such forward moves temporarily outran maintenance capabilities at war rates'. Under the umbrella of Mullik's assurance that the Chinese would not react, Kaul's illogical desire to push forward on all fronts created the recipe for a military disaster that few could even begin to imagine.

During the critical Dhola incident on 8 September 1962, Kaul was on leave, holidaying in the Kashmir Valley. The Dhola incident acted as a catalyst for subsequent events. Brigadier Dalvi was stopped from proceeding on leave at Tezpur, 9 Punjab was pushed into the Nam Ka Chu Valley from its defensive position at Tawang, 1/9 GR who had been relieved by 9 Punjab were told to retrace their steps and 2 Rajput were told to get off the train at Missamari to strengthen the Kameng Frontier Division. With the self-imposed clock now ticking 'to throw the Chinese out', it was again Kaul who was fine with being 'demoted' from CGS to a corps commander and rushed forward to conduct the battle. One would think that in Nehru's army, there was just the one man!

What would have happened had the pickets established as a part of the Forward Policy been better armed and capable of fighting a sustained short defensive war? That question, of course, can never be answered, especially since Kaul almost single-handedly ensured that the men who had extended the line with an almost superhuman effort, simply did not have the means to fight!

Indians would do well to remember that after Kaul had completely botched the army's operational ability in NEFA, he created a similar situation in Assam. The evacuation of Tezpur and the withdrawal of Indian troops by the Kaul-Sen duo from the North Bank was nothing short of an act of panic, especially since the Chinese had at that stage not progressed beyond Chaku and had certainly not entered the foothills. It was Mullik who told the Indian Army that if its commanders were not going to fight, he would do so using State Armed Police, if necessary.

WHERE WERE THE BOYS IN BLUE?

Having failed to read Chinese intent and having created a situation where it was believed by all in high command that the Chinese would react militarily, Mullik's inputs on the use of the IAF as an offensive weapon are even more bewildering. In March 1960, intelligence reports that were with Eastern Command in Lucknow had indicated that the Chinese had constructed a group of airfields north of Lhasa in the region of Yanpachen. This was the main air base in Tibet that could handle the heaviest bombers then in service with the Chinese Air Force (PLAAF). Additional airstrips capable of taking jet fighters had been constructed in and around Rudok, Gartok, Tingri, Shigatse, Gyantse and Tse-la. A number of advance landing grounds from where twin-engine transport aircraft had been reported were Tradom, Khamba Dzong, Tsona Dzong, Lhuntse Dzong, Tithong and Drowagompa. The exact strength of the PLAAF was not known, but during the Republic Day celebrations in Lhasa earlier that year, six to eight bombers along with two squadrons of fighter jets had reportedly participated in the flypast.

By 1962, the imbalance of troops in the Western Sector was a major concern and the use of offensive air support to redress the balance was discussed as early as May. In fact, in a meeting chaired by Krishna Menon on 18 September, Army HQ was in favour of pulling back all available troops for the defence of Leh, but this would have meant abandoning the airfield at Chushul and large tracts of Ladakh—something that the then Chief of Air Staff, Air Marshal Aspy Engineer, vehemently opposed. In turn, the IAF offered to fly in reinforcements and provide interdiction missions against targets in West Tibet in the event of any troop concentrations. The Intelligence Bureau was asked to make a fresh assessment of the Chinese air strength, and the quantum of force that could be brought to bear against India.

The IB's assessment of the Chinese air offensive capability knocked the wind out of any offensive plans the IAF might have had. Mullik in his book claims that accurate intelligence about the PLAAF was passed on to Service HQ even before the 18 September meeting. Despite the withdrawal of support by the USSR, the IB felt that the PLAAF, operating from bases in Tibet, Yunnan and even Sinkiang, would have the run of the subcontinent, their bombers could even get to Madras as the IAF had a paucity of night interceptors. Besides, Chinese MiG-17s and 19s plus the newly acquired MiG-21s would wreak havoc on the Indian Canberra bombers because they all had night capability. The final twist to the projected horror story was that Pakistan was also planning to strike at Kashmir the moment hostilities broke out between India and China.

There were major flaws in what Mullik and the IB were saying. We have already noted that there were no advanced runways for the PLAAF to operate from, especially low-altitude runways from where aircraft could take off with a regular payload. Second, though China had prevailed on the USSR to delay the supply of MiG-21s to India, they themselves did not have any. Third, the IB hadn't taken into account the actual performance of the PLAAF in combat, especially when it had run into US-equipped Chinese National Air Force planes operating over Amoy, Shanghai and Canton. Lastly, the IAF, though numerically inferior to the PLAAF, was equipped with quite an impressive array of aircraft—the Hawker Siddeley Hunter and the Gnat were among the most modern subsonic aircraft at that time. In addition, the IAF had the French Ouragan and the Mystère, mainly based in the Western Sector, from where Ladakh was within relatively easy range. In the Eastern Sector, Ouragans, Vampires and Hunters, apart from the Alize and Sea Hawk naval aircraft were available for hitting targets in NEFA and Tibet.

Apart from Mullik, there were others who played a role in ensuring that the IAF was kept out of the conflict. H. C. Dewan, who was an air commodore in 1962, and the officer in charge of air operations, would later say: 'Everyone talks of General Bijji Kaul and his direct line to Nehru, but few realize that I was equally close to him [Nehru]. It was I who advised him not to use fighters and bombers against the Chinese. As the army got more and more bogged down in NEFA, it became quite difficult to hold Nehru back; he wanted to launch the fighters. Had he done so, it would have had disastrous consequences, which he as a non-military person needed to understand.'

When asked for the rationale behind having advised the prime minister along these lines, Dewan said: 'I flew the Hurricane in the Arakans during World War II. Our job was mainly reconnaissance and I flew hundreds of sorties. I never saw the Japanese, only some smoke from one of their camps once. Hunters, Vampires and the Canberra were faster aircraft; they would have never found the Chinese positions.' Asked if he had ever flown in NEFA, Dewan said no, but claimed that was irrelevant because the terrain in the northeast was similar. 'Besides,' he added, 'if we had used fighters, the Chinese would have retaliated and bombed our troops who were in fixed defensive positions. It would have caused havoc. I also told Nehru that they would bomb Indian cities, including Calcutta. That effectively stopped Nehru from doing anything silly!'

Within the services, Dewan alone probably didn't influence the prime minister; it was the prevailing attitude in Air HQ in 1962 that was shocking. The Chief of Air Staff, Air Marshal Aspy Engineer, simply accepted the IB assessment at face value and rejected all talk of interdiction and close air support for our ground troops. On 20 October 1962, when the Chinese attacked the Rajput positions on the Nam Ka Chu and then attacked 1/9 GR at Tsangdhar, a C-119 Fairchild Packet overflew the drop zone around noon. On returning to Tezpur, the pilots reported to Air Vice Marshal Jaswant Singh, the AOC-in-C, and told him what they had seen from the air. HQ IV Corps at that time had no information as they had been cut off from 4 Division since the morning. Jaswant Singh promptly put in a call to the air chief, and after briefing him on the situation, with his usual dash of humour added 'Well Sir, if the army doesn't know what to do, I will send our fighters into action and I want your permission for it.' Obviously there was an explosion at the other end of the line, for after a while Jaswant Singh spoke again, 'Yes Sir, of course, I know Sir, don't you worry. It was only meant to be a joke.'

In Tibet, unlike the Arakans where the Japanese infantry had plenty of vegetation to cover their tracks, there is excellent visibility and no natural cover available. In fact, on 21 October, AN 12s and Packets flying in the Chushul area had reported a three-kilometre-long Chinese column proceeding towards the Spanggur Gap. The IAF would have had a definite edge over their Chinese counterparts in offensive sweeps over the area, for aircraft taking off from the plains would have operated with full loads while the Chinese would have had to cope with the drawback of operating out of high altitude airfields in Tibet. As for the retaliatory bombing of Indian cities—forget about Calcutta, the Chinese Air Force would have been hard-pressed to get to Gorakhpur. Also, at that time, the Chinese did not have advanced runways in Tibet, nor had they begun to deploy missiles.

Air Chief Marshal S. K. Mehra, confirmed that the IAF was just raring to have a go. A squadron leader at the time, Mehra himself had visited most of the Indian positions in NEFA to work out probable lines of attack and assess the terrain. In addition, fighter pilots were flying in transport aircraft to familiarize themselves with the terrain whenever possible.

According to Jaggi Nath (the Canberra pilot who photographed the

Aksai Chin highway) he met Kaul in Army HQ with photographs of Chinese deployment after a routine sortie over Sinkiang and Tibet. 'We had the run of the skies, there were simply no Chinese aircraft around that could threaten us. We got pictures of everything—vehicles, guns, their defences, especially in the DBO, Qara Qash and Galwan sectors.' However, Kaul showed little interest in what the squadron leader had to say. 'He kept saying how he was just coming from or going to meet the prime minister. For us, not used to the functioning of Army HQ, it looked like a parody.'

The problem probably lay in the difference between availability of intelligence and the ability to interpret it. Mullik's view, that come what may, the Chinese would never attack obviously permeated down ranks in the Intelligence Bureau. No one was willing to rock the boat by offering an opinion contrary to the top man's view. It was a classic case of the tail wagging the dog!

Not only did the IB paint for Nehru a highly exaggerated picture about the PLAAF's strike capability, it was downright dishonest in its overall appreciation. In March 1962, Lieutenant Liu Chengsze of the PLAAF defected to the USA in Formosa (Taiwan). He had earlier approached the Indians seeking political asylum, offering detailed information about the state of the Chinese air capabilities in exchange. The Indians had refused, but the Americans eagerly accepted the offer. However, the gist of Chengsze's information had been shared with the Indian Intelligence Bureau. According to the report, despite having over 2,000 aircraft at their disposal, the Chinese could only utilize a fraction of these against India from Tibet.

The main reason was the complete reliance on the Soviet Union for aviation fuel and spares. While it was true that the Chinese had used fighters and bombers to neutralize Tibetan resistance fighters in 1958, the quantum of aircraft used was miniscule. Subsequently, with Soviet aid drying up in 1960 after a chill in Sino-Soviet relations, the Chinese were hard-pressed to launch aircraft even in China, let alone Sinkiang and Tibet. Why the Intelligence Bureau chose to deliberately mislead the government and why the air chief failed to arrive at an independent assessment will remain another one of the unsolved mysteries of 1962.

On the other hand, the transport wing of the IAF played a major role not just during the operations but from the very beginning. In 1951 No. 11 Squadron was raised, flying Dakotas. At that point, there were already a number of Assam Rifles posts in NEFA, many of which had been completely cut off after the earthquake in 1950. As more and more forward posts were created, the demand for airlifting men and supplies began to escalate rapidly.

More squadrons were raised and in 1954, the first C-119 Packets arrived in India. However, the Packet was not designed for high altitude flying and there were a number of tragic accidents especially in Ladakh. Eventually, an additional engine (known as the jet pack) was fitted to the aircraft and Squadron Leader C. S. K. Raje went on to make aviation history by landing on the airstrip at Daulat Beg Oldi which is situated at 16,614 feet. In 1955, the Soviets presented Nehru with an IL-14 for his personal use, and then followed up with another two dozen aircraft that were flown by No. 42 Squadron.

By then, quite a few short, semi-prepared runways had been laid out by the Assam Rifles for which the DHC-3 Otter Aircraft was the best option; it would soon become the mainstay in the Lohit Frontier Division.

The C-113 seemed to be the frontrunner among heavy lift aircraft the country was looking to buy, until Krishna Menon decided to zero in on to the Soviet AN 12. The deal was signed in 1960, and the first batch of seven aircraft were ordered mainly to airlift heavy machinery for the Border Roads in Ladakh. However, during the initial trial runs the Soviet test pilots, after making the approach, refused to land at either Leh or Chushul, saying it was too risky. Squadron Leader Chandan Singh, who had converted to the aircraft by then, volunteered to take on the task with his crew. Chandan Singh was to later land the first AMX 13 tank at Chushul.

In addition to the AN 12 fleet, Super Constellations from Air India had also been transferred to the IAF fleet and were part of No. 6 Squadron. During October and November 1962, these aircraft clocked 1,000 hours in support of the army, ferrying entire battalions in addition to tons of sand bags and barbed wire.

The Bell-47G-2 light helicopter was the first rotor wing to be inducted into the IAF in 1954. Six Sikorsky S-55s followed shortly, as did Mi-4 helicopters in 1961. Most of the helicopter pilots were thrown into operation right from the moment the machines arrived and it is to the immense credit of the IAF that the helicopter crews performed superbly throughout. By the beginning of November 1962, the first Aloutte III helicopters had also started flying.

THE WILL TO FIGHT

Nehru, Menon, Mullik...these were the three personalities that most influenced events and shaped destiny that year but for those manning the bunkers on the night of 19 October 1962, they were of little relevance. Their officers and their respective COs meant a lot more. For the men, even the likes of Brigadier John Dalvi, the commander of 7 Brigade, and Major General Niranjan Prasad, the GOC of 4 Division, were too far removed from them to impact their fighting capabilities.

Field Marshal William Slim, who had fought the gruelling campaign against the Japanese in what were perhaps equally primitive conditions in the northeast during World War II, would say in his book, *Defeat into Victory*: 'In my experience it is not so much asking men to fight or work with obsolete equipment that lowers morale but the belief that those responsible are accepting such a state of affairs. If men realise that every one above them and behind them is flat out to get the things required for them, they will do wonders, as my men did, with meagre resources they have instead of sitting down moaning for better.'

The key was in Niranjan Prasad and John Dalvi's hands, but the two officers failed to rise to the occasion. Both have since written books putting the entire blame on Kaul who, as we know, gave specific orders not to abandon the positions on the river, regardless of their tactical unsuitability. After the events of 10 October, when the Chinese demonstrated their intention by opening fire, both these officers needed to seize the moment and give their defences some depth. There was simply no Plan A or Plan B, no thinning of the defences or fortification of Hathung-la. Instead, they did absolutely nothing, simply hoping and praying that the Chinese were bluffing.

The bluff had in fact been perpetuated by them. The plan to evict the Chinese from the Thagla Ridge had been drawn up by Dalvi, who subsequently claimed he put up the plan hoping it would be shot down for its sheer absurdity. The sudden appearance of Kaul on the scene as the corps commander and the exit of Umrao Singh had further complicated matters, and set the scene for the Nam Ka Chu tragedy even before the Chinese guns opened up on 20 October.

7 Brigade's collapse was a sign of things to come. Both the commanding officers of 9 Punjab and 4 Grenadiers bolted (there simply is no other word for it), leaving their men to their fate. 1/9 GR abandoned their CO, an unheard of act on the field of battle, while Dalvi himself wandered around until his ordeal ended with his capture. The Chinese hypothesis that if you got behind the Indians they simply would not know what to do was more than amply demonstrated time and again. The PLA commanders also believed that the Indian deployment was not mutually supportive. They could therefore afford to bring overwhelming force against each Indian position and wipe them out one by one.

So focused was Niranjan Prasad on Nam Ka Chu, that the 5 Assam

Rifles platoon and the 1 Sikh company at Bum-la were left more or less on their own to fight screening battles. Despite Bogey Sen's presence on the ground, his complete indifference towards the defence of Tawang was not only shocking, it bordered on callousness. The orders for the garrison to withdraw, the resultant abandonment of tons of stores, equipment and 25-pounder guns should have resulted in the immediate sacking of the army commander. Instead, Bogey Sen got Niranjan Prasad removed for cowardice in the Nam Ka Chu battle.

All organizations, regardless of which country they belong to, have a system of checks and balances. Bijji Kaul may have, by virtue of being Nehru's man, been given the status of the Alpha male, but theoretically he still had two people above him in the chain of command. Both Thapar and Sen had been quick to adopt a submissive posture, realizing that to survive in the existing set-up, they had to take a step back. Thapar, while still the Western Army Commander, had realized that Thorat, by virtue of being cast in the Thimayya mould, was in all probability going to be sidelined once Timmy retired. Thapar's moment of truth came when his subordinate corps commander, Lieutenant General S. D. Verma, took a stand on the situation in Ladakh. As the army commander, Thapar could either back Verma and the men he commanded, thereby ruining his own chances for the top job, or keep silent. The moment Thapar took the second option, he had sold his soul to the Nehru-Menon-Kaul triumvirate and the rest of India paid the price.

Bogey Sen's case was even more intriguing. For many, he was the operational face of the Indian Army in Kashmir in 1947-48. As the commander of 161 Brigade, whose forward elements were airlifted into Srinagar even as the tribal lashkars were just a few miles from the Srinagar airfield, Sen was looked at as a highly capable and competent officer. In many ways, after Nehru and Menon had ridden roughshod over Thimayya and appointed Kaul the QMG in 1959, it was up to Bogey Sen, as the CGS, to draw the line in the sand. Sen was nobody's fool—his book on the J&K Ops, *Slender was the Thread*, showed him to possess a sharp analytical mind. By throwing his hat into Kaul's camp, Sen sounded the death knell of the army as a professional fighting arm.

When Thimayya and Thorat retired, Sen moved from being the CGS to command the Eastern Army. If there was any doubt as to where Sen's loyalty lay, it was dispelled when, in an amazing breach of protocol, Bogey Sen flew to Tezpur to receive Kaul, the newly appointed 4 Corps Commander who was to serve under him.

Thapar and Sen, the two men at the top of the military pyramid, knew that they were under the boot of the ambitious Kaul. It was therefore natural that sooner or later they would both rebel, and when they did, it had equally disastrous implications. When Kaul scuttled back to New Delhi from the Nam Ka Chu Valley on 10 October, having realized the Chinese were firing real bullets, it was perhaps the last chance for the Indians to wake up. At that point, the troops should have been moved out of the riverbed and redeployed on the Tsangdhar Ridge where they would have had a realistic fighting chance. Kaul was shaken enough to realize he had blundered, and was willing to admit it. Nehru agreed, saying he did not want even one man to lose his life, when Sen and Thapar decided to dig in, insisting that 7 Brigade needed to hold its ground.

With the abandoning of Tawang, the sacking of Prasad and the non-availability of Kaul, it was vital that Bogey Sen as the Eastern Army Commander take charge. At this stage, it was imperative that Thorat's defensive line along the Manda-la Heights–Bomdila axis be put into place. Instead, both Thapar and Sen let the histrionics of their DMO take centre stage and, on a whim, declared Se-la the next line of defence. All the new commanders—Major General Anant Pathania, Brigadiers Hoshiar Singh, Cheema and Gurbax Singh—were selected by Thapar and rushed forward.

After the disaster on the Nam Ka Chu, where the Kaul-Sen-Thapar trio successfully helped implode an infantry brigade in a matter of a few hours, Thapar needed to stand up to political interference in matters that were now purely military. The appointment of Lieutenant General Harbaksh Singh as the new corps commander was widely welcomed by the men. By now JCOs and officers (letters home were censored by the IB, and daily reports on the morale of the troops were filed as a matter of routine) were openly critical of Kaul, holding him directly responsible for the Nam Ka Chu fiasco. However, when Nehru told Thapar to reinstate Kaul and send Harbaksh to XXXIII Corps instead of Umrao, Thapar acquiesced without a murmur.

The three weeks spent by the Indians on Se-la told its own story. The new GOC of 4 Division, Anant Pathania, shifted his Division HQ as far back as he could. Kaul having given him permission to do this, no one in Army HQ knew that 4 Division was located at Dirang Dzong. Once again Kaul was guilty of severe misjudgement. He simply assumed that having captured Tawang—or rather having had it presented to them on a platter—the PLA would shut shop for the winter. Palit, who insisted on making Se-la the defence line, on the other hand, seemed to be clueless about the actual state of the alternate routes that linked the Mago Valley with both Dirang Dzong and Bomdila; as we have seen these allowed the Chinese to get behind the Indians.

Brigadier Hoshiar Singh seemed to be an exception to the rule, simply because he was at least talking of fighting the Chinese should they assault Se-la. However, tactically, he needed his GOC and corps commander to help him fight the battle. Since mid-November Kaul had focussed on the Walong Sector and seemed to have forgotten that Se-la existed, while Anant Pathania in Dirang Dzong was too far removed from the front lines to have a realistic appreciation of the situation, let alone contribute positively to its defence. In the near absence of these two personalities, Hoshiar Singh was left more or less on his own. When the Chinese attacked on 17 November, the Garhwalis at Nuranang were outstanding, losing only two men as a single company held the Chinese at bay till 4 p.m. in the afternoon. Instead of reinforcing their success, Hoshiar Singh allowed himself to be browbeaten by HQ 4 Division who ordered him to withdraw.

At the tactical level, there were obviously no rehearsed plans for a fallback, and in reality, there were no real defences to fall back on. Once he decided to withdraw the Garhwalis, Hoshiar Singh pulled the plug on his own plan of holding Se-la to the last man. 2 Sikh LI was the first to lose its nerve, and as its troops bolted, they took the bulk of 1 Sikh with them. Hoshiar Singh tried to stop them, but once panic sets in, the game is over.

The events of 18-19 November were as appalling. 4 Rajput was supposed to cover 62 Brigade's withdrawal from Se-la but the company commander, Major Nair, had upped and gone without orders. Had the Rajputs been in position as they were expected to be, the Chinese could have never ambushed the convoy that was commanded by Major Brahm Sat. In the aftermath of the operations, almost all these men got away scot-free because in the overall collapse, there was no one left to ask any meaningful questions.

The gallant Hoshiar Singh and his officers still tried to get to Bomdila, not aware that the men who were supposed to be behind them were long gone. Eventually, two days after the official ceasefire, Hoshiar Singh was murdered by the Chinese as were quite a few others. The story was much the same in Bomdila where after having the Chinese on the ropes at Thembang, Kaul bullied and threatened Gurbax Singh into thinning his defences and pushing forward with a mobile column to clear the road to Dirang Dzong. What happened afterwards, who ran where, is of little consequence.

We have seen how, on a visit to 2 Rajput in 1959, as the battalion prepared to move to Walong, Thimayya had told the officers assembled in the mess that he hoped they wouldn't be cannon fodder for the Chinese when and if the attack came. At the two extremities of the Indo-Tibet border, if the men felt they were just that, they could be forgiven. 6 Kumaon, having taken over the defence of Walong from 2 Rajput, were abruptly ordered to move to Kibithu which was a screening position held by the Assam Rifles. After the Chinese attacked on 20 October they were ordered to fall back on Walong.

Here, too, a young lieutenant was to distinguish himself, for while falling back, 6 Kumaon's action on the nullah near Ashi Hill halted the Chinese advance for a few days. Lieutenant Bikram Singh was never given his due by way of a gallantry award, despite having distinguished himself yet again in the actual battle of Walong where he was eventually killed. Lieutenant Colonel Madiah, on his return from China where he was a POW, was categorical in saying that Bikram Singh was the one true hero in Walong. It is perhaps fitting, that among those who know of Walong, he is known as the Lion of the Namti Valley.

How ironical that in the Ladakh Sector, the handful of men deployed in penny packets in some of the most inhospitable terrain in the world, flying the flag at DBO, Qara Qash, Galwan and Srijap should put up such a gallant fight when commanders with entire brigades at their disposal should be found wanting in other sectors.

When the final phase of the fighting began on 18 November, despite the stoic resistance of the Kumaonis and the Gorkhas at Rezang-la and Gurung Hill respectively, 114 Brigade capitulated on 19 November, thereby abandoning the Chushul airfield and the entire line of defence on the Rezang Ridge. What saved India from major embarrassment in the Western Sector was the fact that the Chinese did not stay in contact with the retreating Indian troops as had been the case in NEFA. Here too, there was no pre-planned second line of defence, and at the end of the day, the fact is that a retreating army is a defeated army.

So what went wrong in Ladakh? Brigadier Raina had twenty-five days to reorganize himself after Brigade HQ had helplessly watched Dhan Singh Thapa's men get butchered across the Pangong Tso. In the case of Srijap, the massive body of water had isolated the 1/8 GR positions, but the same cannot be said of Rezang-la. The Chinese build-up in the area of Spanggur Tso was clearly visible and it should have been obvious that both the Gurung Hill post and Rezang-la would be targeted. Shaitan Singh's company was deployed at Rezang-la but nothing was done to either give 13 Kumaon's Charlie Company any depth in the eventuality of a Chinese assault or even secure communications for that matter.

Radio Peking's announcement on 24 October after the Chinese had captured all their objectives in the Northern Sector that Chushul was the next target sent both Western Command and Army HQ into a tizzy. To capture Chushul they would have to cross the claim line, which implied that even Leh was being threatened.

On 18 November, Commander 114 Brigade was willing to fight to the finish, yet twenty-four hours later, all fighting posts were called back and the heavy equipment evacuated from the Chushul theatre of operations. Just who pulled the plug in Ladakh continues to remain a mystery. Sometime towards the end of October, Daulet Singh had had an operational briefing in Army HQ wherein he had outlined his plans for the defence of Chushul to Thapar. Subsequently, despite being outranked, Palit, as the DMO, had taken it upon himself to criticize the plan, pointing out what he called the 'strategic weakness of Chushul'. In light of the Chinese stated objective of capturing the Chushul airfield, Palit had quite forcefully argued that the Chinese threat to Leh was even greater than that faced by Tawang. Not only were the Chushul defences tactically poorly sited, the DMO said that, in all likelihood, the Chinese would cut off and isolate the brigade while making straight for Leh along the Indus route. In his opinion, it was necessary to abandon Chushul and fall back on Leh.

With Thapar seemingly buying the argument, the normally unflappable Daulet Singh had become enraged. However, he did not raise his voice but sensibly countered Palit's argument by pointing out that the Chinese had not crossed their claim line either at Srijap or at Demchok; in his opinion, they were unlikely to attack Chushul. Should they do so, the army commander had told Palit and Thapar, the defences at Chushul were quite capable of keeping the Chinese at bay. After Daulet Singh had left, Thapar told Palit that he did not overrule the army commander because he too had a 'gut feeling' that the Chinese would not actually cross the claim line.

Given Daulet Singh's mindset and the stance taken by him against Army HQ's advice to abandon Chushul, the decision to abruptly withdraw 114 Brigade on the night of 19 November is extremely perplexing. For all the noise being created in the Western Sector, if the two Jammu & Kashmir Militia wings were to be excluded, the total number of troops that had actually engaged the Chinese were roughly equivalent to a single infantry battalion: one company of 5 Jat at DBO, Qara Qash and Galwan; one company of 1/8 GR at Srijap and Yula; one company of 13 Kumaon at Rezang-la and one more company of 1/8 GR deployed at Gurung Hill.

Raina had not shown himself to be an imaginative commander,

nevertheless the men under his command had not shown any signs of abandoning their defences. Not only had the Chinese until then scrupulously not crossed the claim line in any of the sectors in Ladakh (including Demchok), even on the evening of 18 November, they had not occupied Gurung Hill after the Gorkhas had pulled out. The only person who could have taken the decision and who clearly outranked Daulet was Thapar. In that case, the order issued by Army HQ to Western Command to fall back from Chushul would be the last operational order issued by Thapar before his resignation came into effect.

Ironically, a few years later, Kaul was to say of the fighting in Ladakh: 'What happened to us in Ladakh—where our debacle was as great in magnitude as in NEFA? As a matter of fact neither the Chushul village nor the airfield were even attacked nor did any battle take place there, though green pictures of fighting in the battle of Chushul have been painted to give the impression that Ladakh (as opposed to NEFA) put up a stout resistance. The saving grace in Ladakh was that Chushul, not being in the claim line, remained intact (because it was never attacked).'

Raina was awarded a Maha Vir Chakra, the country's second highest award for bravery, an award that from any point of view defied logic. Majors Dhan Singh Thapa and Shaitan Singh were given Param Vir Chakras, both perhaps eventually justified, but they were given at a time when there were absolutely no details available about the fighting either at Srijap or at Rezang-la. In the long run this would have repercussions of its own, for exaggerated accounts of the battle were written to justify the awards. There is no taking away from the incredible bravery of 1/8 GR at Srijap or that of 13 Kumaon where 114 men died, each man facing the Chinese until he was killed. Yet, flip through any account of the battle today and the number of Chinese reportedly killed defies any sort of mathematical sense. If we were to go by the projected claims, there would have been hardly any Chinese troops left in the Western Sector.

If awards in the Western Sector were handed out at random, the situation in NEFA was worse. Some MVCs and VrCs were given to individuals who were only interested in self-preservation, while those who had fought and died, especially at Nam Ka Chu and later at Walong, were ignored.

THE SMELL OF DEATH

One of the greatest tragedies of the clash with China in 1962 was India's failure to counter Chinese propaganda.

By 19 November, having ensured that there were no Indian formations left in the Bomdila region that could possibly allow the Indians to counter-attack and re-establish a foothold in the Kameng Frontier Division, the Chinese changed tack. They were fully aware that all the committed Indian formations in NEFA had ceased to exist as cohesive bodies. Having thus achieved their immediate objective, Chou En-lai had called the Indian Charge d'Affaires in Peking and told him that China was declaring an immediate ceasefire from midnight the next day. Owing to the complex cipher procedures—and what must rank as one of the most inexplicable and absurd delays of all times—this information was not transmitted to the Indian government in time, leaving them to learn of the Chinese announcement from the newspapers almost forty hours later.

With only stragglers left in the Kameng Frontier Division, the Chinese field commanders gave specific orders to stop taking prisoners and maximize Indian casualties. The aim obviously was to terrorize the rest of India and brand Chinese supremacy on the Indian psyche for years to come. According to Major Sitaram Johri, who had been the political officer in Bomdila, after the ceasefire 'they ruthlessly indulged in the slaughter of Indians. It is worth noting that the number of Indian casualties after the ceasefire was far more than before it. On the other hand the number of POWs was greater before the ceasefire than after it. Thus the Chinese accomplished their aim.'

Having annihilated the surviving Indian troops (the only organized resistance being put up by Lieutenant Colonel Avasthy's 4 Rajput column at the Lagyala Gompa, where again there were no prisoners taken or any wounded), the Chinese set about their other objective that was to have far-reaching political implications. Says Johri: 'The immediate aim of the Chinese was to reconnoitre the area in the vicinity of the tri-junction of the Assam, Kameng and Bhutan boundaries so that if in the future the People's Republic of China was required to describe the details of the tri-junction it could do so without difficulty. Here it may be pointed out that after the Chinese government pushed the Outer-Inner Tibetan boundary from the north of Rima to the north of Tawang it started claiming NEFA as a part of China. The main objection of the world powers [also repeated ad nauseam by Nehru] against this claim was that as no Chinese had put his foot on the territory, China could not claim it as her own. Chinese patrols, therefore, rushed towards the tri-junction in the vicinity of Kalaktang.'

It is indeed unfortunate that the mass slaughter of Indian troops after 21 November, the date of the ceasefire as declared by the Chinese, could never be taken up at an appropriate forum. With the area immediately south of Tenga being virtually impassable on foot, the bulk of the escaping troops had no option but to try and escape through the Morshing-Kalaktang route, where they were massacred in large numbers. Even the Chinese records brazenly talk of the various actions (including the killing of Brigadier Hoshiar Singh). Despite troops having been ordered to withdraw from the area, Chinese patrols continued to be sighted in the vicinity of Kalaktang even as late as mid-December.

Bertil Lintner in his book *Great Game East* comments: 'As the Tibet issue had its cabal of pro-Chinese Western supporters, so did the Sino-Indian border dispute. Alistair Lamb, a British academic, and the Australian journalist Neville Maxwell both have published books arguing for the Chinese claim. They base their findings mainly on the fact that some British maps place the border at the foothills of the Himalayas, and that the text of the Simla Convention of 27 April 1914 was not included in the Aitchison's Treaties, a 1929 official publication.'

Unfortunately, today there is a tendency among many Indian writers to blindly quote Maxwell in particular, who by virtue of having brought parts of the Henderson Brooks-Bhagat Report into the open is seen in some quarters as being the last word on the Indo-Sino conflict. Adds Lintner: 'In the case of Maxwell, he lost his credibility when in the late 1960s he wrote a series of articles—"India's Disintegrating Democracy"—in which he gives vent to his thundering misjudgements: "The great experiment of developing India within a democratic framework has failed. (Indians will soon vote) in the fourth—and surely last—general election." Maxwell predicted that the Army would soon rule India.'

With the clarity of hindsight it is obvious that Prime Minister Nehru blundered on many counts, his biggest failing being the virtual destruction of his own military thanks to his deep-seated insecurities. From his infamous remark made immediately after Independence—'we do not need the military'—to a systematic downgrading of the Armed Forces in the evolving civil-military structure, Nehru played an active part in weakening the confidence and capability of the military. All this while, China's overtly expansionist moves were never challenged and despite the Rajputs at Nam Ka Chu, the Sikhs at Bum-la, the Garhwalis at Nuranang, the Jats and Gorkhas in DBO and Galwan and Srijap, the Kumaonis at Walong and Rezang-la, when the Chinese finally made their move, the Indian political and military leadership folded. When called upon to defend its own territory, despite the bravery and sacrifice of its junior officers and men, as a result of pathetic leadership and large-scale bungling, the army failed in its mission in battle after battle. 1962, quite simply, was the war that wasn't.

ACKNOWLEDGEMENTS

In acknowledging all those without whose inspiration, encouragement and persistence this book would not have been written, foremost is my publisher, David Davidar, who first broached the subject. Since then, I have been constantly encouraged by him to push the envelope in an attempt to tell the story of what really happened in the folds of the High Himalayas.

Growing up in the insulated world of the army, nothing matters more than the regiment and the battalion, even to the families. The events of 1962 could never ever leave us and impacted us in many different ways. In the immediate aftermath of the tragic events, Lieutenant Colonel Brahmanand Avasthy's family came to stay with us. After the ceasefire, Colonel Avasthy and his entire party of 168 men were intercepted by the Chinese and gunned down in cold blood near the Lagyala Gompa. Over the years, Mrs Avasthy became one of the symbols of the Rajput Regiment and I owe a lot to her for keeping the flame of 1962 burning in me. I also had the benefit of possessing the notes prepared by Lieutenant Colonel Maha Singh Rikh, the commanding officer of 2 Rajput, which he had handed over to my father shortly after his repatriation from the POW camp in China. I am grateful to Lieutenant Colonel Gurdial Singh and Brigadier Bhup Singh, 2 Rajput, for their detailed inputs. Colonel Mustasad Ahmad who wrote a book on the history of the Rajput regiment, also generously shared his notes that helped plug some important gaps in the fighting around Bridge 2 on the Dirang–Se-la axis.

I am particularly indebted to Honorary Captain Dashrath Singh for giving me a ground level perspective of what happened at Nam Ka Chu. This session perhaps prepared me to ask Major General D. K. Palit relevant questions. The general was extremely forthcoming and blunt, even while commenting about his own perceived negative role. Others who I had the occasion to interview and interact with over the decades include H. C. Sarin, the then additional secretary in the Ministry of Defence. I also spoke to Field Marshal Sam Manekshaw, who finally brought about a semblance of sanity when he took over from Lieutenant General Bijji Kaul as the corps commander in Tezpur by issuing a brief statement: 'Gentlemen, there shall be no further withdrawals without my order. And that order shall never be given.'

Among those who fought as young officers and whose recollections have helped in shaping the book are Brigadiers Darshan Khullar who was at Se-la and Amar Jit Singh 'Tiger' Behl who was manning the gun position at Tsangdhar overlooking the Nam Ka Chu Valley. Wing Commander M. Sadatulla who lucidly described the fighting in Tsangdhar as seen from the air and Kaul's last moments in Tezpur, Major Kulwant Singh of 4 Sikh who was wounded in Walong, Major General A. K. 'Chicki' Dewan who commanded the 20 Lancers troop of AMX-13 tanks at Chushul, Lieutenant General Baljeet Singh who was a part of Operation Onkar in the Kumaon Hills, and many others gave me useful insights over the years through their conversations with me as well as published articles.

To Yashwant Thorat I am greatly indebted for searching for and giving me the notes on Exercise Lal Qila, and for sharing stories of his father, Lieutenant General S. P. P. Thorat. Mike Dalvi, twelve years my senior at the Doon School, always responded in a flash whenever I needed to ask him for any input, as did Ashali Varma who talked at length about her father, Lieutenant General Prem Bhagat, the author of the Henderson Brooks-Bhagat Report. I am grateful to Jitender 'Tibu' Daulet Singh, who did the NDC course with my father in 1983, for talking to me about his father, Lieutenant General Daulet Singh, and also making some photographs available. I am grateful to Chitralekha Bakshi, the younger daughter of Lieutenant General Bijji Kaul; Meena Shyam, the daughter of Lieutenant Colonel C. M. Madiah; Ketaki Singh, the granddaughter of Lieutenant General Umrao Singh; Brigadier Mukul Pant, son of Major B. K. Pant; Labella Kathing Gupta and Professor Labrang Khathing, the children of Major Bob Khathing; Colonel N. J. S. Pannu, the son of Lieutenant Colonel Gurdial Singh; Narender Rathore, the younger brother of Lieutenant Bikram Singh; and many others who generously gave me their time. My grateful thanks also to Claude Arpi, the son-in-law of Major General (at the time Lieutenant Colonel) K. K. Tewari, who put me in touch with some of the other families.

My thanks to Wing Commander B. S. Rathee for having made available the photographs of Brigadier Hoshiar Singh's funeral at Phudung and also Karan Thapar for having given me the photograph of his father, General Pran Thapar. My grateful thanks also to Air Marshal Bharat Kumar, Colonel Amandeep Singh Herr of 20 Lancers, Colonel Balbir Singh of 2 Rajput,

Colonel Ankush Thakur of 13 Mechanised Infantry (18 Rajput) and various others who helped source photographs. Colonel Hunny Bakshi shared his photographs of the Nam Ka Chu, having gone into the valley as a young lieutenant some twenty-seven years after the conflict. He had then returned with a fistful of dog tags recovered from the skeletal remains they unearthed from the various bunkers and trenches. Most of the tags had serial numbers beginning with the numerals '29' denoting 2 Rajput.

It was a happy coincidence that my classmate from school, Dr Atul Bahadur Singh, who lives and practises medicine in Najibabad, should be the nephew of Major Sitaram Johri, who painstakingly documented the fighting in both the NEFA and Ladakh theatres during the face-off with the Chinese. Major Johri had served in NEFA as a political officer, but he made three special trips to Ladakh visiting Dungti, Tsaka-la, Chushul, Phobrang, Tangtse, Darbuk and the Shyok village, meeting and interviewing people. It was ironic that he failed to find a publisher and had to eventually self-publish the books that have been extensively quoted, even in the official history of the 1962 operations. I am most grateful to his family for having made available to me his research papers and notes.

There are many officers who are no more with us today, but whose contribution to the book has been immense. Lieutenant General S. K. Pillai, with whom I discussed the various chapters ad nauseam, was a constant source of encouragement. And finally, my father, who generously handed over all the research notes that he had painstakingly put together for his book, *Rivers of Silence*, which first documented 2 Rajput's battle in Nam Ka Chu. In many ways, this is the book he always wanted to write, and I was grateful for the few extra weeks he got in his sickbed that allowed him to read through the manuscript. My big regret is that I could not publish and release the book before he passed away in March 2015.

I owe a debt of gratitude to dozens of young officers and men who acted as my liaison officers and support units as we trudged across Arunachal from one location to the other where the men had stood and died. Lieutenant Colonels I. P. Singh from 5 Rajput, Vinod Chengappa from 19 Mahar and Amit Sharma from the EME are but a few from a list of many. It was a poignant moment when, sitting on top of a bunker looking towards Tawang from Nuranang, I realized that my liaison officer had tears rolling down his cheek. 'Our generals failed us here,' he said, his voice steady despite the obvious emotion, 'they abandoned these defences. If only we had been allowed to fight, we would have avenged 7 Infantry Brigade here itself.'

The writing of the book spanned many months and I must thank

Aienla Ozukum for firmly keeping me on track. Pujitha Krishnan edited the book and I'm grateful to her for her insightful inputs. My thanks to Bena Sareen for designing the cover.

Finally, my grateful thanks to my family—my mother Usha who, as my father loved to say, followed the drum through thick and thin. When 2 Rajput was deployed in Walong, my mother made the epic journey from Ujjain, where my grandfather was posted, all the way to Tezu with me as a three-month-old baby. The last leg of the journey was across the Digaru River on an elephant that belonged to 2 Assam Rifles. While my father was holding me in his lap, sitting comfortably in front, my mother was 'trailing behind, half drowning, desperately holding the tail of the elephant'. Chakoman Gohain, the Tai Khampti raja, had built a bamboo hut for us to live in. I would spend some delightful evenings with him years later while filming the Namdapha Tiger Reserve as a part of the Project Tiger series, listening to his version of the Battle of Walong.

I must thank my wife Dipti, who as usual was a constant sounding board, helped with not just the research and the structure of the narration, but in so many little ways that I happily take for granted. Both my daughters, Vallika and Veeha, worked tirelessly and painstakingly on the dozen maps that appear in the book, going over various references in minute detail, while constantly helping out with various suggestions. And finally, Blaise, our Labrador retriever, who was my constant companion late into the nights—to all of them I owe a huge thank you, for they allowed me 'leave of absence' for more than two years from my other responsibilities while I struggled with the book, which was in many ways an emotional rollercoaster that affected everything around me. It'll be good to return to the present after having lived for so long in the past.

NOTES

These are some of the abbreviations that appear in the book.

2IC	second-in-command
AAG	Assistant Adjutant General
AVM	Air Vice Marshal
BGS	Brigadier General Staff
CGS	Chief of General Staff (today called Vice Chief of Army Staff)
CHM	company havildar major
C-in-C	Commander-in-Chief
CO	commanding officer
COAS	Chief of Army Staff
DMI	Director, Military Intelligence (now called DGMI)
DMO	Director, Military Operations (now called DGMO)
DZ	drop zone
FOO	forward observation officer
FUP	forming-up point
GOC	General Officer Commanding
GPO	gun position officer
GR	Gorkha Rifles
GSO	General Staff Officer
IB	International Boundary
IO	intelligence officer
JCO	junior commissioned officer (Naib Subedar, Subedar, Subedar Major)
MLI	Maratha Light Infantry
MC Bar	Military Cross & Bar
MC	Military Cross
MMG	medium machine gun
MVC	Maha Vir Chakra
NCO	non-commissioned officer (Lance Naik, Naik, Havildar)
OP	observation post
PVC	Param Vir Chakra
QMG	Quarter Master General
RCL	recoilless (anti-tank direct firing weapons)
LI	Light Infantry
Tac HQ	Tactical Headquarters
VrC	Vir Chakra

All photos in the book are courtesy of the author except where indicated.

CHAPTER 1: GOODBYE TIBET, HELLO CHINA

4 Frankly, we were like headless chickens: in an interview to the author, Gurgaon, 2006
4 India was in a quandary: Brigadier John Dalvi, *Himalayan Blunder*, p 6
5 What Cariappa said: B. N. Mullik, *The Chinese Betrayal*
10 did not wish to dispute the validity of the McMahon Line: Correspondence released by the National Archives (Government of India, External affairs Department, File No. 668.C.A. 1946)
10 the third day of the Iron-Haired Year: Major General D. K. Palit, *Sentinels of the Northeast*, p 194
12 the intrusion by the plainsmen: Ibid, p 197
19 Whereas in the case of Pakistan: Major General D. K. Palit, *War in the High Himalaya*, p 80
23 Nehru has finally told Parliament: H. C. Sarin in conversation with the author in 1992, when he confirmed the Ministry of Defence had no prior warning about the prime minister's announcement.
24 No danger threatens: Major General D. K. Palit, *War in the High Himalaya*, p 20; **Rubbish! Total rubbish**: Ibid
25 A thrill has just passed through the Army: Brigadier John Dalvi, *Himalayan Blunder*, p 50
26 a highly excited state of mind: H. C. Sarin in conversation with Lt Gen A. M. Sethna and the author in 1992
27 rather trivial and of no consequence: Nehru's speech in Lok Sabha, 2 September 1959

CHAPTER 2: AN IMPOTENT HQ

30 His posting to Delhi coincided: Neville Maxwell, *India's China War*, p 187
31 There Kaul had emerged: Lieutenant General S. P. P. Thorat, *From Reveille to Retreat*, pp 176-177
32 Every sepoy in the Army knows: Brigadier John Dalvi, *Himalayan Blunder*, p 89
32 one of our brightest and best officers: Ibid, p 88
34 another party under the direction: Notes, Memoranda and Letters Exchanged between the governments of India and China (September-November 1959), White Paper No. II, Ministry of External Affairs, Government of India. Note of the Indian Government (Kongka Pass), 23 October 1959, p 14
36 Well, gentlemen, you have heard the QMG: Brigadier John Dalvi, *Himalayan Blunder*, pp 82-83
41 After my reconnaissance: Major General D. K. Palit, *War in the High Himalaya*, pp 49-50
44 The Aksai Chin area: Notes, Memoranda and Letters Exchanged and agreements signed between the governments of India and China 1954-1959, Ministry of External Affairs, Government of India
48 I argued against: Major General D. K. Palit, *War in the High Himalaya*, pp 50-51
50 a sad and disillusioned man: Brigadier John Dalvi, *Himalayan Blunder*, p 51
51 that they would have every reason: Notes, Memoranda and Letters Exchanged between the governments of India and China (November 1961 and July 1962), White Paper No. VI, Ministry of External affairs, Government of India. Note of the Indian Government, 30 November 1961, p 4

CHAPTER 3: BLANKS ON THE MAP

70 the plunderers: Dipti Bhalla, Kunal Verma, *Brahma's Creation* (Northeast Trilogy-II), p 79

71 if he persists in his old ways: Melvyn C. Goldstein, *The Snow Lion and the Dragon:* p 20

82 Whatever the position of Tibet: Sahdev Vohra, 'Tibet, India and China', *USI Journal, Volume CXVII Journal No.* 494 (October-December 1988), p 338

83 The area from Amra Tala of Tibet: Report of the officials of the Government of India and the People's Republic of China on the Boundary Question (Records of the Survey of India, Volume VUI, Chinese Report Part II), p 25

86 The dividing line between: Ibid, p 28

86 On the western bank: Ibid

86 an overall settlement of the boundary question: Notes, Memoranda and Letters Exchanged between the governments of India and China, November 1959–March 1960 White Paper No. III, p 71

CHAPTER 4: THE VANGUARD

92 high-handed behaviour: Major General D. K. Palit, *Sentinels of the Northeast*, p 27

101 In conformity with the admitted principle: Charles Bell, *Tibet–Past & Present, Anglo-Russian Agreement 1907*, p 290

103 make us a party: Ibid, p 148

105 preliminary and exploratory: Major General D. K. Palit, *Sentinels of the Northeast*, p 96

108 'big insect' eating up the 'smaller insect': Translation of a Tibetan letter dated the 7th of the 3rd Tibetan month Wood, Bird Year (18 April 1945) from the Tibetan Foreign Office to the Officer-in-Charge, British Mission, Lhasa.

CHAPTER 5: THE EYE OF THE STORM

114 Dalvi reached Tawang on 9 September: Conversation with Wing Commander Hoshang Patel (Reaction to Brigadier John Dalvi's 10 September briefing at Tawang and the 7 Brigade/4 Division appreciation), Bharat Rakshak.

On 10 September, Wing Commander Hoshang Patel, who was part of the IAF Tactical Centre attached to 4 Division had accompanied Niranjan Prasad from Tezpur. Patel also knew Dalvi, having been in college with him. After the briefing, while Dalvi was putting away the stick and the chalk and duster, he turned to Patel, 'So Pat, how did it go?'

'John, very nice briefing…very nice briefing. But you know it's all bullshit.'

Dalvi looked thrown for a second, but quickly regained his composure, 'What's bullshit about it?' he asked.

'John. I am not an Army man but even I know that a brigade sector of defence is less than 500 yards per battalion. And you have only two battalions on hand, and that too, under equipped. As it is, I'm cold now and your people are still in cottons and canvas shoes; even the coolie that carried me up to Tawang was grunting because of the very thin air. Moreover, have you forgotten Korea? Have you learnt nothing from the Korean conflict about their tactics? You say they will not come from here, here and here? Well, that is exactly where they will come from. And with their massed-attack tactics you will be swamped.'

What Dalvi had to say to this unsolicited advice from an air force officer will never be known.

114 Our ability to reinforce: Brigadier John Dalvi, *Himalayan Blunder*, p 192

115 Umrao Singh's cautionary note: Lieutenant General Sen, DSO, was a war hero in every sense of the word. He was a King's Commissioned Officer who had served in North Africa before moving to the Burma front as the second-in-command of 6 Baluch. Along with Thimayya and Thorat, he was the only Indian officer to command a battalion in active operations in the war against the Japanese. In October 1947, he had been promoted to the rank of brigadier and given command of 161 Brigade, which had been given the task of rescuing Srinagar from the tribal lashkars that were even then at the outskirts of the city. He had taken over Eastern Command from Lieutenant General S. P. P. Thorat.

116 the Mago Chu (Tawang Chu): The Mago Chu and the Tawang Chu are essentially the same river. West of Bridge 4 that connected Jang with Tawang, the river is referred to as Tawang Chu. To the east, about two kilometres from the bridge, the Nuranang Chu cascades down as a waterfall and joins the Mago Chu. The confluence of the Nuranang Chu and Mago Chu marks the western limit of the Mago region.

116 I watched air drops at Lumpu: Brigadier John Dalvi, *Himalayan Blunder*, p 203

117 reached Bridge 1: Ibid, p 205

118 had been gross over-reaction: Major General D. K. Palit, *War in the High Himalaya*, p 203

118 operational extravaganza: Ibid

120 Dhola was militarily useless: Brigadier John Dalvi, *Himalayan Blunder*, pp 217-218

122 Annexure 1-A: Record of the Meeting in the Defence Minister's Room on Saturday, 22 September chaired by the Minister of State for Defence, K. Raghuramaiah. Ministry of Defence note 11987/JS(G)/62 signed by H. C. Sarin, Joint Secretary. Raghuramaiah, a lawyer by profession, later took over as the Minister of Defence Production in November 1962.

123 My first reaction: Brigadier John Dalvi, *Himalayan Blunder*, pp 217-236

125 When we met the Corps Commander: Major General Ashok Kalyan Verma, *Rivers of Silence*, p 35

128 I asked whether he felt justified: Major General D. K. Palit, *War in the High Himalaya*, p 221

128 This vital piece of information: Decades later, in the afterglow of Scotch whisky (the general had brought his own bottle of Black Dog) and a scrumptious dinner laid out by Dipti, I asked Palit why he had failed to communicate this vital information to Kaul on their way to the airport on 4 October. Palit ignored my question for almost a minute, and just as I began to wonder if I had inadvertently been rude by asking such a sensitive question, he suddenly said: 'You know, it never occurred to me that Mullik had not shared this information with the prime minister or with Bogey Sen and Pran Thapar. I have, as you can imagine, thought about this lapse on my part often. Yet, somehow I believe that even if I had told Kaul what I knew, it would have made no difference. Both Bogey Sen and Kaul were in a zone where they were only hearing what they wanted to hear. It's hard to explain, but it's true.'

129 Look, old boy: Brigadier John Dalvi, *Himalayan Blunder*, p 260

129 senior officers scurrying away: Ibid, p 261

129 Where is GOC 4 Division: Brigade HQ records of 50 Brigade; Brigadier John Dalvi, *Himalayan Blunder*, p 264

132 A variety of astonished gazes: Brigadier John Dalvi, *Himalayan Blunder*, p 288; Lieutenant Colonel Rikh's notes

134 Oh my god, you are right: Brigadier John Dalvi, *Himalayan Blunder*, p 292

Awards (*History of the Conflict with China*, 1962, History Division, Ministry of Defence, pp 457, 458)

Major Mahander Singh Chaudhary (IC-8164) was awarded the Mahavir Chakra posthumously at Nam Ka Chu on 20 October 1962. It is widely believed that the officer was decorated for his outstanding leadership of the Tseng Jong (Nam Ka Chu) patrol on 10 October

Naik Chain Singh (2437390) was awarded the Mahavir Chakra posthumously at Tseng Jong on 10 October 1962

Sepoy Kanshi Ram (2442148) was awarded the Mahavir Chakra at Tseng Jong on 10 October 1962

Havildar Malkiat Singh (2436723) was awarded the Vir Chakra at Tseng Jong on 10 October 1962

Sepoy Suram Chand (2440890) was awarded the Vir Chakra at Tseng Jong on 10 October 1962

CHAPTER 6: THE VALLEY OF DEATH

143 The Gujjar boys of 3 Rajput: Major General Ashok Kalyan Verma, *Rivers of Silence*, p 19

143 It seems they want: Ibid, p 47

143 These men can fight: Lieutenant Colonel Rikh's notes

145 how big the mouth should be opened: *Counter Attack in Self Defence* (Chinese Army version), p 178

146 gallop up: Ibid

146 We were to hold our position: Brigadier John Dalvi, *Himalayan Blunder*, p 296

146 I had seen with my own eyes: Ibid, pp 309-310

148 throwing out the Chinese: Major General D. K. Palit, *War in the High Himalaya*, p 230

149-150 I can no longer stand by: Brigadier John Dalvi, *Himalayan Blunder*, p 340

150 I now think: Dashrath Singh in conversation with author, Varanasi, 2005

151 It could be a deception: Ibid

152 It looks like it is I who will: As narrated by Major General Ian Cardozo to the author

154 The fear of the unknown: Major General Ashok Kalyan Verma, *Rivers of Silence*, pp 52-53

156 The enemy commenced: Ibid, p 60

158 Ab mein kya karu: Ibid, p 62

158 The enemy after having been: Ibid, p 63

159 Make your fire count: Brigadier Rikh's notes

160 the defensive battle: Ibid

161 My god, they are going to: Lieutenant Colonel Gurdial Singh in a conversation with the author in 1992

162 Captain Bhatia and I: Major General Ashok Kalyan Verma, *Rivers of Silence:* pp 68-69

164 I told Subedar Phool Singh: Major General Ashok Kalyan Verma, *Rivers of Silence:*

pp 71-73; Lieutenant Colonel Mustasad Ahmad, *Living up to Heritage: The Rajputs 1947 to 1970*, pp 192-193
164 As a prisoner of war: Major General Ashok Kalyan Verma, *Rivers of Silence:* pp 74-75

Awards (*History of the Conflict with China, 1962*, History Division, Ministry of Defence, p 459)
Captain Gurucharan Singh Bhatia of 2 Rajput (IC-8596) was awarded the Vir Chakra posthumously at Nam Ka Chu on 20 October 1962
Major Gurdial Singh (IC-1880) was awarded the Maha Vir Chakra at Nam Ka Chu on 20 October 1962.
Havildar Saudagar Singh of 2 Rajput (2932655) was awarded the Vir Chakra posthumously at Nam Ka Chu on 20 October 1962
Subedar Brajendra Chandra Roy of 2 Rajput (IC-40451) was awarded the Vir Chakra at the Dhola area on 20 October 1962
Sepoy Jagpal Singh of 2 Rajput (2944566) was awarded the Vir Chakra posthumously at the Dhola area on 20 October 1962
Sepoy (Ambulance Assistant) S. Joseph of 20 Field Ambulance (6797987) was awarded the Vir Chakra posthumously in NEFA on 20 October 1962

CHAPTER 7: FALLBACK ON TAWANG

165 I was alone and lonely: Brigadier John Dalvi, *Himalayan Blunder*, p 357
166 You guys are talking about: Records of 50 Brigade HQ
172 Stragglers and walking wounded: Major General Niranjan Prasad, *The Fall of Towang*, quoted by Major General D. K. Palit in *Sentinels of the North-east*, p 243
174 But it is alleged: Captain Amarinder Singh, *Lest We Forget*, p 177
178 the gunners saw a Bell two-seater helicopter: Second Lieutenant A. J. S Behl in an interview with the author, Chandigarh, 2015: The two-seater Bell helicopter took off from the 4 Division HQ with Major Ram Singh on board. As it approached the vicinity of Tsangdhar, the Chinese engaged it. Second Lieutenant A. J. S Behl, who was commanding the 17 Para Field gun position at Tsangdhar, watched from his position: 'We saw a helicopter approaching the helipad. By that time small arms fire had also started from the black rock area and shelling was also going on. There was no sign of the helicopter taking off again. I sent a patrol of two men to see what had happened. They came back and told me that that the helicopter was there, and two persons; one pilot and another person in a red turban, were lying dead near the helicopter.'
Later in the day, around midday a second helicopter approached Tsangdhar and again came under intense fire from the black rock area. The gunners watched as the helicopter then banked away, after it appeared to have taken a few hits. By 1500 hrs Behl's position was overrun by the Chinese and he along with his men were taken prisoner. The captured men were made to stay at Tsangdhar that night. The next morning, Behl was allowed by the Chinese to bury the two Indian officers. Behl positively could identify them as Squadron Leader Vinod Sehgal and Major Ram Singh of the Corps of Signals.
179 The withdrawal from Tsangdhar: Interview with the author in Chandigarh, 2014
179 They saw a large number: Ibid
180 I decided to go with him: Major General Niranjan Prasad, *The Fall of Towang*, pp 103-104

182 Unbelievably, that was the last: Captain Amarinder Singh, *Lest We Forget*, p 180
185 If only our artillery: Darshan Brigadier Khullar, *When Generals Failed*, p 98, and also in conversation with the author in Ambala in 2015
187 Thapar, Menon, Mullik and Sarin: Major General D. K. Palit, *War in the High Himalaya*, p 244
187 I had at first been regarded: Ibid, p 75
187 After my reconnaissance of the Bum-la region: Ibid, p 65
187 Afterwards I had sent Major Raja Fulay: Ibid, p 66

Awards (*History of the Conflict with China, 1962*, History Division, Ministry of Defence, pp 457-459)
Second Lieutenant Naveen Chand Kohli of 9 Punjab (IC-12955) was awarded the Vir Chakra posthumously at Nam Ka Chu on 20 October 1962
Major Sher Pratap Singh Shrikent of 1/9 GR (IC-5192) awarded Maha Vir Chakra at Tsangdhar
Captain Mahabir Prasad of 1 Sikh attached to 1/9 GR (IC-8423) awarded Maha Vir Chakra posthumously at Tsangdhar
Subedar Bhab Bahadur Katwal of 1/9 GR (JC-5180) awarded the Vir Chakra posthumously at Tsangdhar
Havildar Kaula Singh Thapa of 1/9 GR (5831357) was awarded the Vir Chakra posthumously at Tsangdhar on 20 October 1962
Havildar Ganga Bahadur Rawat of 1/9 GR (5832160) was awarded the Vir Chakra posthumously at Tsangdhar on 20 October 1962
Second Lieutenant Gopalakrishna Venkatesa Prasanna Rao of 4 Grenadiers (IC 13413) was awarded the Mahavir Chakra posthumously at Drokung Samba Bridge, Khenzemane
Lance Naik Sardar Singh of 4 Grenadiers (2640716) was awarded the Vir Chakra posthumously at Drokung Samba Bridge, Khenzemane

CHAPTER 8: WHEN GENERALS FAIL

189 audacious action: Larry M. Wortzel, *The Lessons of History: The Chinese People's Liberation Army at 75*, p 327
194 What is it that you wish to convey: Major General D. K. Palit, *War in the High Himalaya*, p 246
198 the distant sound of artillery fire: Brigadier Darshan Khullar, *When Generals Failed*, p 106
199 To the north of Tawang: *Counter Attack in Self Defence*, Page 202-3
202 unobtrusively pulled him: Major General D. K. Palit, *War in the High Himalaya*, p 251
202 perfunctory and misleading: Ibid, p 252
202 I interrupted to protest: Ibid
203 potential to be the Kohima: Kohima was where the British Indian army stopped the Japanese advance into the plains of Assam during World War II
204 By the time the retreating party: On 2 December 1962, after IV Corps had been reduced to a complete shambles, Lieutenant General (later Field Marshal) Sam Manekshaw took over IV Corps from Bijji Kaul. His first address to his staff in Tezpur took less than fifteen seconds to deliver: 'Gentleman, I have arrived. There will be no more withdrawals in IV Corps. Thank you.' This was followed up by his 'Order of the

Day' to all ranks in the formation: 'From now onwards there will be no withdrawals except on my personal orders which will not be given. We shall stand and fight where we dig in. Remember, we are all expendable; the reputation of the army is not, nor is the honour of the country.' What a pity that none of the commanders in the months leading up to December had the guts to underline this one simple fact. Even if Tawang had fallen eventually, it would have perhaps been better to stand and die there, rather than get picked up by the Chinese like birds frightened by 'the mere twang of the enemy's bow'! (Brigadier Behram M. Panthaki and Zenobia Panthaki, *Field Marshal Sam Manekshaw: The Man and his Times,* p 58)

205 I had received the impression: Major General D. K. Palit, *War in the High Himalaya*, p 259

206 The scene around the convoy: Brigadier Darshan Khullar, *When Generals Failed*, p 113

Awards (*History of the Conflict with China, 1962*, History Division, Ministry of Defence (Appendix VIII, Gallantry Award Winners, pp 457-462)

Subedar Joginder Singh of 1 Sikh (JC-4547) was awarded the Param Vir Chakra at IB Ridge (Bum-la) on 23 October 1962. Joginder Singh was taken prisoner and he was to die in the POW camp later after he refused to have his toes amputated by Chinese doctors

Lieutenant Hari Pal Kaushik of 1 Sikh (IC-11811) was awarded the Vir Chakra at Tongpengla (Bum-la area) on 23 October 1962.

CHAPTER 9: THE BATTLE OF WALONG

213 The Lohit Frontier Division, unlike Kameng: I first saw Walong from the air when I flew in an AN-32 that was dropping a supply load over the runway in 1992. Looking down at the jungle clad hills and the almost uninhabited Lohit Valley, it was fairly obvious that little had changed in the thirty years since the 1962 Indo-China War. In a way, I was retracing the route taken by my father as a young captain, for towards the end of 1959, he had flown into Walong with the first company of 2 Rajput.

216 At Walong the river divided the battalion's deployment: Major General Ashok Kalyan Verma, *Rivers of Silence:* p 22, and from personal notes

217 Monyul, the area of Lower Tsayul: Notes, Memoranda and Letters Exchanged and agreements signed between the Governments of India and China (1954-1959), White Paper, Chinese communication of 28 September 1958, Ministry of External Affairs, Government of India

225 We never thought: Major Kulwant Singh in an interview with the author in New Delhi, 2014

230 I saw the casualties: Lieutenant General Brij Mohan Kaul, *The Untold Story*

239 There were still some of the Gorkhas: In conversation with the author in New Delhi, 2014

239 Since 26 October, their guns had been trying to bracket: Mishmis in Kibithu would recall the daily columns of pack animals brought in from Rima—yaks, dzos and ponies—that would leave for Walong with ammunition and supplies and return with the Chinese dead

242 I overheard several telephone conversations: Lieutenant General Brij Mohan Kaul, *The Untold Story*

244 that he sounded so desperate: Major General D. K. Palit, *War in the High*

Himalaya, pp 301-302

239 The blast lifted me off my feet: Captain Kulwant Singh lay there for two days; despite multiple fractures, the officer was fully conscious. The only thought in his head was to get to the water below. Then a Chinese party came down the track. They fired a single shot and the bullet hit him on the thigh. They checked to see if he was dead and, believing that to be the case, left after taking his identity card. However, since the Chinese were on the lookout for officers, they came back the next day and picked him up. By then Walong had fallen and he was taken to a field hospital near the runway. Two or three weeks later, a Red Cross Otter picked him up and flew him back to Tezu.

Awards (*History of the Conflict with China, 1962*, History Division, Ministry of Defence, pp 459-461)

Naik Bahadur Singh of 6 Kumaon (413962) was awarded the Vir Chakra posthumously at McMahon Ridge, Kibithu area, on 21 October 1962

Rifleman Purna Bahadur Tamang of 2 Assam Rifles (29659) was awarded the Vir Chakra in the Kibithu area on 22 October 1962

Sepoy Kewal Singh of 4 Sikh (3349770) was awarded the Maha Vir Chakra posthumously at Mithun, Walong area, on 26-27 October 1962

Second Lieutenant Pradeep Singh Bhandari (IC-123221) of 71 Heavy Mortar Battery was awarded the Vir Chakra at Green Pimple on 3 November 1962

Subedar Jagandhoy Limbu of 2 Assam Rifles (26460) was awarded the Vir Chakra at Walong on 4 November 1962

Captain Ravi Kumar Mathur of 6 Kumaon (IC-10156) was awarded the Vir Chakra at Walong on 6 November 1962

Captain Balbir Chand Chopra from the AMC (MS6455) was awarded the Vir Chakra at Walong on 14 November 1962

2/Lt Amar Singh Khatri of 6 Kumaon (IC-12970) was awarded the Vir Chakra at Yellow Pimple on 14 November 1962

Captain Prem Nath Bhatia of 6 Kumaon (IC-7077) was awarded the Vir Chakra at Walong on 15 November 1962

Lieutenant Yog Raj Palta of 4 Sikh (IC-11832) was awarded the Vir Chakra posthumously at Walong on 15 November 1962

Havildar Kirpa Ram of 4 Sikh (3330962) was awarded the Vir Chakra posthumously at Walong on 15 November 1962

CHAPTER 10: FORTRESS SE-LA

248 At the time, unaccountably: Major General D. K. Palit, *War in the High Himalaya*, p 50

256 The Chinese knew everything: Tashi Sonam in a conversation with the author in 2009 in Tawang

In 2008 the author met Tashi Sonam, a former Intelligence operative in Tawang. The Intelligence officer accompanying me said: 'He was present in Tawang when the Chinese came here in 1962. He was one of the key people working for the Intelligence Bureau at that time and continued to work for them till he retired.'

Over cups of tea, the old man enthralled us with his stories. I suppose the years he had to spend in silence as a spy, keeping his identity a secret, was having the opposite effect on him now. He spoke lucidly of the many trips he had made to Lhasa as an agent, and the various routes and passes that linked Tibet across the watershed to India. He then mentioned 1942 in passing, referring to it as the first Tibetan invasion. Even though he said it more than once, I presumed the old man had got his dates mixed up by a couple of decades, and did not contradict him. A year later, I was working on the Assam Rifles book. A lot that Tashi Sonam had said in passing now began to make sense. Fortunately, I was again invited by the brigade in Tawang to photograph the flag meeting with the Chinese at Bum-la. Needless to say, I didn't need any prompting, and was back in Tawang in a flash. This was an excellent opportunity to experience the conditions (it was October) and go over the ground on which the battle had been fought by 5 Assam Rifles and 1 Sikh. Though I wasn't properly acclimatized, fortunately, I had little trouble on Bum-la other than the mandatory headache. As soon as we dropped down to Tawang, which is at 10,000 feet, that too disappeared and I went off to find Tashi Sonam again. It was ironical that the old man could not remember our earlier meeting a few months previously, but could recall dates and figures from fifty-sixty years ago without having to refer to any notes. He wanted to go over all the ground we had covered the last time, step by step, but I was in a hurry, so I repeatedly tried to steer him to the two events I was interested in. What happened in 1942 and then in 1950? He would have none of it though, and proceeded at his own pace. Finally, he came around to 1942. 'I was a young boy then,' said the former IB operative, 'but I subsequently joined one of my uncles who marched at the head of the Tibetan column when it came over Tse-la and Posheng-la to Dirang. I did odd jobs in the camp and was quite popular with the soldiers, who would play and joke with me all the time. Where they went and what they did, I had no idea, but I knew quite a few of them after a few days.'

Much later, when working for the IB, it became obvious to Tashi Sonam why the Tibetan Army had come. They knew the boundary treaty had been signed with Britain in 1913, and any concessions on Tawang which was on the Indian side of the line would be difficult as the British were very powerful and determined. Around mid-1942, there was a chance that the momentum of the Japanese invasion would extend through Burma into Assam. Suddenly, cracks had begun to emerge in the Asian mind about British supremacy, and for the watching Tibetans, should Japan be the new masters of Assam, it was necessary to have Tibetan troops present on the ground. The invasion of Tawang, therefore had little or nothing to do with Tawang itself. The objective was to get as far south as possible. In the event of a fresh boundary being drawn up with Imperial Japan, Tibet wanted in on what till just a few years previously was known as 'unadministered area'. Once it became apparent that they could not get across the Naga-Patkai and the Arakan Hills, the Tibetans quietly withdrew.

Tashi Sonam was popular with the Tibetan soldiers, and in later years had maintained his contact with a couple of them. Twenty years later, after the Nam Ka Chu and the Bum-la battles, the Chinese captured Tawang. Though the Chinese were quite averse to pandering to the lamas, the Chinese commanders decided to visit the main Tawang Monastery. Tashi Sonam and other prominent people were present in the monastery where the Chinese were welcomed as honoured guests and were presented scarves by the abbot. Usually it was never easy to identify who were the important Chinese officials. Present with the Chinese commander were a handful of Tibetans. Tashi Sonam recognized one of them—he had been a part of the Tibetan Army in 1942. Twice more in the next few days, Tashi Sonam was to see the Chinese commander. On both occasions, the former soldier was always part of the accompanying group.

The Monpas in 1962 did whatever they could to help in the defence of Tawang. The

Chinese had started infiltrating agents into the area ever since the mid-1950s, and the once the Indian Army moved into the area, 'the Chinese had a far better understanding of their ground reality than our own Indian commanders in Tezpur, Lucknow and Delhi'. For the Chinese operatives, no detail was of little consequence as each bit of information was relayed to their handlers. When the Chinese finally reached Tawang, according to Tashi Sonam, they had interpreters who could speak in almost all the Indian languages.

The icing on the cake, according to Tashi Sonam, was when a Chinese agent managed to attach himself to Lieutenant General B. M. Kaul, even helping to carry the general to Nam Ka Chu on his back. Fluent in both Hindi and English, the man had reported at Le the next day with precise details of the initial conversations between Kaul and Dalvi.

257 We've got those bastards: Dibyesh Anand, *Remembering 1962 Sino Indian Border War*, p 189

259 'the head,' he said, 'is like copper': *Counter Attack in Self Defence*, p 206

262 An officer from 2 Grenadiers: Interview with Colonel C. M. Verma, Gurgaon 2014

262 The terrain along the route: Lieutenant Colonel Mustasad Ahmad, *Living Up To Heritage: The Rajputs 1947 to 1970*, pp 205-206

265 4 Rajput were celebrating: Lieutenant Colonel J.R. Saigal, *The Unfought War of 1962*

266 We saw them moving: Lieutenant Colonel Mustasad Ahmad, *Living up to Heritage: The Rajputs 1947 to 1970*, p 212

Awards (*History of the Conflict with China, 1962*, History Division, Ministry of Defence, pp 457, 461)

Second Lieutenant Vinod Kumar Goswami (IC-12323) was awarded the Vir Chakra posthumously for his action north of the Tawang Chu on 14 November 1962. After volunteering to supply ammunition to the forward platoon of Alpha Company on 17 November, the officer was killed during the withdrawal later in the evening

Rifleman Madan Singh Rawat (4040008) was awarded the Vir Chakra posthumously for the action north of the Tawang Chu

Lieutenant Colonel B. M. Bhattacharjea (IC-1338) was awarded the Maha Vir Chakra at Nuranang on 17 November 1962

Rifleman Jaswant Singh Rawat (4039009) was awarded the Maha Vir Chakra posthumously at Nuranang on 17 November 1962.

Lance Naik Trilok Singh Negi (4037614) was awarded the Vir Chakra posthumously at Nuranang on 17 November 1962

Rifleman Gopal Singh Gusain (4038646) was awarded the Vir Chakra at Nuranang on 17 November 1962

Second Lieutenant Surinder Nath Tandon (IC-12691) was awarded the Vir Chakra at Nuranang on 17 November 1962

Subedar Udai Singh Rawat (JC-12691) was awarded the Vir Chakra at Nuranang on 17 November 1962

Jemadar Jatan Singh Gusain (JC-10921) was awarded the Vir Chakra at Nuranang on 17 November 1962

Havildar Govind Kamble of 7 Mahar (4529486) was awarded the Vir Chakra at Se-la on 17 November 1962

CHAPTER 11: THE IMPLOSION

274 Why were they withdrawn… I hope you will reverse: Major General D. K. Palit, *War in the High Himalaya*, pp 308-309

279 on no account: Dr P. B. Sinha and Colonel A. A. Athale, *History of the Conflict with China*, Official Records, History Division, Ministry of Defence, Chapter 5, Notes 109

280 a very steady and defensive battle: Ibid, p 179

280 The Chinese have ruthlessly: Major General Jaidev Singh Datta, *Recollections of the Se La-Bomdila Debacle 1962*, p 34

281 The General Officer Commanding 4 Infantry Division: Ibid, pp 35-36

283 without waiting for preliminaries: Major General D. K. Palit, *War in the High Himalaya*, p 312

283 he would take off on a description: Ibid and Dr P. B. Sinha and Colonel A. A. Athale, *History of the Conflict with China*, 1962, Official Records, History Division, Ministry of Defence, Chapter 5

284 With a somewhat derisive: Major General D. K. Palit, *War in the High Himalaya*, p 314

286 The imperative of holding: Brigadier Darshan Khullar, *When Generals Failed*, p 127

289 Something awful has happened: Dr P. B. Sinha and Colonel A. A. Athale, *History of the Conflict with China, 1962*, Official Records, History Division, Ministry of Defence, Chapter 5

293 4 Infantry Division has pulled out: Major General D. K. Palit, *War in the High Himalaya*, p 322

296 he fought the rest of the war: Colonel Anil Kaul, Bijji Kaul's nephew in a conversation with the author in Gurgaon, 2015

Awards

Captain Rudolph David Rosario of 2 Sikh LI (IC-8228) was awarded the Vir Chakra posthumously at Jang on 30 October 1962 (He was later killed on Se-la.)

CHAPTER 12: THE FINAL COUNTDOWN

306 There was a strange quietude: Brigadier Darshan Khullar, *When Generals Failed*, p 204

311 As the DMO, Army Headquarters: Major General D. K. Palit, *War in the High Himalaya*, p 328

311 It was nearing dusk: Brigadier Darshan Khullar, *When Generals Failed*, p 221 and in conversation with the author in Ambala, 2015

314 It so happened: Brigadier Darshan Khullar, *When Generals Failed*, p 222

316 When in the late afternoon: Ibid, p 226

318 There was a nightmarish… not put our hands up: Major General D. K. Palit, *War in the High Himalaya*, pp 323-327

CHAPTER 13: THE WESTERN SECTOR

328 We regularly gave them: J. M. Nath in a telephonic conversation with the author

360 At 9 a.m. Ram Singh: The men of Charlie Company of 13 Kumaon were all Ahirs. After the fighting, when Indian troops reached Rezang-la they found that the Chinese had pinned pieces of paper on bayonets with the words 'Brave Indian Soldier' written in blood. The story of 13 Kumaon at Rezang-la, however, has got unnecessarily distorted, with some Indian writers feeling the need to inflate the number of Chinese killed. There is no doubt that the Chinese had severe casualties, but they are highly unlikely to be anywhere close to what is made out by the popular media.

361 no move to occupy these two positions: On 4 December, after the ceasefire, an Indian patrol from 5 Jat went to Foot Hill and the men ran into a minefield. Naib Subedar Balwant Singh had his leg blown off. Since these mines had been laid on the Indian side of the post, it was obvious the Chinese had visited the region and mined it.

362 I consulted Bijji this morning: Major General D. K. Palit, *War in the High Himalaya*, p 330-331

364 I fear that mindlessly: Ibid, p 332

365 It was indeed a pathetic sight: Lieutenant General, S. P. P. Thorat, *From Reveille to Retreat*

367 If we were to withdraw from the South Bank: Major General D. K. Palit, *War in the High Himalaya*, pp 339-340

369 the situation in NEFA Command: Prime Minister Nehru's letters written to the US President J. F. Kennedy on 19 November 1962, Declassified letters, JFK Library, Washington DC

372 There were no staff officers: Wing Commander M. Sadatulla, *1962 War: Supplying from the Air*, p 88

372 slightly drooping, in a crumpled uniform: Ibid, p 90

Awards (*History of the Conflict with China, 1962*, History Division, Ministry of Defence, pp 457, 461)

Subedar Sonam Stopdhan of 14 J&K Militia (9100419) was awarded the Maha Vir Chakra posthumously at Chandani Post on 19 October 1962

Havildar Sarup Singh of 14 J&K Militia (9105087) was awarded the Maha Vir Chakra posthumously at Bhujang Post on 19 October 1962

Captain Raja Amirthalingam from AMC (MS-6497) was awarded the Vir Chakra in Ladakh on 19 October 1962

Jemadar Rigzin Phunchok of 14 J&K Militia (9100488) was awarded the Vir Chakra at Bhujang Post on 19 October 1962

Havildar Tulsi Ram of 14 J&K Militia (9125198) was awarded the Vir Chakra at Ramu Post on 19 October 1962

Sepoy Dorje Phunchok of 14 J&K Militia (9135605) was awarded the Vir Chakra at Chandani Post on 19 October 1962

Brigadier Tapishwar Narain Raina from Kumaon Regiment (IC-1850) was awarded the Maha vir Chakra in Ladakh on 20 October 1962

Major Sardul Singh Randhawa from Rajput Regiment with 14 J&K Militia (IC-2651) was awarded the Maha Vir Chakra at Karakoram Pass and Chip Chap River on 20 October 1962

Subedar Dewan Chand of 14 J&K Militia (JC-25926) was awarded the Vir Chakra at Takkar Post on 20 October 1962

CHM Anant Ram of 14 J&K Militia (9130040) was awarded the Vir Chakra at DBO on 20 October 1962

Sepoy Sonam Wangchuk of 14 J&K Militia (9136074) was awarded the Vir Chakra posthumously in Ladakh on 20 October 1962

Sepoy Sonam Angchok of 14 J&K Militia (9136074) was awarded the Vir Chakra posthumously at Chandani Post on 20 October 1962

Subedar Nihal Singh of 5 Jat (JC-6022) was awarded the Vir Chakra posthumously in the Galwan Area on 20 October 1962

Major Dhan Singh Thapa of 1/8 GR (IC-7990) was awarded the Param Vir Chakra at Srijap on 21 October 1962

Naik Rabi Lal Thapa of 1/8 GR (5733537) was awarded the Maha Vir Chakra at Srijap on 21 October 1962

Lance Naik Raghavan of the Engineer Regiment (1315743) was was awarded the Vir Chakra in Ladakh on 21 October 1962

Rifleman Tulsi Ram Thapa of 1/8 GR (5739236) was awarded the Vir Chakra at Srijap on 21 October 1962

Sepoy Lobrang Chhiring of 14 J&K Militia (9139798) was awarded the Vir Chakra posthumously at Chandani Post on 21 October 1962

Major Ajit Singh of 5 Jat (IC-3276) was awarded the Maha Vir Chakra at Nulla junction on 22 October 1962

Second Lieutenant Harish Chander Gujral of 5 Jat (IC-12920) was awarded the Vir Chakra in Ladakh on 22 October 1962

Havildar Dharam Singh of 5 Jat (3138184) was awarded the Vir Chakra in Ladakh on 22 October 1962

Naik Munshi Ram of 5 Jat (3132623) was awarded the Vir Chakra posthumously in Ladakh on 22 October 1962

Jemadar Ishe Tundup of 7 J&K Militia (9100075) was awarded the Maha Vir Chakra posthumously at Changla Post on 27 October 1962

Havildar Satigian Phunchok of 7 J&K Militia (9100170) was awarded the Maha Vir Chakra posthumously at Changla Post on 27 October 1962

Naik Chhimat Dorje of 7 J&K Militia (9100678) was awarded the Vir Chakra in Ladakh on 27 October 1962

Signalman Dharam Chand Dhilan of the Corps of Signals (6280652) was awarded the Vir Chakra posthumously in Ladakh on 27 October 1962

Sepoy Sonam Rabges of 7 J&K Militia was awarded the Vir Chakra posthumously in Ladakh on 27 October 1962

Major Shaitan Singh of 13 Kumaon (IC-6400) was awarded the Param Vir Chakra at Rezang-la on 18 November 1962

Second Lieutenant Shyamal Dev Goswami from the Regiment of Artillery (IC-12665) was awarded the Maha Vir Chakra at Gurung Hill on 18 November 1962

Captain Purushottam Lal Kher of 1/8 GR (IC-6405) was awarded the Vir Chakra at Gurung Hill on 18 November 1962

Jemadar Tej Bahadur Gurung of 1/8 GR (JC-7024) was awarded the Vir Chakra posthumously at Gurung Hill on 18 November 1962

Captain Ashwani Kumar Dewan of 20 Lancers (IC-7024) was awarded the Vir Chakra at Chushul on 18 November 1962

Gunner (Technical Assistant) Gurdip Singh of Artillery Regiment (1155599) was awarded the Vir Chakra posthumously at Chushul on 18 November 1962

Jemadar Ram Chander of 13 Kumaon (4132072) was awarded the Vir Chakra at Rezang-la on 18 November 1962

Jemadar Surja of 13 Kumaon (4136414) was awarded the Vir Chakra posthumously at Rezang-la on 18 November 1962

Jemadar Hari Ram of 13 Kumaon (4132208) was awarded the Vir Chakra posthumously at Rezang-la on 18 November 1962

Naik Hukam Chand of 13 Kumaon (4140476) was awarded the Vir Chakra posthumously at Rezang-la on 18 November 1962

Naik Gulab Singh of 13 Kumaon (4140983) was awarded the Vir Chakra posthumously at Rezang-la on 18 November 1962

Naik Ram Kumar Yadav of 13 Kumaon (4139673) was awarded the Vir Chakra posthumously at Rezang-la on 18 November 1962

Lance Naik Sing Ram of 13 Kumaon (4134106) was awarded the Vir Chakra posthumously at Rezang-la on 18 November 1962

Sepoy (Nursing Assistant) Dharampal Singh Dahiya of AMC was awarded the Vir Chakra posthumously at Rezang-la on 18 November 1962

EPILOGUE: THE MISSING LINKS

374 He (Gandhi) knew: Jawaharlal Nehru, *The Discovery of India*, p 452

374 We did not realize that whenever China: Interview with former defence minister V. K. Krishna Menon, *the Times of India,* 16 October 1968

375 it did not wish to institute an enquiry: Major General D. K. Palit, *War in High Himalaya*, p 391

375 It did not wish to institute: Ibid

378 occupying the last ridge: Major Sitaram Johri, *Chinese Invasion of NEFA*

379 The Chinese leaders recognized: *The Sino-Indian Border Dispute, Prelude to Negotiations*: Fall 1959 – January 1960, Central Intelligence Agency

382 Every one talks of General Bijji Kaul: In conversation with the author in 1992, New Delhi. The interview was in connection with the making of the historical film, Salt of the Earth, on the IAF's Diamond Jubilee.

382 I flew the Hurricane: Interview with the author in New Delhi, 1992

383 Well Sir, if the army doesn't know what to do: Wing Commander M. Sadatulla, *1962 War: Supplying from the Air*, pp 57-58

384 We had the run of the skies: Interview with the author in New Delhi, 1992

386 In my experience: Field Marshal William Slim, *Defeat into Victory*

392 What happened to us in Ladakh: Ibid

393 they ruthlessly indulged: Major Sitaram Johri, *Chinese Invasion of NEFA*, p 190

393 The immediate aim of the Chinese: Ibid

394 As the Tibet issue had its cabal: Bertil Lintner, *Great Game East*, p 34

394 In the case of Maxwell: Ibid

Awards (*History of the Conflict with China, 1962*, History Division, Ministry of Defence, pp 457, 461)

Squadron Leader Jagmohan Nath (GD(P) 3964) was awarded the Maha Vir Chakra

Squadron Leader Chandan Singh (GD(P) 3460) was awarded the Vir Chakra

BIBLIOGRAPHY

Ahmad, Lieutenant Colonel Mustasad, *Living up to the Heritage: The Rajputs: 1947 to 1970*, New Delhi: Lancer Publishers, 1997

Bell, Charles, *Tibet Past and Present*, London: Asian Educational Services, 1924

Bhutani, Sudarshan, *A Clash of Political Cultures: Sino-Indian Relations (1957–1962)*, New Delhi: Roli Books, 2004

Bowles, Chester, *Promises to Keep: My Years in Public Life, 1941-1969*, New Delhi: BI Publications, 1972

Dalvi, Brigadier J. P., *Himalayan Blunder: The Curtain-raiser to the Sino-Indian War in 1962*, Dehradun: Natraj Publishers, 1997

Das, Colonel Gautam, Understanding the Sino-Indian War 1962, Military Affairs *Series, Har-Anand Publications, New Delhi 2013*

Datta, Major General Jaidev Singh, *Recollections of the Se La Bomdila Debacle 1962*, New Delhi: KWW Publishers, 2013

Elwin, Verrier, *A Philosophy for NEFA*, Itanagar: Government of Arunachal Pradesh, 1958

———, *The Tribal World of Verrier Elwin: An Autobiography*, New York: Oxford University Press, 1964

Evans, Humphrey, *Thimayya of India*, Dehradun: Natraj Publishers, 1988

Fravel, Taylor M., *Strong Borders, Secure Nation: Cooperation and Conflict in China's Territorial Disputes*, Princeton: Princeton University Press, 2008

Fürer-Haimendorf, Christoph von, *Highlanders of Arunachal Pradesh: Anthropological Research in North-East India*, New Delhi: Vikas Publishing House, 1982

———, *Himalayan Barbary*, London: John Murray, 1955.

———, *The APA Tanis and Their Neighbours*, London: Routledge, 1962

———, *Tribes of India: The Struggle for Survival*, California: University of California Press, 1982

Goldstein, Melvyn C., *The Snow Lion and the Dragon: China, Tibet and the Dalai Lama*, California: University of California Press, 1999

Grunfeld, A. Tom, *The Making of Modern Tibet*, New York: M. E. Sharpe, 1996

Halper, Lezlee Brown & Stefan, *Tibet: An Unfinished Story*, London: Oxford University Press, 2014

Hoffmann, Steven A., *India and the China Crisis*, London: University of California Press, 1990

Johri, Major Sitaram, *Chinese Invasion of Ladakh*, Lucknow: Himalaya Publications, 1969

———, *Chinese Invasion of NEFA*, Lucknow: Himalaya Publications, 1968

Kapadia, Harish, *Into the Untraveled Himalaya: Travels, Treks and Climbs*, New Delhi: Indus Publishing, 2005

Kaul, Lieutenant General Brij Mohan, *The Untold Story*, Mumbai: Allied Publishers, 1967

Khullar, Brigadier Darshan, *When Generals Failed: The Chinese Invasion*, New Delhi: Manas Publications, 1999

Kingdon-Ward, Frank, *Land of the Blue Poppy*, London: Cambridge University Press, 1913

———, *Mystery Rivers of Tibet*, London: Seeley Service & Co., 1923

———, *Plant Hunting at the Edge of the World*, London: Victor Gollancz Ltd., 1930

Kumar, Air Marshal Bharat, *Unknown and Unsung: The IAF in Sino-Indian War of 1962* New Delhi: KW Publishers, 2013

Lal, John, *Aksai Chin & Sino-Indian Conflict*, Ahmedabad: Allied Publishers, 1988

Lamb, Alastair, *British India and Tibet, 1766-1910*, London: Taylor & Francis, *1986*

———, *McMahon Line: Hardinge and the Simla Conference*, London: Routledge & K Paul, 1966

Manohar, D. R., *The Guilty Men of 1962*, Mumbai: Tulsi Shah Enterprises, 1968

McKay, Alex, *Tibet and the British Raj: The Frontier Cadre, 1904-1947*, Surrey: Curzon Press, 1997

Mehra, Parshotam, *Essays in Frontier History: India, China, and the Disputed Border*, New Delhi: Oxford University Press, 2007

Mullik, B. N., *My Years with Nehru: The Chinese Betrayal*, New Delhi: Allied Publishers, 1971

Nehru, B. K., *Nice Guys Finish Second*, New Delhi: Viking Penguin India, 1997

O'Connor, W. F. Captain, *Report on Tibet*, Calcutta: Office of the Superintendent of Government Printing–India, 1903

Palit, Major General D. K., *Sentinels of the North-East: the Assam Rifles*, New Delhi: Palit & Palit, 1984

———, *War in the High Himalaya: The Indian Army in Crisis, 1962*, London: C Hurst & Co. Publishers, 1991

Prasad, Major General Niranjan, *The Fall of Towang*, New Delhi: Palit & Palit, 1981

Raghavan, K. N., *Dividing Lines: Contours of India-China Conflict*, Mumbai: Leadstart Publishing, 2012

Rustomji, Nari Kaikhosru, *Enchanted Frontiers: Sikkim, Bhutan and India's North-Eastern Borderlands*, New Delhi: Oxford University Press, 1971

Sadatulla, Wing Commander M., *1962 War Supplying From The Air*, New Delhi: KW Publishers, 2012

Saigal, J. R., *The Unfought War of 1962: The NEFA Debacle*, Mumbai: Allied Publishers, 1979

Singh, Amar Kaur Jasbir, *Himalayan Triangle: Historical Survey of British India's Relations with Tibet, Sikkim and Bhutan*, 1765-1950, London: British Library, 1988

Singh, Captain Amarinder, *Lest We Forget*, Patiala: Regiment of Ludhiana Welfare Association, 1999.

Singh, Major General Jogindar, *Behind the Scenes: An Analysis of India's Military Operations 1947-71*, New Delhi: Lancer Publishers, 1993

Singh, Brigadier Lakshman, *Letters from the Border and Other Less Told Stories*, Noida: BSL Publishers, 2003

Thorat, Lieutenant General S. P. P., *From Reveille to Retreat*, Mumbai: Allied Publishers, 1986

Tsou, Byron N., *China and International Law: The Boundary Dispute*, New York: Praeger Publishers, 1990

Verma, Major General Ashok Kalyan, *Rivers of Silence: Disaster on River Nam Ka Chu, 1962,* New Delhi: Lancer Publishers, 1998

Verma, Kunal and Bhalla, Dipti, *Assam Rifles: 1835-2010*, Gurgaon: KaleidoIndia, *2010*

Wangchuck, Her Majesty Ashi Dorji Wangmo, *Treasures of the Thunder Dragon: A Portrait of Bhutan*, New Delhi: Viking, 2006

White, John Claude, *Sikhim & Bhutan: Twenty-one Years on the North-East Frontier, 1887-1908*, London: Asian Educational Service, 1909

Whiting, Allen S., *The Chinese Calculus of Deterrence: India and Indochina*, Ann Arbor: The University of Michigan Press, 1975

Younghusband, Francis Sir, *India and Tibet*, London: John Murray, 1910

INDEX

Abdullah, Sheikh, 30
Adi Minyong tribe, 85–86
Ahluwalia, Lieutenant Colonel B. S., 52, 54, 125, 141, 167–170
Ahom kingdom, 89–91
Aksai Chin region, 15–18, 21, 26, 33, 75–76, 79, 86, 102–103, 217, 326–329, 338–340
Nehru's directive, 44
Alexander, Major A. O., 281
Amritsar Treaty, 75
Anglo-Russian treaty, 1907, 104
Anglo-Sikh campaign, 77
Anglo-Tibet Convention of 1904, 80
Ao, Naib Subedar, 221
Assam Rifles, 8–9, 20–23, 55, 104–106, 153, 163–164, 170–172, 184, 188–189, 191–193, 195, 197, 204, 210, 213, 215–221, 223–224, 226, 264–267, 296–298, 319, 378, 384–386, 389
  along McMahon Line, 9
  early history, 88–92
  functioning of, 94
  at Khenzemane, 170–173
  at NEFA, 88, 94
  at Tawang, 9–12
Aurora, Brigadier Jagjit Singh, 122, 126
Avasthy, Lieutenant Colonel Brahmanand, 261, 265–266, 306–309, 393

Bahadur, Naib Subedar Dil, 240, 243
Bahadur, Subedar Harka, 169
Bahadur, Subedar Jit, 169
Bahadur, Naik Keshar, 237-238
Bahadur, Subedar Kharak, 237
Bailey, Captain George, 85, 96–97, 99–100, 102–103
Bains, Captain P. P. S., 270
Bakshi, Major, 281
Banon, Lieutenant Colonel R. M., 352
Bavadam, Captain K. N., 237-238, 243
Behl, Second Lieutenant Amar Jit Singh 'Tiger', 177–180, 396
Behl, Lieutenant Colonel A., 218, 222, 225, 230, 236-237, 240
Bell, Sir Charles, 101
Bhagat, Brigadier Premindra Singh, xi-xiii, 23, 374
Bhandari, Second Lieutenant P. S., 226, 241, 407
Bharnagar, Captain G. P., 238–239
Bhatia, Captain Gurucharan Singh, 139, 152, 155–156, 161-162
Bhatia, Captain P. N., 221, 233-234
Bhatia, Prem, 127
Bhattacharjea, Lieutenant Colonel B. M., 197, 271, 280, 303, 409
Bhutan-China relations, 82
Bhutan-Tibet border, 81
Biswas, Jemadar, 152, 161
Bomdila defences, 115, 187, 196, 200, 202–204, 211, 247, 249, 252, 260–261, 264, 273–276, 279, 281, 284, 286–287, 292–300, 309–317
Border Roads Organisation (BRO), 52, 276, 323
Borphukan, Badan Chandra, 89
Bose, Jemadar Jagan Nath 151, 157
Bose, Subhas Chandra, 24
Bowers, General, 94
Brar, Lieutenant Colonel M. S., 296, 316
Brar, Major S. S., 305
Bridge 4, battle for, 205–206
  48 Brigade, 263, 275, 279–280, 282, 321
  at Bomdila, 211, 249–250, 252, 264, 276, 293, 295–298, 309–317
  62 Brigade, 184, 208–210, 249, 258, 277–283, 285–290, 296, 298, 307, 389
  disintegration of, 301–305
Brooks, Lieutenant General Henderson, 374

Brown, Major W. F., 105
Bruce, Robert, 90
Budhwar, Lieutenant Colonel, 250, 281, 304
Bum-la, battle at, 189–193, 197–198
Buragohain, Purnananda, 89

Campbell, Sir Archibald, 90
Cardozo, Ian, 152
Cariappa, General, 5–6, 13, 19, 24
Chai General Hong Tuo, 260
Chand, Dewan Hari, 77–78
Chand, Subedar Diwan, 334
Chand, Jemadar Gian, 151, 159
Chand, Lieutenant Colonel Hari, 329, 347
Chand, Naik Hukum, 357
Chand, Major N. B., 239
Chand, Naib Subedar Ram, 357-358
Chand, Sepoy Suram, 135, 403
Chand, Subedar Surendra, 232
Chander, Subedar Ram, 161
Chander, Lieutenant Subash, 123, 151, 156
Chandran, Lieutenant Colonel K. K., 313, 317
Charak, Major Anant Singh, 168–170
Chatterji, Captain, 337
Chaudhary, Major Mahander Singh, 133–134, 136, 176, 403
Chaudhuri, Lieutenant General Joyanto Nath 'Mucchu', 363, 368-369, 374
Chauhan, Squadron Leader D.W., 351
Chavan, Y. B., 375
Cheema, Brigadier A. S., 211, 262, 265, 291–293, 307, 388
Chen Zhibin, 32
Chetri, Subedar Major Jit Bahadur, 168
China
  Chinese 'claim lines', 45–46
  interaction with India, early evidence, 65
  relationship with Tibet, 65–70
Chinese troops
  counter-attack at Walong, 232–236
  issue of repeated infiltration by, 16–18, 49
  Nam Ka Chu Valley, infiltration and consequences at, 155–164, 173–177
  Nyukamadung, infiltration at, 267
  operational plans, 256–260
  in Tibet, entry of, 4
Chopra, Captain B. C., 234
Choudhary, Second Lieutenant S. S., 297
Chou En-lai, 13–14, 16, 34, 80, 86-87, 371, 393
Chushul Sector, battle for, 348–351
Cooper, Captain, 215
Cornwallis, Governor General Lord, 89
Curzon, Lord, 73

Dagur, Lieutenant Surendra, 255, 302
Dalai Lama (fourteenth), 20, 33, 46, 49, 82, 100-101
Dalvi, Brigadier John, xviii-xix, 4, 51–56, 113–121, 123–124, 126–129, 131–137, 143, 146–150, 153, 165–166, 170, 172–174, 177–178, 180, 256, 386
Dang, Major Shashi, 314–315
Das, Brigadier J. M., 326, 333, 335
Das, Durga, 16, 86
Dass, Jemadar N. P., 152
Datta, Major Jaidev Singh, 281, 290
Daulatram, Jairamdas, 10
Demchok Sector, battle for, 351–354
Desai, M. J., 121, 147, 194, 369
Dewan, Captain A. K., 361
Dewan, Air Commodore H. C., 382–383
Dhillon, Lieutenant Charanjit 'Cherry', 270
Dhillon, Major General Joginder 'Jogi' Singh, 117, 119
Dhingra, Lieutenant Colonel H. S., 331, 359
Dhola incident, 113-118
Din, Sepoy Ganga, 265
Dirang Dzong, xii, 99-100, 105, 107, 114–115, 197–198, 204, 207–208, 221, 249, 257–258, 260–261, 263, 265, 267–268, 273, 276, 284, 291–294, 303-309, 312
Dogra, Second Lieutenant B. D., 168
Doulatram, GovernorJayram Das, 376
Dubey, Second Lieutenant Onkar, 151, 157–158
Dundiya Rebellion, 89
Dzasa, Surkhang, 109

Ehrfing, General Zhao, 94
Eipe, Captain Ravi, 134, 153, 163–164
Elwin, Verrier, 43
Engineer, Air Marshal Aspy, 147, 370, 381, 383
Exercise Lal Qila, xiv, 38, 41, 43, 47–48, 218, 365, 366, 396

Five Principles of Peaceful Co-existence, 13
frontier of India, mapping of, 82, 85, 104–106. *see also* Indo-Tibet boundary

Morshead–Bailey expedition report, 73, 96–101, 263
Frontier Police and expeditions, 91–92
Fulay, Major Raja, 50, 187

Galwan, battle for, 339–344
Gambhir, Major M. M. S., 168
Gandhi, Mahatma, 104
Gill, Brigadier Gurbax Singh (commander 4 Artillery Brigade), 209, 263, 292, 301
Gill, Brigadier G. S. (commander 5 Brigade), 218, 221
Goldstein, Melvyn, 72
Gopal, S., 56
Gorkha Battalion, 165–170
at Gurung Hill, 360–362
Gosal, Captain Gurcharan Singh, 191, 193
Goswami, Major Devinder, 251
Goswami, Lieutenant S. D., 360, 411
Goswami, Lieutenant Vinod Kumar, 253, 270, 409
Government of India Act
1919, 90
1935, 105
Grange, Mr, 91
Grewal, Captain K. J. S, 235
Grewal, Brigadier R. S., 351, 354
Gujral, Lieutenant Harish Chandra, 335
Gupta, Captain Tushar, 149
Gurung, Naib Subedar Jang Bahadur, 339
Gurung, Naik Keshar Bahadur, 237
Gurung, Naib Subedar Teghbahadur, 360
Gurung Hill, battle for, 360–362
Gusain, Rifleman Gopal Singh, 270, 409
Gusain, Naik Ranjit Singh, 270–271
Gyatso, Jamphel, 69
Gyatso, Kelzang, 68
Gyatso, Thubten, 106
Gyatso, Tsayang, 67

Hartley, Brigadier J. C., 222–224
Hasabnis, Major H. S., 330, 339-341
Hastings, Governor General Lord Warren, 69, 89
Henderson Brooks–Bhagat Report, 15, 46, 374–375, 394
Hensman, Major W. N. C., 317
Himmatsinhji, Brigadier, 7
Himmatsinhji Committee (North and Northeast Border Committee), 7
report, 7–8, 14, 18, 23, 44
'Hindi Chini bhai bhai' propaganda, 35
Hopkinson, A. J., 108-109
Hsüan-tsang, 65

Indian subcontinent
geography of, 62–64
influence of Buddhism, 64–65
India's Forward Policy, 8
Indo-Sinkiang Trade Route, 328, 332, 340
Indo-Tibet boundary
central sector, 79–82
eastern sector, 82–87
western sector, 73–79
5 Infantry Brigade, 36, 216, 218, 222
7 Infantry Brigade, 37, 47–54, 56, 114–115, 143, 170, 220, 223, 247
Irani, Lieutenant Colonel A. R., 254, 287, 289
IV Corps, 127–128, 149, 182, 186–187, 201–202, 204, 208–209, 211, 218–219, 221, 223–224, 229, 247, 258, 260, 273–277, 283–285, 317–321

Jai Lal, Sepoy, 334
Jallianwala Bagh incident, 1919, 104
Jamwal, Major S. D. S., 292
Jaspal, Lieutenant Colonel M. S., 332
Jaspal, Major S. S., 254
Johnson, William Henry, 75
Johri, Major Sitaram, 393

Kahlon, Lieutenant R. S., 154
Kale, Lieutenant Colonel G. S., 316
Kameng Frontier Division, 47–48, 50, 54, 70
Kangan, General Fu, 71
Kapila, Lieutenant Akshey, 297
Karakoram Pass, 75–76, 78, 327–328, 332, 372
Kashag, 10, 73, 82, 109
Kathju, Kailash Nath, 25
Kaul, Lieutenant General B. M. 'Bijji,' 28–33, 36, 43, 48, 50–51, 53–54, 117–118, 126–132, 134–136, 146–149, 150, 153, 165–166, 182, 186–188, 194, 201, 204, 209, 212, 218–219, 221, 223–224, 229–230, 232, 242, 244, 247–250, 252, 254, 259, 274, 277, 280-281, 283-287, 293–296, 298, 306, 314, 318–325, 328-329, 331, 362-365, 367–368, 371–372,

376, 379–380, 382-384, 386–389, 392, 395-396
Kaushik, Lieutenant Hari Pal, 189, 191–193, 197
Kennedy, John F., 369-371
Khaira, Lieutenant M. S., 255
Khan, General Ayub, 27
Khan, Kublai, 67
Khan, Lhabsang, 67-68
Khanna, Major, 174–175
Kharbanda, Major Rex, 129–130, 149, 166
Khathing, Major Bob, 10-12, 376, 396
Khatri, Lieutenant A. S., 229, 232–233
Khatwal, Subedar Bhab Bahadur, 170
Khenzemane, 12, 20–21, 23, 26, 33, 36, 41, 47, 49, 54, 56, 100, 107, 116, 124, 139, 141, 144-146, 154, 170–172, 176, 180, 182-185, 201, 203, 214, 377
Kher, Captain P. L., 360
Khera, S. S., 147
Khullar, Brigadier Darshan, 185, 198, 206, 286, 306, 311, 314, 316, 396
Khurnak Fort, 17, 345–347, 372
Kibithu, battle at, 216–221
Kongka Pass, 33-34, 43–44, 327
Kotwal, Captain G., 338-339
Kripalani, J. B., 32
Kuki uprising (1917-1919), 104
Kukrety, Major P. L., 261–262, 268, 307, 309
Kulwant Singh Committee, 13, 15, 23
Kumar, Captain Inder Jit, 237
Kumaramangalam, Lieutenant General P.P., 32
Kutty, Lieutenant, 169

Ladakh Border Commission, 75
Ladakh-Tibet border, 75-76
Lakhanpal, Captain, 315
Lakhimpur Armed Police Battalion, 93, 96
Area of Responsibility (AOR), 104
Lal, Subedar Har, 151, 159
Lal, Subedar Hem, 171
Lal, Naib Subedar Kanhya, 341
Lal, Jemadar Mohan, 152, 161
Lal, Subedar Mohan, 151, 159
Lal, Brigadier Nandi, 184, 208-210
Lall, Joint Secretary (Air) John, 369
Lama, Panchen, 69
Lamb, Alistair, 394
Lhasa, Chinese attack on, 19–20, 74, 77, 81, 326, 379
Lightfoot, Captain G. S., 105–107
1938 expedition, 9, 10
Limbu, Captain H. B., 10
Lintner, Bertil, 394
Liu Bocheng, General, 6, 257
Liu Chengsze, Lieutenant, 384
Liu Gueng, General, 260
Lockhart, General Sir Rob, 24
Log Bridge, xx, 120, 135, 140, 151, 155-156, 159, 160–161
Lohia, Ram Manohar, 35
Longju incident, 3, 20–23, 26–27, 33, 38

MacDonald, Sir Claude, 78
MacDonald line, 78–79
Madiah, Lieutenant Colonel C. N., 180, 218–224, 229–231, 234–235, 243, 390, 396
Mahindra, Lieutenant, 169
Maini, Major, 298
Malik, Major, 223, 236
Manda-la Heights-Bomdila axis, 388
Manekshaw, Major General Sam, 51, 375, 395
Mangat, Captain Mahabir, 139, 152, 156, 161
Manipur Rifles, 8
Mao Zedong (Mao Tse-tung), 4-5, 14, 18, 57,61–62, 80, 189, 326, 373–374, 377, 379
Masilamani, Major G.V. E., 290
Master, Lieutenant Colonel Byram, 52
Mathur, Captain R. K., 226, 228
Maxwell, Neville, 43, 45-46, 88, 394
McMahon, Henry, 101–102
McMahon Line, 9-11, 16, 18, 36, 39–40, 47, 51, 54, 56, 73, 82–83, 85–88, 97, 102–104, 106, 108-109, 152, 183-184, 187, 192, 199, 214–215, 378
Mehra, Chief Marshal S. K., 383
Mehta, Lieutenant Colonel B. M. 'Baij', 52, 55
Menon, K. P. S., 5
Menon, V. K. Krishna, xiv, 23, 25–27, 29-30, 32-33, 38, 42–43, 50, 53, 117–118, 121, 126–127, 147–148, 187–188, 194, 318, 366, 368, 374, 376, 381, 385
Milaktong-la, 196–197, 199
Mi Liu, Marshal, 259
Mills, J. P., 109

Minuwala, Major, 175
Mishmi Exploration Survey of 1912, 96
Mishra, Lieutenant Colonel R. N., 53, 119–120, 133, 136, 174–176, 182
Moamoria Rebellion (1769-1806), 88-89
Molesworth, Colonel, 94
Morshead, S. F., 85, 96-100, 102–103
Morshead–Bailey expedition report, 73, 94, 96–101, 119, 205, 263, 377
Mount Everest, boundary demarcation issue of, 80
Mukdang-la, 184, 198
Mukherjee, Shyama Prasad, 6
Mullik, B. N., 5–6, 13, 16, 43, 48, 118, 124, 126, 147, 182, 187–188, 201-202, 204, 211, 328, 340, 378–385

Naga Hill Tracts Agency (NHTA), 39
Nair, Major K. P. P., 262, 266-267, 307, 389
Namgye, Gyurme, 69
Nam Ka Chu Valley, xii, xiv-xv, xvii-xxi, 55–56, 100, 117, 119, 125, 134, 139, 166–167, 186–188, 380, 383, 388, 392, 394-397
  7 Brigade at, 125
  Chinese infiltration and consequences, 155–164, 173–177
  Indian pull out from, 146–150
  main defences, 140–143
Nanda, Lieutenant Colonel R. B., 207, 303
Nath, Squadron Leader J. M. Jaggi, 328, 383
Nath, Major Trilok, 260
National Highway G219, 14, 16, 18, 20, 23, 26, 45
NATO, 305
Naygam, Major S. G., 220
Negi, Lance Naik Trilok Singh, 270
Nehru, B. K., 370
Nehru, Jawaharlal, 3, 5–7, 11–14, 18, 21–22, 24–26, 29, 43–44, 46–47, 50, 61, 87–88, 94, 118, 121, 126–127, 147–148, 153, 194, 200, 203, 211, 224, 305, 322, 364–366, 368, 370–371, 373, 376, 378, 382, 387, 394
  Forward Policy, 43–46, 51
Nijjar, Major Balraj Singh, 149, 166
North East Frontier Agency (NEFA), 8–9, 11–12, 18, 21–23, 25, 33–34, 36–37, 39, 42–43, 49, 51, 53, 85, 88, 92, 273, 309, 318, 322, 326, 328, 362, 368–371, 380, 382, 384, 392–393
  4 Division at, 35–37
North East Frontier Tracts (NEFT), 96, 106
Nuranang battle of, 303
  4 Garhwal defences at, 207–208, 220, 248–249, 252, 256, 260, 263, 268–272

Oberoi, Lieutenant Colonel M. S., 303
Old Tripura Rifles, 8
Operation Onkar, 53–54

Padmasambhava, 64–65
Pahwa, Lieutenant Pran, 299
Pal, Captain Lakhan, 314-315
Palit, Brigadier D.K. Monty, 4, 41-42, 48–50, 54, 56, 109, 117–118, 124, 127-128, 186–188, 194–195, 200–204, 208–209, 212, 224, 244, 247–248, 252, 273-277, 283–285, 287, 311, 318, 320, 362, 367, 369–370, 375, 380, 388, 391
Pall, Captain T. S., 220
Palta, Lieutenant Yog Raj, 240, 407
Panchsheel Treaty, 3, 13–16, 19, 22, 35–45, 376, 378
Panikkar, Sardar K. M., 5
Pant, Major B. K., 114–116, 151, 157–158, 180
Patel, Sardar Vallabhbhai, 6-9, 11, 24, 30, 373, 378
Pathania, Major General Anant Singh, 204–205, 208–210, 222, 248–249, 261–263, 265, 267, 273–274, 276–277, 279–282, 285–287, 289–292, 295, 305, 372, 388
Pathania, Major General Mohinder S., 208, 224–225, 229-230 , 242
Pathania, Lieutenant Colonel R. S., 232
People's Liberation Army (PLA), 4–5, 19, 22, 31–32, 39, 54, 62, 82, 128, 189, 327–328, 338, 340, 355–356, 386, 388
Pereira, Major, 149
Pholhanas, 68–69
Phunchok, Havildar Satigian, 353, 412
Plassey, battle of, 88
Poshing-la, xv, 99, 107, 188, 203, 205, 209, 252, 263-267, 273, 291, 295-298, 310
Prasad, Captain Mahabir, 55, 119, 169–170
Prasad, Major General Niranjan, xvii-xviii, xix, 53–55, 113–115, 123, 127–129,

131–132, 134–135, 147–150, 165, 171–174, 177, 180–183, 185–186, 188, 195–196, 200–201, 203–205, 208–209, 219, 221, 261, 295, 386, 422
prisoner return ceremony, 34
Pun, Havildar Chandra Bahadur, 238

Radhakrishnan, President Sarvepalli, 368
Raghavan, P. Nedyam, 13
Raghuramaiah, Kotha, 121
Rahim, Lieutenant, 337
Rai, Major Hasta Bahadur, 198, 205, 253
Raina, Brigadier T. N., 329–330, 343, 346–347, 350, 355, 361–362, 390–392, 411
Raj, Subedar Des, 151
Rajan, Major S., 290
Raje, Squadron Leader C. S. K., 385
Rajendrasinhji, General Maharaj Kumar Shri, 13, 18
Rajput, Major, 114
Ram, Naib Subedar Hari, 357
Ram, Havildar Kamal, 151
Ram, Sepoy Kanshi, 136, 403
Ram, Naik Roop, 358
Ram, Sepoy Tale, 334
Randhawa, Major S. S., 335–337, 343
Rao, Lieutenant G.V. P., 171-172, 405
Ratnu, Wazir, 78
Rawat, Rifleman Jaswant Singh, 270
Rawat, Major, 314
Rawat, Subedar Udai Singh, 269
Rawlley, Brigadier N. C., 224–226, 229–230, 232, 235, 242-244
Rezang-la, battle of, 355–359
Rigzen, Lieutenant Chhewang, 332-333, 337
Rikh, Lieutenant Colonel Maha Singh, xii, xiv, xviii, 37, 113–116, 125, 132, 134–135, 139, 146, 152–153, 155–156, 158, 160–165, 180, 216
Rommel, German Field Marshal Erwin, 131
Rosario, Captain R. D., 208, 410
Roshan, Naik, 157–158
Roy, Jemadar A. K., 184, 189, 191
Roy, Subedar B. C., 152, 162
Rustomji, Nari, 257

Saeed, Brigadier G. M., 260
Sagar, Major General Moti, 51
Saigal, Major J. R., 265
Sain, Captain Raghbir, 114
Samvatsar, Major P. M., 222, 236–237
Sandhu, Lieutenant Colonel, 52
Sandhu, Major, 223, 238
Sarin, H. C., 23, 122, 187–188, 364-366, 369–370
Sat, Major Brahm, 250, 301, 389
Sawhney, Captain D. S. R., 337
Saxena, Captain M. K., 251
Sehgal, Major J. R., 305
Sehgal, Vinod, 179-181
Se-la, 42, 47, 50, 187-188, 194-200, 211, 247–250, 257, 277, 285, 363, 365
  battle at, 194–198, 200–203, 207–212, 273–277, 279–290
  deployment of battalions along the flanks of, 260–265
Sen, Lieutenant General L. P. 'Bogey', 43, 48, 50, 54, 115, 118, 122–123, 125–126, 128–129, 147–148, 182, 185–188, 196, 200–204, 208, 210, 212, 247, 257, 274–275, 277, 284, 293, 306, 325, 365, 367, 375, 380, 386–387
Sethi, Major Sharan, 134, 151, 157, 177
Shaikh, Major A. M., 267, 291
Shankar, Lieutenant Vinay, 267, 306–307
Sharma, Major B. N., 220–221, 231
Sharma, Major S. K., 352–354
Shastri, Prime Minister Lal Bahadur, 370
Shatra, Lonchen, 73, 82, 101-103, 377
Shore, Governor General Sir John, 89
Shrikent, Major Sher Pratap Singh, 168–169, 405
Shrinagesh, General S. M., 25
Sibal, Brigadier H. K., 274, 284, 293
Siddhu, Lieutenant, 354
Sikkim-Tibet border, 80–81, 92
Silk Route, 92
Simla Agreement, 9, 16
Simla Convention of 1914, 101–104
Singh, Major Ajit, 330, 342–344
Singh, Captain Amarinder, 182
Singh, Captain Amarjeet, 264, 267, 295
Singh, Major General Amrik, 41, 48, 53
Singh, Sepoy Arjun, 334
Singh, Gunner Avtar, 178
Singh, Sepoy Badan, 334
Singh, Naik Bahadur, 220
Singh, Sepoy Bahadur, 334

Singh, Lieutenant Colonel Bakhtawar, 329-330
Singh, Major Balbir, 154, 176
Singh, Naik Bare, 334
Singh, Subedar Basdeo, 153, 163–164
Singh, Major Bhairon, 329
Singh, Lieutenant Colonel Bhupinder, 114, 139, 152, 161–163, 206, 311, 313–314
Singh, Rifleman Bishan, 172
Singh, Lieutenant General Bikram, 52,325, 328, 333, 347, 350, 362
Singh, Lieutenant Bikram 180, 221-222, 225, 235, 390
Singh, Captain B. N., 231–232
Singh, Major Brij Raj, 297
Singh, Major General Budh, 331, 351
Singh, Naik Chain, 136
Singh, Chamkar, 178
Singh, Naik Chand, 334
Singh, Squadron Leader Chandan, 350, 385
Singh, Lieutenant Chattarpati, 309
Singh, Subedar Dashrath, 134, 136, 150–151, 157–158, 177
Singh, Lieutenant General Daulet, 325, 328, 331, 336, 346, 366, 391
Singh, Havildar Dharam, 335, 412
Singh, Subedar Ganga, 234
Singh, Jemadar Ghanshyam, 153, 163–164
Singh, Jemadar Gian, 174, 177
Singh, Colonel Girdhari, 309
Singh, Subedar Govind, 231–232
Singh, Major G. N., 331
Singh, Gulab, 77–78
Singh, Brigadier Gurbaksh (commander 48 Brigade), 276, 279, 284, 293, 293-298
Singh, Major Gurdial, 114, 139, 142–143, 152–153, 160–162
Singh, Lieutenant Colonel Gurdial, 311, 314–315
Singh, Naib Subedar Gurnam, 230
Singh, Havildar Gurmukh, 241
Singh, Lieutenant General Harbaksh, 201, 204, 207–210, 223–225, 248–249, 388
Singh, Major Harbans, 223, 238, 243
Singh, Lieutenant Colonel Harihar, 174–177
Singh, Subedar Haribaksh, 266
Singh, Major H. P., 171–172
Singh, Brigadier Hoshiar, 209, 250, 253–255, 277–282, 285–287, 289, 301, 304–305, 388–389
Singh, Naik Hoshiar, 151
Singh, Subedar Hoshiar, 341
Singh, Naik Jadunath, 142
Singh, Lieutenant Colonel Jai, 264, 296–297
Singh, Air Vice Marshal Jaswant, 181, 383
Singh, Major Jatar, 358
Singh, Subedar Joginder, 189, 192–193
Singh, Major General Joginder, 366
Singh, Brigadier K. K., 134, 149, 208, 219, 229, 257, 275–276, 280–281, 311
Singh, Brigadier Kalyan, 183–184, 196, 205–206, 209
Singh, Havildar Karam, 33–35, 51, 322, 328
Singh, Lieutenant Kartar, 176
Singh, Sepoy Kewal, 223, 407
Singh, Havildar Kishan, 333
Singh, Lieutenant Colonel K. S. Harihar, 154
Singh, Naik Kuldeep, 243
Singh, Captain Kulwant, 238
Singh, Major General Kulwant, 7, 13, 375
Singh, Major Kulwant, 225
Singh, Captain Lakshman, 149
Singh, Havildar Malkiat, 133–134, 175, 403
Singh, Jemadar Man, 266
Singh, Lieutenant Colonel Manohar, 281, 292
Singh, Lieutenant Manvir, 309
Singh, Sepoy Mela, 237
Singh, Major Nahar, 314
Singh, Subedar Nanak, 289
Singh, Subedar Phool, 163-164, 359
Singh, Havildar Pratap, 193
Singh, Lieutenant Colonel Pritpal, 117
Singh, Purinder, 90
Singh, Havildar Pushkar, 234
Singh, Jemadar Rai, 265
Singh, Havildar Ram, 359-360
Singh, Sepoy Ram, 358
Singh, Major Ram, 179-181
Singh, Subedar Ramjanam, 151
Singh, Maharaja Ranjit, 77
Singh, Lieutenant Colonel Rattan, 171–172
Singh, Major R. D., 12
Singh, Sepoy Salu, 334
Singh, Lance Naik Santok, 237
Singh, Major Shaitan, 357–359, 390, 392
Singh, Lieutenant Surat, 337
Singh, Naib Subedar Surja, 356
Singh, Jemadar Trilok, 232
Singh, Lance Havildar Ujagar, 136

Singh, Havildar Saudagar, 163–164
Singh, Sepoy Tehar, 237
Singh, Subedar Surjit, 343
Singh, Havildar Sucha, 189, 191
Singh, Lance Havildar Ujagar, 136
Singh, Naib Subedar Umaid, 341
Singh, Lieutenant General Umrao, 53, 114–115, 123–129, 218, 224, 248, 386, 388
Singh, Zorawar, 72, 75, 77
Singha, Chandrakanta, 90
Singha, Gaurinath, 88–89
Sinkiang, annexation of, 4
Sino-Indian Trade Agreement of 1954, 79
Sino-Myanmar border, 82
Skyid-Ida-Ngeemagon, 76
Sonam, Rai Sahib, 109
Sonam, Subedar Stopdan, 332, 334
Sonam, Tashi, 256, 409
Stilwell, General 'Vinegar Joe', 37
Subrahmanyam, K., 44-46
Sultan, Tipu, 88
Sun Xiao, 32

Tagin murders, 9–12
Talwar, Captain Harjeet Singh, 149, 177–178
Tandon, Lieutenant Surinder Nath, 269-270
Tawang battle, 199–204
Tawang Monastery, 11, 70, 83, 105, 186
Tawang salient, 9–12, 41, 105
Temporary Bridge, 120, 133–135, 140–141, 146, 160–161
  Indian observation posts at, 148–154
Tewari, Lieutenant Colonel K. K., 149, 167-168, 170
Thagla Ridge, 54–56
  Bogey Sen-Umrao Singh clash, 124–126
  Chinese defences at, 140, 143–146
  Dalvi-Prasad attack plan, 123–124, 126
  Dhola incident, 113–117
  Lieutenant General Bijji Kaul's intervention, 126–137
  Military Operations (MO) at, 117–118
  Operation Leghorn, 118–119, 122
Thapa, Major Dhan Singh, 345, 347–348, 392
Thapa, Naik Rabi Lal, 347-348
Thapa, Naib Subedar Shamsher Bahadur, 171
Thapar, Lieutenant General Pran, xiv, 38, 50–51, 117, 122–123, 126–129, 147–148, 186–188, 194–196, 200–205, 209–212, 248, 274, 277, 283, 285, 306, 319–320, 324, 362, 366–367, 371, 376, 387, 391
Thembang Ridge, 52, 188, 205, 258, 261, 263, 265, 267, 275, 279, 293
Thimayya, General Kodandera Subayya, 18–19, 22-29, 31, 33, 35, 38, 41, 43, 48, 50, 187, 212, 324–325,366, 371, 375–376, 379, 387
  charge of 'treason', 50–51
  resignation of, 26–28
Thomas, Major Oscar, 154, 174, 176, 182
Thorat, Lieutenant General S. P. P, 31–32, 38–40, 47, 50, 128, 187, 202, 212, 324, 365–366, 371
  defensive line, 41-43
Thorat Plan, 39, 41–43, 48, 224, 257, 286
Tibet
  China's relationship with, 65–70
  1914 drawing up of boundary, 104
  India's relationship with, 70–73
  'Inner' and 'Outer', 101
  Lightfoot's expedition, 1938, 105–106
  Morshead–Bailey expedition, 96–101
  Simla Convention of 1914 and, 101–104
  'sovereignty' and China's 'suzerainty' over Tibet, 5–6
Tibetan intrusion in Tawang and Kameng regions, 106–109
Tibet-Mongol treaty, 101
Tongpeng-la, 189-193, 197
Treaty of Betrawati, 79
Tsangdhar Ridge, 47, 56, 100, 119–120, 124–125, 129–131, 135, 140–142, 149–150, 153, 165–169, 173–174, 177–180
Tse-la, 99, 107, 188, 207, 264, 286
Tsona dzongpen, 10–11
Tundup, Jemadar Ishe, 353, 412

Ummat, Major, 268
Usman, Brigadier, 142

Verma, Captain Ashok Kalyan, xi, 114, 216
Verma, Brigadier Inder, 284
Verma, Lieutenant General S. D., 50, 322, 324–325, 387

Wadalia, Lieutenant General K., 366
Wade, Doctor John Peter, 89
Waing, Bodaw U (Bodawpaya), 89
Walong Sector, battle at, 213–217
  Chinese counter-attack, 231–236
  defences at Hayuliang, 243–244
  defences at The Ladders, 239–242
  Indian deployment at, 221–228
  at Kibithu, 217–221
  4 Sikh's Battalion at, 236–239
  at Trijunction, 229–232
  withdrawal of battalions, 242–244
Welsh, Captain Thomas, 89, 91
Western Sector
  Chinese advancing, 332–335
  Chinese plan for, 326–332
  Chushul Sector, 348–351
  DBO Sector, 328–329, 331–332
  Demchok Sector, 351–354
  Galwan, 339–344
  Gurung Hill, 359–362
  14 J&K Militia and, 328, 335–339, 344
  Ladakh, 322–326
  Pangong-Spanggur sector, 344–348
  Rezang-la, 355–359
White, Claude, 102
Williams, A. S., 181
World War II, 61–62, 106–109, 151, 188, 292, 382, 386
Wu-Je incident, 15

Yadav, Lieutenant Colonel, 223, 241–242
Yang Chengiou, General, 32, 373
Yan Xun, Prof., 256
Yonggyap-la, 97, 260, 265
Younghusband, Colonel, 73
Yuan Zhongxian, General, 4
Yu Zhi Guo, General, 260

Zhang Gua Hua, Lieutenant General, 258
Zimithang, 49, 146, 148, 171–172, 174, 180–185